I0062539

Leveling the Playing Field

Scan the QR code to see all the titles in the
Africa Flagships collection

Leveling the Playing Field

Addressing Structural Inequalities to Accelerate Poverty Reduction in Africa

Edited by
Nistha Sinha, Gabriela Inchauste, and Ambar Narayan

WORLD BANK GROUP

© 2024 International Bank for Reconstruction and Development / The World Bank
1818 H Street NW, Washington, DC 20433
Telephone: 202-473-1000; Internet: www.worldbank.org

Some rights reserved

1 2 3 4 27 26 25 24

This work is a product of the staff of The World Bank with external contributions. The findings, interpretations, and conclusions expressed in this work do not necessarily reflect the views of The World Bank, its Board of Executive Directors, or the governments they represent.

The World Bank does not guarantee the accuracy, completeness, or currency of the data included in this work and does not assume responsibility for any errors, omissions, or discrepancies in the information, or liability with respect to the use of or failure to use the information, methods, processes, or conclusions set forth. The boundaries, colors, denominations, links/footnotes, and other information shown in this work do not imply any judgment on the part of The World Bank concerning the legal status of any territory or the endorsement or acceptance of such boundaries. The citation of works authored by others does not mean The World Bank endorses the views expressed by those authors or the content of their works.

Nothing herein shall constitute or be construed or considered to be a limitation upon or waiver of the privileges and immunities of The World Bank, all of which are specifically reserved.

Rights and Permissions

This work is available under the Creative Commons Attribution 3.0 IGO license (CC BY 3.0 IGO) http://creativecommons.org/licenses/by/3.0/igo. Under the Creative Commons Attribution license, you are free to copy, distribute, transmit, and adapt this work, including for commercial purposes, under the following conditions:

Attribution—Please cite the work as follows: Sinha, Nistha, Gabriela lnchauste, and Ambar Narayan, eds. 2024. *Leveling the Playing Field: Addressing Structural Inequalities to Accelerate Poverty Reduction in Africa.* Washington, DC: World Bank. doi: 10.1596/978-1-4648-2160-8. License: Creative Commons Attribution CC BY 3.0 IGO

Translations—If you create a translation of this work, please add the following disclaimer along with the attribution: *This translation was not created by The World Bank and should not be considered an official World Bank translation. The World Bank shall not be liable for any content or error in this translation.*

Adaptations—If you create an adaptation of this work, please add the following disclaimer along with the attribution: *This is an adaptation of an original work by The World Bank. Views and opinions expressed in the adaptation are the sole responsibility of the author or authors of the adaptation and are not endorsed by The World Bank.*

Third-party content—The World Bank does not necessarily own each component of the content contained within the work. The World Bank therefore does not warrant that the use of any third-party-owned individual component or part contained in the work will not infringe on the rights of those third parties. The risk of claims resulting from such infringement rests solely with you. If you wish to re-use a component of the work, it is your responsibility to determine whether permission is needed for that re-use and to obtain permission from the copyright owner. Examples of components can include, but are not limited to, tables, figures, or images.

All queries on rights and licenses should be addressed to World Bank Publications, The World Bank, 1818 H Street NW, Washington, DC 20433, USA; e-mail: pubrights@worldbank.org.

ISBN (paper): 978-1-4648-2160-8
ISBN (electronic): 978-1-4648-2161-5
DOI: 10.1596/978-1-4648-2160-8

Cover image: © Karine Arnou. Used with the permission of Karine Arnou. Further permission required for reuse.
Cover design: Melina Rose Yingling / World Bank Creative Services, Global Corporate Solutions.

Library of Congress Control Number: 2024917591

Contents

CHAPTER 1

Inequality in Africa 1

Nistha Sinha, Gabriela Inchauste, and Ambar Narayan

CHAPTER 2

The Poverty Reduction Challenge in Africa. 25

Ambar Narayan, Liliana Sousa, Haoyu Wu, and Elizabeth Foster

Spotlight 1: Poverty and Inequality Influencers: Climate   **75**
Ruth Hill

CHAPTER 3

People in Africa Face an Unlevel Playing Field for Building Their Productive Capacity 89

Aziz Atamanov, P. Facundo Cuevas, and Jeremy Lebow

Spotlight 2: Poverty and Inequality Influencers: Gender Equality   **155**
Ana Maria Oviedo and Hugo Ñopo

CHAPTER 4

Workers, Firms, and Farms Face an Unlevel Playing Field in Using their Productive Capacities. 165

Nistha Sinha, Elwyn Davies, Alastair Haynes, and Regina Pleninger

Spotlight 3: Poverty and Inequality Influencers: Fragility, Conflict, and Forced Displacement   **217**

Olive Nsababera

CHAPTER 5

Governments Could Do Far More to Level the Playing Field Through Fiscal Policies. **229**

Gabriela Inchauste, Christopher Hoy, Mariano Sosa, and Daniel Valderrama

Spotlight 4: Poverty and Inequality Influencers: Debt   **285**

César Calderón

CHAPTER 6

Policies to Tackle Structural Inequalities and Accelerate Poverty Reduction and Growth **291**

Gabriela Inchauste and Nistha Sinha

BOXES

FIGURES

Foreword

Accelerating progress to eliminate extreme poverty in Africa is possible. To do so, the region must address structural inequalities. Africa has enormous potential; it is rich in natural resources and home to a growing, youthful, vibrant, and entrepreneurial population that can seize opportunities to make the most of innovation, trade, and the global transition to greener technologies. With the region's population forecast to rise from around 1.4 billion today to close to 2.5 billion by 2050, access to these opportunities is crucial for its youth.

The battle against poverty is most urgent in Africa. As of 2022, more than 60 percent of the world's extremely poor population live in Africa. Growth has been slower, more volatile, and vulnerable to exogenous shocks over the past decade as climate change, fragility, and debt pressures have gained importance. Countries in the region also find it more difficult relative to the rest of the world to translate growth into poverty reduction, because the fruits of economic growth all too often do not reach the poorest households. At the heart of this slow progress in bringing people prosperity is inequality. More than half of the countries for which consumption data are available are highly unequal. As of 2022, Africa was the second-most unequal region in the world after Latin America.

This flagship report shows that much of this inequality is structural: instead of differences in individual effort or talent, more than half of income inequality is attributable to circumstances over which individuals have no control. Structural inequalities are the result of laws, institutions, and practices that create advantages for a few but disadvantages for many. They include differences in living standards that come from inherited or unalterable characteristics, such as where people are born and their parents' education, ethnicity, religion, or gender. Moreover, market and institutional distortions, such as lack of competition, give some firms, farms, and workers privileged access to markets, employment, and opportunities while limiting access for the majority, curtailing their productive potential and limiting earning opportunities. Tax and benefit policies are inefficient and ineffective, unable to make up for structural inequality, particularly in a tight fiscal context.

As such, structural inequality slows poverty reduction, curbs social mobility, and hampers sustainable and stable economic growth. But structural inequality is not inevitable: societies can remove and replace barriers to opportunities. Drawing on the latest evidence and global experience, this report revisits the challenges and opportunities to tackle Africa's poverty and inequality and proposes a three-pronged policy framework aimed at leveling the playing field by building up productive capacities, creating jobs and better earning opportunities, and leveraging fair fiscal policy and state effectiveness to invest in people, firms, and farms.

For policy makers focused on helping Africa build a better future, the report's message is that it is possible to alleviate poverty in all its forms if countries strive to create a level playing field. By bringing together comprehensive data, analysis, and country experiences, the report paints a more accurate picture of the complexity of inequality in the region and outlines the best ways to address it. The report advances knowledge of what it will take to achieve the goals of eradicating extreme poverty and boosting shared prosperity on a livable planet.

<table>
<tr><td>Ousmane Diagana</td><td>Victoria Kwakwa</td></tr>
<tr><td>Regional Vice President for Western and Central Africa</td><td>Regional Vice President for Eastern and Southern Africa</td></tr>
<tr><td>The World Bank</td><td>The World Bank</td></tr>
</table>

Acknowledgments

This report is an output of the Poverty and Equity Global Practice in close collaboration with the Africa Chief Economist Office of the World Bank. The preparation of the report was co-led by Nistha Sinha, Gabriela Inchauste, and Ambar Narayan. P. Facundo Cuevas co-led the drafting at the concept stage. The core team included Aziz Atamanov (chapters 1 and 3), Cesar Calderon (debt spotlight), Elwyn Davies (chapter 4), Elizabeth Foster (chapter 2), Alastair Haynes (chapter 4), Ruth Hill (climate spotlight), Christopher Hoy (chapter 5), Jeremy Lebow (chapter 3), Hugo Nopo (gender spotlight), Ana Maria Oviedo (gender spotlight), Regina Pleninger (chapter 4), Mariano Sosa (chapter 5), Liliana Sousa (chapters 1 and 2), Olive Nsababera (conflict spotlight), Daniel Valderrama (chapter 5), and Haoyu Wu (chapter 2). Tom Bundervoet provided key inputs on the elasticity of poverty reduction. Daniel Mahler provided technical advice in calculating inequality of opportunity. Vincenzo Di Maro drafted inputs on top incomes. Walker Kosmidou-Bradley provided geospatial inputs. Valentina Martinez-Pabon and Maria Sarrabayrouse provided key assistance in finalizing the report. Rose-Claire Pakabomba, Santosh Sahoo, Tsehaynesh Seltan, and Arlette Sourou provided administrative support to the team.

This work was conducted under the overall direction of Victoria Kwakwa and Ousmane Diagana, with guidance from Abebe Adugna, Asad Alam (at concept stage), Andrew Dabalen, Luis Felipe Lopez Calva, and Hassan Zaman. The team is also grateful for guidance, advice, and critical inputs from Johan Mistiaen and Pierella Paci.

The team gratefully acknowledges the advice from peer reviewers and external advisers. The report was peer reviewed by Kathleen Beegle, Haroon Bhorat, and Keith Hansen. Mary Hallward Driemeier provided peer review comments at the concept stage. The team also benefited from many helpful discussions with experts across the World Bank Group, including Tom Bundervoet, Luc Christiaensen, Wendy Cunningham, Mitja Del Bono, David Evans, Elena Glinskaya, Aparajita Goyal, Marek Hanusch, Johannes Hoogeveen, Tehmina Khan, Vinny Nagaraj, Ambika Sharma, Venkatesh Sundararaman, Paolo Verme, and Ruslan Yemtsov. Feedback from outside experts, including with the Poverty and Equity Global Practice's Advisory Council, is gratefully acknowledged, with special thanks to Francois Bourguignon, Ashwini Deshpande, Shanta Devarajan, Cecilia Garcia-Peñalosa, Ravi Kanbur, Peter Lanjouw, Santiago Levy, Nora Lustig, and Danielle Resnick. The team also benefited from discussions with Nancy Benjamin.

The report would not have been possible without the support of Beatrice Berman and the communications, editorial, and publishing teams. Paul Gallagher provided key support in the drafting of the Overview. Flore Martinant de Preneuf led the communications strategy. The Overview was edited by Michael Harrup and proofread by Ann O'Malley; the full report was edited by Kathie Porta Baker and proofread by Alfred Imhoff. The Overview and full report were designed by Melina Rose Yingling. Caroline Polk from the World Bank's Publishing Program managed the production of the Overview and full report.

About the Editors and Contributors

Editors

Gabriela Inchauste is a lead economist in the Poverty and Equity Global Practice of the World Bank. Her work focuses on the distributional impact of fiscal policy, ex ante analysis of the distributional impacts of policy reforms, and understanding of the channels through which economic growth improves labor market opportunities for poverty reduction. Before joining the World Bank, she worked at the International Monetary Fund and the Inter-American Development Bank. She has published articles in academic volumes and journals on fiscal policy in low-income countries, decentralization, the distributional impacts of taxes and social spending, macroeconomic shocks and the poor, the informal sector, and the role of remittances in developing countries. She holds a PhD in economics from the University of Texas at Austin.

Ambar Narayan is currently a practice manager of Poverty and Equity in the Europe and Central Asia region of the World Bank. In his current role and previously as lead economist and global lead, he leads and advises teams conducting policy analysis and research in development from a microeconomic perspective. The topics that he has worked on include inequality of opportunity, economic mobility, policy evaluation, economic transformation, and impacts of economic shocks on households. He has been a lead author for several prominent World Bank studies, including a global report on intergenerational mobility and regional reports on inequality of opportunity, and he has coauthored numerous scholarly publications that reflect the eclectic mix of topics he has worked on over the years. He holds a PhD in economics from Brown University.

Nistha Sinha is a senior economist in the Poverty and Equity Global Practice of the World Bank, focusing on the topics of poverty, inequality, and labor markets. She earned a master's degree in economics from the Delhi School of Economics and a PhD in economics from the University of Washington in Seattle. Before joining the World Bank, Nistha was a postdoctoral fellow at Yale University's Economic Growth Center.

Contributors

Aziz Atamanov is a senior economist in the Poverty Global Practice Group of the World Bank. He has worked on poverty measurement and on labor market, gender, and distributional analysis across the Europe and Central Asia, Middle East and North Africa, and Sub-Saharan Africa regions. He has published articles in academic journals and contributed to many edited volumes on topics such as the development impact of international migration and remittances, distributional analysis of subsidy reforms, the role of purchasing power parities in measuring international poverty, and the elasticity of poverty to economic growth. Before joining the World Bank, he worked as a research fellow at the Center for Social and Economic Research. He holds a PhD in development economics from Maastricht University.

César Calderón, a Peruvian national, is lead economist in the Office of the Chief Economist of the Africa Region. He joined the World Bank in 2005 and has worked in the Latin America and the Caribbean Regional Chief Economist Office and the Finance and Private Sector Development Chief Economist Office and was a core member of the 2014 *World Development Report* team. He is the task team leader of *Africa's Pulse*, a regional flagship on recent macroeconomic developments in Sub-Saharan Africa. He has also been a task team leader for regional research projects such as "Africa's Macroeconomic Vulnerabilities" and "Boosting Productivity in Sub-Saharan Africa." César has worked on issues of macroeconomic resilience, growth, and development. He holds a PhD in economics from the University of Rochester.

P. Facundo Cuevas is the lead economist and program leader for the World Bank's Human Development practice groups in Brazil, where he leads and oversees engagements in the education, health, social protection, and labor sectors with national, state, and municipal governments. He joined the World Bank in 2007 and has since provided policy advice, developed operational solutions, delivered technical assistance, and conducted policy research on poverty reduction, equality of opportunity, and social protection. He has published articles in both academic and policy outlets and has worked across low- and middle-income countries in all regions of the world. Before joining the World Bank, he lived in India and worked on community development projects. Facundo is a Fulbright alumnus, and he holds a PhD and a master's degree in economics from the University of California, Los Angeles, and a summa cum laude bachelor's degree from the National University of Cuyo, Mendoza, Argentina.

Elwyn Davies is a senior economist in the Finance, Competitiveness, and Innovation Global Practice of the World Bank, working on firm dynamics, productivity, and innovation in various countries, currently mostly in Africa, Central Asia and Europe. Elwyn's work focuses on constraints on firm growth and productivity as well as on questions related to structural and economic transformation, including the role of services in development. He is an author of the flagship report *At Your Service? The Promise of Services-Led Development*. He has published in the *Journal of*

Development Economics, the *Journal of Economic Behavior & Organization*, the *World Bank Research Observer*, and the *Journal of African Economies*, among other journals. A Dutch and British national, Elwyn joined the World Bank as a Young Professional in 2017. He holds a DPhil degree from the University of Oxford.

Elizabeth Foster is an economist in the Poverty and Equity Global Practice in the West and Central Africa region at the World Bank. She has more than 15 years' experience living and working in West Africa in government, nongovernmental organization, and research roles. She specializes in the technical issues of poverty measurement at national and international poverty lines. She holds a master's degree in public affairs from Princeton University.

Alastair Haynes is an economist in the Poverty and Equity Practice in the Eastern and Southern Africa region at the World Bank. His work has focused on poverty, inequality, labor markets, and social protection. Before joining the World Bank, he worked on monitoring and evaluation and impact evaluations on a range of social protection programs in East Africa. He holds a master's degree in development economics from the University of Nottingham and a bachelor's degree in economics from the University of Sheffield.

Ruth Hill is a lead economist in the Poverty and Equity Global Practice at the World Bank. Ruth has been at the World Bank for 11 years and has led work on the distributional impacts of climate change, fiscal policy, markets, and institutions. She led the report *Poverty and Shared Prosperity 2022* and the development of the Rural Income Diagnostics reports, and she conducted Poverty Assessments and Systematic Country Diagnostics in East Africa and South Asia. From 2019 to 2021, she was on external service as the chief economist at the UK government's Centre for Disaster Protection. Before joining the World Bank in 2013, she was a senior research fellow at the International Food Policy Research Institute, conducting impact evaluations on insurance and market interventions. Ruth has published in the *Journal of Development Economics*, *World Bank Economic Review*, *Economic Development and Cultural Change*, *Experimental Economics*, the *American Journal of Agricultural Economics*, and *World Development*. She has a doctorate in economics from the University of Oxford.

Christopher Hoy is an economist in the Poverty and Equity Global Practice of the World Bank, primarily focusing on fiscal policy. He has published in leading academic journals, including the *American Economic Journal: Economic Policy*, and his work has been featured in top media outlets, such as *The Economist*. Before joining the World Bank as a Young Professional, Christopher worked as an assistant professor at the Australian National University and for a range of organizations, including UNICEF, ODI, the Abdul Latif Jameel Poverty Action Lab / Innovations for Poverty Action, and the Australian Treasury. He has worked throughout the Pacific, Sub-Saharan Africa, and Southeast Asia. He holds a doctorate in economics from the Australian National University.

Jeremy Lebow is an economist in the Social Protection and Jobs Global Practice of the World Bank, working primarily on labor, migration, and skills development. Before this, he was a Young Professional in the Poverty and Equity Practice for East Africa. He has published papers on various topics in academic journals, such as the *Journal of Development Economics*, in particular on the economic and social effects of mass migration in Latin America. He holds a PhD in economics from Duke University.

Hugo Ñopo is a senior poverty economist for Latin America and the Caribbean at the World Bank. He joined the World Bank in 2022, coming from the Group for the Analysis of Development (GRADE) in Peru. Previously, he was the regional economist at the International Labour Organization and lead economist of the Education Division and the Research Department at the Inter-American Development Bank. He was an assistant professor at Middlebury College, an affiliated researcher at GRADE, and an adviser at the Ministry of Labor and Social Promotion in Peru. Hugo works on a broad set of poverty, inequality, education, and labor market issues, with a focus on gender and ethnic inequalities. He is also a research affiliate at the Institute for the Study of Labor in Bonn, Germany, and he was a board member of the Latin American and Caribbean Economic Association. He holds a PhD in economics from Northwestern University and an MSc in mathematical economics from the Instituto de Matemática Pura e Aplicada.

Olive Nsababera is an economist with the Poverty and Equity Global Practice at the World Bank, where she works at the intersection of poverty, inequality, and migration. She joined the World Bank as part of the Young Professionals Program and has since worked on the Eastern and Southern Africa, as well as the Latin America and the Caribbean regions. Before joining the World Bank, she focused on fragile and conflict-affected settings, analyzing the impact of forced displacement on individual welfare, local economic development, and how alternative data sources and machine-learning techniques can be leveraged to inform policy in data-scarce contexts. She holds a BA in economics from Yale University, an MPA from Columbia University, and a PhD in economics from the University of Sussex.

Ana Maria Oviedo is a senior poverty economist in the Eastern and Southern Africa region and co-leads global gender engagement in the Poverty and Equity Global Practice at the World Bank. Her work focuses on intersectoral analytics and lending to improve evidence-based policies and reduce exclusion through targeted fiscal policies and service delivery. She has worked in Latin America and the Caribbean, Türkiye, and the Western Balkans, where she focused on poverty, gender equality in labor markets, social protection, and informality. She holds a PhD in economics from the University of Maryland and a BA in economics from the University of Lausanne, Switzerland.

Regina Pleninger is an economist in the Prosperity Chief Economist Office at the World Bank. Her research interests include inequality, poverty, growth, and jobs. She has worked on the distributional effects of financial development, globalization, and natural disasters. She has published in the *World Bank Economic Review* and in *World Development*, among other journals. Since she joined the World Bank in 2022, she has worked on the *Poverty, Prosperity, and Planet Report 2024* and contributed to the *Central African Republic Poverty Assessment 2023*. Regina holds a PhD in economics from the Swiss Federal Institute of Technology in Zurich.

Mariano Sosa is a consultant for the Poverty and Equity Global Practice of the World Bank, supporting research and knowledge work in the Global Unit and several regions of the practice, including East Asia and Pacific, Europe and Central Asia, and Western and Central Africa. His areas of expertise are public policy, fiscal incidence analysis, social policy, and the redistributive impact of fiscal policy in developing countries. Before joining the World Bank, Mariano was a research fellow for the Research Department of the Inter-American Development Bank. He holds a master's degree in public administration and international development from Harvard Kennedy School.

Liliana Sousa is a senior economist in the Poverty and Equity Practice of the World Bank, currently working in the East Asia and Pacific region. She has previously worked in the Eastern and Southern Africa region and the Latin America and the Caribbean region. She has authored work on various topics, with a particular interest in labor markets and migration. Before joining the World Bank in 2013, she was an economist in the Center for Economic Studies at the U.S. Census Bureau. She holds a PhD in economics from Cornell University and a BA in economics from Vassar College.

Daniel Valderrama is an economist in the Poverty and Equity Global Practice of the World Bank, currently working on the Western and Central Africa region. Before joining the World Bank, he worked at the Colombian National Statistical Office, where he served as a member for the National Committee for Poverty Measurement. As an applied microeconomist, his published research in peer-reviewed academic journals and policy reports lies at the intersection of development and public economics, focusing on the distributional impact of public policies and political distortions. Daniel holds an MA and a PhD in economics from Georgetown University in Washington, DC, as well as an MSc and a BA in economics from Universidad del Rosario and Universidad de Antioquia.

Haoyu Wu is an economist with the Poverty and Equity Global Practice in the Eastern and Southern Africa region at the World Bank. He has worked on topics related to poverty, inequality, welfare distribution, and data systems. He is interested in statistical and methodological research and the development of computational tools for data analysis. He has published articles in academic journals and coauthored several edited volumes and methodology notes on various topics. Haoyu holds a PhD in economics from Clark University.

Key Messages

The state of poverty and inequality in Africa

- **Addressing structural inequality represents one of the continent's best opportunities to accelerate poverty reduction, increase productivity and earnings, and ensure fairness.** Tackling structural inequality requires confronting its many root causes, which include inadequate and inequitable public investments, market failures, and differential exposure to high and uninsurable risks such as conflict and climate change.

- **Africa is the world's second-most-unequal region after Latin America.** More than half of African countries have a Gini index above 40, indicating high levels of inequality. The evidence suggests that the sources of this inequality are structural. Structural inequality results from inherited or unalterable characteristics—such as where people are born; their ethnicity, religion, or gender; and their parents' education—or from market and institutional distortions that privilege some firms, farms, and workers to access markets, employment, and opportunities while limiting access for the majority, curtailing their productive potential and limiting earning opportunities.

- **Poverty reduction in Africa has stalled since the mid-2010s.** Although the incidence of extreme poverty was rapidly reduced to single digits worldwide, the pace in Africa slowed down and flatlined in the past decade. As of 2022, Africa's extreme poverty rate stands at 38 percent, the highest of all regions, and the region is home to more than 60 percent of the global extreme poor population. Tackling high poverty is complicated by the region's high vulnerability to shocks.

- **Economic growth has been low and volatile, with limited impact on poverty reduction.** Since 2014, economic growth has barely kept pace with population growth. Moreover, economic growth has been less efficient in reducing poverty because a 1 percent growth in per capita gross domestic product is associated with only a 1 percent reduction in the poverty rate in Africa, whereas it is associated with a 2.1 percent reduction in the rest of the world. This lower level of efficiency is closely tied to the region's high inequality.

- **This is the region's moment to make a change.** Africa has the talent potential of the 8–11 million youths expected to enter the labor market each year between 2020 and 2050 and the significant revenue potential from green minerals to support a clean energy transition.

A policy framework to level the playing field and accelerate growth and poverty reduction

- **Foster strong economic and institutional foundations.** Promote macroeconomic and fiscal stability, and ensure the institutional framework eliminates barriers to competition, prevents undue privilege, and safeguards property rights to allow productive firms, farms, and workers to prosper.

- **Address inequalities in acquiring human capital and other assets to build productive capacity.** Invest in education, health, and basic infrastructure to significantly enhance workers' productive capacity. Moreover, expand land registration and property rights, encourage investments in natural capital, and improve service delivery to build productive capacities.

- **Enable markets to function well, boost the use of productive capacity, and create jobs and better earnings opportunities for all workers.** Remove market distortions and enable markets to work in ways that expand the access of firms, farms, and household businesses to capital and technology, domestic markets, and global trade while facilitating job searches for workers.

- **Apply fair fiscal policy.** Shift the focus away from subsidies while strengthening social safety nets, promoting progressive taxation, and improving the efficiency and effectiveness of government spending to enhance the redistributive impacts of taxes and transfers.

Abbreviations

ACCESS	Appui aux Communes et Communautés pour l'Expansion des Services Sociaux (Benin)
AfCFTA	African Continental Free Trade Area
AFE	Eastern and Southern Africa
AFR	Africa, Sub-Saharan Africa
AFW	Western and Central Africa
ASP	adaptive social protection
BCG	Bacillus Calmette-Guerin
CEQ	Commitment to Equity
CIT	corporate income tax
CPIA	Country Policy and Institutional Assessment
CT	cash transfer
CT-OVC	cash transfer for orphans and vulnerable children (Kenya)
D-index	dissimilarity index
DTP	diphtheria–tetanus–pertussis
EAP	East Asia and Pacific
ECA	Europe and Central Asia
ECAMS	Enquête Camerounaise Auprès des Ménages
EHCVM	Enquête Harmonise de Conditions de Vie des Ménages
EITI	Extractives Industry Transparency Initiative
FCS	fragile and conflict-affected situations
FDI	foreign direct investment
FGM	female genital mutilation
GDM	Global Database on Intergenerational Mobility
GDP	gross domestic product
GFN	gross financing needs

GGDC	Groningen Growth and Development Centre
GII	Gender Inequality Index
GNI	gross national income
HepB3	three-dose hepatitis B vaccine
HH	household
HIC	high-income countries
HOI	Human Opportunity Index
ICT	information and communication technology
IDA	International Development Association
IDREA	Inquérito Sobre Despesas, Receitas e Emprego em Angola
IPV	intimate partner violence
IGM	intergenerational mobility
ILO	International Labour Organization
IOF	Inquérito sobre Orçamento Familiar
IPCC	Intergovernmental Panel on Climate Change
KIHBS	Kenya Integrated Household Budget Survey
LAC	Latin America and the Caribbean
LAYS	learning-adjusted years of schooling
LIC	low-income countries
LIC-DSF	Low-Income Country Debt Sustainability Framework
LMIC	lower-middle-income countries
MNA	Middle East and North Africa
MSME	micro-, small-, and medium-sized enterprise
NA	North America
OECD	Organisation for Economic Co-operation and Development
OOC	Official Creditor Committee
PC	Paris Club
PISA	Programme for International Student Assessment
PITs	personal income taxes
PMR	product market regulations
PNBSF	Programme National de Bourses de Sécurité familiale (Senegal)

pp	percentage points
PPG	public and publicly guaranteed
PPP	purchasing power parity
PSSB	Basic Social Subsidy Program (Mozambique)
PSSN	Productive Social Safety Net Project (Côte d'Ivoire)
RR	resource rich
SAR	South Asia
SES-HCI	Socioeconomically Disaggregated Human Capital Index
SMEs	small- and medium-sized economies
STRs	simplified tax regimes
TVET	technical and vocational education and training
UBI	universal basic income
UMIC	upper-middle-income countries
VAT	value-added tax
WAEMU	West Africa Economic Monetary Union
WDI	World Development Indicators

All dollar amounts in this report are US dollars unless otherwise indicated. Dollar amounts adjusted for purchasing power parity are noted accordingly in the text.

CHAPTER 1

Inequality in Africa

NISTHA SINHA, GABRIELA INCHAUSTE, AND AMBAR NARAYAN

Chapter highlights

Africa is rebounding from a global pandemic yet is challenged by fiscal constraints and mounting fragility.[1] Policy makers are challenged to revitalize economic growth, strengthen resilience, reduce poverty, and build prosperity. This report profiles inequality in consumption and argues that policies to address high levels of structural inequality in Africa are critical for reigniting, accelerating, and sustaining progress in poverty reduction.

Africa stands out globally not just because it is the region with the highest extreme poverty rate, but also because it is one of the most unequal regions in the world. Of the 725 million people globally living in extreme poverty in 2022, more than 63 percent live in Africa. At the same time, with an average Gini index—a benchmark of inequality—of 40.8 for consumption, Africa is the second-most-unequal region in the world, and inequality in African countries is, on average, 10 Gini points higher than in countries in other regions with similar levels of economic output.

High inequality is both a symptom and a cause of missed opportunities to accelerate poverty reduction and growth and build societies and economies that are more resilient to shocks (Manuelyan Atinc et al. 2005). This report draws on a variety of data sources, including household and enterprise surveys, to analyze structural sources of inequality across the region—which are rooted in laws, institutions, and practices that create advantages for a few but disadvantages for many—and it proposes a triple-pronged policy framework aimed at supporting productive capacity; creating jobs and earning opportunities; and leveraging fair fiscal policy and state effectiveness to invest in people, firms, and farms.

There is reason for optimism. Africa is rich in natural resources and home to a growing, youthful, vibrant, and entrepreneurial population that can seize opportunities to make the most of innovation, trade, and the global economic transition to net zero. With the region's population forecasted to rise from around 1.4 billion today to close to 2.5 billion by 2050, access to these opportunities will be more crucial than ever for its youth.

The time to reignite, accelerate, and sustain progress is now. Over the past 10 years, growth has been slow, volatile, and vulnerable to exogenous shocks. Countries in the region find it difficult to translate growth into poverty reduction. Inequality also remains high, with nearly half of African countries with data reporting a Gini index above 40 percent.

This report focuses on the roots of structural inequality that are at the heart of Africa's slow progress in reducing extreme poverty. Rather than resulting from differences in talent or effort, structural inequalities in living standards are those resulting from either inherited or unalterable characteristics—such as where people are born; their ethnicity, religion, or gender; and their parents' education—or market and institutional distortions that privilege some firms, farms, and workers to access markets, employment, and opportunities while limiting access for the majority, thus curtailing their productive potential and limiting earning opportunities. By one summary measure proposed in this report, structural inequality accounts for one-quarter (Ethiopia) to three-quarters (South Africa) of overall inequality in consumption. Deeply entrenched, uneven chances to learn and earn result in significantly lower poverty reduction than elsewhere in the world.

There is, however, nothing inevitable about structural inequality. Economies that put up barriers to opportunities can also remove and replace them with policies aimed at reducing these inequalities, which also lead to faster growth and poverty reduction. Indeed, across the world, countries in which inequality of opportunity is lower tend to grow faster and have a lower incidence of poverty. Broadening access to opportunities represents one of Africa's key prospects for accelerating poverty reduction by raising productivity and earnings and improving fairness in society. Policy makers can level the playing field to create more opportunities and better jobs, and they can harness fiscal resources more effectively and efficiently.

Africa stands out for its high level of income inequality

Africa as a region stands out for its high level of income inequality. Nearly half (22 of 45) of the countries in Africa with inequality data have a Gini index higher than 40 and are thus classified as being highly unequal, based on the World Bank's new indicator for monitoring high inequality globally.[2] Despite a 9 percent decrease in average inequality relative to the first decade of the 2000s, Africa, with an average Gini index of 40.8, is among the most unequal regions in the world, second only to Latin America and the Caribbean (refer to figure 1.1a).[3] Moreover, as detailed in chapter 5, prefiscal inequality (before taxes and transfers are considered) is even higher, with a Gini index of 46.0.[4] Africa's higher level of inequality relative to other

FIGURE 1.1 Inequality in Africa

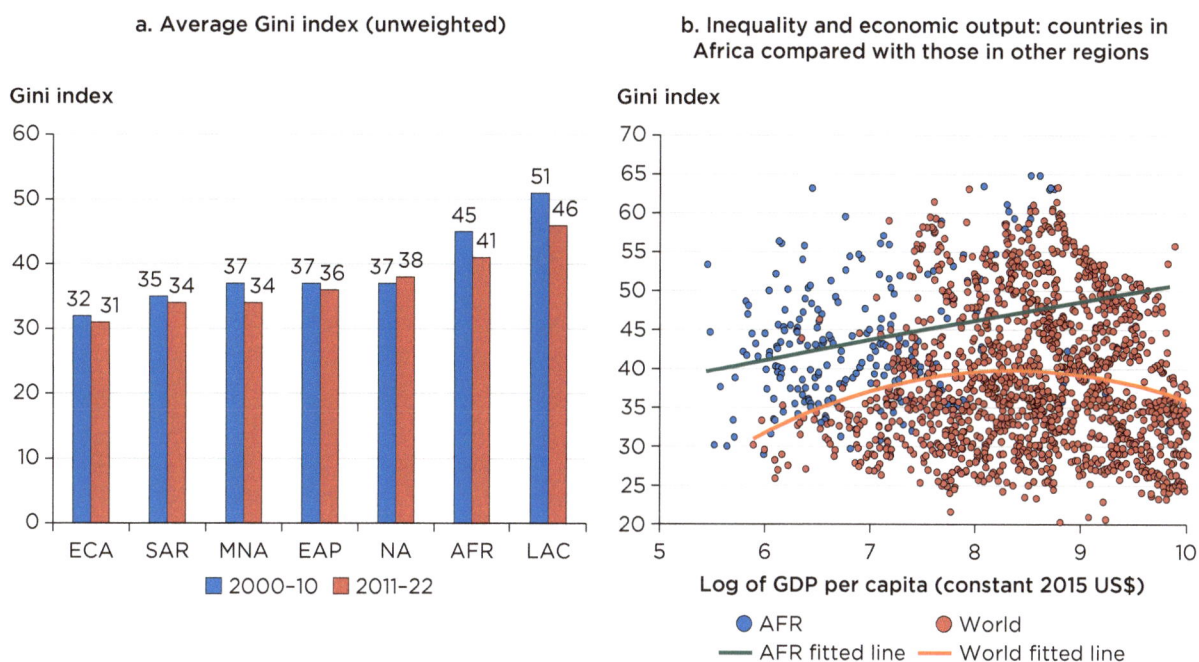

a. Average Gini index (unweighted)

Gini index

b. Inequality and economic output: countries in Africa compared with those in other regions

Gini index

Source: World Bank 2024.

Note: Figure 1.1b is a scatter plot of Gini indexes and logs of GDP per capita between 2000 and 2019. To focus on low- and middle-income countries, only observations with GDP per capita less than $14,000 (2015 US$) are included. The fitted lines reflect the best-fitting polymials of order 2 for the set of African countries and for all other countries. AFR = Sub-Saharan Africa; EAP = East Asia and the Pacific; ECA = Europe and Central Asia; GDP = gross domestic product; LAC = Latin America and the Caribbean; MNA = Middle East and North Africa; NA = North America; SAR = South Asia.

low- and middle-income countries is also reflected in figure 1.1b, which plots inequality levels against gross domestic product (GDP) per capita. Although there is country-specific variation, for a given level of GDP, inequality among countries in Africa is on average 10 Gini points higher than among countries in other regions with similar levels of economic output.

Inequality is associated with higher vulnerability to poverty, especially in the presence of shocks (refer to box 1.1), but, as detailed in this report, it also has significant implications for poverty reduction through growth. First, high inequality is detrimental to growth because it implies an inefficient allocation of resources and lower human capital accumulation and productivity. Even as inequality stifles growth, it also causes growth to become less effective in reducing poverty because large swaths of Africa's population are left out and unable to reinvest the growth into their productive activities. In addition, inequality has been shown to be highly persistent over time because it is associated with a lower degree of social mobility, further complicating Africa's poverty reduction prospects. Progress on the inclusion agenda in Africa will thus determine the success of global poverty reduction efforts in coming decades.

BOX 1.1

Inequality is persistent and reinforces poverty traps: Insights from the literature

Inequality is persistent

Lower intergenerational mobility, a direct consequence of high inequality of opportunity, has a mutually reinforcing relationship with income inequality (Corak 2016; Narayan et al. 2018). Capital market distortions are an important driver of this relationship. In the presence of credit constraints, high income inequality can lead to large differences in parents' investments in their children, which in turn cause income differences to persist or widen across generations.[a] Because wealth can be easily inherited, capital income is more correlated across generations than is labor income, reducing social mobility and widening income inequality. More generally, inequality affects the policies, institutions, and balance of power that shape the opportunities in a society. Unequal opportunities in turn lead to lower social mobility and higher inequality in the next generation (Corak 2013). Moreover, high inequality of opportunity and a lack of social mobility, particularly when the manifestations of these are acute and visible, can erode perceptions of fairness and trust in a society, affecting the social contract that supports growth and social stability.

High levels of inequality tend to amplify the distributional impacts of shocks, increasing the chances for poverty traps to worsen over time

A society with larger preexisting disparities in assets and opportunities is likely to experience more uneven impacts of a crisis, such as the COVID-19 pandemic of 2020, and a more unequal recovery process, with worse implications for poverty and inequality over time (Hill and Narayan 2020; Narayan et al. 2022). When crises occur, they tend to have a larger impact on households that have less access to markets, capital, and basic services (Dercon 2004; Hill and Porter 2017; Lybbert et al. 2004; Thirumurthy, Zivin, and Goldstein 2008). Thus, all other things being equal, crises tend to have larger welfare impacts in economies with greater inequality of opportunity. Because disadvantaged groups experience larger, longer-lasting shocks, they are also more likely to adopt coping mechanisms, such as incurring debt at high interest rates and reducing food intake, that are harmful to their future economic prospects (Hill, Skoufias, and Maher 2019). Preexisting inequalities can thus lead to a crisis having more unequal impacts on human capital formation and productivity. This, in turn, reduces social mobility across generations and causes disparities in income and wealth to widen over time. For example, during the COVID-19 pandemic, unequal access to continued learning during school closures by children from different socioeconomic backgrounds is projected to lead to a long-term decline in intergenerational mobility in low- and middle-income countries (Azevedo et al. 2023).

a. For overviews, see Loury (1981) and Piketty (2000, 2014).

Inequality varies substantially across the region but is particularly pronounced in resource-rich countries that do not suffer from fragility and conflict. On the one hand, most of the countries in Southern Africa are clustered at the top end, accounting for the eight countries with a Gini above 50 in the region (refer to figure 1.2a). On the other hand, countries in West Africa are clustered among the 23 countries with Gini levels below 40. Notably, no country in the region reports a Gini index below 30, compared with 31 countries in other regions.[5] Given the potential for long-term implications of fragility and natural resource wealth for the development and growth trajectories of many countries in Africa, this report groups countries into four distinct groups on the basis of their resource wealth and fragile and conflict-affected situation (FCS) status (refer to box 1.2). The mean Gini index for non-FCS resource-rich countries reached 53.5 in 2022 (refer to figure 1.2b), and expenditures in the top decile were more than 4 times higher than those in the poorest 40 percent (the Palma index—another income inequality metric—was 4.30; refer to figure 1.2c). The high level of inequality in these countries—and the fact that nearly 30 percent of their population remains in extreme poverty—suggests that the deleterious effects of resource reliance may be particularly pronounced in the region: Dutch disease and overreliance on imports result in low economic diversification, constraining economic growth and job opportunities. However, countries with FCS status have lower inequality, both in and outside Africa, likely reflecting the difficulty of capital accumulation in these contexts. Even in these countries, the top decile consumed approximately twice the total amount consumed by the poorest 40 percent.

FIGURE 1.2 Inequality by country, FCS, and resource-rich typologies

a. Inequality levels by country

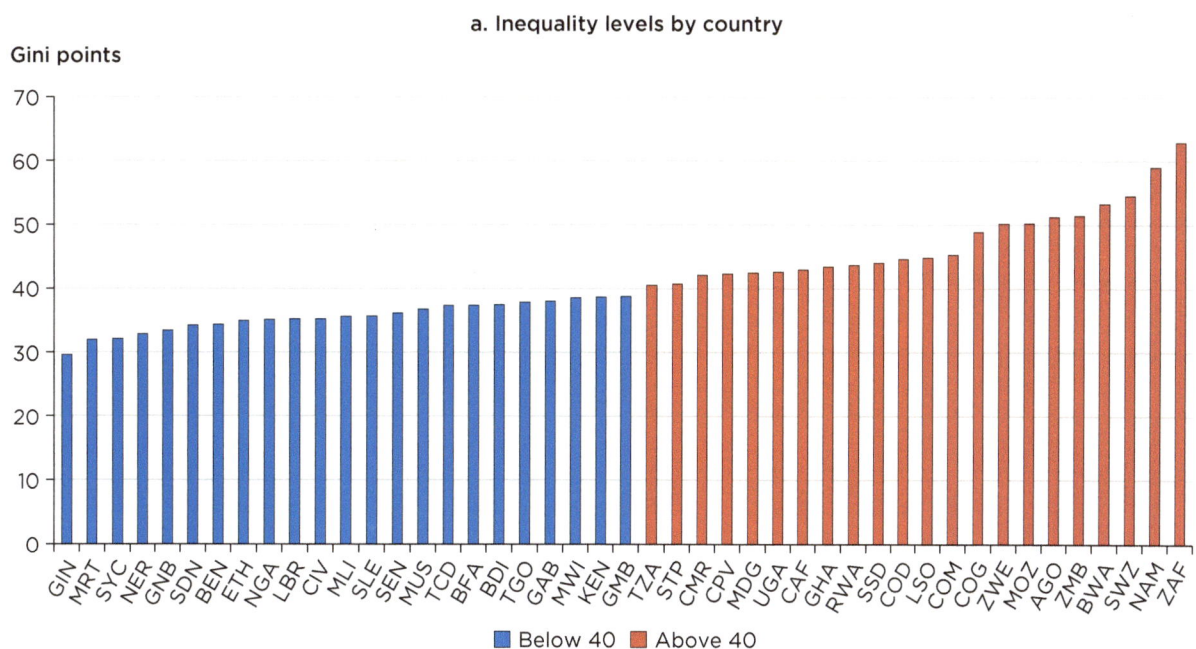

Gini points

Legend: ■ Below 40 ■ Above 40

(continued)

FIGURE 1.2 **Inequality by country, FCS, and resource-rich typologies** *(continued)*

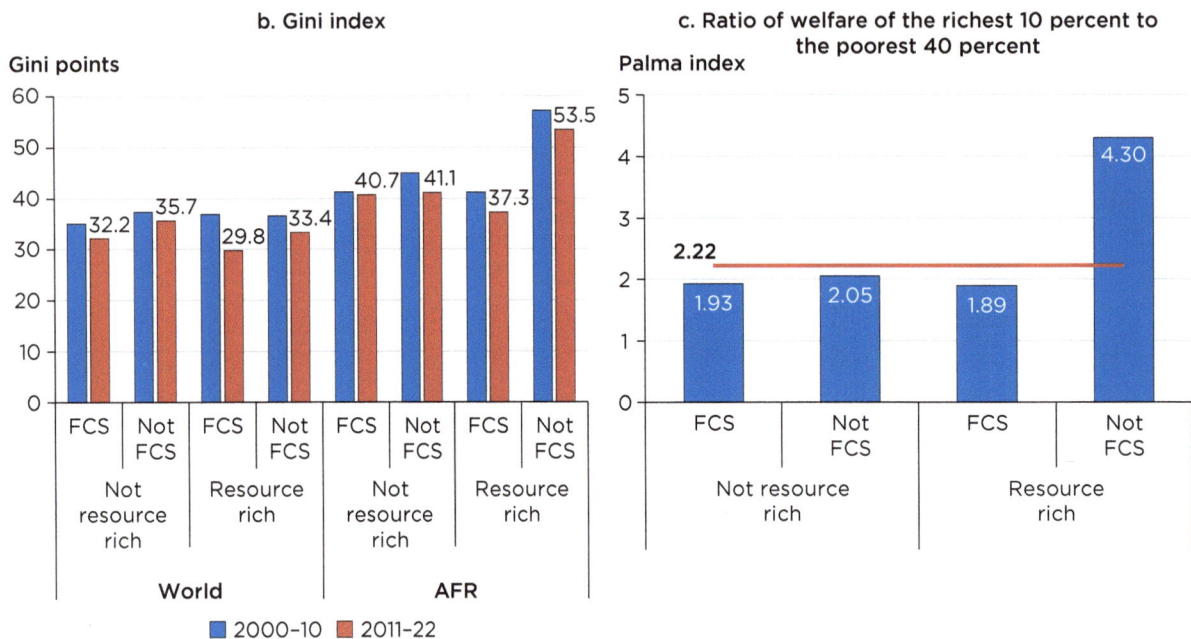

b. Gini index

Gini points

- World
  - Not resource rich: FCS 35.7 (2000–10), 32.2 (2011–22); Not FCS 35.7, 35.7
  - Resource rich: FCS 37.3 (2000–10), 29.8 (2011–22); Not FCS 33.4
- AFR
  - Not resource rich: FCS 40.7, 41.1; Not FCS
  - Resource rich: FCS 37.3; Not FCS 53.5

c. Ratio of welfare of the richest 10 percent to the poorest 40 percent

Palma index

- Not resource rich: FCS 1.93; Not FCS 2.05
- Resource rich: FCS 1.89; Not FCS 4.30
- 2.22 (reference line)

Legend: ■ 2000–10 ■ 2011–22

Source: World Bank 2024 and harmonized household survey data for African countries.
Note: AFR = Sub-Saharan Africa; FCS = countries that have ever experienced fragile and conflict-affected situations. For country abbreviations, refer to https://www.iso.org/obp/ui/#search.

BOX 1.2

Fragility traps and resource curses in Africa's growth and poverty trajectories

Two key characteristics have played a significant role in the different growth and development trends of countries in the region: fragility and natural resource wealth. As noted earlier, Africa is home to a disproportionate share of the world's countries in fragile and conflict-affected situations (FCS) (20 of 39 in 2023), and these countries are themselves home to a disproportionate share of the global poor. Fostering growth and poverty reduction in these contexts is particularly challenging; fragility and conflict have a significant impact on short-term economic growth and capital stock, and, critically, they are also highly persistent because countries can find themselves caught in a fragility trap, in which countries struggle to escape a slow-growth–poor-governance equilibrium (Andrimihaja, Cinyabuguma, and Devarajan 2011). A fragility trap is fed by political instability, violence, and corruption, including insecure property rights. These factors work together to hinder economic growth and development in fragile countries.

Although African countries are not disproportionately wealthy in natural resources compared with other regions, natural resource wealth has been associated with the resource curse in many countries in the region. *Resource curse* refers to the phenomenon whereby countries rich in natural resources, such as minerals, oil, or natural gas, experience negative economic and social outcomes instead of benefiting from their resource wealth. This can occur through a combination of factors—declining

(continued)

BOX 1.2

Fragility traps and resource curses in Africa's growth and poverty trajectories *(continued)*

terms of trade leading to reduced export revenues and high vulnerability to external price fluctuations; Dutch disease stifling economic diversification and job creation; high vulnerability of public revenues to volatility in commodity markets; weak linkages between resource sectors and the rest of the economy; and increased rent seeking that undermines institutional development and may fuel domestic conflict.[a] As a consequence, countries in Africa without resource wealth had higher per-worker growth rates than those with resource wealth, averaging 1.2 percent per year between 1960 and 2017, compared with 0.7 percent in countries with resource wealth (World Bank 2023b). This difference was driven by a significant increase in productivity, as measured by total factor productivity, in those countries without resource wealth, whereas those with resource wealth saw overall declines.

To better explore the extent to which these characteristics have affected trends in Africa, this report uses a categorization that interacts these two dimensions to create four categories (refer to figure B1.2.1). Resource-rich countries are home to 44 percent of the region's population. These 17 countries have rents from natural resources (excluding forests) that exceed 10 percent of gross domestic product over the past decade.[b] FCS status is defined as countries that were ever categorized as FCS by the World Bank between 2006 and 2023. This allows for the potential of long-term effects of the fragility trap even after the country technically exits conflict status. Thirty-one countries in the region are in this category, accounting for 72 percent of the population.

FIGURE B1.2.1 Typology and population share, based on fragility and resource wealth

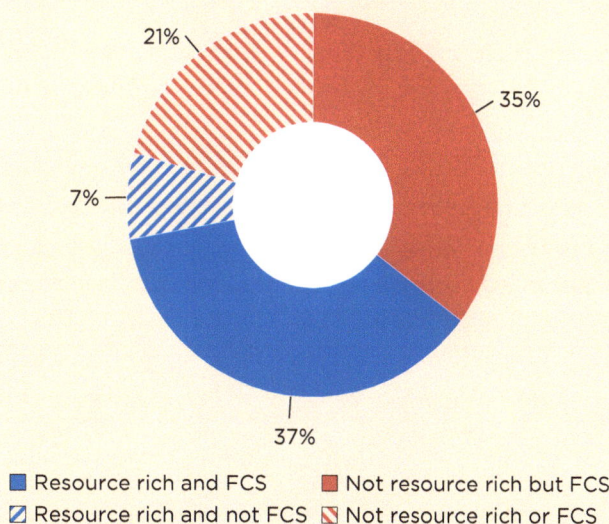

Sources: Tabulations based on World Bank 2023a, 2023b.
Note: FCS = fragile and conflict-affected situation.

a. See Badeeb, Lean, and Clark (2017) for a recent literature review.
b. This definition is based on Calderon (2022).

Structural inequality is a major constraint on Africa's economic growth and poverty reduction

Structural inequality, broadly defined, constitutes a major and multigenerational constraint on growth and poverty reduction in Africa. The concept of structural inequality goes beyond inequality of outcomes, such as income inequality. Rather, structural inequality is the extent to which differences in income across individuals are driven by the circumstances into which people are born and that are beyond their control, including the results of market and institutional distortions, as opposed to differences in individual talent or effort. A well-known example of structural inequality is what the literature refers to as inequality of opportunity, which is inequality between groups differentiated by inherited or unalterable characteristics, such as parental socioeconomic status, location of birth, ethnicity, religion, and gender. These differences lead to the accumulation of disparities in life and in the labor market. However, the concept of structural inequality extends beyond inequality of opportunity to market failures and frictions (Manuelyan Atinc et al. 2005) that systematically limit certain groups' access to higher-productivity income-generating opportunities with severe implications for the region's ability to tackle poverty and promote growth. Inherited circumstances interact with market distortions to create multigenerational cycles of exclusion and poverty—referred to as the *inequality trap* in *World Development Report 2006*—with significant economic costs both for households and for countries' economic prospects (Manuelyan Atinc et al. 2005).

A high degree of structural inequality has severe implications for growth and poverty reduction prospects in Africa. The economic literature provides evidence that sources of structural inequality not only serve to weaken the link between economic growth and improvements in household well-being but also significantly undermine economic growth itself (refer to box 1.3). In this report, three channels stand out as essential to understanding how roots of structural inequality have undermined poverty reduction in Africa. First, structural sources of inequality reduce the region's growth by constraining households' productive capacity and narrowing the pathway of upward mobility across generations. Second, structural sources of inequality have direct implications for the composition of the region's growth itself—in particular, Africa's lack of economic transformation is itself partly attributable to structural inequality. Third, the lower levels of households' productive capacity and economic transformation also undermine the efficiency of growth in reducing poverty. These three channels are discussed in more detail in chapter 2.

BOX 1.3

Sources of structural inequality reduce growth and weaken the link between growth and poverty reduction: Insights from the literature

Sources of structural inequality can weaken the link between economic growth and household well-being by perpetuating a cycle of low social mobility and inequality.[a] When opportunities strongly favor those with advantageous circumstances at birth, poverty and inequality are perpetuated across generations. A high degree of inequality of opportunity in childhood is linked to persistent differences in productivity and earnings, driven by inequality in human capital formation as well as unequal access to capital and jobs because of factor market distortions. This in turn leads to low intergenerational mobility, a well-known indicator of social mobility that is measured by the extent to which individuals' outcomes (such as income or education) are correlated with those of their parents, with a lower correlation indicating greater mobility. Empirical evidence shows that countries characterized by greater inequality of opportunity also tend to exhibit lower intergenerational mobility.

Sources of structural inequality can also adversely affect a country's growth trajectory by reinforcing inefficient allocation of resources. The economic literature theorizes that in economies with credit constraints that disproportionately affect poor individuals, low social mobility (or high inequality of opportunity) and economic growth tend to reinforce each other.[b] Intuitively, lower inequality of opportunity is good for growth in an economy because it leads to more efficient allocation of resources: individuals with higher innate abilities—rather than those who are privileged by birth circumstances—are more likely to obtain more education and more productive jobs. Policies to level the playing field are thus likely to be good for long-run growth as well, by reducing the inefficiencies due to misallocation of human and financial capital, the costs of which accumulate over generations.

Empirical evidence tends to confirm that inequality of opportunity that leads to lower social mobility is damaging to a country's long-term growth prospects. Studies show that realizing human potential by equalizing opportunities would increase the overall stock of human capital in a country, increasing long-term growth.[c] Inequality of opportunity may be particularly harmful to long-term growth because it discourages innovation and human capital investment, in contrast to inequality produced by differences in effort unrelated to circumstances at birth.[d] Cross-country regressions on a global dataset show that a certain cohort or generation being in the top quartile of economies through intergenerational mobility is associated with 10 percent higher gross domestic product (GDP) per capita when the generation reaches adulthood relative to being in the bottom quartile (Narayan et al. 2018).[e]

Moreover, perceptions of high inequality, and particularly inequality of opportunity, can erode support for pro-growth policies and macroeconomic discipline, and they pose a risk to social stability. Behavioral experiments show that people are highly averse to inequality they perceive as unfair (Fehr and Fischbacher 2003; Fleib 2015). Moreover, when expectations of future mobility are higher, people might be more likely to accept reforms that increase prosperity in the long run, but

(continued)

BOX 1.3

Sources of structural inequality reduce growth and weaken the link between growth and poverty reduction: insights from the literature *(continued)*

with some trade-off in inequality today (Benabou and Ok 2001).[f] Perceptions of low social mobility can also lower people's aspirations for the future and thus reduce investments in human capital, reinforcing the cycle of inequality of opportunity and lower growth. In its most extreme form, the vicious cycle of low perceived mobility and low aspirations can lead to marginalization and conflict (Esteban and Ray 1994).

a. In addition to having a negative impact on growth and weakening its impact on poverty reduction, structural inequality was found to be associated with a higher risk of internal armed conflict in low income countries (Ongo Nkoa et al. 2024) and lower subjective well-being (Becchetti et al. 2024).
b. See Narayan et al. (2018) and chapter 1, box 1.3, for an overview of the literature.
c. See, for example, Barro (2001) on the effects of the quantity and quality of schools and Grimm (2011) for an overview of the effects of children's health on long-term growth.
d. For evidence on the contrasting effects of circumstances at birth and effort—the two components of inequality—on growth in Brazil and the United States, see Teyssier (2013) and Marrero and Rodríguez (2013), respectively. Higher inequality of opportunity was also associated with lower growth in the future incomes of poor individuals in the United States between 1960 and 2010 (Marrero, Rodríguez, and van der Weide 2016).
e. This is based on regressions of (logarithm of) GDP or headcount poverty rates on measures of relative intergenerational mobility, at the time when the cohort was about 15 years old, controlling for lagged (log) GDP levels just before the individuals were born and economy or region-specific effects (see Narayan et al. 2018, chap. 3, for details). These results do not necessarily mean a causal relationship, but rather that economies with higher social mobility are also likely to subsequently have higher growth and poverty reduction.
f. This seems to be supported by empirical evidence in several countries (for example, Alesina, Stantcheva, and Teso 2018; Gaviria, Graham, and Braido 2007).

Structural inequality accounts for a large share of income inequality in Africa

Measuring the extent to which structural inequality affects individual outcomes is not straightforward, but estimating inequality of opportunity provides a partial answer. This approach is to decompose observed inequality in the distribution of welfare (consumption) into the part that can be attributed, in a statistical sense, to predetermined circumstances and the part that cannot. This is how inequality of opportunity has often been measured, namely, by quantifying the portion of inequality in per capita consumption that can be attributed to circumstances at birth, including a person's race, gender, ethnicity, place of birth, and parents' level of education. The measure also captures the combined effects of structural inequality across different dimensions for individuals with a set of predetermined circumstances at all stages of the income generation process. It is important to recognize that inequality of opportunity estimated in this manner is likely to underestimate the extent of structural inequality in a society, for reasons that are explained later. The measure, however, still serves as a useful barometer of structural inequality in society for a given set of commonly observable circumstances.

Inequality of opportunity, even when measured with a limited set of circumstances (that likely result in an underestimate), drives overall inequality in Africa. As shown in figure 1.3a, in 13 of 18 analyzed countries in Africa, circumstances at birth (ethnicity, religion, place of birth, parents' level of education, and sector of employment) explain at least half of overall inequality in consumption (Atamanov et al. 2024). Overall, these circumstances explain 26–74 percent of overall inequality in different countries. Inequality of opportunity was lowest in Ethiopia and highest in South Africa. For other countries, inequality of opportunity ranged between 41 and 64 percent. This is higher than many previous estimates for Africa (see, for example, Brunori, Palmisano, and Peragine 2019) and highlights the outsized role of birth circumstances in driving inequality in Africa. Cross-regional comparison suggests that inequality of opportunity in Africa is broadly in the same range as that in Latin America and South Asia, although further evidence is needed, and it is notably higher than in Southeast Asia, Central Asia, and high-income countries (Ferreira et al. 2018). Other analysis using comparable methods has shown that inequality of opportunity is much higher in Africa than in Europe, where it never exceeds 15 percent (Brunori, Palmisano, and Peragine 2019).

FIGURE 1.3 Inequality of opportunity

a. Share of inequality explained by circumstances at birth

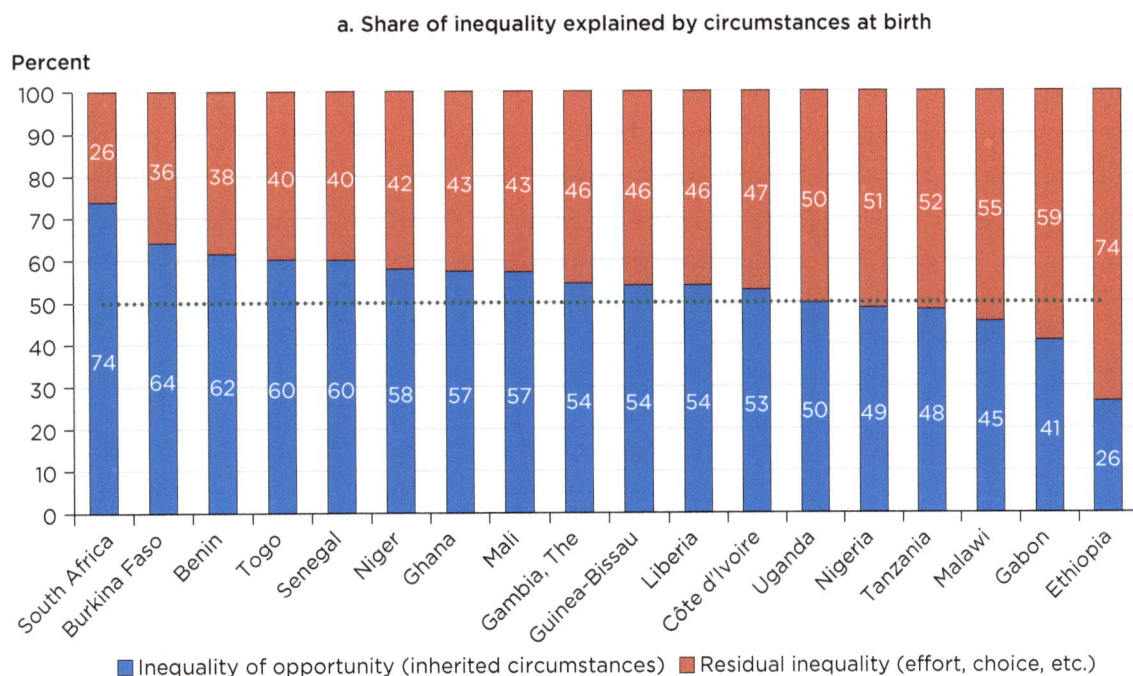

Inequality of opportunity (inherited circumstances) ■ Residual inequality (effort, choice, etc.)

(continued)

FIGURE 1.3 Inequality of opportunity *(continued)*

b. importance of each circumstance for consumption

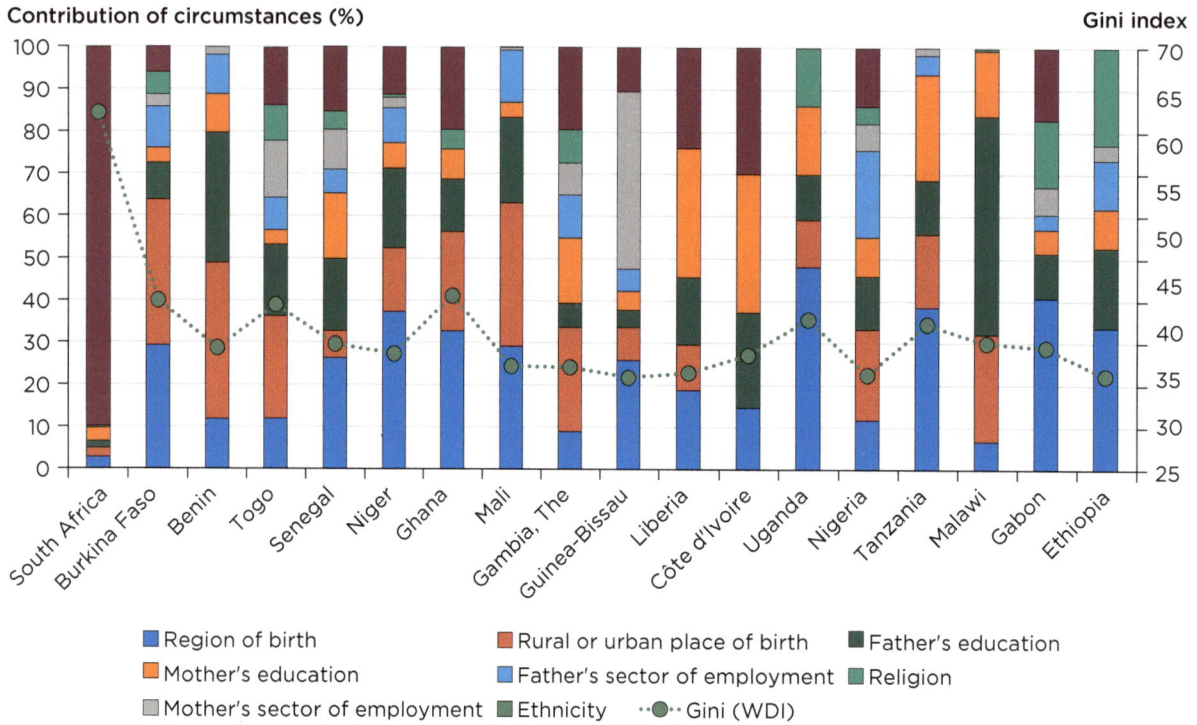

Contribution of circumstances (%) — Gini index

Sources: World Bank tabulations based on household surveys in Atamanov et al. (2024).
Note: In panel a, dotted line indicates 50 percent. For details on the methodology and surveys used, see annex 1.1. Gini is from WDI for the survey year, or if not available, for the most recent year. WDI = World Development Indicators.

Although birthplace is the most relevant circumstance in predicting consumption, there is some variation across countries. Figure 1.3b shows the importance of each circumstance for predicting consumption inequality across countries (Atamanov et al. 2024). Averaging the importance of each factor across countries gives a snapshot of the circumstances most closely associated with household welfare levels. Thus, region of birth is the most important circumstance, followed by ethnicity, although in South Africa this is driven heavily by race. The next circumstances in importance are place of birth (urban versus rural) and father's and mother's education. There is some variation in which circumstances are the most important across countries. Region and place of birth are the most important circumstances in Mali and Burkina Faso. In Malawi, though, father's education is the most important circumstance; mother's education is important in Liberia, Tanzania, and Uganda, and mother's sector of employment is important in Guinea-Bissau. Ethnicity is the second most important circumstance in Côte d'Ivoire and Liberia, as is the case with religion in Ethiopia.[6]

Although these results are useful to illustrate how significant inequality of opportunity is for countries in Africa, they should not be seen as accurate measures of the extent of structural inequality. First, these estimates are not complete measures of inequality of opportunity; it is likely that other circumstances are significant for inequality of opportunity in a particular country but are not included in the measure because of data limitations and the need for a common set of circumstances across countries to enable comparisons. The estimates are thus best seen as lower bounds of the extent of inequality of opportunity in a country and are used for comparison across countries only for the common set of circumstances. Second, the concept of structural inequality goes beyond inequality of opportunity, as explained earlier. Distortions in markets and institutions could lead to inequality in consumption beyond what is reflected in differences by birth circumstances, which are not captured by this measure. For instance, the measure may not capture structural inequality because of the monopsonistic power of large firms that can pay low wages, unrelated to workers' effort or talent, to certain groups of workers with low bargaining power. More generally, to the extent that market distortions lead to an unequal playing field, structural inequality in people's incomes may emerge because of unequal opportunities to use their productive capacities, even in a hypothetical world with no inequality in acquiring productive capacities and skills, in forms that are not associated with birth circumstances. Finally, to the extent that inequality in opportunities and market and institutional distortions can be compounded by fiscal policies, some but not all fiscal interventions are captured in this measure. Consumption, like disposable income, includes the impact of direct taxes and transfers, but not the impact of indirect taxes and subsidies.

Unlocking Africa's potential for accelerated poverty reduction requires addressing structural inequality

Sources of structural inequality act as a major constraint on poverty reduction in Africa through several channels. First, sources of structural inequality lead to wasted human potential, underused productive capacity, and misallocation of resources that affect the long-term trajectory of growth. Second, sources of structural inequality affect the nature and composition of growth in such a way as to weaken the link between economic growth and average household welfare. Third, income inequality arising from structural inequality affects the pace of poverty reduction by lowering the responsiveness of incomes at the bottom of the income distribution to growth in average household welfare. Moreover, perceptions of unequal opportunity, or "fairness" in particular, can weaken the social contract, eroding public support for policies needed for growth and increasing the risk of social instability. Finally, high levels of inequality tend to amplify the regressive distributional impacts of shocks, leading to lower social mobility and more persistent poverty traps over time.

To help identify the policy priorities to realize Africa's potential for accelerated poverty reduction, this report uses a triple-pronged policy framework (refer to figure 1.4). These three prongs should not be interpreted as sequential steps in an individual's life cycle or in the policy-making process. Rather, the three prongs are an analytical construct that facilitates unpacking the various dimensions of structural inequality that affect the income generation process. These prongs interact with each other in multidirectional,

FIGURE 1.4 Triple-pronged policy framework to level the playing field and accelerate growth and poverty reduction

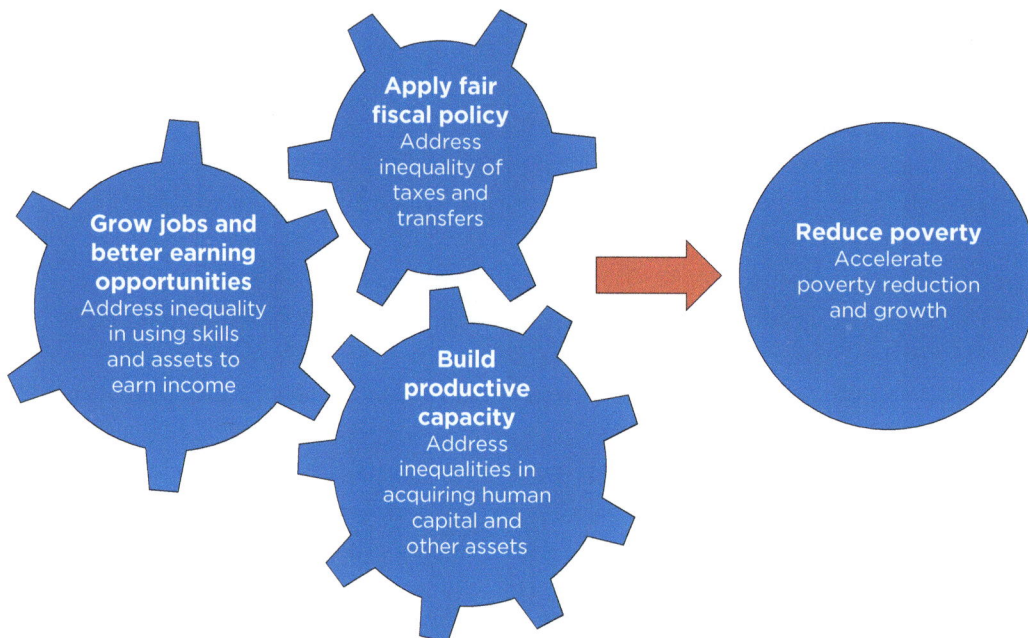

Apply fair fiscal policy
Address inequality of taxes and transfers

Grow jobs and better earning opportunities
Address inequality in using skills and assets to earn income

Build productive capacity
Address inequalities in acquiring human capital and other assets

Reduce poverty
Accelerate poverty reduction and growth

Source: Original figure for this publication.

complex ways that in turn call for policies that take these interactions into account. The three dimensions of the policy framework are defined as follows:

- *Build productive capacity.* Structural inequality in this first dimension is the extent to which differences in productive endowments (such as education and land) across individuals are driven by the circumstances into which people are born and that are beyond their control, as opposed to differences in individual talents or efforts. Chapter 3 examines the nature of disparities in these opportunities through the lens of children to analyze the structural drivers of inequality at this stage.[7] Human capital formation is a substantial part of this opportunity, given its impact on productive capacity. Policies in this dimension would foster endowments, opportunities, and investments that would improve individuals' productive potential.

- *Grow jobs and better earning opportunities.* Structural inequality in this dimension is the income inequality that arises because of market and institutional distortions that affect the performance of workers, firms, and farms and in turn affect the number of good jobs created. These distortions can amplify the effects of structural inequality in building productive capacities, leading to higher income inequality. Distortions also lead to a greater misallocation of resources that is detrimental to growth. Chapter 4 delves into the income inequalities that arise when people engage with markets in the presence of institutional and market imperfections, which leads to policy entry points linked to the microfoundations of firm and farm behavior. Policies in this dimension aim to make markets and institutions function better for firms and farms and thereby foster the creation of well-paying job opportunities.

- *Apply fair fiscal policy.* Structural inequality in this dimension is the extent to which taxes and spending reinforce inequalities in the other dimensions. Chapter 5 focuses on this topic to examine how the system of taxes, benefits, and subsidies can reinforce or reduce inequality and poverty associated with the structural inequalities encountered in the first two prongs. Policies in this dimension would foster redistribution and the protection of poor and vulnerable households. People, firms, and farms also respond to taxes and spending instruments, which implies that the policies in this prong influence those in the other two prongs.

The three prongs of the policy framework are interrelated because actions taken at any stage will have consequences for the other stages. This is most obvious for inequalities in the first prong, which affect the accumulation of capital (human and physical) that influences the distribution of income generated in the job market, which in turn influences taxes collected and subsequent public spending, and thus affects the ability of a society to equitably build and use productive capacities. However, it is equally true when considering inequalities created by tax and benefit policies, which lead to incentives and distortions for workers, firms, and farms that affect investments and outcomes in both building and using productive capacities.

The framework accommodates policies that shape growth and the transmission of growth to poverty reduction. This is because the process of economic growth and its link to people's well-being are products of macroeconomic conditions that interact with a range of microeconomic factors pertaining to households, farms, and firms. Households' earnings are a function of their assets (financial, human, and natural), the rate of utilization of these assets (employment), and returns on assets (wages, profits, and rents). Earnings are generated by farms and firms that make use of human capital and other productive inputs while accessing product and factor markets. These processes are in turn strongly influenced by the sources of structural inequality discussed earlier in this chapter. Income growth and the distribution of growth are therefore jointly determined, to a significant extent, by the drivers of structural inequality.

As the subsequent chapters show, structural inequality in Africa is driven by a wide-ranging set of factors that require a multisectoral perspective to address. These factors include market failures (such as in land and credit), inadequate and inequitable public investment (in education, health, and infrastructure), lack of market size (low population density, lack of market integration), and high and uninsurable risks (including climate change and conflict). Moreover, the scope for using fiscal redistribution policies to close welfare gaps produced at the earlier stages is limited, given the scale of needs relative to the fiscal space that is available in most countries. Reducing welfare gaps therefore requires addressing the drivers of inequality in building and using productive capacities and cannot solely rely on fiscal redistribution. This in turn requires policies and institutions to be guided by objectives that are overlapping and mutually reinforcing—promoting fairness to create a level playing field and enhancing the region's productive capacity. Identifying and prioritizing these policies, this report argues, will promote both equity and prosperity as opposed to trading one for the other.

Road map for the report

The rest of this report is structured as follows. Chapter 2 describes the challenge of poverty reduction in Africa, leveraging the latest available data for the region. This is followed by a spotlight on climate, given the region's exposure and vulnerability to climate events and their link to poverty. Chapter 3 is dedicated to the first prong in the framework presented in this chapter, focusing on structural inequality in building productive capacity. This is followed by a spotlight on gender, given that girls and women often do not enjoy the same opportunities as their male counterparts. Chapter 4 focuses on the second prong of the framework, analyzing structural sources of inequality in using productive capacity, which could pave the way for job growth and better earnings opportunities. This is followed by a spotlight on fragility and conflict in the region and how they affect poverty and well-being. Chapter 5 focuses on the third prong of the framework and analyzes the distributional impact of fiscal policy. This is followed by a spotlight on public debt, outlining the tight fiscal conditions in the region. Chapter 6 concludes, bringing together lessons learned from successful episodes of poverty and inequality reduction in six countries and outlining policy actions across the three policy prongs to tackle structural inequality and accelerate poverty reduction.

Annex 1A: Measuring inequality of opportunity

Estimating an ex ante measure of inequality of opportunity requires two preliminary steps. The first step is to identify the outcome variable and the circumstances that are beyond individual control. The second step is to manipulate the original distribution of the outcome variable, thereby obtaining the counterfactual distribution that reflects inequality of opportunity (Brunori 2016). The selected outcome should satisfy the condition of being equally desirable for all individuals. The typical outcome in the empirical literature is income or consumption, the preferred measures of individual economic well-being.[8] The choice of circumstances is driven by data availability and may include gender, age, ethnicity, race, region of birth, or parental background, which are beyond an individual's control but exogenously affect income-generating capacity.

Once the outcome variable and circumstances are selected, the share of overall inequality related to circumstances needs to be estimated. This is done in two steps. First, the expected outcome is estimated conditional on circumstances, and its inequality will be a measure of inequality of opportunities. The inequality is measured either by mean logarithmic deviation (MLD) or by Gini index.[9] Given that available data often contain only a subset of all circumstances affecting opportunity, there is always an issue of omitted circumstance variables. Therefore, inequality of opportunity estimates are often viewed as lower-bound estimators of the true inequality of opportunity—that is, the inequality that would be captured by observing the full vector of circumstances. Inequality of opportunity estimates can be shown in absolute values or in relative terms as a share of total inequality.

Inequality of economic opportunity has been measured for all world regions, with growing evidence for Africa. For example, Brunori et al. (2019) estimated inequality of opportunity in 10 African countries using 13 household budget surveys conducted in 2003–13. The following circumstances were used: birthplace, parental education, parental occupation, and ethnicity. These circumstances were responsible for about half the observed inequalities in consumption. Ferreira et al. (2018) combined 117 income and expenditure household surveys and 134 Demographic and Health Surveys (DHS), which used wealth index as an outcome, across 42 countries to study the relationship between inequality of opportunity and economic growth. The Africa region was represented by 20 countries, mostly by DHS surveys. Circumstance variables included gender, race, language, ethnicity, birthplace, disability, and immigrant status but did not include parental characteristics. Relative inequality of opportunity ranged from 2 percent to 40 percent. Sulla, Zikhali, and Cuevas (2022) estimated inequality of opportunity for consumption and earnings for five African countries from the Southern African Customs Union using gender, age, and region of residence as circumstances. Relative inequality of opportunity estimates ranged from 12 percent to 22 percent for earnings and from 15 percent to 26 percent for consumption. Race and parental background were included for South Africa, and the inequality of opportunity estimate was much larger, mostly explained by race. Inequality of opportunity has increased over time in all countries except Namibia.

The analysis in this report is conducted for 18 countries in Africa between 2012 and 2019, including countries across West, East, and Southern Africa and large countries from a population point of view, such as Ethiopia, Nigeria, South Africa, Tanzania, and Uganda (table 1A.1). The following circumstances were used across countries: region of birth, birthplace, urban or rural status, parental education, parental industry, religion, and ethnicity (race, in the case of South Africa). Parental education and parental industry were harmonized across countries so that similar categories were defined in the same way. Although most circumstances are not available for every country, we selected these countries with the condition that they all had region of birth and parental education available. These are two of the most important circumstances for inequality of opportunity, and this reflects a large improvement in the available data relative to previous attempts to estimate inequality of opportunity in Africa. We use household consumption per capita as our outcome. To estimate inequality of opportunity, we use a machine learning method that identifies the role of circumstances in a way that requires less ad hoc model selection by the researcher and has been shown to produce more reliable estimates (refer to Atamanov, Cuevas, and Lebow 2024 for details).

TABLE 1A.1 List of surveys used to calculate inequality of opportunity in Sub-Saharan Africa

Country	Year	Survey
Benin	2018–19	Enquête Harmonisée sur le Conditions de Vie des Ménages
Burkina Faso	2018–19	Enquête Harmonisée sur le Conditions de Vie des Ménages
Côte d'Ivoire	2018–19	Enquête Harmonisée sur le Conditions de Vie des Ménages
Ethiopia	2018–19	Ethiopia Socioeconomic Survey
Gabon	2017	Enquête Gabonaise pour l'Évaluation de la Pauvreté
Gambia, The	2015–16	Integrated Household Survey
Ghana	2016–17	Ghana Living Standard Survey
Guinea-Bissau	2018–19	Enquête Harmonisée sur le Conditions de Vie des Ménages
Liberia	2016	Household Income and Expenditure Survey
Malawi	2019–20	Integrated Household Survey
Mali	2018–19	Enquête Harmonisée sur le Conditions de Vie des Ménages
Niger	2018–19	Enquête Harmonisée sur le Conditions de Vie des Ménages
Nigeria	2018–19	Living Standards Survey
Senegal	2018–19	Enquête Harmonisée sur le Conditions de Vie des Ménages
South Africa	2017	National Income Dynamics Study
Tanzania	2017–18	Household Budget Survey
Togo	2018–19	Enquête Harmonisée sur le Conditions de Vie des Ménages
Uganda	2012–13	Uganda National Panel Survey

FIGURE 1A.1 Inequality of opportunity using full or comparable lists of circumstances

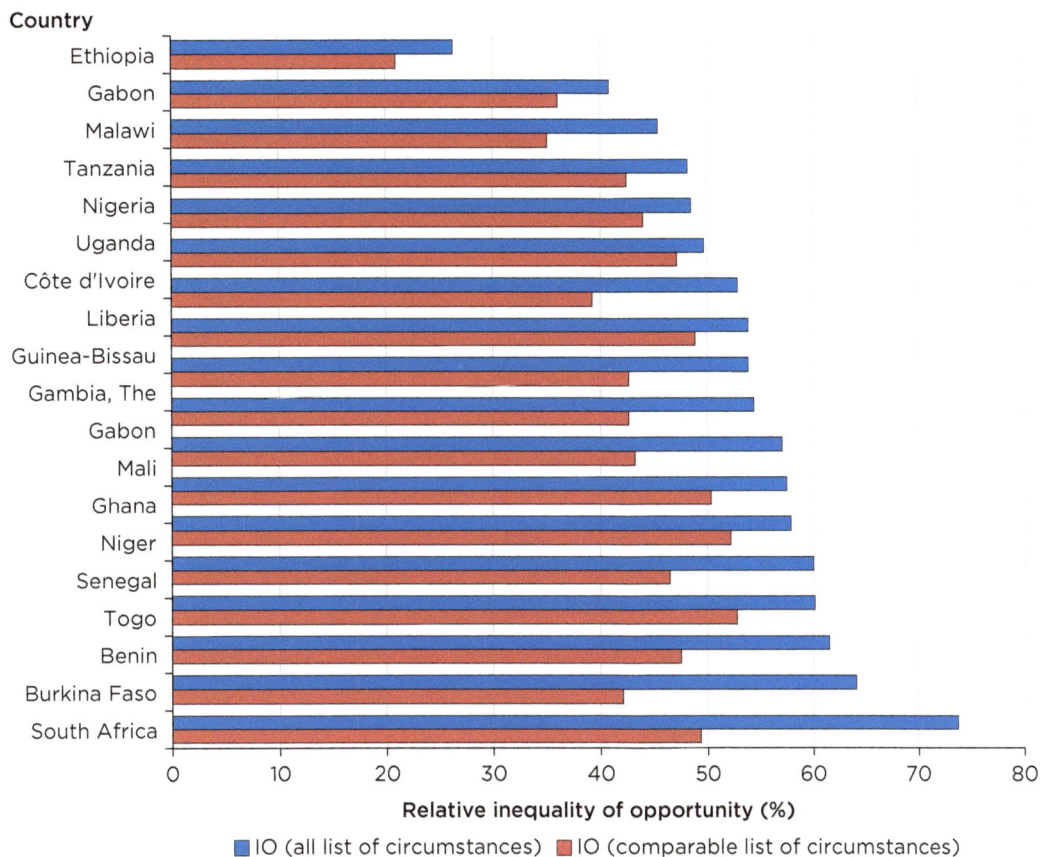

Source: World Bank staff estimates based on household budget surveys.

Note: IO = inequality of opportunity.

Annex 1B: Decomposing inequality of household welfare

This decomposition of inequality in household welfare is based on the methodology of Fields (2003).[10] This methodology is based on a standard income-generating function wherein the log of the outcome of interest (per capita welfare, measured most often by expenditures or consumption) is regressed on a series of household characteristics associated with household welfare. The main drivers of inequality are thus identified on the basis of the contributions of these explanatory variables (such as education, labor market factors, and demographics).

Specifically, the baseline specification of

$$\Delta Log\,(y_i) = \beta \boldsymbol{X}_i + \epsilon_i \tag{1}$$

can be rewritten as a linear model of the form

$$y = \beta_0 + z_1 + z_2 + z_3 + \cdots + z_k + \epsilon, \tag{2}$$

where y_i is household per capita welfare, $\boldsymbol{X}_i$ is a matrix of k household characteristics (including characteristics of the household head or main earner), and z_n is the product of the regression coefficient and the associated variable. Equation 2 is of the same form as that used in Shorrocks (1982) for derivation of the rules for decomposing inequality across factors. Fields (2003) applies Shorrocks's decomposition rule to calculate the contributions of each factor to the inequality of y.

Two approaches are used to calculate the decomposition:

$$y = b_0 + \widehat{z_1} + \widehat{z_2} + \widehat{z_3} + \ldots + \widehat{z_k} + \widehat{\epsilon_1} \tag{3}$$

and

$$\widehat{y} = b_0 + \widehat{z_1} + \widehat{z_2} + \widehat{z_3} + \ldots + \widehat{z_k} \tag{4}$$

Equation 4 models the fitted value of y and hence has no residuals, whereas equation 3 estimates the share of the variable that is unexplained by the factors (that is, the residuals). Chapter 1 includes results from both sets of regressions (with and without the residuals).

Both regressions are run for each of the 43 countries with recent survey data. The results of the decomposition are averaged across countries for the regional aggregate and for the subset of countries for the results by typology.

The factors considered in this analysis include the following:

- *Human capital*: age of household head; gender of household head; whether the household head achieved primary education, secondary education, or tertiary education.

- *Location*: Region or province, rural or urban dummy variables.

- *Household demographics*: share of household members who are children; share of household members who are elderly.

- *Labor market*: sector of employment of household head (industry, service) and head not working (out of labor force or unemployed).

Notes

1. Throughout this report, *Africa* refers to *Sub-Saharan Africa*.
2. Per the 2024 World Bank Scorecard (World Bank 2023c).
3. This refers to the unweighted average of Gini indices of all countries in the region with available data, using the latest survey year for each country during 2011–19. Comparisons across regions come with a significant caveat: inequality in Latin America and the Caribbean is measured on the basis of income (as opposed to consumption or expenditure), and income yields higher inequality. Hence, the difference in levels of inequality between Africa and Latin America and the Caribbean is likely overstated.

4. This estimate is based on a Commitment to Equity analysis of prefiscal inequality, as detailed in chapter 5. Note that these estimates of inequality are likely to be underestimates because household surveys typically do not have good coverage of those who earn very high incomes.

5. Based on Poverty and Inequality Platform (October 2024).

6. A limitation of this approach is that cross-country comparisons of inequality of opportunity are constrained by the availability of data measuring similar circumstance variables across countries. Moreover, variables such as ethnicity and religion have different groups across countries. Inequality of opportunity estimates focusing on variables measured in the same way for every country (birthplace and parental education) are more comparable, with inequality of opportunity remaining high, accounting for 35–53 percent of total inequality for all countries excluding Ethiopia (refer to annex A, figure 1A.1). The ranking between countries is only loosely preserved, with a Spearman correlation coefficient equal to 0.87 and significantly different from zero. Notably, South Africa falls to seventh place once race is excluded. The top six countries are all in West Africa. Ethiopia, Gabon, and Mali remain the countries with the lowest estimates.

7. Prongs 1 and 2 are not perfectly separable, but a broad distinction between them is still useful for a clearer policy discussion. For example, in prong 2, individuals continue accumulating productive capacity through continued accumulation of work experience and other different forms of capital.

8. However, many other measures of inequality of opportunity exist, including access to education, basic infrastructure, health outcomes, and so forth; we discuss these in chapter 3.

9. Mean logarithmic deviation is fully decomposable but sensitive to extreme values and not bounded. Gini is bounded, less sensitive to outliers, but is not perfectly decomposable.

10. This methodological note is also informed by Fiorio and Jenkins (2007), following Fields (2003).

References

Alesina, Alberto, Stefanie Stantcheva, and Edoardo Teso. 2018. "Intergenerational Mobility and Preferences for Redistribution." *American Economic Review* 108 (2): 521–54.

Andrimihaja, Noro Aina, Matthias M. Cinyabuguma, and Shantayanan Devarajan. 2011. "Avoiding the Fragility Trap in Africa." Policy Research Working Paper 5884, World Bank, Washington, DC.

Atamanov, Aziz, Pablo Facundo Cuevas, Jeremy Aaron Lebow, and Daniel Gerszon Mahler. 2024. "New Evidence on Inequality of Opportunity in Sub-Saharan Africa: More Unequal Than We Thought." Policy Research Working Paper 10723, World Bank, Washington, DC. http://documents .worldbank.org/curated/en/099558203182421649/IDU1a3c568111b02514f9d19e221936be7486403.

Azevedo, João Pedro, Alexandru Cojocaru, Veronica Talledo, and Ambar Narayan. 2023. "COVID-19 School Closures, Learning Losses and Intergenerational Mobility." Policy Research Working Paper 10381, World Bank, Washington, DC. http://hdl.handle.net/10986/39607.

Badeeb, Ramez A., Hooi H. Lean, and Jeremy Clark. 2017. "The Evolution of the Natural Resource Curse Thesis: A Critical Literature Survey." *Resources Policy* 51: 123–34.

Barro, Robert J. 2001. "Human Capital and Growth." *American Economic Review* 91 (2): 12–17.

Becchetti, Leonardo, Francesco Colcerasa, Vitorocco Peragine, and Fabio Pisani. 2024. "Inequality of Opportunity and Life Satisfaction." *Oxford Economic Papers*, gpae011. https://doi.org/10.1093/oep /gpae011.

Benabou, Roland, and Efe A. Ok. 2001. "Social Mobility and the Demand for Redistribution: The POUM Hypothesis." *Quarterly Journal of Economics* 116 (2): 447–87.

Brunori, Paolo. 2016. "How to Measure Inequality of Opportunity: A Hands-On Guide." LCC Working Paper 2016-04, Institute for Social Science Research, University of Queensland, Indooroopilly, Queensland, Australia.

Brunori, Paolo, Flaviana Palmisano, and Vitorocco Peragine. 2019. "Inequality of Opportunity in Sub-Saharan Africa." *Applied Economics* 51 (60): 6428–58.

Calderon, Cesar. 2022. *Boosting Productivity in Sub-Saharan Africa: Policies and Institutions to Promote Efficiency*. Washington, DC: World Bank. http://hdl.handle.net/10986/36786.

Corak, Miles. 2013. "Income Inequality, Equality of Opportunity, and Intergenerational Mobility." *Journal of Economic Perspectives* 27 (3): 79–102.

Corak, Miles. 2016. "How Much Social Mobility? More, but Not Without Other Things." In *The US Labor Market: Questions and Challenges for Public Policy*, edited by Michael R. Strain, 2–13. Washington, DC: American Enterprise Institute.

Dercon, Stefan. 2004. "Growth and Shocks: Evidence from Rural Ethiopia." *Journal of Development Economics* 74 (2): 309–29.

Esteban, Joan-Maria, and Debraj Ray. 1994. "On the Measurement of Polarization." *Econometrica: Journal of the Econometric Society* 62 (4): 819–51.

Fehr, Ernst, and Urs Fischbacher. 2003. "The Nature of Human Altruism." *Nature* 425 (6960): 785.

Ferreira, Francisco H. G., Christoph Lakner, Maria Ana Lugo, and Berk Özler, B. 2018. "Inequality of Opportunity and Economic Growth: How Much Can Cross-Country Regressions Really Tell Us?" *Review of Income and Wealth* 64 (4): 800–827.

Fields, Gary S. 2003. "Accounting for Income Inequality and Its Change: A New Method, With Application to the Distribution of Earnings in the United States." In *Worker Well-Being and Public Policy*, edited by S. W. Polachek, 1–38. Vol. 22 of *Research in Labor Economics*. Bingley, UK: Emerald Group Publishing. https://doi.org/10.1016/S0147-9121(03)22001-X.

Fleib, Jurgen. 2015. "Merit Norms in the Ultimatum Game: An Experimental Study of the Effect of Merit on Individual Behavior and Aggregate Outcomes." *Central European Journal of Operations Research* 23 (2): 389–406.

Fiorio, Carlo V., and Stephen P. Jenkins. 2007. "ineqrbd: Regression-Based Inequality Decomposition." PowerPoint presentation. https://www.stata.com/meeting/13uk/fiorio_ineqrbd_UKSUG07.pdf

Gaviria, Alejandro, Carol Graham, and Luis H. B. Braido. 2007. "Social Mobility and Preferences for Redistribution in Latin America." *Economía* 8 (1): 55–96.

Grimm, Michael. 2011. "Does Inequality in Health Impede Economic Growth?" *Oxford Economic Papers* 63 (3): 448–74.

Hill, Ruth Vargas, and Ambar Narayan. 2020. "Covid-19 and Inequality: A Review of the Evidence on Likely Impact and Policy Options." Working Paper 3, Centre for Disaster Protection, London.

Hill, Ruth Vargas, and Catherine Porter. 2017. "Vulnerability to Drought and Food Price Shocks: Evidence from Ethiopia." *World Development* 96: 65–77.

Hill, Ruth, Emmanuel Skoufias, and Barry Maher. 2019. *The Chronology of a Disaster: A Review and Assessment of the Value of Acting Early on Household Welfare*. Washington, DC: World Bank. http://hdl.handle.net/10986/31721.

Loury, Glenn C. 1981. "Intergenerational Transfers and the Distribution of Earnings." *Econometrica* 49 (4): 843–67.

Lybbert, Travis J., Christopher B. Barrett, Solomon Desta, and D. Layne Coppock. 2004. "Stochastic Wealth Dynamics and Risk Management among a Poor Population." *Economic Journal* 114 (498): 750–77.

Manuelyan Atinc, Tamar, Abhijit Banerjee, Francisco H. G. Ferreira, Peter F. Lanjouw, Marta Menendez, Berk Ozler, Giovanna Prennushi, Vijayendra Rao, James Robinson, Michael Walton, and Michael Woolcock. 2005. *World Development Report 2006: Equity and Development*. Washington, DC: World Bank. http://documents.worldbank.org/curated /en/435331468127174418/World-development-report-2006-equity-and-development.

Marrero, Gustavo A., and Juan G. Rodríguez. 2013. "Inequality of Opportunity and Growth." *Journal of Development Economics* 104: 107–22.

Marrero, Gustavo A., Juan Gabriel Rodríguez, and Roy van der Weide. 2016. "Unequal Opportunity, Unequal Growth." Policy Research Working Paper 7853, World Bank, Washington, DC. http://documents.worldbank.org/curated/en/473031476192890227/Unequal-opportunity -unequal-growth.

Narayan, Ambar, Alexandru Cojocaru, Sarthak Agrawal, Tom Bundervoet, Maria Davalos, Natalia Garcia, Christoph Lakner, Daniel Mahler, Veronica Talledo, Andrey Ten, and Nishant Yonzan. 2022. "COVID-19 and Economic Inequality: Short-Term Impacts with Long-Term Consequences." Policy Research Working Paper 9902, World Bank, Washington, DC. https://documents1 .worldbank.org/curated/en/219141642091810115/pdf/COVID-19-and-Economic-Inequality-Short -Term-Impacts-with-Long-Term-Consequences.pdf.

Narayan, Ambar, Roy van der Weide, Alexandru Cojocaru, Christoph Lakner, Silvia Redaelli, Daniel G. Mahler, Rakesh G. N. Ramasubbaiah, and Stefan Thewissen. 2018. *Fair Progress? Economic Mobility across Generations around the World*. Washington, DC: World Bank.

Ongo Nkoa, Bruno Emmanuel, Luis Jacinto Ela Alene, and Ludé Djam'Angai, L. 2024. "New Wave of Internal Armed Conflicts in Developing Countries: Does Inequality of Opportunity Matter?" *African Development Review* 36: 15–29. https://doi.org/10.1111/1467-8268.12738.

Piketty, Thomas. 2000. "Theories of Persistent Inequality and Intergenerational Mobility." In *Handbook of Income Distribution*, vol. 1, edited by Anthony B. Atkinson and François Bourguignon, 429–76. Amsterdam: North Holland.

Piketty, Thomas. 2014. *Capital in the 21st Century*. Cambridge, MA: Harvard University Press.

Shorrocks, A. F. 1982. "Inequality Decomposition by Factor Components." *Econometrica* 50 (1): 193–211. https://doi.org/10.2307/1912537.

Sulla, Victor, Precious Zikhali, and Pablo Facundo Cuevas. 2022. *Inequality in Southern Africa: An Assessment of the Southern African Customs Union—Country Brief: South Africa*. Washington, DC: World Bank. http://documents.worldbank.org/curated/en/099125003072240961/P1649270b73 f1f0b5093fb0e644d33bc6f1.

Teyssier, Geoffrey. 2013. "Inequality, Inequality of Opportunity, and Growth: What Are We Talking about? Theory and Empirical Investigation in Brazil." Ph.D. diss., Université Paris I Pantheón-Sorbonne. https://dumas.ccsd.cnrs.fr/dumas-00906310.

Thirumurthy, Harsha, Joshua Graff Zivin, and Markus Goldstein. 2008. "The Economic Impact of AIDS Treatment: Labor Supply in Western Kenya." *Journal of Human Resources* 43 (3): 511–52.

World Bank. 2023a. Africa's Pulse, No. 28, October: *Delivering Growth to People through Better Jobs*. Washington, DC: World Bank. https://doi.org/10.1596/978-1-4648-2043-4.

World Bank. 2023b. "Classification of Fragile and Conflict-Affected Situations." Updated June 28, 2024. https://www.worldbank.org/en/topic/fragilityconflictviolence/brief/harmonized -list-of-fragile-situations.

World Bank. 2023c. *New World Bank Group Scorecard FY24–FY30: Driving Action, Measuring Results.* Washington, DC: World Bank. http://documents.worldbank.org/curated/en/099121223173511026 /BOSIB1ab32eaff0051a2191da7db5542842.

World Bank. 2024. Poverty and Inequality Platform (version 20240627_2017_01_02_PROD [data set]; accessed July 2024). https://pip.worldbank.org/.

CHAPTER 2

The Poverty Reduction Challenge in Africa

AMBAR NARAYAN, LILIANA SOUSA, HAOYU WU, AND ELIZABETH FOSTER

Chapter highlights

Global poverty is increasingly concentrated in Africa, as the gap in well-being between Africa and the world has widened in the 2000s. Of the 725 million people living in extreme poverty in 2022, more than 60 percent live in the region. Almost one-third of the region's extreme poor live in two countries—the Democratic Republic of Congo and Nigeria. Together with Madagascar, Mozambique, and Tanzania, these countries account for nearly half the poor population living in the region. But poverty extends beyond the 38 percent of the region's population that lives in extreme poverty: more than half the population lives in multidimensional poverty (54 percent), and poverty incidence benchmarked against higher global standards has declined only marginally since 2000. This reflects a significant share of the population that remains highly vulnerable to falling into poverty in the event of a shock. Per the new prosperity gap (PG) indicator, the income (consumption) of individuals in Africa would have to increase, on average, by a factor of 12 to reach the global prosperity income benchmark, compared with a factor of 5 for the rest of the world. The widening PG between Africa and the rest of the world over the past decade is linked to slow growth in average incomes, along with little change in inequality.

Tackling Africa's high poverty is made more complicated by the region's high vulnerability to shocks: it is home to a disproportionate share of countries facing fragility and conflict, and many are among the world's most vulnerable to and least prepared for climate change. Although poverty is particularly pronounced in countries afflicted by fragility or conflict, poverty reduction has been slower in countries with resource wealth. In fact, among all countries, those that were neither fragile nor resource rich saw the biggest gains in poverty reduction during the past 20 years. Resource-rich countries that have experienced fragility or conflict experienced the highest poverty rate—with an average poverty rate of 46 percent in 2022. An additional factor holding back poverty reduction is climate-related shocks: an estimated 42 percent of the region's population is exposed to floods, droughts, and other climate-related shocks.

Additionally, the region's low and volatile aggregate economic growth and its weak linkages to household income growth have also held back poverty reduction. And household income growth matters: poverty reduction in Africa since 2000 has been driven by the growth in average household income (level of income) rather than improvements in the distribution of household income growth (who benefits from income growth). Moreover, aggregate economic growth in the region has faltered in recent years—particularly in resource-rich countries—and since 2014, it has barely kept pace with the region's population growth. At the same time, economic growth in Africa has been less efficient in reducing poverty, as reflected by its median growth elasticity of poverty (GEP) being the lowest among all regions. This lower level of efficiency is closely tied to the region's high inequality in income (consumption), which results from structural inequalities. Taken together, these patterns of growth and poverty reduction in Africa indicate that large potential gains can be made through a more equitable distribution of growth—particularly in resource-rich countries that are not experiencing fragility.

In addition to reducing the efficiency of growth, the presence of structural inequality slows Africa's poverty reduction by limiting people's socioeconomic mobility and the economy's structural transformation. Upward mobility of poor individuals is constrained by a high degree of inequality of opportunities—lower access to education and gainful employment—that also affects the trajectory of economic growth. Poor individuals are also less likely to have access to basic services essential for boosting productivity in microenterprises and self-employment, such as improved water and sanitation, electricity, means of communication, and information. Structural inequality in the region may also have contributed to the slow structural transformation of the economy by misallocating resources across sectors and firms. As a result, Africa remains highly dependent on agriculture for household income, and jobs and manufacturing value added as a share of gross domestic product (GDP) are the lowest globally compared with other regions.

The gap in well-being between Africa and the rest of the world has widened in the 2000s

Africa stands out globally for its high level of extreme poverty, overtaking South Asia in 2011 as the region with the largest number of those who are extremely poor. Of the 725 million people living in extreme poverty in 2022, more than 60 percent—nearly 460 million—lived in Africa (refer to figure 2.1a).[1] At 38 percent, Africa's poverty rate is

FIGURE 2.1 Extreme poverty in the Africa region relative to global poverty, 2000–22

a. Number of extreme poor and Africa's share

b. Rate of extreme poverty

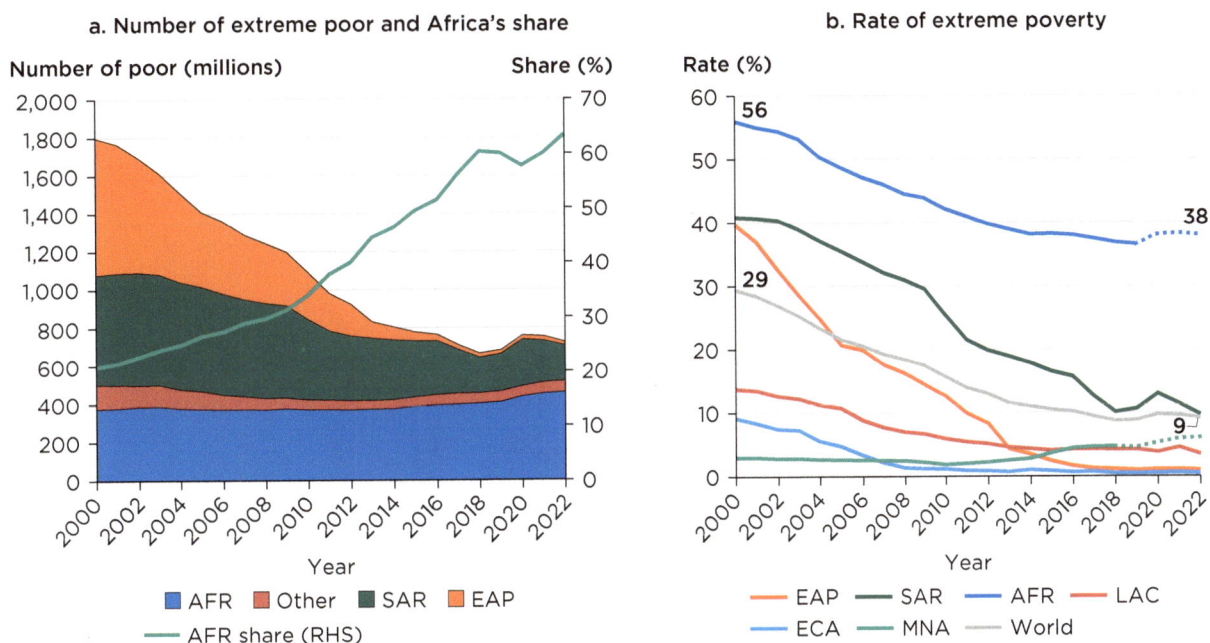

Source: World Bank 2024a.

Note: Estimates based on $2.15/day extreme poverty line (2017 PPP). In the Africa region, population coverage was below 50 percent between 2020 and 2022. In the MNA region, population coverage was below 50 percent between 2019 and 2022. AFR = Sub-Saharan Africa; EAP = East Asia and Pacific; ECA = Europe and Central Asia; LAC = Latin America and the Caribbean; MNA = Middle East and North Africa; PPP = purchasing power parity; RHS = right *y* axis; SAR = South Asia.

the highest of all regions and more than 30 points higher than the next region (South Asia, with a poverty rate of 10 percent; refer to figure 2.1b). Global poverty is likely to become increasingly concentrated in Africa because slow economic growth continues to be accompanied by rapid population growth. Even as Africa's poverty rate fell from 56 percent to 38 percent during years of relatively high growth, its rapid population growth resulted in the number of poor individuals falling by only 2 million, from 376 million in 2000 to 374 million in 2014. For context, this is the period during which the global poor population more than halved. The share of the global poor living in Africa is projected to increase to 87 percent by 2030 (World Bank 2022).

Poverty reduction in Africa has stalled since the mid-2010s

The world has made rapid progress in reducing extreme poverty since the early 1990s, but progress in Africa has been slower and has stalled since the mid-2010s. The global poverty rate, defined by the World Bank's extreme poverty line of $2.15 a day (in 2017 purchasing power parity [PPP]), declined from 38 percent in 1990 to 9 percent in 2022.

This progress was mainly driven by the East Asia and Pacific region and, to a lesser extent, by the South Asia region. Following two largely lost decades, it seemed that Africa would take on the role of engine for global poverty reduction in the early 2000s as growth accelerated beginning in the late 1990s and poverty fell from 56 percent in 2000 to 38 percent by 2014. As growth in the region stalled beginning in 2014, however, the pace of poverty reduction also slowed considerably. The region's high level of extreme poverty had a significant toll on human capabilities, as reflected in continued high rates of food insecurity, malnutrition, and childhood stunting (refer to box 2.1).

BOX 2.1

Health outcomes in the region reflect the human toll of extreme poverty and its long-term implications for human capital

The region's high level of extreme poverty has significant health and long-term human capital implications. As discussed in greater detail in chapter 3 of this report, despite notable progress in health access, key health indicators for the region continue to highlight the human cost of the region's stubbornly high extreme poverty. Africa's life expectancy of 60 years is more than 10 years lower than the average global life expectancy and seven years lower than the next-lowest region (South Asia). About one-third of Africa's children younger than age five, or an estimated 63.1 million in 2022, are affected by stunting (UNICEF, WHO, and World Bank 2023). Stunting is correlated with a higher risk of cognitive deficits and lower economic opportunities, suggesting long-term implications for economic development and the region's human capital stock. Yet food insecurity continues to be widespread and pernicious across the region, driven by conflict as well as climate and economic shocks. Per the *GRFC 2023 Mid-Year Update*, an estimated 156 million people in Africa were experiencing acute food insecurity in 2023, driven by conflict (in countries such as the Democratic Republic of Congo, Nigeria, and Sudan), climate shocks (including severe droughts in Angola, Ethiopia, and Somalia), and high food inflation (exceeding 40 percent in countries such as Burundi, Ghana, Sierra Leone, and Zimbabwe).[a]

a. Acute food insecurity is defined as a status of crisis needing immediate humanitarian assistance, based on the Integrated Food Security Phase Classification (IPC) and Cadre Harmonisé (CH) data (IPC/CH Phase 3 or above; FSIN and GRFC 2023).

Before the global COVID-19 pandemic in 2020, Africa was already experiencing slower progress in poverty reduction than other low-income countries. This slow rate has been attributed to high fertility rates, the low productive capacity of poor individuals, and a quality of growth that did not support growth in household incomes (Beegle and Christiaensen 2019; Beegle et al. 2016). The extreme poverty rate for Africa fell at an annual rate of only 0.8 percent in 2015–19, which was significantly lower than the rate of reduction in 2000–09 (2.7 percent) and 2010–14 (2.8 percent; refer to figure 2.2a). Among the countries that were best able to reduce poverty in the region were Benin,

Guinea, and Namibia, which saw annualized declines in poverty of 14.1 percent (2018–21), 12.6 percent (2007–12), and 8.7 percent (2009–15), respectively.[2] The gap between Africa and the rest of the world in the annual rate of poverty reduction, which was around 4 percentage points in 2000–09, increased to 10 percentage points in 2010–14 and 9 percentage points in 2015–19. Thus, poverty reduction in Africa, which was already lagging the rest of the world before 2010, fell further behind in the 2010s.[3]

FIGURE 2.2 Evolution of poverty in Africa through 2022

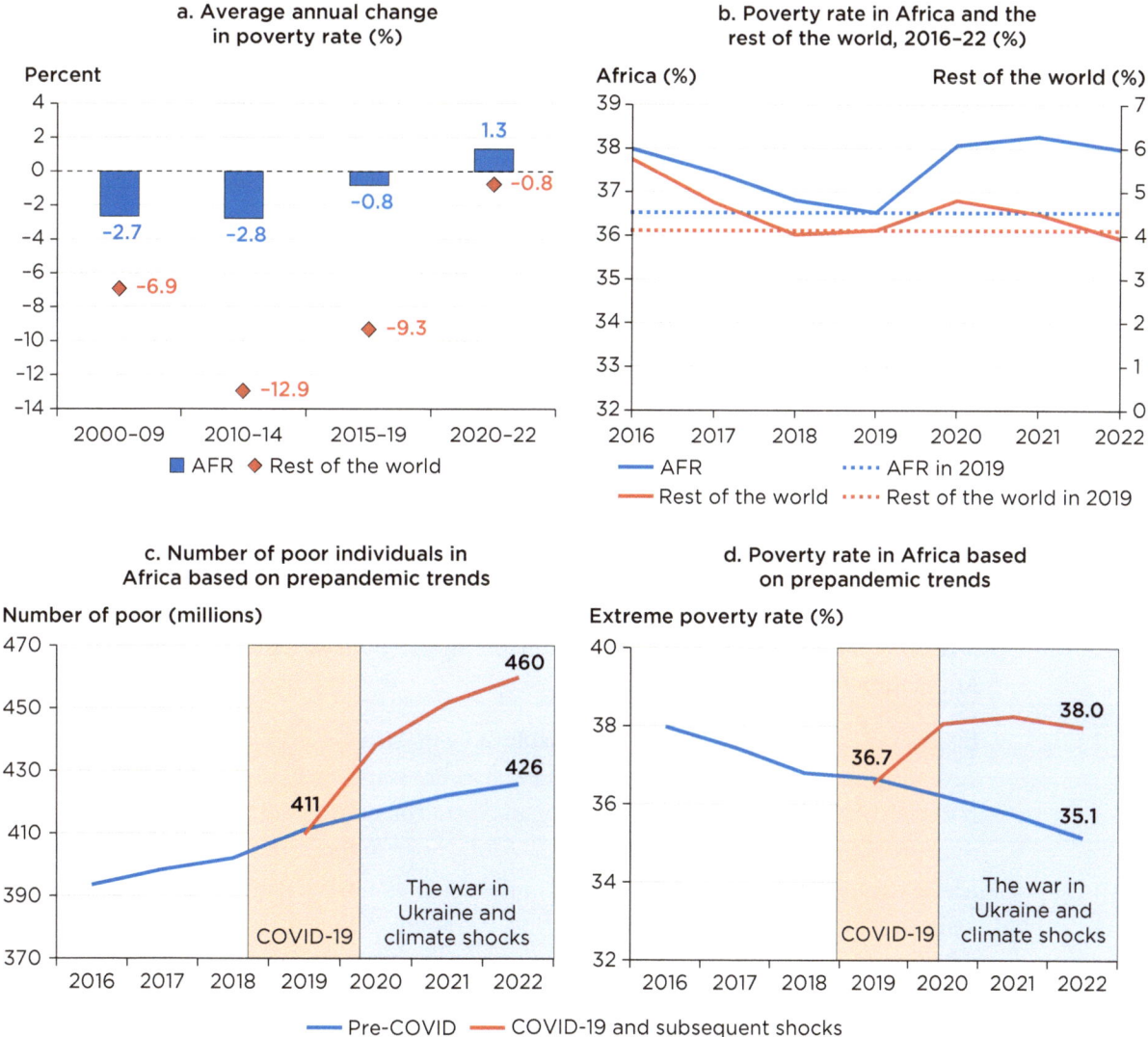

a. Average annual change in poverty rate (%)

b. Poverty rate in Africa and the rest of the world, 2016–22 (%)

c. Number of poor individuals in Africa based on prepandemic trends

d. Poverty rate in Africa based on prepandemic trends

Source: Tabulations based on World Bank 2024a and harmonized household survey data for African countries.
Note: The dashed lines in panel b show 2019 poverty rates. Panels c and d report nowcasting of the number of poor individuals and the poverty rate based on prepandemic trends to the realized trends, based on the methodology of Yonzan, Mahler, and Lakner 2023. Estimates for 2023 are projected on the basis of growth. Nowcasting for 2023 values is based on a distribution-neutral pass-through of 0.7 of gross domestic product growth rates. AFR = Sub-Saharan Africa.

The COVID-19 pandemic and subsequent shocks, including supply chain disruptions, the war in Ukraine, and various climate shocks, have further dampened progress in poverty reduction in the region—poverty in the Africa region remained higher in 2022 than in 2019. Because of a sharp slowdown in economic activity during the pandemic, the region had a two-year increase in extreme poverty of 1.7 percentage points, compared with a one-year increase of 0.9 percentage point in the rest of the world (refer to figure 2.2b). This was followed by a slow and uneven recovery, which resulted in poverty in 2022 remaining higher than it had been before the pandemic. Notably, poverty in the rest of the world recovered to lower-than-prepandemic levels by 2022. In addition to the pandemic and war-related global disruptions, climate-related shocks— including flooding and droughts—affected an estimated 42 percent of the region's population, as discussed in spotlight 1 (climate) of this report. Because of the pandemic and subsequent shocks, an estimated 34 million more people in Africa—an increase of 2.9 percentage points (pp) of the population—are estimated to have been living in extreme poverty in 2022 compared with a scenario in which prepandemic trends had prevailed (refer to figures 2.2c and 2.2d).

Shocks from multiple sources continue to be key contributors to the region's slow rate of poverty reduction. The region has been affected by the accumulated impact of shocks, including conflict and, increasingly, climate-related shocks, contributing to high rates of poverty and acute food insecurity (refer to box 1.2). In fact, 20 of the 39 countries considered to be in fragile and conflict-affected situation (FCS) status in 2023 were in Africa. Overall, the 30 countries in Africa that are or have been in FCS status at some point since 2006 (two-thirds of the region's countries) are home to nearly three-quarters of the region's extremely poor population (74 percent) and more than 70 percent of its population. At the same time, African countries are concentrated among the most vulnerable and least prepared for climate change shocks at a global level—including 13 of the 15 countries ranked lowest globally (Notre Dame Global Adaptation Initiative 2023).

Even as extreme poverty has fallen substantially in Africa, the share of the population not living in poverty by higher global standards has improved only marginally since 2000. As of 2022, just 12 percent of Africans were considered not poor (living on more than $6.85 per day), up from 8 percent in 2000 (refer to figure 2.2b). That is, as many in Africa escaped extreme poverty, most continued to live in poverty, as defined by higher welfare standards. During the same period, the share of the world's population not living in poverty rose from 34 percent to 63 percent—a much faster reduction in poverty even at higher welfare thresholds. The higher thresholds of $3.65 and $6.85 per person/ day (2017 PPP), which are derived from welfare standards typically used in lower- and upper-middle-income countries, are increasingly relevant for Africa because 25 countries—more than half the countries in the region—are lower- or upper-middle income.[4] Poverty in Africa based on these thresholds fell by 13.4 and 4.0 pp, respectively, between 2000 and 2022, compared with 19.0 pp using the extreme poverty threshold of $2.15.

FIGURE 2.3 Composition of population, by poverty status, 2000–22

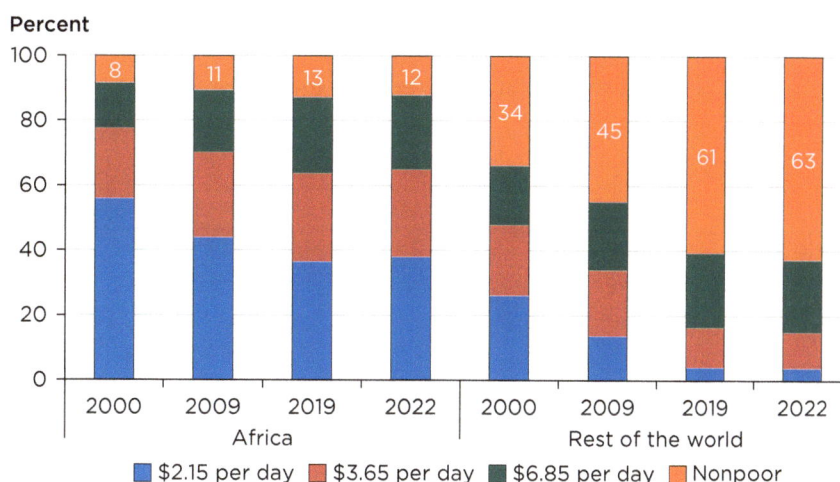

Source: Tabulations based on World Bank 2024a.
Note: Share of population living below the international poverty line (at 2017 purchasing power parity).

Africa's slower reduction in poverty at higher welfare thresholds reflects not just the slow growth of the middle class but also widespread vulnerability to extreme poverty. The share of the population between the $2.15 and $3.65 poverty lines grew from 22 percent in 2000 to 27 percent in 2022, and the share of those between the $2.15 and $6.85 poverty lines increased from 36 to 51 percent (refer to figure 2.3). This has two key implications. First, that the share of population between the higher and lower poverty lines is growing suggests that many of the people who are exiting extreme poverty remain vulnerable to falling back into it. This is because vulnerability, or the risk of falling into extreme poverty, declines (all else being equal) as one moves further away from the poverty line. This trend is of particular concern, given the increased frequency and magnitude of shocks associated with climate change, which are a particular source of vulnerability because households with low assets and lacking insurance and savings can easily be pushed into poverty. Second, the flip side of the first concern is that the middle class in the region is not growing rapidly as a share of the population, if "middle class" is defined in terms of financial security (or low vulnerability), as done in several publications (see, for example, Bussolo et al. 2018; Ferreira et al. 2012; World Bank 2012). A growing and aspiring middle class contributes to social stability and economic prosperity, and the slow expansion of this group can limit progress in different ways, such as the ability of societies to coalesce around good policies and hold politicians accountable.

Poverty varies considerably in the region because of fragility and resource wealth status

Poverty rates vary significantly across the countries of the region, reflecting differences in the development trajectories of countries' economies because of factors such as history, demography, geography, politics, and exposure to shocks. Africa has the twin challenges of areas with a high incidence of poverty and regions with large numbers of poor individuals. Extreme poverty ranges from negligible rates in high-income and upper-middle-income countries (such as Mauritius and the Seychelles) to more than 70 percent in low-income or conflict-affected countries, such as the Democratic Republic of Congo, Madagascar, Mozambique, Malawi, and South Sudan (refer to map 2.1). A few large countries account for a sizable share of the extremely poor population in the region, with nearly 1 in 3 of those living in extreme poverty in the region residing in Africa's two most populous countries—the Democratic Republic of Congo and Nigeria (refer to figure 2.4). These two countries, combined with three others (Madagascar, Mozambique, and Tanzania), account for nearly half the people living in extreme poverty in the region. People living in areas with a high poverty rate are likely to have more difficulty escaping poverty, underscoring the need to focus not just on the regions with the greatest number of poor individuals but also the areas with a high poverty rate (Beegle and Christiaensen 2019).

MAP 2.1 **Poverty rates at the $2.15/day line, 2017 PPP, by country**

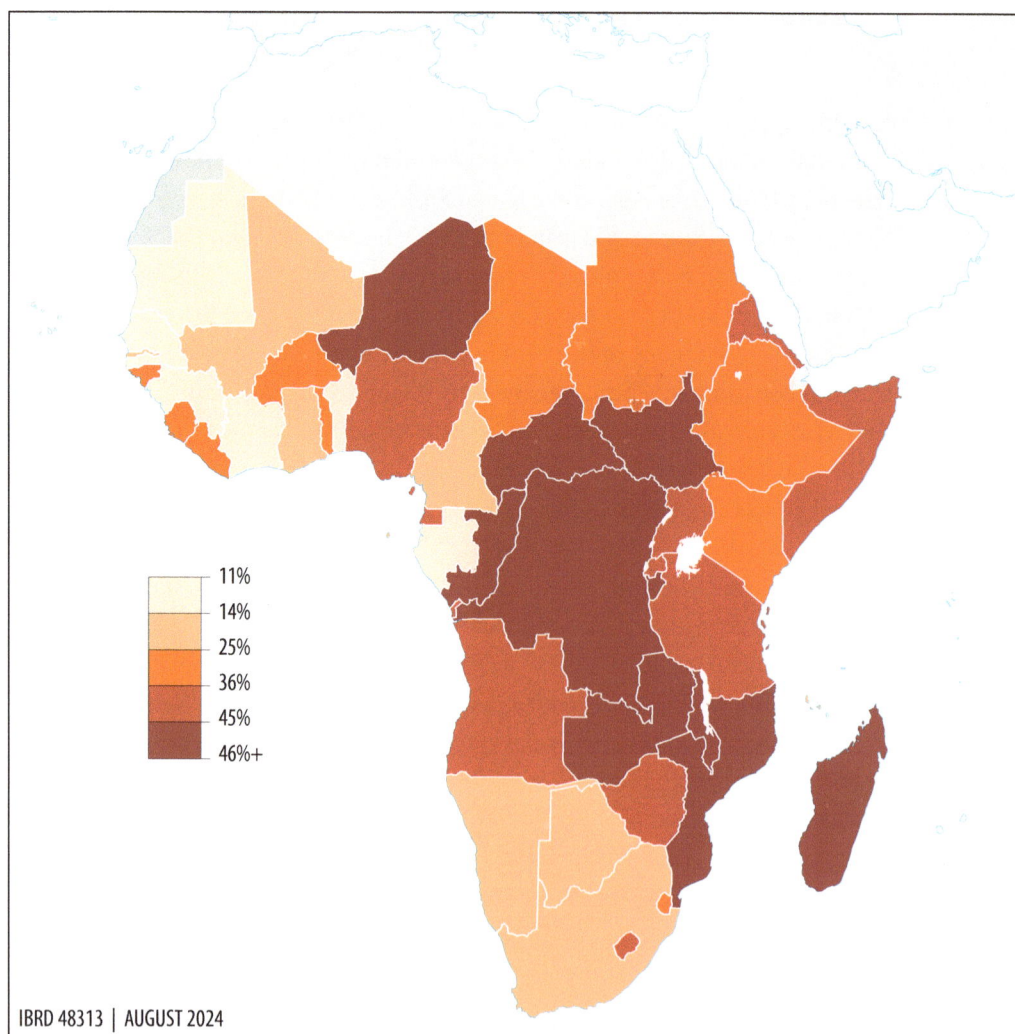

11%
14%
25%
36%
45%
46%+

IBRD 48313 | AUGUST 2024

Note: PPP = purchasing power parity.

FIGURE 2.4 Share of poor individuals at the $2.15/day poverty line in Africa, by country, 2022

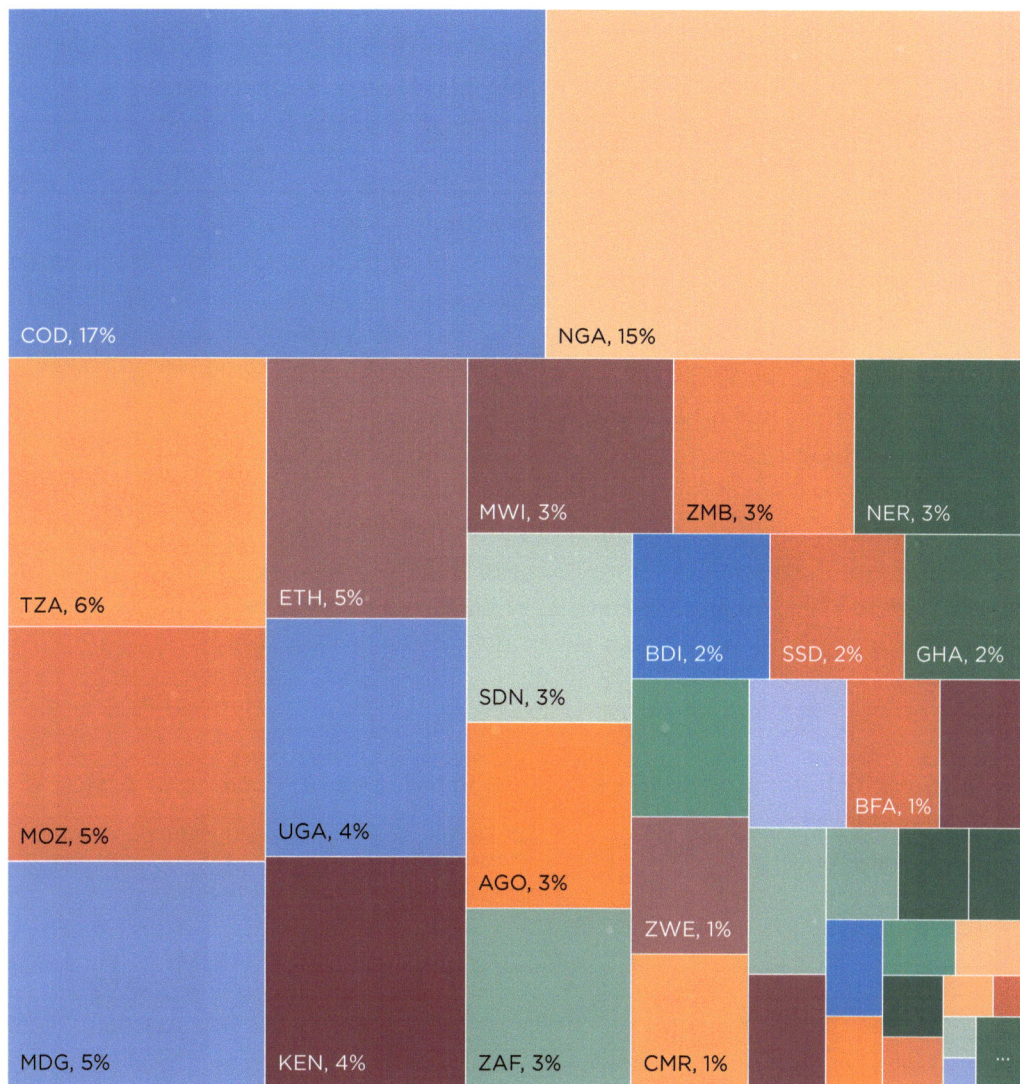

Source: World Bank 2024a.
Note: Africa = Sub-Saharan Africa; PPP = purchasing power parity.

Although poverty rates fell in both urban and rural areas during the first decade of the 2000s, poverty gains after 2010 are more attributable to continued urbanization (the shift of population from rural to urban areas). Africa is the least urbanized region in the world, with about 41 percent of its population living in urban areas as of 2020 (UN DESA, Population Division 2018). On average, the poverty rate in rural areas is more than double that in urban areas: of rural Africans, 50 percent live on less than $2.15/day compared with less than 20 percent of those living in urban areas (refer to figure 2.5a). Given its sizable share, rural poverty reduction drove overall poverty reduction in Africa during the first decade of the 2000s, accounting for two-thirds of total poverty reduction.[5] Reduction in urban poverty rates contributed another one-quarter. Urbanization contributed less than 10 percent. However, during 2010–19, the poverty rate increased marginally in both rural and urban areas—the poverty reduction that did occur came only through continued urbanization (refer to figure 2.5b).

Although most of Africa's population—and poverty—is concentrated in rural areas, the challenges associated with urban poverty are becoming increasingly important in Africa because of rapid urbanization. Africa is the fastest-urbanizing region in the world, with the urban population expected to grow by more than 300 million between 2000 and 2035 to overtake the rural population. The environmental and human challenges associated with this rapid urbanization in the context of a low level of wealth and limited public resources are significant (Lall, Henderson, and Venables 2017). An estimated 60 percent of Africa's urban population lives in informal settlements—typically with poor levels of infrastructure and limited access to basic essential services, such as improved sanitation and water. Tools to tackle urban poverty, improve urban planning, and address urban sprawl are becoming increasingly relevant for policy makers in the region.

FIGURE 2.5 **Evolution of urbanization and poverty in urban and rural areas of Africa**

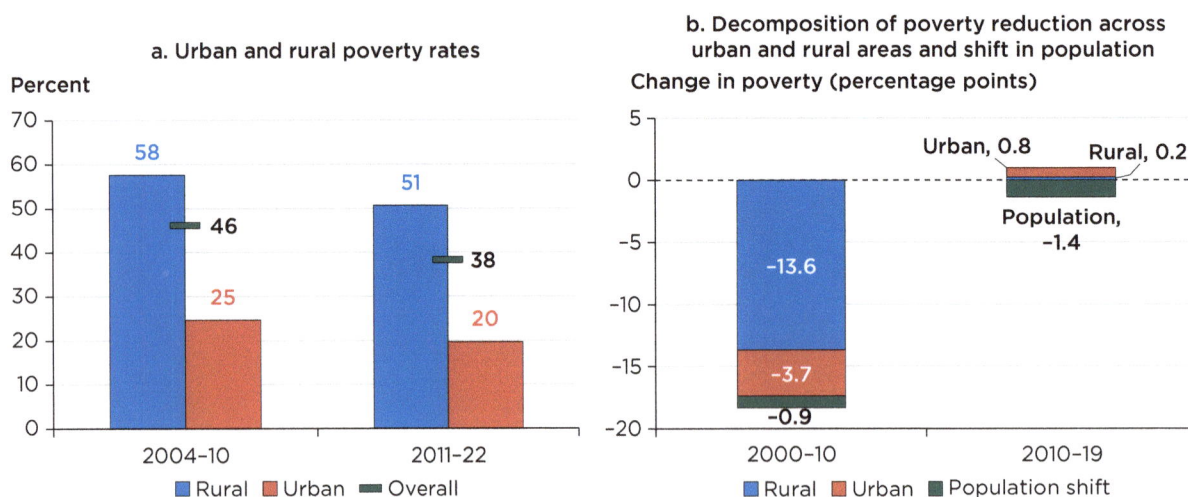

a. Urban and rural poverty rates

b. Decomposition of poverty reduction across urban and rural areas and shift in population

Source: World Bank 2024a and harmonized household survey data for African countries.
Note: Panel a is tabulated using the international poverty line of $2.15/day (2017 PPP). Because of data limitations, urban and rural poverty rates are extrapolated on the basis of a subset of African countries and adjusted to reflect the overall regional poverty rate. Figure b is based on a Huppi–Ravallion decomposition (Ravallion and Huppi 1991), using data from a subset of 17 countries with comparable poverty data for the relevant years of analysis (within three years of 2000, 2010, and 2019). Africa = Sub-Saharan Africa; PPP = purchasing power parity.

Leveling the Playing Field

Poverty in Africa is particularly pronounced in countries experiencing fragility or conflict, whereas the pace of poverty reduction has been slower in countries with resource wealth (refer to figure 2.6a). Figure 2.6 shows that, among countries that are not resource rich, countries that were not fragile achieved faster poverty reduction than those that were, reducing poverty at a rate of 2.5 percent annually compared with 1.8 percent for fragile countries (refer to figure 2.6b). This allowed them to fully close the gap in poverty rates between the two types of countries by 2010. In fact, of the four groups of countries, those that were neither fragile nor resource rich saw the biggest gains in poverty reduction during this period. Resource wealth in the context of fragility or conflict is associated with the highest poverty—an average poverty rate of 46 percent in 2022, 17 percentage points higher than that of countries with resource wealth and not in fragility or conflict. Although this last group—countries with resource wealth that are not in fragility status—have the lowest poverty rates; they have not been able to make substantial gains in poverty reduction since 2007, resulting in an overall decline of only 1.2 percent per year. As noted in chapter 1, this is also the group of countries with the highest level of inequality in the region.

FIGURE 2.6 **Poverty by FCS and resource-rich typologies**

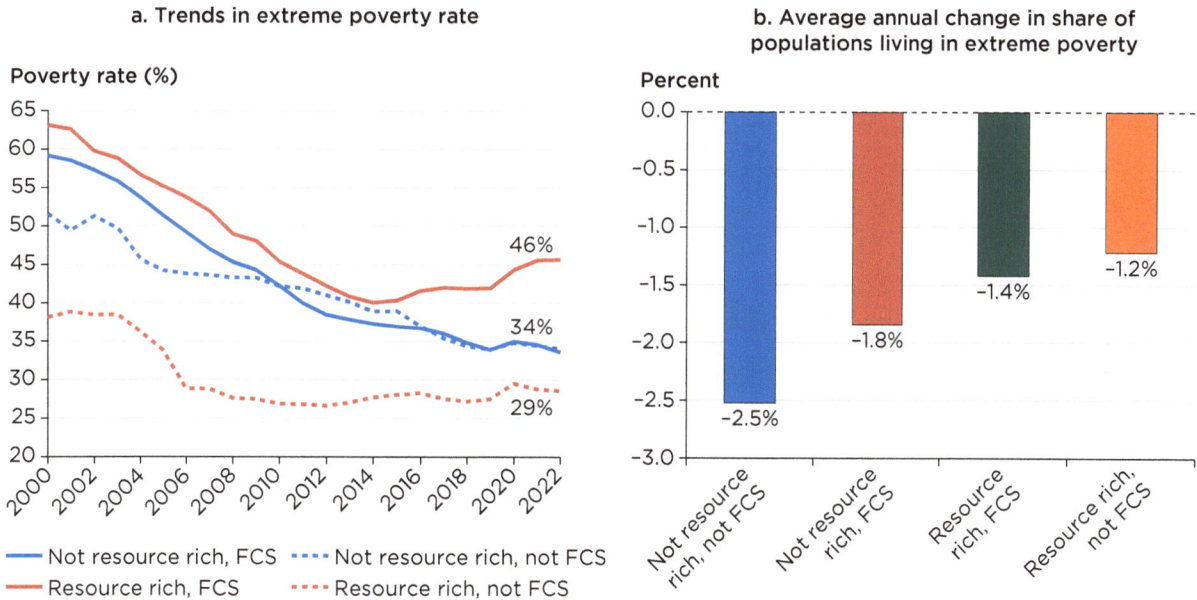

a. Trends in extreme poverty rate

b. Average annual change in share of populations living in extreme poverty

Source: Tabulations based on World Bank 2024a and harmonized household survey data for African countries.
Note: Estimates are based on a poverty line of $2.15 per day (2017 PPP). Countries that have ever experienced fragility or conflict-affected situations. PPP = purchasing power parity.

Deprivation in basic services needed for human capital and productivity growth extends well beyond those living in extreme poverty

Approximately 54 percent of Africa's population lives in multidimensional poverty: in addition to the one-third of Africa's population living in extreme monetary poverty, another 40 percent suffer from deprivations in access to basic services (education and infrastructure). The Multidimensional Poverty Measure (MPM) goes beyond counting the households that are unable to afford a basic bundle of goods (the methodology used to identify the global poor) to also include those experiencing substantial deprivations in access to key services needed for healthy and productive living—education and basic infrastructure (water, sanitation, and electricity).[6] The Africa region substantially underperforms other regions, experiencing significantly higher levels of multidimensional poverty even at similar GDP levels (refer to figure 2.7a). Of the 20 countries in the world with multidimensional poverty rates above 50 percent, only one (Papua New Guinea) is not in Africa. In five countries in the region—Chad, the Democratic Republic of Congo, Madagascar, Mozambique, and South Sudan—more than 80 percent of the population lives in multidimensional poverty. As with monetary poverty, multidimensional poverty is particularly high in countries experiencing fragility and conflict. Those that are fragile and resource wealthy have the highest multidimensional poverty rates, averaging 60 percent of the population with deprivation in access to basic services (refer to figure 2.7b).

High multidimensional poverty in some countries indicates significant unmet needs in basic services beyond those households affected by severe poverty. In half the countries in Africa, multidimensional poverty among those who are not living in monetary poverty affects only a small share of the population (10 percent or less).[7] Cabo Verde and South Africa are overperformers in this respect; their multidimensional poverty rate is significantly lower than expected, given the regional relationship between multidimensional and monetary poverty (refer to figure 2.7d). However, in other countries in the region, the share of the population that is not poor yet faces deprivation of education or basic services is significant: in Chad and Ethiopia, this share reaches 50 percent and 46 percent of the population, respectively (refer to figure 2.7c). Mauritania, one of the least densely populated countries in the world, with a large agropastoral population, is the most significant outlier in this respect, with a low monetary poverty rate of only 5 percent but nearly half its population in multidimensional poverty status (42 percent).[8]

Deprivations occur in multiple nonmonetary dimensions that have considerable (but not perfect) overlap with monetary poverty, with access to improved sanitation particularly lagging. In more than two-thirds of the countries in Africa, the deprivation rate in school enrollment is below monetary poverty rates, indicating that even the poorest individuals have access to schooling (refer to annex 2A). However, access to improved sanitation, another important input for human capital development because of its impact on the spread of disease and illness, is the dimension where most of the population is lagging. Deprivation in access to basic infrastructure—clean water and electricity, in addition to sanitation—is higher than MPM in most countries. In three countries—Burundi, Ethiopia, and Sudan—more than 90 percent of the population lack access to improved sanitation.

FIGURE 2.7 Multidimensional poverty in Africa

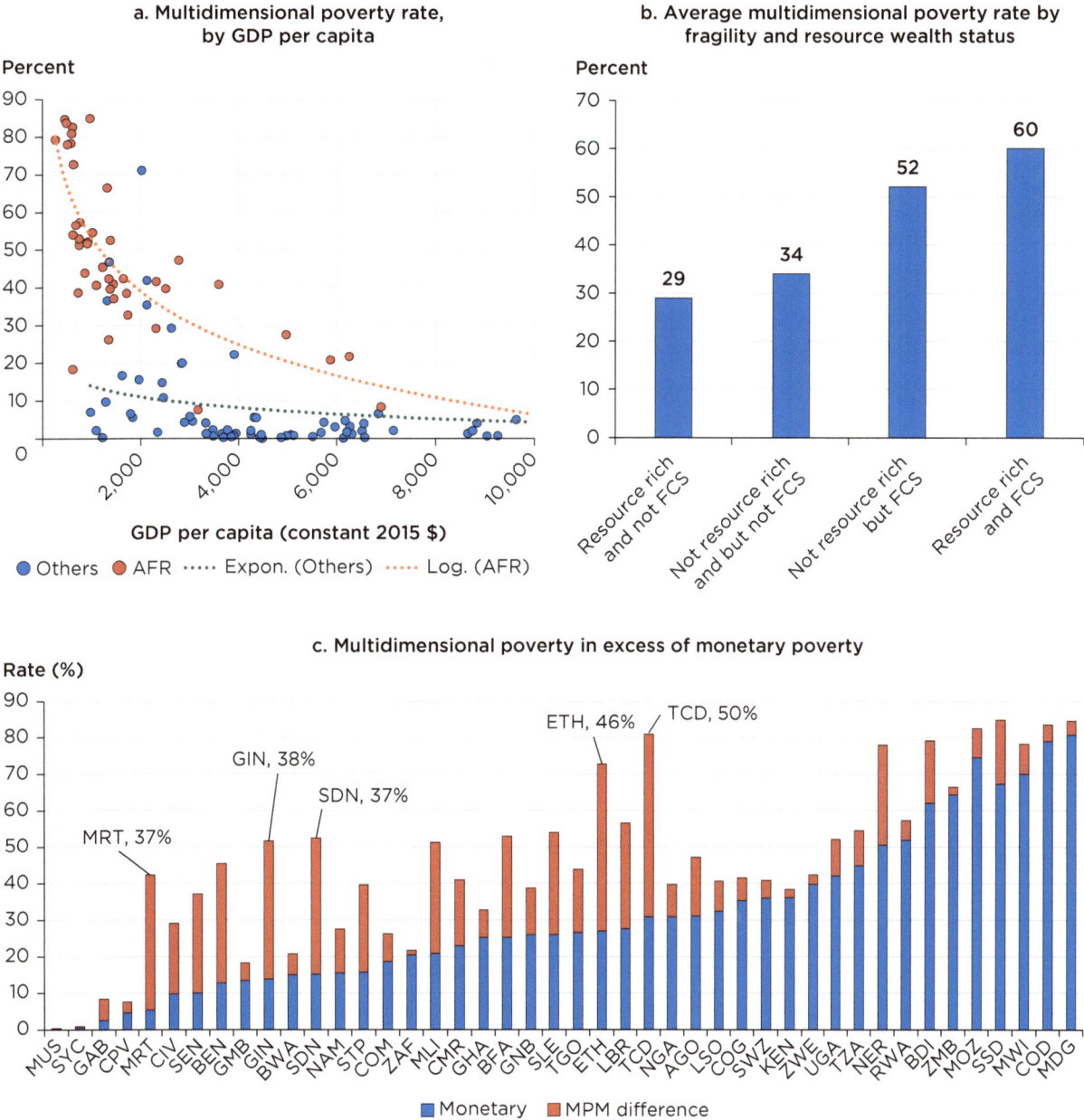

a. Multidimensional poverty rate, by GDP per capita

b. Average multidimensional poverty rate by fragility and resource wealth status

c. Multidimensional poverty in excess of monetary poverty

(continued)

FIGURE 2.7 Multidimensional poverty in Africa *(continued)*

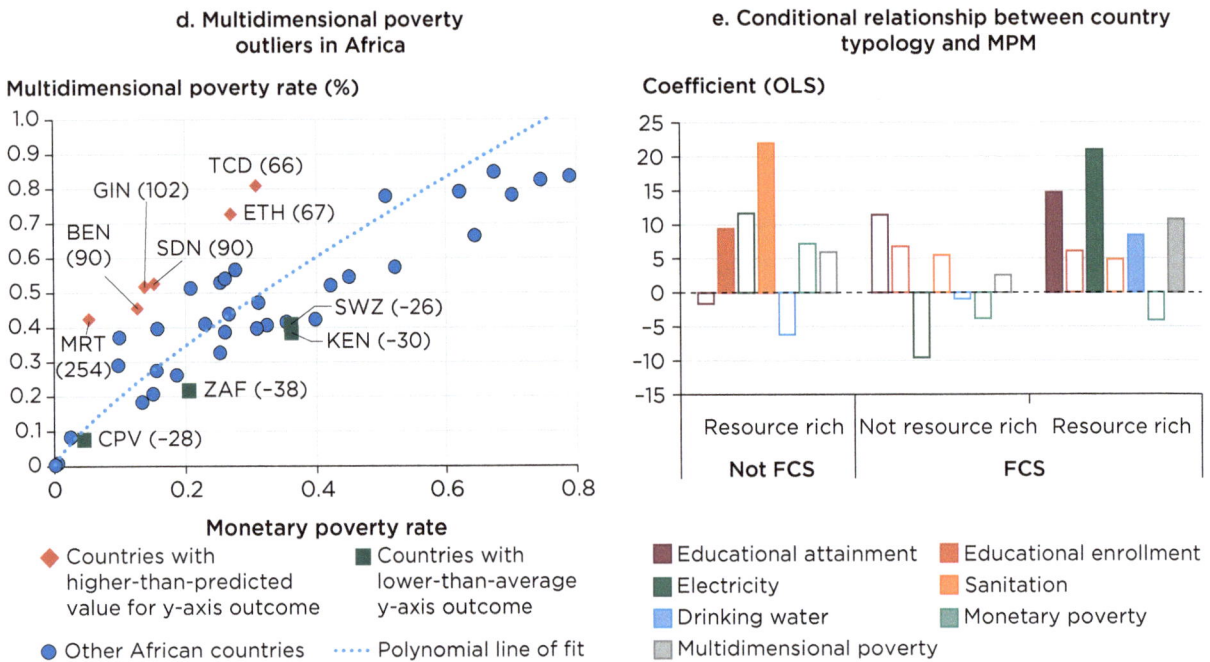

d. Multidimensional poverty outliers in Africa

Multidimensional poverty rate (%)

e. Conditional relationship between country typology and MPM

Coefficient (OLS)

Legend (panel d):
- ◆ Countries with higher-than-predicted value for y-axis outcome
- ■ Countries with lower-than-average y-axis outcome
- ● Other African countries
- ⋯⋯ Polynomial line of fit

Legend (panel e):
- ■ Educational attainment
- ■ Educational enrollment
- ■ Electricity
- ■ Sanitation
- ■ Drinking water
- ■ Monetary poverty
- ■ Multidimensional poverty

Source: Tabulations based on World Bank 2024a and harmonized household survey data for African countries.
Note: The MPM analysis is limited to the subset of countries with sufficiently detailed surveys to estimate MPM. MPM outliers in panel d are identified on the basis of a polynomial fit. Panel e reports the coefficients from a series of OLS linear regressions in which the dependent variable is each of the dimensions of the MPM (which includes monetary poverty) and the overall MPM (refer to annex 2B). The bars report the conditional effect of country typology on each outcome relative to the baseline of countries that are neither FCS nor resource rich, controlling for the natural logarithm of GDP, whether a country is landlocked, and whether the outcome is in the first or second decade of the 2000s. A positive coefficient indicates higher levels of deprivation. Solid bars reflect coefficients that are statistically significantly different from zero. AFR = Sub-Saharan Africa; Expon. = exponential; FCS = fragile and conflict-affected situation; GDP = gross domestic product; Log. = natural logarithm; MPM = Multidimensional Poverty Measure; OLS = ordinary least squares. For country abbreviations, refer to https://www.iso.org/obp/ui/#search.

Deprivation levels in resource-rich countries suggest lower-than-expected access to basic services given their level of economic output; this is particularly true for those countries that are also afflicted by fragility (refer to figure 2.7e). Considering a country's level of GDP, resource-rich countries that do not have a recent history of fragility have higher-than-expected deprivation in school enrollment rates and sanitation. For those that are fragile or have a recent history of fragility, multidimensional poverty is higher than expected, as is the rate of deprivation of educational attainment of the adult population, electricity, and drinking water. This provides further evidence of the extent to which the resource curse may be affecting poverty reduction in the region.

No significant relationship is found with fragility status, suggesting that outcomes are largely aligned with levels of economic output.

Monetary well-being in Africa has grown but remains far from levels attained by the rest of the world

The prosperity gap shows the limited progress Africa has made in lifting people's incomes to a global prosperity standard, relative to the rest of the world. The prosperity gap represents the average factor by which income (or consumption) of all individuals in a country or region needs to be multiplied to reach the global prosperity standard of $25 per person daily (at 2017 PPP; refer to box 2.2). In 2023, the income of individuals in Africa would have had to increase, on average, by a scale-up factor of 12 to reach the global prosperity standard, compared with a scale-up factor of 5 for the world as a whole (refer to figure 2.8a). Although these scale-up factors are smaller than in 2000, when they were 17 and 9, respectively, the difference in the scale-up factors for Africa and the world increased from 87 percent in 2000 to 144 percent in 2023. Countries afflicted by fragility—particularly those that are also resource rich—have worse outcomes than other groups of countries, as reflected by their disproportionate role in Africa's prosperity gap (refer to annex 2A).

The widening difference in the prosperity gap between Africa and the world over the past decade is linked to slow growth in average incomes along with little change in inequality. After a rapid decline in the prosperity gap over the first decade of the 2000s, progress in Africa has stalled since the middle of the 2010s. This trend largely mirrors what was seen for poverty rates. The prosperity gap for Africa improved only slightly between 2010 and 2019, from 13.0 to 11.9. The economic impact of COVID-19 and subsequent slow recovery led to the prosperity gap remaining unchanged between 2019 and 2022. Most of the reduction in the region's prosperity in the first decade of the 2000s was driven by growth in average (mean) incomes (refer to figure 2.8b). Change in inequality had a small contribution to the rapid decline of the prosperity gap in this period. The next decade saw a smaller contribution of inequality and much lower growth in mean income, which led to a much smaller decline in prosperity gap. Further analysis shows that whatever contribution (changes in) inequality made to the decline in prosperity gap was due to a small decline in inequality between countries in Africa, because within-country inequality remained almost unchanged. Reductions in inequality have decreased the prosperity gap since 2019 but were offset by a reduction in average incomes.

BOX 2.2

The prosperity gap: An intuitive measure of what it will take to achieve prosperity for all

Although the term *shared prosperity* lacks a commonly agreed-on definition, a new measure named the prosperity gap (PG), introduced by Kraay et al. (2023), gives it an intuitive interpretation—combining the idea of distance from a fixed prosperity standard with distribution sensitivity in how individuals are weighted according to their distance from the standard. The PG measures the global average shortfall in income from a standard of prosperity set at $25 per day (adjusted for differences in purchasing power parity across countries). This is the typical (median) poverty line in high-income countries today, which is an aspirational benchmark for most low-income countries. The PG is defined as the average factor by which incomes need to be multiplied to bring everyone to the prosperity standard. A PG value greater than 1 signals a shortfall in prosperity, indicating the need for incomes to increase by an average multiple equal to the PG to attain the prosperity standard.

The PG narrows (or improves) when incomes anywhere in the world increase, but it improves more when the incomes of those who are poorest increase. For example, in figure B2.2.1, person A, with an income of $2.50, contributes to the PG 5 times more than person B, who has an income of $12.50, and 10 times more than person C, with income of $25.00. Thus, the PG would improve more if A's income were to grow by a given rate than it would if B's or C's income were to grow by the same rate.

The PG can be decomposed across subgroups (such as geographic areas or demographic groups) within a country or region in a consistent manner, making it a useful tool for evaluating shared prosperity for countries and regions in a way that is consistent with the global measure. The PG can also be decomposed into average income and inequality, which allows the quantification of how reductions in inequality and increases in average income separately contribute to improvements in the PG.

FIGURE B2.2.1 The prosperity gap improves more when incomes of the poorest increase

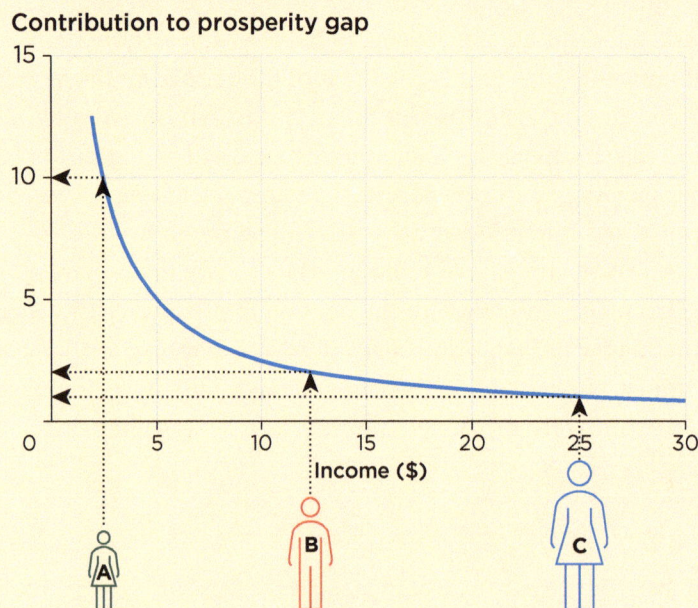

Source: Based on Kraay et al. 2023.

FIGURE 2.8 **Prosperity gap: A new measure of shared prosperity**

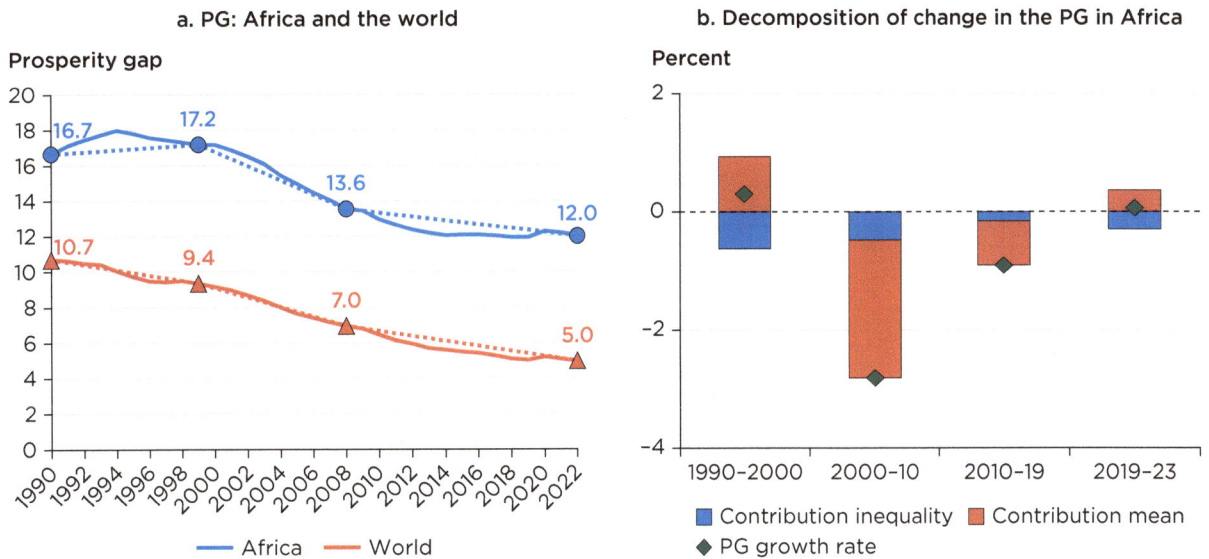

a. PG: Africa and the world

Prosperity gap

b. Decomposition of change in the PG in Africa

Percent

— Africa   — World

■ Contribution inequality   ■ Contribution mean
◆ PG growth rate

Sources: Tabulations based on World Bank 2024a and Kraay et al. 2023.
Note: PG refers to the average factor by which incomes need to be multiplied to reach the global prosperity standard of $25/person/day (2017 PPP). Refer to annex 2A for additional figures. Africa = Sub-Saharan Africa; PG = prosperity gap; PPP = purchasing power parity.

The region's slow rate of poverty reduction is linked to low, inequitable, and inefficient growth

Household income growth, rather than more equitable distribution of incomes, has driven poverty reduction

Since 2000, poverty reduction in Africa has been driven primarily by growth in average household income as opposed to distributional changes in household income that would arise from faster income growth of those living in poverty. The Datt–Ravallion decomposition calculates the contribution to poverty reduction from two channels: the growth component measures the contribution of changes in the mean of the welfare (income or consumption) distribution, and the redistribution component measures the contribution of changes in the inequality of the welfare distribution. As an illustration, poverty could be reduced with no change in the average income level if income from the top of the distribution were to be reallocated to those living in poverty at the bottom of the distribution. This decomposition shows that growth in the average level of welfare accounted for

FIGURE 2.9 Decomposition of poverty reduction through income growth versus income redistribution, 2000–19

Change in poverty (percentage points)

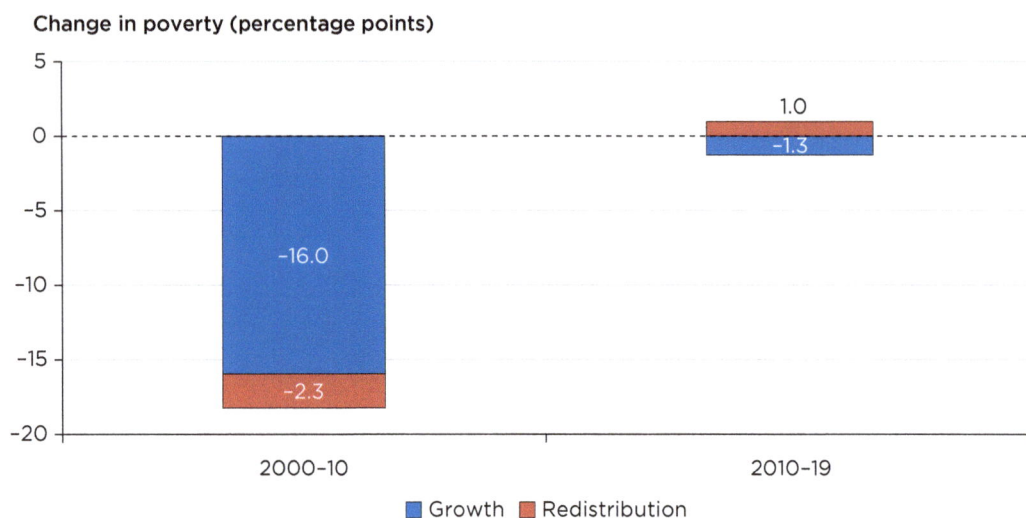

Source: This figure is based on a Datt–Ravallion decomposition (Datt and Ravallion 1992), using harmonized household survey data from a subset of 17 African countries with comparable poverty data for the relevant years of analysis (within three years of 2000, 2010, and 2019).

87 percent of the reduction in poverty between 2000 and 2010 (refer to figure 2.9). Redistribution, in the form of reduced inequality in welfare, accounted for the remaining 13 percent. During the lower growth period from 2010 to 2019, growth accounted for all the poverty reduction seen across the region, and increased inequality worked in the opposite direction, reducing the extent to which poverty was reduced during this period. Although growth has been the key driver of poverty reduction in the region, the lack of redistribution is a lost opportunity for furthering poverty reduction. The region's high inequality suggests, however, that there are big potential gains to be made through redistribution—particularly in resource-rich countries not experiencing fragility.

Poverty reduction has been limited by low economic growth

The slowdown in poverty reduction since the mid-2010s tracks closely with slower GDP growth in the region—including an extended period of negative per capita growth (refer to figure 2.10). After nearly two decades of fast-paced economic expansion (1996–2014), growth in the region started to falter in the years leading up to the COVID-19 pandemic. GDP growth fell from an annual average rate of 5 percent over 2000–14 to 2.4 percent over 2014–19. Several factors played a role, including volatile commodity prices and

FIGURE 2.10 **GDP and population growth in Africa**

Percent

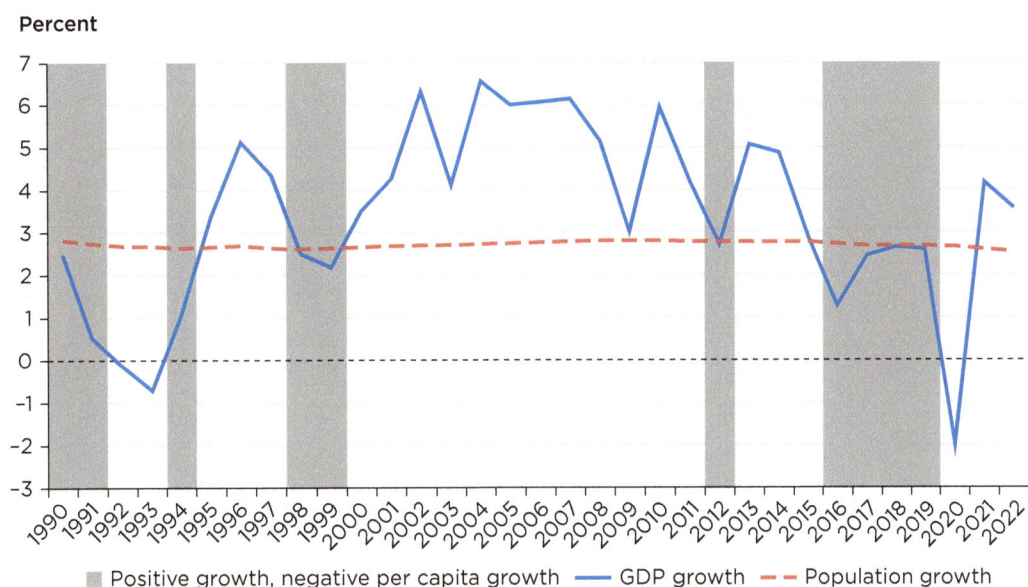

Legend: Positive growth, negative per capita growth — GDP growth – – Population growth

Source: Tabulations based on the World Bank's World Development Indicators.
Note: Africa = Sub-Saharan Africa; GDP = gross domestic product.

weak export performance, which particularly affected resource-rich countries (World Bank 2019a). A more long-standing challenge on the supply side has been the relatively low labor productivity growth in the region, with growth mainly coming from factor accumulation and the limited contribution of total factor productivity growth (Calderón 2021). Relatedly, although public capital accumulation was an important driver of labor productivity growth in the region, there is evidence that such public investment was inefficient (Calderón 2021).

The region's rapid population growth has slowed the eradication of poverty and contributed to the lower rate of convergence in per capita GDP. In short, the region needs average growth above 3 percent per year just to keep up with population growth. Since 2014, growth has barely kept pace with population growth, such that the regional real per capita GDP in 2021 was 5 percent below that in 2014. As a result, in 2000–19, when the gap in per capita GDP between low-income countries and advanced economies was closing, convergence was slower for African countries than for the developing world as a whole. Recent research shows that although poorer countries have been catching up with richer countries in per capita GDP since the mid-1990s (unconditional convergence), the convergence coefficient without African countries is substantially greater than with these countries, indicating that these countries are a drag on overall convergence (Patel, Sandefur, and Subramanian 2021).

Large economies in the region—particularly those that are resource rich—saw growth fall substantially in the 2010s. Analyzing countries' growth resilience by comparing GDP growth in 1995–2008 with that in 2015–19, the World Bank (2019) finds that 21 countries in the region, accounting for 64 percent of Africa's GDP and 42 percent of the region's population, experienced a slippage in performance. This group includes countries of Southern Africa along with Nigeria, the region's largest economy and home to 16 percent of the poor population in the region. In fact, the biggest reduction in growth was experienced by resource-rich countries that do not suffer from fragility, reflecting both their significant success at the beginning of the 2000s as well as their reliance on commodity prices for growth (refer to figure 2.11). These countries averaged per capita growth of more than 3 percent per year before the 2009 crisis, but the recovery after the 2009 crisis was short-lived because growth rates plummeted again in 2015, resulting in negative per capita growth between 2012 and 2019. The trend was similar, although less severe, for resource-rich countries with fragility. On average, only the non–resource-rich countries in Africa were able to achieve positive per capita growth in the 2010s—with fragile countries in this group seeing an increase in growth relative to the first decade.

FIGURE 2.11 **GDP per capita growth by typology, 2000–22**

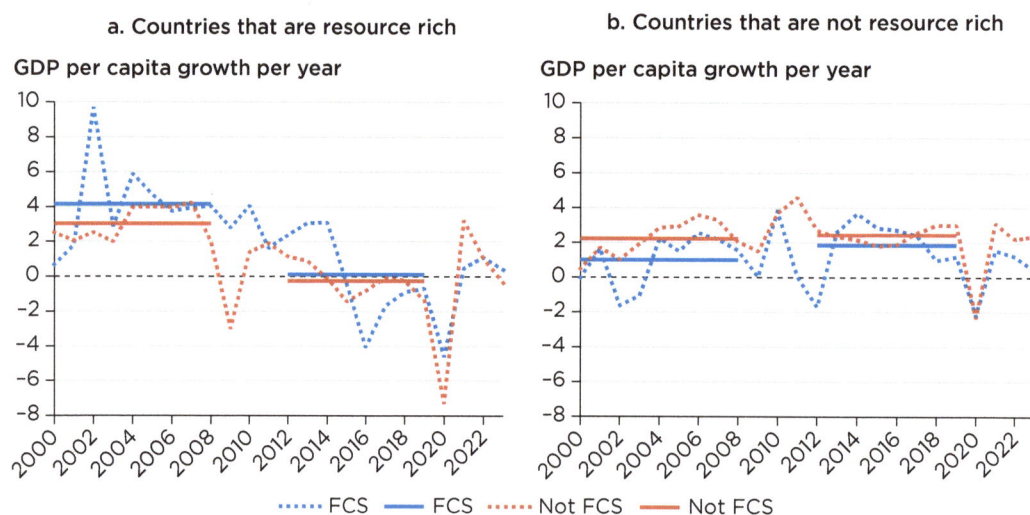

a. Countries that are resource rich

b. Countries that are not resource rich

Source: World Development Indicators.
Note: The thick lines show average per capita growth over the following two sets of years: 2000–08 and 2012–19. FCS = fragile and conflict-affected situation; GDP = gross domestic product.

Poverty reduction has been limited by growth that is also less effective in reducing poverty

Poverty reduction is driven not only by per capita economic growth rates but also by the extent to which growth is translated into welfare improvements at the bottom of the income distribution (that is, its efficiency in reducing poverty). In this sense, growth in the region has not been very efficient in reducing poverty. On average, economic growth in the countries of Africa has been less effective in reducing poverty than in the rest of the world. Even during Africa's high-growth period, there were concerns about the limited extent to which this growth benefited the poor population (see, for example, Bhorat and Naidoo 2018; Fosu 2023; Thorbecke 2023). A comprehensive analysis of the period between 1981 and 2021, based on a sample of 575 successive and comparable growth episodes for countries across the world between 1981 and 2021, reveals that economic growth in Africa has been less poverty reducing relative to other regions because the GEP has been systematically lower (Wu et al. 2024).[9] The median GEP in Africa is found to be the lowest among all regions for both growth in household consumption and per capita GDP (refer to figure 2.12a). The difference is larger for GEP for growth in per capita GDP, in which Africa ranks the lowest among all regions by a considerable margin.[10] The elasticity of poverty to per capita GDP growth has not changed significantly over time, providing further evidence supporting the slowdown in growth as being the key driver behind the recent slowdown in poverty reduction, globally and in Africa.

The GEP for GDP growth is lower in Africa relative to other regions even after controlling for initial differences in poverty, income levels, and inequality. Although average GEPs for African countries are lower (as shown earlier), this could occur because of differences in certain initial conditions of countries. Poorer countries, for example, are likely to have lower GEPs because the poverty rate would need to change more to produce the same percentage change in poverty than a country with a lower initial poverty rate. After controlling for initial poverty rates, initial welfare means, and initial inequality for every country's growth episode, however, growth in GDP per capita in Africa is still found to be associated with a significantly slower pace of poverty reduction compared with other regions.[11] Grouping countries by typology reveals that countries in the region lag countries of the same group in the rest of the world in elasticity of poverty reduction (refer to figure 2.12b). The only exception is for resource-rich countries that are in fragility status, in which African countries outperform those outside the region.

FIGURE 2.12 Elasticity of poverty reduction to growth

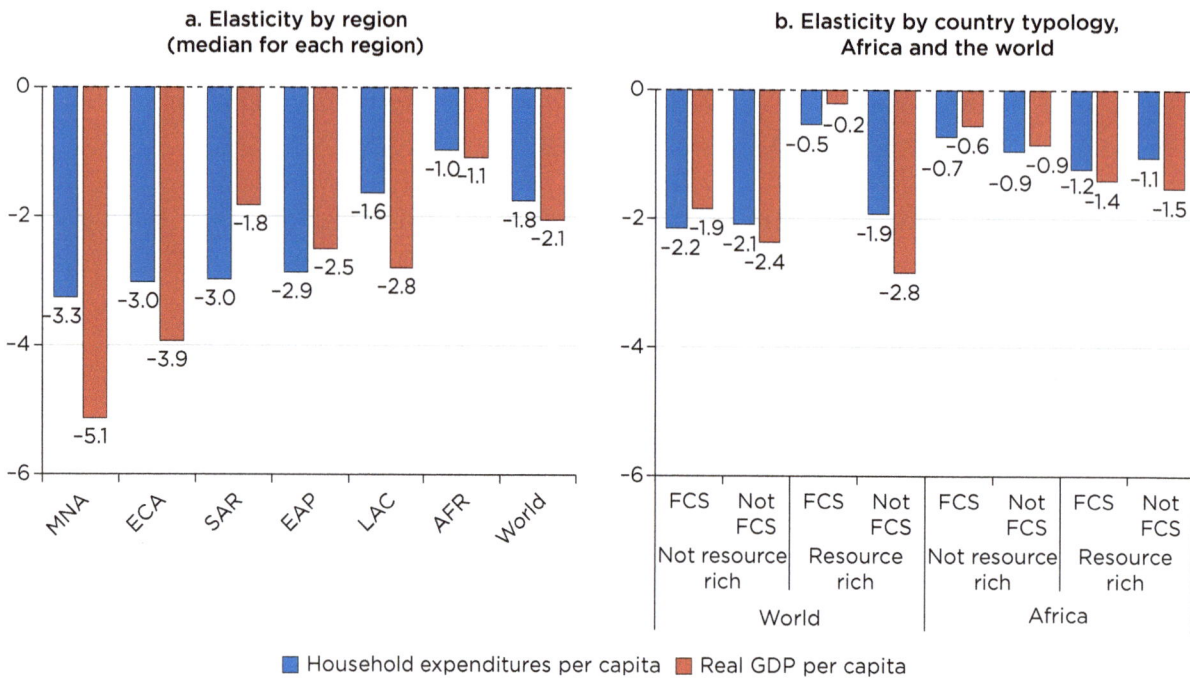

a. Elasticity by region
(median for each region)

b. Elasticity by country typology,
Africa and the world

■ Household expenditures per capita ■ Real GDP per capita

Source: Wu et al. 2024. Refer to annex 2C for methodological details.
Note: Based on elasticity of poverty change to growth in household expenditures and per capita GDP, across all nonoverlapping episodes with available data for each country, between 1990 and 2019 (limited to cases with poverty rate > 2 percent and winsorizing to remove outliers). Africa = Sub-Saharan Africa; EAP = East Asia and Pacific; ECA = Europe and Central Asia; FCS = fragile and conflict-affected situation; GDP = gross domestic product; LAC = Latin America and the Caribbean; MNA = Middle East and Northern Africa; SAR = South Asia.

On the basis of the cross-country growth literature and research on the determinants of household welfare, three broad categories of variables—human capital, economic structure, and dependency on natural resources—are found to influence the link between economic growth and household welfare.[12] The findings suggest the importance of human capital development, structural transformation, and economic diversification in spreading the benefits of economic growth more widely. Improving primary education, along with basic sanitation and clean drinking water that are likely to reduce the disease burden, can promote upward mobility of poor individuals through human capital improvements, and structural transformation increases workers' opportunities to shift into higher-productivity activities. These effects are in addition to the direct positive effects of structural transformation and human capital improvements on economic growth itself. Greater diversification of the economy away from reliance on natural resources is associated with growth being more welfare improving, potentially because natural resource–led growth may have more limited effects in job creation and income spillovers to other sectors.

In general, countries in Africa lag the rest of the world in the factors that are associated with poverty reduction being more responsive to growth. On average, variables that amplify the effect of economic growth—such as primary school enrollment, literacy rates, and access to electricity and drinking water—are scarcer in African countries, and variables that inhibit the poverty-reducing effect of growth—employment and value added in agriculture, natural resource dependency—are more abundant (refer to annex 2D, table D2.4).

Structural inequality slows Africa's poverty reduction by limiting mobility, structural transformation, and the efficiency of growth

A significant portion of inequality in outcomes across households in the region is attributable to long-standing structural inequality resulting from market failures, uneven access to human capital, and lack of opportunities for women. A cross-country decomposition analysis based on Fields (2003) reflects the relative importance of these key sources of structural inequalities.[13] This analysis shows that, of the 40 percent of inequality that can be explained through basic household characteristics (refer to the note to figure 2.13), three characteristics account for two-thirds:[14] the higher fertility rate of poorer households, significant spatial inequality within countries, and limited access to tertiary education.

FIGURE 2.13 **Factors contributing to inequality in Africa**

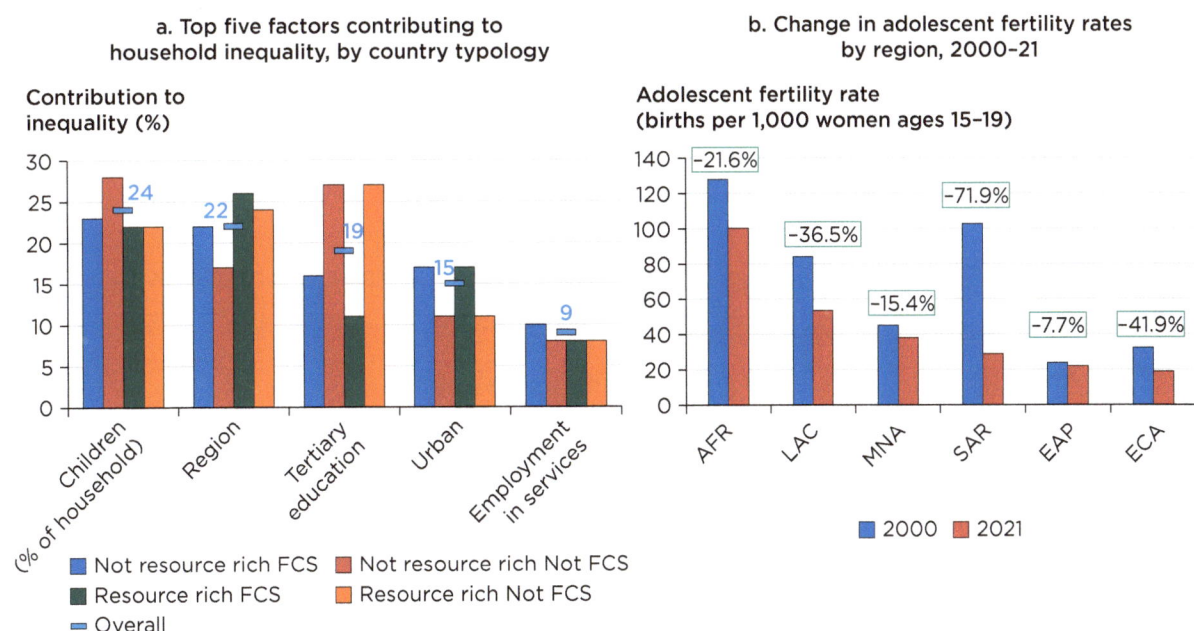

a. Top five factors contributing to household inequality, by country typology

b. Change in adolescent fertility rates by region, 2000–21

Sources: Panel a based on World Bank 2024a panel b based on World Development Indicators.
Note: Panel a reports the results of regression-based decompositions averaged across a set of countries. Refer to annex 1F for methodological details. Figure b reports the change in adolescent fertility rates between 2000 and 2021 by region for countries that are members of the International Bank for Reconstruction and Development or International Development Association. AFR = Sub-Saharan Africa; EAP = East Asia and Pacific; ECA = Europe and Central Asia; FCS = fragile and conflict-affected situation; MNA = Middle East and Northern Africa; SAR = South Asia.

- Structural barriers limiting women's and girls' opportunities and agency contribute to the region's high fertility, including high rates of adolescent births closely linked to early marriage. Regionwide, adolescent girls experience 100.4 births per 1,000 (compared with 53.4 for Latin America and the Caribbean, the next-highest region) as of 2021. This is an area of particular concern because Africa has not made the sizable reductions seen in other regions that had high adolescent fertility in 2000—notably, South Asia and Latin America and the Caribbean. The resulting high dependency ratios of poorer households (the relative number of children to adults) is the single strongest contributor to income inequality overall, accounting for nearly one-quarter of inequality.

- Spatial inequality across regions explains another 22 percent of inequality, which is particularly important in resource-rich countries. This reflects market failures and frictions that lead to spatial concentration of commercial activities and higher-wage jobs in certain regions while other regions struggle because of a lack of access to markets and infrastructure (such as a lack of roads). This effect is in addition to inequality driven by the urban/rural divide, which on its own accounts for 15 percent of inequality. Hence, regional and urban/rural inequality combined account for one-third of inequality.

- Limited access to tertiary education explains another 19 percent. The countries of Africa see large premiums associated with tertiary education, particularly in non-FCS countries. This can reflect a combination of two channels. Higher wages can reflect higher productivity, but they can also reflect a higher skill premium because of the low supply of skilled labor driven by the region's high intergenerational wealth inequality and extremely limited access to education beyond basic schooling, particularly at the university level.

Chapter 1 introduced the concept of structural inequality and established its importance for economic growth and poverty reduction in Africa. Three channels were identified through which structural inequality has undermined Africa's poverty reduction:

- By narrowing the pathway of upward mobility,

- By undermining the region's structural transformation, and

- Through lower efficiency of growth to reduce poverty.

These three channels are explored in more detail here.

Structural inequality limits upward mobility and reinforces low-income traps

Poor individuals' low productive capacity reduces the economic growth potential of the region while limiting pathways out of low-income traps for much of Africa's population. Some of the key constraints across the region are apparent from cross-tabulating the characteristics of different income segments of the African population (refer to figure 2.14). These are strongly associated with the sources of structural inequality

FIGURE 2.14 Profiles of poverty and inequality, by demography, education, and livelihood

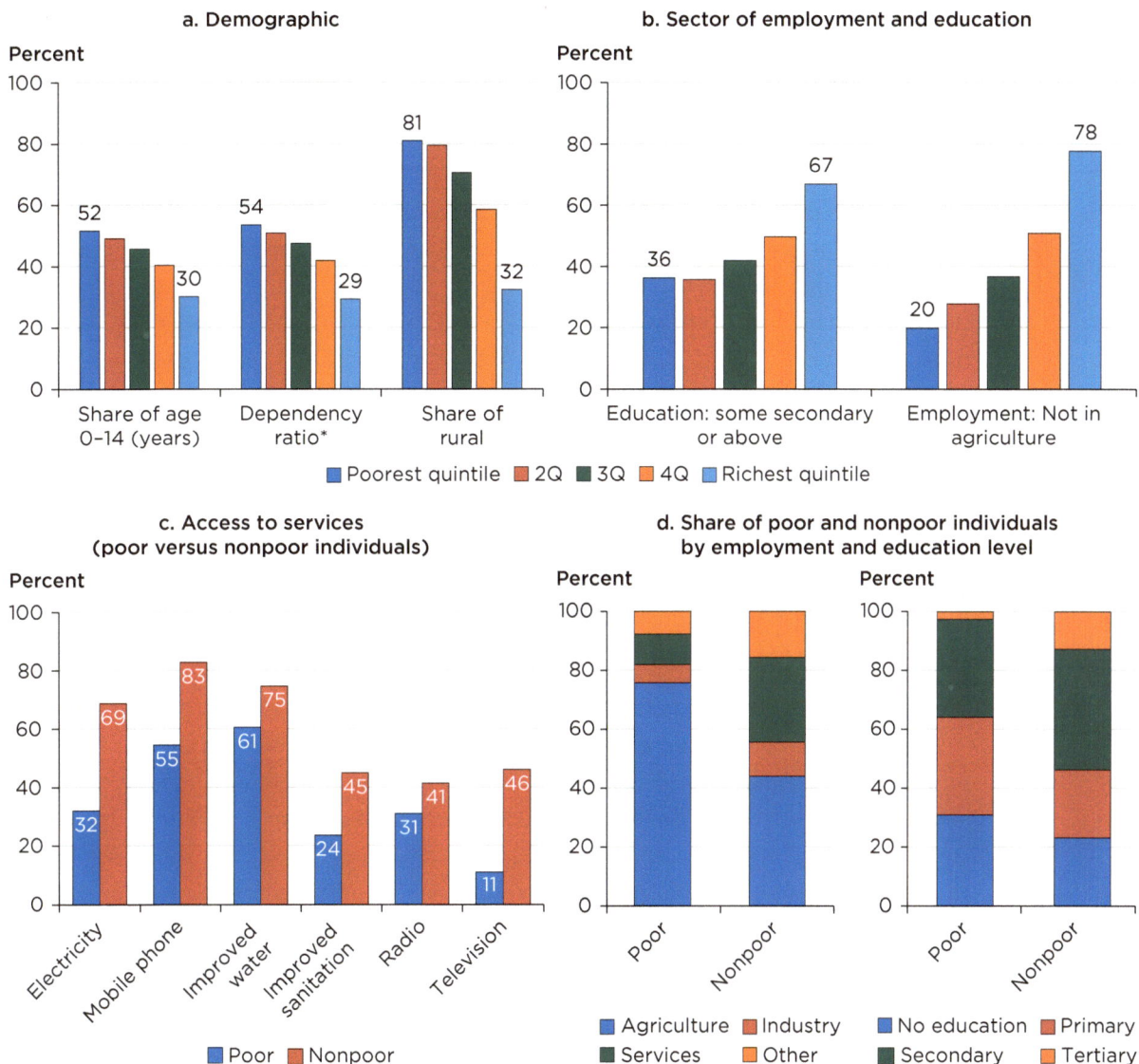

a. Demographic

Percent

b. Sector of employment and education

Percent

Legend: ■ Poorest quintile ■ 2Q ■ 3Q ■ 4Q ■ Richest quintile

c. Access to services (poor versus nonpoor individuals)

Percent

Legend: ■ Poor ■ Nonpoor

d. Share of poor and nonpoor individuals by employment and education level

Percent

Percent

Legend:
■ Agriculture ■ Industry
■ Services ■ Other

■ No education ■ Primary
■ Secondary ■ Tertiary

Sources: Tabulations based on Global Monitoring Database and World Development Indicators.
Note: Quintiles by per capita consumption for Sub-Saharan Africa as a whole. For dependency ratio, quintiles of households; for the rest, quintiles of total population. Poor versus nonpoor by $2.15/day (2017 PPP). PPP = purchasing power parity; Q = quintile.

identified earlier: those based on gender, on location, and on access to services, especially higher education. Household demographics matter—the number of children in the household and the dependency ratio tend to be progressively higher for households lower down the economic scale. Having less than secondary education, employment in agriculture, and location in rural areas are likewise associated with lower welfare status of households. Poor individuals are also less likely to have access to basic services such as improved water and sanitation and, in particular, electricity, as well as to means of communication and information, such as mobile phones, radio, and television. These are not just critical inputs into human capital formation but are also labor productivity and economic opportunities, including in the region's substantial employment in agriculture and microenterprises.

Upward mobility of poor individuals is constrained by a high degree of inequality of opportunities that also affects the trajectory of economic growth. For African countries, intergenerational mobility in education, a direct outcome of inequality of opportunity in childhood, is on average well below that of the developing world, with several countries in the bottom quintile of the world (Narayan et al. 2018; van der Weide et al. 2024; refer also to Suarez et al. 2015). Thus, in most Africa countries, the social status of parents (proxied by education) has a strong influence on the educational attainment of offspring, indicating a lack of social mobility that is in some countries among the lowest in the world. Global cross-country evidence shows that lower intergenerational mobility is strongly associated with higher income inequality and that higher intergenerational mobility in education among a generation is associated with higher economic growth and lower poverty when that generation reaches adulthood (Narayan et al. 2018). The extent of intergenerational mobility is further analyzed in detail in chapter 3 of this report.

A source of structural inequality that has a particularly strong effect on poverty reduction and growth in the region is gender-based inequality. Gender inequality in opportunities for women and girls undermines their human capital accumulation and prospects for intergenerational mobility (Delprato, Akyeampong, and Dunne 2017). Certain social norms, and in some cases legal restrictions, also result in inequities in the intrahousehold allocation of resources and time, which further limits women's agency and economic independence. Perhaps most concretely for growth and poverty reduction, these inequities have a direct effect on the region's high adolescent fertility. All these factors result in important gender gaps in economic outcomes, such as in returns to entrepreneurship (a 31 percent gap in profits in Malawi, a 49 percent gap in the Democratic Republic of Congo, and a 45 percent gap in Ethiopia) (Banerjee et al. 2014; World Bank 2019b) and in agricultural yields (13 percent in Uganda, 25 percent in Malawi, and 23 percent in Ethiopia). The extent to which gender inequalities affect poverty and outcomes in Africa is explored in more detail in spotlight 2 (gender) of this report.

The region significantly trails the rest of the world in building human capital, providing quality education, and closing gender gaps (as shown in chapter 3), despite significant progress in most countries in the region, as reflected by the low rate of deprivation in school enrollment of school-age children relative to that of older generations. This represents a significant intergenerational shift in access to basic schooling and potential for building human capital—especially for women. Although a significant gender gap

FIGURE 2.15 Gender gap in deprivation from access to education

Gender gap (pp)

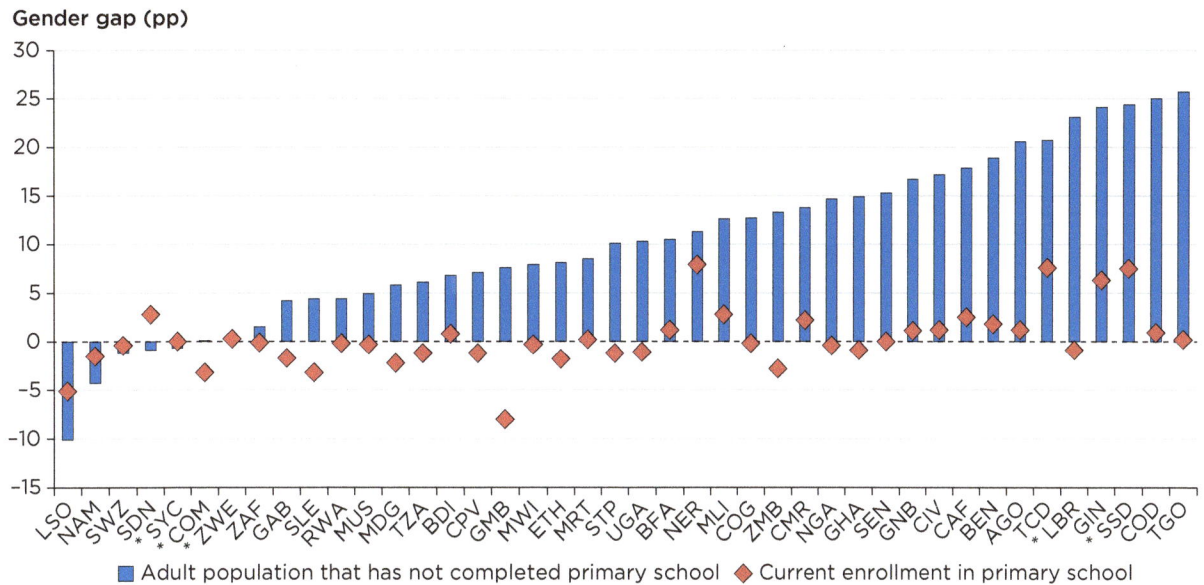

■ Adult population that has not completed primary school ◆ Current enrollment in primary school

Sources: Tabulations based on World Bank 2024a and World Development Indicators.
Note: Gender gap is defined as the deprivation rate for women and girls in excess of that for men and boys. Negative values indicate that men and boys have a higher deprivation rate than women and girls. Because of differences in surveys, an asterisk denotes countries in which the indicator used was adult population with any education rather than adult population with primary school completed. pp = percentage point. For country abbreviations, refer to https://www.iso.org/obp/ui/#search.

among adults exists in primary school completion in most countries of the region, recent primary school enrollment rates tend to have significantly lower gender gaps (refer to figure 2.15). Critically, for the region's growth and inclusion prospects, increased access to basic schooling does not automatically translate to learning and increased skills. This is explored in more detail in chapter 3.

Structural inequality contributes to slow structural transformation and limited job creation

Structural inequality in the region may also have contributed to the region's slow structural transformation and the resulting low growth of labor productivity. Building on the analysis by Duclos and O'Connell (2015), two clear channels through which poverty-inducing structural inequality can affect the region's composition of growth are, first, regressive market imperfections, such as credit being limited to lending to those with wealth (for collateral) because of information and enforcement failures and, second, politically generated distortions, such as institutions that favor incumbent firms through the allocation of public resources or policies designed to thwart competition.

These lead to a misallocation of resources across sectors and firms, thus influencing the composition of growth and the rate of structural transformation. These distortions would help explain the low growth of productivity and slow structural transformation seen in the region today.

Africa's economic growth is dominated by low-productivity services, and agriculture remains the region's largest employer. This services-driven growth and large dependence on low-productivity agriculture limit households' opportunities to use their productive capacity to raise incomes, even in growing economies. The share of agriculture (in terms of value added) in GDP, although much lower than that of services and industry, is still higher in Africa than for any other region except for South Asia (refer to figure 2.16b). The sector employs the highest share of workers, even as value added per worker, or labor productivity, in agriculture is the lowest among the three sectors, which is evident from the high share of agricultural households among those who are poor (refer to figure 2.14d). The reliance on agriculture for livelihoods implies significant household dependence on natural resources and rainfall, leaving many households highly vulnerable to the effects of climate change. As noted earlier, globally across countries, higher shares of employment and value added in agriculture are associated with a weaker link between growth in GDP and average living standards of households.

FIGURE 2.16 Sectoral composition of growth and value added

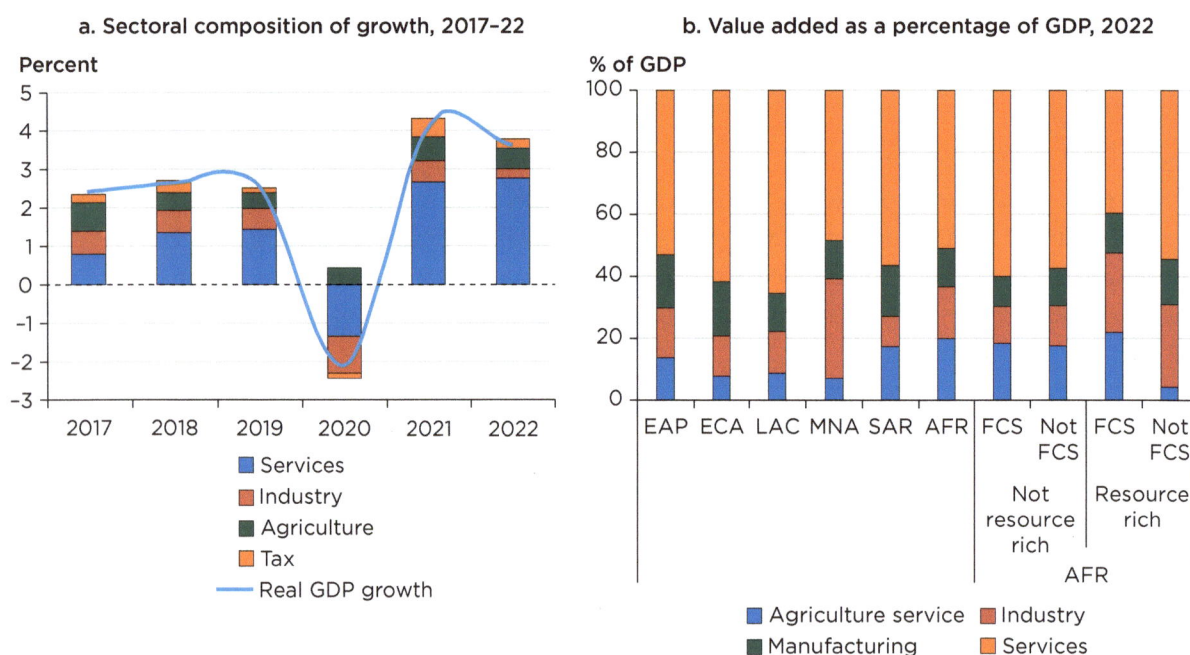

a. Sectoral composition of growth, 2017–22

b. Value added as a percentage of GDP, 2022

Services
Industry
Agriculture
Tax
Real GDP growth

Agriculture service   Industry
Manufacturing   Services

Sources: Panel a, World Bank 2024b; panel b, World Development Indicators.
Note: In panel b, regional aggregates exclude high-income countries. AFR = Sub-Saharan Africa; EAP = East Asia and Pacific; ECA = Europe and Central Asia; FCS = fragile and conflict-affected situation; GDP = gross domestic product; LAC = Latin America and the Caribbean; MNA = Middle East and North Africa; SAR = South Asia.

Africa's manufacturing value added as a share of GDP is the lowest globally compared with other regions, consistent with what has been referred to as Africa's "premature deindustrialization" (McMillan and Zeufack 2022; refer to figure 2.16b). This limits the potential for job creation, because manufacturing is widely considered to be a source of good jobs for low-income countries, based on East Asia's experience. In fact, Africa is experiencing a peak in the employment share of manufacturing at much lower levels of GDP per capita, according to the research literature. Studies find that this is due to a combination of factors related to changes in demand, globalization, and technological advances (Goldberg and Reed 2023; Rodrik 2016). Instead, structural transformation in the region has taken the shape of shifting workers from agriculture into services. This shift may be increasing inequality: evidence from cross-country analysis suggests that a shift in employment share from agriculture to services is associated with an increase in income inequality, whereas a similar shift from agriculture to industry is not (Baymul and Sen 2019, using data from the Groningen Growth and Development Center and inequality data from the World Income Inequality Database).

The structural shifts in employment that have occurred have not brought about the expected boost to labor productivity in Africa. Diao, McMillan, and Rodrik (2017) show that growth-promoting structural change has been significant in Africa, but it has been accompanied by mostly negative labor productivity growth in nonagricultural sectors. This is the result of small firms absorbing a large majority of the growth of employment in African countries (Baymul and Sen 2019). Therefore, although there are gains to households' income in moving from agriculture to other, more productive sectors, within-sector labor productivity growth in the nonagricultural sector is not substantial, which brings down overall labor productivity growth. In some resource-rich countries in the region, the industry sector is dominated by the capital-intensive sectors of mining and extractives. Growth of industry, therefore, need not necessarily lead to a higher rate of creation of good jobs if the growth occurred primarily in the mining and extractive industries.

Structural inequality reduces the efficiency of growth for poverty reduction

Weak transmission of macroeconomic growth to average household welfare is the main driver of the region's significantly weaker link between GDP growth and poverty reduction relative to other regions, as shown earlier in this chapter (Wu et al. 2024). Intuitively, the elasticity (responsiveness) of poverty to per capita GDP growth is the product of two components: first, the transmission from growth in GDP per capita to growth in average (per capita) household welfare, as measured with surveys and, second, the transmission from growth in average household welfare to change in poverty. The first component is the main factor contributing to the lower GEP for Africa.[15] The association between GDP and household consumption growth is found to be significantly weaker in Africa, suggesting that, relative to other regions, African countries need higher GDP growth to achieve similar improvements in average monetary household welfare. This finding also validates the robustness of the earlier headline result (refer to figure 2.12) that GEP for GDP growth is significantly lower in Africa than in other low-income regions.[16] As shown earlier, weak transmission of growth to household welfare is associated with lower levels of human capital development, structural transformation, and economic diversification.

Africa's higher levels of income inequality, a consequence of high structural inequality, also result in a weaker link between growth in average household welfare and poverty reduction. Higher initial inequality (at the beginning of a growth episode) has a significant and positive effect on the relationship between growth in average household consumption and poverty change, confirming that high levels of inequality weaken the transmission from growth to poverty reduction, as other studies have found (Bergstrom 2022; Bourguignon 2003). To the extent that current measures of inequality do not capture incomes at the top of the distribution, this effect may be even larger (refer to box 2.3). To illustrate, the average GEP amounts to −2.3 for episodes with an initial Gini index lower than 40 but weakens to −1.4 when the initial Gini is 40 or higher.[17] As a result, countries with higher levels of inequality need to achieve faster growth in average household consumption to reduce poverty by the same factor. A close look at the welfare trends in Botswana and Chad illustrates this point. Both countries were able to reduce their severe poverty rate by about one-third (39.3 percent for Botswana and 36.6 percent for Chad) during comparable periods. However, because of its reduction in inequality, Botswana was able to accomplish this with average household welfare growth at only 2 percent per year, compared with Chad's growth in excess of 5 percent per year (refer to figure 2.17).[18] That is, Botswana achieved the same level of poverty reduction through a combination of reduction in inequality and lower growth as Chad did through higher growth accompanied by increased inequality.

FIGURE 2.17 Growth incidence curves for Botswana and Chad

a. Botswana (2002–09)

Growth in per capita household consumption (%)

b. Chad (2003–11)

Growth in per capita household consumption (%)

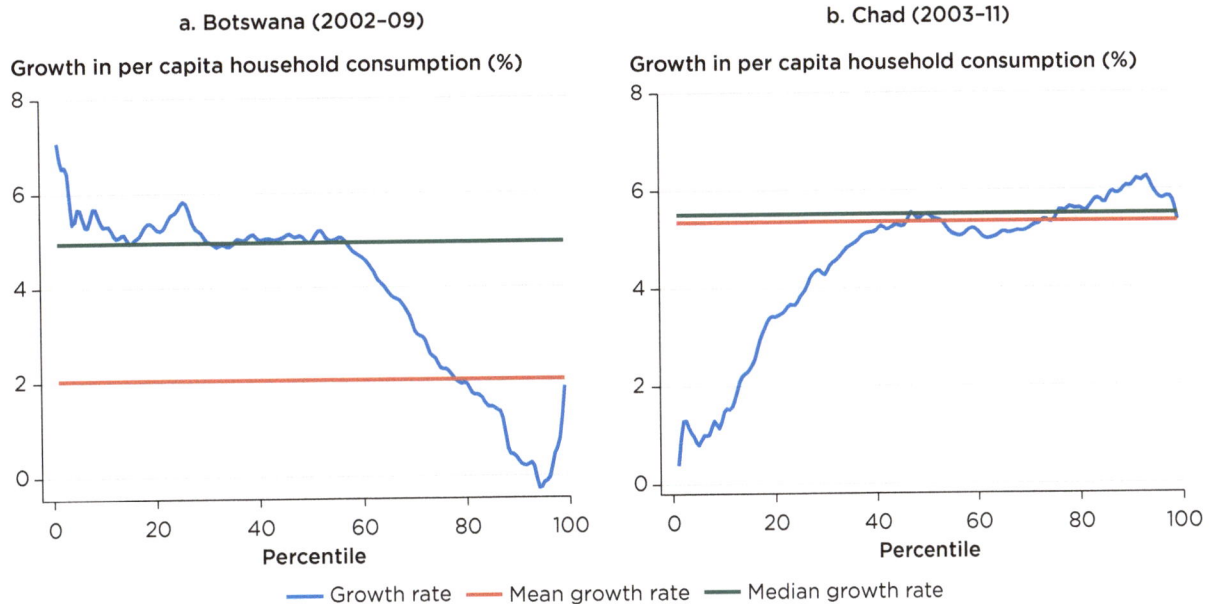

—— Growth rate —— Mean growth rate —— Median growth rate

Source: Tabulations based on World Bank 2024a.
Note: The growth incidence curve shows the rate of growth at each percentile of the income or consumption distribution between two years.

BOX 2.3

Top incomes in Africa

Inequality in Africa could be higher than estimated through household survey data. The first reason is that inequality in Africa is mostly measured using consumption as a proxy for welfare, which typically leads to a lower estimated inequality compared with inequality measured with income because consumption does not capture the role of savings or wealth (Blundell et al. 2008; World Bank 2016). Another important reason is the difficulty in measuring incomes at the top of the distribution, either because wealthy individuals do not respond to surveys or because they underreport their income when they do respond.[a] A large literature has looked at these challenges and proposed solutions (Choumert-Nkolo et al. 2023; JEI 2022; Kerr and Zondi 2024; Lustig 2020; Ravallion 2022). Recent advances involve combining household survey data with national accounts data and administrative data, such as tax records (refer to the Distributional National Accounts, Blanchet 2024, Piketty et al. 2022, and the World Inequality Database [https://wid.world/]). A recent paper using this approach focuses on Africa and shows that it is the region with the highest top-10-percent-to-bottom-50-percent income ratio in the world (Chancel et al. 2023). Moreover, 55 percent of total regional income goes to the regional top 10 percent of the distribution, on par with regions or countries characterized by extreme inequality, such as Latin America and the Caribbean or India.

(continued)

The Poverty Reduction Challenge in Africa

55

BOX 2.3
Top Incomes in Africa *(continued)*

FIGURE B2.3.1 **Global income–consumption distribution versus Africa's**

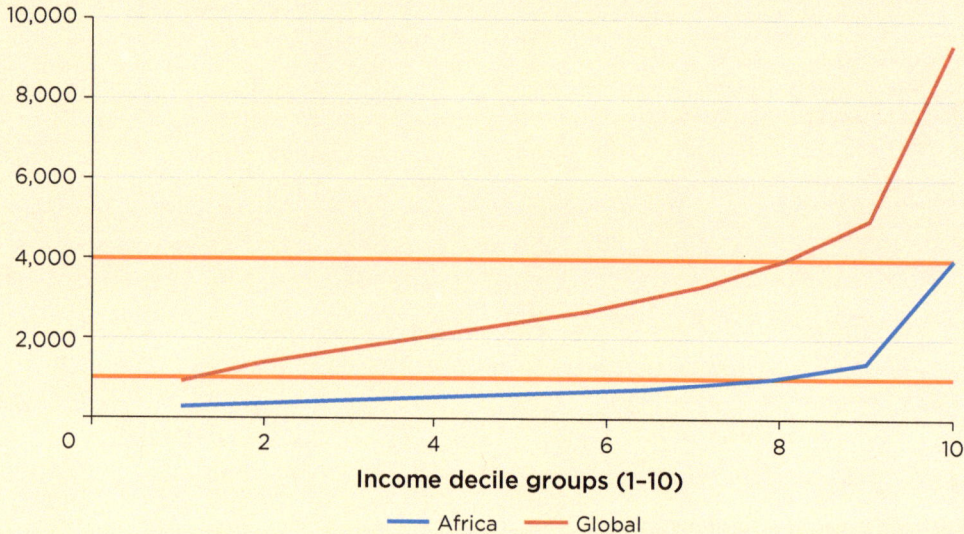

Sources: World Bank staff estimates based on data from Lakner and Milanovic 2016. The data are available in the World Bank Data Catalog or at https://stonecenter.gc.cuny.edu/research/lakner-milanovic-world-panel-income -distribution/.
Note: The top orange horizontal line is the average per capita income or consumption for decile 10 in Africa, and the bottom orange horizontal line is the average per capita income or consumption for decile 8 in Africa.

Top incomes in Africa are not too far away from those of the super rich elsewhere. Although in the 1990s almost nobody in Africa was richer than people with the median income in the poorest country in the Organisation for Economic Co-operation and Development, in 2018 this group grew only slightly, to 1.1 percent (Milanovic 2024). This indicates that only the richest individuals in Africa might have benefited from the growth in the past 30 years or so, and indeed estimates suggest that (consumption) growth has been very unequal, such that the richest 5 percent of Africans received around 40 percent of the total gains (Jirasavetakul and Lakner 2020). Figure B2.3.1 shows that all decile groups in Africa are well below the corresponding decile for the global income distribution, which means that people in Africa are overall poorer than those in the rest of the world at any point in the global distribution. However, top incomes in Africa fare extremely well compared with their African peers, at least in relative terms. For instance, the top decile in Africa would still be in the top part of the global distribution (around decile 8; see the top red line in figure B2.3.1). However, other rich deciles in Africa would be among the poorest in the world; for instance, decile 8 in Africa would be around decile 1 globally (see the bottom red line in figure B2.3.1). Overall, although poorer than the super rich at the same decile globally, top incomes in Africa are not too far away from those of the super rich elsewhere. This is completely different for the rest of the deciles in Africa, which are among the poorest in global terms.

a. Measuring the upper tail of the distribution using household surveys has proven difficult for a variety of reasons, including unit nonresponse (top-income individuals are more likely not to respond to surveys) and item (income questions are not responded to), underreporting of income, and sparseness (only few observations in top tail if income is highly concentrated).

Conclusion

Successfully reducing poverty in the region requires tackling structural inequality. As the subsequent chapters show, structural inequality in Africa is driven by a wide-ranging set of factors, and addressing them requires a multisectoral perspective. These factors include inadequate and inequitable public investment (in education, health, and infrastructure), market failures (such as in land and credit) and lack of market size (low population density and lack of market integration), and high and uninsurable risks (including climate change and conflict). Lower levels of human capital development and access to basic services, for example, are linked to a high degree of inequality of opportunity, and the lack of structural transformation and economic diversification is associated with inequalities in access to productivity-enhancing factors, such as finance and market access. The next chapter delves into how structural inequalities work to limit many Africans' access to basic opportunities, namely, through human capital accumulation, thus ensuring an uneven playing field right from birth.

Annex 2A: Additional data for chapter 2

TABLE 2A.1 Poverty rate (US$2.15/day, 2017 PPP), by region and world average, 2000–22

Year	EAP	SAR	AFR	LAC	ECA	MNA	World
2000	39.7	40.9	56.0	13.7	9.2	3.0	29.4
2001	37.0	40.7	55.0	13.5	8.3	3.0	28.4
2002	32.5	40.4	54.4	12.6	7.4	2.8	26.9
2003	28.5	38.9	53.2	12.2	7.3	2.8	25.3
2004	24.9	37.2	50.4	11.3	5.5	2.7	23.4
2005	20.7	35.5	48.7	10.7	4.7	2.7	21.6
2006	19.9	33.8	47.2	8.8	3.3	2.6	20.6
2007	17.6	32.1	46.0	7.7	2.2	2.5	19.3
2008	16.2	30.9	44.5	7.0	1.4	2.5	18.4
2009	14.5	29.5	43.9	6.7	1.2	2.2	17.5
2010	12.6	25.4	42.1	5.9	1.2	1.9	15.7
2011	9.9	21.6	41.0	5.4	0.9	2.0	13.9
2012	8.3	19.8	39.8	5.1	0.9	2.2	13.0
2013	4.3	18.9	38.9	4.5	0.7	2.5	11.6
2014	3.4	17.8	38.1	4.3	1.0	2.8	11.0
2015	2.3	16.6	38.2	4.0	0.8	3.7	10.5

(continued)

TABLE 2A.1 Poverty rate (US$2.15/day, 2017 PPP), by region and world average, 2000–22 *(continued)*

Year	EAP	SAR	AFR	LAC	ECA	MNA	World
2016	1.7	15.7	38.0	4.2	0.7	4.4	10.2
2017	1.2	12.6	37.5	4.3	0.7	4.7	9.4
2018	1.2	10.1	36.8	4.2	0.4	4.7	8.7
2019	1.0	10.6	36.5	4.2	0.5	4.6	8.8
2020	1.1	13.0	38.1	3.8	0.5	5.3	9.7
2021	1.1	11.4	38.3	4.5	0.5	5.9	9.6
2022	1.0	9.7	38.0	3.4	0.5	6.1	9.1

Source: Poverty and Inequality Platform, World Bank (October 2024; https://pip.worldbank.org/home).
Note: AFR = Sub-Saharan Africa; EAP = East Asia and Pacific; ECP = Europe and Central Asia; MNA = Middle East and North Africa; PPP = purchasing power parity; SAR = South Asia.

TABLE 2A.2 Poverty rate for Africa, by international poverty line, 2000–22

Year	$2.15/day	$3.65/day	$6.85/day
2000	56.0	77.6	91.6
2001	55.0	77.2	91.6
2002	54.4	76.9	91.6
2003	53.2	76.6	91.7
2004	50.4	74.9	91.3
2005	48.7	73.7	91.0
2006	47.2	72.4	90.3
2007	46.0	71.6	90.0
2008	44.5	70.6	89.5
2009	43.9	70.2	89.4
2010	42.1	69.0	88.9
2011	41.0	68.2	88.7
2012	39.8	67.4	88.4
2013	38.9	66.6	88.1
2014	38.1	65.8	87.7
2015	38.2	65.7	87.5
2016	38.0	65.4	87.5
2017	37.5	64.8	87.4

(continued)

TABLE 2A.2 **Poverty rate for Africa, by international poverty line, 2000–22** *(continued)*

Year	$2.15/day	$3.65/day	$6.85/day
2018	36.8	64.2	87.3
2019	36.5	63.7	87.2
2020	38.1	65.2	87.9
2021	38.3	65.2	87.8
2022	38.0	65.0	87.8

Source: Poverty and Inequality Platform, World Bank (October 2024; https://pip.worldbank.org /home).

TABLE 2A.3 **Multidimensional poverty, by country**

Economy	Year	Deprivation dimension (%)					MPM rate (%)	Monetary poverty rate (%)
		Education completed	School enrollment	Electricity	Sanitation	Water		
Angola	2018	30	27	53	54	32	47	31
Benin	2021	49	32	35	77	24	45	13
Botswana	2015	8	4	35	52	4	21	15
Burkina Faso	2021	48	51	35	59	17	53	25
Burundi	2020	45	34	91	91	12	79	62
Cabo Verde	2015	12	3	10	30	11	8	5
Cameroon	2021	56	24	37	52	19	41	23
Chad	2022	49	53	94	96	43	81	31
Comoros	2014	15	7	28	67	6	26	19
Congo, Dem. Rep.	2020	22	10	69	82	36	84	79
Congo, Rep.	2011	13	2	30	47	23	42	35
Côte d'Ivoire	2021	44	25	9	60	17	29	10
Eswatini	2016	11	0	36	46	28	41	36
Ethiopia	2015	67	31	64	96	43	73	27
Gabon	2017	11	8	9	68	12	8	2
Gambia, The	2020	29	40	29	53	13	36	17
Ghana	2016	15	9	19	80	41	33	25
Guinea	2018	61	25	56	71	21	52	14
Guinea-Bissau	2021	20	31	28	60	21	39	26

(continued)

TABLE 2A.3 Multidimensional poverty, by country *(continued)*

Economy	Year	Deprivation dimension (%)					MPM rate (%)	Monetary poverty rate (%)
		Education completed	School enrollment	Electricity	Sanitation	Water		
Kenya	2021	10	1	25	22	36	38	36
Lesotho	2017	18	5	59	55	14	41	32
Liberia	2016	31	54	80	62	26	57	28
Madagascar	2012	82	35	13	77	60	85	81
Malawi	2019	54	4	89	75	11	78	70
Mali	2021	64	46	16	48	19	51	21
Mauritania	2019	56	34	20	56	38	42	5
Mauritius	2017	7	0	0	.	.	0	0
Mozambique	2019	47	7	68	72	49	82	75
Namibia	2015	11	6	54	68	9	28	16
Niger	2021	72	47	74	83	34	78	51
Nigeria	2018	18	9	39	45	33	40	31
Rwanda	2016	37	4	64	28	25	57	52
São Tomé and Príncipe	2017	11	4	31	62	88	40	16
Senegal	2021	39	33	30	32	11	37	10
Seychelles	2018	0	.	0	0	5	1	1
Sierra Leone	2018	29	19	69	87	34	54	26
South Africa	2014	2	2	4	35	10	22	21
South Sudan	2016	39	62	.	88	14	85	67
Sudan	2014	40	23	49	93	45	53	15
Tanzania	2018	13	19	44	72	29	55	45
Togo	2021	30	12	32	86	26	44	27
Uganda	2019	31	12	41	71	24	52	42
Zambia	2022	16	23	45	54	27	67	64
Zimbabwe	2019	1	6	38	38	19	42	40

Source: Poverty and Inequality Platform, World Bank (October 2024; https://pip.worldbank.org/home).
Note: MPM = Multidimensional Poverty Measure.

TABLE 2A.4 Averages of selected development indicators, Africa and the World, 2022

Indicator	2022	
	AFR	**World**
Literacy rate, youth total (% of people ages 15–24)	67.7	87.0
Access to electricity (% of population)	51.4	91.4
People using at least basic drinking water services (% of population)	50.6	83.8
People using at least basic sanitation services (% of population)	34.6	80.6
Agriculture, value added (% of GDP)	17.3	4.3
Forest rents (% of GDP)	2.4	0.1
Employment in services (% of total employment) (modeled ILO estimate)	36.8	49.7

Source: World Development Indicators (October 2024).
Note: AFR = Sub-Saharan Africa; GDP = gross domestic product; ILO = International Labour Organization.

TABLE 2A.5 Typology of countries, by FCS and resource-rich status

Not resource rich and never FCS	Resource rich and never FCS	Not resource rich and FCS	Resource rich and FCS
Benin	Botswana	Burkina Faso	Angola
Cabo Verde	Equatorial Guinea	Burundi	Chad
Eswatini	Gabon	Cameroon	Congo, Dem. Rep.
Ghana	Namibia	Central African Republic	Guinea
Kenya	South Africa	Comoros	Liberia
Lesotho	Zambia	Côte d'Ivoire	Mauritania
Mauritius		Eritrea	Niger
Rwanda		Ethiopia	Nigeria
Senegal		Gambia, The	Sierra Leone
Seychelles		Guinea-Bissau	South Sudan
Tanzania		Madagascar	Congo, Rep.
Uganda		Malawi	
		Mali	
		Mozambique	
		São Tomé and Príncipe	
		Somalia	

(continued)

TABLE 2A.5 Typology of countries, by FCS and resource-rich status (continued)

Not resource rich and never FCS	Resource rich and never FCS	Not resource rich and FCS	Resource rich and FCS
		Sudan	
		Togo	
		Zimbabwe	

Source: Original for this publication based on World Bank 2023a, 2023b.
Note: FCS = fragile and conflict-affected situation.

FIGURE 2A.1 Deprivation rates in school enrollment and access to improved sanitation, by poverty rate

Share of population (%)

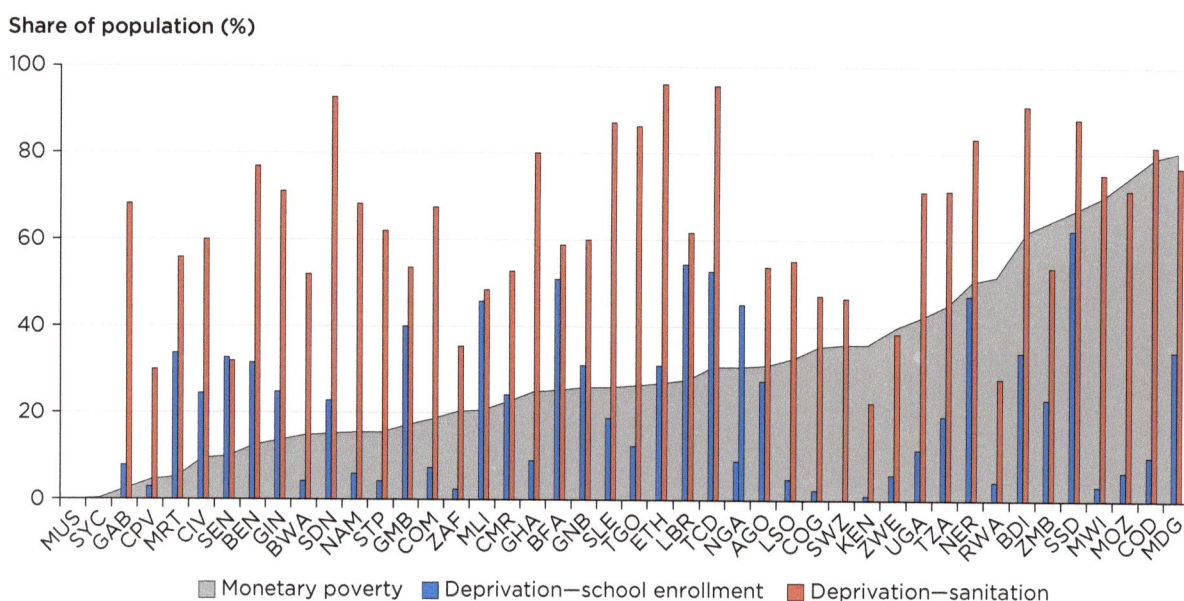

Monetary poverty Deprivation—school enrollment Deprivation—sanitation

Source: Tabulations based on Poverty and Inequality Platform (October 2024).
Note: Using international poverty line of $2.15/day (2017 purchasing power parity). MPM analysis is limited to the subset of countries with sufficiently detailed surveys to estimate MPM. MPM = Multidimensional Poverty Measure.

FIGURE 2A.2 Prosperity gap: Additional figures

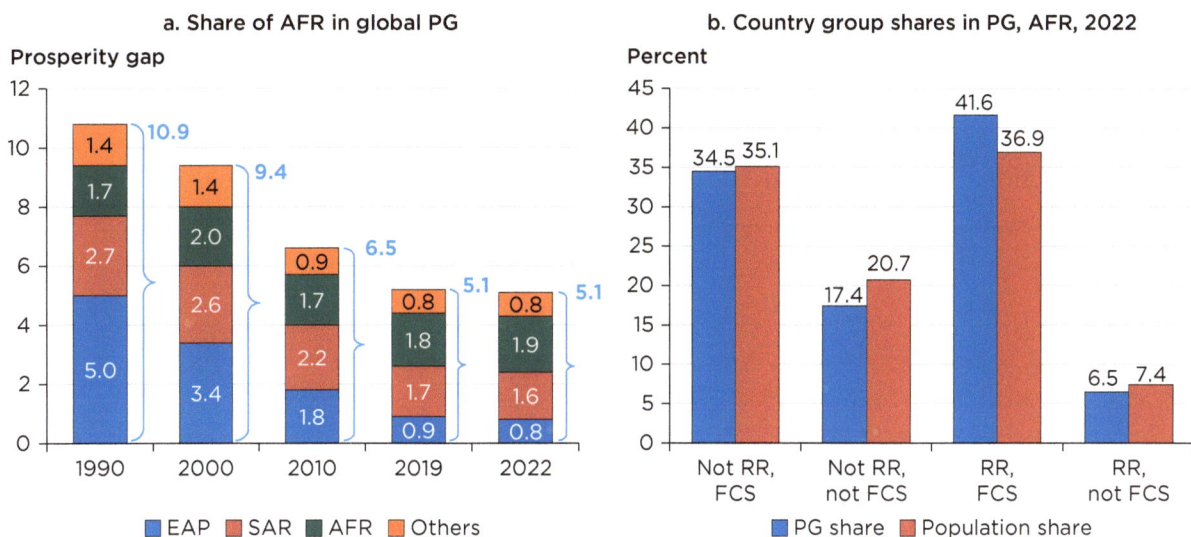

a. Share of AFR in global PG

Prosperity gap

b. Country group shares in PG, AFR, 2022

Percent

Legend (chart a): EAP, SAR, AFR, Others

Legend (chart b): PG share, Population share

Source: Poverty and Inequality Platform (October 2024).
Notes: AFR = Sub-Saharan Africa; EAP = East Asia and Pacific; FCS = fragile and conflict-affected situation; PG = prosperity gap; RR = resource rich; SAR = South Asia.

Annex 2B: Estimating the conditional relationship between country typology and the Multidimensional Poverty Measure

This annex describes the process for estimating the relationship between country typology and poverty, as defined by the Multidimensional Poverty Measure.

Data description

This analysis uses two data sets. The first is the World Bank's (2023c) Multidimensional Poverty Measure (MPM). This data set contains results from the most recent survey for each country conducted between 2011 and 2020. The second is the World Development Indicators (October 26, 2023, update), which includes data on gross domestic product (GDP) per capita in current US dollars. In addition, all countries are classified on the basis of the resource-rich and fragile and conflict-affected situation typology used in this report, as well as on whether they are landlocked (Botswana, Burkina Faso, Burundi, Chad, Ethiopia, Eswatini, Lesotho, Malawi, Mali, Niger, Ruanda, South Sudan, Uganda, Zambia, and Zimbabwe).[19]

Regression

The methodology is an extension of the one used for figure O.4 in Beegle et al. (2016). In turn, each of the dimensions of the MPM (which includes monetary poverty) and the overall measure are regressed on indicators for the four typologies, controlling for log of

GDP per capita (in the year when the survey was conducted), whether the country is landlocked, and whether the survey is from 2011–16 or 2017–20. Figure 2.7e in the current report shows the value of the coefficients and their statistical significance.

Annex 2C: Estimating the elasticity of poverty to economic growth

This annex presents an overview of the data and methodology used by Wu et al. (2024b).

Data description

The data used for the Wu et al. (2024b) analysis are from the Poverty and Inequality Platform (World Bank 2022a), the World Bank's database for monitoring global poverty (refer to World Bank 2022b for a description of the data sources and methods used). It contains household welfare distributions (either income or consumption, depending on the survey) from nationally representative household surveys used for national and international poverty monitoring.

Following the traditional approach of research on the growth elasticity of poverty (GEP), a database of episodes is created by combining each pair of comparable consecutive surveys in every country. For each episode, the mean household welfare per capita (in 2017 purchasing power parity) and the $2.15/day poverty rate at both the start and the end of the episode are calculated. Each of the country–episode years is merged with national accounts data (gross domestic product [GDP] and household final consumption expenditures [HFCE], expressed in constant dollars and per capita terms) from the World Development Indicators.[20] Because of the sensitivity of elasticity estimates to outliers of a small magnitude, episodes for which both the initial-year and end-year poverty rate are below 2 percent were eliminated from the sample.[21] This results in a sample of 575 comparable episodes between 1981 and 2021, based on 715 nationally representative household surveys for 89 countries, representing more than 92 percent of the population of low- and middle-income countries.

Finally, to correct the bias toward countries with many surveys, observations are weighted equal to the inverse number of episodes in each country. This results in equal weight given to each country regardless of the number of episodes available and changes the regional distribution of episodes by giving more weight to countries with fewer observations.

Regression analysis

Wu et al. (2024a) use the following base specification from Ravallion and Chen (1997) to estimate the GEP and test for differences across regions and time periods:

$$\Delta Log\, P_{it} = \alpha + \beta \Delta Log\, \mu_{it} + \Delta \epsilon_{it}, \tag{2C.1}$$

where the rate of poverty reduction is regressed on the rate of growth (in household consumption per capita, GDP per capita, or HFCE per capita). $\Delta Log\,P_{it}$ denotes the change in log poverty rates during episode t in country i (expressed in annual terms), whereas $\Delta Log\,\mu_{it}$ is the change in real GDP per capita (or real per capita survey means) in the same country during the same period. This basic specification is estimated with and without country fixed effects.

Although equation 2C.1 forms the core of the analysis, several variables are added sequentially to control for initial differences (in poverty rates, inequality, and so forth) and to assess whether elasticities differ significantly across regions or time periods.

To test whether Africa has lower elasticities than other regions, whether elasticities have changed over time, and whether the effect of growth on poverty reduction is mediated by the level of inequality, Wu et al. (2024a) augment equation 2C.1 as follows:

$$\Delta Log\,P_{it} = \alpha + \beta\,\Delta Log\,\mu_{it} + \gamma X_{i0} + \delta\,(\Delta Log\,\mu_{it} * X_{i0}) + \in_{it}, \qquad (2C.2)$$

where X_{i0} is the relevant characteristic whose mediating influence is being tested (region, time period, or initial inequality) and δ is the coefficient of the interaction between household consumption growth and the relevant characteristic. If δ is statistically significant, characteristic X_{i0} has an influence on the extent to which growth translates into poverty reduction.

As a final step in the analysis, Wu et al. (2024a) assess which factors mediate the effect of economic growth (measured by GDP per capita or HFCE per capita) on household welfare using the following equation:

$$\Delta Log\,Y_{it} = \alpha + \beta\,\Delta LogGDP\_Cap_{it} + \gamma X_{i0} + \delta\,(\Delta LogGDP\_Cap_{it} * X_{i0}) + \in_{it}, \qquad (2C.3)$$

where $Log\,Y_{it}$ is the change in household welfare during episode t, $\Delta LogGDP\_Cap_{it}$ is the change in GDP per capita (from national accounts) during the time period, and X_{i0} is the variable that potentially mediates the effect of GDP growth on household welfare growth.[22] This regression is run separately for each of the 68 variables tested.[23] To test for Type I errors, Wu et al. (2024a) control for the expected false discovery rate by calculating sharpened q values (rather than ordinary p values), as proposed by Benjamini, Krieger, and Yekutieli (2006) and Anderson (2008).

Annex 2D: Decomposing inequality of household welfare

This decomposition of inequality in household welfare is based on Fields's (2003) methodology.[24] This methodology is based on a standard income-generating function wherein the log of the outcome of interest (per capita welfare, measured most often by expenditures or consumption) is regressed on a series of household characteristics associated with household welfare. The main drivers of inequality are thus identified on the basis of the contributions of these explanatory variables (such as education, labor market factors, and demographics).

Specifically, the baseline specification of

$$\Delta Log\,(y_i) = \beta \boldsymbol{X}_i + \in_i \qquad \text{(2D.1)}$$

can be rewritten as a linear model of the form

$$y = \beta_0 + z_1 + z_2 + z_3 + \cdots + z_k + \in, \qquad \text{(2D.2)}$$

where y_i is household per capita welfare, $\boldsymbol{X}_i$ is a matrix of k household characteristics (including characteristics of the household head or main earner), and z_n is the product of the regression coefficient and the associated variable. Equation 2D.2 is of the same form as that used by Shorrocks (1982) to derive the rules for decomposing inequality across factors. Fields (2023) applies Shorrocks's decomposition rule to calculate the contributions of each factor to the inequality of y.

Two approaches are used to calculate the decomposition:

$$y = b_0 + \widehat{z_1} + \widehat{z_2} + \widehat{z_3} + \ldots + \widehat{z_k} + \widehat{\in_l} \qquad \text{(2D.3)}$$

and

$$\hat{y} = b_0 + \widehat{z_1} + \widehat{z_2} + \widehat{z_3} + \ldots + \widehat{z_k}. \qquad \text{(2D.4)}$$

Equation 2D.4 models the fitted value of y and hence has no residuals, whereas equation 2D.3 estimates the share of variable that is unexplained by the factors (that is, the residuals). Chapter 1 includes results from both sets of regressions (with and without the residuals).

Both regressions are run for each of the 43 countries with recent survey data. The results of the decomposition are averaged across countries for the regional aggregate and for the subset of countries for the results by typology.

The factors considered in this analysis include the following:

- *Human capital*: age of household head; gender of household head; and whether the household head achieved primary education, secondary education, or tertiary education

- *Location*: Region–province and rural–urban dummy variables

- *Household demographics*: share of household members who are children and share of household members who are elderly

- *Labor market*: sector of employment of head (industry, service) and whether head is not working (out of labor force or unemployed).

Notes

1. Extreme poverty measured using International Poverty Line, which amounts to $2.15 per person per day at 2017 PPP.

2. These are the best performers from the set of countries in the region that have multiple and comparable surveys during the period of analysis. The analysis excludes Mauritius and the Seychelles because of very low initial poverty rates.

3. In terms of percentage point (pp) changes instead of percent changes, poverty fell at an annual average rate of 0.54 pp in 2014–19 compared with 1.35 pp in 2000–14, whereas global poverty fell at the average rates of 1.30 pp and 0.53 pp in the corresponding periods. Given that global poverty rate was much lower throughout the period, the fact that change in Africa was close to that for the world implies that Africa has progressively fallen behind the rest of the world in proportionate terms.

4. In addition to the 25 countries that are middle income, the Seychelles is Africa's only high-income country, and the remaining 22 countries are low income.

5. This is limited to the subset of countries with sufficient information to look at trends between the beginning and end of the decade.

6. The Multidimensional Poverty Measure (MPM) is based on deprivations in three equally weighted dimensions: consumption (household falls under the international poverty line of $2.15/day [2017 purchasing power parity]); lack of education (no adult has completed primary school, at least one school-age child is not enrolled in school); and lack of access to basic infrastructure (limited standard drinking water, limited standard sanitation, and electricity). Because all households living in monetary poverty are considered deprived under the MPM, this indicator of multidimensional poverty is, by construction, at least as high as the poverty rate. Individuals are considered multidimensionally deprived if they fall short on at least one dimension or a combination of indicators equal in weight to a full dimension.

7. Mauritius and the Seychelles are excluded from this analysis because of data limitations.

8. Mauritania's low population density and significant population spread over pastoral land likely contribute to relatively high deprivations in access to basic infrastructure services.

9. Growth elasticity of poverty (GEP) is the percentage change in poverty rate for a percentage change in a per capita indicator of welfare. Compared with earlier research on GEP (such as Ravallion 2004; Ravallion and Chen 1997), this report takes advantage of the rapid increase in the number of household surveys since the early 2000s to increase sample size and cover a larger share of low-income countries' population. The curated sample consists of 575 comparable episodes between 1981 and 2021, where both start- and end-year poverty rates are above 2 percent, based on household surveys for 89 countries representing 92 percent of the population of low-income countries. Africa accounts for 80 of those episodes, a share of 36 percent of all episodes (weighted by the inverse of number of episodes for each country to ensure equal representation).

10. On average, across all countries globally, a 1 percent increase in household per capita consumption (or income) as measured from surveys is associated with a 2 percent decline in the poverty rate, which implies an average GEP of −2. This is similar to what was found by Ravallion (2004) with a far smaller sample. A 1 percent increase in gross domestic product (GDP) per capita is associated with a 2.8 percent decrease in the poverty rate, on average. The average GEP is estimated as the coefficient from the regression of rate of poverty reduction on rate of growth (in household consumption per capita or GDP per capita) in the same country during the same period, for all nonoverlapping growth episodes and countries, with country fixed effects. For more details, see Wu et al. (2024).

11. These results are significantly different from those obtained by Beegle and Christiaensen (2019), which show that Africa's low GEP is similar to that of comparably poor countries outside the region and that most of the intraregional differences in GEP can be attributed to high initial poverty levels in Africa. The results reported here (from Wu et al. 2024) are based on a much larger and updated sample of countries and growth episodes, which leads to strong confidence in their robustness. The results are derived from the regression of the rate of poverty reduction on the rate of growth (in household consumption or GDP per capita) for all countries and growth episodes, with additional controls for poverty rate, welfare mean, and inequality at the beginning of each episode for every country, and the interaction of rate of growth and the region a country belongs to. Positive and significant coefficients for the interaction with the Africa region indicate that growth in Africa is associated with a significantly slower pace of poverty reduction relative to other regions, especially when growth is measured by GDP. A series of robustness tests and limiting the sample to only low-income countries does not change the results. In addition, to get around the concern with the base effects (the high baseline poverty rates in Africa), Wu et al. (2024) also estimated the elasticity between change in GDP and change in household consumption (as opposed to change in GDP and change in poverty). The results are similar, in that the pass-through between growth in GDP and growth in household consumption is significantly lower in Africa, controlling for baseline welfare levels. Finally, nearest-neighbor matching estimation, following Beegle and Christiaensen (2019), also yields a significant difference between Africa and other comparably poor countries.

12. Specifically, as reported by Wu et al. (2024), human capital—better basic education (higher net primary enrollment rate and youth literacy)—is associated with a stronger transmission from per capita GDP growth to change in poverty but not to growth in average household welfare, and access to basic infrastructure—higher levels of electrification, safe drinking water, and basic sanitation—amplifies the effect of economic growth on average household welfare, poverty, or both. With respect to economic structure, higher shares of employment and value added in agriculture are associated with a weaker link between GDP growth and average household welfare, whereas more employment in services and industry is associated with stronger transmission from growth to welfare. Regarding dependency on natural resources, a higher share of mineral and forest rents in GDP appears to weaken the link between GDP growth and household welfare. In contrast, rents from oil, natural gas, or coal are not robustly associated with transmission from economic growth to household welfare.

13. Sulla, Zikhali, and Cuevas (2022) used this methodology to assess drivers of inequality in Southern Africa. Fields (2003) uses a regression-based approach to estimate standard income- or consumption-generating equations. The relative contributions to inequality are calculated on the basis of the composite value of the explanatory variables (such as education, labor market factors, and demographics) and their coefficients. Fields (2003) is based on the fitted outcome; hence, it yields no residual. This is the set of results reported in figure 2.13.

14. Based on a version of Fields (2003) allowing for residuals, 57 percent of inequality is not explained by the model.

15. This relationship is estimated by regressing changes in survey mean consumption or income per capita during an episode of growth in GDP per capita, controlling for initial differences. The results are qualitatively similar when regressing household consumption expenditures from surveys on household final consumption expenditures (HFCE), as measured by national accounts.

16. Some would argue that the lower GEP in Africa should not be a surprise, given that elasticities tend to be lower in countries with high baseline poverty rates, as an artifact of the way the GEP is calculated. Even though the regressions control for initial poverty rates, one could still argue that

these controls are insufficient. However, this argument cannot be extended to the regressions of survey means on GDP per capita or HFCE—because both these variables have a similar low base in Africa—that show economic growth to have a significantly weaker link with household welfare in Africa relative to other regions. Because poverty is measured by household welfare (consumption or income), one would therefore expect GDP per capita growth to have a weaker effect on poverty reduction in Africa relative to other regions.

17. Initial inequality, however, does not affect the extent to which growth in GDP per capita translates into poverty reduction in the sample of growth episodes considered by Wu et al. (2024). The balance of evidence, therefore, suggests that the initial distribution of welfare does not affect how macroeconomic growth translates to changes in household welfare, but it does affect how growth in average welfare translates to growth at the bottom.

18. In Botswana, inequality fell from 64.7 to 60.5 Gini points, whereas in Chad it increased from 39.8 to 43.3 Gini points.

19. The Central African Republic is also landlocked, but it is not in the MPM data and thus is not included in the analysis.

20. Whenever a survey spans two years, we use weighted GDP across both years as our measure of GDP per capita.

21. Small absolute changes in poverty where baseline poverty rates are low tend to be large in relative terms, mechanically pushing up the absolute value of the estimated elasticities.

22. All regressions also include regional dummies (to control for time-invariant omitted variables at the regional level), the mean household welfare at the start of the episode, and a dummy indicating the type of welfare aggregate variable used in the survey (consumption or income).

23. Refer to Wu et al. (2024a) for the full list of variables.

24. This methodological note is also informed by Fiorio and Jenkins (2007), following Fields (2003).

References

Anderson, Michael L. 2008. "Multiple Inference and Gender Differences in the Effects of Early Intervention: A Reevaluation of the Abecedarian, Perry Preschool, and Early Training Projects." *Journal of the American Statistical Association* 103 (484): 1481–95.

Banerjee, Raka, Kajal Gulati, Michael B. O'Sullivan, Arathi S. Rao, and Margaux L. Vinez. 2014. "Levelling the Field: Improving Opportunities for Women Farmers in Africa." World Bank, Washington, DC.

Baymul, Cinar, and Kunal Sen. 2019. "Kuznets Revisited: What Do We Know About the Relationship Between Structural Transformation and Inequality?" *Asian Development Review* 36 (1): 136–67.

Beegle, Kathleen, Luc Christiaensen, Andrew Dabalen, and Isis Gaddis. 2016. *Poverty in a Rising Africa*. Washington, DC: World Bank.

Beegle, Kathleen, and Luc Christiaensen, eds. 2019. *Accelerating Poverty Reduction in Africa*. Washington, DC: World Bank. https://hdl.handle.net/10986/32354.

Benjamini, Yoav, Abba M. Krieger, and Daniel Yekutieli. 2006. "Adaptive Linear Step-Up Procedures That Control the False Discovery Rate." *Biometrika* 93 (3): 491–507.

Bergstrom, Katy. 2022. "The Role of Income Inequality for Poverty Reduction." *World Bank Economic Review* 36 (3): 583–604. https://doi.org/10.1093/wber/lhab026.

Bhorat, Haroon, and Karmen Naidoo. 2018. "Economic Growth and the Pursuit of Inequality Reduction in Africa." Working Paper, Group of 24 and Friedrich Ebert Stiftung, New York. https://g24.org/economic-growth-and-pursuit-of-inequality-reduction-in-africa/.

Blanchet, T., L. Chancel, I. Flores, and M. Morgan. 2024. "Distributional National Accounts Guidelines, Methods and Concepts Used in the World Inequality Database." World Inequality Lab. https://wid .world/document/distributional-national-accounts-guidelines-2020-concepts-and-methods-used -in-the-world-inequality-database/.

Blundell, Richard, Luigi Pistaferri, and Ian Preston. 2008. "Consumption Inequality and Partial Insurance." *American Economic Review* 98 (5): 1887–1921.

Bourguignon, François. 2003. "The Growth Elasticity of Poverty Reduction: Explaining Heterogeneity Across Countries and Time Periods." In *Inequality and Growth: Theory and Policy Implications*, edited by Theo S. Eicher and Stephen J. Turnovsky, 3–26. Cambridge, MA: MIT Press. https://doi .org/10.7551/mitpress/3750.003.0004.

Bussolo, Maurizio, María E. Dávalos, Vito Peragine, and Ramya Sundaram. 2018. *Toward a New Social Contract: Taking on Distributional Tensions in Europe and Central Asia*. Washington, DC: World Bank. http://hdl.handle.net/10986/30393.

Calderón, César. 2021. *Boosting Productivity in Sub-Saharan Africa: Policies and Institutions to Promote Efficiency*. Washington, DC: World Bank. http://hdl.handle.net/10986/36786.

Chancel, L., D. Cogneau, A. Gethin, A. Myczkowski, and A. S. Robilliard. 2023. "Income Inequality in Africa, 1990–2019: Measurement, Patterns, Determinants." *World Development* 163: 106162. https://doi.org/10.1016/j.worlddev.2022.106162.

Choumert-Nkolo, J., G. Santana Tavera, and P. Saxena. 2023. "Addressing Non-Response Bias in Surveys of Wealthy Households in Low- and Middle-Income Countries: Strategies and Implementation." *Journal of Development Studies* 59 (9): 1427–42. https://doi.org/10.1080/0022038 8.2023.2217998.

Datt, Gaurav, and Martin Ravallion. 1992. "Growth and Redistribution Components of Changes in Poverty Measures: A Decomposition with Applications to Brazil and India in the 1980s." *Journal of Development Economics* 38 (2): 275–95.

Delprato, Marcos, Kwame Akyeampong, and Máiréad Dunne. 2017. "Intergenerational Education Effects of Early Marriage in Sub-Saharan Africa." *World Development* 91: 173–92. https://doi .org/10.1016/j.worlddev.2016.11.010.

Diao, Xinshen, Margaret McMillan, and Dani Rodrik. 2017. "The Recent Growth Boom in Developing Economies: A Structural Change Perspective." Working Paper 23132, National Bureau of Economic Research, Cambridge, MA.

Duclos, Jean-Yves, and Stephen A. O'Connell. 2015. "Is Poverty a Binding Constraint on Growth in Sub-Saharan Africa?" In *Economic Growth and Poverty Reduction in Sub-Saharan Africa: Current and Emerging Issues*, edited by Andrew McKay and Erik Thorbecke, 54–90. Oxford: Oxford University Press. https://doi.org/10.1093/acprof:oso/9780198728450.003.0003.

Ferreira, Francisco H. G., Julian Messina, Jamele Rigolini, Luis-Felipe López-Calva, Maria Ana Lugo, and Renos Vakis. 2012. *Economic Mobility and the Rise of the Latin American Middle Class*. Washington, DC: World Bank.

Fields, Gary S. 2003. "Accounting for Income Inequality and Its Change: A New Method, With Application to the Distribution of Earnings in the United States." In *Worker Well-Being and Public Policy*, edited by S. W. Polachek, 1–38. Vol. 22 of *Research in Labor Economics*. Bingley, UK: Emerald Group Publishing. https://doi.org/10.1016/S0147-9121(03)22001-X.

Fiorio, Carlo V., and Stephen P. Jenkins. 2007. "ineqrbd: Regression-Based Inequality Decomposition." PowerPoint presentation. https://www.stata.com/meeting/13uk/fiorio_ineqrbd_UKSUG07.pdf.

Fosu, Augustin Kwasi. 2023. "Progress on Poverty in Africa: The Importance of Growth and Inequality." *Journal of African Economies* 32 (Supplement 2): ii164–82. https://doi.org/10.1093/jae/ejac047.

FSIN (Food Security Information Network) and GRFC (Global Network Against Food Crises). 2023. *GRFC 2023 Mid-Year Update*. Rome: FSIN. https://www.fsinplatform.org/sites/default/files /resources/files/GRFC2023-MYU.pdf.

Goldberg, Pinelopi Koujianou, and Tristan Reed. 2023. "Presidential Address: Demand-Side Constraints in Development—The Role of Market Size, Trade, and (In)Equality." *Econometrica* 91 (6): 1915–50. https://doi.org/10.3982/ecta20787.

JEI. 2022. *Journal of Economic Inequality*, "Special Issue: Finding the Upper Tail." https://link.springer .com/journal/10888/volumes-and-issues/20-1.

Jirasavetakul, La-Bhus Fah, and Christoph Lakner 2020. "The Distribution of Consumption Expenditure in Sub-Saharan Africa: The Inequality Among All Africans." *Journal of African Economies* 29 (1): 1–25. https://doi.org/10.1093/jae/ejz016.

Kerr, Andrew, and Mxolisi Zondi. 2024. "Measuring the Upper Tail of the Income and Wealth Distributions," Unpublished, paper commissioned by World Bank, Data for Policy initiative, Global Solutions Group.

Kraay, Aart, Christoph Lakner, Berk Ozler, Benoit Marie A. Decerf, Dean Mitchell Jolliffe, Olivier Christian Brigitte Sterck, and Nishant Yonzan. 2023. "A New Distribution Sensitive Index for Measuring Welfare, Poverty, and Inequality." Policy Research Working Paper 10470, World Bank, Washington, DC.

Lakner, Christoph, and Branko Milanovic. 2016. "Global Income Distribution: From the Fall of the Berlin Wall to the Great Recession." *World Bank Economic Review* 30 (2): 203–32.

Lall, Somik Vinay, J. Vernon Henderson, and Anthony J. Venables. 2017. *Africa's Cities: Opening Doors to the World*. Washington, DC: World Bank.

Lustig, N. 2020. "The 'Missing Rich' in Household Surveys: Causes and Correction Approaches," Vol. 520. ECINEQ, Society for the Study of Economic Inequality.

McMillan, Margaret, and Albert Zeufack. 2022. "Labor Productivity Growth and Industrialization in Africa." *Journal of Economic Perspectives* 36 (1): 3–32. https://doi.org/10.1257/jep.36.1.3.

Milanovic, B. 2024. "The Three Eras of Global Inequality, 1820–2020 with the Focus on the Past Thirty Years." *World Development* 177.

Narayan, Ambar, Roy Van der Weide, Alexandru Cojocaru, Christoph Lakner, Silvia Redaelli, Daniel Gerszon Mahler, Rakesh Gupta N. Ramasubbaiah, and Stefan Thewissen. 2018. *Fair Progress? Economic Mobility Across Generations Around the World*. Washington, DC: World Bank. https://hdl .handle.net/10986/28428.

Notre Dame Global Adaptation Initiative. 2023. *ND-GAIN Country Index*. https://gain.nd.edu/ our-work/country-index/rankings/.

Patel, Dev, Justin Sandefur, and Arvind Subramanian. 2021. "The New Era of Unconditional Convergence." *Journal of Development Economics* 152: 102687.

Piketty, T., E. Saez, and G. Zucman. 2022. "Twenty Years and Counting: Thoughts about Measuring the Upper Tail." *Journal of Economic Inequality* 20 (1): 255–64.

Ravallion, Martin. 2004. "Pro-Poor Growth: A Primer." Policy Research Working Paper 3242, World Bank, Washington DC.

Ravallion, Martin. 2022. "Missing Top Income Recipients." *Journal of Economic Inequality* 20: 205–22.

Ravallion, Martin, and Shaohua Chen. 1997. "What Can New Survey Data Tell Us about Recent Changes in Distribution and Poverty?" *World Bank Economic Review* 11 (2): 357–82. https://doi .org/10.1093/wber/11.2.357.

Ravallion, Martin, and Monika Huppi. 1991. "Measuring Changes in Poverty: A Methodological Case Study of Indonesia during an Adjustment Period." *World Bank Economic Review* 5 (1): 57–82. https://doi.org/10.1093/wber/5.1.57.

Rodrik, Dani. 2016. "Premature Deindustrialization." *Journal of Economic Growth* 21 (1): 1–33. https://doi.org/10.1007/s10887-015-9122-3.

Shorrocks, A. F. 1982. "Inequality Decomposition by Factor Components." *Econometrica* 50 (1): 193–211. https://doi.org/10.2307/1912537.

Suarez, Alejandro Hoyos, Andrew Dabalen, Ambar Narayan, Jaime Saavedra-Chanduvi, Alejandro Hoyos Suarez, Ana Abras, and Sailesh Tiwari. 2015. *Do African Children Have an Equal Chance? A Human Opportunity Report for Sub-Saharan Africa*. Washington, DC: World Bank. http://hdl.handle.net/10986/20458.

Sulla, Victor, Precious Zikhali, and Pablo F. Cuevas. 2022. *Inequality in Southern Africa: An Assessment of the Southern African Customs Union*. Washington, DC: World Bank.

Thorbecke, E. 2023. "The Interrelationships among Growth, Inequality and Poverty in Africa." *Journal of African Economies* 32 (Supplement 2): ii81–86. https://doi.org/10.1093/jae/ejac055.

UN DESA (United Nations, Department of Economic and Social Affairs), Population Division. 2018. *World Urbanization Prospects: The 2018 Revision, Online Edition*. New York: United Nations. https://population.un.org/wup/Publications/Files/WUP2018-Report.pdf.

UNICEF (United Nations Children's Fund), WHO (World Health Organization), and World Bank. 2023. *Levels and Trends in Child Malnutrition: UNICEF / WHO / World Bank Group Joint Child Malnutrition Estimates—Key Findings of the 2023 Edition*. New York: UNICEF and WHO. https://iris.who.int/bitstream/handle/10665/368038/9789240073791-eng.pdf?sequence=1.

Van der Weide, Roy, Christoph Lakner, Daniel Gerszon Mahler, Ambar Narayan, and Rakesh Gupta. 2024. "Intergenerational Mobility around the World: A New Database." *Journal of Development Economics* 166: 103167. https://doi.org/10.1016/j.jdeveco.2023.103167.

World Bank. 2012. *World Development Report 2012: Gender Equality and Development*. Washington, DC: World Bank.

World Bank. 2016. *Poverty and Shared Prosperity 2016: Taking on Inequality*. Washington, DC: World Bank. https://doi.org/10.1596/978-1-4648-0958-3.

World Bank. 2019a. *An Analysis of Issues Shaping Africa's Economic Future*. Africa's Pulse 19 (April). Washington, DC: World Bank. https://hdl.handle.net/10986/31499.

World Bank. 2019b. "Profiting from Parity: Unlocking the Potential of Women's Business in Africa." World Bank, Washington, DC.

World Bank. 2022a. "Poverty and Inequality Platform." Washington, DC: World Bank. Version 20220909_2017_01_02_ PROD, accessed September 2022. https://www.pip.worldbank.org.

World Bank. 2022b. *Poverty and Inequality Platform Methodology Handbook*. Washington, DC: World Bank.

World Bank. 2022c. *Poverty and Shared Prosperity 2022: Correcting Course*. Washington DC: World Bank.

World Bank. 2023a. "Delivering Growth to People Through Better Jobs." *Africa's Pulse* 28 (October). https://doi.org/10.1596/978-1-4648-2043-4.

World Bank. 2023b. "Classification of Fragile and Conflict-Affected Situations." Updated June 28, 2024. https://www.worldbank.org/en/topic/fragilityconflictviolence/brief/harmonized-list-of-fragile-situations.

World Bank. 2023c. "Multidimensional Poverty Measure." 5th ed. Updated April 2024. https://www
.worldbank.org/en/topic/poverty/brief/multidimensional-poverty-measure.

World Bank. 2024a. Poverty and Inequality Platform (version 20240627_2017_01_02_PROD) [dataset],
accessed July 2024, https://pip.worldbank.org/.

World Bank. 2024b. "Tackling Inequality to Revitalize Growth and Reduce Poverty in Africa." *Africa's
Pulse* 29. World Bank, Washington, DC. https://doi.org/10.1596/978-1-4648-2109-7.

Wu, Haoyu, Aziz Atamanov, Tom Bundervoet, and Pierella Paci. (2024a). "Is Economic Growth Less
Welfare Enhancing in Africa? Evidence From the Last Forty Years." *World Development* 184:
106759. https://doi.org/10.1016/j.worlddev.2024.106759

Wu, Haoyu, Aziz Atamanov, Tom Bundervoet, and Pierella Paci. (2024b). "The Growth Elasticity of
Poverty: Is Africa Any Different?" Policy Research Working Paper 10690, World Bank, Washington, DC.
https://hdl.handle.net/10986/40997.

Yonzan, Nishant, Daniel Gerszon Mahler, and Christoph Lakner. 2023. "Poverty Is Back to Pre-COVID
Levels Globally, but Not for Low-Income Countries." *Data Blog*. World Bank, October 3.
https://blogs.worldbank.org/en/opendata/poverty-back-pre-covid-levels-globally-not-low
-income-countries.

Poverty and Inequality Influencers: Climate

RUTH HILL

Climate, poverty, and inequality in Africa

Lifting people out of poverty requires helping households to acquire and use capital—financial, physical, human, social, and natural—and ensuring that they earn a good return from it. The livelihoods of poor households are often based on the use of natural capital, such as farming, pastoralism, or fishing. At the global extreme poverty line, 81 percent of households live in rural areas (compared with 51 percent of the population globally), and 62 percent are predominantly engaged in agriculture (World Bank 2020, 2022).

This is, however, not the only reason why climate change is particularly challenging for poor households. The lack of capital that accompanies a life in poverty makes hazards more costly. Inadequate insulation, lack of weatherproofing, and substandard construction materials are common characteristics of houses inhabited by poor households, rendering them more susceptible to weather extremes (refer to figure S1.1a). Because poor people often live in remote locations, the prices of the goods they buy are more likely to be affected by local weather events. They are less likely to be able to rely on savings, access to credit, or insurance to manage their loss of income or assets (refer to figure S1.1b); less likely to be covered by social insurance; and less likely to be able to switch to another livelihood because of low levels of education, financial resources, and market access. As a result, poor households often cope with shocks by depleting the few assets they hold, which turns temporary shocks into permanent losses. The impacts can be long-lasting, and as a result shocks cause inequality to be amplified (refer to figure S1.2).

However, the subtler welfare impact occurs not when disasters strike but in the costly behavior driven by the anticipation of shocks that households are ill-placed to cope with. Although quieter, in some contexts this can be the larger constraint on accelerating poverty reduction. In Zimbabwe, the lack of investment because of climate risk was found to have twice as large an impact on income growth (Elbers, Gunning, and Kinsey 2007). Ten well-identified studies across contexts show that when households have higher access to climate risk management instruments, there is a 15–30 percent increase in investment regardless of whether shocks occur (refer to Mobarak and Rosenzweig 2013 for rainfall index insurance in India; Elabed and Carter 2018 for area yield insurance in Mali; Karlan et al. 2014 for rainfall index insurance in Ghana; Cai et al. 2015 for swine insurance in China; Cai 2016 for area-yield insurance in China; Fuchs Tarlovsky and Wolff 2016 for rainfall index insurance in Mexico; Jensen, Barrett, and Mude 2017 for livestock insurance in Kenya; Hill et al. 2019 for rainfall and area yield insurance in Bangladesh; Stoeffler et al. 2022 for area yield in Burkina Faso; and Bulte et al. 2020 for multiperil crop insurance in Kenya).

Climate change, characterized by higher temperatures, rainfall extremes, and storms, alters natural capital and thus especially affects the ability of poor people to earn an income. Recent estimates of the number of people exposed, vulnerable, and at risk for extreme weather quantify and underscore the challenge Africa faces (Doan et al. 2023). Table S1.1 presents the size and share of the population exposed to extreme weather events globally and in Africa. It also presents the share of the population that is both exposed and in poverty, at both the $2.15 and $6.85 international poverty lines. In 2019, 42 percent of the population of Africa was exposed to the probability of experiencing at least one of the extreme weather events considered: floods, droughts, heat waves, and cyclones. This is very similar to the global average of 55 percent; however, a higher share of the population of South Asia and East Asia and the Pacific are exposed. Drought is the shock that the largest share of the African population is exposed to, followed by floods and heat waves. The rate of exposure to droughts in Africa is much higher than in other regions in the world.

FIGURE S1.1 Climate hazards across the income distribution, Africa

a. Households in Accra, Ghana,
affected by flooding

Percent of households

b. Losses in income and consumption
due to droughts in Uganda

Percent reduction

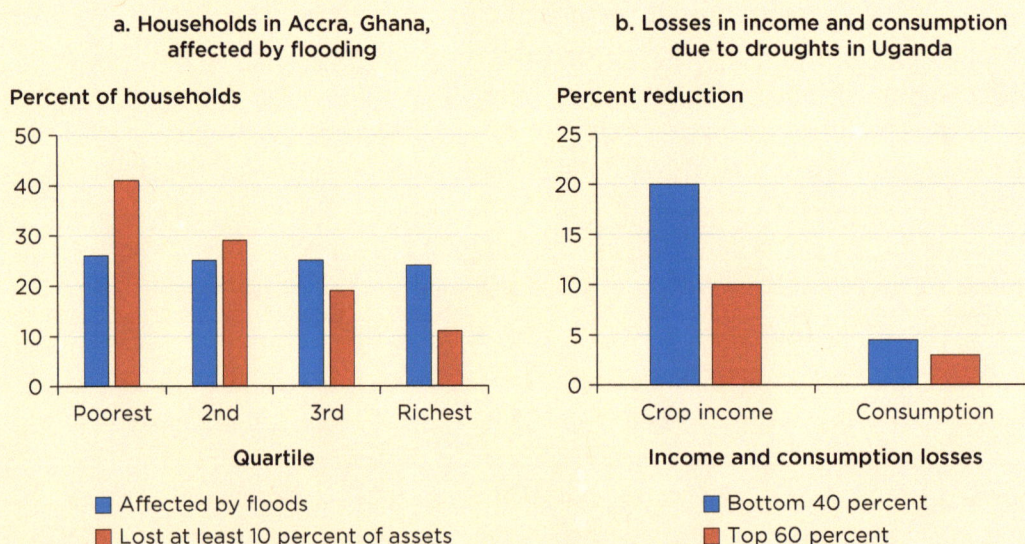

Sources: Panel a, Erman et al. 2018; panel b, World Bank 2016.

FIGURE S1.2 Inequality and weather shocks: A vicious cycle

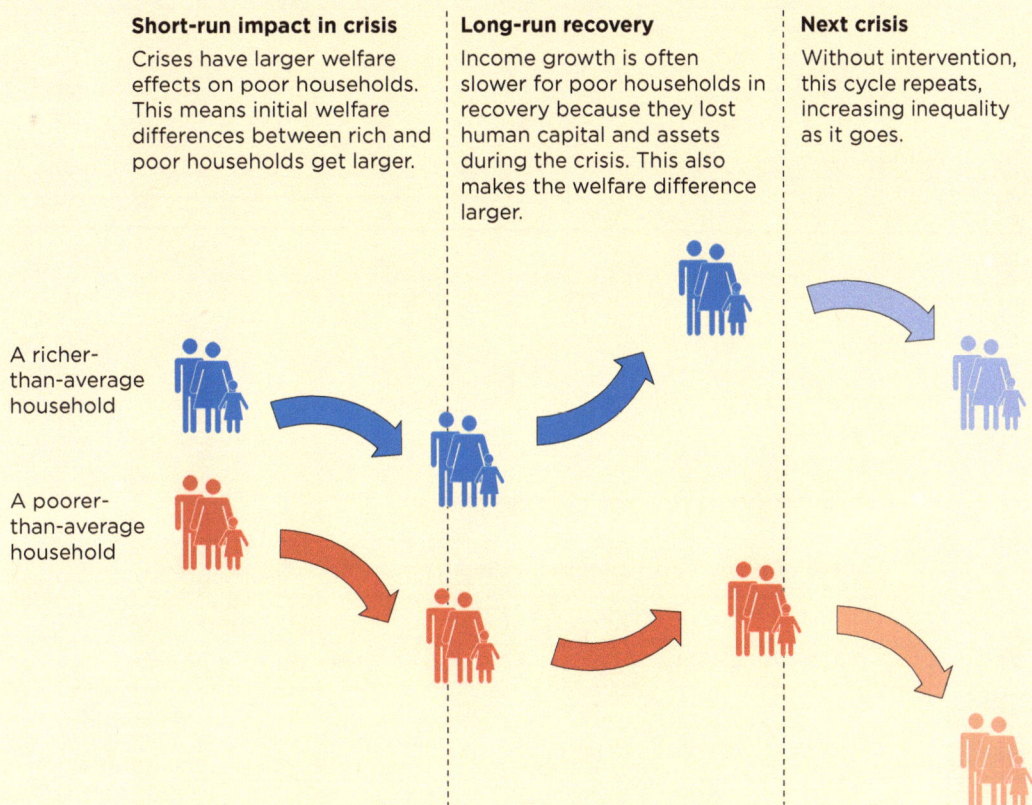

Short-run impact in crisis
Crises have larger welfare effects on poor households. This means initial welfare differences between rich and poor households get larger.

Long-run recovery
Income growth is often slower for poor households in recovery because they lost human capital and assets during the crisis. This also makes the welfare difference larger.

Next crisis
Without intervention, this cycle repeats, increasing inequality as it goes.

A richer-than-average household

A poorer-than-average household

Source: Hill and Narayan 2020.

When the share of the population that is both exposed and poor is considered, the challenge of climate risk to Africa is seen much more clearly. Although 29 percent of the world's population is both exposed and poor (when measured against the $6.85 poverty line), this rate is 38 percent in Africa. At the extreme poverty line of $2.15, the difference is even starker—5 percent of the world's population is exposed and poor, but in Africa the rate is slightly more than three times as high, at 16 percent.

Table S1.2 looks at vulnerability to extreme weather events in a multidimensional way. It documents the share of the population that is both exposed and vulnerable along six dimensions: lacking safe water, lacking electricity (both infrastructure assets that can help reduce the initial impact of extreme weather events), lacking income to manage the shock, lacking education to help adapt to the shock's impacts, lacking social protection, or lacking access to finance (a mobile money account or other bank account) to aid in receiving transfers. This table highlights again that the challenge facing Africa is not just its exposure to extreme weather, but the high levels of vulnerability of African households that put them at risk. If being at risk is considered as being vulnerable in one dimension, nearly all—90 percent of the exposed population—are at risk.[1] This is identical to the share at risk globally, even though global exposure rates are higher.

TABLE S1.1 Exposure to extreme climate shocks in Africa

	Global				Africa			
	Exposed		**Exposed and poor (%)**		**Exposed**		**Exposed and poor (%)**	
Shock	**Millions**	**%**	**$2.15**	**$6.85**	**Millions**	**%**	**$2.15**	**$6.85**
Flood	962	12	1	5	66	6	2	5
Drought	1,383	18	2	9	314	28	11	26
Heat wave	2,737	35	3	21	186	17	6	15
Cyclone	601	8	0	3	5	0	0	0
Any shock	4,335	55	5	29	471	42	16	38

Source: Doan et al. 2023.

TABLE S1.2 Population at risk for climate shocks

	Share of population exposed to any shock and vulnerable (%)							
Population	**Water**	**Electricity**	**Income**	**Education**	**Social protection**	**Access to finance**	**≥1**	**≥2**
Africa	14	22	25	18	29	23	42	9
World	6	17	12	16	31	18	42	12

Source: Doan et al. 2023.
Note: Table includes only countries for which there are data on all dimensions of vulnerability.

An eight-country analysis of the impacts of droughts on welfare in Africa using survey data from close to 100,000 households quantifies the impact of historical weather conditions on poverty and highlights the risk to poverty outcomes that weather variability causes (Gascoigne et al. 2024). Poverty is 1–12 percent higher under the worst weather conditions relative to the best conditions observed in the past 13 years. This amounts to an increase in the total poverty gap that ranges from US$4 million to US$2.4 billion (2011 purchasing power parity).

The poverty and inequality impact of a world with increased climate extremes in Africa cannot be overestimated. Additionally, a world that is on average hotter every year, and in some parts of the continent drier, has a big impact for Africa. Map S1.1 shows the expected poverty cost of climate change as a result of the lower growth projected because of climate change by Burke, Hsaing, and Miguel (2015). The poverty impact in Africa is very large (accounting for projected demographic changes).

MAP S1.1 Increases in poverty caused by climate change in Africa

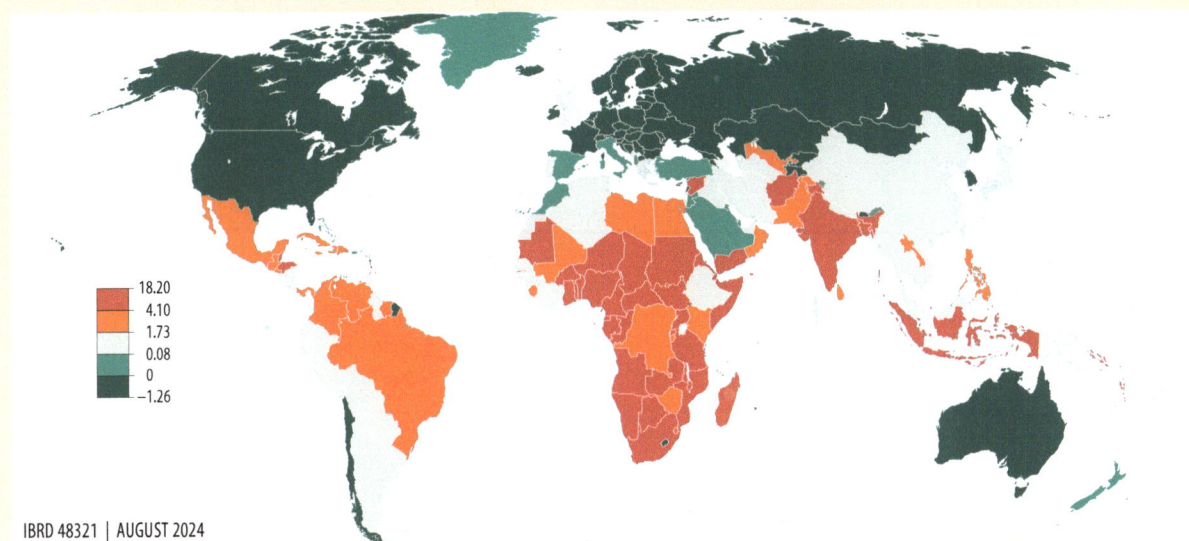

18.20
4.10
1.73
0.08
0
−1.26

IBRD 48321 | AUGUST 2024

Source: Burke, Hsiang, and Miguel 2015.
Note: These poverty projections use the growth estimates presented by Burke, Hsiang, and Miguel (2015) to estimate poverty in 2050 by applying growth rates to the income distribution in each country. These estimates also take into account demographic changes between now and 2050. Growth estimates with and without climate change are used to project poverty with and without climate change and calculate the difference. See Corral and Nguyen forthcoming for more details.

Hallegatte et al. (2016) estimate that the impact of climate change on agricultural incomes and food prices will be one of the biggest drivers of the impact of climate change on poverty. New work using a household survey–based trade model of the impacts of climate change quantifies the large reductions in income as a result of lower yields (Artuc, Porto, and Rijkers 2023). This model shows that this will be the largest impact of climate change on poverty, much larger than indirect price effects as a result of food shortages, consistent with findings from the spatial economics literature on the impact of climate change. The household income losses projected are particularly large for some African countries (refer to figure S1.3), but some countries will see yields and agricultural incomes increase on average. When losses are present, they are consistently larger at the bottom of the distribution—19 percent for the poorest quarter of households, compared with 16 percent on average and 14 percent for the richest quarter of households—highlighting the impact that climate change will have on both poverty and inequality unless action is taken to address it.

FIGURE S1.3 Distribution of the income effects of climate change, by country

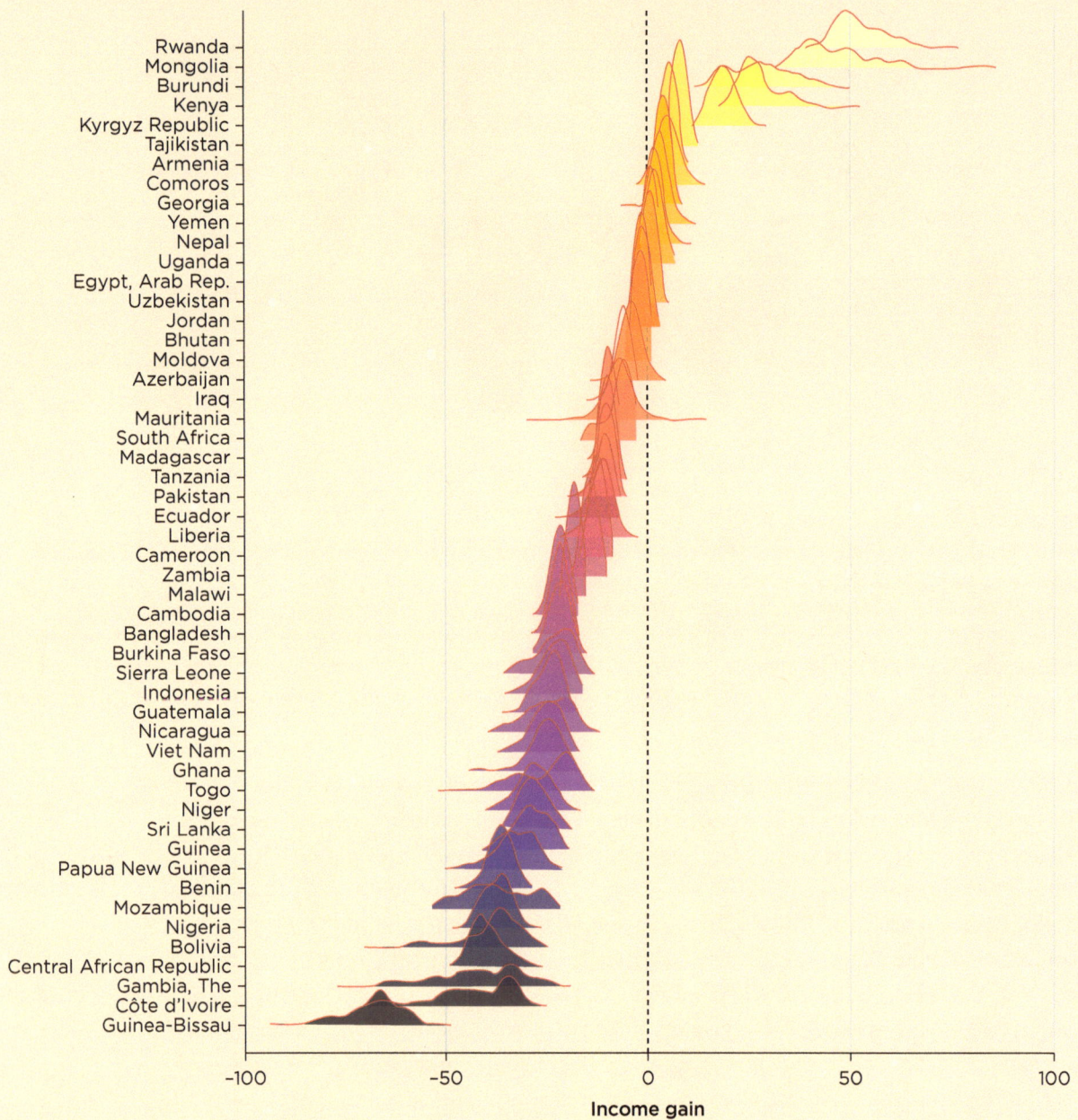

Source: Artuc, Porto, and Rijkers 2024.

Reducing poverty and inequality and improving livability in Africa

Reducing the impact of climate change on poor and vulnerable households is essential to hastening poverty reduction. When it comes to thinking about policies that do this, it is useful to use the same hazard, exposure, and vulnerability framework that is used to understand the physical impacts of climate change (IPCC 2022). *Hazard* refers to climate-related physical events and trends that may cause damage and welfare losses, *exposure* indicates the presence of people and livelihoods in places that could be adversely affected, and *vulnerability* captures how much exposure to a given hazard affects a household's income or well-being. Climate-related hazards include, but are not limited to, droughts, heat waves, floods, severe storms, landslides, wildfires, and sea-level rise. As noted, poor households are particularly vulnerable to these hazards because they disproportionately rely on natural capital to earn income and because their lack of other assets makes it much harder to manage the impacts.

Policies are needed in each of these areas. The probability distribution of hazards in the future can be altered through mitigation policies in the long run, because the accumulation of greenhouse gas emissions at a global level is causing climate change. An example is carbon taxes, which reduce emissions, particularly in high-emitting countries (see Rafaty, Dolphin, and Pretis 2021; for Europe, Lin and Li 2011; for the United Kingdom, Martin, de Preux, and Wagner 2014; for Canada, Rivers and Schaufele 2015 and Metcalf 2019; and for Sweden, Andersson 2019). However, other policies, such as those that encourage increasing tree cover, can also bring more immediate changes in local weather conditions (see, for example, Harlan et al. 2006, Schwaab et al. 2021, and Ziter et al. 2019).

Exposure can be altered by policies that enable households to move themselves or their assets to locations less affected by hazards. Policies that change a household's vulnerability to hazards range from those focused on adaptation, such as encouraging households to invest in water management and soil quality or in better-quality housing, to more general development policies that increase the capital of poor households, thereby allowing them to better cope with climate shocks or earn more income from activities less affected by hazards. For example, increasing the quality of education, building better roads that connect households to markets, improving city planning, adopting early warning and evacuation systems, and facilitating financial inclusion can all contribute to reducing a household's vulnerability.

The reality is that, for Africa, reductions in emissions will have a negligible impact on the distribution of hazards faced as a result of climate change. Africa has contributed very little to either the stock of or current emissions that are causing climate change (refer to Chancel, Both, and Voituriez 2023; Ritchie, Rosado, and Roser 2023). With the exception of some countries, such as South Africa, reducing emissions in Africa will have very little impact on total global emissions. Ending extreme poverty in Africa will also have very little impact on emissions (Wollburg, Hallegatte, and Mahler 2023). However, this does not necessarily mean that development strategies should not consider emissions reduction. There are two reasons why emissions reduction may still be a focus. First, policies that reduce emissions can have locally beneficial effects by reducing air pollution and investing in nature more broadly (for example, an increased tree cover that reduces temperatures). Second, locking into emissions-intensive energy production will have a larger contribution to global emissions in the future, an increase in emissions that the world cannot afford, given that high-income economies have burned through more than their fair share of the world's carbon. For this reason, it is wise to consider a green energy transition now for Africa. However, this is asking African countries to do something earlier in their development process than high-income economies had to do, and African countries should be compensated for doing this). This could be done by valuing the potential carbon emissions reduced and using the social cost of carbon to value this global public good to which African countries are contributing (Kanbur 2023). As energy transitions are planned, it is essential to ensure that households at the bottom end of the consumption distribution are compensated for higher energy (and fertilizer) costs, or poverty will increase.

In most cases, the priority for countries in Africa will be policies that both bring income growth and reduce vulnerability for poor households—double wins, as it were. Supporting income growth while protecting against the setbacks of extreme weather events becomes increasingly important as Africa's risk of extreme weather events increases.

Many policies that increase households' ability to earn income also reduce the impact of extreme climate events on welfare. For example, mobile money spurs development, thereby increasing welfare (Batista and Vicente forthcoming). When a weather crisis strikes, mobile money also allows households to quickly receive transfers or remittances from relatives or migrant family members who live elsewhere (Jack and Suri 2014). Similarly, better access to roads in remote areas increases access to markets, goods, and services, thereby bringing development. When drought reduces local food availability, improved access to markets reduces the impact of this weather shock on local food prices (Burgess and Donaldson 2010). Education increases a household's ability to earn income, but it also allows households to switch sectors when climate shocks reduce returns in the sector in which they are engaged (Hill and Mejia-Mantilla 2017). None of these policies, or policies similar to them, would be considered adaptation investments designed to reduce the vulnerability of households to climate events, but they can be highly effective in reducing vulnerability.

Vulnerability to climate change—vulnerability to both extreme shocks and the yearly reductions in income that a changing climate will bring—can be reduced through investments in infrastructure and changes in production practices that reduce the initial impact of a climate hazard on income or assets. For example, investments in irrigation and access to safe or improved water can reduce the immediate impact of water scarcity on incomes and health. Additionally, changes in production practices can reduce this impact; in addition to the investments in soil conservation mentioned in box S1.1, investments in drought-resistant varieties, both research and development investments and investments by households in adopting drought-resistant varieties, reduce the impact of water deficits on crop production. Similar examples exist for floods (for example, investing in flood defenses, flood-resilient roads and bridges, better housing stock) and heat waves (for example, electricity for fans, refrigeration and air conditioning, or planting trees to reduce local temperatures). These types of investments are often the most cost-effective way of reducing the welfare impact of climate events.

However, not all risk can be reduced, and the residual risk needs to be managed well to reduce its welfare impacts. Residual risk can be managed by transferring risk across time through savings and credit markets and transferring risk across space through insurance (public safety nets and private markets) and informal transfers between family and friends (the geographic reach of these types of transfers is greatly aided by mobile money). The most appropriate means of strengthening households' ability to manage risk will vary from context to context and for different types of households. For very poor households in some areas, adaptive social protection may be the only means by which the risk of extreme shocks can be managed. For more commercially oriented farmers, insurance may play a role.

Crucially, reducing and managing risk requires investments to be made both by households and by the state. Understanding the constraints on household investments in risk reduction and management and addressing these constraints can unlock private household investment in these areas, and given the large adaptation needs Africa faces, this will be a priority. Box S1.1 highlights some evidence on the constraints on soil conservation investments in the Sahel—knowledge—and public investments in this area can address this by providing training. Evidence on smallholder irrigation for Africa shows that it very often brings a return, but households do not often invest in it. This may in part be due to lack of access to knowledge and equipment, but in large part it reflects a lack of access to the type of long-run financing for households that is needed for this type of investment because the cost is incurred well in advance of returns being recouped. Findings from innovative loans for asset purchases offer considerable promise for unlocking investments in irrigation assets.

In some cases, however, public investment will be needed, and the investment needs are large. As Chancel, Bothe, and Voituriez (2023) underscore, not only did Africa contribute the least to climate change, it is also least able to afford the needed adaptation investments. Additional public financing of resilience-increasing investments is needed in Africa.

Furthermore, some policies not only support income growth and reduce vulnerability but also improve future climate outcomes by reducing emissions or improving the local environment (triple wins, as it were). For example, soil conservation practices in agriculture, tree planting, and investing in mangroves are all policies that bring returns in good and bad years, reduce vulnerability to climate shocks, sequester carbon, and reduce emissions and local temperature. The available evidence base for these types of actions can help prioritize those that carry significant benefits. Box S1.1 details the evidence that already exists.

BOX S1.1

Triple wins

The IPCC's (2022) Sixth Assessment Report, *Climate Change 2022: Impacts, Adaptation, and Vulnerability*, reviews the evidence on policies that reduce vulnerability and poverty while bringing ecosystem services. It highlights sustainable aquaculture and fisheries, improved cropland management, green infrastructure and ecosystem services in urban areas, and climate services, including early warning systems.

In the Sahel, farmers use low-cost, efficient traditional practices, such as agroforestry and conventional rainwater harvesting techniques, to capture rainfall, reduce runoff, and restore soils. Soils play an important role as passive agents in removing atmospheric carbon dioxide (Manning 2008). In Niger, these practices were found to increase yields (Aker and Jack 2021), which is consistent with the findings of older studies that showed that yields were 16–30 percent higher for farmers implementing these techniques, with similar yield gains in Burkina Faso (Matlon 1985). These practices also reduce vulnerability to low rainfall, allowing yield increases in low rainfall years (Hill and Baquié 2023). Training increases adoption of these practices (Aker and Jack 2021).

Reducing inefficiency in trade is another way in which policy reform can support income growth while reducing vulnerability and current emissions. Inefficiencies in trucking are a large challenge in many African countries. Regulations that limit competition often encourage inefficient fleet or empty cargos (Teravaninthorn and Raballand 2009). Regulatory reform, by increasing the incentive to invest in more efficient trucking fleet and trucking practices, reduces inefficiencies in trade and the emissions content of trade in the continent.

Social safety nets are highlighted as being particularly beneficial for poor households, but they are not in general strongly beneficial for the environment. They can be, however, when combined with conditionality that increases investment in the local environment, such as through planting trees in Ethiopia's Productive Safety Net Program (Hirvonen et al. 2022).

Note

1. The share of households exposed in countries for which vulnerability data are available is higher than the overall exposure numbers presented in this spotlight. In countries for which vulnerability data are available, 47 percent of the population is exposed.

References

Aker, Jenny C., and Kelsey Jack. 2021. "Harvesting the Rain: The Adoption of Environmental Technologies in the Sahel." Working Paper 29518, National Bureau of Economic Research, Cambridge, MA. https://doi.org/10.3386/w29518.

Andersson, Julius J. 2019. "Carbon Taxes and CO_2 Emissions: Sweden as a Case Study." *American Economic Journal: Economic Policy* 11 (4): 1–30.

Artuc, Erhan, Guido Porto, and Bob Rijkers. 2024. "Crops, Conflict and Climate Change." Unpublished manuscript. Last modified August 15, 2023. https://www.colorado.edu/economics/sites/default /files/attached-files/artuc.pdf.

Batista, Cátia, and Pedro C. Vicente. Forthcoming. "Is Mobile Money Changing Rural Africa? Evidence from a Field Experiment." *Review of Economics and Statistics*. https://doi.org/10.1162/rest_a_01333.

Bulte, Erwin, Francesco Cecchi, Robert Lensink, Ana Marr, and Marcel van Asseldonk. 2020. "Does Bundling Crop Insurance with Certified Seeds Crowd-in Investments? Experimental Evidence from Kenya." *Journal of Economic Behavior & Organization* 180: 744–57. https://doi.org/10.1016 /j.jebo.2019.07.006.

Burgess, Robin, and Dave Donaldson. 2010. "Can Openness Mitigate the Effects of Weather Shocks? Evidence from India's Famine Era." *American Economic Review: Papers & Proceedings* 100 (2): 449–53.

Burke, Marshall, Solomon M. Hsiang, and Edward Miguel. 2015. "Global Non-Linear Effect of Temperature on Economic Production." *Nature* 527 (7577): 235–39.

Cai, Hongbin, Yuyu Chen, Hanming Fang, and Li-An Zhou. 2015. "The Effect of Microinsurance on Economic Activities: Evidence from a Randomized Field Experiment." *Review of Economics and Statistics* 97 (2): 287–300.

Cai, Jing. 2016. "The Impact of Insurance Provision on Household Production and Financial Decisions." *American Economic Journal: Economic Policy* 8 (2): 44–88.

Chancel, Lucas, Philipp Bothe, and Tancrède Voituriez. 2023. *Climate Inequality Report 2023*. World Inequality Lab Study 2023/1. Paris: World Inequality Lab.

Corral, P., and M. Nguyen. Forthcoming. *The Future of Poverty: Projecting the Impact of Climate Change on Global Poverty through 2050*. Washington, DC: World Bank.

Doan, Miki Khan, Ruth Hill, Stephane Hallegatte, Paul Corral, Ben Brunckhorst, Minh Nguyen, Samuel Freije-Rodriguez, and Esther Naikal. 2023. "Counting People Exposed to, Vulnerable to, or at High Risk from Climate Shocks: A Methodology." Policy Research Working Paper 10619, World Bank, Washington, DC. http://documents.worldbank.org/curated/en/099602511292336760/IDU07 639ca570f3cb048db09bf60fc2cc82df22d.

Elabed, Ghada, and Michael Carter. 2018. "*Ex-Ante* Impacts of Agricultural Insurance: Evidence from a Field Experiment in Mali." https://arefiles.ucdavis.edu/uploads/filer_public/2c/e8/2ce82578-e1d3 -4aeb-9ca1-62b8bec093eb/impact_evaluation_nov_2018.pdf.

Elbers, Chris, Jan Willem Gunning, and Bill Kinsey. 2007. "Growth and Risk: Methodology and Micro Evidence." *World Bank Economic Review* 21 (1): 1–20. https://doi.org/40282230.

Erman, Alvina, Elliot Motte, Radhika Goyal, Aakosua Asare, Shinya Takamatsu, Xiaomeng Chen, Silvia Malgioglio, Alexander Skinner, Nobuo Yoshida, and Stephane Hallegatte. 2018. "The Road to Recovery: The Role of Poverty in the Exposure, Vulnerability and Resilience to Floods in Accra." Policy Research Working Paper 8469, World Bank, Washington, DC.

Fuchs Tarlovsky, Alan, and Hendrik Wolff. 2016. "Drought and Retribution: Evidence from a Large-Scale Rainfall-Indexed Insurance Program in Mexico." Policy Research Working Paper 7565, World Bank, Washington, DC. http://documents.worldbank.org/curated/en/458801467991945790/Drought-and-retribution-evidence-from-a-large-scale-rainfall-indexed-insurance-program-in-Mexico.

Gascoigne, Jon, Sandra Baquie, Katja Vinha, Emmanuel Skoufias, Evie Calcutt, Varun Sridhar Kshirsagar, Conor Meenan, and Ruth Hill. 2024. "The Welfare Cost of Drought in Sub-Saharan Africa." Policy Research Working Paper 10683, World Bank, Washington, DC. http://documents.worldbank.org/curated/en/099325301292478621/IDU1ae0eac0e145d214c6218002156b672eb8155

Hallegatte, Stephane, Mook Bangalore, Laura Bonzanigo, Marianne Fay, Tamaro Kane, Ulf Narloch, Julie Rozenberg, David Treguer, and Adrien Vogt-Schilb. 2016. *Shock Waves: Managing the Impacts of Climate Change on Poverty*. Climate Change and Development Series. Washington, DC: World Bank. https://doi.org/10.1596/978-1-4648-0673-5.

Harlan, Sharon L., Anthony J. Brazel, Lela Prashad, William L. Stefanov, and Larissa Larsen. 2006. "Neighborhood Microclimates and Vulnerability to Heat Stress." *Social Science & Medicine* 63 (11): 2847–63. https://doi.org/10.1016/j.socscimed.2006.07.030.

Hill, Ruth, and Sandra Baquié. 2023. "Case Study 11: Improving Water Availability and Restoring Soil Fertility in the Sahel." In *Decarbonization Policy Implementation: Illustrative Case Studies*, 89–93. Washington, DC: World Bank. https://api.knack.com/v1/applications/5b23f04fd240aa37e01fa362/download/asset/6566307b904dc70028106796/thesahelimprovingwateravailabilityandrestoringsoilfertilityworldbank2023.pdf.

Hill, Ruth Vargas, Neha Kumar, Nicholas Magnan, Simrin Makhija, Francesca de Nicola, David J. Spielman, and Patrick S. Ward. 2019. "Ex Ante and Ex Post Effects of Hybrid Index Insurance in Bangladesh." *Journal of Development Economics* 136 1–17. https://doi.org/10.1016/j.jdeveco.2018.09.003.

Hill, Ruth, and Carolina Mejia-Mantilla. 2017. "With a Little Help: Shocks, Agricultural Income, and Welfare in Uganda." Policy Research Working Paper 7935, World Bank, Washington, DC. http://hdl.handle.net/10986/25944.

Hill, Ruth Vargas, and Ambar Narayan. 2020. "Covid-19 and Inequality: A Review of the Evidence on Likely Impact and Policy Options." Working Paper 3, Centre for Disaster Protection, London.

Hirvonen, Kalle, Elia A. Machado, Andrew M. Simons, and Vis Taraz. 2022. "More Than a Safety Net: Ethiopia's Flagship Public Works Program Increases Tree Cover." *Global Environmental Change* 75: 102549. https://doi.org/10.1016/j.gloenvcha.2022.102549.

IPCC (Intergovernmental Panel on Climate Change). 2022: "Summary for Policymakers." Edited by H.-O. Pörtner, D. C. Roberts, E. S. Poloczanska, K. Mintenbeck, M. Tignor, A. Alegría, M. Craig, S. Langsdorf, S. Löschke, V. Möller, and A. Okem. In *Climate Change 2022: Impacts, Adaptation, and Vulnerability*, edited by H.-O. Pörtner, D. C. Roberts, M. Tignor, E. S. Poloczanska, K. Mintenbeck, A. Alegría, M. Craig, S. Langsdorf, S. Löschke, V. Möller, A. Okem, and B. Rama, 3–33. Contribution of Working Group II to the Sixth Assessment Report of the Intergovernmental Panel on Climate Change. New York: Cambridge University Press. https://doi.org/10.1017/9781009325844.001.

Jack, William, and Tavneet Suri. 2014. "Risk Sharing and Transactions Costs: Evidence from Kenya's Mobile Money Revolution." *American Economic Review* 104 (1): 183–223.

Jensen, Nathaniel D., Christopher B. Barrett, and Andrew G. Mude. 2017. "Cash Transfers and Index Insurance: A Comparative Impact Analysis from Northern Kenya." *Journal of Development Economics* 129: 14-28.

Kanbur, R. 2023. "What Is the World Bank Good for?" Paper presented at the EFI Africa Directors Inspirational Breakfast Series, Washington, DC, November 28.

Karlan, Dean, Robert Osei, Isaac Osei-Akoto, and Christopher Udry. 2014. "Agricultural Decisions after Relaxing Credit and Risk Constraints." *Quarterly Journal of Economics* 129 (2): 597–652. https://www.jstor.org/stable/26372558.

Lin, Boqiang, and Xuehui Li. 2011. "The Effect of Carbon Tax on Per Capita CO_2 Emissions." *Energy Policy* 39 (9): 5137–46.

Manning, D. A. C. 2008. "Biological Enhancement of Soil Carbonate Precipitation: Passive Removal of Atmospheric CO_2." *Mineralogical Magazine* 72 (2): 639–49.

Martin, Ralf, Laure B. de Preux, and Ulrich B. Wagner. 2014. "The Impact of a Carbon Tax on Manufacturing: Evidence from Microdata." *Journal of Public Economics* 117: 1–14.

Matlon, P. J. 1985. *Annual Report of ICRISAT/Burkina Economics Program.* Ouagadougou, Burkina Faso: International Crops Research Institute for the Semi-Arid Tropics.

Metcalf, Gilbert E. 2019. "On the Economics of a Carbon Tax for the United States." *Brookings Papers on Economic Activity*, Brookings Institution, Washington, DC.

Mobarak, Ahmed Mushfiq, and Mark R. Rosenzweig. 2013. "Informal Risk Sharing, Index Insurance, and Risk Taking in Developing Countries." *American Economic Review* 103 (3): 375–80.

Rafaty, Ryan, Geoffroy Dolphin, and Felix Pretis. 2021. "Carbon Pricing and the Elasticity of CO_2 Emissions." Working Paper 21-33, Resources for the Future, Washington, DC.

Ritchie, Hannah, Pablo Rosado, and Max Roser. 2023. "CO_2 and Greenhouse Gase Emissions." OurWorldInData.org. https://ourworldindata.org/co2-and-greenhouse-gas-emissions.

Rivers, Nicholas, and Brandon Schaufele. 2015. "Salience of Carbon Taxes in the Gasoline Market." *Journal of Environmental Economics and Management* 74: 23–36.

Schwaab, Jonas, Ronny Meier, Gianluca Mussetti, Sonia Seneviratne, Christine Bürgi, and Edouard L. Davin. 2021. "The Role of Urban Trees in Reducing Land Surface Temperatures in European Cities." *Nature Communications* 12 (1): 1–11. https://doi.org/10.1038/s41467-021-26768-w.

Stoeffler, Quentin, Michael Carter, Catherine Guirkinger, and Wouter Gelade. 2022. "The Spillover Impact of Index Insurance on Agricultural Investment by Cotton Farmers in Burkina Faso." *World Bank Economic Review* 36 (1): 114–40. https://doi.org/10.1093/wber/lhab011.

Teravaninthorn, Supee, and Gaël Raballand. 2009. *Transport Prices and Costs in Africa: A Review of the International Corridors.* Directions in Development; Infrastructure. Washington, DC: World Bank. http://hdl.handle.net/10986/6610.

Wollburg, Philip, Stephane Hallegatte, and Daniel Gerszon Mahler. 2023. "Ending Extreme Poverty Has a Negligible Impact on Global Greenhouse Gas Emissions." *Nature* 623 (7989): 982–86.

World Bank. 2016. *The Uganda Poverty Assessment Report 2016: Farms, Cities, and Good Fortune—Assessing Poverty Reduction in Uganda from 2006 to 2014.* Washington, DC: World Bank.

World Bank. 2020. *Poverty and Shared Prosperity Report 2020: Reversals of Fortune.* Washington, DC: World Bank.

World Bank. 2022. *Poverty and Shared Prosperity Report 2022: Correcting Course.* Washington, DC: World Bank.

Ziter, Carly D., Eric J. Pedersen, Christopher J. Kucharik, and Monica G. Turner. 2019. "Scale-Dependent Interactions between Tree Canopy Cover and Impervious Surfaces Reduce Daytime Urban Heat during Summer." *Proceedings of the National Academy of Sciences* 116 (15): 7575–80. https://doi.org/10.1073/pnas.1817561116.

CHAPTER 3

People in Africa Face an Unlevel Playing Field for Building Their Productive Capacity

AZIZ ATAMANOV, P. FACUNDO CUEVAS, AND JEREMY LEBOW

Chapter highlights

Productive assets and access to basic opportunities, such as health and education, are important drivers of people's income-earning potential. In Africa, these productive capacities and basic opportunities are unequally distributed, especially in countries in fragile or conflict-affected situations (FCS). This chapter focuses on the structural drivers of inequality in building productive capacity. Structural inequality arises from the outsized role of inherited circumstances and characteristics, and it shapes who gets an education, owns assets, or has access to basic services. Unequal access to assets, basic infrastructure, and acquisition of human capital affects lifelong income-earning potential and the ability to connect to an economy's growth engine and escape poverty. Structural inequality resulting from inherited characteristics or circumstances outside a person's control is socially unfair, leads to suboptimal allocation of resources, and limits economic growth. It also implies lower economic mobility, making poverty and inequality persistent over time.

The presence of structural inequality is evident in children's access to basic opportunities. Children's unequal access to basic services is also driven to a large extent by the circumstances to which a child is born, such as the location of their household. Africa has made significant gains in school enrollment since the late 1990s, although inequalities in quality persist. Data on individuals who were not exposed to this expansion suggest that children's education prospects are most closely tied to their parents' education. Children in Africa, especially girls, had the lowest probability of surpassing their parents' education. Rising enrollments in the past two decades may have enhanced mobility among subsequent generations, but it is still difficult to verify because of the lack of more recent data.

Climate shocks, an expanding working-age population, and intensifying conflicts have the potential to exacerbate these structural inequalities. Poor and vulnerable populations are often more likely to experience shocks. At the same time, they have the least capacity to cope with them. For example, children from poorer families living in rural areas had less or no access to learning opportunities during school closures related to the COVID-19 pandemic. Higher learning losses among children with lower school enrollment will exacerbate existing inequalities in human capital and future productive capacity. In a similar manner, climate shocks are likely to affect poor households the most because they are typically engaged in agricultural activities that depend on rain and other forces of nature. At the same time, poor households have the lowest resilience because of a low capacity to adapt and cope with weather shocks.

Addressing existing structural inequalities in building productive capacities requires prioritizing poor individuals and targeting underserved populations in lagging areas. An explicit focus on equity, along with higher coverage, may bring the best results in the case of services with the lowest and most unequal coverage, such as electricity, sanitation, and ensuring that children start and finish primary school on time. However, just sustaining the current level of access to basic services will require more resources than most countries can currently afford because of the fast-growing population and stalled economic growth. Revenue mobilization and improving the efficiency of budget spending in areas that contribute to human capital accumulation will be necessary to address current and future inequalities.

Structural inequality in building productive capacity

Inequality in access to factors that affect individuals' income-generating capacity (or productive capacity) starts to accumulate early in life. This section examines the extent to which children have universal access to a broad range of basic opportunities and productive capacities, such as education, health, access to electricity, and information and communication technology (ICT) services. The analysis then discusses the extent to which inequality in access is driven by the circumstances to which a child is born and the extent to which these inequalities could lead to low intergenerational mobility (IGM). Finally, the section concludes with an analysis of available data on land ownership in the region.

Africa has made progress in building productive capacity

Impressive progress has been made in health services for children over the past two decades, but progress on education and skills has been more mixed. Progress has been achieved in Africa regarding health outcomes such as measles and hepatitis immunization and the reduction of stunting prevalence (refer to figure 3.1 for Africa and figure 3A.4 in annex 3A for other regions). For example, stunting prevalence in Africa was reduced to 32 percent in 2020—remarkably close to the 28 percent average for lower-middle-income countries. Immunization against measles (children ages

12–23 months) and hepatitis (children age one year) reached more than 70 percent, still lower than but close to the averages observed in lower-middle-income countries (83 percent and 81 percent, respectively). In terms of education, although Africa made impressive progress and caught up with other regions in universal primary school enrollment, it continues to lag in other indicators (refer to figure 3.1 for Africa and figure 3A.2 in annex 3A for other regions). Access to preprimary schooling was the lowest, reaching 28 percent in 2020 compared with 58 percent in lower-middle-income countries. In 2020, the primary school completion rate in Africa reached 71 percent, increasing by more than 15 percentage points since 2000, but it was still lower than the 92 percent average for low-income countries in other regions. Secondary school enrollment rates also increased, reaching 44 percent in 2020 compared with 71 percent in lower-middle-income countries. Beyond differences in enrollment and completion rates, performance on learning outcomes suggests that the region lags in building skills for children who do attend school (Arias Diaz, Evans, and Santos 2019).

Despite significant progress in improving access to basic infrastructure in the past decade, such as access to basic drinking water, electricity, and unshared improved sanitation, Africa has not reached the level of lower-middle-income countries in 2020 and lags other regions. With respect to access to infrastructure, the most striking differences are in access to electricity and basic sanitation (refer to figure 3.1 for Africa and figure 3A.1 for other regions). Access to basic unshared sanitation reached almost 70 percent in

FIGURE 3.1 Selected basic services in Africa in 2000 and 2020 compared with the average level observed in lower-middle-income countries in 2020

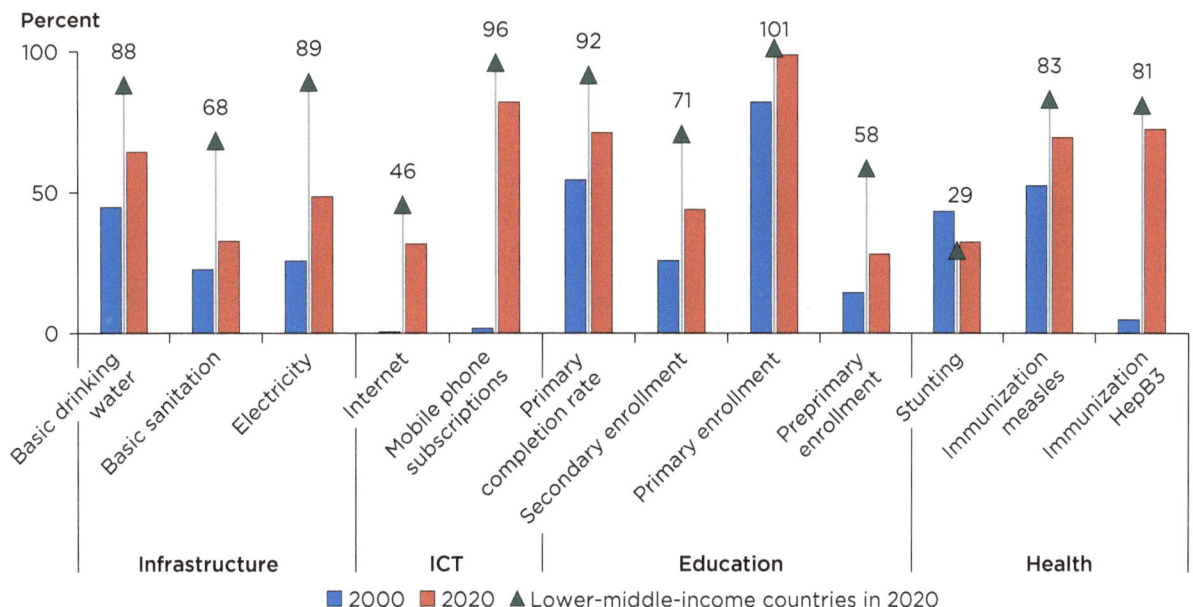

Source: World Bank staff calculations using data from World Development Indicators (https://databank.worldbank .org/source/world-development-indicators).
Note: HepB3 = hepatitis B, three dose; ICT = information and communication technology.

lower-middle-income countries in 2020 but remained almost half that (33 percent) in Africa in the same year. Access to electricity in Africa increased from 26 percent to 48 percent between 2000 and 2020 but was much lower than the near 90 percent average for lower-middle-income countries. Lower-middle-income countries are used here not as a benchmark, because they have higher economic development,[1] but rather as an aspirational goal. However, it is worth mentioning that in 2000 basic sanitation was even lower in South Asia than in Africa, and it has improved substantially since then and caught up with the average in lower-middle-income countries by 2020.

Finally, access to ICT services measured by mobile phone subscriptions and access to the internet grew exponentially in all regions, including Africa. Access to the internet increased in Africa from zero in 2000 to 32 percent in 2020, and mobile phone subscriptions increased from zero to 82 percent. Despite this, average access rates in Africa were still below average values in lower-middle-income countries in 2020; however, in terms of regional performance, Africa was on par with South Asia.

Leading and lagging countries in Africa converged with regard to most selected indicators measuring access to basic services during 2000–20. Countries with lower initial access to basic drinking water, electricity, secondary school enrollment, and primary school completion exhibited higher growth in 2000–20 (refer to figure 3A.5). Sanitation was a notable exception; countries with low access to sanitation in 2000 have not improved access faster than countries with high initial access.

Regional and country-level trends in access to basic infrastructure, health, and ICT services mask the gaps in access across different population groups. Figure 3.2 shows selected indicators for the poorest 20 percent and richest 20 percent of the population based on consumption per capita. The divide between the two groups is extremely large and is particularly pronounced for finishing primary school on time among children ages 13–16 years and for having access to electricity. For example, in Cameroon in 2014, access to electricity among the richest top quintile of the population was more than 90 percent compared with slightly higher than 10 percent among the poorest bottom quintile. There is also a substantial divide in access to basic services across rural and urban areas of African countries. These differences are partly driven by the time it takes to get to service providers, as detailed in box 3.1. This descriptive analysis signals that despite the progress achieved in service delivery, these opportunities may not be accessible to all and differ across socioeconomic characteristics (refer to figure 3A.3).

FIGURE 3.2 Access to basic services for the poorest and richest 20 percent of the population

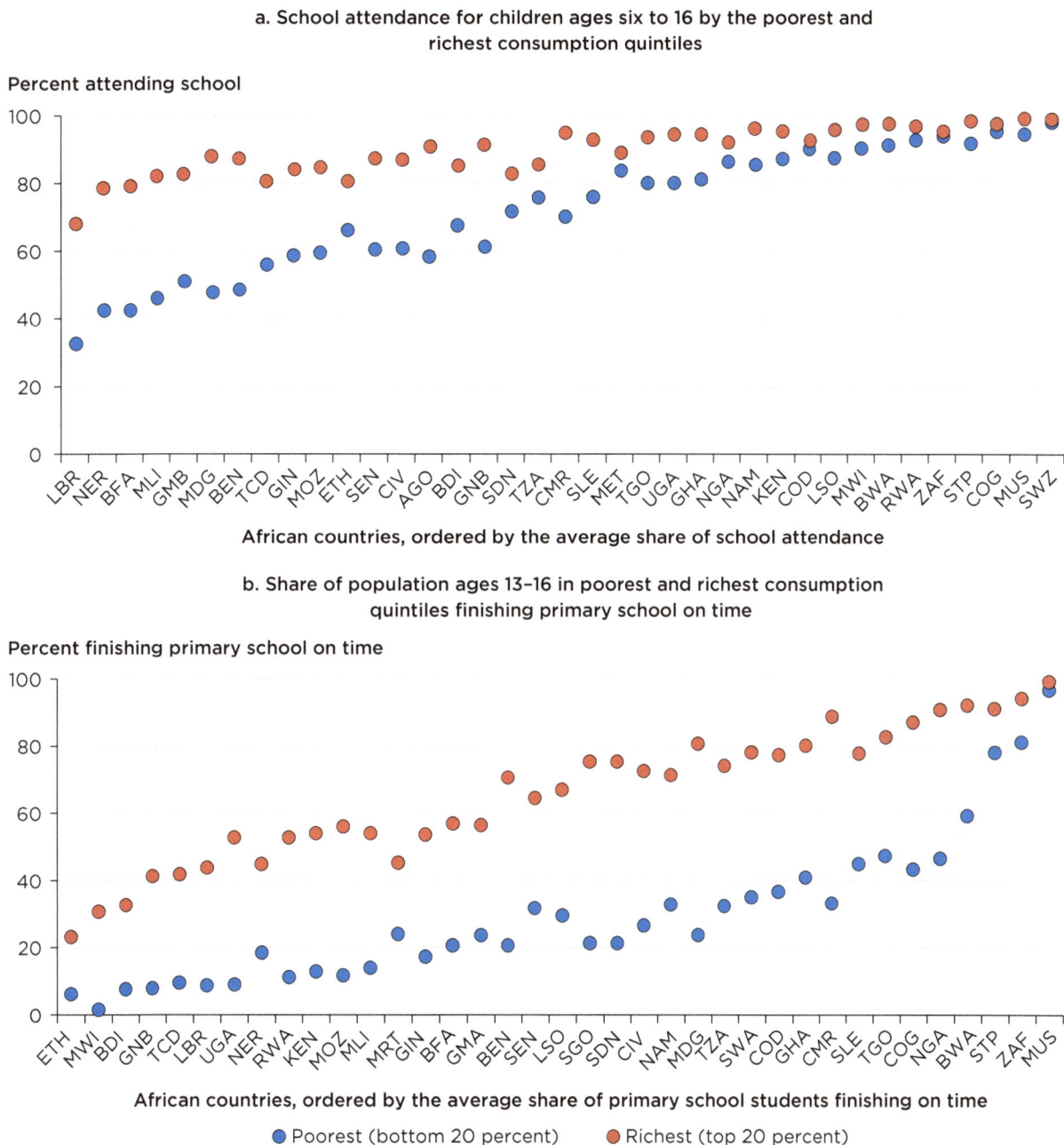

a. School attendance for children ages six to 16 by the poorest and richest consumption quintiles

Percent attending school

African countries, ordered by the average share of school attendance

b. Share of population ages 13–16 in poorest and richest consumption quintiles finishing primary school on time

Percent finishing primary school on time

African countries, ordered by the average share of primary school students finishing on time

● Poorest (bottom 20 percent)   ● Richest (top 20 percent)

(continued)

FIGURE 3.2 Access to basic services for the poorest and richest 20 percent of the population *(continued)*

c. Access to electricity among the poorest and richest consumption quintiles

Percent of population with access to electricity

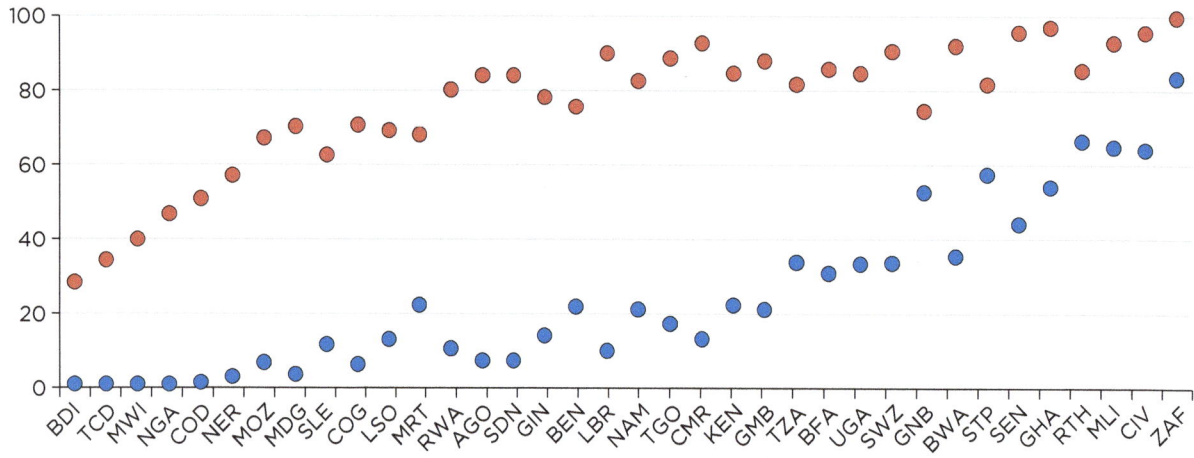

African countries, ordered by the average share with access to electricity

d. Access to mobile phone for individuals ages 15 and older by the poorest and richest consumption quintiles

Percent of population with access to mobile phone

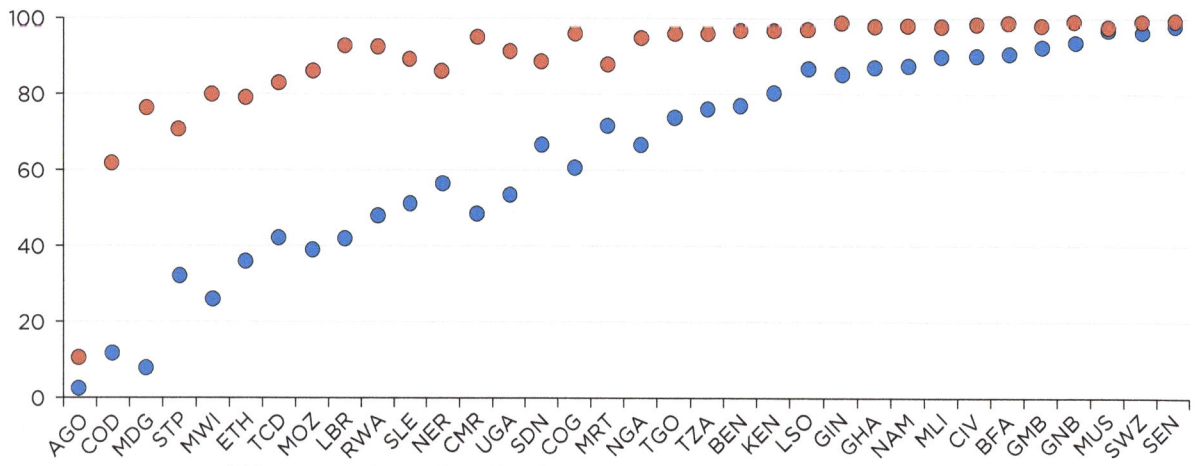

African countries, ordered by the average share with access to mobile phones

● Poorest (bottom 20 percent) ● Richest (top 20 percent)

Source: World Bank staff calculations using data from the World Bank's Global Monitoring Database.
Note: For country abbreviations, refer to https://www.iso.org/obp/ui/#search.

BOX 3.1

Urban versus rural access to health

Physical access of the population to health facilities is an important factor affecting access to health outcomes and contributing to regional and rural–urban disparities. To show this, population-weighted travel distance to any health facility is reported for rural and urban areas in African countries (refer to figure B3.1.1). Travel distance time is split into four categories: shorter than 60 minutes (benchmark), one to two hours, two to three hours, and longer than four hours. Even though a lot of variation within countries is hidden, the difference between rural and urban areas is stark. It takes less than an hour to get to any health facility in 43 of 47 African countries in urban areas. However, in rural areas, this is true for only 20 of 47 African countries.

Regional variation in physical access of populations to health facilities is substantial and is correlated with health outcomes (figure 3A.10 in annex 3A). Longer distance to health facilities is associated with a lower share of births attended by skilled health personnel, a lower share of newborns receiving postnatal care within two days of delivery, and lower immunization among one-year-old children with the diphtheria–tetanus–pertussis and Bacillus Calmette-Guérin vaccines.

MAP B3.1.1 Population-weighted average walking distance time to any health facility across rural and urban areas of African countries

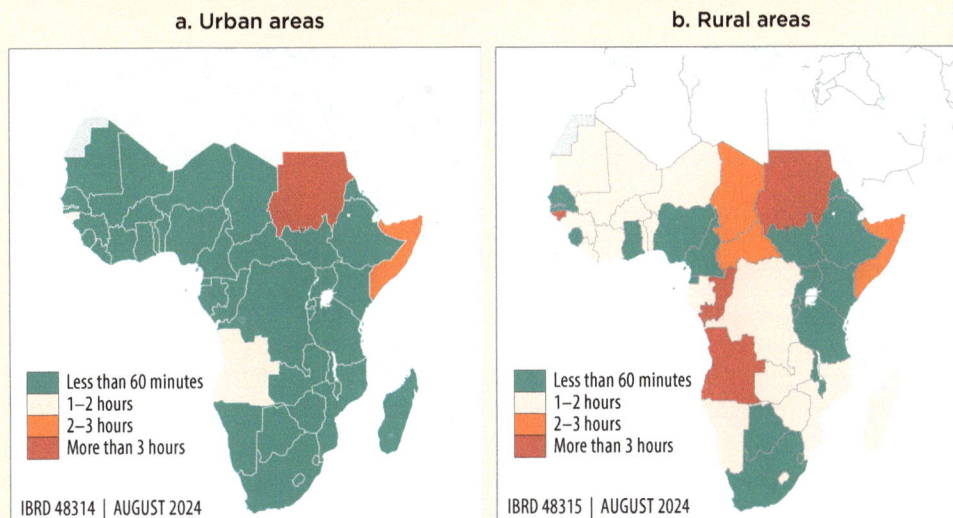

a. Urban areas

b. Rural areas

Less than 60 minutes
1–2 hours
2–3 hours
More than 3 hours

IBRD 48314 | AUGUST 2024

IBRD 48315 | AUGUST 2024

Source: World Bank staff calculations using the database of health facilities from Maina et al. (2019).

Despite progress, inequality in access to services for children persists

Measuring inequality in access to basic services and identifying disadvantaged groups can provide important information for policy makers. This can be done using the Human Opportunity Index (HOI), a composite indicator estimated for children, which combines two elements:

1. The level of coverage of basic opportunities necessary for human development and

2. The degree to which the distribution of those opportunities is conditional on children's circumstances, as measured by the dissimilarity index (D-index), a proxy for inequality of opportunity that penalizes the HOI for unfairly distributed access to services.

This penalty implies that if the HOI is below the coverage rate, inequalities in access to services exist. A detailed explanation of the index and how it was constructed for this study is described in annex 3B.

Children living in countries not affected by fragility and conflict have higher and more equal access to most opportunities. Figure 3.3 shows average coverage rates and HOIs for different opportunities, averaged for groups of countries depending on their resource and fragility status. Overall, for almost all opportunities, living in countries characterized by FCS results in lower coverage rates and HOI regardless of whether those countries are resource rich or not. Starting primary school on time is an exception, but it may be related to differences in the official starting school age. Thus, for example, the average HOI for finishing primary school on time in resource-rich and FCS countries is about 40 percent, which is much lower than the 62 percent in resource-rich and non-FCS countries. The average HOI in access to electricity in resource-rich and FCS countries is about 25 percent, compared with 57 percent in resource-rich but non-FCS countries. Consistently, average inequality of opportunity, measured by the D-index, also tends to be lower in non-FCS countries for all opportunities, as shown in figure 3.4.

Access to education is limited and unequal. Figure 3A.6 shows country-level coverage rates and the HOI for several education opportunities, such as school attendance and starting and finishing primary school on time. Coverage for education opportunities is much less than universal in most countries. Moreover, average coverage is higher than average HOI, pointing to large inequalities in access. For example, the coverage rate for finishing primary school on time is on average about 46 percent compared with an average HOI of 39 percent. In addition, a significant cross-country correlation across education HOIs signals that progress in one education opportunity is correlated with that in other education opportunities. Finally, and most importantly, there is a stark difference between HOI and coverage rates for opportunities related to school attendance and opportunities related to starting and finishing primary school on time. The latter captures the quality of schooling, albeit imperfectly. Thus, HOI for school attendance rates is higher than HOI for school completion rates, signaling higher inequality in finishing school on time. For example, the average HOI for school attendance (ages 13–16 years) was close to 76 percent, whereas the average HOI for primary school completion was 39 percent. This is consistent with the widely documented gap between rapid growth in enrollment and lagging learning outcomes in Africa, and it points to high inequality in learning outcomes (Bashir et al. 2018). Better measures for quality of education point to more severe inequalities in learning opportunities, as discussed in box 3.2.

FIGURE 3.3 **Coverage and HOI across African countries, by resource and FCS status**

Average value of indicator (%)

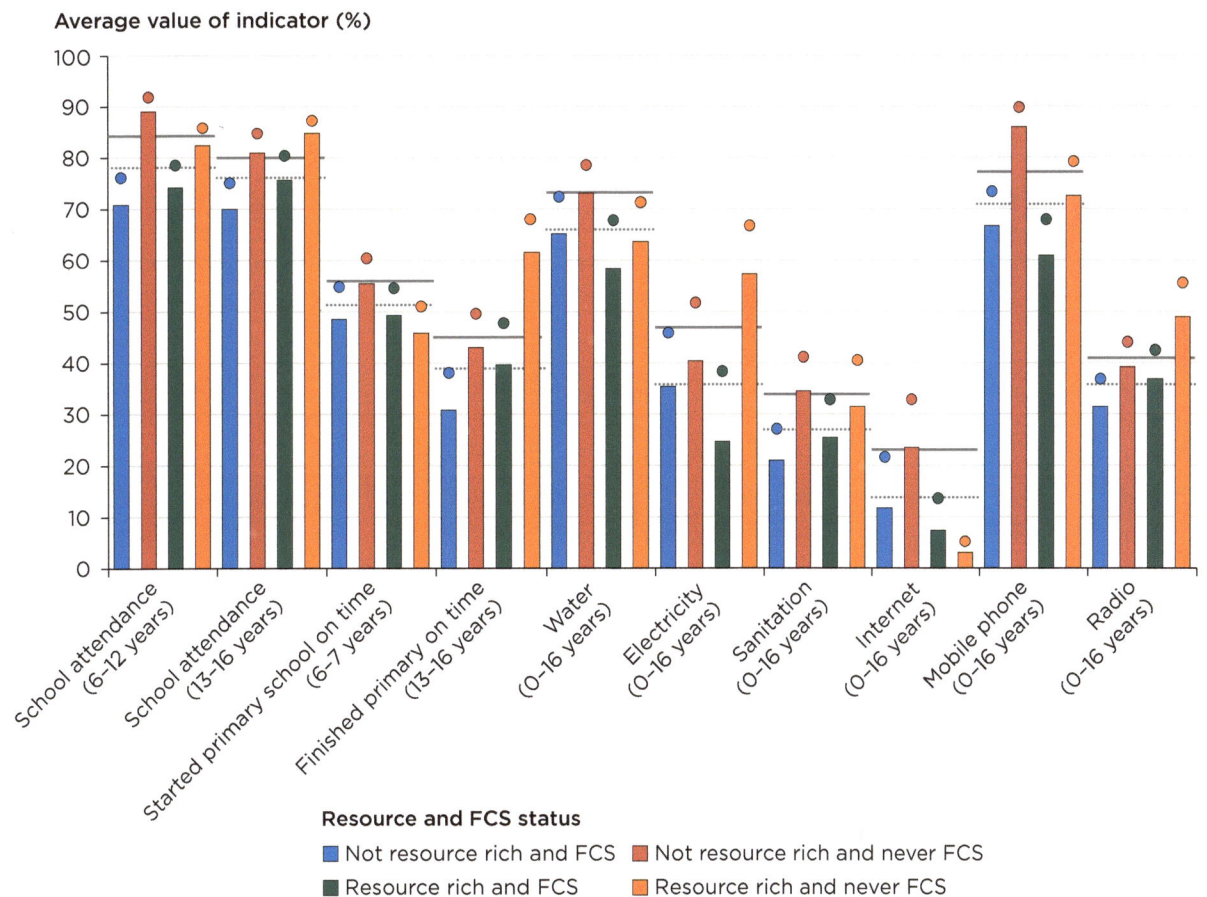

Resource and FCS status
- Not resource rich and FCS
- Not resource rich and never FCS
- Resource rich and FCS
- Resource rich and never FCS

Source: World Bank staff calculations using data from the World Bank's Global Monitoring Database.
Note: Dark gray lines show average coverage for each opportunity, and dotted lines show average HOI for all countries. Dots represent coverage, and bars indicate HOI. FCS = fragile and conflict-affected situations; HOI = Human Opportunity Index.

FIGURE 3.4 Average D-index (inequality of opportunity) across African countries, by resource and FCS status

D-index (%)

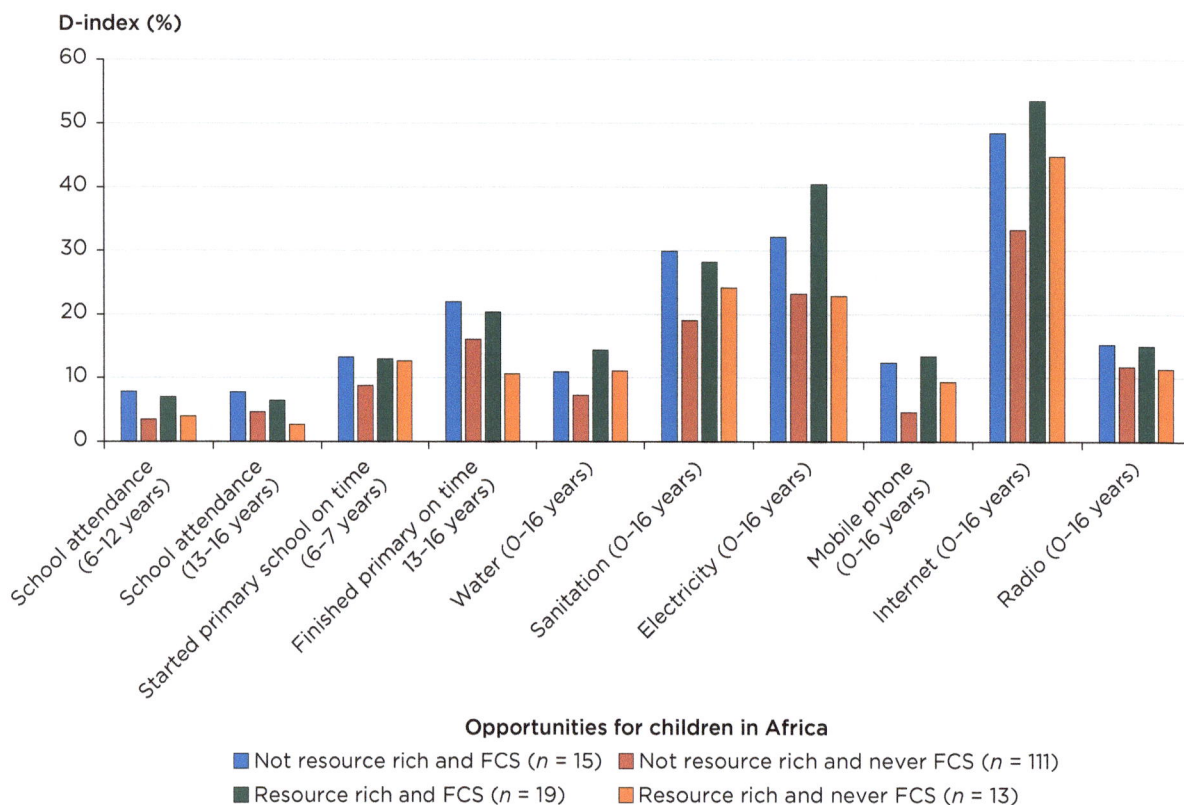

Opportunities for children in Africa

■ Not resource rich and FCS (*n* = 15)   ■ Not resource rich and never FCS (*n* = 111)
■ Resource rich and FCS (*n* = 19)   ■ Resource rich and never FCS (*n* = 13)

Source: World Bank staff calculations using data from the World Bank's Global Monitoring Database.
Note: D-index = dissimilarity index; FCS = fragile and conflict-affected situations.

Access to basic services ranges from relatively high access to improved water (simple average HOI of 66 percent) to low and unequal access to electricity (36 percent) and even lower access to improved sanitation (27 percent). Using stricter criteria accounting for the quality of water and electricity services results in even lower and more unequal access, as shown in box 3.2. Moreover, countries with similar coverage rates may differ on inequality in access. For example, access to basic drinking water was similar in Ethiopia and Mauritania (55 percent versus 57 percent, respectively), but the HOI is higher in Ethiopia (50 percent versus 42 percent), signaling much lower inequality (refer to figure 3A.7). Indeed, checking only one dimension shows that the gap in access rates to drinking water between rural and urban areas was much higher in Mauritania (35 percent versus 87 percent, respectively) than in Ethiopia (51 percent versus 79 percent, respectively). Although it is not possible to construct HOI indicators for health services using standard household surveys, evidence from other surveys points to inequalities in access as well (refer to box 3.3). Similarly, recent analysis focused on horizontal inequalities in child well-being (child mortality, stunting, and years of schooling) across groups—spatial, ethnic, gender, or religious—finds significantly higher inequalities in Africa than in other low- and middle-income countries (Tetteh-Baah et al. 2024).

Mobile phone penetration is relatively high in Africa, with the average HOI being close to 71 percent, which is higher than access to basic services.[2] Average access to the internet in Africa was measured in only a handful of countries. Nevertheless, existing numbers show that it was low and very unequal, with HOI equal to 14 percent. Such low access to the internet may look contradictory to high mobile phone penetration numbers, but it is important to remember that many people in Africa own basic phones without access to the internet (see, for example, Atamanov et al. 2022).

BOX 3.2

Changes in the Human Opportunity Index with quality dimension

One important limitation of the current analysis using the Human Opportunity Index (HOI) is that access to services does not reflect the quality of these services. For example, indicators on access to electricity do not consider the hours of supply provided, and indicators on access to basic drinking water do not consider the time needed to reach the source of water. This box provides some illustrative examples of changes in HOI when adding additional information on the quality of services provided. Figure B3.2.1a shows coverage, HOI, and the dissimilarity index (D-index, or inequality of opportunity) for water and electricity opportunities in Ghana in 2016. Original indicators on water were expanded by considering the distance to the water source and the quality of water. Once both factors are accounted for, the HOI for drinking water falls from 54 to 42 percent, with a slight increase in inequality. Opportunity in access to electricity was expanded by controlling for whether the supply of electricity was available 24 hours per day. This reduced HOI in access to electricity by slightly more than half (from 70 percent to 37 percent), with a substantial increase in inequality. Figure B3.2.1b shows coverage, HOI, and D-index for water and electricity opportunities in Nigeria in 2018. As in the case of Ghana, HOI substantially declines once information on distance to and availability of water supply are added. However, the most striking difference occurs for electricity when duration of supply is factored in. It turns out that almost nobody has access to electricity for 24 hours a day, compared with 57 percent electricity coverage without this additional information.

(continued)

BOX 3.2

Changes in the Human Opportunity Index with quality dimension *(continued)*

FIGURE B3.2.1 Human Opportunity Index, coverage, and D-index for extended opportunities

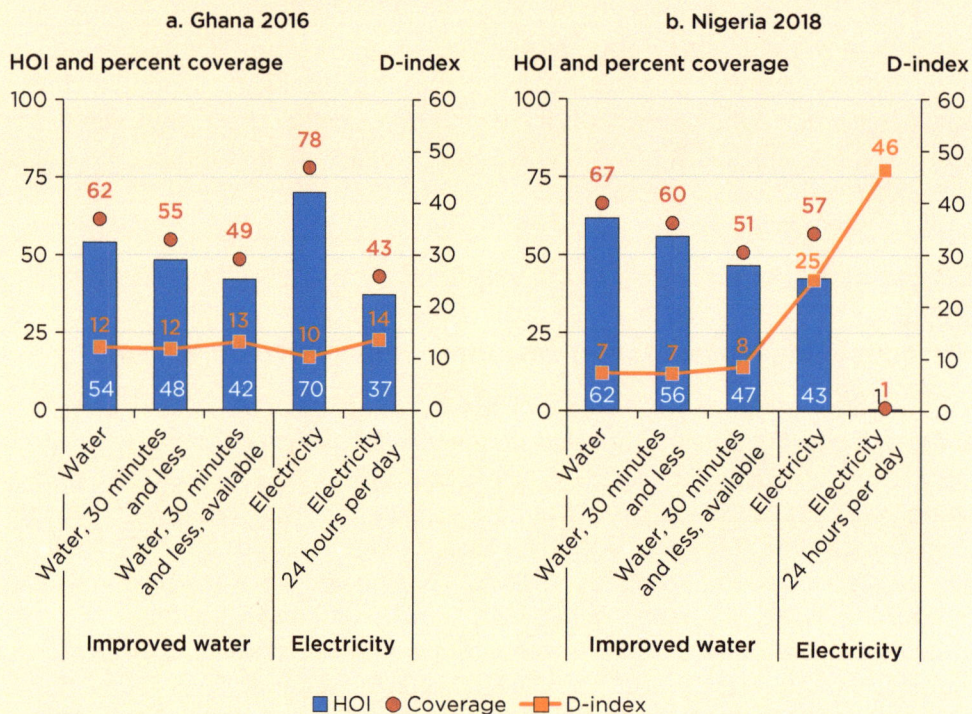

a. Ghana 2016

b. Nigeria 2018

Source: World Bank staff calculations using data from the World Bank's Global Monitoring Database.
Note: D-index = dissimilarity index; HOI = Human Opportunity Index.

Similarly, measuring the quality of education has so far been limited by using on-time progression through school. A better indicator is a direct measure of learning through standardized test scores. Household budget surveys do not collect this information, and different surveys that specifically measure learning should be used. A school subcomponent of the Human Capital Index, standardized test scores, is used to illustrate how test scores vary across just one dimension related to

(continued)

BOX 3.2
Changes in the Human Opportunity Index with quality dimension (continued)

household welfare (refer to figure B3.2.2). Overall, Africa has the lowest average standardized score, 374, on par with that of South Asia. Note that 400 corresponds to the benchmark of low proficiency in the Trends in International Mathematics and Science Study at the student level, whereas 625 corresponds to advanced proficiency. Country-level numbers in Africa vary a lot, in particular if they are reported for the poorest and richest quintiles (refer to figure B3.2.3). For example, the average test score of students from the poorest quintile in Tanzania was about 331, whereas for the richest quintile it was 407. Using test scores confirms that quality of education and inequality in learning are an important source of concern in majority of Africa countries for which data are available.

FIGURE B3.2.2 Harmonized test scores circa 2020, averages by World Bank regions

Harmonized test score

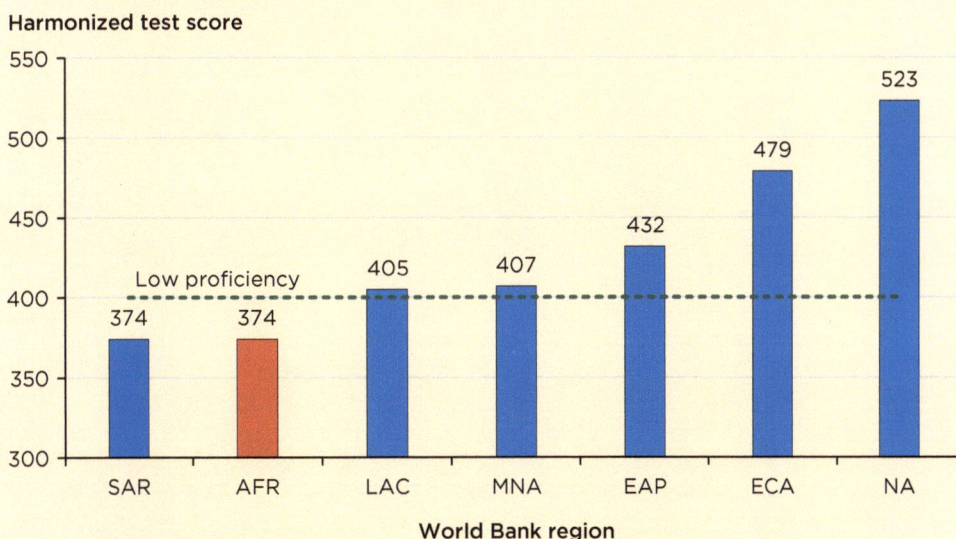

Source: World Bank 2021.
Note: Dashed line indicates the benchmark of low proficiency in the Trends in International Mathematics and Science Study at the student level. AFR = Sub-Saharan Africa; EAP = East Asia and Pacific; ECA = Europe and Central Asia; LAC = Latin America and the Caribbean; MNA = Middle East and North Africa; SAR = South Asia.

(continued)

BOX 3.2

Changes in the Human Opportunity Index with quality dimension
(continued)

FIGURE B3.2.3 Harmonized test scores circa 2020 across the poorest
and richest welfare quintiles

Harmonized test score

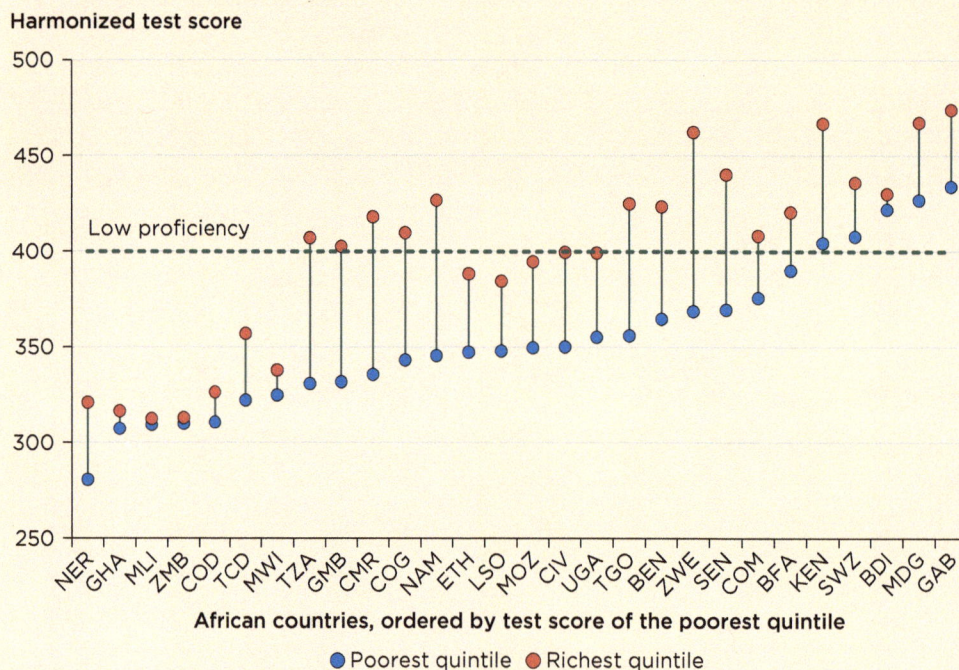

African countries, ordered by test score of the poorest quintile

● Poorest quintile   ● Richest quintile

Source: SES-HCI.
Note: SES-HCI data at the quintile level, and averaged to the national level, are not fully
comparable or consistent with the global HCI. Dashed line indicates the benchmark of low
proficiency in the Trends in International Mathematics and Science Study at the student level.
SES-HCI = Socioeconomically Disaggregated Human Capital Index. For country abbreviations,
refer to https://www.iso.org/obp/ui/#search.

BOX 3.3
Inequality in access to health opportunities

A previous regional study of Africa (Dabalen et al. 2015) used Demographic and Health Surveys to construct the Human Opportunity Index (HOI) for health opportunities and found that wealth and mother's education were the most important contributors to inequality in immunization, explaining 56 percent of the dissimilarity index. Wealth and child's gender were the two most important contributors (with similar magnitude) to the opportunity of not being stunted, followed by mother's education and location. This report does not construct HOI for health opportunities because these data are not typically collected in the household budget surveys used here to measure HOI. Instead, for illustrative purposes, the most recent measles immunization and stunting rates are reported, with the first indicator split by mother's education and the second by wealth quintiles.

Despite the high level of immunization against measles at the country and regional levels, many countries have substantial disparities in immunization rates based on mother's education. On average, the immunization rate among children with uneducated mothers was about 68 percent, compared with 85 percent among children with mothers having secondary or higher education (refer to figure B3.3.1).

Stunting prevalence rates among children younger than age five years are also quite different across wealth quintiles. Figure B3.3.2 reports the most recent stunting rates for the poorest and richest wealth quintiles in African countries. On average, stunting prevalence is more than two times lower among children from the top richest wealth quintile compared with children from the poorest bottom quintile: 16 percent versus 37 percent. In some countries, the wealth gap turns to be extremely high—four times higher in Cameroon or five times higher in Gabon.

(continued)

BOX 3.3

Inequality in access to health opportunities *(continued)*

FIGURE B3.3.1 Measles immunization coverage among two-year-olds in African countries, by mother's education level

a. No education

African countries, ordered by share of
immunized children with uneducated mothers

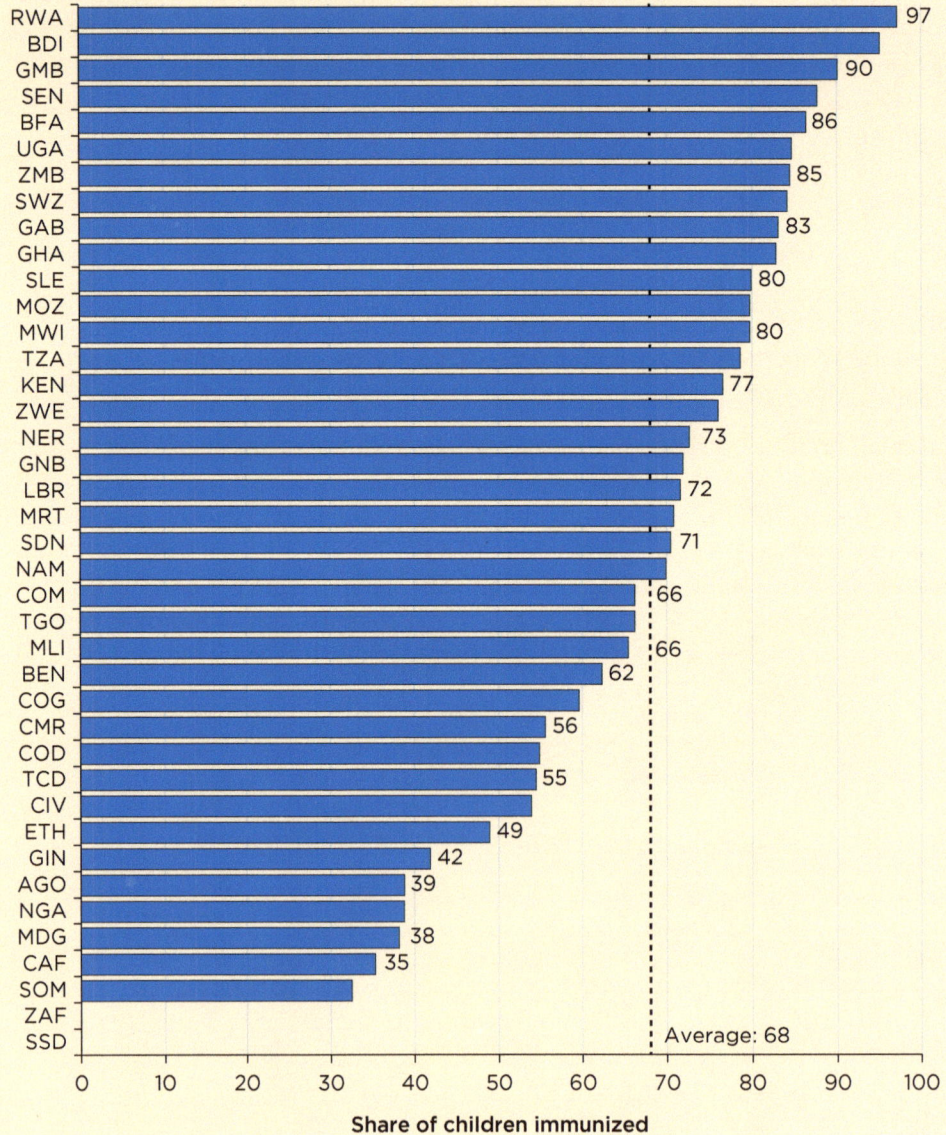

Share of children immunized

(continued)

BOX 3.3

Inequality in access to health opportunities *(continued)*

FIGURE B3.3.1 Measles immunization coverage among two-year-olds in African countries by mother's education level *(continued)*

b. Secondary or higher education

African countries, ordered by share of immunized children with uneducated mothers

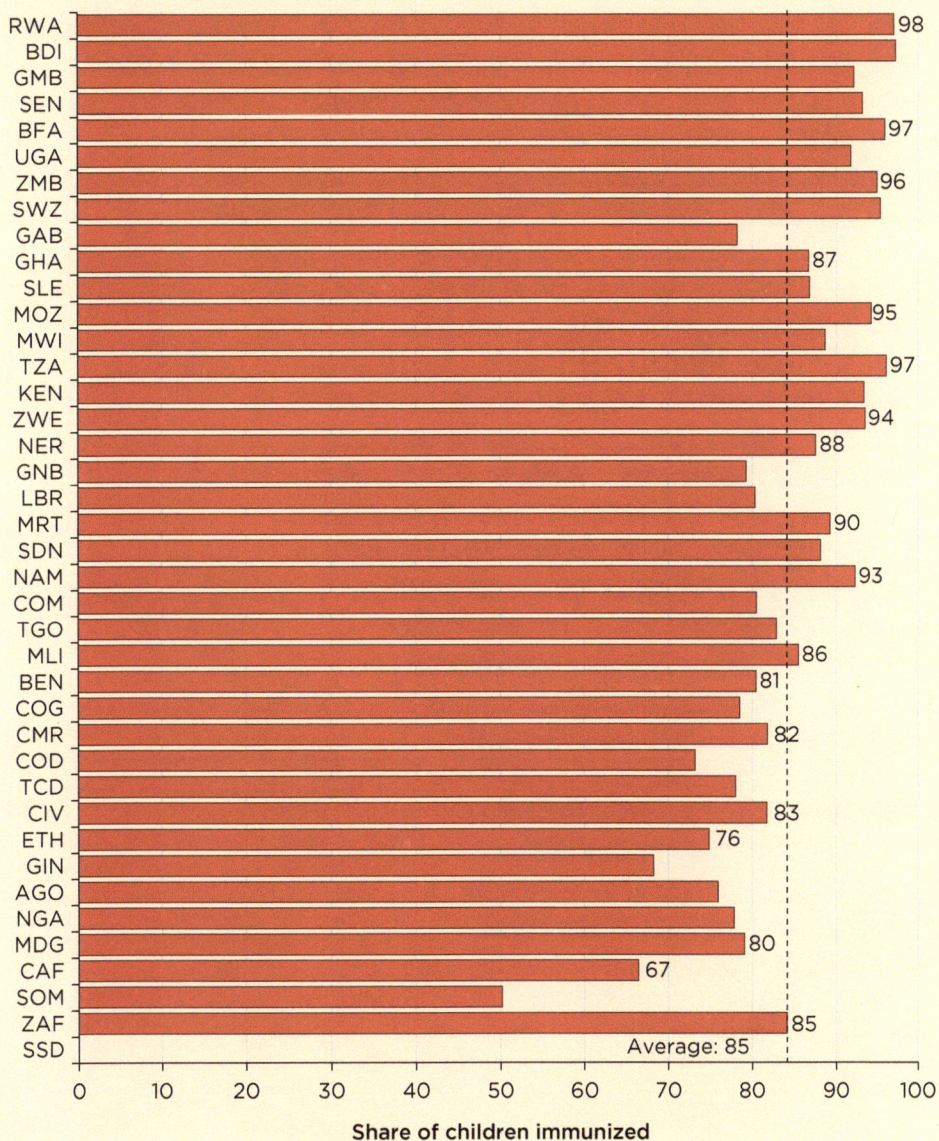

Share of children immunized

Source: WHO Health Inequality Data Repository, World Health Organization (https://www.who.int/data/inequality-monitor/data). Accessed July 2023.
Note: For country abbreviations, refer to https://www.iso.org/obp/ui/#search.

(continued)

BOX 3.3

Inequality in access to health opportunities *(continued)*

FIGURE B3.3.2 Stunting prevalence among children younger than 5 years in African countries across the poorest and richest wealth quintiles

a. Quintile 1 (poorest)

African countries, ordered by stunting prevalence in the poorest quintile

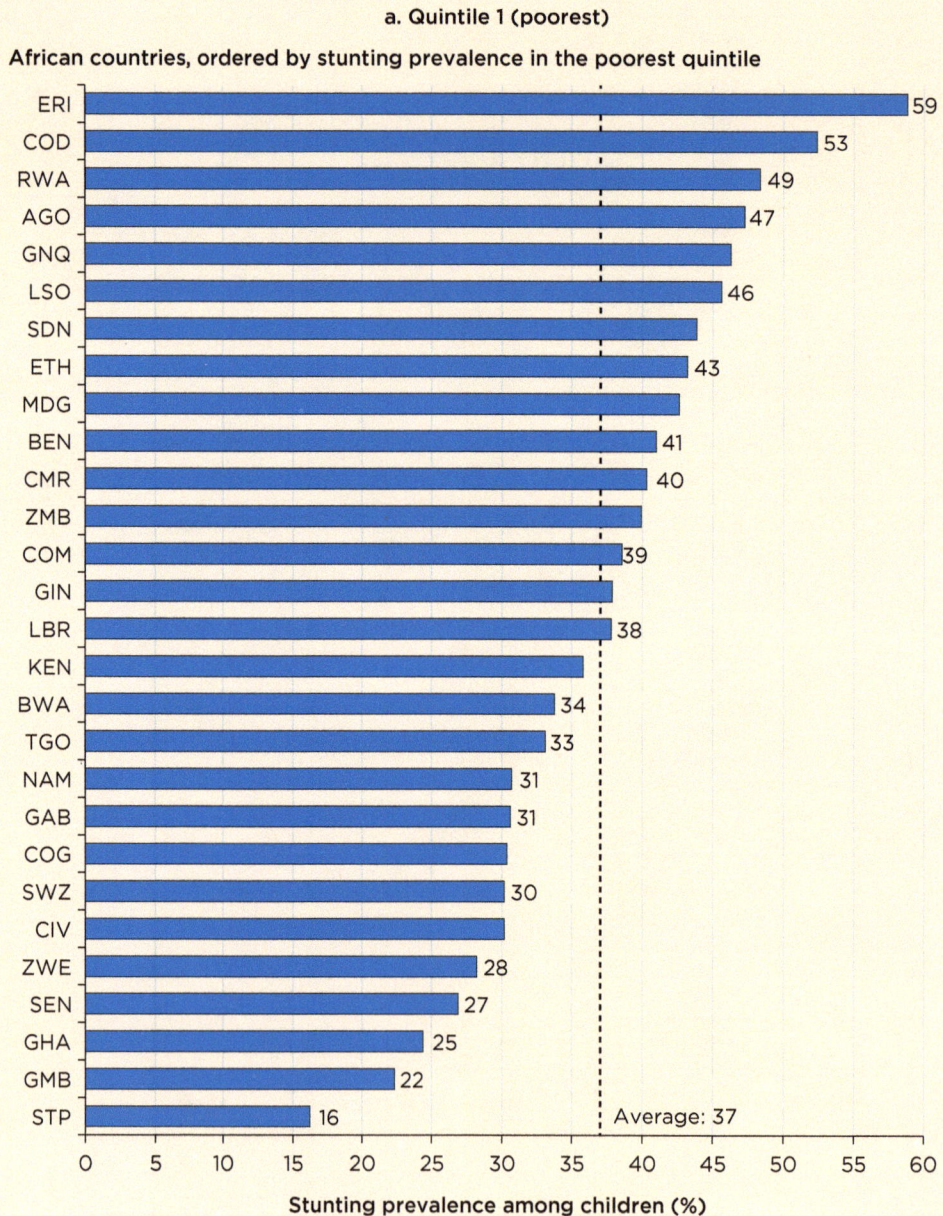

Country	Value
ERI	59
COD	53
RWA	49
AGO	47
GNQ	
LSO	46
SDN	
ETH	43
MDG	
BEN	41
CMR	40
ZMB	
COM	39
GIN	
LBR	38
KEN	
BWA	34
TGO	33
NAM	31
GAB	31
COG	
SWZ	30
CIV	
ZWE	28
SEN	27
GHA	25
GMB	22
STP	16

Average: 37

Stunting prevalence among children (%)

(continued)

BOX 3.3

Inequality in access to health opportunities *(continued)*

FIGURE B3.3.2 **Stunting prevalence among children younger than 5 years in African countries across the poorest and richest wealth quintiles *(continued)***

b. Quintile 5 (richest)

African countries, ordered by stunting prevalence in the poorest quintile

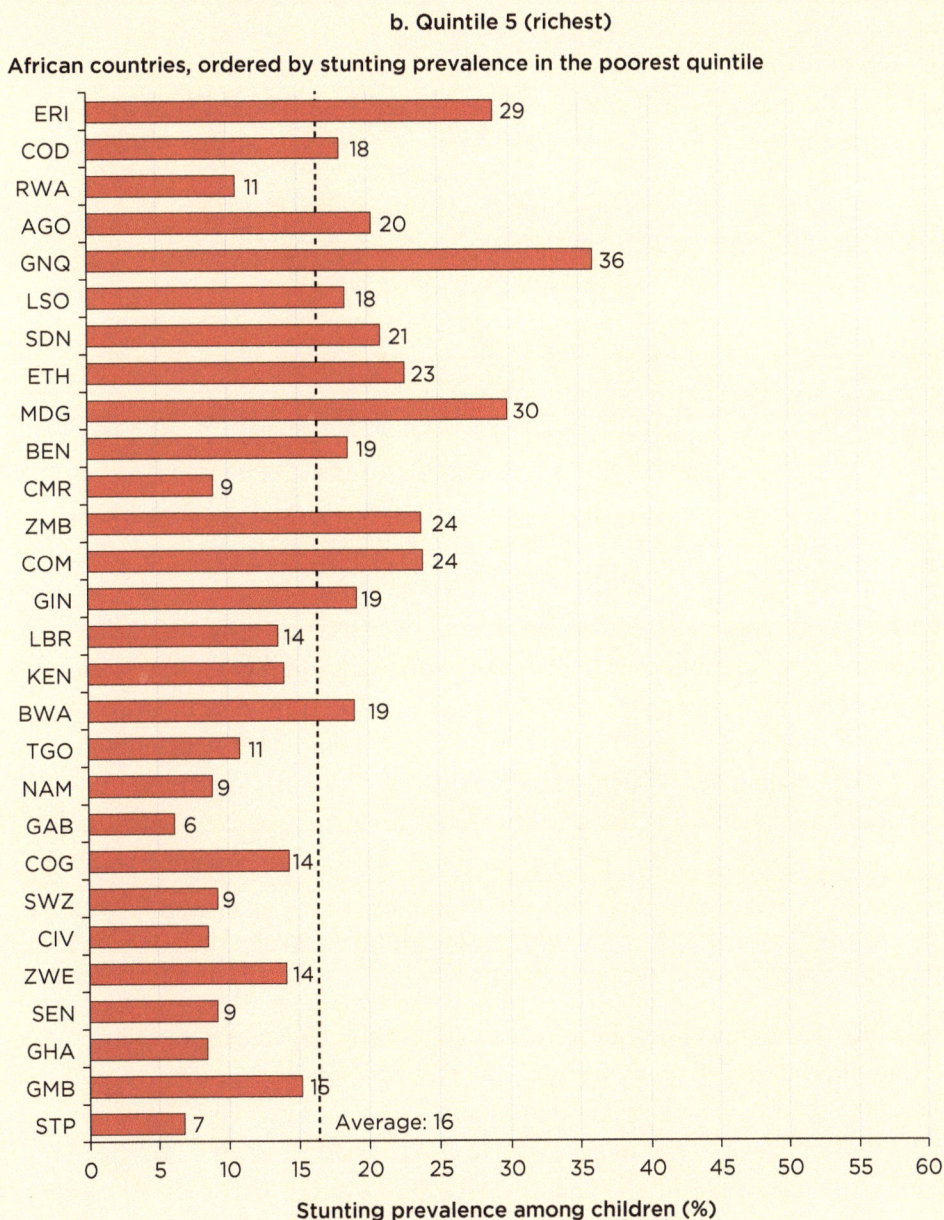

Stunting prevalence among children (%)

Source: WHO Health Inequality Data Repository, World Health Organization (https://www.who.int/data/inequality-monitor/data). Accessed July 2023.

Note: For country abbreviations, refer to https://www.iso.org/obp/ui/#search.

Inequality in access to services is heavily influenced by the circumstances to which a child is born

Having established earlier in this chapter that important inequalities exist in access to services for children, this report assesses the extent to which those inequalities are driven by the circumstances in which a child is born. The report identifies the circumstances of children that contribute the most to the observed inequality of opportunity. In presenting the results, the focus is primarily on the average contribution of each circumstance to inequality of opportunities, where the average is computed over all or a subset of countries in the sample. While checking and interpreting the results, it is important to keep in mind that the level of inequality is quite different across opportunities.

On average, a child's location (rural–urban and region) is responsible for more than half of the inequality in access to basic services (water, electricity, and sanitation). For some countries, location accounts for more than 75 percent of the inequality of opportunity (D-index). However, the relative contributions of rural–urban and regional disparities vary widely across countries and opportunities. Regional disparities account for 73 percent of inequality in access to basic water in Burundi, whereas rural–urban disparities account for more than half of inequality in access to electricity in Mozambique. For other opportunities, location effects still account for more than 40 percent of inequality. Inequality in access to such opportunities as starting primary school on time and primary and secondary school attendance was associated with regional disparities to a much larger extent than with the rural–urban divide. These findings are consistent with recent work finding that spatial inequality is higher than ethnic, gender, and religious inequality when it comes to other indicators of well-being, including child mortality, child stunting, and years of schooling (Tetteh-Baah et al. 2024). However, there are important differences across countries. The combined location effect (urban and regional) is particularly pronounced when measuring the D-index in resource-rich countries, especially FCS ones. Thus, for example, urban and regional disparities accounted, on average, for 54 percent of inequality across all opportunities in resource-rich and FCS countries, significantly higher than the 42 percent in not-resource-rich and never-FCS countries (refer to figure 3.5).

Affordability is a key constraint for access to mobile phones, electricity, internet, and sanitation. Household monetary well-being measured by consumption per capita is the largest contributor to inequality in access to mobile phones—accounting, on average, for 24 percent of inequality (refer to table 3.1). In some countries, such as Malawi, Mauritius, and Rwanda, consumption disparities account for more than 40 percent of inequality in access to mobile phones, signaling that the cost of mobile phone service is still an important barrier to higher penetration rates. Household monetary well-being measured by consumption also plays an important role in inequality in access to electricity, internet, and sanitation as well, highlighting the issue of affordability.

FIGURE 3.5 **Average contributions of circumstances to inequality of opportunities (D-index)**

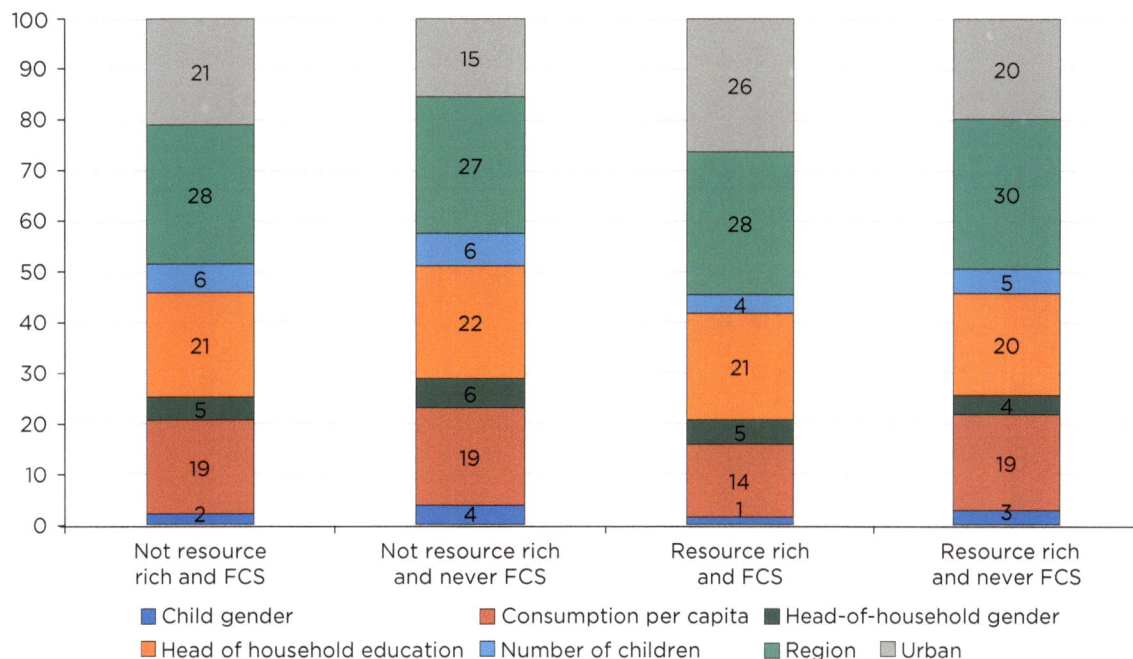

Source: World Bank staff calculations using data from the World Bank's Global Monitoring Database.
Note: D-index = dissimilarity index; FCS = fragile and conflict-affected situations.

Head-of-household education was an important contributor to inequality in education opportunities, accounting on average for 26 percent of inequality in school attendance rates, 24 percent of inequality in access to internet and primary school completion rates, and 23 percent of inequality in access to mobile phones. Head-of-household gender was not an important contributor to inequality in access to any opportunities except a radio, where it accounted for 20 percent of overall inequality. Country-level data show that female heads of household are significantly less likely to own a radio than male heads, even after controlling for other factors such as head-of-household education, welfare status, and so forth. For example, in Mozambique access to a radio among children from households with a female head was about 27 percent, compared with 49 percent among households with a male head. Child gender was not found to be an important contributor to inequality, but it was a noticeable contributor to inequality of opportunities related to finishing primary school on time and school enrollment for children ages 13–16.

TABLE 3.1 Average contributions of circumstances to inequality of opportunities (D-index)

Circumstances	Opportunities									
	Education				Basic services			ICT		
	School attendance (6-12 years)	School attendance (13-16 years)	Started primary school on time (6-7 years)	Finished primary on time (13-16 years)	Water (0-16 Years)	Sanitation (0-16 Years)	Electricity (0-16 years)	Mobile phone (0-16 years)	Internet (0-16 years)	Radio (0-16 years)
Child gender	4	6	3	7	0	1	0	0	1	1
Consumption per capita	16	15	15	16	14	22	24	24	21	12
Head-of-household gender	4	4	2	2	3	3	2	5	3	20
Head-of-household education	26	26	24	23	13	18	17	23	24	18
Number of children	5	5	6	6	4	6	4	6	4	9
Region	29	28	31	23	36	28	25	21	24	30
Urban	17	16	17	23	29	24	28	20	24	10
Total	100	100	100	100	100	100	100	100	100	100

Source: World Bank staff calculations using data from the World Bank's Global Monitoring Database.
Note: D-index = dissimilarity index; ICT = information and communication technology.

Countries with lower dissimilarity have higher gross domestic product (GDP) per capita and lower poverty rates. Countries with higher economic development, measured by GDP per capita in 2017 US$ purchasing power parity (PPP), tend to have lower D-index,[3] calculated as a simple average across all opportunities. Similarly, international poverty measured using the 2017 US$2.15 PPP poverty line was positively correlated with average D-index.[4] It is not clear, however, how the correlation between per capita GDP and the D-index works. It may be that richer countries are able to reduce disparities in access to education and basic services, or it may be that persistent inequality in access leads to inefficiencies in investment and utilization of physical and human capital, limiting economic growth. Nevertheless, Molina, Narayan, and Saavedra-Chanduvi (2013) found that inequality of opportunities in Programme for International Student Assessment (PISA) test scores hindered development measured by GDP per capita in a cross-country study.

Before the expansion in schooling, the probability that a child in Africa surpassed their parents' education was lowest among all regions, with little progress over time and a gap between boys and girls

To what extent is inequality in educational opportunities perpetuated across generations? The previous section established that access to basic services that are critical for children, such as education, is far from universal and remains very unequal. Moreover, this inequality often depends on parental characteristics. This is problematic not just at the individual level but also because it has implications for the overall economy because it jeopardizes the productive capacity of those children in the future. Moreover, to the extent that unequal educational opportunities limit economic mobility, it could perpetuate poverty and inequality across generations. This section measures IGM by using information about the educational attainment of children and their parents before the recent expansion in schooling. Measuring changes in IGM across cohorts is only possible for a limited set of 19 African countries, and the most accurate cross-regional comparison is possible only for the 1980s cohort, with results being derived from 43 African countries. Detailed information on the Global Database on Intergenerational Mobility (GDIM; World Bank 2023a) and its limitations are provided in annex 3C.

Educational mobility is usually measured using two distinct but related indicators: absolute and relative IGM. *Absolute upward IGM* is the extent to which a generation's education is higher than that of their parents. This reflects a universal human aspiration of parents hoping for a better life for their children. *Relative IGM* is the extent to which an individual's education is independent of their parents' education.[5] Higher relative mobility (lower intergenerational persistence in education) across generations is associated with lower inequality of opportunity. Both indicators are interrelated and important for economic progress. Without absolute mobility, it is difficult to increase living standards. Lack of relative mobility is unfair and constrains absolute upward mobility (van der Weide et al. 2021).

The probability that a child in Africa surpasses their parents' education is much lower and much slower to progress than in other regions. Sadly, educational achievement has not changed much in Africa across the 1960s and 1980s cohorts (refer to figure 3.6a). This is in sharp contrast to the East Asia and Pacific, Latin America and Caribbean, and Middle East and North Africa regions, where absolute IGM increased across generations and in which the 1980s cohort's educational achievement is now on par or even above the level of high-income countries (refer to figure 3.6b).[6]

FIGURE 3.6 Changes in absolute upward mobility over time

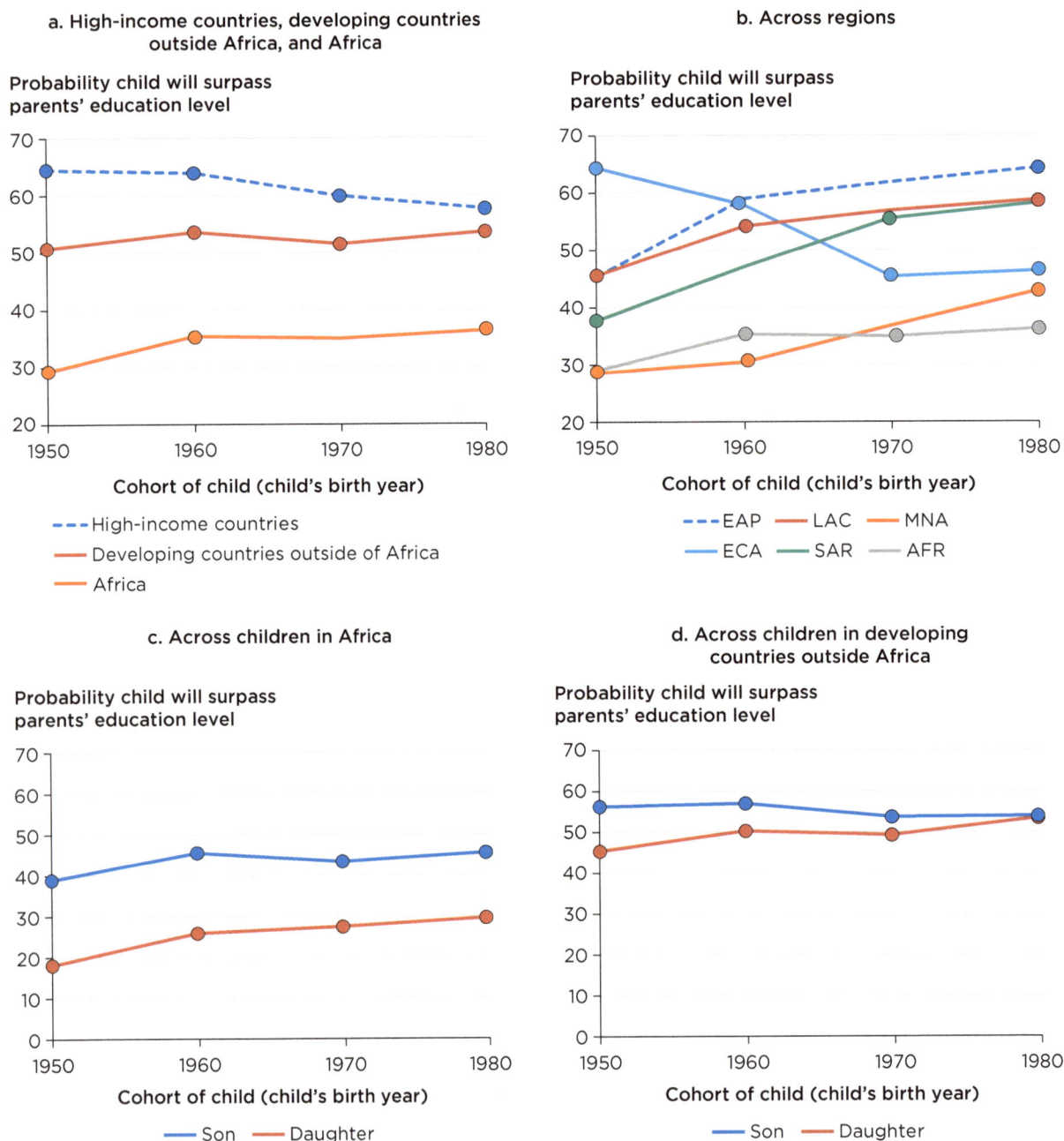

a. High-income countries, developing countries outside Africa, and Africa

Probability child will surpass parents' education level

- High-income countries
- Developing countries outside of Africa
- Africa

b. Across regions

Probability child will surpass parents' education level

- EAP
- ECA
- LAC
- SAR
- MNA
- AFR

c. Across children in Africa

Probability child will surpass parents' education level

- Son
- Daughter

d. Across children in developing countries outside Africa

Probability child will surpass parents' education level

- Son
- Daughter

Source: World Bank staff calculations using data from the Global Database on Intergenerational Mobility (March 2023).
Note: Using surveys with retrospective questions only. AFR = Sub-Saharan Africa; EAP = East Asia and Pacific; ECA = Europe and Central Asia; LAC = Latin America and the Caribbean; MNA = Middle East and North Africa; SAR = Sourth Asia.

Girls have moved ahead of boys in absolute IGM and have been rapidly closing the gap in developing economies, except in Africa, where the gap narrowed but remained substantial. Figure 3.6d shows that in developing countries excluding Africa, girls had a disadvantage in absolute mobility over boys until the 1980s, when it fully converged. In contrast, the gender gap in absolute mobility in Africa narrowed in the 1960s but remained significant (figure 3.6c). The gender gap in Africa for the 1980s cohort turns out to be smaller, though, if all surveys are used, regardless of how parental education is measured (refer to figure 3A.8).

Absolute mobility in Africa is particularly low in countries affected by violent conflicts and with high levels of institutional and social fragility. Figure 3.7a shows no significant difference between resource-rich and not-resource-rich countries in the region in the probability that a child surpasses their parents' educational category. However, FCS countries have significantly lower absolute mobility. FCS significantly reduces absolute mobility across countries, regardless of their natural resources (refer to figure 3.7b). Thus, the probability that a child surpasses their parents' educational category is about 50 percent in resource-rich never-FCS countries, but only 32 percent among resource-rich FCS countries.

FIGURE 3.7 **Absolute upward mobility, 1980s cohort**

a. Depending on resource and FCS status

b. Across FCS status

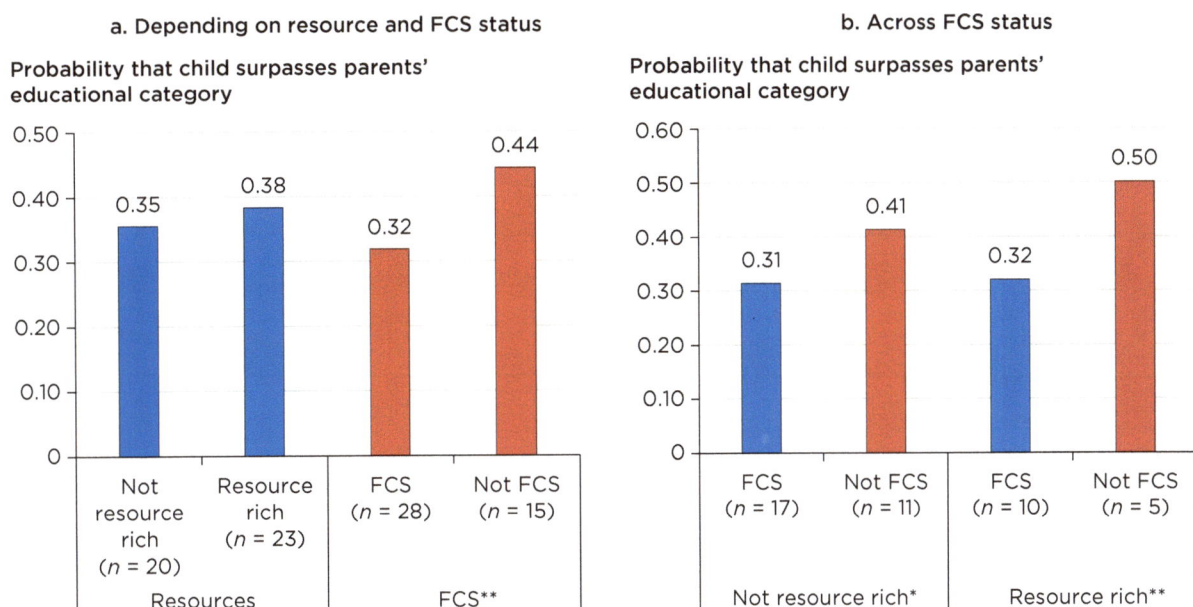

Source: World Bank staff calculations using data from the Global Database on Intergenerational Mobility (March 2023).
Note: Using all surveys with retrospective and coresident questions. FCS = fragile and conflict-affected situations.
* Significant at 10 percent; ** significant at 5 percent.

As with stagnant absolute mobility, relative mobility in Africa has not changed much between the 1960s and 1980s cohorts. Relative mobility, measured here by the coefficient obtained from regressing children's number of years of education on parents' number of years of education, also shows that Africa is behind other developing countries but doing better than South Asia (refer to figure 3.8). This implies that children's prospects will continue to be tied to parental educational attainment. In sum, the regions with the lowest GDP per capita and the highest poverty rates, South Asia and Africa, are the regions in which parental background—whether in education or income—matters the most for their children's prospects.

Intergenerational persistence in education is also higher in FCS countries. Figure 3.9a shows no statistically significant difference in relative mobility between resource-rich and not-resource-rich countries. However, on average, FCS countries have significantly higher intergenerational persistence (or lower relative mobility). This finding holds across countries regardless of resources (refer to figure 3.9b).

FIGURE 3.8 Changes in relative mobility over time

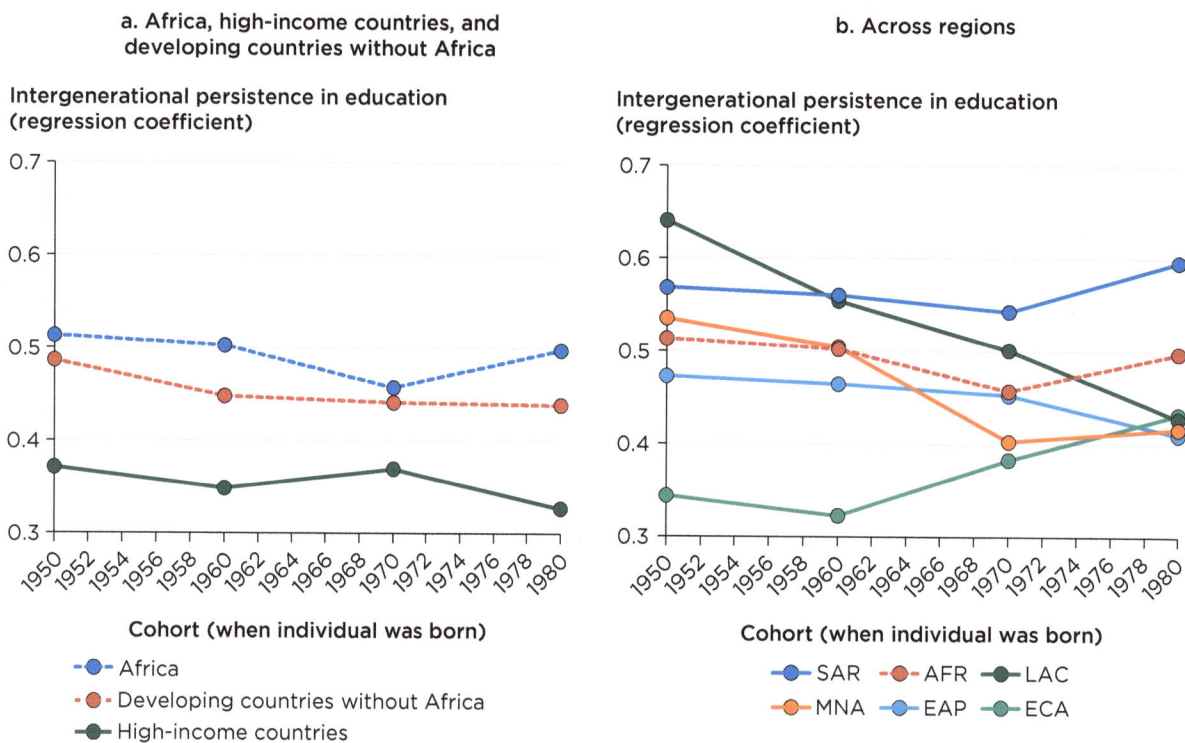

a. Africa, high-income countries, and developing countries without Africa

Intergenerational persistence in education (regression coefficient)

b. Across regions

Intergenerational persistence in education (regression coefficient)

Cohort (when individual was born)

- - ● - - Africa
- - ● - - Developing countries without Africa
- ● - High-income countries

- ● - SAR - - ● - - AFR - ● - LAC
- ● - MNA - ● - EAP - ● - ECA

Source: World Bank staff calculations using data from the Global Database on Intergenerational Mobility (March 2023).
Note: Using surveys with retrospective questions only. Higher persistence indicates lower mobility. AFR = Sub-Saharan Africa; EAP = East Asia and Pacific; ECA = Europe and Central Asia; LAC = Latin America and the Caribbean; MNA = Middle East and North Africa; SAR = South Asia.

FIGURE 3.9 Relative mobility, 1980s cohort

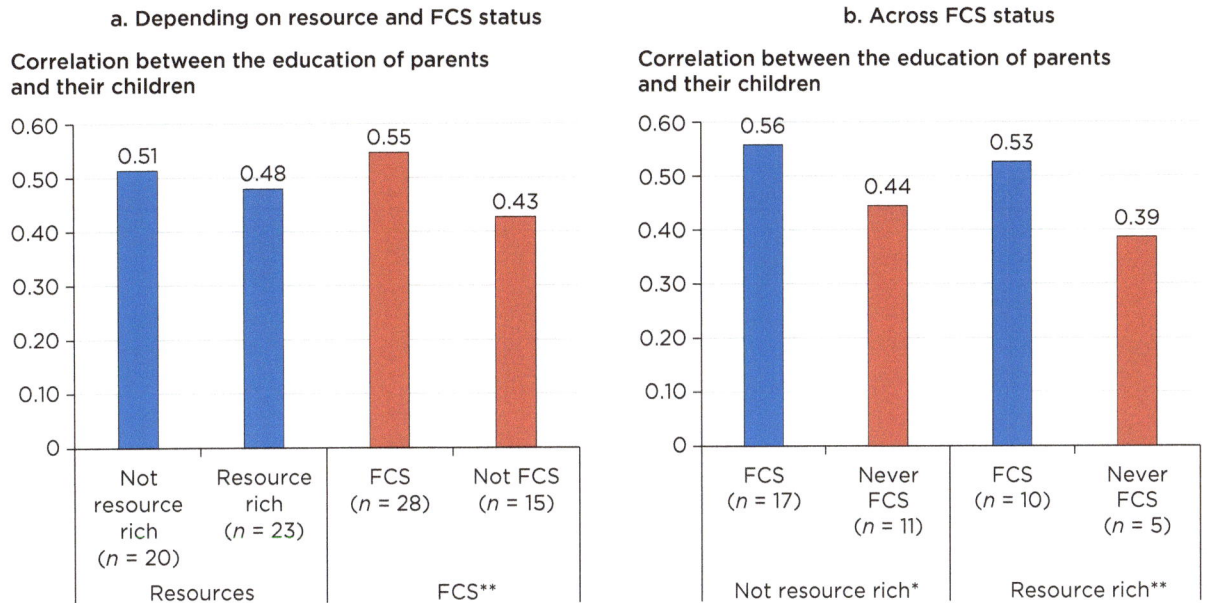

a. Depending on resource and FCS status

Correlation between the education of parents and their children

Not resource rich (*n* = 20)	0.51	
Resource rich (*n* = 23)	0.48	
FCS (*n* = 28)	0.55	
Not FCS (*n* = 15)	0.43	

Resources | FCS**

b. Across FCS status

Correlation between the education of parents and their children

FCS (*n* = 17)	0.56	
Never FCS (*n* = 11)	0.44	
FCS (*n* = 10)	0.53	
Never FCS (*n* = 5)	0.39	

Not resource rich* | Resource rich**

Source: World Bank staff calculations using data from the Global Database on Intergenerational Mobility (March 2023).
Note: Using all surveys with retrospective and co-resident questions. Higher persistence indicates lower mobility. FCS = fragile and conflict-affected situations.
* Significant at 10 percent; ** significant at 5 percent.

Cross-country analysis demonstrates that higher education mobility is associated with better economic outcomes. Narayan et al. (2018) use global data to show that greater mobility is associated with higher levels of GDP, although with some important differences across relative and absolute mobility. Relative IGM starts to increase with GDP per capita only after the latter exceeds $2,500 per capita (1990 PPP), whereas absolute IGM starts increasing at low income levels and continues to grow until GDP per capita reaches $5,000 per capita. They explain the observed pattern for relative mobility by the fact that infrastructure to equalize opportunities may remain unaffordable even if the country grows. For example, the fiscal space necessary to fund the type of public interventions to equalize opportunities may not be there yet.

Focusing on African countries seems to produce similar findings. There is a high positive correlation of 0.66 between GDP per capita and absolute IGM for the 1980s cohort (refer to figure 3.10a), but a less strong negative correlation of –0.48 with relative mobility or intergenerational education persistence, potentially signaling that countries in Africa may not have reached a sufficiently high level of economic development to reduce the correlation between the educational outcomes of parents and their children (refer to figure 3.10b). Indeed, if countries with high GDP per capita (Gabon, Mauritius, and South Africa) are dropped out, the correlation between GDP per capita and relative mobility is not significantly different from zero, whereas the correlation between GDP per capita and absolute mobility still remains significant.

FIGURE 3.10 Mobility in Africa, 1980s cohort, by GDP per capita

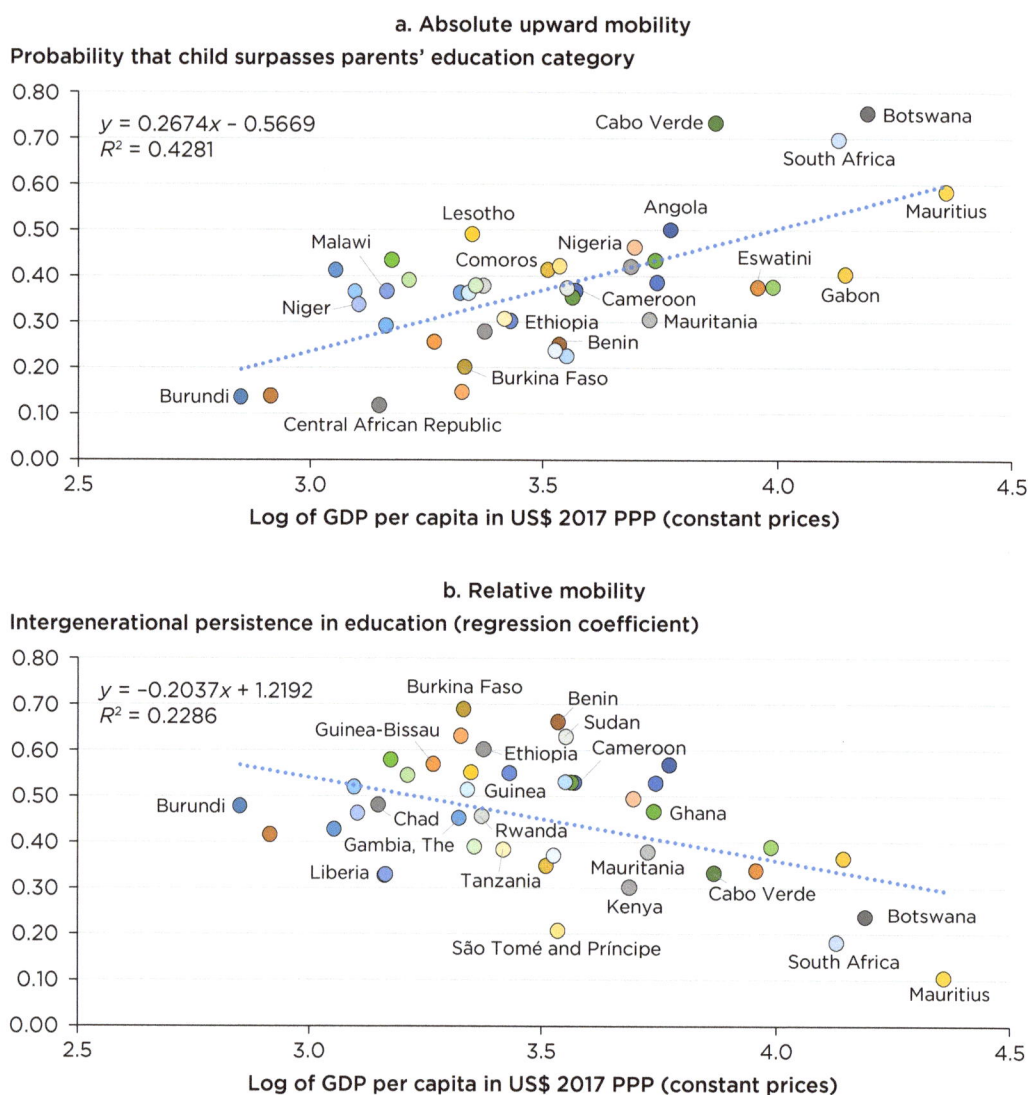

a. Absolute upward mobility

b. Relative mobility

Source: World Bank staff calculations using data from the Global Database on Intergenerational Mobility (March 2023) and World Development Indicators for latest GDP per capita numbers. *Note:* GDP = gross domestic product; PPP = purchasing power parity.

A positive relationship between IGM and economic outcomes observed once countries reach a particular development level means that both phenomena reinforce each other, but institutional fragility and conflicts may weaken these links in Africa. The economic literature shows that greater mobility may promote the accumulation of human capital, whereas greater relative mobility may stimulate a more efficient allocation of human capital, contributing to growth. Wealthier countries, in turn, may have higher levels of public spending, equalizing disparities in opportunities and facilitating IGM. However, as discussed earlier and in line with findings presented in chapter 5, being a resource-rich country in Africa does not guarantee that government dedicates resources to improving IGM, especially in fragile and conflict-affected environments.

Access to land is concentrated, adding to structural inequality

Available household survey data show that land ownership and registration are unevenly distributed globally as well as in Africa. Bauluz, Govind, and Novokmet (2020) report Gini coefficients of 50 and higher for the area of agricultural land owned in 10 African countries (refer to figure 3.11).[7] In a subset of the African countries studied, agricultural landlessness ranges from 40 percent (Ethiopia) to 21 percent (Tanzania). Their global comparison of inequality in agricultural land area owned and the market value of the land shows that inequality is high in Africa but not as high as in countries in Latin America and South Asia. These authors also show that inequality in the market value of agricultural land owned (valued at prevailing market prices) is much higher than the inequality in land area, indicating that ownership of valuable land is concentrated. In Ethiopia, The Gambia, Malawi, Niger, Nigeria, and Tanzania, the top 10 percent of landowners own more than 30 percent of land area and 40 percent or more by land value. In the cases of Ethiopia and Tanzania, the richest 10 percent own close to 60 percent of the total land value. Accounting for the landless population increases the measured inequality. Beyond self-reported ownership, the share of households with registered land is low and highly unequal in terms of income distribution and gender of the owner (Deininger and Goyal 2023, using household survey data from West African Economic and Monetary Union countries).

FIGURE 3.11 **Access to land among the top 10 percent: Land value versus land area**

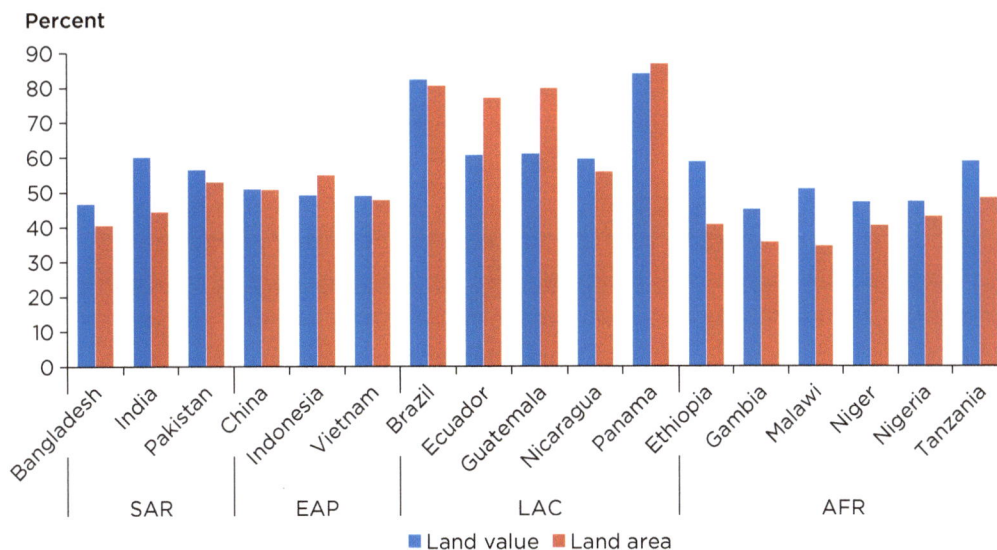

Source: Bauluz, Govind, and Novokmet 2020, figure 3. © World Inequality Lab. Adapted with permission from the World Inequality Lab; further permission required for reuse.
Note: Figure is based on household survey data and includes estimates of the share of area and value held by the top 10 percent of owners (from both urban and rural areas) or of those with land user rights. AFR = Sub-Saharan Africa; EAP = East Asia and Pacific; LAC = Latin America and the Caribbean; SAR = South Asia.

Southern Africa's colonial legacy has resulted in unequal land ownership patterns (Sulla, Zikhali, and Cuevas 2022). Land ownership is particularly unequal in Namibia and South Africa. Race is an important dimension of this inequality. Sulla, Zikhali, and Cuevas (2022) report that, in 2018, 70 percent of Namibia's commercial farmland was owned by those of European descent; only 16 percent was owned by Black Namibians.

Ongoing and future trends: Implications for inequality in building productive capacity

In the presence of structural inequalities, recent and future risks could further increase inequality in building productive capacity. COVID-19, climate shocks, an expanding working-age population, and intensifying conflicts have the potential to increase inequality of opportunity in Africa. Poor and vulnerable populations are often more likely to experience shocks. At the same time, they have the least capacity to cope with them. This section discusses how these risks could alter inequality of opportunity and IGM.

Learning losses resulting from COVID-19 are expected to widen existing inequalities in education and foundational skills

On top of the immediate impact on mortality, economic growth, and poverty, the COVID-19 pandemic eroded human capital accumulation, affecting the education and health of children who missed schooling, nutrition, and health care. Such earlier life crises may have negative effects across multiple generations. School closures affected educational outcomes across countries by increasing dropouts and preventing learning. Figure 3.12 shows simulated losses in learning-adjusted years of schooling (LAYS) for all regions,[8] distinguishing between losses from school closures and losses from school dropouts (Schady et al. 2023). Africa saw smaller impacts of COVID-19 on learning losses because, on average, schools were closed for shorter durations compared with other regions (although there is variation across countries) and because schools produced less learning (on average) to begin with. Simulated loss in LAYS for Africa was about half a year—close to losses in East Asia and Pacific and the Middle East and North Africa but much lower than in South Asia and Latin America and Caribbean. However, in terms of the share of prepandemic LAYS, Africa was doing worse. This is shown in figure 3.13, in which many African countries stand out as having low LAYS losses because of the pandemic but remarkably high relative losses compared with prepandemic LAYS. Africa also stands out as having the largest relative losses because of dropouts, who accounted for 21 percent of all losses; in other regions, the contribution of dropouts to overall losses did not exceed 9 percent.

FIGURE 3.12 **LAYS lost because of the pandemic by learning loss and dropouts by region**

LAYS lost from pandemic (years)

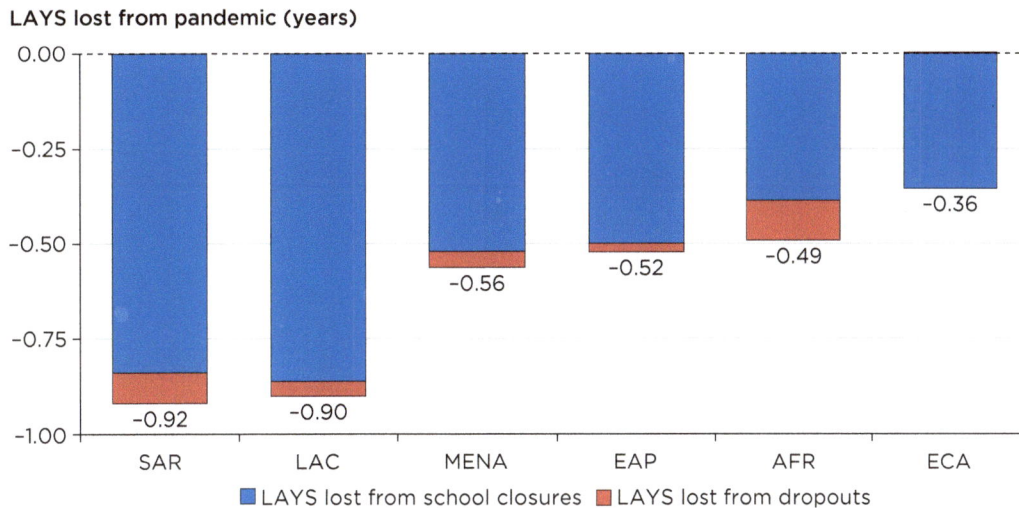

■ LAYS lost from school closures ■ LAYS lost from dropouts

Source: Preliminary estimates from Schady et al. 2023. Data on the duration of school closures are from UNESCO Global Monitoring of School Closures Caused by the COVID-19 Pandemic (https://covid19.uis.unesco.org/global-monitoring-school-closures-covid19/). Data on enrollment rates are simulated for each country using data on log GDP per capita and the duration of school closures. *Note:* AFR = Sub-Saharan Africa; EAP = East Asia and Pacific; ECA = Europe and Central Asia; LAC = Latin America and the Caribbean; LAYS = learning-adjusted years of schooling; MNA = Middle East and North Africa; SAR = South Asia.

Phone surveys conducted to measure the impact of COVID-19 provide some evidence that children from the poorest households were those most likely to be affected by school closures. In Ethiopia, for example, 91 percent of households with school-age children had them enrolled in school before the pandemic (Wieser et al. 2020). However, after school closures, only about 20 percent of these households reported that children were engaged in any learning or education activities, and this share was much higher among urban than rural households (39 versus 12 percent, respectively). In Uganda, 92 percent of households with at least one child in the 3–18 age group had at least one child enrolled in school before the closures (World Bank 2020). After the closures, the share of households with any child attending any remote learning activity was about 60 percent and distributed very unequally. For example, it ranged from 44 percent among the poorest pre–COVID-19 consumption quintile to 74 percent among the richest top quintile. This signals that learning losses during COVID-19 were distributed unequally, further widening the existing inequality of opportunities.

FIGURE 3.13 **LAYS lost because of the pandemic versus prepandemic shares of LAYS**

Share of prepandemic LAYS lost (%)

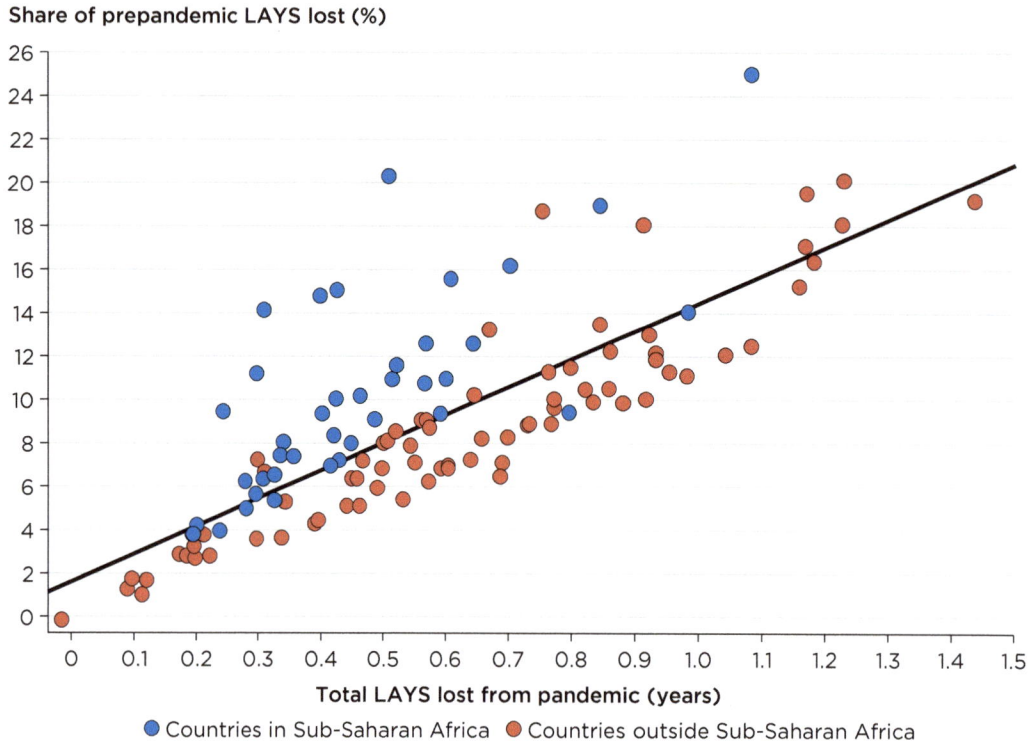

● Countries in Sub-Saharan Africa ● Countries outside Sub-Saharan Africa

Source: Preliminary estimates from Schady et al. 2023. Data on the duration of school closures are from UNESCO Global Monitoring of School Closures Caused by the COVID-19 Pandemic (https://covid19.uis.unesco.org/global-monitoring-school-closures-covid19/). Data on enrollment rates are simulated for each country using data on log GDP per capita and the duration of school closures. *Note:* LAYS = learning-adjusted years of schooling.

Rapid population growth and limited fiscal space will make reduction of inequality in access to basic services more challenging

As a continent with a very young population, Africa's economies can tap into the talent potential of the 8–11 million youth expected to enter the labor market across the region every year. Africa is experiencing rapid population growth triggered by a combination of declining mortality and some of the highest birthrates in the world. By 2050, Africa's population will make up close to 25 percent of the world's population (UN DESA 2022). Four of the eight countries expected to account for more than half of global population growth to 2050 are in Africa, with Nigeria forecast to become the world's third-most-populous country.[9] By 2060, Africa will be the only region with an increasing share of the population being working-age (refer to figure 3.14). These population shifts are expected to be accompanied by

FIGURE 3.14 Actual and forecast share of working-age population (ages 15–64) across regions, 2020–60

Share of working-age population (percent)

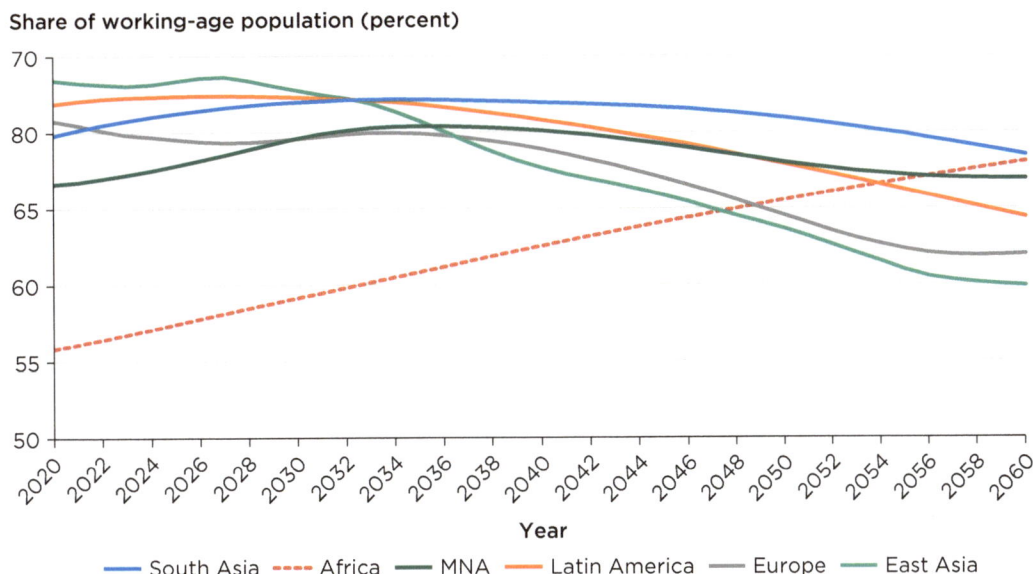

Source: World Bank staff calculations using UN population numbers.
Note: Regional numbers include only developing countries using World Bank methodology. MNA = Middle East and North Africa.

urbanization—another megatrend for the region. This presents both a challenge and an opportunity. The growing working-age population will be able to contribute to growth and productivity if they are provided with the right skills and opportunities. However, it also poses challenges given the sheer number of children (ages 0–14 years) entering the schooling system, who will later enter the labor market. To the extent that structural inequalities in building productive capacities are not addressed, they would place a large share of the workforce at a disadvantage, with consequences for future growth and poverty reduction.

Public spending on education and health is low. Taking as an example the education sector, Africa meets common international benchmarks on education spending (4–6 percent of GDP), but it still spends very little per school-age child because of small budgets and a large young population (Arias Diaz and Kheyfets 2023). Figure 3.15a illustrates this by showing overall education expenditures (private and public) as a share of GDP and in per capita terms expressed in 2017 US$ PPPs (using PPP values helps to account for differences in education prices across countries) across regions. Even though the share of education expenditures in GDP in Africa was higher than the world average, education expenditures in per capita terms were at least three times

FIGURE 3.15 Education and health care expenditures, Africa versus other regions

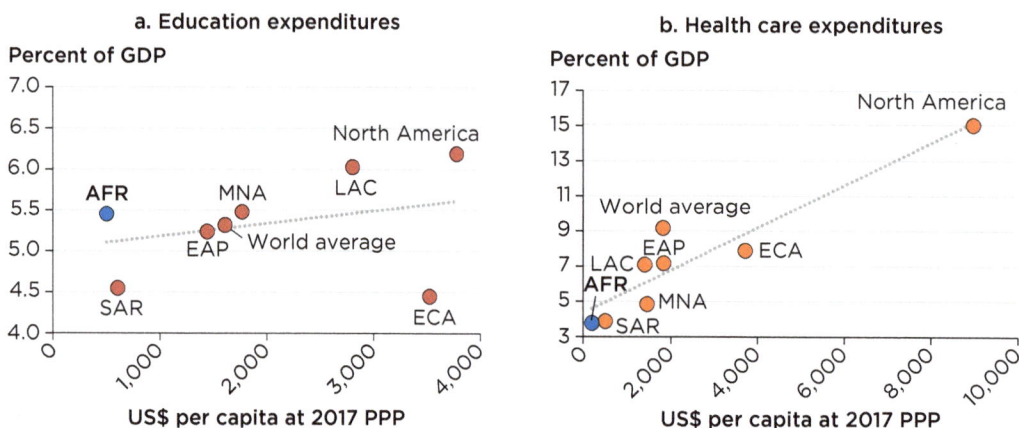

Source: World Bank staff calculations using data from the 2017 International Comparison Program and World Development Indicators.
Note: Dotted line represents simple correlation. AFR = Sub-Saharan Africa; EAP = East Asia and Pacific; ECA = Europe and Central Asia; GDP = gross domestic product; LAC = Latin America and the Caribbean; MNA = Middle East and North Africa; PPP = purchasing power parity; SAR = South Asia.

lower than what was spent on average in the world and were the lowest across all regions. Further increases in education spending to account for the growing young population and to improve the quality of education will require higher domestic resource mobilization. Figure 3.15b shows health expenditures as a share of GDP and in per capita terms. For both measures, Africa has the lowest numbers across comparators. Health spending accounted for 3.8 percent of GDP in 2017, whereas average health expenditures in per capita terms were equal to $201 in 2017 PPP—two times lower than the average in South Asia.

Moreover, spending on education and health in Africa is less equalizing compared with other regions. Although spending on education and health reduces inequality across countries in Africa, this is especially the case in southern African countries (refer to figure 3.16). The equalizing impact of health spending is especially small for countries outside of southern Africa, compared with other low- and middle-income countries, despite its relevance for growth, equality of opportunities, and long-term poverty reduction. Health facilities often lack necessities, including essential medicines, simple diagnostic equipment, and adequate water and sanitation (Gatti et al. 2021).

FIGURE 3.16 Public spending and marginal contributions to equity

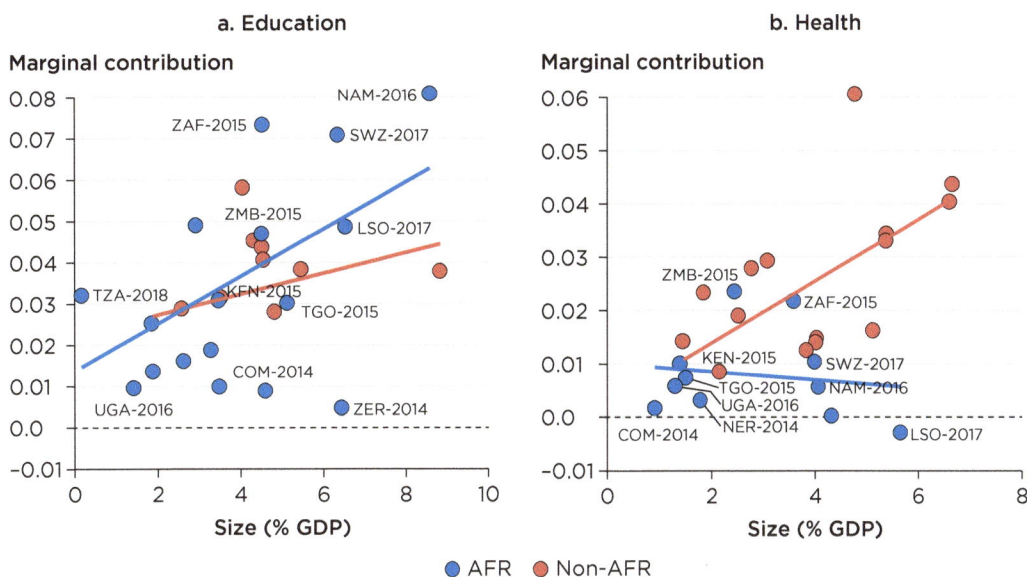

a. Education

b. Health

Source: Staff estimates based on CEQ studies conducted by the World Bank and the CEQ Institute, Tulane University.
Note: AFR = Sub-Saharan Africa; CEQ = Commitment to Equity; GDP = gross domestic product. For country abbreviations, refer to https://www.iso.org/obp/ui/#search.

Spending in these sectors could have more impact by improving within-sector allocations. For instance, not only is health sector spending lower than in other regions, but government expenditures are also skewed toward tertiary services, which are disproportionately used by wealthy individuals. In Senegal, the incidence of public health benefits based on reported use of services suggests a regressive concentration in 2019, with the richest 40 percent of the population receiving 50 percent of basic health benefits and the poorest 40 percent receiving only 30 percent. In Tanzania, 60 percent of health care spending was allocated to inpatient services in 2018. The richest 20 percent of the population received 41 percent of these inpatient benefits, and the poorest 20 percent received only 6 percent. This allocation of benefits contrasts with that of outpatient care, for which the richest 20 percent received a proportionate 20 percent of spending, the same as the poorest 20 percent. Although everyone is eligible to receive these health benefits, rich individuals use them more, suggesting access problems related to information asymmetries, financial constraints in affording the copayments, or distance to health care centers. In education, few students from the lowest quintiles attain upper secondary or tertiary education (Bashir et al. 2018). According to UNICEF (2021), a child from the wealthiest quintile can benefit from as much as 12 times more government resources than a child from the poorest quintile. Inequality comes mostly from secondary education and above, and expenditures on primary education are much more equal. Moreover, in some countries, more public resources go to schools in wealthier, more urban areas. For example, 72 percent of tertiary education spending in Côte d'Ivoire goes to the richest 20 percent of the population, compared with 11 and 24 percent of the budget for primary and secondary education, respectively, benefiting the top two deciles. This partly reflects that the distribution of trained and experienced teachers is biased toward urban schools, as well as the fact that urban public schools often have better infrastructure and learning materials (Beegle and de la Fuente 2019; Gatti et al. 2021). Moreover, although primary education is especially important for equality of opportunity and does the most in terms of reducing postfiscal inequality (refer to figure 3.17), spending per child is higher in tertiary education. Because children from low-income households are less likely to attend university, spending on tertiary education increases postmarket inequality.[10]

FIGURE 3.17 **Marginal contributions to reducing inequality are highest for primary education**

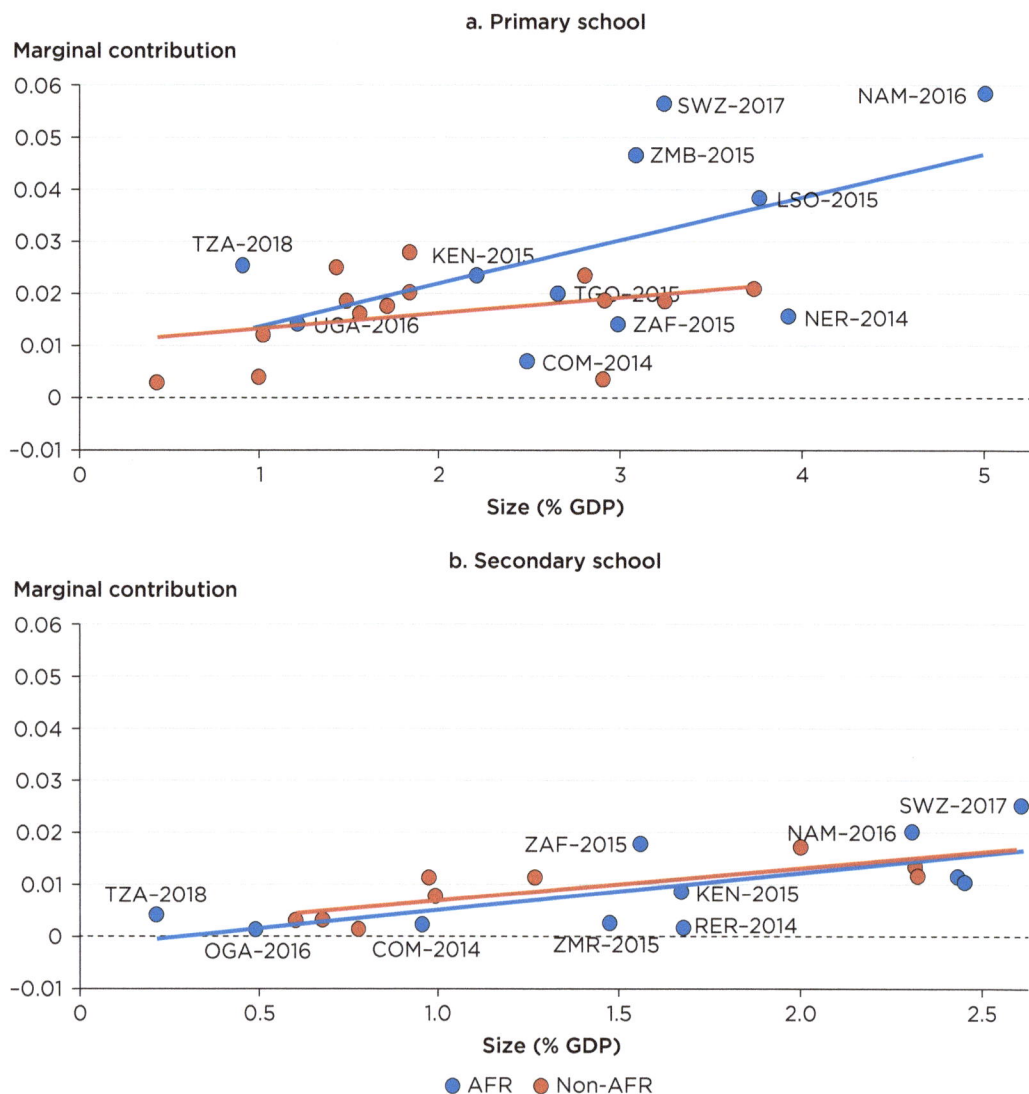

a. Primary school

b. Secondary school

● AFR ● Non-AFR

(continued)

FIGURE 3.17 **Marginal contributions to reducing inequality are highest for primary education** *(continued)*

c. Tertiary school

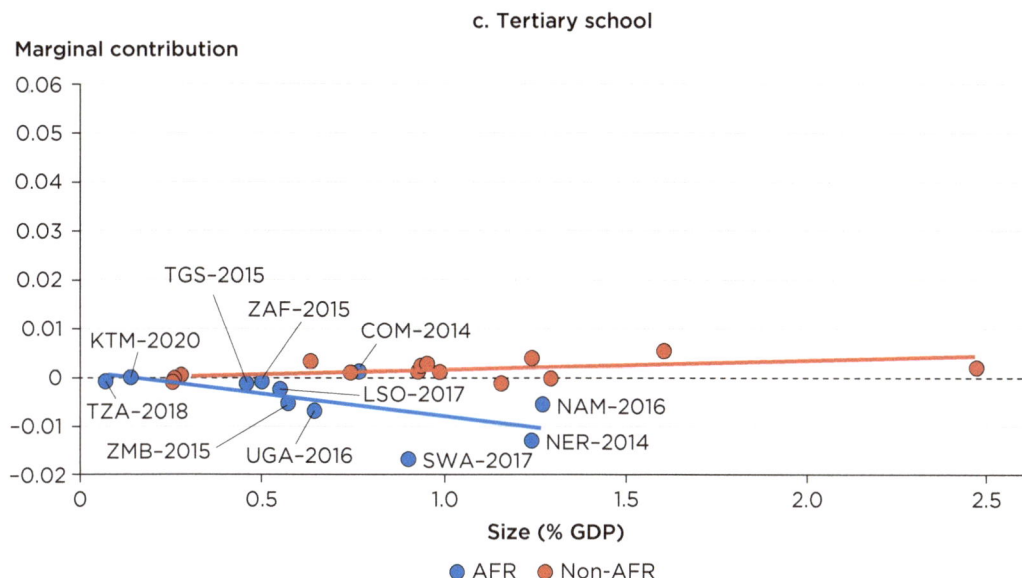

Source: Staff estimates based on CEQ studies conducted by the World Bank and the CEQ Institute, Tulane University.
Note: The size of each education spending level (primary, secondary, tertiary) is estimated as the product of two components: (1) total education spending in percentage of GDP and (2) an adjustment factor computed as the ratio of the incidence of each education level and the incidence of total education spending. AFR = Sub-Saharan Africa; CEQ = Commitment to Equity; GDP = gross domestic product. For country abbreviations, refer to https://www.iso.org/obp/ui/#search.

The efficiency and quality of education and health spending could also be improved. The quality of public education, health, and other services is generally low, even when adjusted for spending levels. For instance, measured student learning is low across countries in Africa, with fewer than half of students able to read a simple sentence or perform basic mathematical operations (Gatti et al. 2021). However, differences in learning are large, both between and within countries, with the lowest-performing schools concentrated in rural areas. There are several reasons for this, including the fact that teacher skills are low, in both content knowledge and pedagogy, and almost one-quarter of teachers can be expected to be absent on any given day. Similarly, more than 20 percent of health care providers can be expected to be absent, and their clinical abilities, measured as their diagnostic and treatment accuracy, are especially bad at low-level facilities (Gatti et al. 2021). These findings bolster the case for within-sector reforms that would improve competencies, ensure an adequate mix of inputs (such as medicines, learning materials, and water and sanitation investments), and improve financial accountability and transparency. Moreover, there may be room for policies that could improve outcomes while improving the efficiency of spending.[11] For instance, assigning more students to better teachers could potentially lead to better learning outcomes and substantial cost savings, even if there are negative class size effects (Bold et al. 2019). Ensuring that all incoming teachers have the officially mandated effective years of education, along with increasing the time spent on teaching to the officially mandated schedule, could almost double student learning within the next 30 years.

Intensifying conflicts may exacerbate existing structural inequalities in building productive capacity and reverse fragile gains Africa made in human capital and access to basic services

Being in conflict has a profound impact on socioeconomic well-being. As noted earlier, extreme poverty is increasingly concentrated in fragile and conflict-affected situations (FCS). On top of high monetary poverty, people in FCS are more likely to be deprived in terms of educational outcomes and lack access to basic services such as improved water, sanitation, and electricity. Using the World Bank's multidimensional poverty measure, Corral et al. (2020) show that about half of all individuals in FCS countries were multidimensionally poor compared with one in five in non-FCS economies. Indeed, previous sections of this chapter show that children in FCS countries have, on average, lower access to basic services and higher inequality.

On top of the immediate negative impact on well-being, exposure to conflict may have a long-term negative impact through human capital channels and reduce IGM. Exposure to conflict is associated with higher neonatal and infant and child mortality and higher rates of stunting and underweight (Corral et al. 2020). Moreover, there are second-generation effects on the health of children whose mothers were exposed to conflicts. Conflicts also have a negative impact on educational attainment and disruption of cognitive development. Individuals exposed to high degrees of violence[12] have around a 40 percent chance of surpassing both of their parents' education, whereas those not exposed to such violence during their childhood have, on average, more than a 55 percent chance of doing so (Corral et al. 2020).

The increase in the number of state-based conflicts in Africa may reverse the fragile gains made in building productive capacities in Africa. Between 2017 and 2022 alone, the number of conflict events more than tripled, reaching more than 28,000 in 2022. Compared with other regions, Africa experienced the largest relative and absolute gain in conflicts in the past decade (Palik, Obermeier, and Rustad 2022). Intensifying conflicts may reverse the fragile gains Africa has made in human capital and exacerbate existing structural inequality in the ability of countries to build their productive capacity, thus affecting their short-term and long-term development paths.

Climate change will exacerbate existing structural inequalities in building productive capacity in the region because of high exposure and sensitivity coupled with low adaptive capacity

Climate change will affect health outcomes through economic, social, and environmental determinants of health, such as clean air, safe drinking water, sufficient food, and secure shelter. Extreme weather events may reduce the availability of safe drinking water, compromise sanitation, and increase the incidence of disease, leading to absenteeism and possible withdrawal of children from school and older individuals from work (Caruso, de Marcos, and Noy 2024). Similarly, droughts and increasing temperatures lead to poor harvests and food insecurity, negatively affecting the incomes of agricultural households and increasing the risk of infant mortality, stunting, and permanent effects on cognitive development (Dimitrova and Bora 2020; Le and Nguyen 2022; Miller 2017). With warming by 1.2–1.9°C by 2050, the proportion of the population undernourished in Africa is projected to increase by 25–90 percent (World Bank 2013). Impacts for children in utero to early childhood can be particularly severe and long-lasting (Andrabi, Daniels, and Das 2023 Almond and Currie 2011). Other impacts include higher mortality and morbidity resulting from events such as extreme heat and flooding. For instance, recent work on West Africa has shown that extreme heat exposure increases the prevalence of both chronic and acute malnutrition among children ages 3–36 months (Blom, Ortiz-Bobea, and Hoddinott 2022). Extreme temperatures are also expected to increase the risks of noncommunicable diseases, physiological heat strain, and heat-related illnesses. Finally, climate hazards can also affect health facilities because of increases in temperature, flooding, wind damage, and transportation disruptions.

Climate change is also expected to affect education outcomes. Heat exposure affects the rate of skill formation and school enrollment. For instance, a cross-country study using data from 58 countries on the Organisation for Economic Co-operation and Development's PISA exam found that 15-year-old students perform worse on exams taken after hotter-than-average years (Park, Behrer, and Goodman 2021). The effects were stronger in low-income countries and among poor students and minority groups, who may lack access to effective adaptations. Higher temperatures may affect students and their ability to study. Higher-than-average temperatures are also associated with fewer years of schooling (Randell and Gray 2019), school graduation status (Park 2022), and performance on college entrance exams (Zivin et al. 2020). Older school-age children may also suffer more from the long-term consequences of not being able to attend school or from dropping out of the formal education system altogether (Garg, Jagnani, and Taraz 2020; Shah and Steinberg 2017). These findings indicate that the increase in extreme temperatures may worsen existing inequalities in the education sector. Finally, extreme weather events are also likely to damage educational facilities with potential consequences for educational outcomes (Baéz, de la Fuente, and Santos 2010).

Policies to build productive capacity with equity

The focus of this chapter was on assessing and quantifying disparities that occur when people are building their productive capacity prior to entering markets. Children's access to basic services that are key to building productive capacity was found to be far from universal and very unequal, with substantial gaps across different circumstances that children cannot control for. This has important implications: if not addressed, inequality of opportunity accumulated early in life will result in inequality of economic opportunities, later on such as employment options and earnings, creating an environment in which poverty and inequality are perpetuated across generations. This concluding section outlines policy options that countries can pursue to level the playing field and reduce inequality of opportunity. They can be summarized as follows:

- Invest in disadvantaged children's health and education, which not only yields future returns in the labor market but also has positive externalities for other outcomes such climate change adaptation and mitigation, violence prevention, age at first marriage, and teen pregnancy, among others;

- Invest in basic infrastructure to reduce the coverage gap of electricity, water, and sanitation services in underserved regions; and

- Improve land and asset registration and property rights.

Each of these three policy pathways is discussed in turn.

First, it is crucial to strengthen the efficacy and efficiency of investments in health and education to accelerate human capital accumulation by underserved populations. The analysis in this chapter shows that African countries have achieved universal access to primary school and have attained important gains in health outcomes. However, the quality of education and health services remains thin and unequal. Addressing this will take concerted action on both the demand side (that is, children and their households) and the supply side (that is, the service providers). In terms of education, it is important to invest in targeted policies to ensure that disadvantaged children not only go to school but are also ready to learn. Social protection programs, such as (conditional and unconditional) cash transfers and school feeding programs, are a sharp instrument for that.

On the supply side, improving service delivery will require investing in teachers, improving school management and infrastructure, and increasing parental involvement for community-based monitoring. The most effective interventions to improve learning outcomes in Africa have been those that combine teacher training with ongoing teacher support and classroom learning materials for students (Bashir et al. 2018). Across the region, deficient learning is correlated with teachers' low levels of content knowledge and subpar pedagogy skills. Some schools are also missing crucial inputs, such as blackboards or private and gendered toilets, and struggle with high pupil–teacher ratios (Gatti et al. 2021). For instance, in The Gambia, 14 percent of teachers were absent from school at least once a week in 2019, with higher absences in rural than in urban schools. Moreover, 10 percent of teachers reported classroom absence while in school, and another 10 percent reported limited time on task (UNICEF Innocenti Research Centre 2021). The pandemic created additional challenges; in August 2021, two-thirds of phone survey respondents reported that the quality of teaching and learning was worse than before the start of the pandemic (World Bank 2022).

However, even if efforts are in place to train, monitor, and support teachers, they may be insufficient. Power relationships and norms prevent laws and policies from being implemented as written. For example, policy makers may have a mandate to ensure teachers deliver better learning, but they may at the same time depend on teachers for political support, which can diminish their willingness to monitor and enforce performance. There are several ways to change the incentives and norms. Improving public awareness of the unacceptably low levels of learning in selected areas of a country may be used to change the incentives for teachers and policy makers to improve the quality of education. Adding new actors—for example, parents—can also change power dynamics if parents can credibly enforce sanctions. Promoting norms that support better behavior and attract teachers who share these norms, such as teacher professionalism and a sense of duty, may help to enhance service delivery (World Bank 2017).

Improving the delivery of health services is also challenging, but similar policy principles can help guide more effective health care reform. Health facilities lack essential medicines, basic diagnostic equipment, and adequate water and sanitation. Moreover, health care providers' absences are a concern, as is their low ability to diagnose and treat common health conditions correctly, particularly in rural areas (Gatti et al. 2021). As in the case of education, better training, improved supervision, and provision of water and sanitation services can help. However, this alone will not guarantee improved health outcomes. Involving more impartial actors in the practice of hiring health workers may help to break patronage, when appointments are made based on personal connections and networks. Involving communities with clear mandates and tools to monitor providers can help to strengthen the quality of medical care. Properly implemented decentralization can increase the accountability of policy makers because voters can better observe the effects of health policies (World Bank 2017).

A focus on women's health warrants special attention, and it should include interventions to improve reproductive health and eliminate child marriage and other harmful practices, such as female genital mutilation (FGM). FGM remains prevalent in 33 African countries, with high rates in The Gambia, Guinea, Mali, and Somalia, affecting more than 70 percent of women ages 15 to 19 (UNICEF 2024). FGM not only is a health risk but has long-term consequences for girls' ability to study, work, and be come productive members of society (WHO 2023).

Investments in reproductive health can lead to future health care savings, equalize the labor market, and boost economic growth (Canning and Schultz 2012). Increasing the age at first marriage has also been shown to be effective, but only 13 countries in Africa have set the legal age for marriage at 18; 17 have no minimum age; and the others set a minimum age younger than 18 (World Bank 2023b). Overall, investments in girls' education and health have a high payoff and far-reaching impacts, influencing factors such as age at first marriage, fertility, productivity, and intergenerational poverty transmission.

A final recommendation on the human capital dimension is that it is a high-return strategy to focus on early childhood interventions. With respect to education, a focus on high-quality early childhood development should be an integral part of national plans to accelerate learning (Bendini and Devercelli 2022). Early childhood education programs have consistently shown a positive impact on long-term outcomes among children in low-income families (Narayan et al. 2018). Improving access to preprimary enrollment, prioritizing rural and poor communities, could lead to improved success in primary school (Bashir et al. 2018; Schütz, Ursprung, and Wößmann 2008). Similarly, early health interventions should be prioritized, because they are crucial for physical and mental development. Basic health interventions, such as deworming and providing vitamin A supplements, are known to generate large impacts relative to up-front costs (Bhula, Mahoney, and Murphy 2020). Similarly, a recent randomized trial found substantial improvements in child health from a program in Mali that delivered free care for children, followed up with community health worker visits (Dean and Sautmann 2022).

Second, the findings of this chapter highlight the importance of investing in basic infrastructure targeting underserved populations and regions. The key rationale for public spending on basic services such as electricity, water and sanitation is that these are investments that the private sector will likely not make. An explicit focus on equity, along with coverage, will be needed to achieve the desired results. Inequality in access to and in quality of electricity, water, and sanitation services will become more acute and more expensive to tackle with the growing population. Achieving universal access to piped water and electricity by providing heavily subsidized services in Africa has not worked and has largely bypassed the groups most in need (Foster and Briceño-Garmendia 2010). Four key strategies for service expansion are suggested. First, before rolling out new networks, the focus should be on understanding the barriers to connecting to existing networks. Second, increasing coverage can be done in a more efficient way by focusing on underserved populations living physically close to infrastructure networks. Third, a better understanding of community needs and demand-side barriers is crucial for expanding coverage. Fourth, the way connection costs are recovered needs to be rethought, potentially shifting them from one-time upfront connection charges to repaying them over several years, recovering them through general tariffs shared across the entire customer base, or directly subsidizing them. Limiting subsidies to connections in new network rollouts rather than densifying the existing network would improve targeting.

Given rural-to-urban population movements, it is crucial to focus on how the provision of basic services can be made more efficient and equitable in urban areas and, in particular, on avoiding fragmentation through sound urban planning. Urban plans define the pattern in which the future population will settle, in either defined expansion areas or unoccupied land in an urban area. However, in many cities, inadequate legal frameworks, coupled with poor planning policy, have resulted in ad hoc urban development, grabbing of public land, the capture of benefit by private actors, and conflict between communities and government over the use of public space (Kaw, Lee, and Wahba 2020). Moreover, cities in most developing countries pay little attention, if any, to accommodating an unexpected rise in population. As a result, an estimated 55 percent of the urban population of Africa lives in slums, far above the estimated 30 percent in South Asia and 20 percent in Latin America, partly because of inadequate urban planning but also because of housing and land markets (Rains and Krishna 2021).

Third, it is important to improve land and asset registration and property rights. Serious issues for urban land management include restricted zoning, unregulated construction, and unclear property rights and their enforcement. In particular, land use planning and zoning are critical for making cities livable and for building their resilience to shocks. To enhance the resilience of individuals, a core task for city authorities is to provide accurate information to enable land, housing, and insurance markets to operate efficiently (Lall et al. 2023). More broadly, land registries are important for optimal use of land resources in both urban and rural areas. Deininger and Goyal (2023) discuss the potential for expanding registration, citing successful cases from the region, such as Ethiopia and Rwanda. Public policies in these countries have facilitated registration and formalization of use rights, which in turn have had significant payoffs through higher individual earnings and greater revenue mobilization from property taxation. Last, but not least, a special focus on women is necessary; across 37 countries, only around 8 percent of married women own land or housing, compared with about 25 percent of married men (World Bank 2023b). Eliminating regulatory barriers for female asset ownership, including through inheritance and family laws, would go a long way toward reducing inequality of opportunities for women.

FIGURE 3A.1 Access to basic infrastructure across regions and years

a. People using at least basic drinking water services

b. People using at least basic sanitation services

c. Access to electricity

d. Mobile cellular subscriptions (per 100 people)

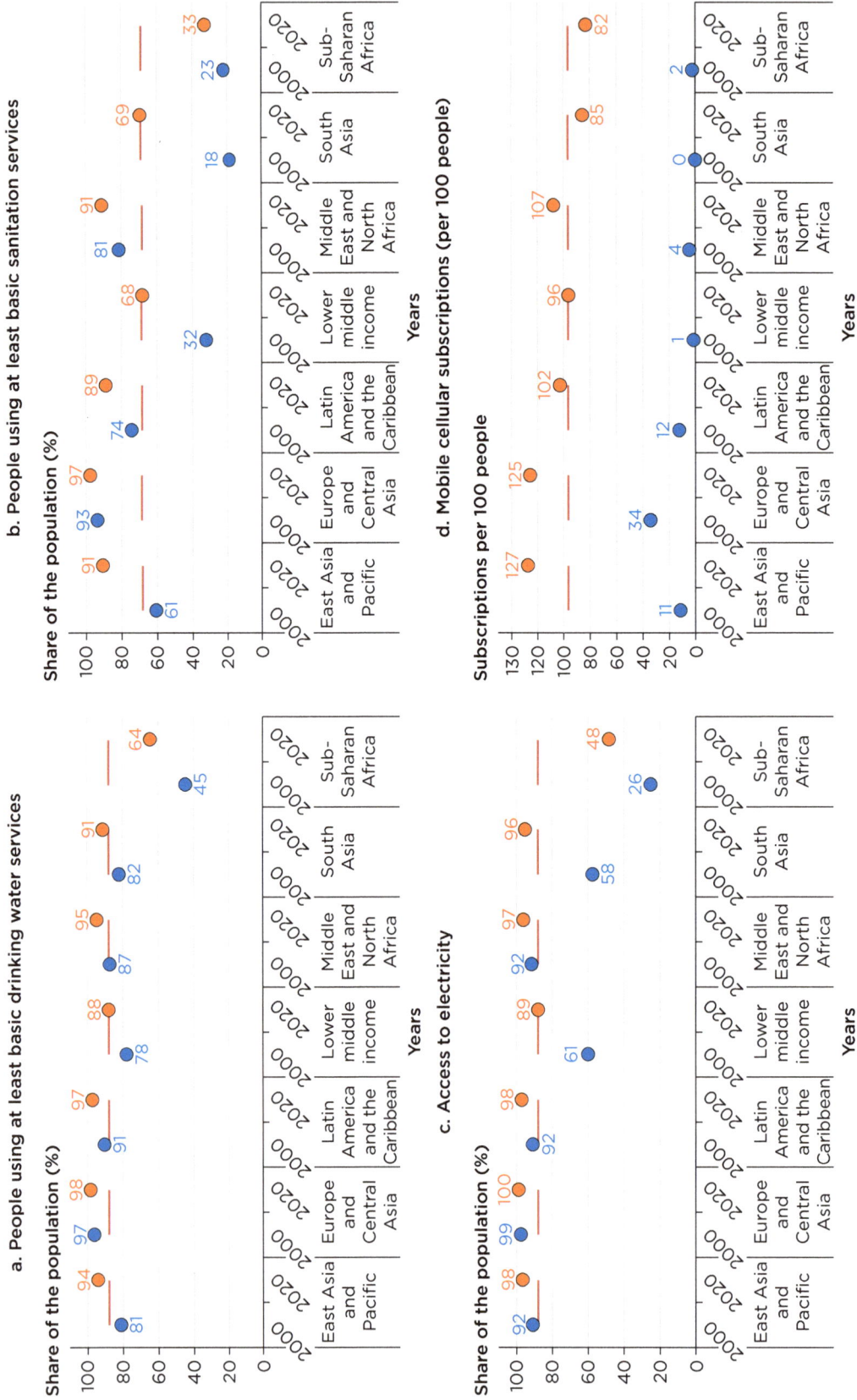

Source: World Bank staff calculations using World Development Indicators.

FIGURE 3A.2 Access to education across regions and years

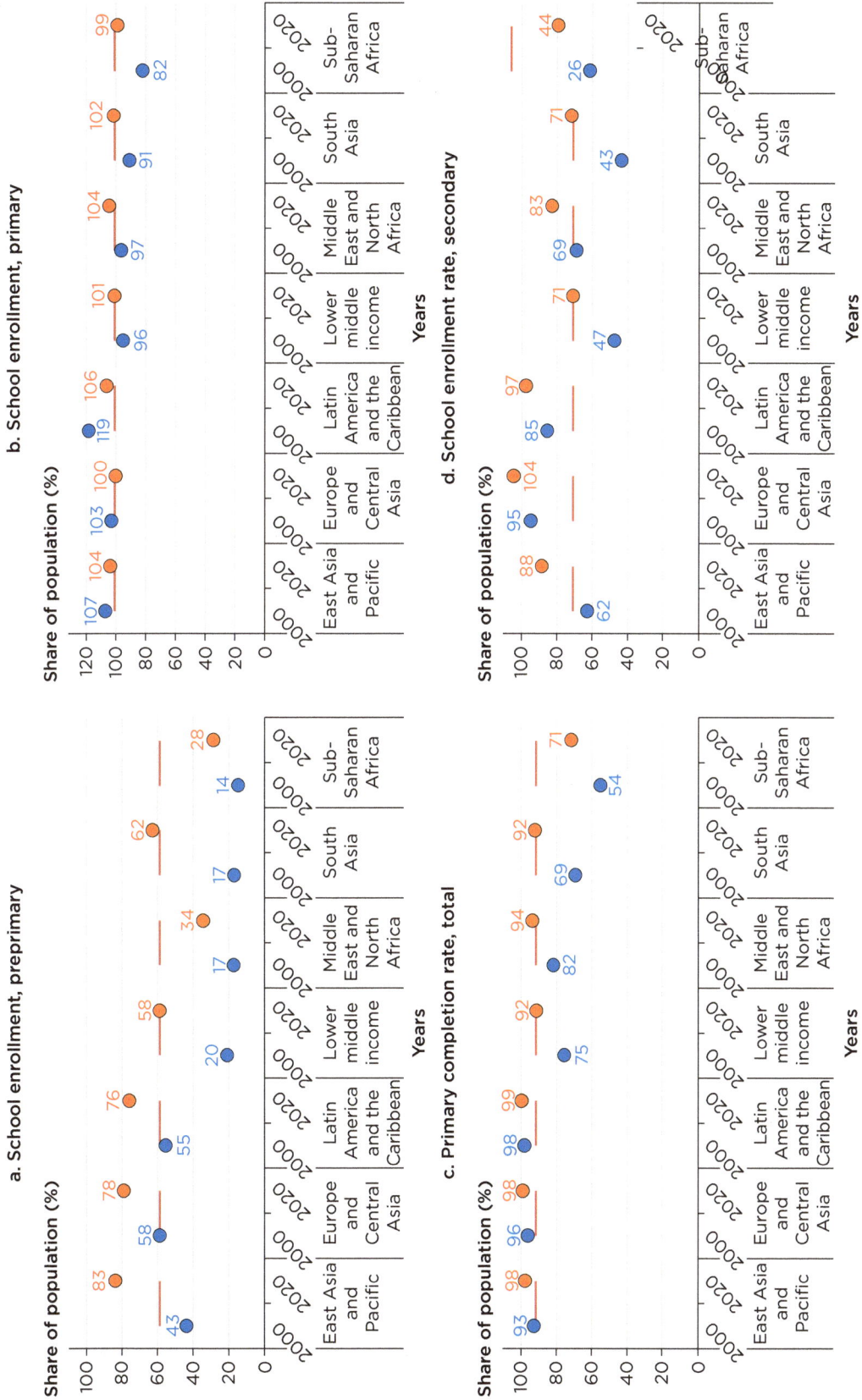

a. School enrollment, preprimary

b. School enrollment, primary

c. Primary completion rate, total

d. School enrollment rate, secondary

Source: World Bank staff calculations using World Development Indicators.

FIGURE 3A.3 Urban–rural divide in access to water and sanitation services across regions and years

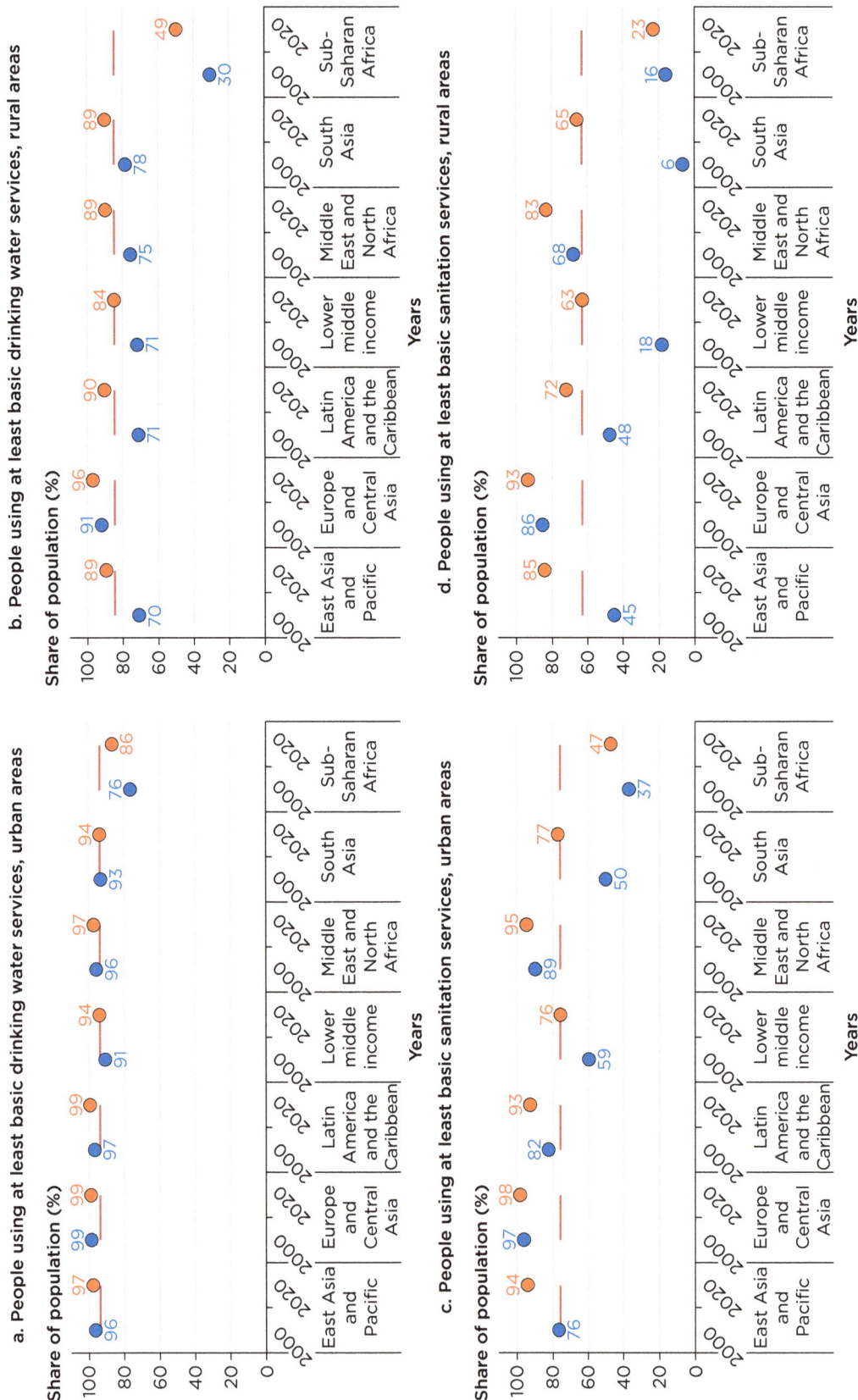

a. People using at least basic drinking water services, urban areas

Share of population (%)

	East Asia and Pacific	Europe and Central Asia	Latin America and the Caribbean	Lower middle income	Middle East and North Africa	South Asia	Sub-Saharan Africa
Orange	97	99	99	94	97	94	86
Blue	96	99	97	91	96	93	76

Years

b. People using at least basic drinking water services, rural areas

Share of population (%)

	East Asia and Pacific	Europe and Central Asia	Latin America and the Caribbean	Lower middle income	Middle East and North Africa	South Asia	Sub-Saharan Africa
Orange	89	96	90	84	89	89	49
Blue	70	91	71	71	75	78	30

Years

c. People using at least basic sanitation services, urban areas

Share of population (%)

	East Asia and Pacific	Europe and Central Asia	Latin America and the Caribbean	Lower middle income	Middle East and North Africa	South Asia	Sub-Saharan Africa
Orange	94	98	93	76	95	77	47
Blue	76	97	82	59	89	50	37

Years

d. People using at least basic sanitation services, rural areas

Share of population (%)

	East Asia and Pacific	Europe and Central Asia	Latin America and the Caribbean	Lower middle income	Middle East and North Africa	South Asia	Sub-Saharan Africa
Orange	85	93	72	63	83	65	23
Blue	45	86	48	18	68	6	16

Years

Source: World Bank staff calculations using World Development Indicators.

Leveling the Playing Field

Access to health services using proxy indicators across regions and years

a. Modeled estimate, share of children younger than five (%)

b. Share of children ages 12–23 months

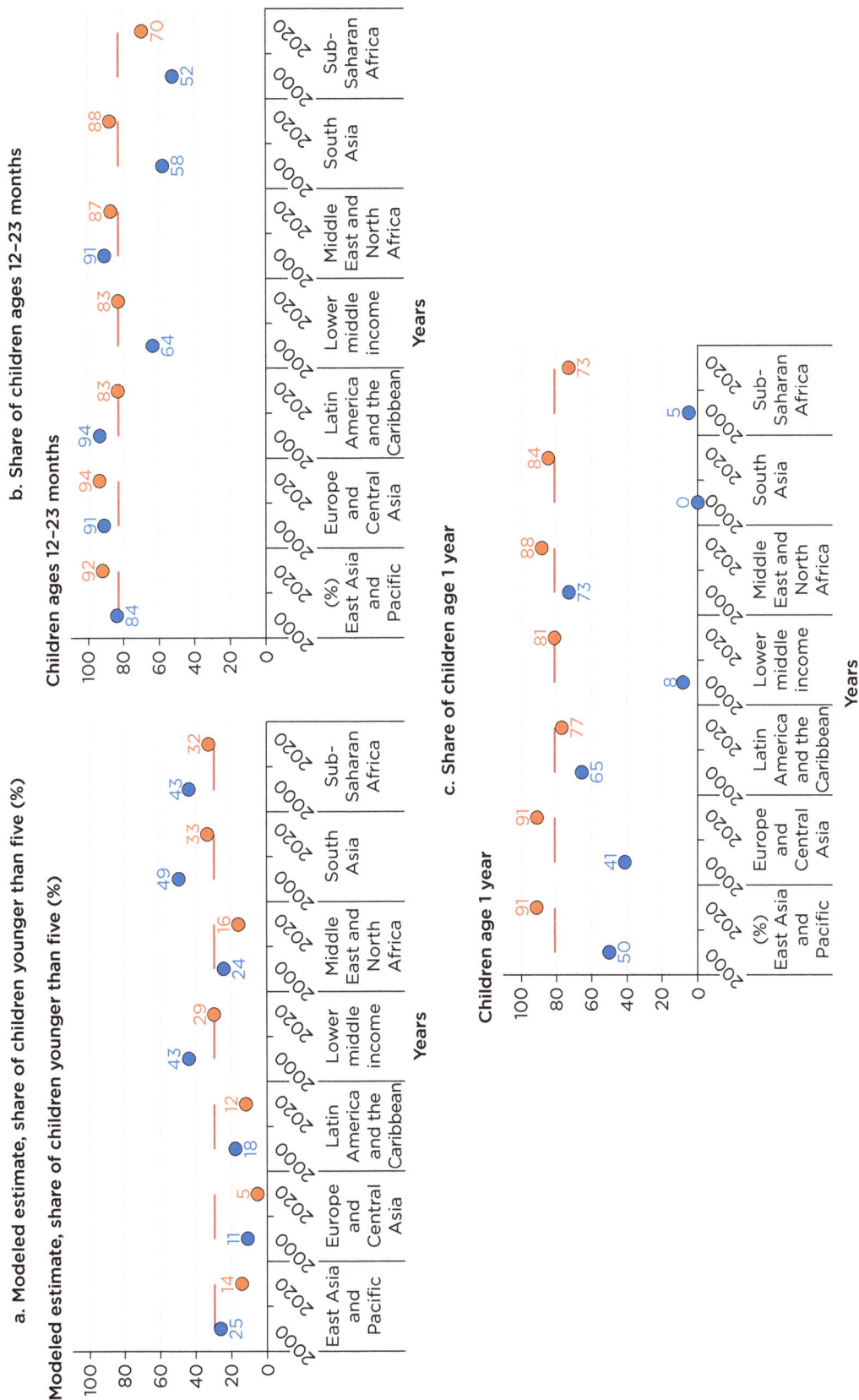

Children ages 12–23 months

c. Share of children age 1 year

Children age 1 year

Modeled estimate, share of children younger than five (%)

Source: World Bank staff calculations using World Development Indicators.
Note: HepB3 = three-dose hepatitis B vaccine.

People in Africa Face an Unlevel Playing Field for Building Their Productive Capacity

FIGURE 3A.5 Changes in access to selected basic services in AFR in percentage points during 2000–20 conditional on performance in 2000

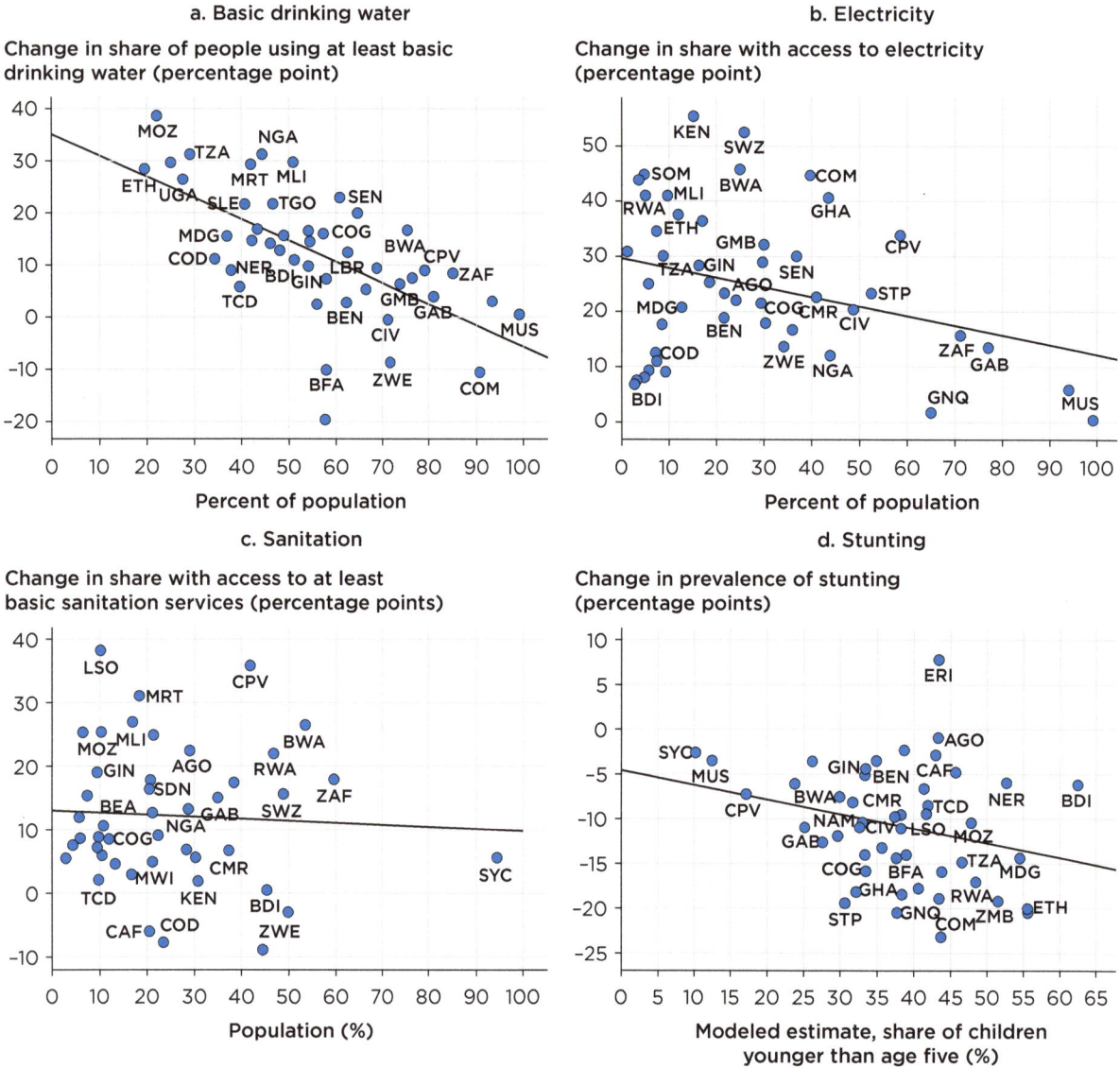

a. Basic drinking water

Change in share of people using at least basic drinking water (percentage point)

b. Electricity

Change in share with access to electricity (percentage point)

c. Sanitation

Change in share with access to at least basic sanitation services (percentage points)

d. Stunting

Change in prevalence of stunting (percentage points)

FIGURE 3A.5 Changes in access to selected basic services in AFR in percentage points during 2000–20 conditional on performance in 2000 *(continued)*

e. Secondary school enrollment

f. Primary school completion

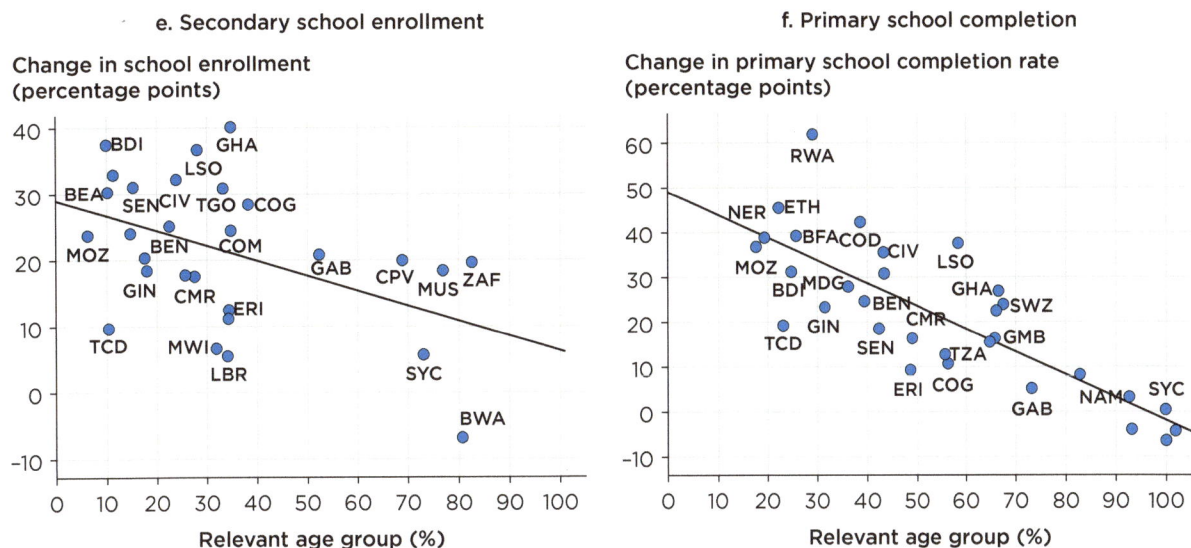

Source: World Bank staff calculations using World Development Indicators.
Note: Numbers of 2000 and 2020 are calculated using the median for values during 1998–2002 and 2018–20, respectively. For country abbreviations, refer to https://www.iso.org/obp/ui/#search.

FIGURE 3A.6 HOI and coverage rates for education across countries

a. School attendance (6–12 years)

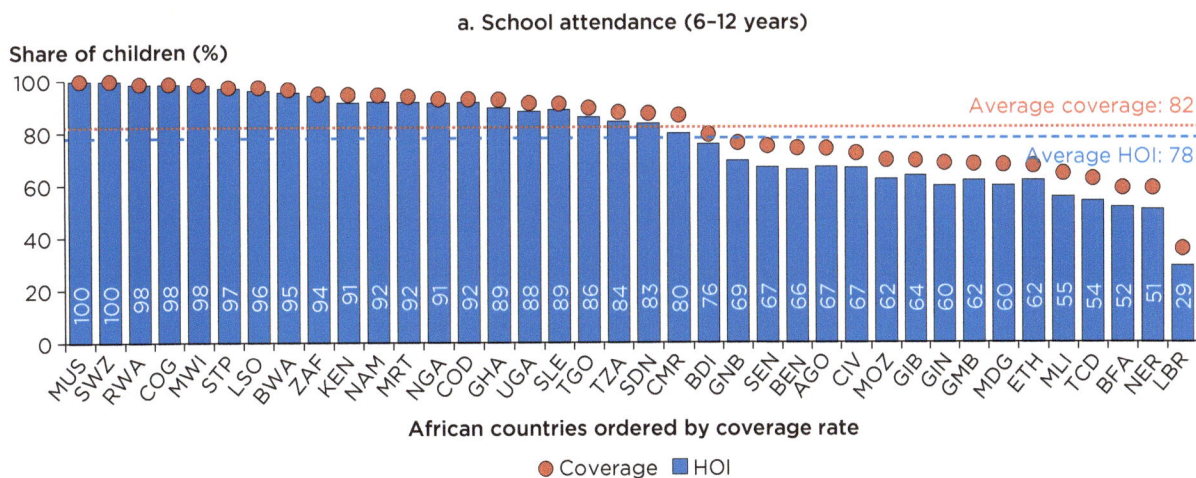

(continued)

FIGURE 3A.6 HOI and coverage rates for education across countries *(continued)*

b. School attendance (13-16 years)

Share of children (%)

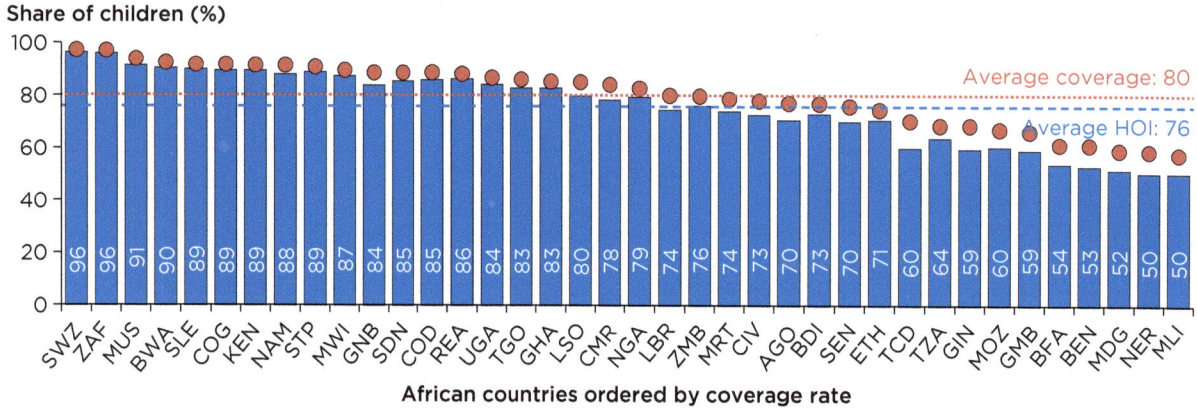

Average coverage: 80

Average HOI: 76

96 96 91 90 89 89 89 88 89 87 84 85 85 86 84 83 83 80 78 79 74 76 74 73 70 73 70 71 60 64 59 60 59 54 53 52 50 50

SWZ ZAF MUS BWA SLE COG KEN NAM STP MWI GNB SDN COD REA UGA TGO GHA LSO CMR NGA LBR ZMB MRT CIV AGO BDI SEN ETH TCD TZA GIN MOZ GMB BFA BEN MDG NER MLI

African countries ordered by coverage rate

c. Started primary school on time (6-7) years

Share of children (%)

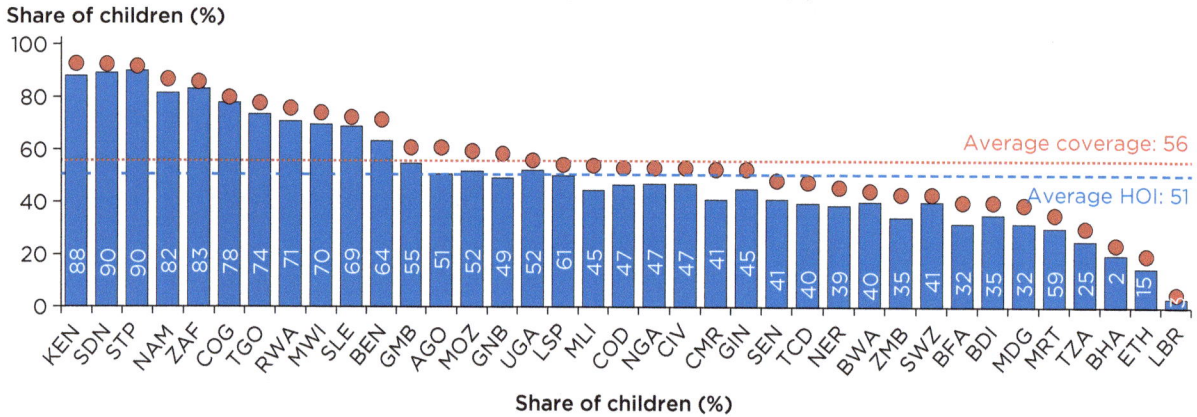

Average coverage: 56

Average HOI: 51

88 90 90 82 83 78 74 71 70 69 64 55 51 52 49 52 61 45 47 47 47 41 45 41 40 39 40 35 41 32 35 32 59 25 2 15

KEN SDN STP NAM ZAF COG TGO RWA MWI SLE BEN GMB AGO MOZ GNB UGA LSP MLI COD NGA CIV CMR GIN SEN TCD NER BWA ZMB SWZ BFA BDI MDG MRT TZA BHA ETH LBR

Share of children (%)

d. Finished primary school on time (13-16 years)

Share of children (%)

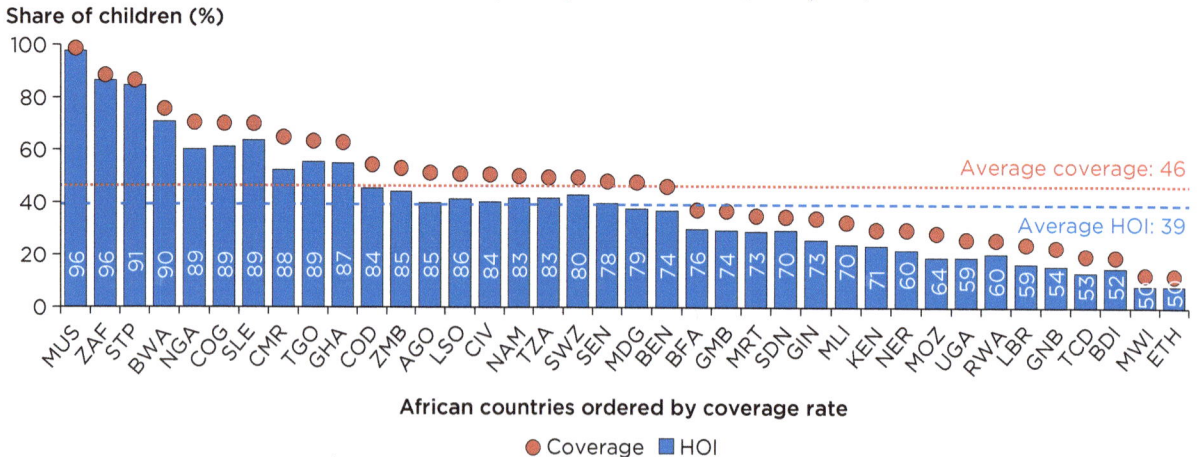

Average coverage: 46

Average HOI: 39

96 96 91 90 89 89 89 88 89 87 84 85 85 86 84 83 83 80 78 79 74 76 74 73 70 73 70 71 60 64 59 60 59 54 53 52 50 50

MUS ZAF STP BWA NGA COG SLE CMR TGO GHA COD ZMB AGO LSO CIV NAM TZA SWZ SEN MDG BEN BFA GMB MRT SDN GIN MLI KEN NER MOZ UGA RWA LBR GNB TCD BDI MWI ETH

African countries ordered by coverage rate

● Coverage ■ HOI

Source: World Bank staff calculations using the Global Monitoring Database.
Note: HOI = Human Opportunity Index. For country abbreviations, refer to https://www.iso.org/obp/ui/#search.

FIGURE 3A.7 HOI and coverage rates for basic services across countries

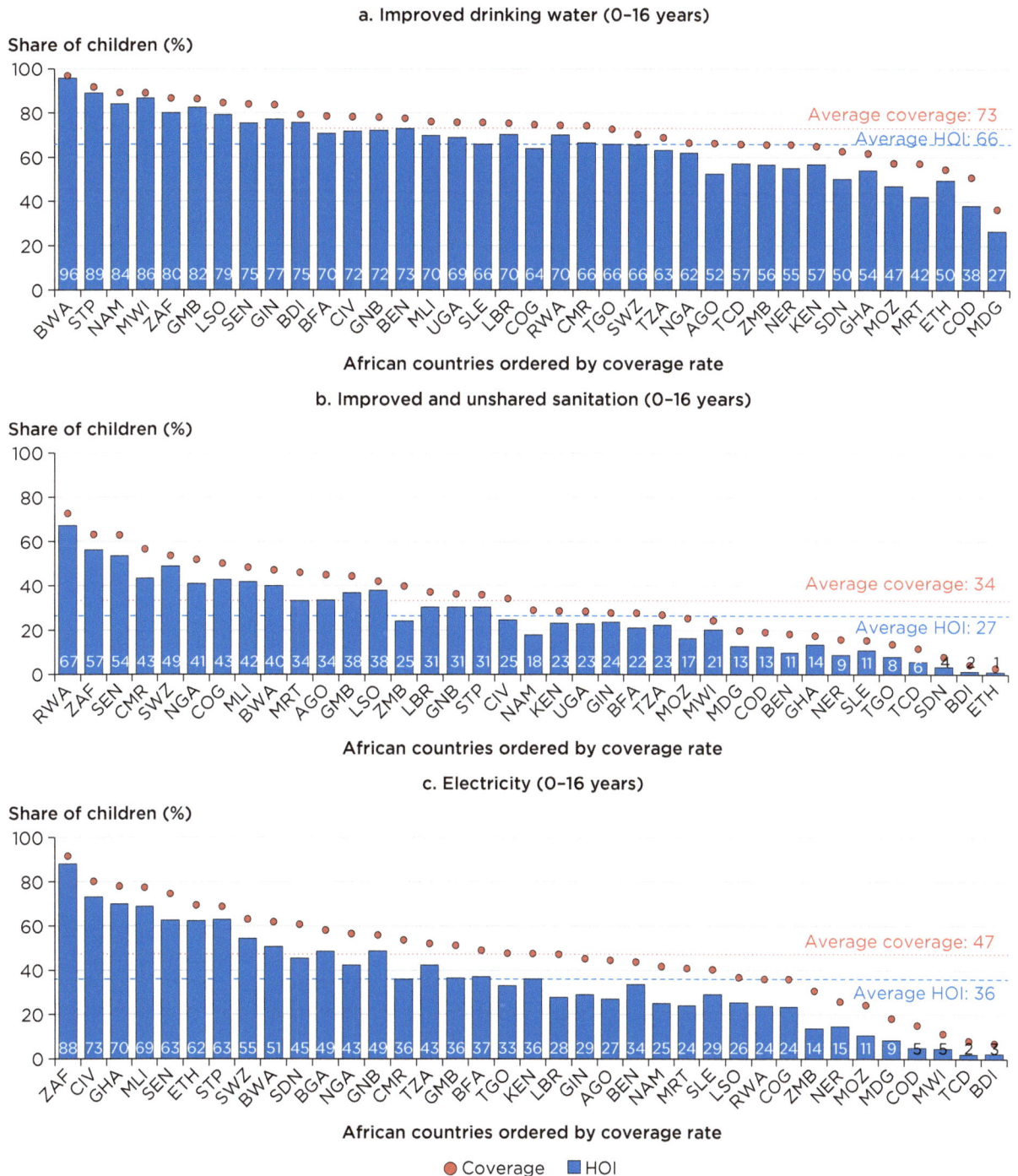

a. Improved drinking water (0–16 years)

Share of children (%)

Average coverage: 73
Average HOI: 66

African countries ordered by coverage rate

Bar values (HOI): BWA 96, STP 89, NAM 84, MWI 86, ZAF 80, GMB 82, LSO 79, SEN 75, GIN 77, BDI 75, BFA 70, CIV 72, GNB 72, BEN 73, MLI 70, UGA 69, SLE 66, LBR 70, COG 64, RWA 70, CMR 66, TGO 66, SWZ 66, TZA 63, NGA 62, AGO 52, TCD 57, ZMB 56, NER 55, KEN 57, SDN 50, GHA 54, MOZ 47, MRT 42, ETH 50, COD 38, MDG 27

b. Improved and unshared sanitation (0–16 years)

Share of children (%)

Average coverage: 34
Average HOI: 27

African countries ordered by coverage rate

Bar values (HOI): RWA 67, ZAF 57, SEN 54, CMR 43, SWZ 49, NGA 41, COG 43, MLI 42, BWA 40, MRT 34, AGO 34, GMB 38, LSO 38, ZMB 25, LBR 31, GNB 31, STP 31, CIV 25, NAM 18, KEN 23, UGA 23, GIN 24, BFA 22, TZA 23, MOZ 17, MWI 21, MDG 13, COD 13, BEN 11, GHA 14, NER 9, SLE 11, TGO 8, TCD 6, SDN 4, BDI 2, ETH 1

c. Electricity (0–16 years)

Share of children (%)

Average coverage: 47
Average HOI: 36

African countries ordered by coverage rate

Bar values (HOI): ZAF 88, CIV 73, GHA 70, MLI 69, SEN 63, ETH 62, STP 63, SWZ 55, BWA 51, SDN 45, BGA 49, NGA 43, GNB 49, CMR 36, TZA 43, GMB 36, BFA 37, TGO 33, KEN 36, LBR 28, GIN 29, AGO 27, BEN 34, NAM 25, MRT 24, SLE 29, LSO 26, RWA 24, COG 24, ZMB 14, NER 15, MOZ 11, MDG 9, COD 5, MWI 5, TCD 2, BDI 3

● Coverage   ■ HOI

(continued)

FIGURE 3A.7 HOI and coverage rates for basic services across countries *(continued)*

e. Access to internet (0–16 years)

Share of children (%)

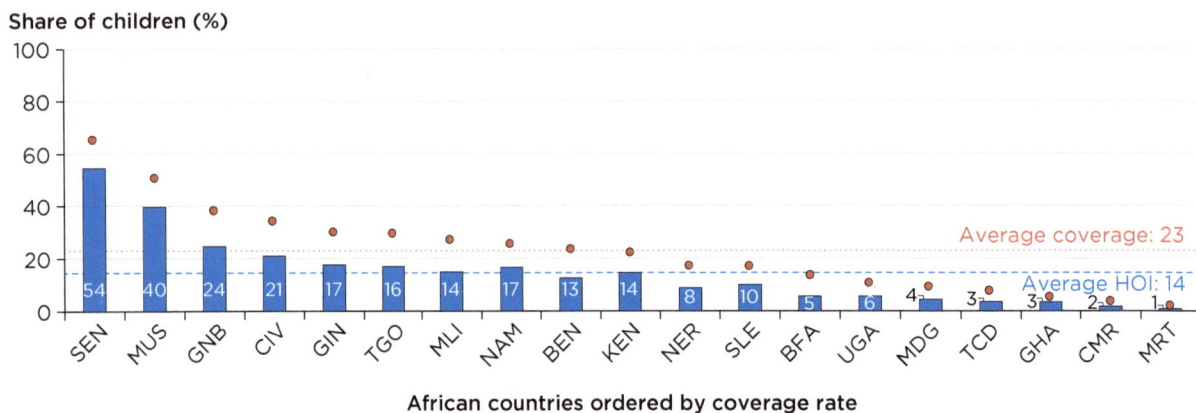

Average coverage: 23

Average HOI: 14

Bars (HOI values): SEN 54, MUS 40, GNB 24, CIV 21, GIN 17, TGO 16, MLI 14, NAM 17, BEN 13, KEN 14, NER 8, SLE 10, BFA 5, UGA 6, MDG 4, TCD 3, GHA 3, CMR 2, MRT 1

African countries ordered by coverage rate

f. Access to radio (0–16 years)

Share of children (%)

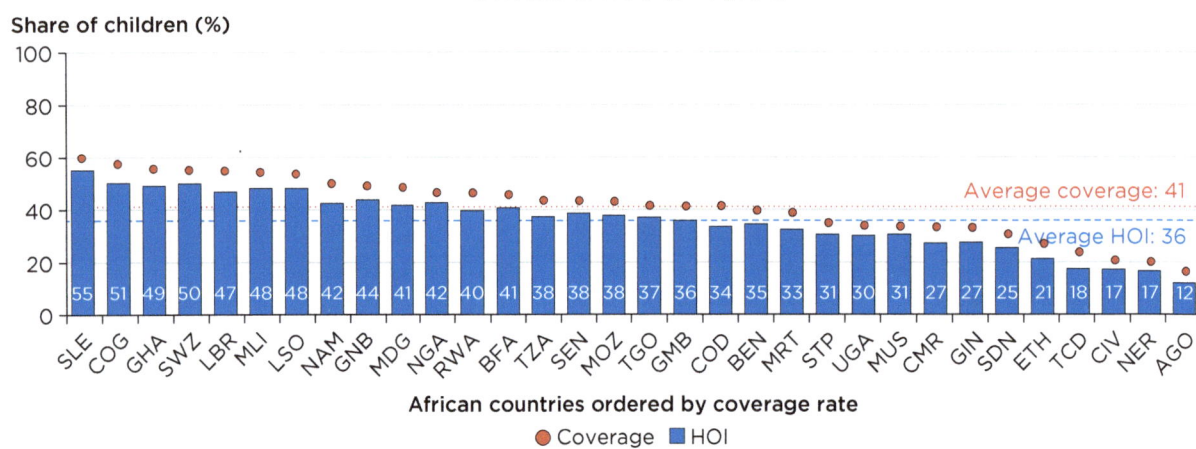

Average coverage: 41

Average HOI: 36

Bars (HOI values): SLE 55, COG 51, GHA 49, SWZ 50, LBR 47, MLI 48, LSO 48, NAM 42, GNB 44, MDG 41, NGA 42, RWA 40, BFA 41, TZA 38, SEN 38, MOZ 38, TGO 37, GMB 36, COD 34, BEN 35, MRT 33, STP 31, UGA 30, MUS 31, CMR 27, GIN 27, SDN 25, ETH 21, TCD 18, CIV 17, NER 17, AGO 12

African countries ordered by coverage rate

● Coverage ■ HOI

Source: World Bank staff calculations using the Global Monitoring Database.

Note: HOI = Human Opportunity Index. For country abbreviations, refer to https://www.iso.org/obp/ui/#search.

FIGURE 3A.8 **Absolute upward mobility, 1980s cohort**

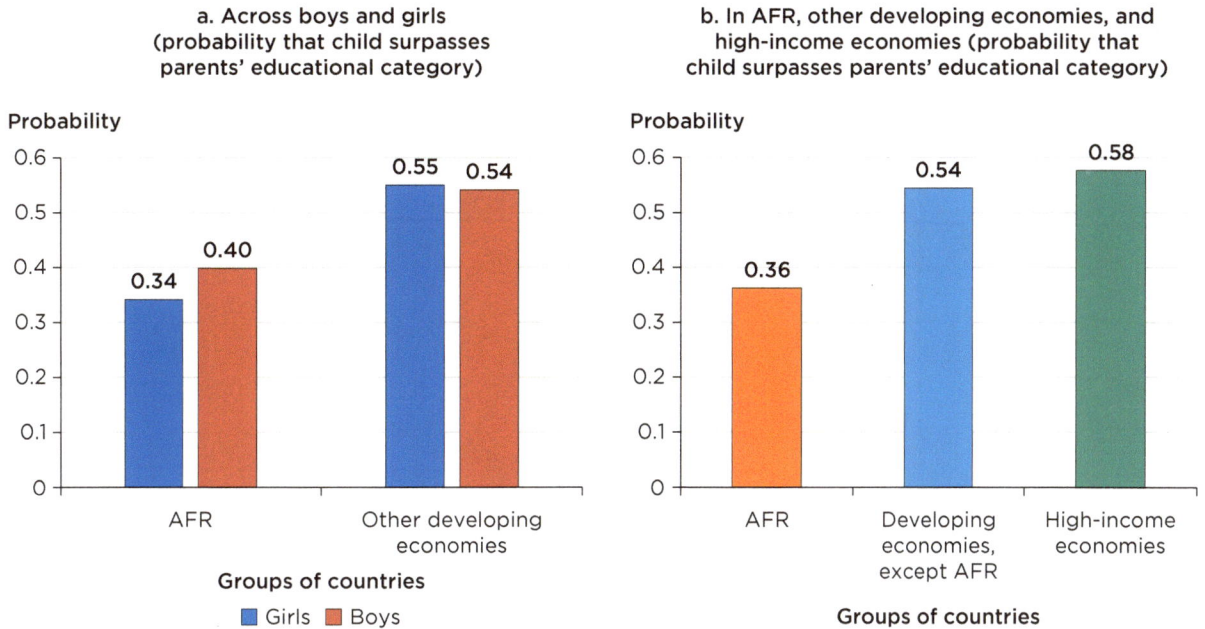

a. Across boys and girls
(probability that child surpasses
parents' educational category)

b. In AFR, other developing economies, and
high-income economies (probability that
child surpasses parents' educational category)

Probability

AFR: Girls 0.34, Boys 0.40	Other developing economies: Girls 0.55, Boys 0.54

Groups of countries

■ Girls ■ Boys

Probability

AFR 0.36 | Developing economies, except AFR 0.54 | High-income economies 0.58

Groups of countries

Source: IGM database from March 2023, World Bank staff calculations.
Note: Using all surveys with retrospective and coresident questions. AFR = Sub-Saharan Africa.

FIGURE 3A.9 **Relative mobility, 1980s cohort**

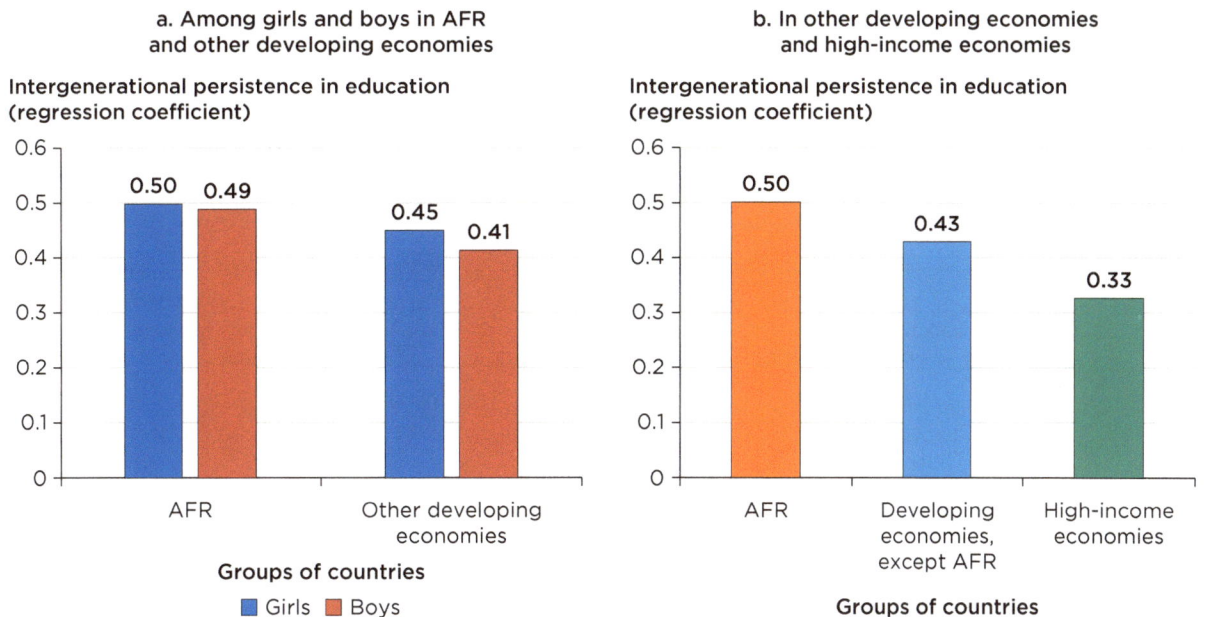

a. Among girls and boys in AFR
and other developing economies

b. In other developing economies
and high-income economies

Intergenerational persistence in education
(regression coefficient)

AFR: Girls 0.50, Boys 0.49	Other developing economies: Girls 0.45, Boys 0.41

Groups of countries

■ Girls ■ Boys

Intergenerational persistence in education
(regression coefficient)

AFR 0.50 | Developing economies, except AFR 0.43 | High-income economies 0.33

Groups of countries

Source: IGM database from March 2023, World Bank staff calculations.
Note: Higher persistence indicates lower mobility. Using all surveys with retrospective and coresident questions. AFR = Sub-Saharan Africa.

FIGURE 3A.10 Distance to health facilities

a. Versus births attended by skilled health personnel in the five years preceding the survey

WHO estimate (%)

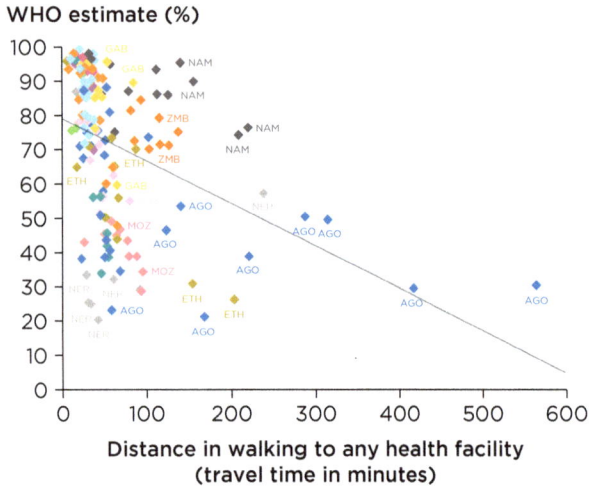

Distance in walking to any health facility (travel time in minutes)

b. Versus share of newborns who received postnatal care within two days of delivery

WHO estimate (%)

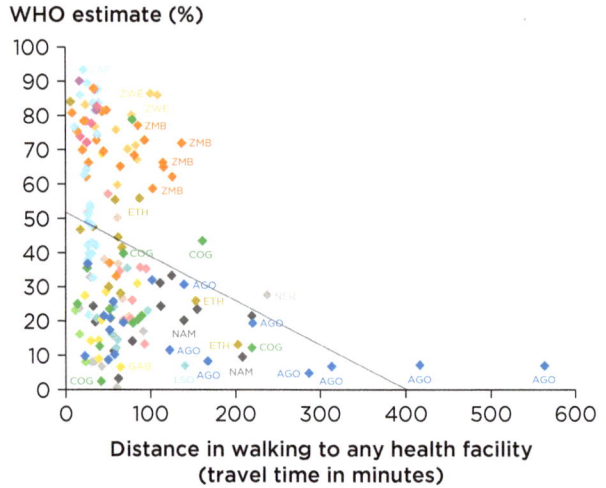

Distance in walking to any health facility (travel time in minutes)

c. Versus BCG immunization coverage among 1-year-olds

WHO estimate (%)

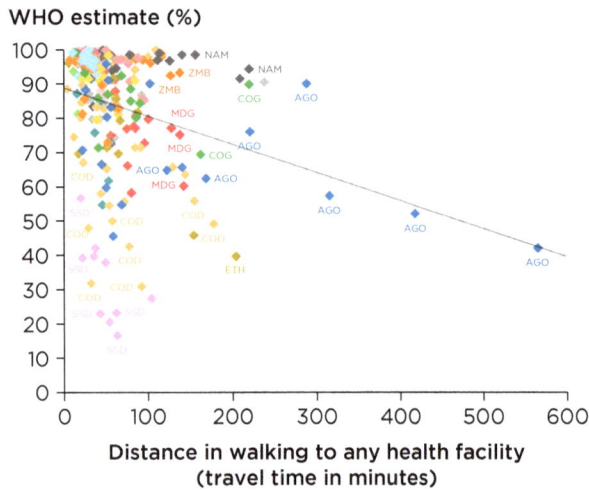

Distance in walking to any health facility (travel time in minutes)

d. Versus the share of 1-year-old children who did not receive any doses of the DTP vaccine

WHO estimate (%)

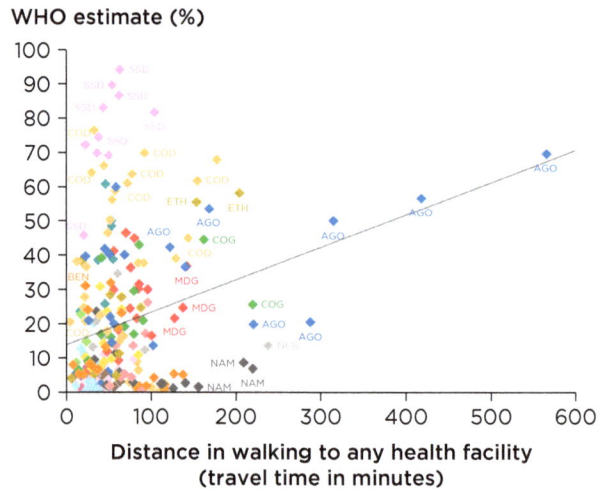

Distance in walking to any health facility (travel time in minutes)

Source: Health Inequality Monitor, WHO (https://www.who.int/data/inequality-monitor/data).
Note: BCG = Bacillus Calmette-Guerin; DTP = diphtheria–tetanus–pertussis; WHO = World Health Organization.

Annex 3B: Measuring the Human Opportunity Index

Conceptually, the Human Opportunity Index (HOI) is based on idea that there is a set of basic opportunities that are necessary to achieve society's economic potential and that should universally be provided to everyone regardless of the circumstances. Opportunities are operationalized as access to basic goods and services, which makes it easy to measure them.[13] Because HOI is calculated for children, it limits the issue of endogeneity, making sure that all observed inequality can be safely assumed to be inequality of opportunity because a child cannot be held responsible for their actions, and access to opportunity is controlled by family or society. Focusing on childhood also limits the space of opportunities to those that are critical for human development and affordable. Typically, these opportunities include access to education, basic infrastructure, immunizations, minimum nutritional levels, and a birth certificate.

Measuring HOI in its simplest interpretation involves calculating the coverage rate for services necessary to progress in life (C), discounted or "penalized" by how unfairly the services are distributed among the population (P). HOI can range from 0 to 100, with 100 percent being universal provision:

$$HOI = C - P.$$

Alternatively, HOI can be computed as

$$HOI = C(1 - P/C),$$

where P/C is called the dissimilarity index (D-index), which can be viewed as a proxy measure of inequality of opportunity. It shows a share of the total number of opportunities that should be reallocated among all groups of the population with different circumstances to ensure equality of opportunity. Consider the simple example in table 3B.1 to illustrate how the HOI and D-index are constructed.

TABLE 3B.1 Hypothetical example for HOI: Number of children ages 6 to 10 enrolled in primary school in countries A and B, by welfare group

Groups by circumstance	Country A	Country B
Group 1, top 50 percent richest households	40	35
Group 2, bottom 50 percent poorest households	20	25
Total	60	60

Source: World Bank.
Note: HOI = Human Opportunity Index.

Imagine two countries, each having a population of 100 primary-school-age children. The average primary enrollment rate in both countries is 60 percent; however, education opportunity is not distributed equally across groups. In each country, children are grouped into the 50 poorest and 50 richest groups based on per capita household income. The principle of equality will hold only if each group has 30 children enrolled in primary school and the same coverage rate (50 percent). However, only 20 children from the bottom 50 percent of income in country A are enrolled in primary school, and only 25 children from the bottom 50 percent of income in country B are enrolled in primary school. This suggests inequality in opportunity in both countries and that country A is more unequal than country B. More formally, the D-index for country A is 10/60 (10 opportunities need to be reallocated from group 1 to group 2 to achieve parity) and 5/60 for country B (five opportunities need to be reallocated from group 1 to group 2 to achieve parity). Therefore, for country A the HOI index is equal to 0.50, and for country B it is equal to 0.55. In sum, despite equal coverage rates, the HOI is lower and the D-index is higher for country A, signaling that inequality in access to education opportunities is higher than in country B:

$$HOI_a = C_a\,(1 - D_a) = 0.6 \times (10/60) = 0.50 \text{ and}$$

$$HOI_b = C_b\,(1 - D_b) = 0.6 \times (1 - 5/60) = 0.55.$$

Calculating the D-index when there are multiple circumstances becomes more complex and is done econometrically. The HOI has several appealing features. For example, the HOI will increase by a factor k if coverage for all groups increases by a factor k. If coverage for one group increases without coverage for other groups decreasing, the HOI increases. If inequality declines and overall coverage remains constant, or overall coverage increases while inequality remains constant, the HOI will always improve.

HOI was constructed for the first time for 19 countries of the Latin American and Caribbean region (Paes de Barros et al. 2009) for the following set of opportunities: completion of sixth grade at age 13; school attendance for children ages 10–14; and access to water, sanitation services, and electricity for children ages 0–16. HOI was lower for sanitation than for water services, with a regional average of 67 percent in the case of water and 43 percent in the case of sanitation. Regarding electricity, only several countries have reached universal access, and many others had HOI scores of around 50 percent. In terms of the role of different circumstances, parental education was an important divide in educational opportunity in Latin America and the Caribbean. Location was the most important circumstance in explaining inequality of opportunity in housing conditions for children.

HOI has been constructed for African countries as well. A regional study (Dabalen et al. 2015) constructed HOI for 20 African countries, using Demographic and Health Survey data from the late 2000s. HOI was estimated for the following opportunities: school attendance rates; starting and finishing primary school on time; access to water, sanitation, and electricity; and being fully immunized and not being stunted. Circumstances included gender of the child, presence of children and elderly people in the household, rural or urban location, education of the head of household, and wealth index quintiles. Dabalen et al. (2015) found that school attendance in most countries was much higher than indicators of achievement such as primary school completion. Depending on the standard used to define adequacy, access to safe water, sanitation, and electricity in African countries ranged from uneven to poor. Inequality of opportunity was higher for immunization than for nutrition in most countries, with a caveat that nutrition depended on many factors other than just access to health care. During the period considered, the 1990–2000s, HOI increased for many countries and for most opportunities. In terms of circumstances, a child's socioeconomic background (wealth and parental education) was crucial in explaining their chances of accessing basic services and goods, followed by location (rural or urban) of the household. For all opportunities, being in a richer, urban household with educated parents was favorable. Mother's education was important in explaining inequality of opportunities in health.

In this report, HOI is constructed for the most recent household budget surveys of 38 African countries (20 of them were conducted in 2017 and later).[14] Following previous regional studies, three broad groups of opportunities were selected for HOI: education, basic infrastructure, and telecommunication services. The full list of opportunities with definitions and age groups considered is provided in table 3B.2.

TABLE 3B.2 Opportunities to construct the HOI for African countries

Opportunity	Definition
Education	School attendance (6–12 years)
	School attendance (13–16 years)
	Started primary school on time (6–7 years)
	Finished primary on time (13–16 years)
Basic services	Improved drinking water (0–16 years)
	Improved and unshared sanitation (0–16 years)
	Electricity (0–16 years)
Access to information and communication technology	Mobile phone in the household (0–16 years)
	Internet (0–16 years)
	Radio (0–16 years)

Source: World Bank.
Note: HOI = Human Opportunity Index.

For education, two indicators measure school attendance, and other two aim to capture achievements for school quality and a child's ability to use education to attain a basic level of learning. Age groups for school attendance broadly capture primary and secondary school ages. This distinction is important because in most countries primary school is compulsory and fully free, whereas access to secondary school is associated with costs even in countries where secondary education is free. Starting and completing primary school on time are equally important and reinforce one another. Children starting primary school on time are more likely to get the necessary educational inputs at an early age. Starting school later than official entry age was one of the factors for overenrollment in first grade in Africa. Children who complete primary school on time are more likely to have achieved the minimum learning to progress through grades without repetition, which is another common problem in many African countries (Bashir et al. 2018).

Access to basic infrastructure is captured by indicators of access to improved drinking water, improved and unshared sanitation, and electricity. Access to clean drinking water and improved sanitation are key drivers of public health that reduce the incidence of diarrhea and other preventable diseases, malnutrition, and other health issues. Access to electricity is an important determinant of the quality of life and facilitates access to other opportunities, including access to digital technologies, information, and studying. Households' access to information and communication technology (ICT) is believed to bring large economic gains in Africa (Calderón and Cantu 2021). However, access to ICT was not typically used in measuring HOI in previous studies, mostly because few surveys collected this information. Nowadays, most surveys include questions about access to digital services. Three indicators were selected to measure ICT opportunities: access to mobile phones, internet, and radio. Inclusion of radio makes sense in Africa because it is one of the most-used mass communication mediums.[15]

Given that HOI in this report is based on household budget surveys, which do not typically measure health opportunities and access very well, secondary sources are used to illustrate discrepancies for selected indicators such as immunization and stunting (low height for age). The opportunity to be adequately nourished is a key factor affecting human capital and lifelong earnings. In contrast to other indicators, it is not an input indicator but an outcome of multiple different policies, including access to water, sanitation, health services, and so forth.

The circumstances, defined as exogenous characteristics of the child, are not supposed to affect access to selected opportunities. The following set of circumstances were used: household demographic composition measured by the number of children in the household, child's gender, head of household's education level, monetary well-being, and location captured by rural–urban and regional dimensions (refer to table 3B.3). It is important to remember that the HOI changes if circumstances change, so the results of this study hold for a selected set of circumstances and are subject to change if circumstances are changed. If new circumstances are added, the HOI will always be lower and inequality higher, meaning that HOI and inequality always serve as an upper and lower bound of the "true" HOI and inequality based on all circumstances.

TABLE 3B.3 List of circumstances used to construct the HOI for African countries

Circumstance	Definition
Household member characteristics	Number of children in the household (ages 0–16 years)
Child characteristics	Gender
Head-of-household characteristics	Gender
	Education level
Monetary well-being	Average household consumption per capita in 2017 US$ PPP
Location	Urban–rural areas
	Regions

Source: World Bank.
Note: HOI = Human Opportunity Index; PPP = purchasing power parity.

Annex 3C: Measuring intergenerational mobility

Parental characteristics are often included as potential factors contributing to inequality of opportunity and inequality in access to basic services. Inequality will be transmitted across generations if a child's outcome depends on parental characteristics. Intergenerational mobility (IGM) directly measures whether people's life outcomes, such as earnings, education, and occupation, depend on those of their parents. In a society with more equal opportunities, the link between the children and parental outcomes would be weak, and people would be more socially mobile. Given that education is a key dimension of human progress—in particular, of earnings—educational mobility is important on its own and is an essential element of economic mobility. There are other reasons for using information on intergenerational education instead of intergenerational income to measure economic mobility. First, education data across generations are much more widely available. Second, it is easier for respondents to report parental education with high-level precision than it is their income. Third, adult education level does not vary much over the life cycle, and one survey round can capture all necessary information, whereas accurate tracking of individual income will require panel data.

To measure IGM, this report relies on the World Bank's (2023a) Global Database on Intergenerational Mobility (GDIM), used in van der Weide et al. (2021, 2024).[16] This is the largest database covering 153 countries of the world and representing 97 percent of the global population. The database contains estimates of IGM in education by 10-year cohorts, covering individuals born between 1940 and 1989 and using mostly representative household budget surveys. The estimates of IGM for the generation born between 1980 and 1989 contains IGM estimates by the type (subpopulation) of parental educational attainment (mothers, fathers, average, maximum) and the type (subpopulation) of child's educational attainment (sons, daughters, all respondents to the surveys). This allows more granular estimation between, for example, the relationship of mother's to daughter's IGM.

Depending on each survey, parental education is measured differently. Some surveys measure parental education asking all adult respondents retrospective questions on the education of their parents, as well as their own education. Some surveys do not collect retrospective data, and coresident data are considered instead. In these surveys, the information on parental educational attainment is obtained for the subset of all respondents ages 21–25 who coreside with their parents. This limits information from these surveys to only one cohort: the 1980s. The largest number of coresident surveys is observed among African countries: 21 of 43. This makes it challenging to measure intergenerational mobility over time in Africa. Therefore, the most accurate comparison of Africa with other regions can be done for the latest 1980s cohort, whereas IGM estimates over time in Africa are based on only a limited set of surveys with retrospective questions.

Notes

1. All dollar amounts are US dollars unless otherwise indicated. Dollar amounts adjusted for purchasing power parity are noted in the text. For example, gross domestic product (GDP) per capita in 2017 purchasing power parity constant prices was US$6,544 in lower-middle-income countries in 2020 compared with US$3,655 in Africa (developing countries only).
2. An important caveat here is the difference in the period in which data were collected in different countries, which may have a significant impact on the results.
3. The rank correlation coefficient between GDP per capita and the average dissimilarity index (D-index) was -0.56 ($p = 0.0003$).
4. The rank correlation coefficient between international poverty and the average D-index was 0.4732 ($p = 0.0027$).
5. Relative intergenerational mobility can be measured by using correlation coefficients between children's and parents' years of schooling, coefficients from regressing children's on parents' years of schooling, or both.
6. The results remain qualitatively the same for the 1980s cohort if all surveys are used, regardless of how parental education is measured.
7. Determined through Living Standard Measurement Surveys for Burkina Faso, Ethiopia, The Gambia, Ghana, Malawi, Mali, Niger, Nigeria, Tanzania, and Uganda.
8. Learning-adjusted years of schooling is simply the product of a country's expected years of schooling and its harmonized learning measure (test scores) benchmarked against a standard.
9. The four countries are the Democratic Republic of Congo, Ethiopia, Nigeria, and Tanzania. See Stanley (2023).
10. Tertiary education spending is undoubtedly important for skill development and potential economic growth; however, additional efforts are needed to ensure that this spending is more inclusive, including through scholarships aimed at talented low-income children.
11. Kerwin and Thornton (2021) warn, though, that reducing the costs of a highly effective program can make it less effective, leaving some students worse off.

12. That is, 10,000 conflict deaths per 100,000 people in the setting of their formative years.

13. By using access as a synonym for opportunities, we assume that access implies usage of a services. Having a school nearby does not imply access, but school attendance will be viewed as access (opportunity). It is also important to make sure that quality is taken into consideration in defining access by having a minimum threshold of quality for each basic good or service.

14. This is not the full list of countries with surveys available, but the list of countries with surveys for which it was possible to construct all selected opportunities and create all circumstances.

15. For illustrative purposes, the Human Opportunity Index for basic services will be expanded to account for the quality of services. For example, access to electricity will consider hours of services available and access to drinking water will consider the distance to the source. This is done for several countries for which this information was collected.

16. The database is being constantly updated, and this report uses version 3 (March 2023).

References

Almond, Douglas, and Janet Currie. 2011. "Human Capital Development before Age Five." In *Handbook of Labor Economics*, vol. 4, part B, edited by Orley C. Ashenfelter and David E. Card, 1315–1486. Amsterdam: North-Holland.

Andrabi, Tahir, Benjamin Daniels, and Jishnu Das. 2023. "Human Capital Accumulation and Disasters: Evidence from the Pakistan Earthquake of 2005." *Journal of Human Resources* 58 (4): 1057–96. https://doi.org/10.3368/jhr.59.2.0520-10887R1.

Arias Diaz, Omar, David Evans, and Indhira Vanessa Santos. 2019. *The Skills Balancing Act in Sub-Saharan Africa: Investing in Skills for Productivity, Inclusivity, and Adaptability*. Washington, DC: World Bank. http://documents.worldbank.org/curated/en/558991560840574354/The-Skills-Balancing-Act-in-Sub-Saharan-Africa-Investing-in-Skills-for-Productivity-Inclusivity-and-Adaptability.

Arias Diaz, Omar S., and Igor Kheyfets. 2023. *The Adequacy of Public Expenditure on Education and the Needs Post-Covid-19*. Washington, DC: World Bank http://documents.worldbank.org/curated/en/099103123163731570/P1781350d855aa0170ab8f0f8644bd8efd7.

Atamanov, Aziz, Eduardo Alonso Malsquez Carbonel, Takaaki Masaki, Cara Ann Myers, Rogelio Granguillhome Ochoa, and Nistha Sinha. 2022. *Uganda Poverty Assessment: Strengthening Resilience to Accelerate Poverty Reduction*. Washington, DC: World Bank. http://documents.worldbank.org/curated/en/099135006292235162/P17761605286900b10899b0798dcd703d85.

Báez, Javier E., Alejandro de la Fuente, and Indhira Vanessa Santos. 2010. "Do Natural Disasters Affect Human Capital? An Assessment Based on Existing Empirical Evidence." Discussion Paper 5164, Institute of Labor Economics, Bonn.

Bashir, Sajitha, Marlaine Lockheed, Elizabeth Ninan, and Jee-Peng Tan. 2018. *Facing Forward: Schooling for Learning in Africa*. Africa Development Forum series. Washington, DC: World Bank. https://doi.org/10.1596/978-1-46481260-6.

Bauluz, Luis, Yajna Govind, and Filip Novokmet. 2020. "Global Land Inequality." Working Paper 10, World Inequality Database. https://wid.world/document/global-land-inequality-world-inequality-lab-wp-2020-10/.

Beegle, Kathleen, and Alejandro de la Fuente. 2019. "Mobilizing Resources for the Poor." In *Accelerating Poverty Reduction in Africa*, edited by Kathleen Beegle and Luc Christiaensen, 247–85. Washington, DC: World Bank.

Bendini, Magdalena, and Amanda E. Devercelli. 2022. *Quality Early Learning: Nurturing Children's Potential*. Washington, DC: World Bank. https://www.worldbank.org/en/topic/education/publication/quality-early-learning-nurturing-children-s-potential.

Bhula, Radhika, Meghan Mahoney, and Kyle Murphy. 2020. "Conducting Cost-Effectiveness Analysis (CEA)." Cambridge, MA: Abdul Latif Jameel Poverty Action Lab. https://www.povertyactionlab.org/resource/conducting-cost-effectiveness-analysis-cea.

Blom, Sylvia, Ariel Ortiz-Bobea, and John F. Hoddinott. 2022. "Heat Exposure and Child Nutrition: Evidence from West Africa." *Journal of Environmental Economics and Management* 115: 102698.

Bold, Tessa, Deon Filmer, Ezequiel Molina, and Jakob Svensson. 2019. "The Lost Human Capital: Teacher Knowledge and Student Achievement in Africa." Policy Research Working Paper 8849, World Bank, Washington, DC. http://hdl.handle.net/10986/31673.

Calderón, Cesar, and Catalina Cantu. 2021. "The Impact of Digital Infrastructure on African Development." Policy Research Working Paper 9853, World Bank, Washington, DC. https://documents1.worldbank.org/curated/en/382651637242152978/pdf/The-Impact-of-Digital-Infrastructure-on-African-Development.pdf.

Canning, D., and T. P. Schultz. 2012. "The Economic Consequences of Reproductive Health and Family Planning." *Lancet* 380 (9837): 165–71.

Caruso, Germán, Inés de Marcos, and Ilan Noy. 2024. "Climate Changes Affect Human Capital." *Economics of Disasters and Climate Change* 8: 157–96. https://doi.org/10.1007/s41885-023-00140-2.

Corral, Paul, Alexander Irwin, Nandini Krishnan, Daniel Gerszon Mahler, and Tara Vishwanath. 2020. *Fragility and Conflict: On the Front Lines of the Fight against Poverty*. Washington, DC: World Bank. https://doi.org/10.1596/978-1-4648-1540-9.

Dabalen, Andrew, Ambar Narayan, Jaime Saavedra-Chanduvi, Alejandro Hoyos Suarez, Ana Abras, and Sailesh Tiwari. 2015. *Do African Children Have an Equal Chance? A Human Opportunity Report for Sub-Saharan Africa*. Directions in Development—Poverty. Washington, DC: World Bank.

Dean, Mark, and Anja Sautmann. 2022. "The Effects of Community Health Worker Visits and Primary Care Subsidies on Health Behavior and Health Outcomes for Children in Urban Mali." Policy Research Working Paper 9986, World Bank, Washington, DC. http://hdl.handle.net/10986/37245.

Deininger, Klaus, and Aparajita Goyal. 2023. "Land Institutions to Address New Challenges in Africa: Implications for the World Bank's Land Policy." Policy Research Working Paper 10389, World Bank, Washington, DC. http://hdl.handle.net/10986/39634.

Dimitrova, Anna, and Jayanta Kumar Bora. 2020. "Monsoon Weather and Early Childhood Health in India." *PLOS ONE* 15 (4): e0231479.

Foster, Vivien, and Cecilia Briceño-Garmendia, eds. 2010. *Africa's Infrastructure: A Time for Transformation*. Washington, DC: World Bank.

Garg, Teevrat, Maulik Jagnani, and Vis Taraz. 2020. "Temperature and Human Capital in India." *Journal of the Association of Environmental and Resource Economists* 7 (6): 1113–50.

Gatti, Roberta, Kathryn Andrews, Ciro Avitabile, Ruben Conner, Jigyasa Sharma, and Andres Yi Chang. 2021. *The Quality of Health and Education Systems Across Africa: Evidence from a Decade of Service Delivery Indicators Surveys*. Washington, DC: World Bank. http://hdl.handle.net/10986/36234.

Kaw, Jon Kher, Hyunji Lee, and Sameh Wahba. 2020. *The Hidden Wealth of Cities: Creating, Financing, and Managing Public Spaces*. Washington, DC: World Bank. http://hdl.handle.net/10986/33186.

Kerwin, J., and Thornton, R. 2021. "Making the Grade: The Sensitivity of Education Program Effectiveness to Input Choices and Outcome Measures." *Review of Economics and Statistics* 103 (2): 251–64. https://doi.org/10.1162/rest_a_00911.

Lall, Somik V., Jon Kher Kaw, Forhad Shilpi, and Sally Beth Murray. 2023. *Vibrant Cities—On the Bedrock of Stability, Prosperity, and Sustainability*. Washington, DC: World Bank. http://hdl.handle .net/10986/40712.

Le, Kien, and My Nguyen. 2021. "In-Utero Exposure to Rainfall Variability and Early Childhood Health." *World Development* 144: 105485.

Maina, Joseph, Paul O Ouma, Peter M. Macharia, Victor A. Alegana, Benard Mitto, Ibrahimo Socé Fall, Abdisalan M. Noor, Robert W. Snow, and Emelda A. Okiro. 2019. "A Spatial Database of Health Facilities Managed by the Public Health Sector in Sub-Saharan Africa." *Scientific Data* 6: 134.

Miller, Ray. 2017. "Childhood Health and Prenatal Exposure to Seasonal Food Scarcity in Ethiopia." *World Development* 99: 350–76.

Molina, Ezequiel, Ambar Narayan, and Jaime Saavedra-Chanduvi. 2013. "Outcomes, Opportunity and Development: Why Unequal Opportunities and not Outcomes Hinder Economic Development." Policy Research Working Paper 6735, World Bank, Washington, DC.

Narayan, Ambar, Roy van der Weide, Alexandru Cojocaru, Christoph Lakner, Silvia Redaelli, Daniel Gerszon Mahler, Rakesh Gupta N. Ramasubbaiah, and Stefan Thewissen. 2018. *Fair Progress? Economic Mobility across Generations around the World*. Washington, DC: World Bank. https://hdl .handle.net/10986/28428.

Paes de Barros, Ricardo, Francisco H. G. Ferreira, Jose R. Molinas Vega, Jaime Saavedra Chanduvi, Mirela De Carvalho, Samuel Franco, Samuel Freije-Rodriguez, and Jeremie Gignoux. 2009. *Measuring Inequality of Opportunities in Latin America and the Caribbean*. Latin American Development Forum. Washington, DC: World Bank. http://documents.worldbank.org/curated/en /219971468045038979/Measuring-inequality-of-opportunities-in-Latin-America-and-the -Caribbean.

Palik, Júlia, Anna Marie Obermeier, and Siri Aas Rustad. 2022. "Conflict Trends in Africa, 1989–2021." PRIO Paper. Oslo: Peace Research Institute Oslo.

Park, R. Jisung. 2022. "Hot Temperature and High-Stakes Performance." *Journal of Human Resources* 57 (2): 400–34.

Park, R. Jisung, A. Patrick Behrer, and Joshua Goodman. 2021. "Learning Is Inhibited by Heat Exposure, Both Internationally and within the United States." *Nature Human Behavior* 5 (1): 19–27. https://doi.org/10.1038/s41562-020-00959-9.

Rains, Emily, and Anirudh Krishna. 2021. "Informalities, Volatility, and Precarious Social Mobility in Urban Slums." In *Social Mobility in Developing Countries: Concepts, Methods, and Determinants*, edited by Vegard Iversen, Anirudh Krishna, and Kunal Sen, 351–73. Oxford: Oxford University Press.

Randell, Heather, and Clark Gray. 2019. "Climate Change and Educational Attainment in the Global Tropics." *Proceedings of the National Academy of Sciences* 116 (18): 8840–45.

Schady, Norbert, Alaka Holla, Shwetlena Sabarwal, Joana Silva, and Andres Yi Chang. 2023. *Collapse and Recovery: How the COVID-19 Pandemic Eroded Human Capital and What to Do about It*. Washington, DC: World Bank. https://hdl.handle.net/10986/39403

Schütz, Gabriela, Heinrich W. Ursprung, and Ludger Wößmann. 2008. "Education Policy and Equality of Opportunity." *Kyklos* 61 (2): 279–308.

Shah, Manisha, and Bryce Millett Steinberg. 2017. "Drought of Opportunities: Contemporaneous and Long-Term Impacts of Rainfall Shocks on Human Capital." *Journal of Political Economy* 125 (2): 527–61.

Stanley, Andrew. 2023. *African Century: A Demographic Transformation in Africa Has the Potential to Alter the World Order*. Washington, DC: International Monetary Fund. https://www.imf.org/en/Publications/fandd/issues/2023/09/PT-african-century

Sulla, Victor, Precious Zikhali, and Pablo Facundo Cuevas. 2022. *Inequality in Southern Africa: An Assessment of the Southern African Customs Union*. Washington, DC: World Bank. http://documents.worldbank.org/curated/en/099125303072236903/P1649270c02a1f06b0a3ae02e57eadd7a82

Tetteh-Baah, Samuel, Kenneth Harttgen, Rahul Lahoti, and Isabel Günther. 2024. "Horizontal Inequalities in Africa." *Review of Income and Wealth*. https://doi.org/10.1111/roiw.12669

UN DESA (United Nations Department of Economic and Social Affairs), Population Division. 2022. "World Population Prospects 2022: Summary of Results." UN DESA/POP/2022/TR/NO. 3.

UNICEF (United Nations Children's Fund). 2021. "Analysis of Education Spending in the West and Central Africa Region: A Policy Brief for Ministers of Education and Finance." New York: UNICEF.

UNICEF (United Nations Children's Fund). 2024. "At Least 200 Million Girls and Women Alive Today Living in 31 Countries Have Undergone FGM." New York: UNICEF. https://data.unicef.org/topic/child-protection/female-genital-mutilation/.

UNICEF Innocenti Research Centre. 2021. *Time to Teach: Teacher Attendance and Time on Task in Primary Schools in The Gambia*. Florence: UNICEF Office of Research—Innocenti. https://www.unicef-irc.org/publications/1233-time-to-teach-teacher-attendance-and-time-on-task-in-primary-schools-in-the-gambia.html.

van der Weide, Roy, Christoph Lakner, Daniel Gerszon Mahler, Ambar Narayan, and Rakesh Gupta. 2024. "Intergenerational Mobility around the World: A New Database." *Journal of Development Economics* 166: 103167.

van der Weide, Roy, Christoph Lakner, Daniel Gerszon Mahler, Ambar Narayan, and Rakesh Ramasubbaiah. 2021. "Intergenerational Mobility around the World," Policy Research Working Paper 9707, World Bank, Washington, DC. https://documents1.worldbank.org/curated/en/817351624329601595/pdf/Intergenerational-Mobility-around-the-World.pdf.

WHO (World Health Organization). 2023. "Female Genital Mutilation." Fact sheet. https://www.who.int/news-room/fact-sheets/detail/female-genital-mutilation.

Wieser, Christina, Alemayehu A. Ambel, Tom Bundervoet, and Asmelash Haile Tsegay. 2020. "Monitoring COVID-19 Impacts on Households in Ethiopia (Vol. 3): Results from a High-Frequency Phone Survey of Households." Washington, DC: World Bank.

World Bank. 2013. *Turn Down the Heat: Climate Extremes, Regional Impacts, and the Case for Resilience*. Washington, DC: World Bank.

World Bank. 2017. *World Bank Development Report 2017: Governance and the Law*. Washington, DC: World Bank.

World Bank. 2020. *COVID-19 Impact Monitoring: Uganda, Round 1*. Washington, DC: World Bank. http://hdl.handle.net/10986/34395.

World Bank. 2021. *The Human Capital Index 2020 Update: Human Capital in the Time of COVID-19*. Washington, DC: World Bank. http://hdl.handle.net/10986/34432.

World Bank. 2022. *The Gambia Poverty and Gender Assessment 2022: Securing a Robust and Inclusive Recovery*. Washington, DC: World Bank. http://hdl.handle.net/10986/38310.

World Bank. 2023a. "Global Database on Intergenerational Mobility." Washington, DC: World Bank Group. https://datacatalog.worldbank.org/search/dataset/0050771/Global-Database-on -Intergenerational-Mobility

World Bank. 2023b. *What Works to Narrow Gender Gaps and Empower Women in Sub-Saharan Africa? An Evidence-Review of Selected Impact Evaluation Studies.* Washington, DC: World Bank. https://documents1.worldbank.org/curated/en/099061623110030316/pdf/P1804940a8a04e0ab0988e0e 90727152914.pdf.

Zivin, Joshua Graff, Yingquan Song, Qu Tang, and Peng Zhang. 2020. "Temperature and High-Stakes Cognitive Performance: Evidence from the National College Entrance Examination in China." *Journal of Environmental Economics and Management* 104: 102365.

Poverty and Inequality Influencers: Gender Equality

ANA MARIA OVIEDO AND HUGO ÑOPO

> Every woman shall have the right to respect as a person and to the free development of her personality.
>
> —Article III.2, *Protocol to the African Charter on Human and People's Rights on the Rights of Women in Africa* (African Union 2003)

Gender equality is a fundamental tenet of social justice and a driver of economic development. It fosters a fair playing field while contributing to equal access to opportunities and resources. Equality of opportunities allows the full use of human capital by broadening the talent pool and stimulating innovation and entrepreneurship, all of which contribute to a more robust, inclusive, and sustainable economy (World Bank 2012). However, in Africa, gender equality is still far from a reality, with varying progress across the region (AfDB and UNECA 2020; Beegle and Christiaensen 2019; Broccolini, Fruttero, and Jain 2023).

The basics: equality before the law, social norms, and early investments

By 2022, 47 countries had signed the *Protocol to the African Charter on Human and People's Rights on the Rights of Women in Africa*, or Maputo Protocol (African Union 2003), committing to equalize women's rights. However, many legal barriers persist. *Women, Business and the Law 2024* (World Bank 2024) indicates that, of 2.5 billion working-age women lacking equal legal rights globally, 346 million are in Africa. Although the region has recently made notable progress, there is wide cross-country variation in women's legal rights, with 24 economies scoring below the global average (77.9) and four scoring below 50, meaning that in these countries, women have fewer than half of men's rights in the domains considered. The 2021–23 period deserves special attention because it has witnessed a notable surge in reforms aimed at fostering gender equality in Africa. *Women, Business and the Law 2024* shows a 1.15-point increase in the region's average score since October 2022, reaching a score of 74, higher than that for East Asia and the Pacific. This positive trend can be credited to the substantial contributions in the past two years of Benin, Côte d'Ivoire, Equatorial Guinea, Gabon, Lesotho, Malawi, the Republic of Congo, Rwanda, Senegal, Sierra Leone, Togo, and Uganda. Over time, Rwanda, Sierra Leone, and Togo implemented multiple reforms that resulted in scores above 90. Recent reforms encompass diverse and crucial measures, including legal adjustments to enhance women's involvement in all sectors, the implementation of parental leave policies, ensuring equal pay for equal work, and the prohibition of gender-based discrimination in accessing credit, among other significant steps.

Gender inequality manifests throughout the life cycle, disproportionately affecting impoverished women (Beegle and Christiaensen 2019). Intrahousehold disparities subject women to human rights abuses, such as female genital mutilation (FGM), early family formation, and increased household work. These factors consistently hinder human capital accumulation and limit opportunities, perpetuating poverty across generations. Concerningly, FGM persists in 33 African countries, with high prevalence in The Gambia, Guinea, Mali, and Somalia, affecting more than 7 in 10 women ages 15–19 (UNICEF 2024). Positive trends have emerged in Burkina Faso, Chad, Côte d'Ivoire, Ethiopia, Mauritania, and Sierra Leone, where advocacy, legal reforms, and changing social norms have lowered the prevalence in younger cohorts.

Weak legal protections, cultural norms, and limited access to education and economic opportunities contribute to prevalent early marriages and parenthood among young women in Africa (Melesse et al. 2021; Parsons et al. 2015). In the region, a minority of countries (13) have enacted legislation setting the legal age for marriage at 18, whereas 17 countries have no minimum age, and the rest have set a minimum age younger than 18 (Costa et al. 2023). In Western Africa, 40–60 percent of women ages 15–19 are in unions or married; this is also prevalent in high-poverty countries, such as Madagascar and Mozambique, trapping poor girls in a cycle of poverty (Melesse et al. 2021; Parsons et al. 2015).

Notwithstanding the expansion of primary education since 1990, children in the poorest quintile consistently show lower attendance and completion. Secondary education gender gaps widen toward the end of lower secondary school, most notably in West Africa, Ethiopia, and Madagascar. Moreover, in the Sahel region, post-2010 Demographic and Health Survey data reveal that significant proportions of women ages 15–24 in all wealth quintiles lack any education (refer to figure S2.1). Additionally, increased hours of unpaid household work during adolescence negatively affect job quality and earnings in adult years (Carmichael et al. 2023).

FIGURE S2.1 Share of women ages 15–24 with no education, by wealth quintile, Africa

Percentage with no education

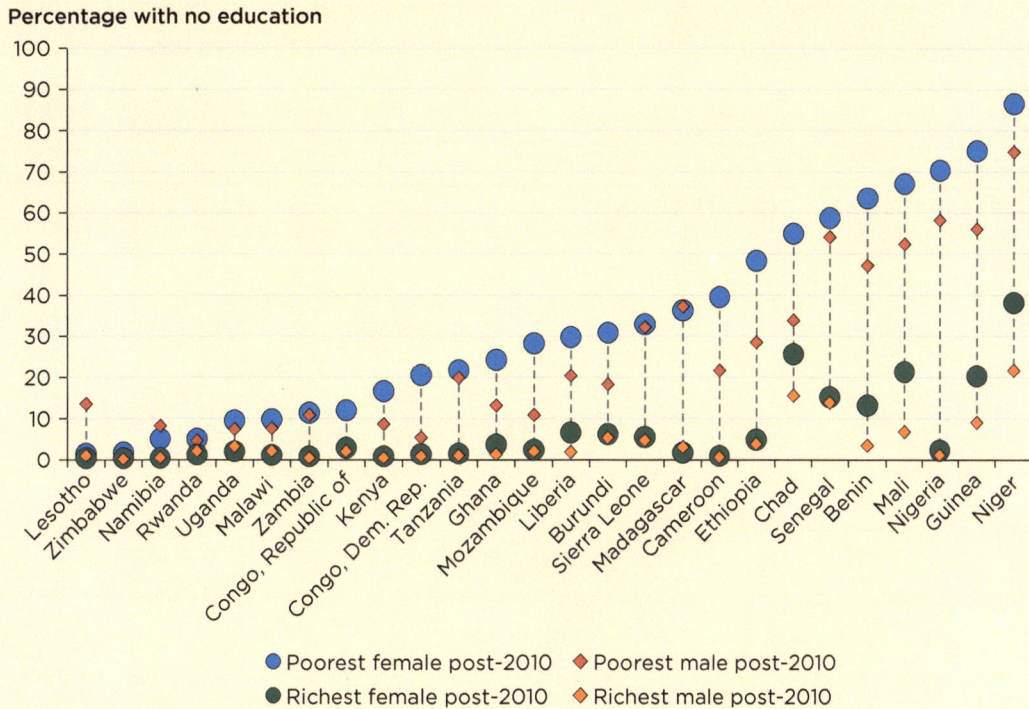

● Poorest female post-2010   ◆ Poorest male post-2010
● Richest female post-2010   ◆ Richest male post-2010

Source: World Bank, Demographic and Health Survey data, various years (https://dhsprogram.com/).

Development outcomes: the elusive economic parity

Although progress on the legal front is visible, gender gaps in human development and economic outcomes remain so wide in Africa that it is now the most gender-unequal continent (refer to map S2.1). The UN Gender Inequality Index for 2022 places the region below all others and shows little progress over time (UNDP 2022a, 2022b). Women in Africa are more active in the labor force and public services than women in other regions, but their human development indicators, such as secondary education, maternal mortality, and adolescent fertility, significantly lag those of other regions (Costa et al. 2023).

Moreover, women in Africa predominantly work in vulnerable jobs, and their productivity and earnings trail those of men (Costa et al. 2023). The documented gender differences in employment quality, productivity, and earnings contribute to a heterogeneous gender pay gap, closely linked to countries' stage of structural transformation and economic development. Indeed, in wealthier countries workers have greater access to wage employment (generally superior to self-employment), and the gender gap is narrower. This is also true for earnings (Van den Broeck, Kilic, and Pieters 2023). For example, Nigeria, at a more advanced stage, exhibits a smaller gender pay gap compared with Malawi and Tanzania. Educational discrepancies, occupational segregation, and location (urban versus rural) also explain the earnings gap.

MAP S2.1 Gender inequality across the world

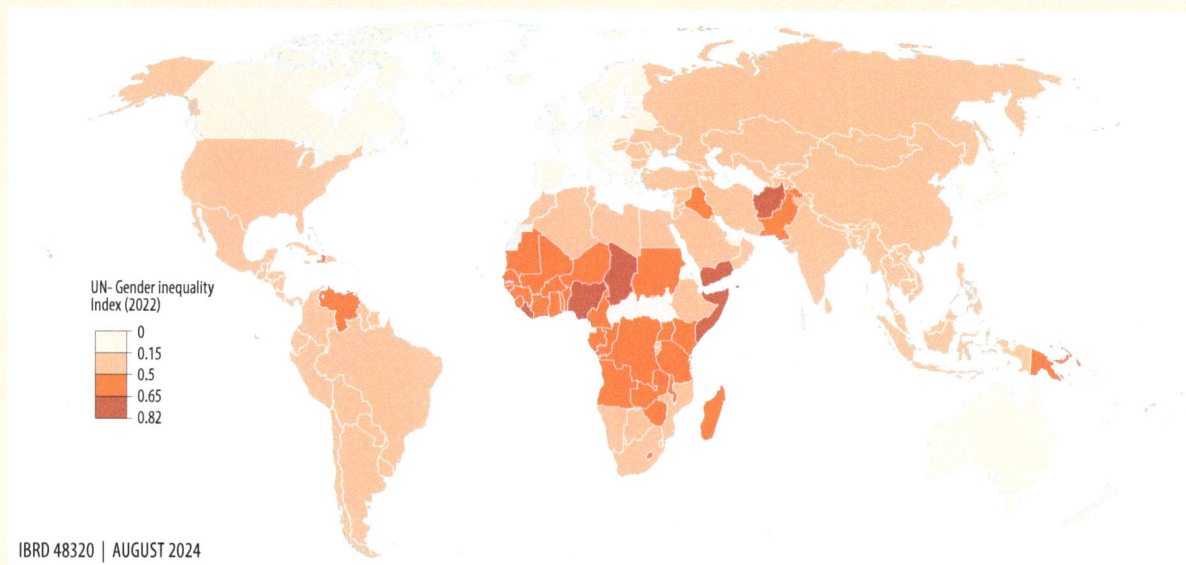

IBRD 48320 | AUGUST 2024

Source: UNDP 2022b.

Productivity gaps affect entrepreneurs and agricultural workers alike. Female-owned businesses consistently underperform male-owned ones, facing challenges such as fewer employees, lower sales, and less value added (World Bank 2019). Agricultural productivity is similarly estimated to be 13–25 percent lower for women-controlled plots, even when accounting for size and region (World Bank and ONE 2014).

For these outcomes, equality before the law is crucial. For women entrepreneurs, legal constraints and societal norms pose obstacles, limiting business ownership and perpetuating discriminatory practices (World Bank 2019). Gender-based violence further impedes well-being and managerial capacities (Morrison and Orlando 2004; Ouedraogo and Stenzel 2021). Education and skills gaps undermine women's confidence and resources to compete in male-dominated sectors (Carranza, Dhakal, and Love 2018; World Bank 2022). Limited access to financial resources hampers investment capacity (Suri and Jack 2016). In agriculture, factors such as land tenure systems, control issues, and restricted access to social networks undermine productivity for women, who also contend with reduced authority over household resource allocation (Gaddis, Lahoti, and Li 2018; World Bank and ONE 2014) and substantial time dedicated to nonremunerated activities (Dinkelman and Ngai 2022).

Social norms and the legal framework perpetuate a key inequality: agency

In Africa, gender gaps are largely fueled by disparities in agency, which are particularly evident in legal constraints surrounding marriage and divorce. Notably, four countries—Equatorial Guinea, Mali, Mauritania, and Sudan—have legal provisions mandating wives to obey husbands, and nine countries impede women from assuming head-of-household roles similar to those of men (World Bank 2024). Dissimilar divorce procedures for men and women exist in 10 countries, and 25 nations maintain distinct remarriage procedures. Shockingly, 12 countries lack specific legislation addressing domestic violence.

Legal recognition of women's nonmonetary contributions to households remains absent in 40 percent of African economies, limiting their economic autonomy. Nine economies deny women equal ownership rights to immovable property, and the same number restrict women from controlling jointly owned assets. Property inheritance rights are also unequal in 12 economies, favoring sons over daughters. Not surprisingly, systematic gender disparities persist in property ownership (refer to figure S2.2), with around 8 percent of married women owning land or housing alone, compared with about 25 percent of married men across 37 countries. These gender gaps are most pronounced in West Africa, whereas Southern Africa exhibits more even ownership.

FIGURE S2.2 **Sole ownership of assets among women and men**

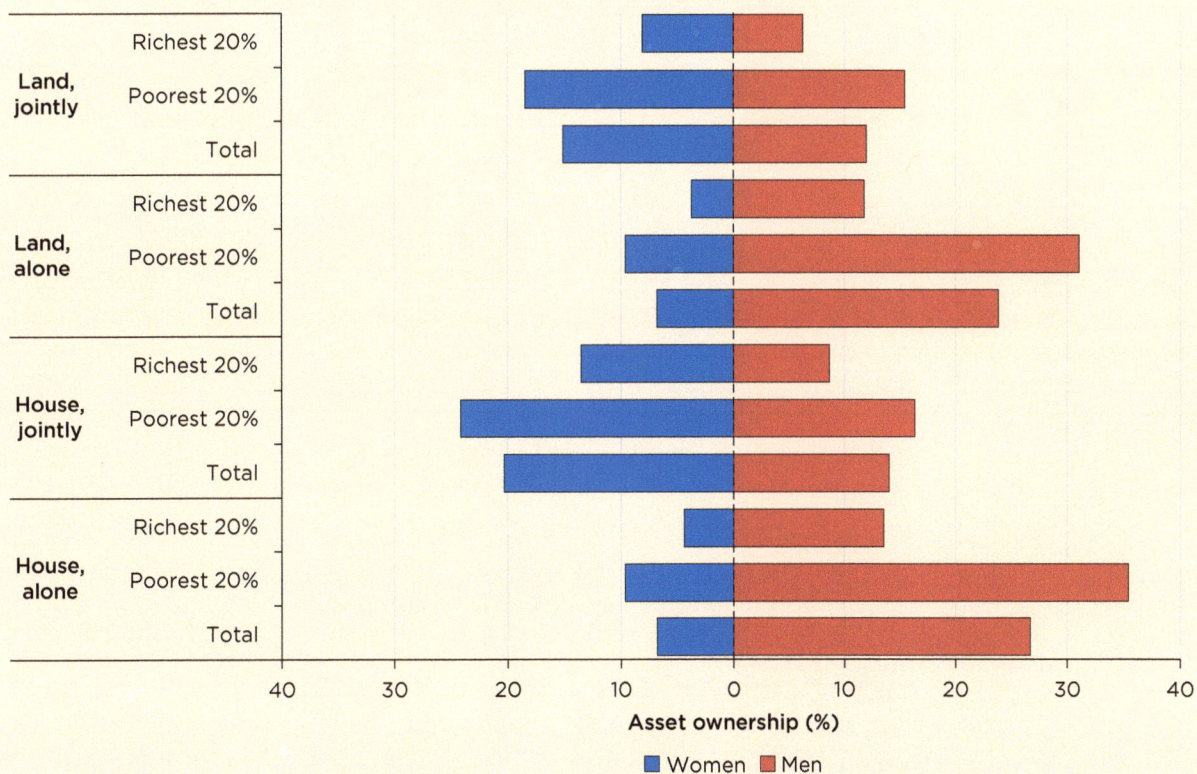

Source: World Bank, Demographic and Health Survey data, latest year available.

Studies underscore the pivotal role of women's asset ownership for household-level outcomes, affecting decision-making power, consumption, human capital investment, and intergenerational transfers. Maternal status significantly influences the well-being of the next generation, shaping nutrition, health, and overall development. However, an observed trade-off between women's increased agency and intimate partner violence (IPV) indicates a positive association between women's employment and both acceptance and experience of IPV, especially in areas with higher abuse tolerance and economic inequality (Cools and Kotsadam 2017; González-Brenes 2004).

Gender and the unrealized economic potential

The impact of gender inequality on a country's economic potential is often underestimated, particularly when focusing on poverty as the primary dimension. In Senegal, gender disparities in nonfood consumption within households were found to increase overall consumption inequality by 14 percent (De Vreyer and Lambert 2021), highlighting the significance of intrahousehold gender inequality in identifying vulnerable populations. Notably, nonmonetary deprivations persist among women, even in households not categorized as poor (Brown, Ravallion, and van de Walle 2019).

Addressing gender disparities is not only a matter of social justice but also a crucial step toward unlocking the full economic potential of the region. Several studies emphasize the economic benefits of addressing gender disparities, particularly in the labor market. Global estimates suggest that gender gaps in economic activity, including labor force participation, occupational segregation, and wage disparities, contribute to an average income loss of 15 percent, with 40 percent attributed to entrepreneurship disparities, disproportionately affecting developing countries (Cuberes and Teignier 2016). Conversely, enhancing women's labor market opportunities, measured by their increased share of employment, enhances aggregate technical efficiency and fosters economic growth, particularly in developing economies (Bargain and Lo Bue 2022; Bertay, Dordevic, and Sever 2020; Hazarika, Khraiche, and Kutlu 2023; Pervaiz et al. 2023).

The way forward: breaking the inertia of slow progress

Although gender disparities are prevalent across the region, some progress can be seen in recent years, especially on the legal front. A key fact conveys both good and bad news: most of the legal progress of the region is explained by about one-fourth of the countries. A pessimistic view is that most legislative bodies in the region have taken no action toward gender equality. An optimistic one is that there are about a half-dozen interesting models to follow. What did these countries do? What sparked the action? Are there replicable experiences? The answers to these questions will be valuable in paving the way for action on the legal front, reducing unnecessary barriers impeding equal opportunities for men and women.

However, the much-needed change must transcend the law, converting the vicious cycle that links norms and laws into a virtuous one (Benabou and Tirole 2011). This involves addressing inequality both in households (human rights abuses, gender roles, and human capital investments, among others) and in public spaces (equal opportunities in the labor market, in business developments, and in assets accumulation, among others). For most of these issues, single interventions and policies are not enough, and recent evidence clearly shows that the most significant progress results from multisectoral approaches that combine addressing financial barriers, building skills, increasing access to sexual and reproductive health, and changing the narrative around gender roles for men and women (Costa et al. 2023; Starrs et al. 2023).

Investing in women's human capital, reforming laws to ensure basic rights, and influencing social norm changes will boost the sustainability of incipient progress in human capital and economic outcomes, in this way expanding the virtuous cycle and realizing the potential of more egalitarian societies on their path to development.

References

AfDB (African Development Bank) and UNECA (United Nations Economic Commission for Africa). 2020. *Africa Gender Index Report 2019*. Abidjan, Côte d'Ivoire: African Development Bank Group.

African Union. 2003. *Protocol to the African Charter on Human and People's Rights on the Rights of Women in Africa*. Maputo, Mozambique: African Union. https://au.int/sites/default/files/treaties /37077-treaty-charter_on_rights_of_women_in_africa.pdf.

Bargain, Olivier, and Maria C. Lo Bue. 2021. "The Economic Gains of Closing the Employment Gender Gap: Evidence from Morocco." Working Paper 2021-79, World Institute for Development Economic Research, Helsinki.

Beegle, Kathleen, and Luc Christiaensen. 2019. *Accelerating Poverty Reduction in Africa*. Washington, DC: World Bank. http://hdl.handle.net/10986/32354.

Benabou, Roland, and Jean Tirole. 2011. "Laws and Norms." Working Paper 17579, National Bureau of Economic Research, Cambridge, MA.https://www.nber.org/system/files/working_papers/w17579 /w17579.pdf.

Bertay, Ata Can, Ljubica Dordevic, and Can Sever. 2020. "Gender Inequality and Economic Growth: Evidence from Industry-Level Data." Working Paper 20/119, International Monetary Fund, Washington, DC.

Broccolini, Chiara, Anna Fruttero, and Saanya Jain. 2023. "Revisiting Trends in Gender Equality." In *Gender Equality and Economic Development in Sub-Saharan Africa*, edited by Lisa L. Kolovich and Monique Newiak, 9–42. Washington, DC: International Monetary Fund.

Brown, Caitlin, Martin Ravallion, and Dominique van de Walle. 2019. "Most of Africa's Nutritionally Deprived Women and Children Are Not Found in Poor Households." *Review of Economics and Statistics* 101 (4): 631–44.

Carmichael, Fiona, Christian Darko, Shireen Kanji, and Nicholas Vasilakos. 2023. "The Contribution of Girls' Longer Hours in Unpaid Work to Gender Gaps in Early Adult Employment: Evidence from Ethiopia, India, Peru and Vietnam." *Feminist Economics* 29 (1): 1–37.

Carranza, Eliana, Chandra Dhakal, and Inessa Love. 2018. "Female Entrepreneurs: How and Why Are They Different?" Jobs Working Paper 20, World Bank, Washington, DC.

Cools, Sara, and Andreas Kotsadam. 2017. "Resources and Intimate Partner Violence in Sub-Saharan Africa," *World Development* 95, issue C, 211–30.

Costa, Rita D., Alina Kalle, Diana Milena Lopez Avila, Marilia Castelo Magalhaes, Miriam Muller, and Elizabeth Salazar. 2023. *What Works to Narrow Gender Gaps and Empower Women in Sub-Saharan Africa? An Evidence-Review of Selected Impact Evaluation Studies*. Washington, DC: World Bank. http://documents.worldbank.org/curated/en/099061623110030316/P1804940a8a04e0ab0988e 0e90727152914.

Cuberes, David, and Marc Teignier. 2016. "Aggregate Effects of Gender Gaps in the Labor Market: A Quantitative Estimate." *Journal of Human Capital* 10 (1): 1–32.

De Vreyer, Philippe, and Sylvie Lambert. 2021. "Inequality, Poverty, and the Intra-Household Allocation of Consumption in Senegal," *World Bank Economic Review*, 35 (2): 414–435. https://doi.org/10.1093/wber/lhz052.

Dinkelman, Taryn, and L. Rachel Ngai. 2022. "Time Use and Gender in Africa in Times of Structural Transformation." *Journal of Economic Perspectives* 36 (1): 57–80.

González-Brenes, M. 2004. "Domestic Violence and Household Decision-Making: Evidence from East Africa." Unpublished manuscript, University of Massachusetts, Amherst. https://www.sscnet.ucla .edu/polisci/wgape/papers/7_Gonzalez.pdf.

Gaddis, Isis, Rahul Lahoti, and Wenjie Li. 2018. "Gender Gaps in Property Ownership in Sub-Saharan Africa." Policy Research Working Paper 8573, World Bank, Washington, DC.

Hazarika, Gautam, Maroula Khraiche, and Levant Kutlu. 2023. "Gender Equity in Labor Market Opportunities and Aggregate Technical Efficiency: A Case of Equity Promoting Efficiency." *Applied Economics* 56 (23): 2806–17. https://doi.org/10.1080/00036846.2023.2203451.

Melesse, Dessalegn, Réka M. Cane, Aveneni Mangombe, Macellina Y. Ijadunola, Adom Manu, Eniola Bamgboye, Abdu Mohiddin, Rornald M. Kananura, Elsie Akwara, Elsabé du Plessis, Yohannes D. Wado, Martin K. Mutua, Wubegzier Mekonnen, Cheikh M. Faye, Sarah Neal, and Ties Boerma. 2021. "Inequalities in Early Marriage, Childbearing and Sexual Debut among Adolescents in Sub-Saharan Africa." *Reproductive Health* 18 (Supplement 1): 117. https://doi.org/10.1186/s12978 -021-01125-8.

Morrison, Andrew R., and Maria Beatriz Orlando. 2004. "The Costs and Impacts of Gender-Based Violence in Developing Countries: Methodological Considerations and New Evidence." Working Paper. Washington, DC: World Bank. http://documents.worldbank.org/curated/en/4422814 68339624395/The-cost-and-impacts-of-gender-based-violence-in-developing-countries -methodological-considerations-and-new-evidence.

Ouedraogo, Rasmané, and David Stenzel. 2021. "The Heavy Economic Toll of Gender-Based Violence: Evidence from Sub-Saharan Africa." Working Paper 21/277, International Monetary Fund, Washington, DC.

Parsons, J., J. Edmeades, A. Kes, S. Petroni, M. Sexton, and Q. Wodon. 2015. Economic Impacts of Child Marriage: A Review of the Literature." *Review of Faith & International Affairs* 13 (3): 12–22. https://doi.org/10.1080/15570274.2015.1075757.

Pervaiz, Zahid, Shahla Akram, Sajjad Ahmad Jan, and Amatul R. Chaudhary. 2023. "Is Gender Equality Conducive to Economic Growth of Developing Countries?" *Cogent Social Sciences* 9: 2. https://doi .org/10.1080/23311886.2023.2243713.

Starrs, Ann, Alex Ezeh, Gilda Sedgh, and Susheela Singh. 2023. "To Achieve Development Goals, Advance Sexual and Reproductive Health and Rights." *Lancet* 403 (10429): 787–89. https://doi .org/10.1016/S0140-6736(23)02360-7.

Suri, Tavneet, and William Jack. 2016. "The Long-Run Poverty and Gender Impacts of Mobile Money." *Science* 354 (6317): 1288–92.

UNDP (United Nations Development Programme). 2022a. "Gender Development Index (GDI)." Human Development Reports. New York: UNDP. https://hdr.undp.org/gender-development -index#/indicies/GDI.

UNDP (United Nations Development Programme). 2022b. "Gender Inequality Index (GII)." Human Development Reports. New York: UNDP. https://hdr.undp.org/data-center/thematic-composite -indices/gender-inequality-index#/indicies/GII.

UNICEF (United Nations Children's Fund). 2024. "Over 230 Million Girls and Women Worldwide Have Undergone Female Genital Mutilation." https://data.unicef.org/topic/child-protection /female-genital-mutilation/.

Van den Broeck, Goedele, Talip Kilic, and Janneke Pieters. 2023. "Structural Transformation and the Gender Pay Gap in Sub-Saharan Africa." *PLoS ONE* 18 (4): e0278188. https://doi.org/10.1371 /journal.pone.0278188.

World Bank. 2012. *World Development Report 2012: Gender Equality and Development*. Washington, DC: World Bank. https://openknowledge.worldbank.org/entities/publication/51c285f6 -0200-590c-97d3-95b937be3271.

World Bank. 2019. *Profiting from Parity. Unlocking the Potential of Women's Businesses in Africa*. Washington, DC: World Bank. https://documents1.worldbank.org/curated/en /501971553025918098/pdf/Main-Report.pdf.

World Bank. 2022. *Breaking Barriers: Female Entrepreneurs Who Cross Over to Male-Dominated Sectors*. Washington, DC: World Bank. http://hdl.handle.net/10986/36940.

World Bank. 2024. *Women, Business and the Law 2024*. Washington, DC: World Bank. https://doi .org/10.1596/978-1-4648-2063-2.

World Bank and ONE. 2014. *Levelling the Field: Improving Opportunities for Women Farmers in Africa*. Washington, DC: World Bank. https://documents1.worldbank.org/curated/en /579161468007198488/pdf/860390WP0WB0ON0osure0date0March0180.pdf.

CHAPTER 4

Workers, Firms, and Farms Face an Unlevel Playing Field in Using Their Productive Capacities

NISTHA SINHA, ELWYN DAVIES, ALASTAIR HAYNES, AND REGINA PLENINGER

Chapter highlights

Incomes in the Africa region are highly unequal because people face an unlevel playing field in using their productive capacities. This unlevel playing field creates structural sources of income inequality. Distortions faced by firms and farms create unequal access to good earning opportunities in two ways: first, they curb the creation of high-quality and well-paying wage jobs, making them accessible to only a few workers, largely in the public sector; and second, they constrain the productivity and profitability of firms and farms, dampening earnings for those engaged in these activities. As a result, many end up in low-productivity and low-paying fallback activities. An understanding of the distortions that create an unlevel playing field for firms and farms opens policy entry points to address inequality from the production side of the economy:

- Promoting market-based innovations to improve firms' and farms' access to capital and technology

- Expanding their market access

- Facilitating the matching of workers and employers

- Promoting competition, gender-equal labor laws, macroeconomic stability, and access to justice.

Pursuing these policies could also pay off in spurring economy-wide growth in productivity.

Structural inequality in using productive capacity is linked to market distortions

Studies of income inequality usually focus on billionaires and top income earners; however, this chapter focuses on income inequality among the majority of the population. Data on Africa's billionaires are scarce, but survey data on African households' income are available for several countries since 2010. People deploy their productive capacity to earn income from three sources: wage work in firms or the public sector, running household enterprises, and wage or self-employment in agriculture. African households typically have members who bring in income from multiple sources. Total household income resulting from these earned and nonearned sources (remittances, social safety transfers) displays high levels of inequality. In 12 countries studied for this report, the Gini indexes of per capita total incomes exceed 50 (refer to figure 4.1). A decomposition of total income inequality shows that wage income and household enterprise income account for almost all income disparities; whereas wages and household enterprise incomes push up inequality, agricultural incomes tend to have an equalizing effect.[1]

Where people use their productive capacity and the type of job they have varies across the income distribution (refer to figures 4.2a and 4.2b). Household incomes in the lowest deciles are dominated by agricultural earnings. Incomes in the top deciles are dominated by wage earnings. Wage employment in productive establishments tends to

FIGURE 4.1 Inequality in total and wage income: Gini index

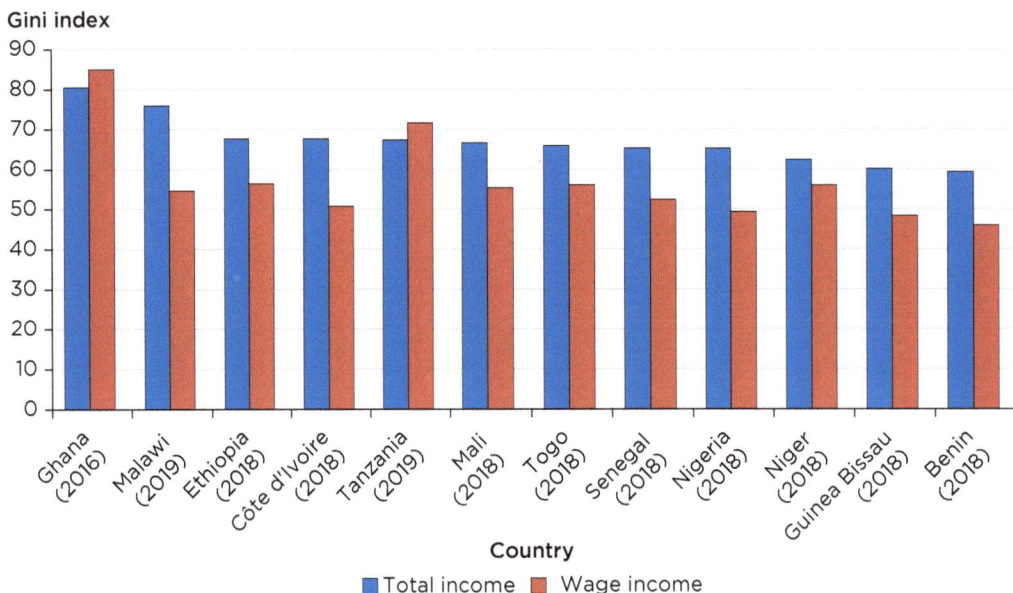

Sources: World Bank calculations based on Living Standards Measurement Study (https://www
.worldbank.org/en/programs/lsms) and West Africa Economic Monetary Union surveys for
respective countries (ANSD 2022).
Note: Total household income is per capita; wage income is at the individual level.

FIGURE 4.2 Share of households with the largest income source from agriculture, household enterprises, or wage jobs, by consumption deciles

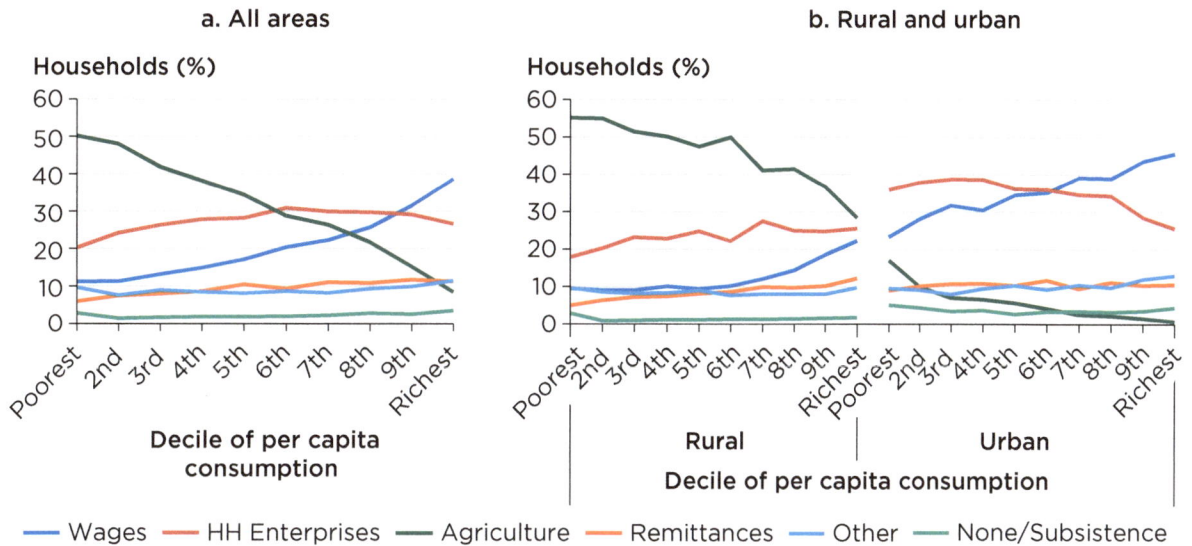

a. All areas

b. Rural and urban

Wages — HH Enterprises — Agriculture — Remittances — Other — None/Subsistence

Sources: World Bank calculations based on Living Standards Measurement Study surveys (https://www.worldbank .org/en/programs/lsms) from Ethiopia, Ghana, Malawi, Nigeria, Tanzania, and Uganda and the West Africa Economic Monetary Union (ANSD 2022).
Note: Household (HH) enterprises include own-account workers. The shares presented are the cross-country average for each consumption decile.

provide the highest and most robust earning opportunities. Nonfarm household enterprises—which include own-account workers—contribute to incomes across the consumption distribution. After agriculture, rural families rely on earnings from nonfarm household enterprises. The contribution of wage earnings is rather limited in rural areas, but its contribution to total income rises with consumption deciles. Urban families derive income mainly from own-account work, household enterprises, and wage work. Among the poorest urban families, income from own-account work and household enterprises is the largest income source for just under 40 percent of households. Urban families' reliance on wage earnings rises sharply with income, with wages forming the largest source of total income for the richest 40 percent of families (sixth decile and higher).

The rich/poor disparities in income sources arise from a number of sources, including how much productive capacities people own, gender norms about work, and the skills intensity of production technology. This chapter focuses on the role of structural conditions—distortions faced by firms and farms during the production process—in shaping the distribution of incomes in the region. Evidence suggests that such distortions are large in Africa region (Calderón 2022). These distortions create unequal access to good earnings opportunities in two ways. First, they curb the creation of high-quality and well-paying wage jobs, making them accessible to only a few workers. Such jobs are often mainly found in the public sector. Second, they constrain the productivity and profitability

FIGURE 4.3 Cross-country correlation between Gini index and size of the wage sector

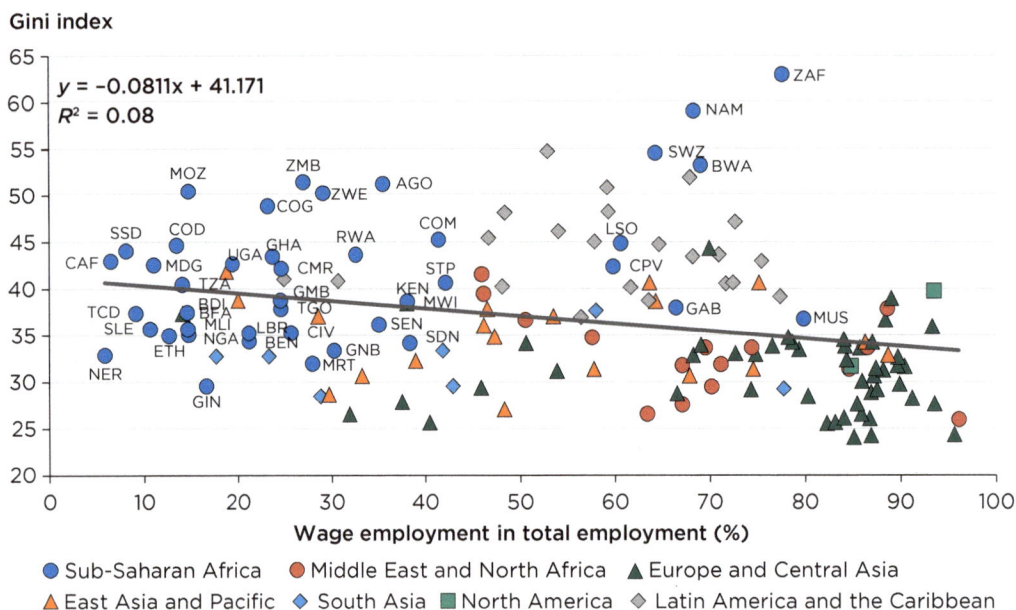

Source: Original figure for this publication based on estimates using data from the World Bank's World Development Indicators (https://databank.worldbank.org/source/world-development-indicators).
Note: Gray line represents correlation. Gini index for consumption distribution except for countries in Latin America and Caribbean. For country abbreviations, refer to https://www.iso.org/obp /ui/#search.

of firms and farms, dampening earnings for those engaged in these activities. As a result, many end up in low-productivity and low-paying fallback activities. Looking across the globe, country-level consumption inequality tends to be higher in countries with a low share of employment in wage jobs (and a corresponding higher share of self-employment; refer to figure 4.3). Within Africa itself, the negative correlation between consumption inequality and wage share of employment is less evident because of Southern African countries that are resource rich and have historically had high inequality levels.

An understanding of the distortions that create an unlevel playing field for firms and farms opens policy entry points to address income inequality. An important consequence of these distortions is that differences in productivity across firms and farms are driven by the way markets function, as opposed to differences in firm talents, management capacities, and efforts. For example, a wage worker in a firm that is unable to sell to new customers because of unfair market access might see a lower return to their labor than a wage worker in a firm that has privileged market access. Labor market frictions might prevent a worker from moving to the better-paying firm. Another consequence of the distortions is that most firms and farms are smaller in scale than they could be in the absence of distortions, resulting in less wage job creation and therefore fewer opportunities for income mobility. If the unprivileged firm cannot expand because of these market frictions, it might forgo recruiting a new worker, who might then end up in self-employment and likely achieve lower productivity—and lower earnings—in that activity. Even if these workers have similar productive potential, these market distortions will likely create inequalities in outcomes. To the extent that market and institutional distortions create an unequal playing field, some firms and farms will be prevented from reaching their productive potential. These distortions also lead to misallocation of resources in the economy, which hurts growth (Restuccia and Rogerson 2017). Tackling these market distortions would therefore have an additional payoff in spurring productivity growth.

The rest of the chapter is organized in three sections. A description of the jobs landscape in the region details the characteristics of income sources—the firms and farms where people use their productive capacities. This is followed by a diagnostic of how market distortions in input, product, and labor markets affect firm and farm performance. Although the historical origins of Africa's weak productivity performance have been well documented, this report focuses on examining these disparities as they exist today and their implications looking ahead (refer to, for example, Nunn 2007, 2014). Using these diagnostic findings, the last section concludes the chapter with a discussion of four policy directions that the countries in the region could pursue to level the playing field for firms and farms.

Africa's jobs and earnings challenge lies in where people work, not in whether they work

Nonwage income is the most important earning source in the region. Most employment is also concentrated in nonwage activities. Because the process of economic development is typically accompanied by a rise in wage employment, this report refers to agriculture and nonfarm household enterprises as fallback sectors. Given the limited wage employment opportunities, these fallback sectors play a vital role in providing earning opportunities, particularly for those with low or no education. Household enterprises are an important part of the process of structural transformation in the region, providing nonfarm earning sources, especially in urban areas (Beegle and Christiaensen 2019). The important role played by household enterprises as a source of nonagricultural employment could diminish if wage sector employment expands, as has been found to be the case in Viet Nam (Oostendorp, Trung, and Tung 2009). The region's jobs and earnings challenge stems from the fact that the average scale of firms, including household enterprises and farms, tends to be small, and this in turn contributes to the income inequality described in the previous section. Nevertheless, workers in fallback sectors tend to be heterogeneous in both potential and performance; some might have the capabilities to transition out but face constraints in doing so, whereas others opt for self-employment out of preference rather than necessity.

Labor force participation is high and mostly in nonwage work

A large share of the region's working-age population participates in the labor force. In globally comparable estimates, the share of 15- to 64-year-olds (that is, those of working age) in 2022 who participated in economic activities in Africa is among the highest, at 68 percent, similar to Latin America (69 percent) and higher than South Asia (55 percent) and the Middle East and North Africa (45 percent).[2] In Africa, labor force participation rates do not vary by poverty status, and employment status (whether someone works) is itself not a major driver of poverty or income inequality (refer to figure 4.4a).[3] There are nevertheless some differences across countries. Employment as a percentage of the total working-age population is below 50 percent in resource-rich but nonfragile countries, a group that includes Southern African countries (refer to figure 4.4b). These countries also have high unemployment rates because of structural distortions that affect both the demand and the supply sides of the labor market (Sulla, Zikhali, and Cuevas 2022). Southern African countries' labor force participation rates are also in line with those of upper-middle-income countries because richer countries tend to have lower employment rates. Poorer countries tend to have higher labor force participation rates because many must rely on necessity employment. Accordingly, labor force participation rates are highest in resource-rich and fragile countries, a group of countries with the lowest per capita gross domestic product and high extreme poverty.

FIGURE 4.4 Characteristics of the labor force, ages 15–64, Africa region

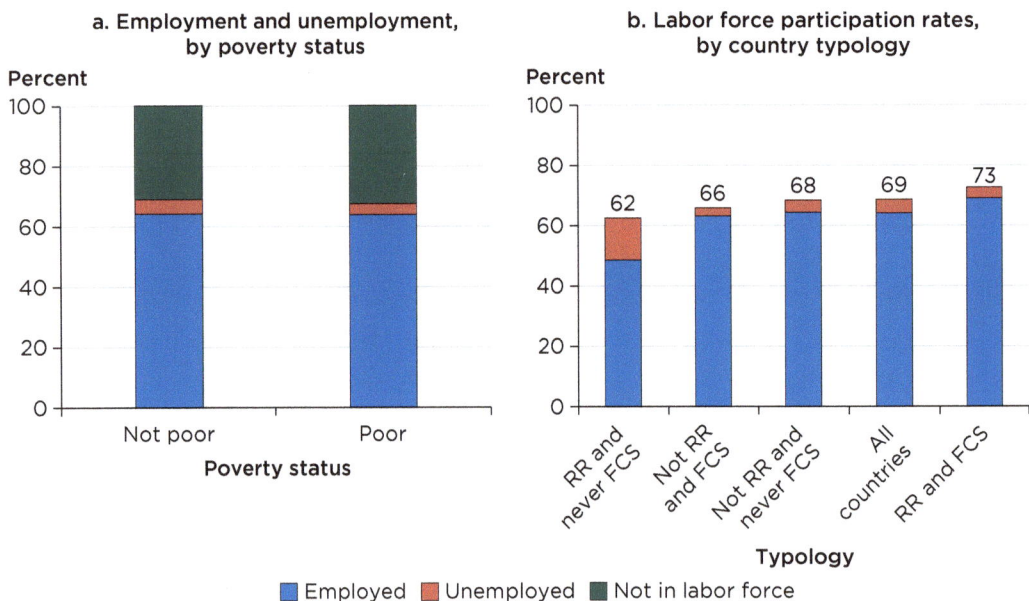

a. Employment and unemployment, by poverty status

b. Labor force participation rates, by country typology

Legend: ■ Employed ■ Unemployed ■ Not in labor force

Source: Harmonized household survey data for African countries (2013–19).
Note: Panel a shows shares of those who are employed, unemployed, and not engaged in either activity among the working-age population who are poor and nonpoor using the $2.15 international poverty line (2017 purchasing power parity). Unemployed individuals are those seeking work but not employed. In panel b, labor force participation consists of those who are employed in economic activities and those who are seeking work but not employed.
FCS = countries that have ever experienced fragility, conflict, and violence situation;
RR = countries that are resource rich.

Most workers are engaged in nonwage employment, a reliance on fallback sectors that is higher than in other regions. According to globally comparable estimates, just less than one-quarter (22 percent) of workers are in wage employment across African countries. This share remains below that of South Asia (27 percent) and less than half of that seen in the East Asia and Pacific (52 percent), Latin America and Caribbean (63 percent), and Middle East and North Africa (65 percent) regions (World Development Indicators and International LO Modelled Estimates Database.[4] Household surveys in the region show that about half of workers are self-employed. The share of wage employment rises with income, but self-employment in household enterprises or agricultural work remains important (refer to figure 4.5a). Unpaid work on family farms and household enterprises, mostly carried out by women, declines sharply with income. Women are more likely to be self-employed (particularly in running household enterprises) and are less likely to be in wage work. The share of economic activity that is in wage jobs is the highest in countries that have not experienced fragility or conflict; for this group of countries, the share of wage jobs is close to 30 percent (refer to figure 4.5b). Fragile and conflict-affected countries, regardless of their reliance on natural resources, have less wage employment. Reliance on agriculture as a main source of income is high. On average, close to 60 percent of all workers in fragile and conflict-affected situation (FCS) countries and 40 percent in non-FCS countries are engaged in agriculture. Over time, the average share of employment in agriculture has declined in Africa because many workers have moved to nonfarm work, especially in nonfarm household enterprises (Christiaensen and Maertens 2022).

FIGURE 4.5 Structure of employment, Africa region

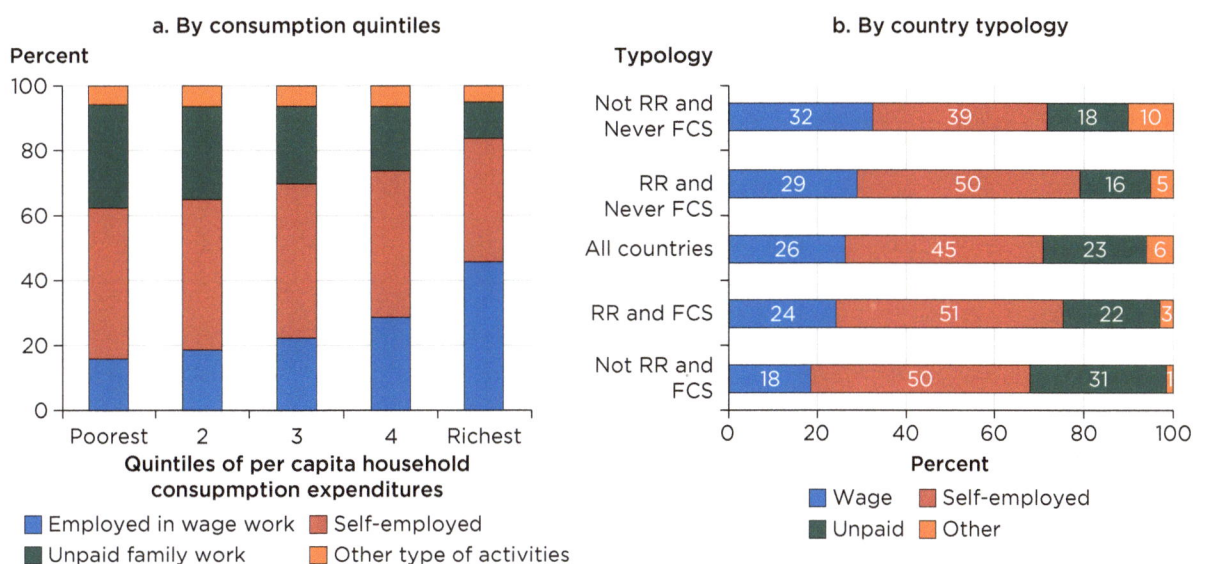

a. By consumption quintiles

Percent

Quintiles of per capita household consupmtion expenditures

- Employed in wage work
- Self-employed
- Unpaid family work
- Other type of activities

b. By country typology

Typology

Typology	Wage	Self-employed	Unpaid	Other
Not RR and Never FCS	32	39	18	10
RR and Never FCS	29	50	16	5
All countries	26	45	23	6
RR and FCS	24	51	22	3
Not RR and FCS	18	50	31	

Percent

- Wage
- Self-employed
- Unpaid
- Other

Source: Harmonized household survey data for African countries (2013–19).
Note: Data reflect share of those employed ages 15 to 64 who are in wage employment, self-employment, unpaid work, and uncategorized activities. Self-employment includes work in agriculture. FCS = countries that have ever experienced fragility, conflict, and violence situations; RR = countries that are resource rich.

Workers, Firms, and Farms Face an Unlevel Playing Field in Using Their Productive Capacities

FIGURE 4.6 Share of wage employment in the public sector

Percent

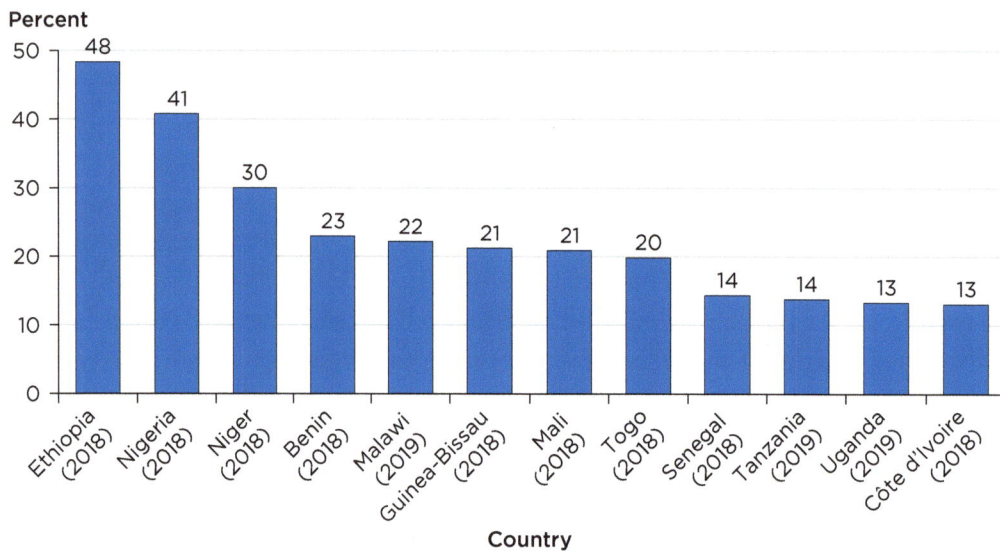

Sources: Estimates based on Living Standards Measurement Study (https://www.worldbank.org/en/programs/lsms) and West Africa Economic Monetary Union surveys for 2018–19 (ANSD 2022).

The public sector is an important source of wage employment, but its share varies (refer to figure 4.6). In countries such as Ethiopia and Nigeria, more than 40 percent of all wage workers are employed in the public sector as administrators, teachers, and doctors. However, the share of the public sector in wage employment is less than 15 percent in countries such as Côte d'Ivoire, Senegal, Tanzania, and Uganda. Where the public sector accounts for a large share of wage workers, it is also a large employer of tertiary-educated workers: more than 60 percent of tertiary-educated workers in Ethiopia, Nigeria, and Niger are in the public sector. Across countries, it is mainly the better-off households that rely on public sector wages. Unequal opportunities for people to access public wage employment can be another source of inequality.

There is heterogeneity in earnings from each of the income sources

Because workers' movement between wage and nonwage sectors tends to be limited, productivity within the wage and fallback sectors matters for the distribution of earnings. Across the globe, longitudinal household data on workers' employment transitions show limited transitions between household firms or farms and larger organized economic structures (Donovan, Lu, and Schoellman 2023). Data from a longitudinal household survey in Uganda also show little movement of workers from family enterprises to the wage job sector between 2016 and 2018, but those in wage jobs were likely to move to agriculture or household enterprises; workers were more likely to move between farm work and work in household enterprises. Studies from Ghana, South Africa, Tanzania, and Uganda have also documented little movement between self-employment and wage work, a pattern unlike those found for Latin American countries (Danquah, Schotte, and Sen 2019).

FIGURE 4.7 Distribution of per capita wage, household enterprise, and agricultural revenues

Probability density

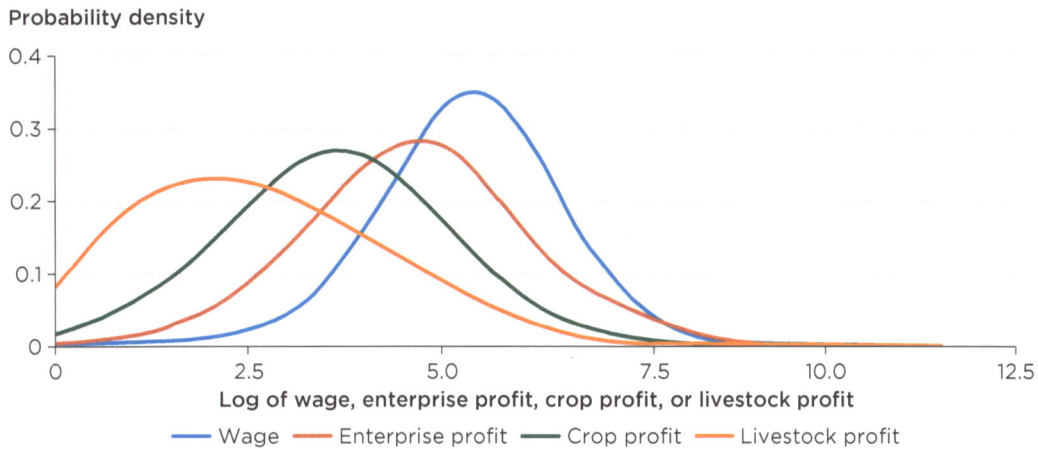

Sources: Based on harmonized Living Standards Measurement Study and West Africa Economic Monetary Union surveys.
Note: Figure shows probability density functions of each income source (wage, enterprise profit, crop profit, livestock profit) expressed in purchasing power parity ($). Log refers to natural logarithm.

Although average wages are higher, household enterprise owners do not necessarily earn less than wage workers, and the distribution of enterprise revenues overlaps to a considerable extent with the distribution of wages (refer to figure 4.7). Revenues from these enterprises show a high degree of dispersion. The significant contribution of household enterprises to the total income of richer urban households suggests that some of these businesses may be highly productive. A survey from Côte d'Ivoire shows that for most urban informal enterprise owners, the activity is a preferred option; 30 percent report that this preference is due to better earnings relative to salaried work, and another 35 percent report that they value the independence (Karlen et al. 2023). Studies of factories in Ethiopia's industrial parks also confirm that workers face poor working conditions that also affect worker retention (Abebe, Buehren, and Goldstein 2020). Crop and livestock earnings of family farms tend to be the lowest among all household income sources. This finding is consistent with the lower productivity in the farm sector. A study of six countries (Ethiopia, Malawi, Mali, Niger, Nigeria, and Tanzania) found that from 2008 to 2019, there was virtually no productivity growth among smallholder crop growers (Wollburg et al. 2024).

The scale of operations is small, which affects productivity and earnings

Much of the economic activity in Africa takes place in small-scale firms and farms, even in the organized formal sector firms. The average African manufacturing establishment employs six workers, compared with 19 workers in East Asia and 16 workers in high-income countries. A similar pattern can be seen in the services sector. There are few large firms: business establishment censuses in four countries that cover both registered and unregistered establishments across the size distribution suggest that only 5 percent of business establishments employ 10 or more employees (Abreha et al. 2022). This is much lower than in developed economies. For example, in the United States, 28 percent of establishments employ 10 or more employees (refer to figure 4.8). Only one-quarter (26 percent) of workers in Africa are employed in firms with more than 100 employees, compared with 45 percent in the United States. Household surveys show a similar picture of limited wage employment in larger-scale firms. For example, in Nigeria and Uganda, only 5 and 6 percent of all workers, respectively, are employed in an establishment with more than 20 employees.

FIGURE 4.8 Firm size and employment distribution in Africa and the United States

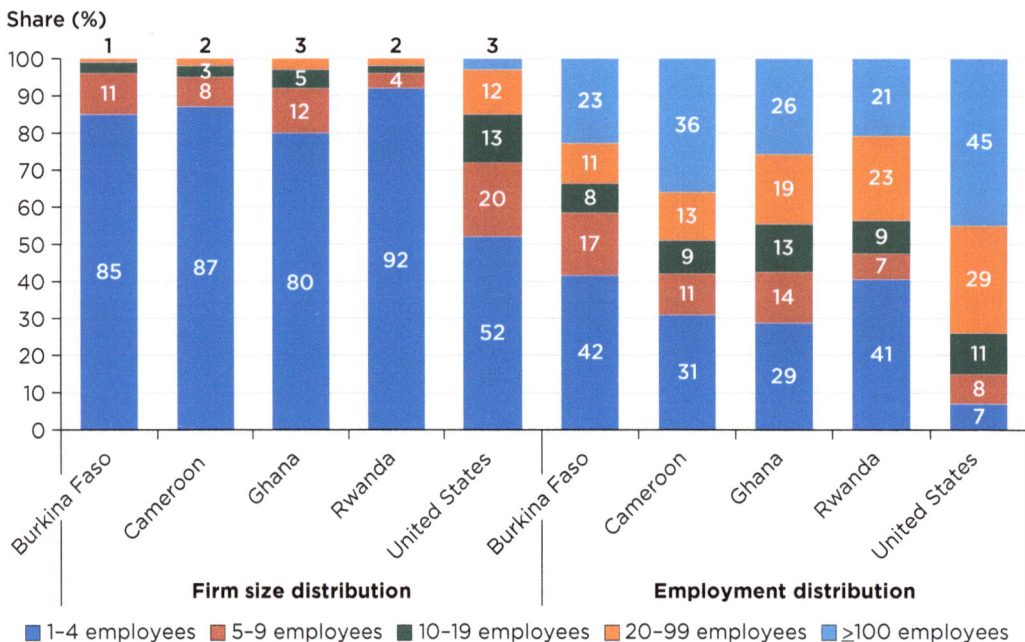

Source: Abreha et al. (2022), based on establishment census data and U.S. Business Dynamics Statistics.
Note: Firm size is measured by number of employees. Figure shows share of firms by size of firm and share of employment across firms by size of firm. Data for Africa are based on census data covering both registered and unregistered business establishments, across all sectors in the economy. Year of coverage is as follows: Burkina Faso, 2015; Cameroon, 2008; Ghana, 2013; Rwanda, 2013; and the United States, 2013.

FIGURE 4.9 Average firm size over the firm life cycle

Number of employees

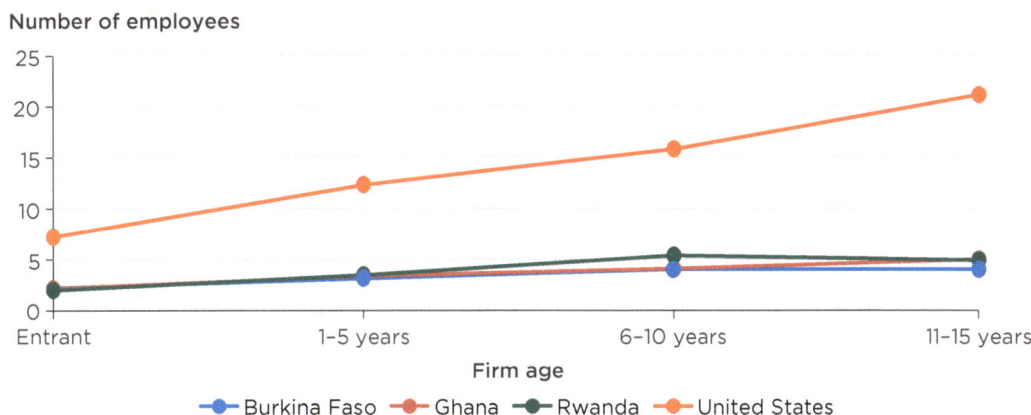

Source: Abreha et al. (2022), based on establishment census data and U.S. Business Dynamics Statistics.
Note: Employment distributions for Africa are based on census data covering both registered and unregistered business establishments in the manufacturing sector. Year of coverage is as follows: Burkina Faso, 2015; Cameroon, 2008; Ghana, 2013; Rwanda, 2013; and the United States, 2013.

Limited transitions between firm types and employment and limited growth of firms lead to significant gaps between frontier firms and the rest of the economy. In many African countries, there are significant gaps in productivity between the most productive frontier firms in the economy and the rest of the economy. Distributions of employment in firms as well as productivity distributions in farms appear to have a "missing middle"—an overrepresentation of small-scale firms, few mid-sized firms, and a small but important group of frontier firms (see, for example, Abreha et al. 2022).[5] This is the result not only of a preponderance of many small-scale, often informal enterprises but also of a general lack of growth of firms. Whereas a mature manufacturing firm (one between 11 and 15 years old) in the United States employs about 15 more employees than an entrant firm and is three times larger, mature manufacturing firms in Burkina Faso, Ghana, and Rwanda employ only two or three more workers and are only slightly more than double in size (refer to figure 4.9).

As in the organized sector, household-owned and -managed enterprises tend to be small. In a sample of 12 countries with comparable definitions of household enterprises, between 60 percent and 80 percent of enterprises are solo operated (refer to figure 4.10). Between 12 and 30 percent have two or more people working in them (including the owner). A small share of the enterprises, ranging from 9 percent in Guinea-Bissau, Malawi, and Uganda to 20 percent in Niger, report hiring labor—a factor that matters for their productivity. Household enterprises are typically unorganized and unregistered, relying mainly on family labor and operating out of homes or mobile locations. This group of enterprises is often associated with informality, although informality covers many different practices and is a sector with considerable

FIGURE 4.10 Size distribution of household enterprises by number of workers, including owner-operator

Percent

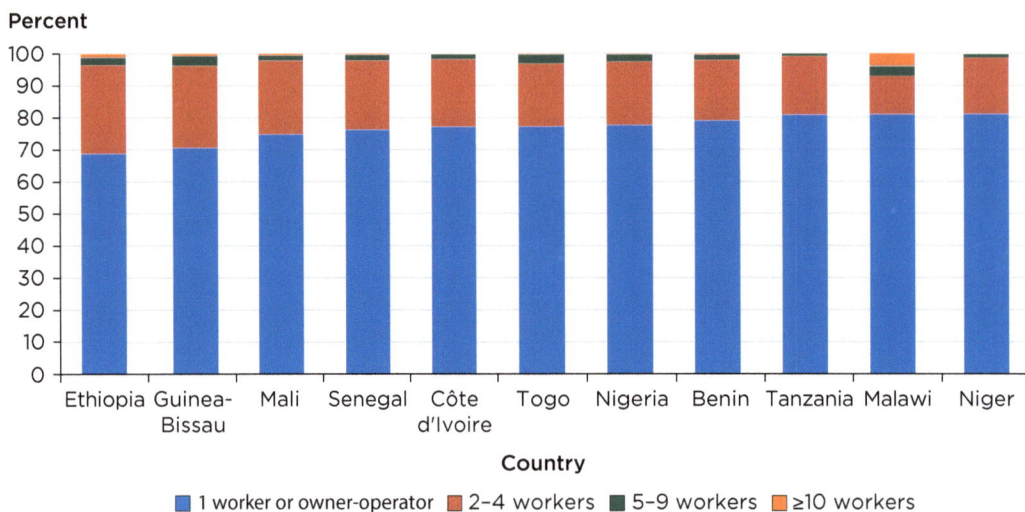

Sources: World Bank calculations using household survey data from Living Standards Measurement Study (https://www.worldbank.org/en/programs/lsms) and West Africa Economic Monetary Union surveys (ANSD 2022).
Note: Figures do not add up to 100% because some households did not report number of workers.

heterogeneity (refer to box 4.1). These enterprises are also quite heterogeneous, as recently conducted surveys in West Africa Economic Monetary Union (WAEMU) countries demonstrate. Both poor and nonpoor households operate household enterprises. In Guinea-Bissau, Senegal, and Togo, more than 60 percent of both poor and nonpoor households run enterprises. Across the WAEMU countries, for instance, 60 percent or more of household enterprises are owned by women (except in Mali and Niger). Qualitative studies from Angola and Liberia show that for women, this fallback activity is an opportunity to flexibly earn an income and look after their families (World Bank 2023c). Enterprises owned by women are more likely to be solo operated than those owned by men.

Family farms are small scale, with holdings under 2 hectares. According to a global estimation of the number and size of farms, in 2000 there were 570 million farms, 475 million of which were smaller than 2 hectares and 500 million of which were family farms that relied entirely on family labor (Lowder, Skoet, and Raney 2016). In line with these figures, an estimated 70–80 percent of farms in Africa were smaller than 2 hectares. In Ethiopia, for example, the average landholding in rural areas is close to 1 hectare (World Bank 2022). The process of structural transformation is expected to bring some farmland consolidation and the emergence of wage labor in agriculture. Some evidence has shown that African countries such as Ghana, Kenya, Tanzania, and Zambia have started to experience farmland consolidation, with a rise in the share of farmland holdings larger than 5 hectares, raising concerns about a rise in inequality in rural areas (Jayne et al. 2016). The impetus for this consolidation appears to be land acquisition by urban households.

BOX 4.1

Informality: A driver or a symptom of low performance?

Many of the economic activities in Africa—and especially those in which poor individuals are engaged—are characterized by informality. Informality usually describes a whole range of practices that are not compliant with the law, including businesses that lack registration or licenses (business informality), workers who are employed without a contract or for whom no social security contributions are made (employment informality), and tax avoidance (tax informality). In some cases, informality is taken as being synonymous with a lack of organization (for example, not keeping records) or firms being of a small scale (refer to, for example, La Porta and Shleifer 2014).

Informal status is generally associated with lower revenue, profits, employment, and productivity. The literature has raised the question of whether informality is a driver of low performance or whether it is mostly a symptom of it. La Porta and Shleifer (2014) describe three views of informality: one that emphasizes that informality is holding back firms (commonly associated with De Soto 2007), one that emphasizes the unfair competition of the informal sector for firms in the formal sector (the parasite view), and one that emphasizes informality as the consequence of low capabilities (the survival view).

There is a growing understanding of the heterogeneity of the informal sector. Ulyssea (2018) argues that the three views described by La Porta and Shleifer (2014) are not contradictory but instead describe the heterogeneity of the informal sector: some firms could thrive in the formal sector, some might take advantage of not having to comply with all regulations, and others might be the result of "necessity entrepreneurship." Diao, Kweka, and Mcmillan (2016) use firm-level data from Tanzania to argue that although many informal firms perform below formal firms, there is a substantial "in-between" sector of informal firms whose productivity overlaps that of formal and informal firms. Analyses of World Bank Enterprise Surveys data on informal firms, collected using an adaptive cluster sampling approach, show important heterogeneity of both characteristics and performance of informal firms. Aga et al. (2021) show that although most informal firms underperform their formal counterparts, a group of 7.6 percent of informal firms exists that in their characteristics and productivity levels resemble formal firms.

Interventions focusing on formalization have shown some success in increasing registration rates by simplifying the procedure (Kaplan, Piedra, and Seira 2011; Mullainathan, and Schnabl 2010), providing information to increase transparency (Campos, Goldstein, and McKenzie 2023), increasing enforcement (De Andrade, Bruhn, and McKenzie 2014), or providing financial incentives (De Mel, McKenzie, and Woodruff 2013). However, the evidence on whether formalization also increases business performance is more mixed. For example, the field experiment in Malawi by Campos, Goldstein, and McKenzie (2023) resulted in 70 percent of targeted firms registering, but there was no impact on business performance. More success has been had with complementary interventions—for example, combining formalization with facilitating access to finance (Campos et al. 2018)—or when the focus is limited to specific high-potential groups of firms. De Mel et al. (2013) highlight that formalization after a financial incentive increased performance significantly for about 5 percent of firms.

(continued)

BOX 4.1

Informality: a driver or a symptom of low performance? *(continued)*

Given the heterogeneity of the informal sector, the context specificity of local formalization requirements, and correlations with other explanatory factors, this report does not use informality as a key organizing characteristic for firms but rather focuses on employment types (wage vs. nonwage employment) and firm size (including whether the firm is a sole entrepreneur or a larger business). This is not to say that informality is not important: it often correlates strongly with employment type, firm size, and firm performance, and as the literature has shown, formalization can be meaningful for certain groups of firms or when combined with other interventions.

For firms, the scale of operations matters for productivity and for the earnings of workers employed by them. The limited role of larger-scale establishments in Africa has ramifications for productivity and earnings. Size is an important determinant of productivity: economies of scale increase the efficiency of firms' production. A large manufacturing firm in a low- or middle-income country is about 2.4 times more productive than a micro-sized one, and in the services sector it is about 1.6 times more productive (Nayyar, Hallward-Driemeier, and Davies 2021).[6] Controlling for workers' gender and education level, wage workers in larger firms (≥20 employees) in a sample of African countries, including Ethiopia and Nigeria, earn significantly more (refer to figure 4.11a). This is also the case with household enterprises—businesses with more two or more workers earn significantly higher revenues than those that are solo operated (refer to figure 4.11b). Household enterprises that hire workers could be a select group (greater entrepreneurial talent, higher start-up capital, or other unobserved characteristics) that is hard to account for. Completing primary or a higher level of education brings higher wage earnings as well as higher enterprise revenues. Taken together, these results show that scale paired with more education can significantly boost earnings. Inequality of opportunities to scale up or obtain more education could therefore translate into unequal distribution of earnings.

Women fare worse than men in earnings. All else being equal, male-run household enterprises earn significantly more than female-run enterprises, and male wage workers earn more than female wage workers. These gender gaps arise from inequality in the use of inputs and access to customers and also from discrimination in the labor market. Overall, for women additional obstacles are posed not only by market distortions but also by social norms, attitudes toward women's work, and gender differences in norms about marriage and care responsibilities. Such inequality is not only unfair but also inefficient—it can lead to a misallocation of talent and dampen economic growth (refer to Cuberes and Teignier 2016).

FIGURE 4.11 Returns to gender of owner, education, and firm size

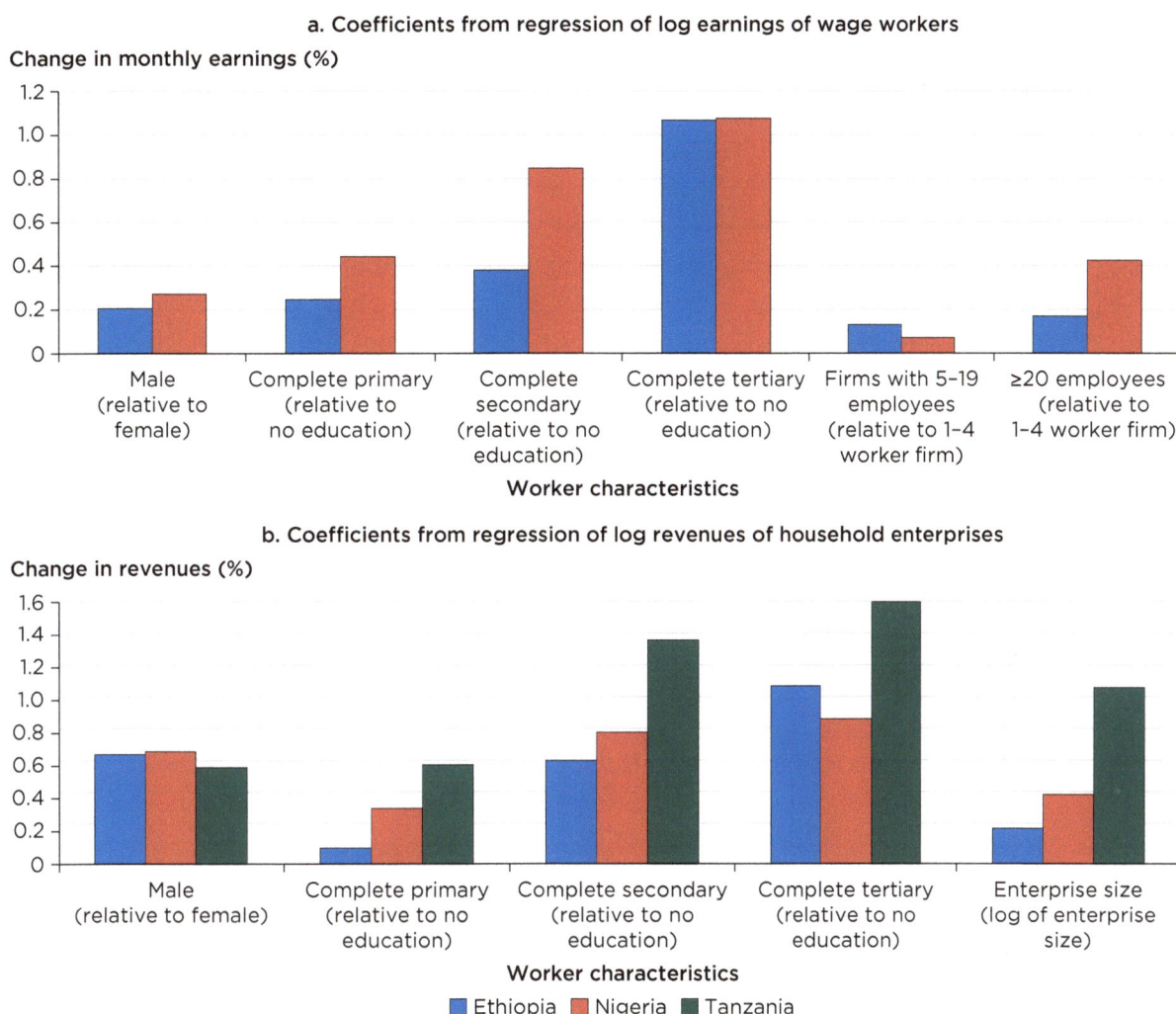

a. Coefficients from regression of log earnings of wage workers

Change in monthly earnings (%)

Worker characteristics

b. Coefficients from regression of log revenues of household enterprises

Change in revenues (%)

Worker characteristics

■ Ethiopia ■ Nigeria ■ Tanzania

Source: World Bank calculations based on Living Standards Measurement Study (https://www.worldbank.org/en/programs/lsms) surveys for respective countries.
Note: Panel a: Coefficients are from a regression of log monthly earnings on worker characteristics, including gender, education, firm size, public sector, and sector (agriculture, industry, services). The coefficient for firm size 5–19 is statistically not significant. The coefficient for completed primary school is not statistically significant for Ethiopia. Panel b: Coefficients are from a regression of log revenues of household enterprises on characteristics of the enterprise owner and enterprise size.

For farms, the relationship between scale and productivity is not as clear as is the case with firms. In emerging economies in general and in Africa in particular, larger farms tend to be less productive than smaller farms. The reason for this is the presence of transaction costs and labor market imperfections that hinder the deployment of labor and inputs when needed and therefore dampen the returns to scale (Dillon and Barrett 2017; Foster and Rosenzweig 2022). This contrasts with developed country settings, where an increase in farm scale is associated with higher productivity. The roles that market imperfections and failures play in affecting firm and farm performance are the focus of the next section.

Distortions in three markets matter for structural income inequality

By limiting scale-up and hiring, market distortions exacerbate income inequality. Global evidence suggests that the behavior of producers and allocation of resources across them matters for income distribution. Several studies have analyzed the role of firm-specific factors in driving wage dispersions that contribute to overall wage inequality. Drawing on research from the United States and other developed countries, Lazear and Shaw (2018) discuss the role of firms in shaping income inequality. Some income inequality stems from differences in the firms in which workers are employed, such that similarly qualified workers can earn different amounts depending on their firm. Kurz (2023) highlights how market power held by firms in the United States canlead to wage differentials and income inequality.[7] In a study tailored to the production landscape of Africa, Rud and Trapeznikova (2021) show that the presence of firm entry costs discourages the reallocation of workers from self-employment to wage work and allows both high- and low-productivity firms to coexist, which results in lower aggregate productivity, lower wages, and high wage dispersion. In the case of developing countries, large firms can also exercise monopsonistic power to drive down wages and thus exacerbate income inequality (Abebe, Buehren, and Goldstein 2020; Amodio, Medina, and Morlacco 2022). In this framing, similar to Restuccia and Rogerson (2017), market distortions lead to misallocation of resources, coexistence of low- and high-productivity enterprises, and income inequality (refer to annex 4A).

The report focuses on four types of distortion that affect the scale of firms and farms, job creation, and earnings and ultimately shape the distribution of income. Four types of distortions matter (Restuccia and Rogerson 2017; also refer to chapter 3):

- Inequality of opportunity, in which an individual's inherited characteristics, not their effort or talent, affect how much human capital or physical capital they acquire (refer to chapter 3)

- Market imperfections, such as monopoly and monopsonistic power, market frictions, low contestability, and weak contract enforcement

- Regulations that vary by size (or age or sector), such as special credit policies; industrial parks; regulations that restrict market access, such as product market regulations; and legal provisions that restrict market access for women, such as restrictions on sector of work

- Discretionary provisions that treat similar producers differently because of political connections.

Distortions can be caused by tax and labor policies, which this chapter does not cover. Tax design of both direct and indirect taxes, for example, can affect firms' performance and growth, which is discussed in more detail in chapter 5. Labor laws can also affect producers.

Almost all countries in Africa have adopted minimum wage laws for wage workers; however, impacts on employment and earnings are available from only a few countries, such as South Africa (Bhorat, Kanbur, and Stanwix 2017). In line with the experience of other developing countries, evidence from the region shows that the introduction of minimum wage laws has only a small negative impact on employment, although the size of the impacts varies across countries depending on the stringency of enforcement and where the wage floor is set relative to the average wage (Bhorat, Kanbur, and Stanwix 2017; Neumark and Munguía Corella 2021).

Distortions in input and product markets appear to be higher in Africa than in other regions. International Comparison Program data show that prices in Africa (and low-income countries) tend to be higher than in other regions because of low competition and small market sizes (Beirne and Kirchberger 2021; Leone, Macchiavello, and Reed 2021). Global indicators of competition also show African countries to be lagging other regions in the extent of market competition (Reda Cherif et al. 2020; World Bank 2023b). For example, according to the Bertelsmann Stiftung's Transformation Index 2024, a majority of African countries have among the lowest scores globally on market organization, competition policy, protection of private property, legal guarantees for private enterprise, and equal opportunity. Firms in Africa tend to have higher markups—an indicator of market power—than firms in other regions (Reda Cherif et al. 2020) Competition has an important effect on the reallocation of resources to more productive firms. Evidence from high-income countries suggests that allowing productive firms to grow is the key channel through which productivity growth leads to employment growth: although productivity gains might be labor-saving, these losses are outweighed by employment gains as a result of these firms being able to expand their market share (Calligaris et al. 2023).[8] Fostering productivity with employment growth therefore requires contestability in markets, which appears to be low in Africa.

Across different country groupings, those exposed to conflict are likely to experience additional distortions and constraints. Conflict can have large impacts on firms' performance because of security concerns, supply chain and trade disruptions, and the destruction of physical capital. Conflict in Côte d'Ivoire reduced firm productivity by an average of 16–23 percent (Klapper, Richmond, and Tran 2013), with many of these impacts lasting for several years (Léon and Dosso 2022). Armed conflict in the Democratic Republic of Congo and Uganda (Eberhard-Ruiz 2022) and postelection violence in Kenya (Ksoll, Macchiavello, and Morjaria 2022) led to reductions in exports. Evidence from conflicts outside Africa—in, for example, Libya, the Syrian Arab Republic, and West Bank and Gaza—shows similar disruptive impacts on firms.[9] Although conflict itself has major impacts on a firm's productivity, growth, and overall performance, climatic factors can have large impacts on the occurrence of conflict. The literature suggests that droughts increase the probability of conflicts (Couttenier and Soubeyran 2014; Hsiang, Burke, and Miguel 2013; Jia 2014; Miguel, Satyanath, and Sergenti 2004). Similarly, adverse weather shocks during the growing season of local crops persistently affect conflict incidences in Africa (Harari and La Ferrara 2018).

Analytical framework: distortions and behavior of firms and farms

Market distortions are present in different market interactions, preventing the growth of firms and farms and the expansion of productive earning opportunities and reinforcing structural inequality.[10] Market distortions that prevent the expansion of productive earnings opportunities work through three key channels (refer to figure 4.12):

- Market distortions in capital and input markets prevent firms from acquiring productive capacities. These include the inputs that farms use, the physical capital that firms possess, the technology that firms use, and also the managerial and organizational practices that firms adopt.

- Limited and unfair access to product markets domestically and abroad prevents firms from achieving scale economies. This constrains returns to productive capacity and the ability of firms and farms to expand. The lack of contestability in domestic markets—including those driven by the presence of state-owned enterprises—and limited integration with regional and global value chains limit the scale that can be achieved.

- Frictions in the labor market limit hiring of workers and thereby reduce the creation of wage jobs, whether on farms or in firms. Costly job searches, high transport costs, lack of information about workers, and costly screening of workers can cause frictions in the labor market.

FIGURE 4.12 **Markets and performance of firms and farms: Analytical framework**

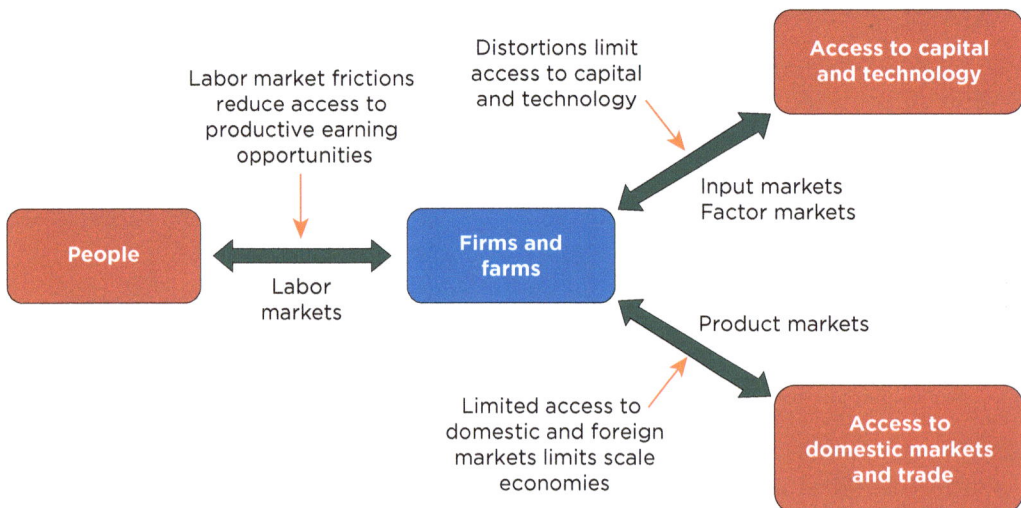

Source: Original figure for this publication.

Constrained access to capital and technology

The first channel dampening the growth of firms and farms is distortions surrounding accessing capital and technologies, which reduces their productive capabilities and investments. Although some productive capacities, such as education and skills, are acquired before working, firms and farms acquire important productive capacities while operating. These include the inputs that farms use, the physical capital that firms possess, the technology that they use, and the managerial and organizational practices that firms adopt (Sutton 2012). Developing these productive capabilities requires investment—either in tangible resources, such as machinery, equipment, and buildings, or in intangible forms of capital, such as the capabilities of workers and managers. Impact evaluations and other studies in African countries and elsewhere suggest that there are large returns to investment among some microentrepreneurs (Banerjee and Duflo 2005).[11] The acquisition of productive capacities depends on well-functioning markets for credit and capital, but it is often constrained by market failures, including information asymmetries (for example, on the creditworthiness of borrowers, information gaps on business practices or technologies), leading to underinvestment in and a lack of adoption of appropriate technologies and organizational practices. Information asymmetries raise financial institutions' cost of lending to this segment via market-driven products. Institutional challenges also affect credit provision; the high cost of using judicial systems in case of default is another thing holding back the flow of credit (Fafchamps 2001, 2003).

Credit market distortions disproportionately affect those who are less well off and worsen inequality. Lenders overcome limited information on borrowers' repayment abilities by requiring information and collateral. Microcredit institutions that do not require collateral have used approaches such as group lending to overcome the lack of information on poor borrowers' productivity and creditworthiness, but these have been effective only in certain cases (Cai et al. 2023). In the case of formal finance via banks, reliance on traditional collateral remains high in Africa. Inequality in ownership of assets such as land, discussed in chapter 3, therefore not only exacerbates income inequality but also leads to resource misallocation and productivity loss because there is no a priori reason that those who are better off are always more efficient at making use of capital than those who are poor. Cumulatively, low productive capabilities restrict the earning opportunities of firms as well as the scale they can achieve.

Moreover, there is evidence that farmers and firms face credit constraints. For example, farmers tend to sell their produce immediately after harvest when prices are low and return later during the lean season to buy produce when prices are high ("sell low, buy high"); this may be the result of a lack of credit. Burke, Bergquist, and Miguel (2019) study the case of grain farmers in Kenya and find that farmers sell right after harvest to meet cash needs (such as paying school fees). Lack of credit or savings opportunities prevents farmers from moving sales of grains from times of low prices (harvest time) to times of high prices (lean season). This reduces farmers' incomes considerably and contributes to large seasonal price variations. It has been well documented that farmers in the region enter into relational contractual agreements with traders to get access to credit and other inputs in return for sales at a set price (see discussion in the next section). For firms, several studies, including from Africa, have documented large returns to investment among some microentrepreneurs (Banerjee and Duflo 2005). For example, programs that provide grants to microentrepreneurs in Ghana and to aspiring entrepreneurs in Nigeria have shown positive returns to receipt of financing (Fafchamps et al. 2014; McKenzie 2017). An analysis of firms in Ethiopia shows that small firms in the services sector that obtained a loan were also more likely to experience employment growth (World Bank 2017).

Reflecting the challenges of credit markets, firms' use of external sources of finance is low. Most own-account workers and household enterprises rely on their own resources, resources from family and friends, or informal sources to obtain the capital to start up their business (refer to figure 4.13). Across five countries with suitable data from household surveys, on average 85 percent of own-account workers and household enterprises indicate that own resources or those from family and friends were the main source. Small firms in the region might prefer to borrow from friends and family—lower transaction costs and personal relationships provide a better opportunity to enforce repayments (Fafchamps 1994). Many nonhousehold enterprises, including larger ones, rely on nonbank resources as the main source of finance for their day-to-day operations (refer to figure 4.14). For firms with fewer than 19 employees, only about 1 in 10 firms rely on bank financing. These firms are also more likely to report accessing credit to be a major constraint. About one-third of larger firms rely on banks for financing. Cusolito and Didier (forthcoming) highlight that the gap in financing between middle- and high-income countries is especially pertinent for nonlarge firms (that is, those with fewer than 100 employees).

FIGURE 4.13 **Sources of start-up capital for household enterprises**

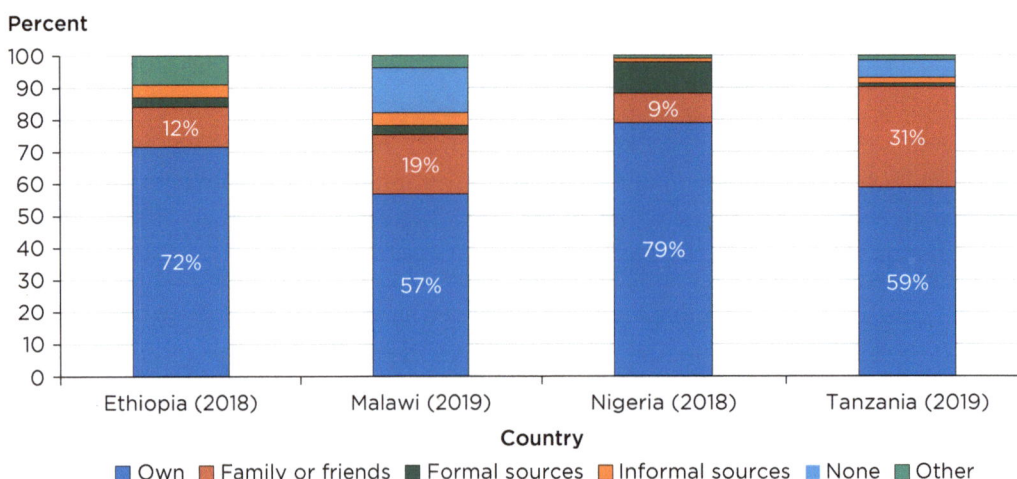

Percent

| Country | Own | Family or friends | Formal sources | Informal sources | None | Other |

Ethiopia (2018): Own 72%, Family or friends 12%
Malawi (2019): Own 57%, Family or friends 19%
Nigeria (2018): Own 79%, None 9%
Tanzania (2019): Own 59%, Family or friends 31%

Legend: ■ Own ■ Family or friends ■ Formal sources ■ Informal sources ■ None ■ Other

Source: World Bank calculations using household survey data on household enterprises from Living Standards Measurement Study (https://www.worldbank.org/en/programs/lsms) for respective countries.

FIGURE 4.14 Financial sources for day-to-day operations

Firms with source of finance (%)

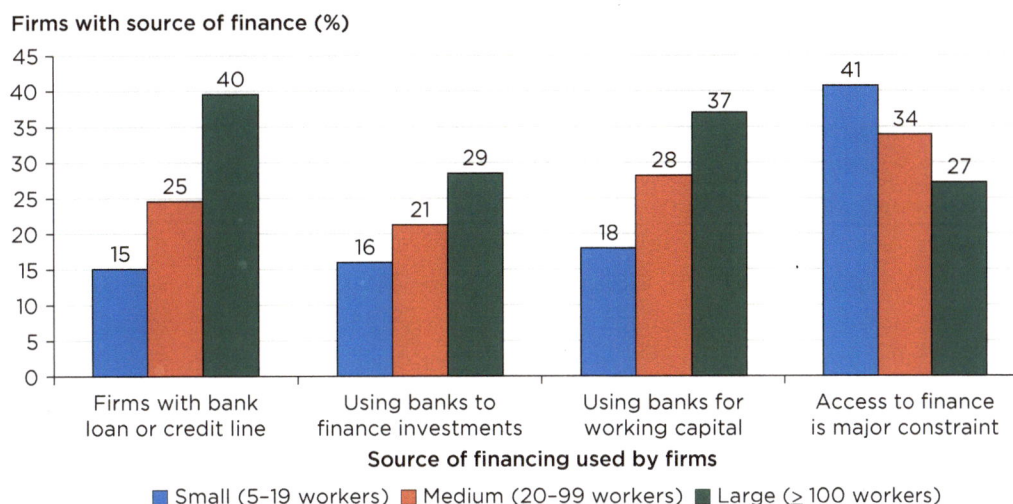

Source of financing used by firms

■ Small (5–19 workers) ■ Medium (20–99 workers) ■ Large (≥ 100 workers)

Source: Analysis based on World Bank Enterprise Surveys from the Africa region (https://www
.enterprisesurveys.org/en/enterprisesurveys).
Note: Firms can select multiple options.

In addition to credit market challenges, inadequate business practices and a low
degree of technological sophistication also affect productivity. The adoption of
structured management practices in marketing, record keeping, and financial
planning remains low in many micro- and small enterprises, although the adoption of
such practices correlates strongly with business performance (McKenzie and
Woodruff 2017). In larger firms, the adoption of structured management practices,
such as target setting, monitoring, or the use of incentives, is lower in African
countries (Bloom et al. 2014). The World Bank's Firm-level Adoption of Technology
survey—also conducted in five African countries—highlights that the degree of
technological sophistication in African firms is low, thereby harming productivity
(Cirera, Comin, and Cruz 2022). Information asymmetries—firm owners not knowing
what type of technology or practice would be beneficial for their business—are an
important constraint to adopting more sophisticated technologies and more
structured organizational practices.

Technology adoption by farmers is affected by several factors (Suri and Udry 2022).
Productivity of African agriculture suffers from the limited availability of
technologies that have been developed for commonly grown crops, such as cassava,
sweet potatoes, and yams (Gollin 2015). Large variations in production
environments across agroecological zones in the region also make it difficult to
develop replicable agricultural technologies. Use of technologies such as
mechanization, irrigation, and fertilizer is also low in the region (Suri and Udry
2022). Low skills, adverse climate and geography, and reliance on rain-fed
agriculture are additional factors that contribute to low crop productivity in the
region (Gollin 2015; Suri and Udry 2022).

In Africa, the cost of inputs such as cement and fertilizers are higher than could be the case because the markets for these inputs tend to be characterized by low levels of competition and weak contestability. Using data from the 2017 round of the International Comparison Program, Beirne and Kirchberger (2021) report that the price of cement in Africa is 1.5 times the price of cement in the United States at market exchange rates and 3.6 times the price in terms of purchasing power parity. Because cement is a homogeneous good produced in process manufacturing plants, price differences across regions are indicative of the market power of producers rather than differences in quality. Low demand and small domestic market size could also play a role, as discussed by Leone, Macchiavello, and Reed (2021), yet booming construction in many African cities suggests rising demand. Unlike cement, which is nontradable, fertilizer is a tradable good. Fertilizer prices in the region are also affected by low competition among importers and bulk suppliers (the region relies on fertilizer imports). Roberts et al. (2023) document the presence of oligopoly and low contestability in fertilizer imports in Eastern and Southern Africa, where the price of fertilizers rose in 2021–23 but did not drop in line with global prices.

Access to markets is often impeded, effectively reducing the size of product markets

The second channel affecting the growth and productivity of firms and farms is distortions that restrict access to markets. These distortions largely reflect high transportation costs and weak competition in product markets that create barriers to firm entry. Participation in value chains, domestically and regionally, and global markets is low.

The region's firms have limited participation in global or regional value chains. The AUC and OECD (2022) estimate that Africa accounted for 1.7 percent of participation in global value chains in 2019, and regional value chains accounted for only 2.7 percent of Africa's global value chain participation, compared with 26.4 percent for Latin America and Caribbean and 42.9 percent for Asia (refer to figure 4.15). Responding to the opportunities to expand exports requires regional integration, improving subregional connectivity (physical and digital), and addressing nontariff barriers. There is concern that the monopsonistic power of buyer-driven foreign firms could lead to poor working conditions (in the case of factories) or low farmer earnings (for example, coffee value chains) if there are no complementary regulations to enforce labor standards (Abebe, Buehren, and Goldstein 2020; Boudreau, Cajal-Grossi, and Macchiavello 2023).

Within countries, a growing urban population is a market-expanding opportunity for farmers, yet high transportation costs have cascading effects on limiting domestic market integration, encouraging producers to serve local customers, and conferring market power on local traders. The agriculture and food sector is an important source of demand. In Ethiopia, Malawi, Nigeria, Tanzania, and Uganda, it is estimated that food processing, food trading, and food service account for

FIGURE 4.15 Share of participation in regional value chains as a percentage of participation in global value chains, 2019

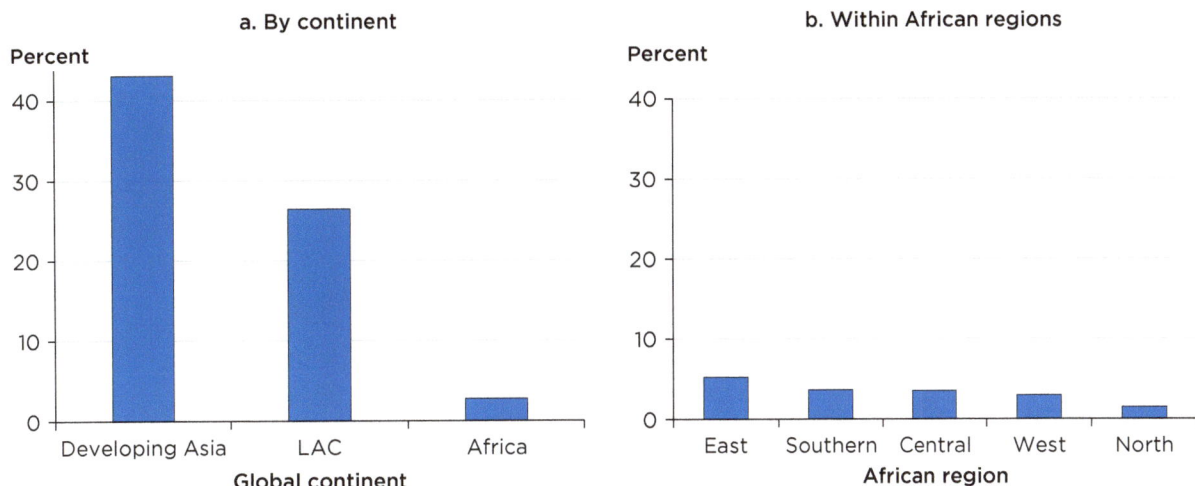

a. By continent

Percent

b. Within African regions

Percent

Source: Based on AUC and OECD (2022).
Note: LAC = Latin America and the Caribbean.

24 percent of rural employment (full-time equivalent) and 41 percent of all rural off-farm employment (Christiaensen and Maertens 2022). The rise of supermarkets in Africa is an important channel for farmers and those in the food value chain to tap into growing demand (Barrett et al. 2022). However, a study of spatial price differences in Ethiopia and Nigeria by Atkin and Donaldson (2015) found that within-country trade costs are four to five times higher than in the United States. This high trade cost is consistent with the high transportation costs estimated for the region by Teravaninthorn and Raballand (2009).

The high transportation costs in turn reflect several factors. These include poor road infrastructure, low competition in the transportation sector, topography, and insecurity that additionally raise the costs of moving goods to far-off locations. Close to 25 percent of firms in the World Bank's Enterprise Surveys reported transportation to be a major constraint, one of the highest shares across all regions (refer to figure 4.16). Transport prices are particularly high in West and Central Africa because of low competition in the sector (Bove et al. 2018). Studies of the Africa region consistently find spatial differences in prices of imported goods (food and nonfood) as well as in nontraded agricultural staples, indicating that markets are not well integrated and that retail prices of products are affected by distance (Abdulai 2006; Fackler and Goodwin 2001).[12] Agricultural markets are also not integrated, and prices vary spatially such that smallholders earn less at the farm gate and consumers pay higher prices. There is evidence that in the case of some crops, traders have market power (Bergquist and Dinerstein 2020).

FIGURE 4.16 **Firms identifying transportation as a major constraint**

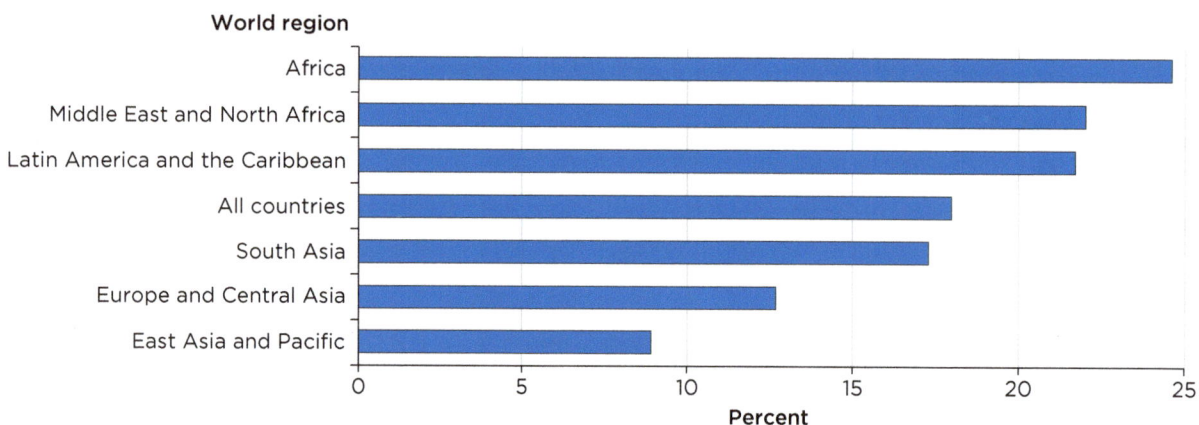

Source: World Bank Enterprise Surveys (https://www.enterprisesurveys.org/en/enterprisesurveys).

FIGURE 4.17 **Main customers for own-account workers and household enterprises**

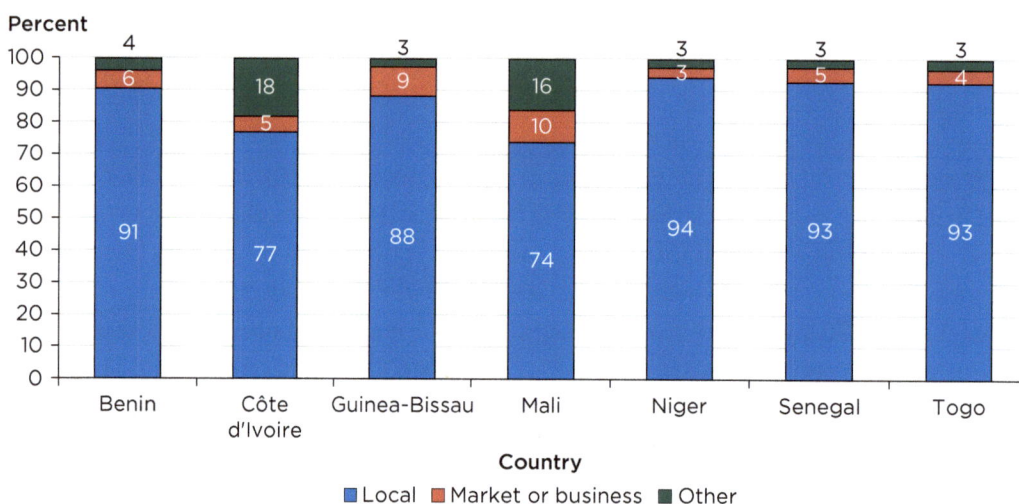

Source: Calculations based on household surveys.
Note: Figures are based on own-account workers and household enterprises.

The majority of African enterprises and farmers therefore sell locally, mostly to nearby consumers, with few firms being exposed to global markets through exports. For roughly 9 in 10 own-account workers and household enterprises, local customers form the most important source of demand (refer to figure 4.17). Among larger firms with at least five employees, about 14 percent of African firms export directly or indirectly compared with 17 percent of firms globally. Smallholder farmers who have market surplus sell their produce in nearby markets. In Ethiopia, the share of smallholders relying on local markets increases the further away they are from an urban center. In Malawi and Nigeria, the main buyers are friends and family and local markets, regardless of how far the smallholder is from an urban area.

FIGURE 4.18 Firms directly or indirectly exporting

Percent

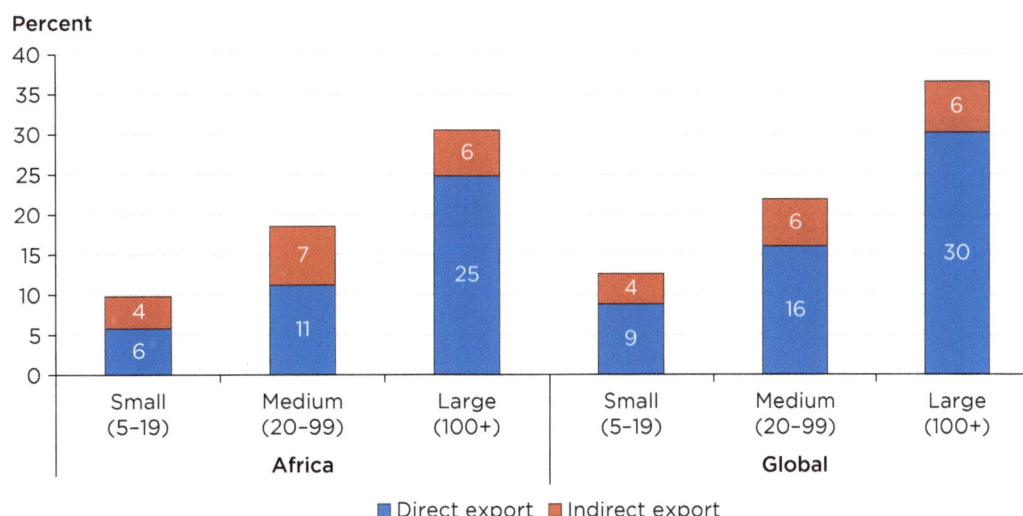

Source: Enterprise Surveys, World Bank (https://www.enterprisesurveys.org/en/enterprisesurveys).
Note: A firm is considered an exporter (direct or indirect) if at least 10 percent of sales are exported.

Limited contestability of domestic markets is an additional constraining factor that raises firm entry costs. Global analysis of World Bank and OECD Product Market Regulation Statistics indices suggest that between 2013 and 2018, barriers to competition in product markets tended to be higher in African countries because of a high degree of state involvement in markets, administrative barriers to entrepreneurship, and barriers to trade and investment (refer to figure 4.19). State participation in markets that can be effectively served by the private sector limits the prospects further. Recent data from the World Bank's Business of the State database show that by 2023, in countries such as Ghana, Kenya, and Uganda, close to or more than half of sectors had businesses with state ownership operating in them, often in sectors in which the private sector could provide products and services efficiently, such as hospitality sectors, manufacturing, and wholesale and retail (refer to figure 4.20). Ethiopia, Kenya, and South Africa have examples of state-owned businesses that benefit disproportionately from favorable regulations, creating an unlevel playing field for firms (World Bank 2023a). In agriculture, state involvement via crop boards and price supports to stabilize food prices and the provision of subsidized inputs serve to discourage private sector participation in food imports and sales of inputs (Jayne 2012; Mather and Jayne 2018).

FIGURE 4.19 Product market regulations in Africa, indexes

PMR score (0–6)

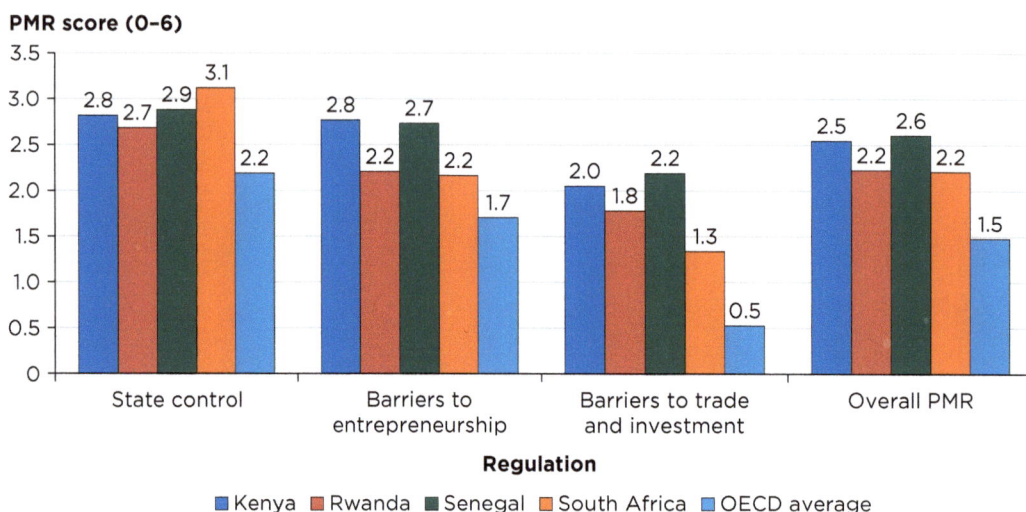

Source: OECD and World Bank Product Market Regulations.
Note: Time period is the latest available year between 2013 and 2018. Higher PMR scores mean that markets are more restricted. OECD = Organisation for Economic Co-operation and Development; PMR = product market regulations.

FIGURE 4.20 Presence of business with state ownership in competitive markets

Business with state ownership (%)

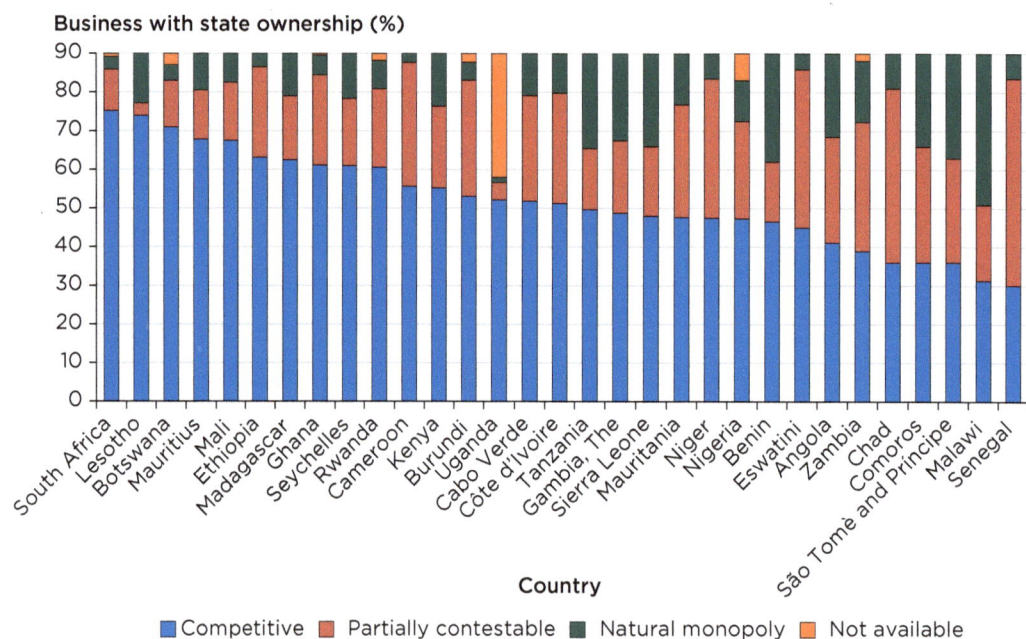

Sources: World Bank (2023a), based on the World Bank Business of the State database.
Note: Includes businesses with at least 10 percent state ownership.

Access to productive work opportunities is curbed

The third channel concerns frictions in labor markets that make it difficult for firms and farms to find workers when they need them and prevent workers from finding jobs for which they would be a good match. Labor markets are characterized by frictions, preventing workers from accessing productive earnings opportunities and firms and farms from recruiting workers needed for expansion. On the worker side (labor supply), such frictions include high transportation costs and costly job searches. On the firm side (labor demand), frictions include information asymmetries and costly screening of workers. The lack of spatial integration discussed earlier also creates frictions in the labor market. Another source of friction is legal restrictions on women's work—typically, laws that restrict hours or sectors of work.

Frictions in the labor market prevent workers from accessing productive work opportunities.[13] The friction faced by firms arises from unequal access to information about potential employees and costly screening of workers. A fact well recognized by job seekers across the globe is that networks and whom one knows matter in finding a job—such networks help reduce information frictions. For small firms, it can be costly to recruit and train workers, particularly youth with no work experience. A study of an apprenticeship placement program in Ghana found that small firms that received apprentices grew in size, revenues, and profits because the program reduced the firms' cost to screen workers (Hardy and McCasland 2023). Similarly, for farms, hiring labor when needed may be difficult, given the low population density in the region's rural areas. For agricultural households, reliance on family labor rather than wage labor addresses the difficulty of finding workers, and having such restricted ability to hire workers can hamper farmers' ability to reap the benefits of technology adoption (Dillon and Barrett 2017; Suri and Udry 2022).

Connectivity and transportation can be another source of labor market frictions. On the worker side, the cost of commuting and the distance to firms' location can be sources of friction that lock them out of good-quality jobs. Franklin (2018) illustrates the effect of costly commuting using 2013 Labor Force Survey data from Ethiopia. The further away workers are from the center of Addis Ababa, the more likely they are to be in less-skilled occupations, and the share of medium- and high-skill jobs declines with distance. Thus, accessing good jobs will mean being able to travel to jobs closer to the city center. The low rates of internal migration observed in many countries despite the productivity differences between agriculture and nonagriculture sectors is also a reflection of labor market frictions.

For women, these labor market frictions also interact with access to affordable childcare. Because of social norms, time spent on care and household chores and maintenance is an important determinant of time spent by women in economic activities. Studies from across the globe show that the presence of children in the household is associated with a lower probability of women working (Ahmed et al. 2023).

Legal barriers can further exacerbate frictions. For women, such frictions may be aggravated by restrictive, gendered legal provisions. Although Africa performs well globally, discriminatory laws exist in several countries. For example, in 2022 women in Cameroon, Chad, Equatorial Guinea, Guinea-Bissau, Mauritania, and Niger could not get a job without their husband's permission.

Cumulative effects

Cumulatively, these features exacerbate income inequality by adversely affecting firm growth, limiting expansion in wage employment opportunities and growth in farm productivity, and they give rise to the composition of employment seen in Africa. These distortions also enable top income earners to thrive, especially in "rent-thick" sectors (real estate, oil, mining, telecommunications, and cement, among others). In general, politically connected wealth accumulation can have a negative effect on growth (Burgis 2015; Gandhi and Walton 2012). Specifically for Africa, the nexus between higher resource rents and more corruption, especially in less democratic countries, has been documented (Rabah and Gylfason 2013). Removing market and institutional structural distortions is therefore essential to tackling income inequalities from both the bottom and top ends of the income distribution.

Opening policy portals to grow jobs and better earning opportunities for all workers

For workers in Africa who find themselves in small firms or farms and fallback sectors, the availability of jobs and better earning opportunities rests on removing market distortions and allowing the market to work. Markets must work to expand access to capital and technology, domestic markets, and global trade and facilitate workers' job searches. When access to these opportunities is universalized in ways that are not distortionary, structural sources of income inequality will be removed. Of course, the effectiveness of these policies depends on sound macrofiscal policies, fair fiscal policy (refer to chapter 5), and strong market institutions.

A payoff from leveling the playing field is that it can unlock economic growth as well. Policies that allow the market to function well also unlock many of the constraints on firm and farm growth, both on the side of efficiency of production (supply side) and in the size of markets in which firms and farms participate (demand side). As Goldberg and Reed (2023) emphasize, gains on both fronts are needed for progress in development. From a sectoral transformation perspective, they can remove barriers faced by manufacturing and services firms in accessing inputs, product markets, and workers, because these are the sectors that are well placed to create good jobs and earnings opportunities for more workers (refer to box 4.2). When implemented in a coordinated manner, these policy actions can also pay off in strengthening the microfoundations of growth and reducing resource misallocation, thereby strengthening the relationship between economy-wide growth and people's income growth. This potential win–win of tackling inequality and realizing growth gains is important for a region that has struggled to raise productivity, create jobs, and spur structural transformation.

BOX 4.2

Job creation, structural transformation, and the role of manufacturing and services

Manufacturing has played in an important role in driving growth and job creation in the current high-income countries as well as in East Asian countries. In Africa, the role has been more limited, because most of the growth has been in less-productive services sectors. Developing the manufacturing sector in Africa will require increasing the productivity of the sector and access to global markets that facilitate participation in global value chains. This includes addressing important frictions highlighted in this chapter, including transportation frictions.

The choice between manufacturing and services might be a false dilemma. Many of the current growing economies are relying much less on manufacturing than in the past (refer to figure B4.2.1). Enabling service sectors—such as transportation, logistics, and administrative and support services—plays an important role in facilitating the growth of other sectors—including manufacturing and agriculture—and employing workers across the spectrum of skills. Digitization is creating new productive employment opportunities. Although some of these digital services depend on a high level of skill, many tasks within digital services require a more basic level of skills, such as literacy and basic computing skills, that might be within the reach of many more people.

FIGURE B4.2.1. Long-run GDP per capita and industrial sector employment shares, 1801–2021

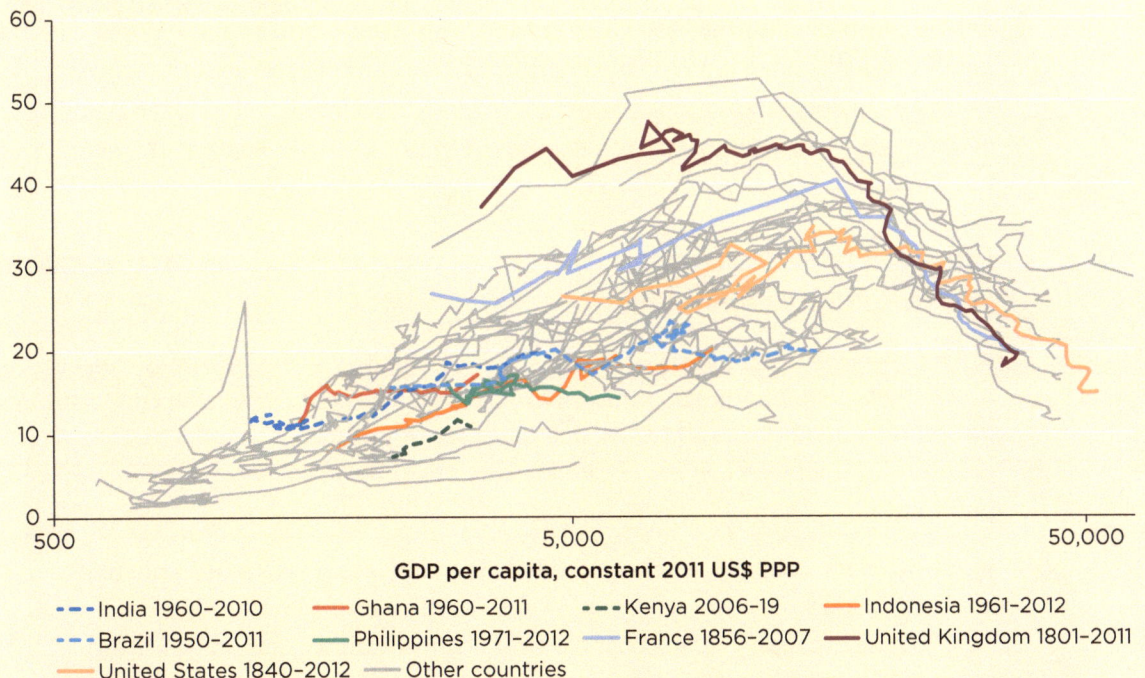

Share of employment in industrial sectors (%)

GDP per capita, constant 2011 US$ PPP

- - - India 1960–2010 — Ghana 1960–2011 - - - Kenya 2006-19 — Indonesia 1961–2012
- - - Brazil 1950–2011 — Philippines 1971–2012 — France 1856–2007 — United Kingdom 1801–2011
— United States 1840–2012 — Other countries

Sources: Adapted from World Bank (2023d), based on Herrendorf, Rogerson, and Valentinyi (2014), the GGDC 10-Sector Database (https://www.rug.nl/ggdc/structuralchange/), and the GGDC's Maddison Project (Bolt and Van Zanden 2024). Kenyan data are estimates modeled by the International Labour Organization on the basis of Kenya National Bureau of Statistics statistics.
Note: GDP = gross domestic product; GGDC = Groningen Growth and Development Centre; PPP = purchasing power parity.

Removal of market distortions must be accompanied by appropriate institutions to ensure healthy functioning, as well as monitoring of impacts as reforms unfold. However, positive impacts on inequality or poverty reduction only materialize after a longer period or in an appropriate redistributive policy environment. For example, increasing competition in product markets can lead to short-term losses in earnings and employment for those working in incumbent firms that face increased market pressures. Trade liberalization can generate more productive job opportunities but might benefit skilled workers more than others. It is crucial that market reforms be accompanied by strong institutions that ensure that anticompetitive practices do not take root, as well as by a transition plan defining the appropriate timing and sequencing of reform and, where appropriate, redistributive policies (refer to chapter 5) to ensure that the removal of distortions does indeed lead to improved livelihoods across the earnings distribution.

Country-specific circumstances, such as the presence of resource sectors or fragility, also determine what policies are feasible. In countries with resource-rich sectors, there tend to be few linkages, except for consumption linkages, between the resource sectors and other sectors of the economy, limiting the potential for productivity spillovers. Building such linkages by, for example, encouraging domestic firms to provide inputs to this sector can be promising. In the case of countries with fragility, market institutions will be constrained by the local situation and high levels of uncertainty. When possible, policies should aim to increase the predictability of the business environment, especially in domains that can be influenced by policy. Digital technologies could also be leveraged to get around market imperfections (for example, sharing price information).

Promote market-based innovations to provide better access to capital and to suitable technology

Financial sector policy and credit infrastructure can be designed to facilitate innovative financial products that can increase the take-up of formal finance by household enterprises and firms. Innovations offer alternative ways to collateralize loans and leverage information about borrowers' repayment potential.

Asset-based microfinance lends for a fixed asset that also serves as the collateral and has been found to be improve firm performance when tested in Kenya and Pakistan. Supply chain financing for microborrowers, such as retailers, has not yet been scientifically tested. An example from Kenya suggests that supply chain financing structures can fulfill and overcome working capital needs and bottlenecks, allowing for faster inventory turnover and an increase in sales. In Kenya, Unilever and Mastercard worked with KCB Bank to offer supply chain credit to microretailers, leveraging Unilever's information about retailers' performance.

For farmers, tailored loan products can help improve take-up. For example, harvest time microcredit to smallholder farmers can help them smooth seasonal variations in incomes. An impact evaluation of group microloans to maize farmers in Kenya's Bungoma County offered via the One Acre Fund right after harvest season (tied to grain storage) significantly raised revenues and general equilibrium effects, showing that this intervention also stabilized seasonal price shifts (Burke, Bergquist, and Miguel 2019).

Financial technology (fintech) and digital financial loan products for working capital or investment needs are another promising approach, particularly for microbusinesses. Kenya's M-Shwari is a digital bank account (savings and credit services) that is linked to M-PESA, mobile money services provided by Safaricom. Suri, Bharadwaj, and Jack (2021) show that M-Shwari loans helped households mitigate shocks, were largely used to pay for short-term needs but were not for business purposes. More important, these loans did not substitute for other loan sources or informal borrowing. On the bank side, the introduction of M-Shwari appears to have increased competition and led to the introduction of similar products in the market (Suri, Bharadwaj, and Jack 2021). As more countries expand digital infrastructure and fintech facilitates the introduction of loan products, it will be important to put in place adequate financial consumer protection regulations (Boeddu and Chien 2022).

Equity financing and venture capital can play an important role in providing essential capital to start-ups and growing businesses that may not have access to traditional bank loans due to a lack of collateral or a proven track record.[14] Nevertheless, there is a limited offering of equity financing and venture capital funds in African countries. Improving regulatory frameworks (for example, to allow for legal partnership structures common in venture capital financing), building investor confidence through improvements in the investment climate, capacity building of entrepreneurs and investors, and strengthening financial infrastructure can help the development of equity financing and venture capital.

Complementary approaches that use the credit infrastructure to overcome the lack of information about borrowers are also crucial. Credit infrastructure, such as reporting systems and collateral registries, can enhance access to finance for firms and farms. Credit reporting systems can be made comprehensive by incorporating information on financial transactions from entities such as microfinance institutions and mobile telephone operators. By obtaining reliable credit information, lenders can better assess the creditworthiness of borrowers, reducing the risks associated with lending and potentially lowering interest rates. Collateral registries can help secure property rights, enabling firms to use their assets as security for loans, which can be particularly empowering for small- and medium-sized enterprises that may not have other forms of collateral.

Interventions aimed at increasing the capabilities of entrepreneurs and firms can offset inequality in skills acquisition and lead to higher productivity, when provided with the right targeting and the right degree of intensity. A meta-analysis of randomized controlled trials of training programs aimed at improving business practices conducted between 2002 and 2017 suggests an estimated improvement of 4.7 percent in sales and 10.1 percent in profits (McKenzie 2021). The program's success depends not only on the delivery and intensity but also on how firms are selected, because returns to training programs tend to be heterogeneous. Nevertheless, targeting the right beneficiaries remains a challenge, with traditional scoring methods as well as more sophisticated machine learning efforts having low predictable power (McKenzie and Sansone 2017).

For microentrepreneurs, combining traditional business skills training with soft skills training and aiming to build an entrepreneurial mind-set has shown promising results (for example, Campos et al. 2017 for Togo and Glaub et al. 2014 for Uganda), including for female entrepreneurs, although the impacts of such programs have been heterogeneous and also depend on the quality of the trainers (Alibhai et al. 2019; McKenzie and Puerto 2021). Interventions offering business development services, such as consulting services, can increase firm performance across the firm-size distribution (for example, Bloom et al. 2013 for large firms in India; Iacovone, Maloney, and McKenzie 2022 for smaller firms in Colombia; and Anderson and McKenzie 2022 for Nigeria).

Government financing support for firms can be effective if it is delivered via a modality that is transparent, promotes competition, and does not crowd out private sector innovations in loan products (McKenzie 2023). A concern with direct financing offered to firms is that governments have no more information than private lenders about whether a firm is credit constrained or not. This information gap can be overcome via competitive calls, such as business plan competition in Nigeria for aspiring entrepreneurs, which was found to be effective in selecting growth-oriented firms that experienced significant improvements in firm performance (McKenzie 2017). Ensuring transparency and competitive selection are important for the success of such initiatives. Ways of strengthening oversight and monitoring and evaluating effects will be important.

A package of coordinated interventions can help address multiple constraints faced by farmers—including knowledge gaps, input access, and technology access; complementary public investments in irrigation infrastructure; and research and development—are also required. An example of a package of interventions is One Acre Funds' initiative in Kenya; however, the effectiveness of these interventions has not been proven. Different elements of such packages have been found to be effective. Well-designed training for farmers, along with agricultural research and development investments, can help. In-depth training was effective in building farmers' capability to adopt technology and use it to manage threats to production, such as limited water. An impact evaluation in Niger found that one day's training on how to build rainwater harvesting technology had a significant impact on the adoption of this technology and agricultural output (Aker and Jack 2021). Light touch training for livestock, however, was found to have only a limited impact in Burkina Faso (Leight et al. 2021). Research and development spending is important for supporting technology adoption, as India's experience has shown. Average public spending in Southern and Eastern Africa has grown quickly, particularly in Uganda and Ethiopia. However, public spending on research and development has lagged in other parts of the region, and the private sector has not stepped in to fill the gap (Suri and Udry 2022).

Enabling smallholders to manage and cope with risks could also enhance technology adoption. Exposure to climate shocks, conflict, and other related shocks is ubiquitous in the region, particularly in the Horn of Africa and the Sahel (see spotlights 1 and 3 on climate and conflict, respectively). Farmers may cope with such risks by choosing suboptimal investment strategies, which is one explanation for why farmers might not adopt a new variety of seeds. Market-based insurance products, subsidized or otherwise, have not been proven to be effective, and this remains an important area of policy research, given the rising frequency of shocks. In such contexts, investments to protect against shocks, such as improvements in irrigation and soil conservation, will be important to enable the large share of farm households to cope with weather-related risks.

Adopt policies for better market access for firms and farms, domestically and globally

Improving market access requires a focus both on integration of domestic markets— through improving connectivity and contestability—and on integration with regional and global value chains. This chapter has shown that markets in the region are segmented because of high transport costs and the market power of traders serving consumers and producers, particularly in distant locations. Investing in roads, especially rural roads (and their maintenance), and in digital infrastructure and making the transport sector competitive will facilitate market integration. These investments will need to be accompanied by further reforms that increase domestic contestability, including competition policies. Such integration can help reduce in-market sources of inequality. Better infrastructure can also help reduce inequality in premarket incomes. Investment from abroad and participation in regional global value chains by fostering intersectoral linkages can help connect firms and farms to markets abroad.

There are strong returns to investing in roads (construction and upgrading), digital infrastructure, electricity, and affordable transport (Ali et al. 2015).[15] In the case of roads, the relative returns to investing in highways and rural roads differ because they serve different populations.[16] Investments in rural roads have been found to have unambiguously favorable effects on development indicators in Africa, with the greatest benefits accruing to the most remote locations (Foster et al. 2023). In Ethiopia, rural road development increased household consumption by 16–28 percent, reduced the incidence of poverty by 14 percent in drought-affected areas (Nakamura et al. 2020), and increased agricultural incomes of connected villages (Kebede 2024). In Cameroon, it increased the number of economic activities in the most isolated households (Gachassin 2013). Similarly, electrification has contributed to agricultural production, employment, better health and education outcomes, and higher household income and consumption (Foster et al. 2023). In fact, the absence of electricity can negatively affect jobs because firms affected by power outages respond to productivity losses by cutting jobs (Mensah 2023).[17] Investments in digital technology have also been shown to boost economic growth, contribute to education and labor market outcomes, and reduce inequality (Foster et al. 2023). There are important complementarities. For example, in India, investment in rural feeder roads significantly raised middle school enrollment and test scores in newly connected villages (Adukia, Asher, and Novosad 2020). Evidence from 27 countries highlights positive and significant combined effects of better access to roads and grid electricity, leading to better employment outcomes in urban areas and a shift to more skilled occupations in rural areas (Abbasi et al. 2022).

Making transport affordable requires complementary policy efforts to ensure competition in the trucking services sector (Bove et al. 2018; Teravaninthorn and Raballand 2009). Trucks are the dominant mode of transport within and across countries, and the industry is particularly prone to noncompetitive behavior by firms. There are successful cases of deregulation in the trucking sector, where breaking cartels results in lower prices. In West and Central Africa, inadequate regulatory frameworks, weak implementation, collusive business practices in the trucking industry, and the prevalence of illegal road blocks all contribute to raising transport prices (Bove et al. 2018). It is important to ensure a comprehensive and functioning regulatory framework, facilitating competition in the sector and professionalization of the trucking market.

Participation in value chains—domestically, regionally, and globally—can be an important opportunity to boost market access and incomes. For some enterprises, especially in agriculture, the focus should be on participating in domestic integrated value chains. For others, the focus should be on direct or indirect participation in global value chains. When firms have access to larger markets, they can increase their production volumes and achieve economies of scale. Local cross-border trade is an important factor as well, especially for small traders in the region, and it is estimated to account for 30–40 percent of total intraregional trade in Africa (Eberhard-Ruiz 2022).

For smallholder farmers who are already part of the food system, participating in integrated agricultural value chains can be an important opportunity to boost market access and incomes (Christiaensen 2020). Agricultural value chains, such as those for dairy products, allow participants to add value at each step of the process to deliver the product to the buyer, typically a large business or retailer. Smallholders who are part of integrated value chains are contractually connected to other participants in the chain and in return receive credit, agronomic information, and an ability to reduce risks. This arrangement therefore overcomes distortions at the input and market access stages identified earlier. Integrated value chains are more likely to be effective for nonstaple crops and agricultural products with high potential for adding value (dairy and meat) than for staple crops. Poor individuals can still directly benefit by participating as producers or being employed on larger farms or in the agri-food sector or through spillover effects to the local economy.

Producer organizations can help increase the bargaining power of smallholders, allowing them to claim a larger share of value added. Integrated agricultural value chains are increasingly being implemented, and Christiaensen (2020) identifies several areas where more experimentation and learning are needed, along with continued policy attention to raising labor productivity in agriculture:

- Identifying which organizational and contracting arrangements are the most effective, including testing the role of producer organizations for crops such as staples where such organizations typically do not exist

- Upskilling participants in the value chain

- Determining how best to incentivize financial institutional participation and the modality that can then be used (for example, grants).

Increasing trade opportunities can yield growth opportunities. Firms that export tend to be more productive, reflecting both selection effects (Melitz 2003) and learning by exporting (De Loecker 2013). Firms that export are more exposed to international markets through their trading partners as well as through their competitors, fostering knowledge and technology spillovers. They are also more exposed to international standards, which can encourage upgrading. Atkin, Khandelwal, and Osman (2017) show how increasing access to rug producers in Egypt increases quality, productivity, and profits.

The region stands to gain significantly if the goal of regional integration via the African Continental Free Trade Area (AfCFTA) is realized. International trade agreements and programs, such as Economic Partnership Agreements with the European Union and the United States' African Growth and Opportunity Act, provide important pathways for African countries to obtain access to international markets. The AfCFTA agreement will create the largest free trade area in the world, as measured by the number of countries participating. The pact connects 1.3 billion people—equivalent to the population size of India—across 55 countries and has the potential to increase employment opportunities and lift millions out of extreme poverty (World Bank 2020). World Bank modeling estimates suggest that implementing the AfCFTA agreement could raise income by 7 percent and reduce the number of people living in extreme poverty by 40 million, and even better results could be obtained under more ambitious scenarios that depend on deep integration (Echandi, Maliszewska, and Steenbergen 2022).

Achieving the full potential of trade programs such as AfCFTA will require removing distortions to enable the free flow of goods, capital, and information across borders; create competitive business environments that can boost productivity and investment, especially in agricultural value chains, in which many are engaged; enforce labor standards to ensure good working conditions; and promote increased foreign competition and foreign direct investment that can raise productivity and innovation for domestic firms. It will be important to monitor the distributional effects of more regional trade to ensure that benefits do not end up being regionally concentrated.

Foreign direct investment (FDI) can be a source of growth, and it can foster participation in global value chains, including in local firms. Workers can benefit, too, provided labor standards are enforced. Fostering participation in global value chains also requires further opening up FDI, which can help establish links between the domestic economy and global markets. Firms that set up subsidiaries abroad tend to be closer to the productivity frontier than those that do not (Helpman, Melitz, and Yeaple 2004). FDI has the potential to contribute to job creation through a combination of new capital, improved access to global markets, the adoption of higher-quality technology and management practices, and better training of workers (Alfaro 2017). FDI firms can also contribute to technological spillovers to other sectors, either through supply or demand linkages or through competition effects (Alfaro Ureña, Manelici, and Vasquez 2019; Bajgar and Javorcik 2020; Iacovone et al. 2015; Javorcik 2004). Nevertheless, in many African countries, FDI has traditionally been concentrated in resource-rich sectors, which have relatively limited scope for creating linkages with firms in the host economy, although FDI flows to sectors such as food and beverages and communications and information technology have recently increased (Morgan, Farris, and Johnson 2022). Fostering linkages with suppliers also requires that supplying firms have the productive capacities necessary to be able to supply the FDI-receiving firm.

The green transition will provide new opportunities as well. Africa is endowed with plentiful natural resources, including green minerals that are in high demand to support a global clean energy transition. Africa can capitalize on its mineral endowments to drive transformative sustainable growth, economic diversification, and local and regional development through value-added processing and manufacturing. At the same time, it is crucial to ensure that the global shift to clean technologies does not reinforce existing structural inequalities, burdening local communities with environmental damage and increased rent seeking or corrupt practices. Additional challenges stem from the fact that substantial reserves of critical minerals are in areas with vulnerable biodiversity as well as affected by fragility and conflict.

Facilitate the matching of workers and employers

Growing evidence documents the presence of job-finding frictions in Africa, yet the solutions to this problem are still an area of active policy research (Caria et al. 2024; Carranza and McKenzie 2023). Reducing transport costs is a promising solution, but the effects on improved employment outcomes do not appear to last. Job search platforms are widely available for both skilled and unskilled workers; however, available studies do not find these platforms to be effective in improving employment outcomes, and there are concerns about their ability to attract low-skilled and less-educated workers. One solution that has been found to be effective is jobs skills certification, which works for both workers and firms. The effectiveness of this intervention is unsurprising, given the low learning outcomes of school graduates in the region and the important role of social networks in job searches.

Transport subsidies have been tested in a variety of settings, including Africa, but have so far been found to have only limited effects on employment (Abebe et al. 2021; Caria et al. 2024; Franklin 2018). Studies have tested the impacts of a small cash transfer to young people in Ethiopia and South Africa to travel to urban centers and learn about job openings. Although this cash subsidy had no employment impacts in South Africa, the experience in Ethiopia shows some effects. In Ethiopia, transport subsidies boosted job searches and raised the probability of job seekers finding contracted wage jobs. However, these effects lasted only in the short term and dissipated over time.

Job skills certification interventions are the most promising, and studies show that they can be a cost-effective intervention. Experimental studies from a variety of settings, including Africa, have found that skills certification is an effective intervention for both job seekers and firms that want to hire (Caria et al. 2024). In Africa, where education quality is low, job skills certification plays an important role in providing credible information to firms on workers' skills. Abebe et al. (2021) study the effects of a skills certification program for young people in Addis Ababa. They find that having skills certification significantly raised young people's probability of finding contract wage employment and led to a significant increase in earnings four years after they received the intervention. Hardy and McCasland (2023) studied the impact of an apprenticeship placement program in Ghana that connected unemployed youth with placement in small firms. The program prioritized unemployed youth who were poor and enabled them to access apprenticeships without the entrance fees. As a result of the program, firm size increased by about half a worker in the manufacturing firms that received an apprentice. In-depth analysis shows that the mechanism behind the impact is that the program eased firms' costs for screening low-ability workers and reduced the cost of hiring and training first-time labor market entrants.

For women, access to affordable and convenient-to-reach childcare services can complement the efforts mentioned earlier. Center-based care provided by infant nurseries, preschools, and community-based centers can be effective in raising women's employment in Africa, as studies from Burkina Faso and the Democratic Republic of Congo suggest (Ahmed et al. 2023). In Uganda, provision of childcare subsidies was found to be effective in increasing women's participation in the labor force. A further complementarity is that access to high-quality childcare can additionally improve the inequalities in children's access to build human capital.

Enhance legal certainty for firms and farms, promote competition, adopt gender-equal labor laws, and ensure strong macrofiscal frameworks

The effectiveness of in-market policies depends crucially on an adequate macrofiscal framework, contestability, and strong institutions. Contestability facilitates the fair allocation of resources in the economy. Strong institutions for enforcing contracts that are fit for purpose can facilitate market transactions and investments by firms and farms. Another important dimension of strong institutions is legislation guaranteeing equal treatment of women in the workplace and business.

An adequate macrofiscal framework and monetary policy are crucial for macroeconomic stability and promoting business confidence to invest and hire. Macroeconomic instability can drive inflation with potentially deleterious effects. Inflation in particular taxes the earnings of informal sector workers, who have no protections against cost-of-living or input price increases. Input price inflation can also adversely affect the decisions of businesses and farmers operating in low-income settings.

Increasing contestability of markets via regulatory reform, rebalancing the role of state-owned enterprises, and using competition policy will be crucial to supporting innovation and expanding access to capital, technology, and markets. Ensuring a level playing field by removing barriers to competition will help more productive firms expand their employment. This often involves reforming licensing and permitting programs, reforming regulations limiting ownership, and rethinking price controls. Evidence from studies that focus on opening up competition suggests that there are large benefits to consumers from lower prices.[18] Firms that source inputs can also benefit from competition, especially those depending on inputs from the services sector (Arnold, Javorcik, and Mattoo 2011; Fernandes and Paunov 2012). Similarly, increasing the contestability of telecommunications and transportation sectors, complemented by a strong regulatory framework, can enhance the affordability of these services essential to market integration. Increasing market contestability also means addressing the dominance of state-owned enterprises in many markets, especially in markets where private sector provision is viable. Reassessing the role of state involvement in competitive markets, as well as governance arrangements to minimize distortive impacts of business with state involvement, is important to increase market contestability. Almost all countries in the region have adopted a competition law to govern the market and promote and protect competition (Büthe and Kigwiru 2020).

Strong contract enforcement institutions provide legal certainty in case of commercial disputes and can therefore unlock investments by firms and farms. Strong state capacity is needed to ensure an effective justice system, and special mechanisms are needed in fragile contexts (Bosio 2023a, 2023b; Büthe and Kigwiru 2020; Lichand and Soares 2014; Rao 2024). The small scale of firms and farms in the region calls for fit-for-purpose mechanisms that can offer a speedy resolution to disputes. Good practices in contract enforcement identified by the World Bank include dedicated and specialized commercial courts, divisions, or judges; having small claims courts or simplified procedures; and the use of alternative dispute resolution mechanisms to complement the traditional court system (World Bank n.d.). Although research on the effectiveness of these measures is limited, there is evidence of smallholder farmers in Ethiopia, Rwanda, and South Sudan engaging in relational contracts with traders and mills when formal contract enforcement is weak (Boudreau, Cajal-Grossi, and Macchiavello 2023; Bulte, Do Nascimento Miguel, and Anissa 2024; Macchiavello and Morjaria 2021). Smallholders' reliance on relational contracts reduces competition in agricultural product markets. Strong and accessible contract enforcement systems can therefore unlock additional benefits in the form of greater competition and better prices for smallholders.

Legal reforms that remove institutional barriers to women's economic participation can be effective in reducing gender differences in labor market outcomes (Roy 2019). Recently, Côte d'Ivoire, Gabon, and Togo removed legal restrictions on women's economic participation (Tavares and Benetatos 2023; refer also to spotlight 2 on gender equality). Côte d'Ivoire and Gabon, for example, removed legal restrictions on women's employment. In Gabon, the 1972 Civil Code was revised so that, like men, women could be recognized as the official head of household, choose where they live, and own and manage property (Tavares 2022). As a result of the reform, women can also open bank accounts. Reforms were also introduced to ensure that women cannot be discriminated against when accessing credit.

Annex 4A: Analytical foundations: Links between income inequality, market distortions, and producers

To map out how the distribution of earned income is linked to markets and the production side of the economy, it useful to follow Restuccia and Rogerson (2017) and consider an economy in which each producer i (firm or farm) generates output using the following production function: $y_i = a_i f(l_i, k_i)$, where a_i is productivity of each producer i, l_i is labor employed by the producer, and k_i is capital used. L and K are the total labor (workers, farmers, household enterprise workers) and capital, respectively, in the economy.

Each worker earns a wage that is equal to the marginal product for given levels of capital; entrepreneurs, farms, and household enterprise owners earn returns to their labor and capital. This gives rise to a dispersion of wages and earnings for each producer. Taken together, the incomes earned affect the level and distribution of personal income in the economy.

Aggregate output is affected by the availability of technology (a_i); producer entry, survival, and exit; and how total labor (L) and capital (K) resources are allocated across firms and farms.

When allocation of resources is efficient, producers with higher productivity receive more labor and capital. This gives rise to a distribution of producer sizes and the equalization of the marginal product of labor and capital across all producers.[19] Combining insights from Restuccia and Rogerson (2017), Rud and Trapeznikova (2021), and Lazear and Shaw (2018) suggests that the personal income distribution in this economy is affected by all three channels that also affect aggregate output.

Distortions result in inefficient allocation of labor and capital across different producers and thus adversely affect both the distribution of income and the level of income. In this way, distortions lead to inequality and poverty. They also misallocate labor and capital across producers, and this misallocation reduces aggregate output. Distortions also affect the size distribution of producers. Correcting distortions can therefore reduce poverty and inequality, boost growth, and affect the size and scale of firms and farms.

Source: World Bank elaboration.

Notes

1. Following Fields (1979), total household income inequality is decomposed by the different income sources. These income sources are wages, enterprise income, agriculture income, remittances, and other income sources. This analysis was done using the *descogini* command in Stata (Lopez-Feldman 2006) for total household income and per capita household income.

2. International Labour Organization Modelled Estimates Database.

3. The 31 percent who are neither working nor unemployed consist mainly of those attending school or young women. There is gender gap in economic participation rates, but it is not large (about 65 percent of women and 70 percent of men).

4. International Labour Organization Modelled Estimates Database. Figures exclude high-income countries.

5. There is an academic debate on whether firm distributions in developing countries can be characterized by a missing middle or not. Tybout (2000) highlights an underrepresentation of mid-sized firms in the employment distribution of developing economies compared with high-income countries. Hsieh and Olken (2014) argue that there is no missing middle because firm distributions do not exhibit them, and the underrepresentation of mid-sized firms is not robust to different size classifications. Abreha et al. (2022) confirm the underrepresentation of mid-sized firms in the employment distribution in African countries but relate it to the existence of mostly informal small-scale enterprises and argue that a distribution with a missing middle can point to distortions across the size distribution: a lack of growth of small-scale firms and a limited absorption of self-employed workers by larger firms.

6. Estimates based on firm-level data from 20 low- and middle-income countries. In this analysis, a large firm is defined as having 250 or more employees, a microfirm as having fewer than 10 employees.

7. Kurz (2023) analyzes the role that proprietary innovative technology has played in driving income inequality in the United States by enabling innovating firms to gain substantial market power and earn abnormally high profits, which in turn get distributed to the few who own or work in these firms.

8. Employment growth does not have to occur in the same productive firm. An expansion, even when labor saving for that particular firm, will create opportunities in other firms.

9. In Libya, conflict has led to a decline in revenues for 51 percent of firms (Rahman and Di Maio 2020). Studying firm exit in the Syrian Arab Republic from 2009 to 2017, Salmon, Assaf, and Francis (2018) suggest that higher-productivity firms were more likely to stay in business, except for firms in the most affected city, Aleppo, where productive firms mostly relocated. In West Bank and Gaza, during the Second Intifada, firms substituted domestically produced materials with

imports, leading to a more than 70 percent fall in output value in high-conflict districts (Amodio and Di Maio 2018).

10. To reflect the diversity of economic activity in Africa, this analytical framework refers to both household enterprises and those businesses that operate as entities independently of their households as firms. The former are usually considered as necessity or survivalist and the latter as opportunity- or growth-oriented firms, but, as shown later in the chapter, some household enterprises display the potential of growth orientation.

11. Returns to capital nevertheless depend on several factors, including factors related to the household. For example, female entrepreneurs in Ghana did not see returns to grants given as a cash but did see returns to grants that were given in kind (Fafchamps et al. 2014). Lack of instruments to manage risks could also lead potentially high-return firms to underinvest in capital.

12. In integrated markets, because of spatial arbitrage, prices of goods converge across locations, and global changes in the price of imported goods are passed on to domestic prices.

13. Recent research has also documented unrealistic expectations about wage offers and jobs among young labor market entrants as another source of job-matching friction.

14. Equity financing allows entrepreneurs to access funds without incurring debt in exchange for a share of ownership in their company. Venture capital, a subset of equity financing, is often directed toward companies with high growth potential, bringing not only capital but also strategic guidance, mentorship, and access to networks.

15. The bigger bottlenecks to investments lie in implementation, state capacity, and efficiency of public spending (Calderon et al. 2018).

16. India's upgrading of a network of national highways resulted in significant improvement in firm performance, whereas investments in rural road networks had positive but limited impacts in the short term (Asher and Novosad 2020; Ghani, Goswami, and Kerr 2016).

17. Mensah 2023 analyzed causal impacts in African countries.

18. For example, in Mexico, opening up competition by allowing foreign entry in the retail sector lowered consumer prices (Atkin, Faber, and Gonzalez-Navarro 2018).

19. In a dynamic economy, in response to a shock such as trade, marginal products might not equalize as the economy adjusts and resources shift across sectors and producers.

References

Abbasi, Mansoureh, Mathilde Lebrand, Arcady Bluette Mongoue, Roland Pongou, and Fan Zhang. 2022. "Roads, Electricity, and Jobs Evidence of Infrastructure Complementarity in Sub-Saharan Africa." Policy Research Working Paper 9976, World Bank, Washington, DC. http://documents .worldbank.org/curated/en/970271647884335950/ Roads-Electricity-and-Jobs-Evidence-of-Infrastructure-Complementarity-in-Sub-Saharan-Africa.

Abdulai, Awudu. 2006. "Spatial Integration and Price Transmission in Agricultural Commodity Markets in Sub-Saharan Africa." In *Agricultural Commodity Markets and Trade: New Approaches to Analyzing Market Structure and Instability*, edited by Alexander Sarris and David Hallan, 163–86. Cheltenham, UK: Edward Elgar.

Abebe, Girum, Niklas Buehren, and Markus Goldstein. 2020. "Short-Run Welfare Impacts of Factory Jobs Experimental Evidence from Ethiopia." Policy Research Working Paper 9325, World Bank, Washington, DC. http://documents.worldbank.org/curated/en/400881595340716051/Short-Run -Welfare-Impacts-of-Factory-Jobs-Experimental-Evidence-from-Ethiopia.

Abebe, Girum, A. Stefano Caria, Marcel Fafchamps, Paolo Falco, Simon Franklin, and Simon Quinn. 2021. "Anonymity or Distance? Job Search and Labour Market Exclusion in a Growing African City." *Review of Economic Studies* 88 (3): 1279–310. https://doi.org/10.1093/restud/rdaa057.

Abreha, Kaleb, Xavier Cirera, Elwyn Davies, Roberto Fattal Jaef, and Hibret Maemir. 2022. "Deconstructing the Missing Middle: Informality and Growth of Firms in Sub-Saharan Africa." Policy Research Working Paper 10233, World Bank, Washington, DC. https://documents .worldbank.org/en/publication/documents-reports/documentdetail/099924211162242314 /idu0b070c6340f4d10403d08bd90f758ec6dcf49.

Adukia, Anjali, Sam Asher, and Paul Novosad. 2020. "Educational Investment Responses to Economic Opportunity: Evidence from Indian Road Construction." *American Economic Journal: Applied Economics* 12 (1): 348–76. https://doi.org/10.1257/app.20180036.

Aga, Gemechu, Francisco Campos, Adriana Conconi, Elwyn Davies, and Carolin Geginat. 2021. "Informal Firms in Mozambique: Status and Potential." Policy Research Working Paper 9712, World Bank, Washington, DC. https://documents1.worldbank.org/curated/en /728261624545269477/pdf/Informal-Firms-in-Mozambique-Status-and-Potential.pdf.

Ahmed, Tanima, Amanda Devercelli, Elena Glinskaya, Rudaba Nasir, and Laura B. Rawlings. 2023. "Addressing Care to Accelerate Equality." World Bank Group Gender Thematic Policy Notes Series, World Bank, Washington, DC. https://openknowledge.worldbank.org/handle/10986/40184.

Aker, Jenny C., and Kelsey Jack. 2021. "Harvesting the Rain: The Adoption of Environmental Technologies in the Sahel." Working Paper 29518, National Bureau of Economic Research, Cambridge, MA. http://www.nber.org/papers/w29518.

Alfaro, Laura. 2017. "Gains from Foreign Direct Investment: Macro and Micro Approaches." *World Bank Economic Review* 30 (Supplement 1): S2–S15.

Alfaro Ureña, Alonso, Isabela Manelici, and Jose P. Vasquez. 2019. "The Effects of Multinationals on Workers: Evidence from Costa Rica." Working Paper 285, Griswold Center for Economic Policy Studies, Princeton, NJ. https://gceps.princeton.edu/wp-content/uploads/2021/06/285_Valdez.pdf.

Ali, Rubaba, A. Federico Barra, Claudia Berg, Richard Damania, John Nash, and Jason Russ. 2015. *Highways to Success or Byways to Waste.* Washington, DC: World Bank.

Alibhai, Salman, Niklas Buehren, Michael Frese, Markus Goldstein, Sreelakshmi Papineni, and Kathrin Wolf. 2019. "Full Esteem Ahead: Mindset-Oriented Business Training in Ethiopia." World Bank Policy Research Working Paper 8892, World Bank, Washington, DC. https://hdl.handle.net/10986/31905.

Amodio, Francesco, and Michele Di Maio. 2018. "Making Do With What You Have: Conflict, Input Misallocation and Firm Performance." *Economic Journal* 128 (615): 2559–612. https://doi.org /10.1111/ecoj.12518.

Amodio, Francesco, Pamela Medina, and Monica Morlacco. 2022. "Labor Market Power, Self-Employment, and Development." Working Paper, Private Enterprise Development in Low-Income Countries, London. https://pedl.cepr.org/sites/default/files/WP%206500%20 AmodioMedinaMorlacco%20LabourMarketPowerSelfEmploymentDevelopment_v4.pdf.

Anderson, Stephen J., and David McKenzie. 2022 "Improving Business Practices and the Boundary of the Entrepreneur: A Randomized Experiment Comparing Training, Consulting, Insourcing, and Outsourcing." *Journal of Political Economy* 130 (1): 157–209.

ANSD (Agence National de la Statistique et de la Démographie). 2022. "Enquête Harmonisée sur le Conditions de Vie des Ménages 2018-2019." Data set. Washington, DC: World Bank. https://doi .org/10.48529/HHHX-J012.

Arnold, Jens M., Beata S. Javorcik, and Aaditya Mattoo. 2011. "Does Services Liberalization Benefit Manufacturing Firms? Evidence from the Czech Republic." *Journal of International Economics* 85 (1): 136–46.

Asher, Sam, and Paul Novosad. 2020. "Rural Roads and Local Economic Development." *American Economic Review* 110 (3): 797–823. https://doi.org/10.1257/aer.20180268.

Atkin, David, and Dave Donaldson. 2015. "Who's Getting Globalized? The Size and Implications of Intra-National Trade Costs." Working Paper 21439, National Bureau of Economic Research, Cambridge, MA. https://doi.org/10.3386/w21439

Atkin, David, Amit K. Khandelwal, and Adam Osman. 2017. "Exporting and Firm Performance: Evidence from a Randomized Trial." *Quarterly Journal of Economics* 132 (2): 551–615.

AUC (African Union Commission) and OECD (Organisation for Economic Co-operation and Development). 2022. *Africa's Development Dynamics 2022: Regional Value Chains for a Sustainable Recovery*. Africa's Development Dynamics. Paris: OECD. https://doi.org/10.1787/2e3b97fd-en.

Bajgar, Matej, and Beata Javorcik. 2020. "Climbing the Rungs of the Quality Ladder: FDI and Domestic Exporters in Romania." *Economic Journal* 130 (628): 937–55.

Banerjee, Abhijit V., and Esther Duflo. 2005. "Growth Theory through the Lens of Development Economics." *Handbook of Economic Growth*, Vol. 1, Part A, edited by Philippe Aghion and Steven N. Durlauf, 473–552. https://doi.org/10.1016/S1574-0684(05)01007-5.

Barrett, Christopher B., Thomas Reardon, Johan Swinnen, and David Zilberman. 2022. "Agri-Food Value Chain Revolutions in Low- and Middle-Income Countries." *Journal of Economic Literature* 60 (4): 1316–77. https://doi.org/10.1257/jel.20201539.

Beegle, Kathleen, and Luc Christiaensen. 2019. *Poverty Reduction in Africa*. Washington, DC: World Bank.

Beirne, Keelan, and Martina Kirchberger. 2021. "Concrete Thinking about Development." Trinity Economics Paper tep0621, Trinity College Dublin, Dublin.

Bergquist, Lauren Falcao, and Michael Dinerstein. 2020. "Competition and Entry in Agricultural Markets: Experimental Evidence from Kenya." *American Economic Review* 110 (12): 3705–47. https://doi.org/10.1257/AER.20171397.

Bhorat, Haroon, Ravi Kanbur, and Benjamin Stanwix. 2017. "Minimum Wages in Sub-Saharan Africa: A Primer." *World Bank Research Observer* 32 (1): 21–74. https://doi.org/10.1093/wbro/lkw007.

Bloom, Nicholas, Benn Eifert, Aprajit Mahajan, David McKenzie, and John Roberts. 2013. "Does Management Matter? Evidence From India." *Quarterly Journal of Economics* 128 (1): 1–51.

Bloom, Nicholas, Renata Lemos, Raffaella Sadun, Daniela Scur, and John Van Reenen. 2014. "JEEA-FBBVA Lecture 2013: The New Empirical Economics of Management." *Journal of the European Economic Association* 12 (4): 835–76.

Boeddu, Gian, and Jennifer Chien. 2022. "Financial Consumer Protection and Fintech: An Overview of New Manifestations of Consumer Risks and Emerging Regulatory Approaches." Fintech and the Future of Finance Overview Paper, World Bank, Washington, DC. https://thedocs.worldbank.org/en/doc/11ea23266a1f65d9a08cbe0e9b072c89-0430012022/related/Note-5.pdf.

Bolt, Jutta, and Jan Luiten Van Zanden. 2024. "Maddison–Style Estimates of the Evolution of the World Economy: A New 2023 Update." *Journal of Economic Surveys*.

Bosio, Erica. 2023a. *Increasing Access to Justice in Fragile Settings*. Washington, DC: World Bank. http://documents.worldbank.org/curated/en/099101123141530374/P17955108fb2a104e0a55e04b0257738ea3.

Bosio, Erica. 2023b. "A Survey of Judicial Effectiveness: The Last Quarter Century of Empirical Evidence." Policy Research Working Paper 10501, World Bank, Washington, DC. http://documents .worldbank.org/curated/en/099330206262335739/IDU0c20eb45a08f4504cee09199072bada1c4771.

Boudreau, Laura, Julia Cajal-Grossi, and Rocco Macchiavello. 2023. "Global Value Chains in Developing Countries: A Relational Perspective from Coffee and Garments." *Journal of Economic Perspectives* 37 (3): 59–86. https://doi.org/10.1257/jep.37.3.59.

Bove, Abel, Olivier Hartmann, Aiga Stokenberga, Vincent Vesin, and Yaya Yedan. 2018. "West and Central Africa Trucking Competitiveness." Working Paper 108, Africa Transport Policy Program, World Bank, Washington, DC. https://www.ssatp.org/publication/west-and-central -africa-trucking-competitiveness.

Bulte, Erwin, Jérémy Do Nascimento Miguel, and Banawe Plambou Anissa. 2024. "Competition on Agricultural Markets and Quality of Smallholder Supply: The Role of Relational Contracting and Input Provision by Traders." *Economic Development and Cultural Change* 72 (2): 603–32. https://doi.org/10.1086/721024.

Burgis, Tom. 2015. *The Looting Machine. Warlords, Oligarchs, Corporations, Smugglers, and the Theft of Africa's Wealth.* New York: Public Affairs.

Burke, Marshall, Lauren Falcao Bergquist, and Edward Miguel. 2019. "Sell Low and Buy High: Arbitrage and Local Price Effects in Kenyan Markets." *Quarterly Journal of Economics* 134 (2): 785–842. https://doi.org/10.1093/qje/qjy034.

Büthe, Tim, and Vellah Kedogo Kigwiru. 2020. "The Spread of Competition Law and Policy in Africa: A Research Agenda." *African Journal of International Economic Law* 1 (Fall): 41–83. https://www .afronomicslaw.org/sites/default/files/journal/2021/Bu%C3%8C%C2%88theKigwiru-Spread-of -Competition-Policy-in-Africa-1-AfJIEL-41-2020-2.pdf.

Cai, Jing, Muhammad Meki, Simon Quinn, Erica Field, Cynthia Kinnan, Jonathan Morduch, and Jonathan De Quidt. 2023. "Microfinance." *VoxDev Lit* 3 (2).

Calderón, César. 2022. *Boosting Productivity in Sub-Saharan Africa: Policies and Institutions to Promote Efficiency.* Washington, DC: World Bank.

Calderón, César, Catalina Cantú, and Punam Chuhan-Pole. 2018. "Infrastructure Development in Sub-Saharan Africa: A Scorecard." Policy Research Working Paper 8425, World Bank, Washington, DC. http://www.worldbank.org/research.

Calligaris, Sara, Flavio Calvino, Rudy Verlhac, and Martin Reinhard. 2023. "Is There a Trade-Off Between Productivity and Employment? A Cross-Country Micro-to-Macro Study." OECD Science, Technology and Industry Policy Paper 157, OECD Publishing, Paris. https://doi.org/10.1787/99bede51-en.

Campos, Francisco, Michael Frese, Markus Goldstein, Leonardo Iacovone, Hillary C. Johnson, David McKenzie, and Mona Mensmann. 2017. "Teaching Personal Initiative Beats Traditional Training in Boosting Small Business in West Africa." *Science* 357 (6357): 1287–90.

Campos, Francisco, Markus Goldstein, and David McKenzie. 2023. "How Should the Government Bring Small Firms Into the Formal System? Experimental Evidence From Malawi." *Journal of Development Economics* 161: 103045.

Caria, Stefano, Kate Orkin, Alison Andrew, Robert Garlick, Rachel Heath, and Niharika Singh. 2024. "Barriers to Search and Hiring in Urban Labour Markets." *VoxDevLit* 10 (1).

Carranza, Eliana, and David McKenzie. 2023. "Job Training and Job Search Assistance Policies in Developing Countries." Policy Research Working Paper 10576, World Bank, Washington, DC. http://documents.worldbank.org/curated/en/099648409282314225/IDU0376203a30f7ac04 c690bd9900b63d1dbfd80.

Christiaensen, Luc. 2020. "Agriculture, Jobs, and Value Chains in Africa." World Bank *Jobs Note* 9. https://documents1.worldbank.org/curated/en/766801588571083740/pdf/Agriculture-Jobs-and -Value-Chains-in-Africa.pdf.

Christiaensen, Luc, and Miet Maertens. 2022. "Rural Employment in Africa: Trends and Challenges." *Annual Review of Resource Economics* 14: 267–89. https://doi.org/10.1146/annurev-resource -111820-014312.

Cirera, Xavier, Diego Comin, and Marcio Cruz. 2022. *Bridging the Technological Divide: Technology Adoption by Firms in Developing Countries*. Washington, DC: World Bank.

Couttenier, Mathieu, and Raphael Soubeyran. 2014. "Drought and Civil War in Sub-Saharan Africa." *Economic Journal* 124 (575): 201–44. https://doi.org/10.1111/ecoj.12042.

Cuberes, David, and Marc Teignier. 2016. "Aggregate Effects of Gender Gaps in the Labor Market: A Quantitative Estimate." *Journal of Human Capital* 10 (1): 1–32. https://doi.org/10.1086/683847.

Cusolito, Ana P., and Tatiana Didier. forthcoming. *Unleashing Productivity Through Firm Financing*. Washington, DC: World Bank.

Danquah, Michael, Simone Schotte, and Kunal Sen. 2019. "Informal Work in Sub-Saharan Africa: Dead End or Steppingstone?" Working Paper 2019/107, UNU-WIDER, Helsinki. https://doi.org/10.35188 /UNU-WIDER/2019/743-9.

De Andrade, Gustavo Henrique, Miriam Bruhn, and David McKenzie. 2013. "A Helping Hand or the Long Arm of the Law: Experimental Evidence on What Governments Can Do to Formalize Firms." Policy Research Working Paper 6435, World Bank, Washington, DC. http://documents.worldbank .org/curated/en/802931502348707678/A-helping-hand-or-the-long-arm-of-the-law-experimental -evidence-on-what-governments-can-do-to-formalize-firms.

De Loecker, Jan. 2013. "Detecting Learning by Exporting." *American Economic Journal: Microeconomics* 5 (3): 1–21.

De Mel, Suresh, David McKenzie, and Christopher Woodruff. 2013. "The Demand for, and Consequences of, Formalization Among Informal Firms in Sri Lanka." *American Economic Journal: Applied Economics* 5 (2): 122–50.

De Soto, Hernando. 2007. *The Mystery of Capital: Why Capitalism Triumphs in the West and Fails Everywhere Else*. New York: Basic Books.

Diao, Xinshen, Josaphat Kweka, and Margaret Mcmillan. 2016. "Economic Transformation in Africa from the Bottom Up: Evidence from Tanzania." Working Paper 22889, National Bureau of Economic Research, Cambridge, MA. http://www.nber.org/papers/w22889.

Dillon, Brian, and Christopher B. Barrett. 2017. "Agricultural Factor Markets in Sub-Saharan Africa: An Updated View with Formal Tests for Market Failure." *Food Policy* 67: 64–77. https://doi.org/10.1016 /j.foodpol.2016.09.015.

Donovan, Kevin, Will Jianyu Lu, and Todd Schoellman. 2023. "Labor Market Dynamics and Development." *Quarterly Journal of Economics* 138 (4): 2287–325. https://doi.org/10.1093/qje/qjad019.

Eberhard-Ruiz, Andreas. 2022. "The Impact of Armed Conflict Shocks on Local Cross-Border Trade: Evidence from the Border Between Uganda and the Democratic Republic of Congo." *Economic Development and Cultural Change* 72 (3): 1151–87. https://doi.org/10.1086/722967.

Echandi, Roberto, Maryla Maliszewska, and Victor Steenbergen. 2022. *Making the Most of the African Continental Free Trade Area: Leveraging Trade and Foreign Direct Investment to Boost Growth and Reduce Poverty*. Washington, DC: World Bank.

Fackler, Paul L., and Barry K. Goodwin. 2001. "Spatial Price Analysis." In *Handbook of Agricultural Economics*, Vol. 1, Part B, edited by B. Gardner and G. Rausser, 971–1024. New York: Elsevier Science.

Fafchamps, Marcel. 1994. "Industrial Structure and Microenterprises in Africa." *Journal of Developing Areas* 29 (1): 1–30.

Fafchamps, Marcel. 2001. "Networks, Communities and Markets in Sub-Saharan Africa: Implications for Firm Growth and Investment." *Journal of African Economies* 10 (Supplement 2): 109–42. https://doi.org/10.1093/jae/10.Suppl2.109.

Fafchamps, Marcel. 2003. *Market Institutions in Sub-Saharan Africa.* Cambridge, MA: MIT Press. https://doi.org/10.7551/mitpress/4445.001.0001.

Fafchamps, Marcel, David McKenzie, Simon Quinn, and Christopher Woodruff. 2014. "Microenterprise Growth and the Flypaper Effect: Evidence from a Randomized Experiment in Ghana." *Journal of Development Economics* 106: 211–26. https://doi.org/10.1016/j.jdeveco.2013.09.010.

Fernandes, Ana M., and Caroline Paunov. 2012. "Foreign Direct Investment in Services and Manufacturing Productivity: Evidence for Chile." *Journal of Development Economics* 97 (2): 305–21.

Foster, Andrew D., and Mark R. Rosenzweig. 2022. "Are There Too Many Farms in the World? Labor Market Transaction Costs, Machine Capacities, and Optimal Farm Size." *Journal of Political Economy* 130 (3): 636–80. https://doi.org/10.1086/717890.

Foster, Vivien, Nisan Gorgulu, Stéphane Straub, and Maria Vagliasindi. 2023. "The Impact of Infrastructure on Development Outcomes: A Qualitative Review of Four Decades of Literature." Policy Research Working Paper 10343, World Bank, Washington, DC. https://documents1 .worldbank.org/curated/en/099529203062342252/pdf/IDU0e42ae32f0048304f74086d102b6d7 a900223.pdf.

Franklin, Simon. 2018. "Location, Search Costs and Youth Unemployment: Experimental Evidence from Transport Subsidies." *Economic Journal* 128 (614): 2353–79. https://doi.org/10.1111/ecoj.12509.

Gandhi, Aditi, and Michael Walton. 2012. "Where Do India's Billionaires Get Their Wealth?" *Economic & Political Weekly* 47 (40): 10–14.

Ghani, Ejaz, Arti Grover Goswami, and William R. Kerr. 2016. "Highway to Success: The Impact of the Golden Quadrilateral Project for the Location and Performance of Indian Manufacturing." *Economic Journal* 126 (591): 317–57. https://doi.org/10.1111/ecoj.12207.

Glaub, Matthias E., Michael Frese, Sebastian Fischer, and Maria Hoppe. 2014 "Increasing Personal Initiative in Small Business Managers or Owners Leads to Entrepreneurial Success: A Theory-Based Controlled Randomized Field Intervention for Evidence-Based Management." *Academy of Management Learning & Education* 13 (3): 354–79.

Goldberg, Pinelopi Koujianou, and Tristan Reed. 2023. "Presidential Address: Demand-Side Constraints in Development: The Role of Market Size, Trade, and (In)Equality." *Econometrica* 91 (6): 1915–50. https://doi.org/10.3982/ecta20787.

Gollin, Douglas. 2015. "Agriculture as an Engine of Growth and Poverty Reduction: Lessons for Africa." In *Economic Growth and Poverty Reduction in Sub-Saharan Africa*, edited by Andrew McKay and Erik Thorbeck, 91–121. New York: Oxford Academic. https://doi.org/10.1093/acprof :oso/9780198728450.003.0004.

Harari, Mariaflavia, and Eliana La Ferrara. 2018. "Conflict, Climate, and Cells: A Disaggregated Analysis." *Review of Economics and Statistics* 100 (4): 594–608. https://doi.org/10.1162/rest_a_00730.

Hardy, Morgan, and Jamie McCasland. 2023. "Are Small Firms Labor Constrained? Experimental Evidence from Ghana." *American Economic Journal: Applied Economics* 15 (2): 253–84. https://doi .org/10.1257/app.20200503.

Helpman, Elhanan, Marc J. Melitz, and Stephen R. Yeaple. 2004. "Export Versus FDI with Heterogeneous Firms." *American Economic Review* 94 (1): 300–16.

Herrendorf, Berthold, Richard Rogerson, and Akos Valentinyi. 2014. "Growth and Structural Transformation." In *Handbook of Economic Growth*, Vol. 2, edited by Philippe Aghion and Steven N. Durlauf, 855–941. Amsterdam: Elsevier.

Hsiang, Solomon M., Marshall Burke, and Edward Miguel. 2013. "Quantifying the Influence of Climate on Human Conflict." *Science* 341 (6151): 1235367. https://doi.org/10.1126/science.1235367.

Hsieh, Chang Tai, and Benjamin A. Olken. 2014. "The Missing 'Missing Middle.'" *Journal of Economic Perspectives* 28 (3): 89–108. https://doi.org/10.1257/jep.28.3.89.

Iacovone, Leonardo, Beata Javorcik, Wolfgang Keller, and James Tybout. 2015. "Supplier Responses to Walmart's Invasion in Mexico." *Journal of International Economics* 95 (1): 1–15.

Iacovone, Leonardo, William Maloney, and David McKenzie. 2022. "Improving Management with Individual and Group-Based Consulting: Results from a Randomized Experiment in Colombia." *Review of Economic Studies* 89 (1): 346–71.

Javorcik, Beata Smarzynska. 2004. "Does Foreign Direct Investment Increase the Productivity of Domestic Firms? In Search of Spillovers Through Backward Linkages." *American Economic Review* 94 (3): 605–27.

Jayne, T. S. 2012. "Managing Food Price Instability in East and Southern Africa." *Global Food Security* 1 (2): 143–49. https://doi.org/10.1016/j.gfs.2012.10.002.

Jayne, T. S., Jordan Chamberlin, Lulama Traub, Nicholas Sitko, Milu Muyanga, Felix K. Yeboah, Ward Anseeuw, Antony Chapoto, Ayala Wineman, Chewe Nkonde, and Richard Kachule. 2016. "Africa's Changing Farm Size Distribution Patterns: The Rise of Medium-Scale Farms." *Agricultural Economics* 47 (S1): 197–214. https://doi.org/10.1111/agec.12308.

Jia, Ruixue. 2014. "Weather Shocks, Sweet Potatoes and Peasant Revolts in Historical China." *Economic Journal* 124 (575): 92–118. https://doi.org/10.1111/ecoj.12037.

Kaplan, David S., Eduardo Piedra, and Enrique Seira. 2011. "Entry Regulation and Business Start-Ups: Evidence From Mexico." *Journal of Public Economics* 95 (11–12): 1501–15. https://doi.org/10.1016/j.jpubeco.2011.03.007.

Karlen, Raphaela Beatrice, Solene Marie Paule Rougeaux, Sara Johansson de Silva, and Simon Serge Barraud. 2023. *Resilience and Productivity: Keys to a Better Future for Urban Informal Sector Workers in Côte d'Ivoire*. Washington, DC: World Bank. https://openknowledge.worldbank.org/handle/10986/40435.

Kebede, Hundanol A. 2024. "Gains from Market Integration: Welfare Effects of New Rural Roads in Ethiopia." *Journal of Development Economics* 168: 103252. https://doi.org/10.1016/j.jdeveco.2024.103252.

Klapper, Leora, Christine Richmond, and Trang Tran. 2013. "Civil Conflict and Firm Performance Evidence from Côte d'Ivoire." Policy Research Working Paper 6640, World Bank, Washington, DC. http://hdl.handle.net/10986/16857.

Ksoll, Christopher, Rocco Macchiavello, and Ameet Morjaria. 2022. "Electoral Violence and Supply Chain Disruptions in Kenya's Floriculture Industry." *Review of Economics and Statistics* 105 (6): 1335–51. https://doi.org/10.1162/rest_a_01185.

Kurz, Mordecai. 2023. *The Market Power of Technology*. New York: Columbia University Press. https://doi.org/10.7312/kurz20652.

La Porta, Rafael, and Andrei Shleifer. 2014. "Informality and Development." *Journal of Economic Perspectives* 28 (3): 109–26. https://doi.org/10.1257/jep.28.3.109.

Lazear, Edward P., and Kathryn L. Shaw. 2018. "Introduction: Firms and the Distribution of Income: The Roles of Productivity and Luck." *Journal of Labor Economics* 36 (S1): S1–S12.

Leight, Jessica, Josué Awonon, Abdoulaye Pedehombga, Rasmané Ganaba, and Aulo Gelli. 2021. "How Light Is Too Light Touch: The Effect of a Short Training-Based Intervention on Household Poultry Production in Burkina Faso." *Journal of Development Economics* 155: 102776. https://doi.org /10.1016/J.JDEVECO.2021.102776.

Léon, Florian, and Ibrahima Dosso. 2022. "Civil Conflict and Firm Recovery: Evidence from Côte d'Ivoire." *Journal of Development Studies* 58 (11): 2263–89. https://doi.org/10.1080/00220388.2022.2094255.

Leone, Fabrizio, Rocco Macchiavello, and Tristan Reed. 2021. "The Falling Price of Cement in Africa." Policy Research Working Paper 9706, World Bank, Washington, DC. https://documents1 .worldbank.org/curated/en/727041624328488778/pdf/The-Falling-Price-of-Cement-in-Africa.pdf.

Lichand, Guilherme, and Rodrigo R. Soares. 2014. "Access to Justice and Entrepreneurship: Evidence from Brazil's Special Civil Tribunals." *Journal of Law and Economics* 57 (2): 459–99. https://doi .org/10.1086/675087.

Lopez-Feldman, Alejandro. 2006. "Decomposing Inequality and Obtaining Marginal Effects." *Stata Journal* 6 (1): 106–11.

Lowder, Sarah K., Jakob Skoet, and Terri Raney. 2016. "The Number, Size, and Distribution of Farms, Smallholder Farms, and Family Farms Worldwide." *World Development* 87: 16–29. https://doi .org/10.1016/j.worlddev.2015.10.041.

Macchiavello, Rocco, and Ameet Morjaria. 2021. "Competition and Relational Contracts in the Rwanda Coffee Chain." *Quarterly Journal of Economics* 136 (2): 1089–143. https://doi .org/10.1093/qje/qjaa048.

Mather, David L., and Thomas S. Jayne. 2018. "Fertilizer Subsidies and the Role of Targeting in Crowding Out: Evidence from Kenya." *Food Security* 10 (2): 397–417. https://doi.org/10.1007/s12571 -018-0773-8.

McKenzie, David. 2017. "Identifying and Spurring High-Growth Entrepreneurship: Experimental Evidence from a Business Plan Competition." *American Economic Review* 107 (8): 2278–307.

McKenzie, David. 2023. "Is There Still A Role for Direct Government Support to Firms in Developing Countries?" Policy Research Working Paper 10628, World Bank, Washington, DC. https://documents1.worldbank.org/curated/en/099601212052338958/pdf /IDU0b34e6a2d01a52049ec09e66091587f19bc5e.pdf.

McKenzie, David, and Susana Puerto. 2021. "Growing Markets through Business Training for Female Entrepreneurs: A Market-Level Randomized Experiment in Kenya." *American Economic Journal: Applied Economics* 13 (2): 297–332. https://doi.org/10.1257/app.20180340.

McKenzie, David, and Dario Sansone. 2017. "Man vs. Machine in Predicting Successful Entrepreneurs: Evidence from a Business Plan Competition in Nigeria." Policy Research Working Paper 8271, World Bank, Washington, DC. https://documents1.worldbank.org/curated/en/968231513116778571 /pdf/WPS8271.pdf.

McKenzie, David, and Christopher Woodruff. 2017. "Business Practices in Small Firms in Developing Countries." *Management Science* 63 (9): 2967–81.

Melitz, Marc J. 2003. "The Impact of Trade on Intra-Industry Reallocations and Aggregate Industry Productivity." *Econometrica* 71 (6): 1695–725.

Mensah, Justice Tei. 2023. "Jobs! Electricity Shortages and Unemployment in Africa." *Journal of Development Economics* 167: 103231. https://doi.org/10.1016/j.jdeveco.2023.103231.

Miguel, Edward, Shanker Satyanath, and Ernest Sergenti. 2004. "Economic Shocks and Civil Conflict: An Instrumental Variables Approach." *Journal of Political Economy* 112 (4): 725–53. https://doi .org/10.1086/421174.

Morgan, Stephen, Jarrad Farris, and Michael E. Johnson. 2022. *Foreign Direct Investment in Africa: Recent Trends Leading up to the African Continental Free Trade Area (AfCFTA)*. Economic Information Bulletin 242. Washington, DC: U.S. Department of Agriculture, Economic Research Service. https://www.ers.usda.gov/webdocs/publications/104996/eib-242.pdf?v=6185.1.

Mullainathan, Sendhil, and Philipp Schnabl. 2010. "Does Less Market Entry Regulation Generate More Entrepreneurs? Evidence From a Regulatory Reform in Peru." In *International Differences in Entrepreneurship*, edited by Josh Lerner and Antoinette Schoar, 159–77. Chicago: University of Chicago Press.

Nakamura, Shohei, Tom Bundervoet, and Mohammed Nuru. 2020. "Rural Roads, Poverty, and Resilience: Evidence From Ethiopia." *Journal of Development Studies* 56 (10): 1838–55.

Nayyar, Gaurav, Mary Hallward-Driemeier, and Elwyn Davies. 2021. *At Your Service? The Promise of Services-Led Development*. Washington, DC: World Bank. https://worldbank.org/services-led-development.

Neumark, David, and Luis Felipe Munguía Corella. 2021. "Do Minimum Wages Reduce Employment in Developing Countries? A Survey and Exploration of Conflicting Evidence." *World Development* 137: 105165. https://doi.org/10.1016/j.worlddev.2020.105165.

Nunn, Nathan. 2007. "Historical Legacies: A Model Linking Africa's Past to Its Current Underdevelopment." *Journal of Development Economics* 83 (1): 157–75. https://doi.org/10.1016/j.jdeveco.2005.12.003.

Nunn, Nathan. 2014. "Historical Development." In *Handbook of Economic Growth*, Vol. 2, edited by Philippe Aghion and Staven N. Durlauf, 347–402. New York: Elsevier. https://doi.org/10.1016/B978-0-444-53538-2.00007-1.

Oostendorp, Remco H., Tran Quoc Trung, and Nguyen Thanh Tung. 2009. "The Changing Role of Non-Farm Household Enterprises in Vietnam." *World Development* 37 (3): 632–44. https://doi.org/10.1016/j.worlddev.2008.07.007.

Rabah, Arezki, and Thorvaldur Gylfason. 2013. "Resource Rents, Democracy, Corruption and Conflict: Evidence from Sub-Saharan Africa." *Journal of African Economies* 22 (4): 552–69. https://doi.org/10.1093/jae/ejs036.

Rahman, Aminur, and Michele Di Maio. 2020. "Conflict Effects on Firm Performance." In *The Private Sector amid Conflict: The Case of Libya*, 29–38. Washington, DC: World Bank. https://doi.org/10.1596/978-1-4648-1644-4_ch4.

Rao, Manaswini. 2024. "Front-Line Courts as State Capacity: Evidence from India." Working Paper, Department of Economics, University of Delaware, Newark. http://dx.doi.org/10.2139/ssrn.4854161.

Reda Cherif, Sandesh Dhungana, Xiangming Fang, Jesus Gonzalez-Garcia, Miguel Mendes, Yuanchen Yang, Mustafa Yenice, and Jung Eun Yoon. 2020. "Competition, Competitiveness and Growth in Sub-Saharan Africa." Working Paper WP/20/30, International Monetary Fund, Washington, DC.

Restuccia, Diego, and Richard Rogerson. 2017. "The Causes and Costs of Misallocation." *Journal of Economic Perspectives* 31 (3): 151–74. https://doi.org/10.1257/jep.31.3.151.

Roberts, Simon, Olwethu Shedi, Isaac Tausha, Kondwani Kaongo, Grace Nsomba, and Ntombifuthi Tshabalala. 2023. "Concentration, Competition and Market Outcomes in Fertiliser Markets in East and Southern Africa." Working Paper 2023/15, African Market Observatory, Centre for Competition, Regulation, and Economic Development, Johannesburg. https://static1.squarespace.com/static/52246331e4b0a46e5f1b8ce5/t/65e6e0a3926b7c65ab22acf2/1709629609329/AMO%2BCCC2023+Fert+WP_20240304_REV_Final.pdf.

Roy, Sanchari. 2019. "Discriminatory Laws against Women: A Survey of the Literature." Policy Research Working Paper 8719, World Bank, Washington, DC. https://documents1.worldbank.org /curated/ar/393191548685944435/pdf/WPS8719.pdf.

Rud, Juan Pablo, and Ija Trapeznikova. 2021. "Job Creation and Wages in Least Developed Countries: Evidence from Sub-Saharan Africa." *Economic Journal* 131 (635): 1331–64. https://doi.org/10.1093 /ej/ueaa110.

Salmon, Kinley, Nabila Assaf, and David Francis. 2018. "Surviving Firms of the Syrian Arab Republic: A Rapid Assessment." Policy Research Paper 8397, World Bank, Washington, DC. http://hdl.handle .net/10986/29610.

Sulla, Victor, Precious Zikhali, and Pablo Facundo Cuevas. 2022. *Inequality in Southern Africa: An Assessment of the Southern African Customs Union.* Washington, DC: World Bank. http://documents.worldbank.org/curated/en/099125303072236903 /P1649270c02a1f06b0a3ae02e57eadd7a82.

Suri, Tavneet, Prashant Bharadwaj, and William Jack. 2021. "Fintech and Household Resilience to Shocks: Evidence from Digital Loans in Kenya." *Journal of Development Economics* 153: 102697. https://doi.org/10.1016/j.jdeveco.2021.102697.

Suri, Tavneet, and Christopher Udry. 2022. "Agricultural Technology in Africa." *Journal of Economic Perspectives* 36 (1): 33–56. https://doi.org/10.1257/JEP.36.1.33.

Sutton, John. 2012. *Competing in Capabilities: The Globalization Process.* Oxford: Oxford University Press.

Tavares, Paula. 2022. "Gabon Revises Legislations to Protect Women and Increase Their Economic Role." *Africa Can End Poverty* (blog), March 2. https://blogs.worldbank.org/en/africacan/gabon -revises-legislation-protect-women-and-increase-their-economic-role

Tavares, Paula, and Dion Benetatos. 2023. "Gender Equality Gains Momentum in Sub-Saharan Africa." *Let's Talk Development* (blog), November 14. https://blogs.worldbank.org/en/developmenttalk /gender-equality-gains-momentum-sub-saharan-africa.

Teravaninthorn, Supee, and Gaël Raballand. 2009. *Infrastructure Transport Prices and Costs in Africa: A Review of the International Corridors.* Washington, DC: World Bank. http://documents .worldbank.org/curated/en/278561468201609212/Transport-prices-and-costs-in-Africa-a-review -of-the-international-corridors.

Tybout, James R. 2000. "Manufacturing Firms in Developing Countries: How Well Do They Do, And Why?" *Journal of Economic Literature* 38 (1): 11–44.

Ulyssea, Gabriel. 2018. "Firms, Informality, and Development: Theory and Evidence From Brazil." *American Economic Review* 108 (8): 2015–47.

Wollburg, Philip, Thomas Bentze, Yuchen Lu, Christopher Udry, and Douglas Gollin. 2024. "Crop Yields Fail to Rise in Smallholder Farming Systems in Sub-Saharan Africa." *Proceedings of the National Academy of Sciences of the United States of America* 121 (21): e2312519121. https://doi.org/10.1073 /pnas.2312519121.

Wollburg, Philip, Thomas Bentze, Yuchen Lu, Christopher Udry, and Douglas Gollin. n.d. "Agricultural Productivity Growth in Africa: New Evidence from Microdata." Unpublished manuscript, World Bank, Washington, DC. https://thedocs.worldbank.org/en/doc/ccfc87d5ab2c6c4af0ba501f1887d887 -0050022023/original/Agricultural-Productivity-Growth-in-Africa.pdf.

World Bank. 2017. "Ethiopia Employment and Jobs Study." World Bank, Washington, DC. https:// documents1.worldbank.org/curated/en/443391562238337443/pdf/Ethiopia-Employment-and -Jobs-Study.pdf.

World Bank. 2020. *The African Continental Free Trade Area : Economic and Distributional Effects.* Washington, DC: World Bank. https://documents.worldbank.org/en/publication/documents -reports/documentdetail/216831595998182418/the-african-continental-free-trade-area-economic -and-distributional-effects.

World Bank. 2022. "Ethiopia—Rural Income Diagnostics Study: Leveraging the Transformation in the Agri-Food System and Global Trade to Expand Rural Incomes." World Bank, Washington, DC. http://hdl.handle.net/10986/37954.

World Bank. 2023a. *The Business of the State.* Washington, DC: World Bank.

World Bank. 2023b. "Delivering Growth to People through Better Jobs." *Africa's Pulse* 28 (October). https://openknowledge.worldbank.org/handle/10986/40388.

World Bank. 2023c. *Navigating Education, Motherhood, and Informal Labor: The Experiences of Young Women in Luanda.* Washington, DC: World Bank. http://hdl.handle.net/10986/40401.

World Bank. 2023d. "Seizing Kenya's Services Momentum." Country Economic Memorandum for Kenya. Washington, DC: World Bank. https://www.worldbank.org/en/country/kenya/publication /kenya-country-economic-memorandum-afe-seizing-kenya-s-services-momentum.

World Bank. n.d. "Enforcing Contracts." Washington, DC: World Bank. https://subnational .doingbusiness.org/en/data/exploretopics/enforcing-contracts/good-practices#Using.

Poverty and Inequality Influencers: Fragility, Conflict, and Forced Displacement

OLIVE NSABABERA

Conflict and violence have been rising in Africa. After a period of relative stability in the early 2000s, the number of events associated with all types of conflict—battles, explosions, protests, riots, and violence against civilians—has increased sharply since 2010. In the years between 2018 and 2023 alone, the number of conflict events nearly doubled, reaching more than 27,000 in 2023 (refer to figure S3.1a). This has been driven by events in the Democratic Republic of Congo, Ethiopia, Nigeria, the Sahel, and Sudan (refer to figure S3.1b). The proliferation of communal and ethnic militias and nonstate actors has exacerbated conflicts over territory and resources, contributing to instability in these countries. The Sahel region, particularly Burkina Faso and Mali, has seen a dramatic escalation in violence since 2012, marked by military coups and increasing influence of external actors, that has intensified the conflict and civilian casualties. Jihadist groups have significantly expanded their operations, contributing to regional instability and a surge in violent incidents, challenging government control in several areas (ACLED 2023).

Fragility is persistent in parts of the region (refer to map S3.1). *Fragility* is defined as a "systemic condition or situation characterized by an extremely low level of institutional and governance capacity which significantly impedes the state's ability to function effectively, maintain peace and foster economic and social development" (World Bank 2024b, 1). Aside from new countries becoming fragile, some countries have persistently remained fragile, underscoring the considerable challenges of successfully exiting from the cycle of economic and political instability, weak governance and institutional capacity, and limited political and social inclusion that locks countries in a fragility trap (Akanbi et al. 2021; Collier 2021). Conflict significantly increases the likelihood of new, prolonged, recurrent, or escalating conflict episodes (Collier, Hoeffler, and Söderbom 2008; Hegre, Nygård, and Ræder 2017). The persistence of conflict on the continent is evident. Using the World Bank's (2023c) harmonized classification of fragile and conflict-affected situations, we examine whether a country was never fragile, always fragile, or transitioned in and out of fragility.[1] Of the 48 countries in Africa, in 2010–19 fewer than half were never fragile throughout the period, and 25 were classified as fragile at least once during that period. Of these, only seven exited the list completely, five moved in and out of fragility status, and 13 remained fragile for the entire period.

FIGURE S3.1 **Conflict events, 2000–23**

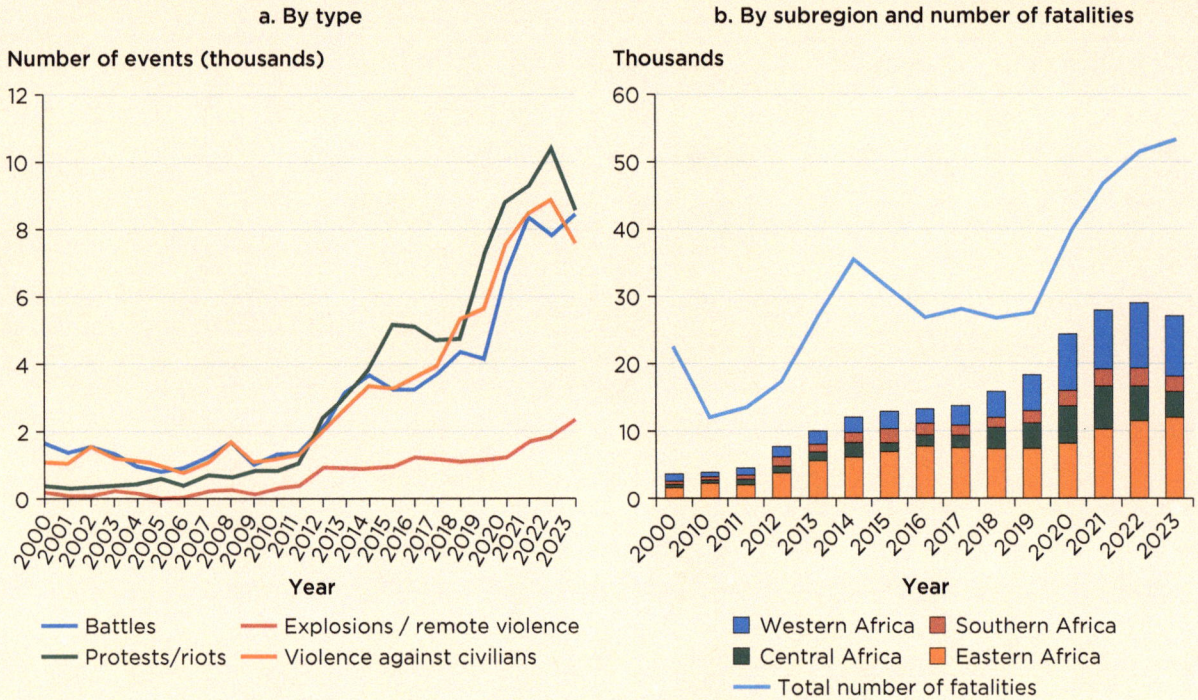

a. By type

Number of events (thousands)

b. By subregion and number of fatalities

Thousands

Legend (a):
- Battles
- Explosions / remote violence
- Protests/riots
- Violence against civilians

Legend (b):
- Western Africa
- Southern Africa
- Central Africa
- Eastern Africa
- Total number of fatalities

Source: Armed Conflict Location and Event Data Project database (https://www.acleddata.com/).
Note: Bars represent number of conflict events by region; figure excludes Cabo Verde, Comoros, Mauritius, São Tomé and Príncipe, and Seychelles because no data are available before 2020.

MAP S3.1 **Persistence of fragile situations, 2010 and 2019**

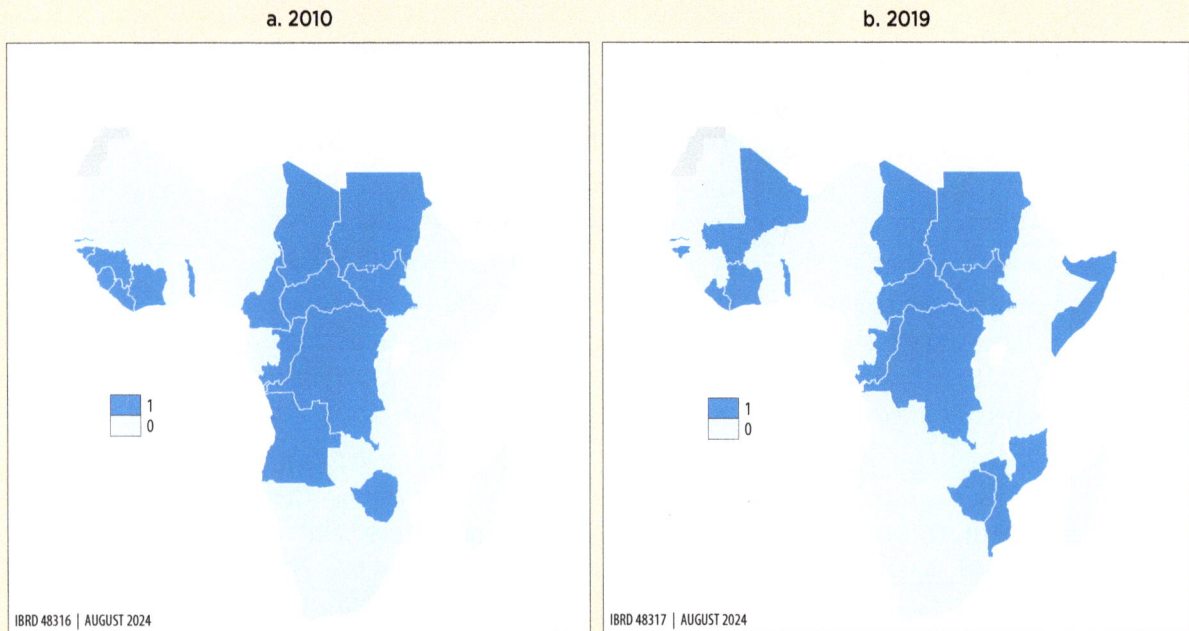

a. 2010

IBRD 48316 | AUGUST 2024

b. 2019

IBRD 48317 | AUGUST 2024

Source: World Bank staff illustration based on harmonized list of fragile situations; World Bank 2024b.

In addition to the loss of human life, conflict destroys physical capital and affects household and individual behavior. Conflict disrupts normal economic activities and may cause households and individuals to resort to survival strategies that prioritize immediate needs over long-term investments, thus perpetuating a cycle of poverty (Beegle and Christiaensen 2019). Changes in consumption patterns, labor market participation, and risk preferences are some possible channels through which conflict can affect behavior and a country's long-term economic development (Braun and Stuhler 2023; Brown et al. 2019; Jakiela and Ozier 2019; Parigi 2024). Additionally, exposure to conflict undermines trust and social cohesion and reduces the likelihood of engaging in impersonal exchanges (Cassar, Grosjean, and Whitt 2013; Fiedler 2023). War and violence also limit the accumulation of human capital (Blattman and Annan 2010).

Fragility, conflict, and violence have constrained progress in poverty reduction in Africa, with fragile countries having higher poverty rates. On average, countries that were fragile during 2010–19 had a higher poverty rate (refer to figure S3.2a). Additionally, analysis using data on comparative episodes of growth and changes in extreme poverty (US$2.15 poverty line at 2017 purchasing power parity) between 2010 and 2019 to examine the percentage reduction in the poverty rate associated with a percentage change in gross domestic product (GDP) per capita (refer to chapter 2) suggests that although the elasticity of poverty to GDP per capita is low overall for all countries in Africa, it is lower in fragile countries. Specifically, a 1.0 percent increase in GDP per capita is associated with a 0.5 percent reduction in poverty in fragile countries, compared with a reduction of 0.8 percent in countries that were never fragile (refer to figure S3.2b). Although the precision of the estimates is limited by the sample size, the findings are consistent with existing evidence that fragile countries have higher poverty rates and that fragility is associated with lower growth (Baah and Lakner 2023; Beegle et al. 2016; Corral et al. 2020; Mueller 2016).

FIGURE S3.2 Poverty and fragility nexus

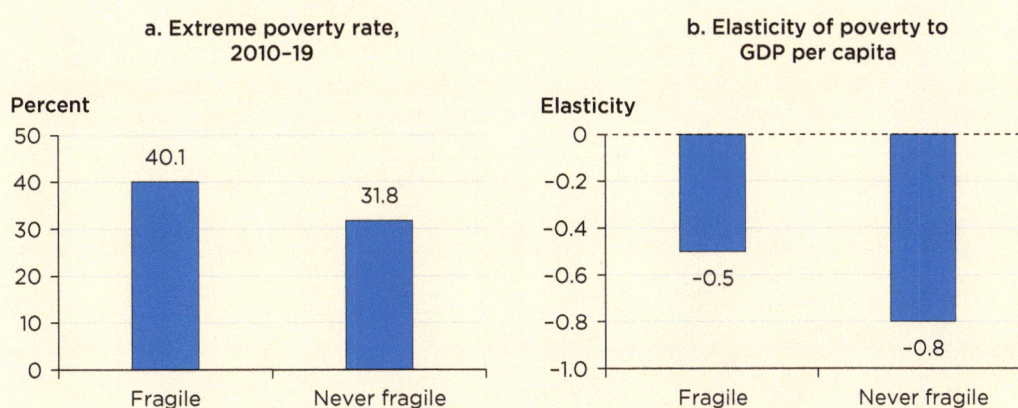

a. Extreme poverty rate, 2010–19

b. Elasticity of poverty to GDP per capita

Sources: Original calculations using data from the Poverty and Inequality Platform, World Bank 2024b harmonized list of fragile situations, and data from Wu et al. 2024.
Note: Panel b shows the median of all episodes within the period. GDP = gross domestic product.

Displacement further exacerbates the challenge, with significant humanitarian, social, and economic consequences for both displaced populations and host communities. Africa is home to some of the world's largest and most protracted displacement crises. As of 2023, more than 41 million forcibly displaced individuals resided in the region, approximately more than one-third of the global forcibly displaced population. The number of displaced individuals in the region has more than doubled in the past decade alone (refer to figure S3.3). Armed conflicts, civil wars, political instability, and persecution are the major drivers of displacement in Africa (IDMC 2023). At the same time, conflict is often interconnected with and reinforced by other causes, such as natural disasters, environmental factors, poverty, and economic factors, that can push people to search for safer and better prospects (World Bank 2023c). Those left behind may fare worse because those who are displaced are not necessarily those who are poorest (Beegle and Christiaensen 2019).

A distinctive feature of forced displacement in Africa is that the majority of those who are displaced remain internally displaced (refer to figure S3.3). The largest share of displaced individuals in Africa, estimated at nearly 80 percent in 2023, are displaced within their own country. The Democratic Republic of Congo, Nigeria, Ethiopia, Somalia, South Sudan, and Sudan are the top countries generating displacement, with an estimated 80 percent of the stock of all displaced individuals in Africa in 2023 having originated from just these six countries. The first four are home to more than one-third of the poor population in the region.

FIGURE S3.3 **Forced displacement trend in Africa, 2013–23**

Number forcibly displaced (millions)

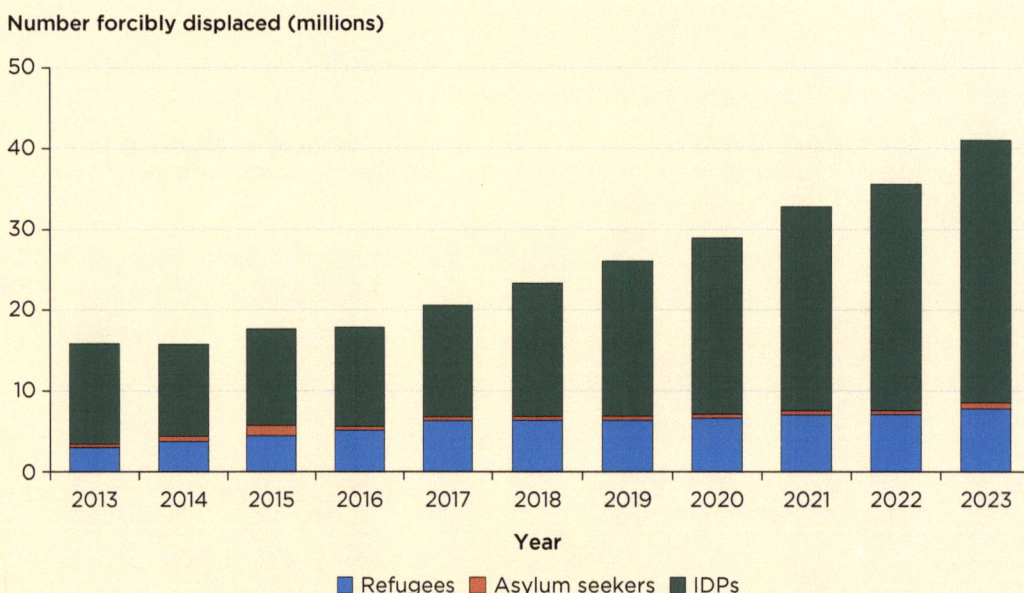

Source: Authors' calculation from UNHCR 2024.
Note: IDPs = internally displaced persons.

FIGURE S3.4 Hotspots for displacement in Africa

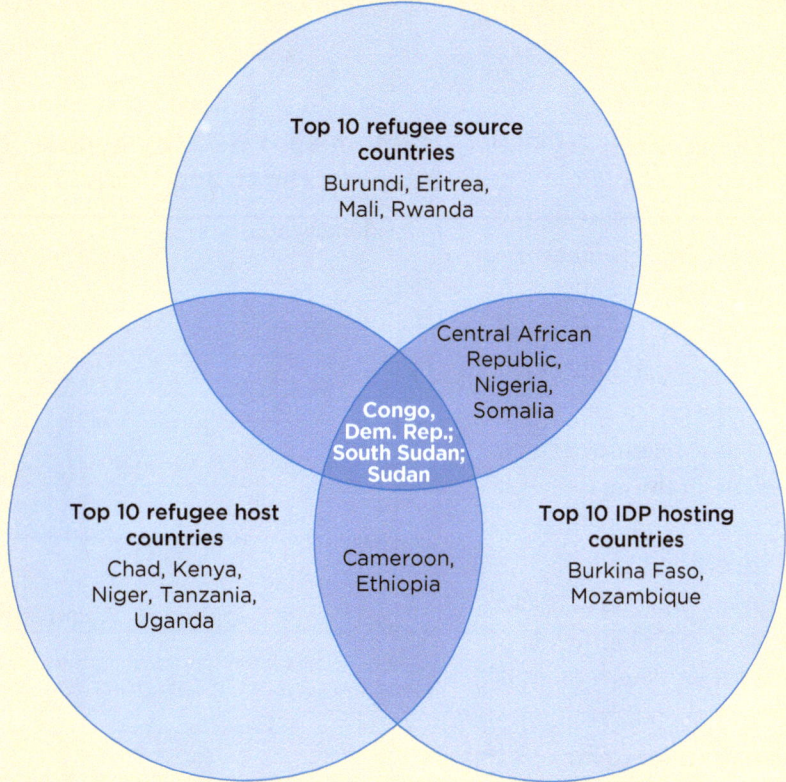

Top 10 refugee source countries
Burundi, Eritrea, Mali, Rwanda

Central African Republic, Nigeria, Somalia

Congo, Dem. Rep.; South Sudan; Sudan

Top 10 refugee host countries
Chad, Kenya, Niger, Tanzania, Uganda

Cameroon, Ethiopia

Top 10 IDP hosting countries
Burkina Faso, Mozambique

Source: Original calculation from UNHCR 2024.
Note: IDPs = internally displaced persons.

In 2023, more than 7 million individuals, equivalent to nearly one-fifth of all people displaced across borders globally, resided in Africa, predominantly in three countries: Chad, Ethiopia, and Uganda. The source of refugees is also highly concentrated, with three countries (Democratic Republic of Congo, South Sudan, and Sudan) being the origin of more than 50 percent of all refugees hosted in the region (refer to figure S3.4). Children are disproportionately represented among the displaced, necessitating urgent interventions given the potential long-term impacts of displacement on their welfare (Baez 2011; Nsababera 2020; Sarzin and Nsababera 2024; Sonne and Verme 2019).

Forced displacement risks increasing the inequality of opportunity because of challenges in accessing basic services and economic opportunities. Displaced individuals encounter significant hurdles in accessing basic services, such as education, health care, and economic opportunities, because of their displacement status. They may also face other challenges, such as language barriers, discrimination and stigma in host communities, physical and mental health issues, and lack of social networks (Gardi 2021; Schuettler and Caron 2020; UNHCR 2022). Although internally displaced persons are nationals of the country in which they are displaced and have de jure rights as other nationals, they often face similar hurdles in accessing opportunities and services and can face greater risk of exclusion because they have less visibility to both humanitarian and development responses (UNHCR 2022).

African countries perform relatively well in granting refugees access to basic services, but in practice inclusion in national systems is weak. For host countries for which data on access are available, a review of the status of inclusion by Ginn et al. (2022) suggests that most African countries (10 of 11 examined) perform well on granting de facto access to primary school equal to nationals (a score of 4 or 5 on a five-point scale). However, de facto access is poorer at higher levels of education, with only two countries (Cameroon and Rwanda) obtaining a score of 4 or 5 (refer to map S3.2). African countries also perform

FIGURE S3.5 **School attendance of children ages 6–12, by gender, in Chad, Ethiopia, Niger, and Uganda**

Percent of children ages six to 12

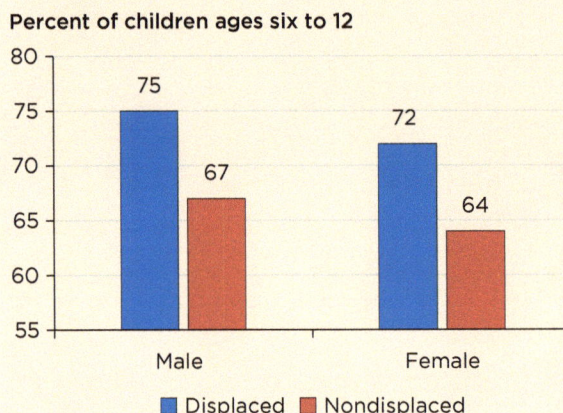

Sources: World Bank staff calculations, using harmonized data for Chad (2018), Ethiopia (2017), Niger (2018), and Uganda (2018).

moderately well in terms of de jure work rights for refugees, with 8 of 11 countries considered receiving a score of 4 or 5 on a five-point scale. Three countries—Chad, Rwanda, and Uganda—received the highest score of 5, indicating the existence of fully functioning national policies supporting refugees' right to work without restrictions. However, there is a divergence between the law and its implementation; only two countries—Rwanda and Uganda—receive a score of 4 for labor market access in practice, which is nevertheless lower than their de jure scores. Chad is a prime example of the divergence between law and implementation. Although it has national policies fully supporting refugees' right to work without restrictions, in practice refugees face significantly restricted rights to work (Ginn et al. 2022). Health interventions are typically more expensive compared with other forms of assistance. Consequently, compared with other opportunities, such as education, provision of inclusive health care has seen fewer investments and slower progress (UNHCR 2022).

MAP S3.2 Status of refugees' access to education in Africa

a. Primary

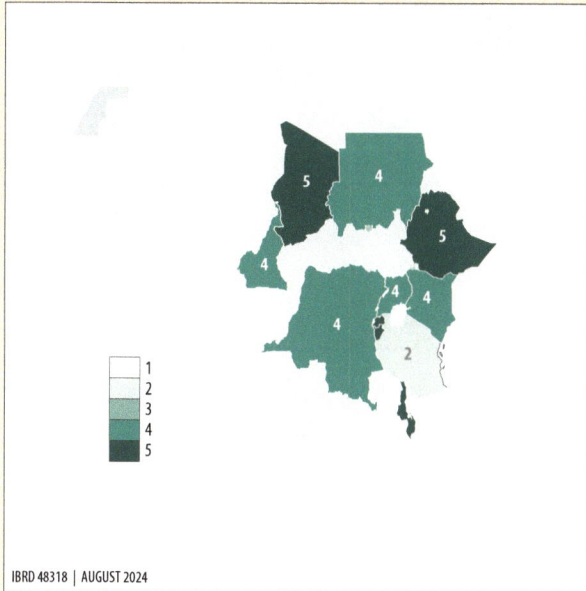

IBRD 48318 | AUGUST 2024

b. Secondary

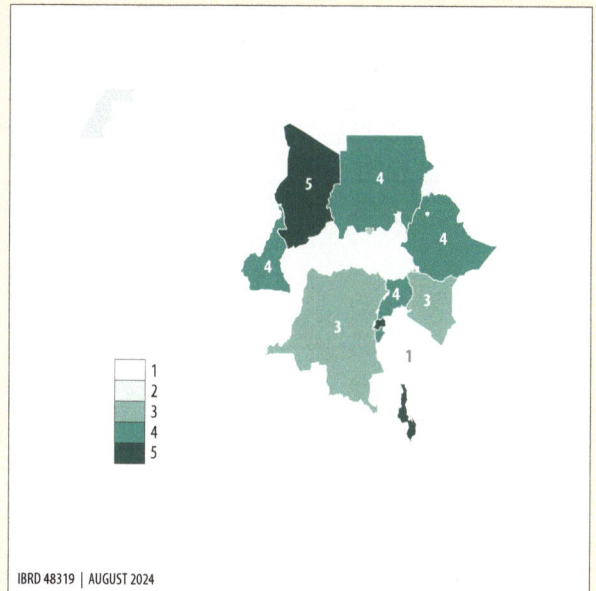

IBRD 48319 | AUGUST 2024

c. Tertiary

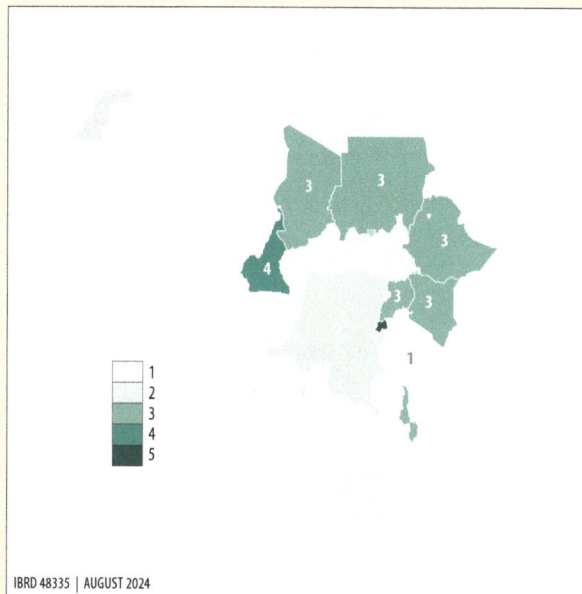

IBRD 48335 | AUGUST 2024

Source: World Bank staff, using data from Ginn et al. 2022.
Note: Scores range from 1 to 5, with 5 being highest and denoting access equal to that of nationals.

In some contexts, displaced individuals are in places where access to services remains out of reach for the host population, underscoring the importance of integrated service delivery (refer to figures S3.5 and S3.6). Although findings on the welfare of displaced persons vary across contexts, a striking finding for Kenya is that host populations in Turkana County, which hosts both the Kakuma refugee camp and Kalobeyei integrated settlement, fall below the national average and have lower primary school attendance rates than the refugee population (World Bank 2024a). Only about half of primary-school-age Turkana host children are enrolled in primary education, which may be due to the greater focus of development organizations on refugees' education needs (World Bank 2024a). Additionally, although the secondary school attendance rate is lower than the primary school rate across the country, Turkana host communities also have a lower secondary school attendance rate than refugees, indicating a need to understand the barriers to transition to secondary education for refugees as well as for the host community (Fix et al. 2019; World Bank 2024a). Comparable data for Chad, Ethiopia, Niger, and Uganda also show that both nondisplaced and displaced households have poor dwelling conditions and access to improved sanitation (refer to figure S3.6).

Reducing poverty and inequality in countries experiencing fragility, conflict, and violence necessitates a multifaceted approach centered on bolstering institutional capacity and integrated service delivery. Strengthening governance structures, enhancing public service delivery mechanisms, and promoting inclusive economic policies are crucial steps toward mitigating conflict and the adverse effects of forced displacement. Although for decades refugee assistance was delivered in parallel systems aligned with countries of origin with the aim to prepare refugees for eventual return, there is a growing consensus that integrating displaced individuals into

FIGURE S3.6 Living conditions and access to basic services in four African countries

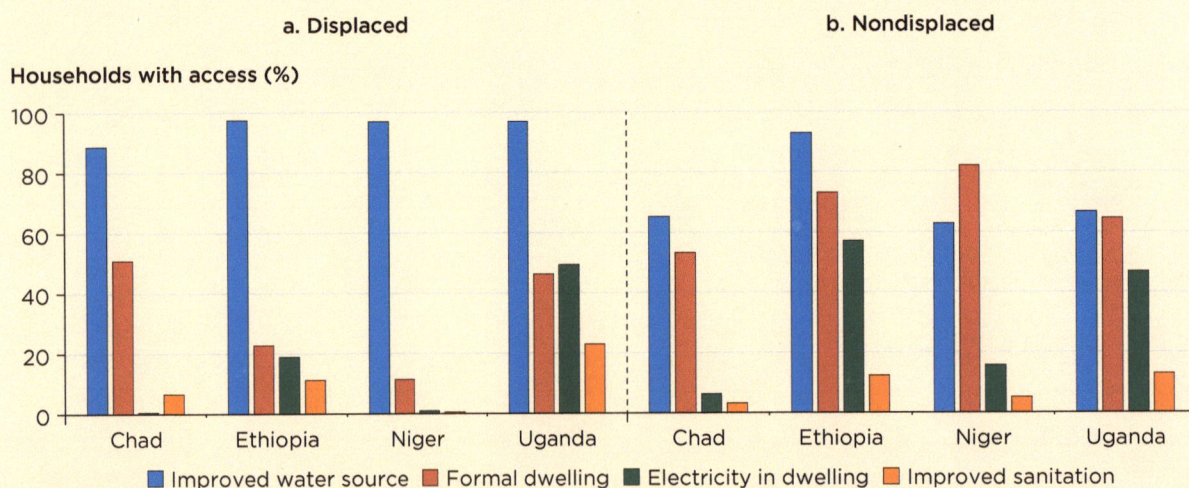

a. Displaced

b. Nondisplaced

Households with access (%)

Improved water source   Formal dwelling   Electricity in dwelling   Improved sanitation

Source: World Bank 2023a.

national systems is the most sustainable solution (UNHCR 2022). Inclusive systems allow for equal access to services, such as education, and can lead to efficiency gains in resource allocation and improved quality of teaching and learning environments (Abu-Ghaida and Silva 2021). Furthermore, services offered exclusively to displaced persons may sometimes be better than those available to hosting communities, creating unequal outcomes and potential tensions. By contrast, integration can lead to improved service delivery for underserved hosting communities (World Bank 2023c; World Bank and UNHCR 2021).

To improve the access of forcibly displaced persons to employment and economic opportunities, the starting point will depend on the state of economic inclusion in a country. For countries in which the legal framework for worker rights is not conducive to refugee integration, ensuring that national laws grant refugees fair and equitable right to work and labor protection is crucial. Relaxing legal restrictions related to the right to work, freedom of movement, and obtaining permanent residency status significantly improves labor market outcomes for those who are forcibly displaced (Schuettler and Caron 2020). Facilitating internal mobility, or freedom of movement within the host country, can transform the management of refugee situations and their outcomes, ensuring better alignment with the needs of the destination society, reducing pressure on communities in areas of first arrival, and reducing financial costs (World Bank 2023c). There is some evidence that the refugees living under liberal policy regimes in terms of the right to work are more likely to be employed, and freedom of movement is an especially important driver of better employment outcomes for refugees (World Bank 2023b). Host communities are unlikely to lose out when there is increased refugee economic inclusion (Aksoy and Ginn 2022). For countries in which the legal framework is conducive but implementation is weak, addressing systemic barriers that prevent displaced individuals from accessing employment and economic opportunities is necessary. Countries that perform moderately well to high in both law and practice will also need to continue addressing lurking systemic barriers. Last, in all countries, interventions should be based on reliable, context-specific data and analysis.

Note

1. Countries or territories in a situation of fragility are identified by the combination of (1) the Country Policy and Institutional Assessment (CPIA) score for International Development Association countries for which CPIA scores are disclosed that is below 3.2 and (2) the presence of a UN peacekeeping operation during the past three years.

References

Abu-Ghaida, Dina, and Karishma Silva. 2021. "Educating the Forcibly Displaced: Key Challenges and Opportunities." Reference Paper for the 70th Anniversary of the 1951 Refugee Convention, United Nations High Commissioner for Refugees, Geneva.

ACLED (Armed Conflict Location and Event Data Project). 2023. "The Sahel: Geopolitical Transition at the Center of an Ever-Worsening Crisis." Conflict Watchlist 2023. https://acleddata.com/conflict-watchlist-2023/sahel/.

Akanbi, Olusegun, Nikolay Gueorguiev, Jiro Honda, Paulomi Mehta, Kenji Moriyama, Keyra Primus, and Mouhamadou Sy. 2021. "Avoid a Fall or Fly Again: Turning Points of State Fragility." Working Paper 2021/133, International Monetary Fund, Washington, DC.

Aksoy, Cevat Giray, and Thomas Ginn. 2022. "Attitudes and Policies toward Refugees: Evidence from Low- and Middle-Income Countries." Policy Research Working Paper 9985, World Bank, Washington, DC.

Baah, Samuel Kofi Tetteh, and Christoph Lakner. 2023. "Fragility and Poverty in Sub-Saharan Africa: Two Sides of the Same Coin." *Data* (blog), *World Bank*, August 15. https://blogs.worldbank.org /opendata/fragility-and-poverty-sub-saharan-africa-two-sides-same-coin.

Baez, Javier E. 2011. "Civil Wars beyond Their Borders: The Human Capital and Health Consequences of Hosting Refugees." *Journal of Development Economics* 96 (2): 391–408.

Beegle, Kathleen, and Luc Christiaensen. 2019. *Accelerating Poverty Reduction in Africa*. Washington, DC: World Bank. http://hdl.handle.net/10986/32354.

Beegle, Kathleen, Luc Christiaensen, Andrew Dabalen, and Isis Gaddis. 2016. *Poverty in a Rising Africa*. Washington, DC: World Bank. http://hdl.handle.net/10986/22575.

Blattman, Christopher, and Jeannie Annan. 2010. "The Consequences of Child Soldiering." *Review of Economics and Statistics* 92 (4): 882–98.

Braun, Sebastian T., and Jan Stuhler. 2023. "Exposure to War and Its Labor Market Consequences over the Life Cycle." Discussion Paper 16040, Institute of Labor Economics, Bonn.

Brown, Ryan, Verónica Montalva, Duncan Thomas, and Andrea Velásquez. 2019. "Impact of Violent Crime on Risk Aversion: Evidence from the Mexican Drug War." *Review of Economics and Statistics* 101 (5): 892–904.

Cassar, Alessandra, Pauline Grosjean, and Sam Whitt. 2013. "Legacies of Violence: Trust and Market Development." *Journal of Economic Growth* 18: 285–318.

Collier, Paul. 2021. "Transition Programs: A Theory of the Scaffolding Needed to Build out of Fragility." In *Macroeconomic Policy in Fragile States*, edited by Ralph Chami, Raphael Espinoza, and Peter J. Montiel, 58–81. Oxford: Oxford University Press. https://doi.org/10.1093/oso/9780198853091.003.0003.

Collier, Paul, Anke Hoeffler, and Måns Söderbom. 2008. "Post-Conflict Risks." *Journal of Peace Research* 45 (4): 461–78.

Corral, Paul, Alexander Irwin, Nandini Krishnan, Daniel Gerszon Mahler, and Tara Vishwanath. 2020. *Fragility and Conflict: On the Front Lines of the Fight against Poverty*. Washington, DC: World Bank. http://hdl.handle.net/10986/33324.

Fiedler, Charlotte. 2023. "What Do We Know about How Armed Conflict Affects Social Cohesion? A Review of the Empirical Literature." *International Studies Review* 25 (3): viad030.

Fix, Jedidiah Rooney, Utz Johann Pape, Felix Konstantin Appler, Theresa Parrish Beltramo, Florence Nana Pokuaah Nimoh, Laura Abril Ríos Rivera, Felix Schmieding, and Nduati Maina Kariuki. 2019. *Understanding the Socioeconomic Conditions of Refugees in Kenya: Volume A—Kalobeyei Settlement: Results from the 2018 Kalobeyei Socioeconomic Survey*. Washington, DC: World Bank.

Gardi, Rez. 2021. "Reference Paper for the 70th Anniversary of the 1951 Refugee Convention: Access to Higher Education for Forcibly Displaced Persons: Challenges, Good Practices, and Suggestions for the Future." United Nations High Commissioner for Refugees, Geneva.

Ginn, Thomas, Reva Resstack, Helen Dempster, Emily Arnold-Fernández, Sarah Miller, Marta Guerrero Ble, and Bahati Kanyamanza. 2022. *2022 Global Refugee Work Rights Report*. Washington, DC: Center for Global Development, Asylum Access, and Refugees International. https://www .cgdev.org/publication/2022-global-refugee-work-rights-report.

Hegre, H., H. M. Nygård, and R. F .Ræder. 2017. "Evaluating the Scope and Intensity of the Conflict Trap: A Dynamic Simulation Approach." *Journal of Peace Research* 54 (2): 243–61. https://doi .org/10.1177/0022343316684917.

IDMC (Internal Displacement Monitoring Centre). 2023. *2023 Global Report on Internal Displacement*. Geneva: IDMC.

Jakiela, Pamela, and Owen Ozier. 2019. "The Impact of Violence on Individual Risk Preferences: Evidence from a Natural Experiment." *Review of Economics and Statistics* 101 (3): 547–59.

Mueller, Hannes. 2016. "Growth and Violence: Argument for a Per Capita Measure of Civil War." *Economica* 83 (331): 473–97.

Nsababera, O. 2020. "Refugee Camps—A Lasting Legacy? Evidence on Long-Term Health Impact." *Economics and Human Biology* 39: 100926. https://doi.org/10.1016/j.ehb.2020.100926.

Parigi, Marta. 2024. "The Effect of Violent Conflict on Calorie Consumption and Dietary Quality in Iraq." *Journal of Agricultural Economics* 75 (1): 341–61.

Sarzin, Z., and Nsababera, O. 2024. "Forced Displacement: A Stocktaking of Evidence." Background paper, Africa companion report to *World Development Report 2023: Migrants, Refugees, and Societies*. World Bank, Washington, DC.

Schuettler, Kirsten, and Laura Caron. 2020. "Jobs Interventions for Refugees and Internally Displaced Persons." Jobs Working Paper 47, World Bank, Washington, DC.

Sonne, Soazie Elise Wang, and Paolo Verme. 2019. "Intergenerational Impact of Population Shocks on Children's Health: Evidence from the 1993–2001 Refugee Crisis in Tanzania." Policy Research Working Paper 9075, World Bank, Washington, DC. https://doi.org/10.1596/1813-9450-9075.

UNHCR (United Nations High Commissioner for Refugees). 2022. *People Forced to Flee: History, Change and Challenge*. Oxford: Oxford University Press.

UNHCR (United Nations High Commissioner for Refugees). 2024. Refugee Data Finder. https://www .unhcr.org/refugee-statistics/download/?url=IAr67y.

World Bank. 2023a. *Brief 1: A Profile of Forcibly Displaced Populations and Their Hosts: Leveraging Harmonized Data to Improve Welfare among Forcibly Displaced Populations and Their Hosts: A Technical Brief Series*. Washington, DC: World Bank.

World Bank. 2023b. Brief 2: Do Legal Restrictions Affect Refugees' Labor Market and Education Outcomes? Evidence from Harmonized Data *Leveraging Harmonized Data to Improve Welfare among Forcibly Displaced Populations and Their Hosts: A Technical Brief Series*. Washington, DC: World Bank.

World Bank. 2023c. *World Development Report 2023: Migrants, Refugees, and Societies*. Washington, DC: World Bank. https://www.worldbank.org/en/publication/wdr2023.

World Bank. 2024a. *Building Evidence to Enhance the Welfare of Refugees and Host Communities: Insights from the Kenya Longitudinal Socioeconomic Study of Refugees and Host Communities*. Washington, DC: World Bank.

World Bank. 2024b. "Classification of Fragile and Conflict-Affected Situations." Washington, DC: World Bank. https://www.worldbank.org/en/topic/fragilityconflictviolence/brief /harmonized-list-of-fragile-situations.

World Bank and UNHCR (United Nations High Commissioner for Refugees). 2021. *The Global Cost of Inclusive Refugee Education*. Washington, DC: World Bank.

Wu, Haoyu, Aziz Atamanov, Tom Bundervoet, and Pierella Paci. 2024. "Is Economic Growth Less Welfare Enhancing in Africa? Evidence from the Last Forty Years. *World Development* 184: 106759. https://doi.org/10.1016/j.worlddev.2024.106759.

CHAPTER 5

Governments Could Do Far More to Level the Playing Field Through Fiscal Policies

GABRIELA INCHAUSTE, CHRISTOPHER HOY, MARIANO SOSA, AND DANIEL VALDERRAMA

Chapter highlights

Taxes, transfers, and subsidies do not directly tackle the root causes of inequality. Rather, they are an ex post instrument to make up for unequal opportunities and market imperfections and affect the distribution of income. Fiscal redistribution is greater in Africa compared with similar-income countries in the rest of the world, but it is not enough to overcome higher levels of prefiscal inequality. Moreover, most African households pay far more in taxes than they receive in transfers and subsidies, leading to increases in short-term poverty.

The objective of reducing poverty and inequality through fiscal interventions has become increasingly challenging in the context of limited fiscal space and, in some cases, the high risk of debt distress across the continent. Given the increasingly constrained fiscal environment in the region, this chapter proposes four policy shifts that could make a real difference in leveling the playing field through fair fiscal policy.

The first is a shift away from subsidies. The currently high subsidy expenditures mostly benefit high-income households, increase inequality, and have a limited impact on poverty. The second is to strengthen social safety nets. For instance, adaptive social safety nets and school feeding programs are effective and efficient in reducing poverty and in providing timely assistance in times of crisis.

The third is a shift toward more progressive taxation. This includes placing greater focus on collecting property taxes, reducing corporate tax incentives, eliminating value-added tax (VAT) exemptions that largely benefit rich individuals, and being careful in designing simplified tax regimes. Furthermore, in resource-rich countries, tax instruments should be directly linked to the profitability of the sector, and if extractive industries are bad for the environment, they should be taxed appropriately. However, in the poorest and most fragile contexts, international development assistance will continue to be critical for poverty reduction, even with improvements in domestic resource mobilization.

The fourth is a shift toward improved state effectiveness on taxes and spending. Improving tax compliance among high-income taxpayers would support efforts for progressive revenue mobilization, and promoting regional cooperation on multinational firms would avoid a race to the bottom. Improving public expenditure management would reduce gaps between the budget allocation process and the actual execution of government spending. Better debt management would reduce the cost of finance and allow for more pro-poor spending. Critically, better financial planning for disaster response can ensure that financing would be available quickly and cost-effectively should a crisis hit.

Fiscal redistribution in a tight macro-fiscal context

Taxes, transfers, and subsidies do not directly tackle the root causes of inequality. Rather, they are an ex post instrument that can be leveraged to protect the population from shocks and, to some extent, to make up for unequal opportunities and market imperfections. As such, they can be a powerful redistributive tool at the end of the production process. However, they are also interrelated with the process of building and using productive capacities. To the extent that government revenues are used to finance access to health, education, and basic services, tax and spending policies contribute to human capital accumulation, which will in turn reduce structural inequality in building productive capacities in the future. Similarly, tax and spending interventions place incentives on workers, farms, and firms during the production process and, as such, affect how productive capacities are used. More generally, tax and spending policies can help moderate extreme differences in wealth (particularly inherited wealth) that drive extreme forms of inequality of opportunities and intergenerational persistence.

The collective desire among governments across countries for tax and spending policies to contribute to reducing both inequality and poverty is embodied by the inclusion of target 10.4 in the Sustainable Development Goals.[1] How much do African countries redistribute, and what difference does this make in inequality? What is the combined impact of taxes and social spending on poverty? How much more redistribution could be expected given the current fiscal and country contexts? This chapter addresses these questions.

African countries redistribute more than countries with similar income levels, but this is still not enough to overcome their high levels of prefiscal inequality

Fiscal incidence analysis can help to understand which population segments bear the burdens and reap the benefits of domestic resource mobilization and government spending. Using detailed country-level fiscal incidence analysis, it is possible to assess the level of inequality before and after taxes, transfers, and subsidies (refer to box 5.1) and thus measure the distributional impact of fiscal policies. It is then useful to compare country results across income levels, as well as fragile and conflict-affected situations (FCS) and natural resource wealth status, because each of these factors influences a country's capacity to redistribute.

BOX 5.1

The Commitment to Equity methodology to assess the progressivity and regressivity of fiscal policy

The Commitment to Equity (CEQ) assessment is a diagnostic tool that uses fiscal incidence analysis to determine the extent to which fiscal policy alleviates inequality and poverty, enabling the study of individual fiscal interventions and of the system as a whole.[a] It has become a standard tool, with 110 studies applied to 81 countries in the past decade. In this chapter, we use results for 70 countries at various income levels; 22 of the 70 are in Africa.[b]

For each country, household survey microdata are used to calculate household income before and after fiscal interventions. Prefiscal income or market income is defined as the sum of all factor income from wages and earnings from formal and informal labor markets and income from capital (such as rents, profits, dividends, or interest).[c] From here, disposable income is constructed by adding income from direct transfers and discounting the amounts paid in direct taxes given country-specific tax and benefit policies (refer to figure B5.1.1). Consumable income is defined as disposable income plus indirect subsidies, minus indirect taxes paid on consumption. Final income is obtained by adding the estimated value of public education and public health. Each of these measures is estimated at the household level. As such, the difference between prefiscal (market) income and consumable income can be used to measure the extent to which policies reduce inequality as an ex post instrument—after the income generation process and without considering the impact of policies on health and education.

FIGURE B5.1.1 Commitment to Equity core income concepts

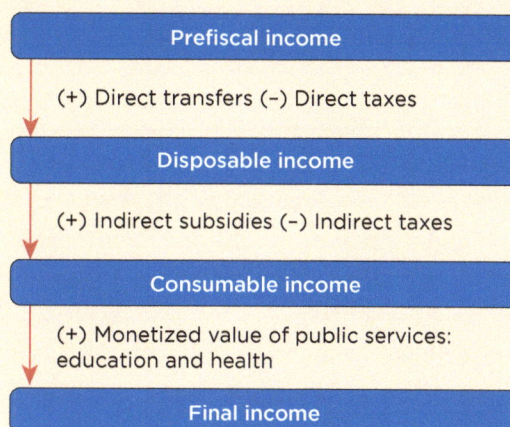

Prefiscal income

(+) Direct transfers (–) Direct taxes

Disposable income

(+) Indirect subsidies (–) Indirect taxes

Consumable income

(+) Monetized value of public services: education and health

Final income

Source: Lustig 2022.

(continued)

BOX 5.1

The Commitment to Equity methodology to assess the progressivity and regressivity of fiscal policy (continued)

The impact of individual tax or benefit policies is measured by the marginal contribution to redistribution, which is calculated as the difference between the Gini with and without the policy of interest.

The relative incidence of a tax or transfer is defined as the value of that policy relative to household income. A spending policy is progressive with respect to income if poorer households receive a larger benefit relative to their income compared with wealthier households. A tax is progressive in relative terms if the tax burden relative to income is larger for rich than for poor households. The absolute incidence of a policy is the distribution of the total budget (or revenue) of the policy across the income distribution. A spending policy is pro-poor or progressive in absolute terms if the share of the spending budget going to poor households is larger than that going to rich households. A tax is progressive in absolute terms if the share of tax revenue collected from rich households is larger than what is collected from poor households. Ideally, policies should be progressive in both absolute and relative terms.

a. Led by Nora Lustig since 2008, the CEQ project is an initiative of the Center for Inter-American Policy and Research; the Department of Economics at Tulane University; and the Center for Global Development and the Inter-American Dialogue. The CEQ project is housed in the CEQ Institute at Tulane University. For more details and a full description of the methodology developed by the CEQ Institute at Tulane University, visit https://www.commitmentoequity.org.
b. The data used in this chapter come from CEQ studies conducted by the World Bank and staff estimates based on older studies undertaken in collaboration with and by the CEQ Institute at Tulane University. The studies included in the analysis use survey data from 2014 or later, which leaves out 11 older CEQ assessments. Data from the CEQ Institute at Tulane University are available at https://commitmentoequity.org/datacenter. The analysis relies mainly on household income and expenditure surveys, which limits the model's capacity to incorporate relevant taxes, such as corporate income tax and expenditures on public goods, whose benefit is diffuse. Additionally, the CEQ analysis is a point-in-time study, excluding general equilibrium effects.
c. Market income is difficult to measure in most low-income settings. Instead, total household consumption is set equal to disposable income. From here, it is possible to derive market income by subtracting direct transfers and adding imputed direct taxes. See Lustig (2022).

Figure 5.1 compares the level of inequality before any fiscal intervention with market income with a measure of disposable income that accounts for the impact of direct taxes and transfers and a measure of consumable income that also accounts for the impact of indirect taxes and subsidies. First, note that, on average, prefiscal levels of inequality in Africa are higher than the prefiscal levels of inequality of comparable countries in other regions. For instance, although the prefiscal (market income) Gini in Africa is 46 on average, it is 41 for non-African countries.[2] Second, although

FIGURE 5.1 **Fiscal redistribution in Africa**

Gini index (higher values indicate higher levels of inequality)

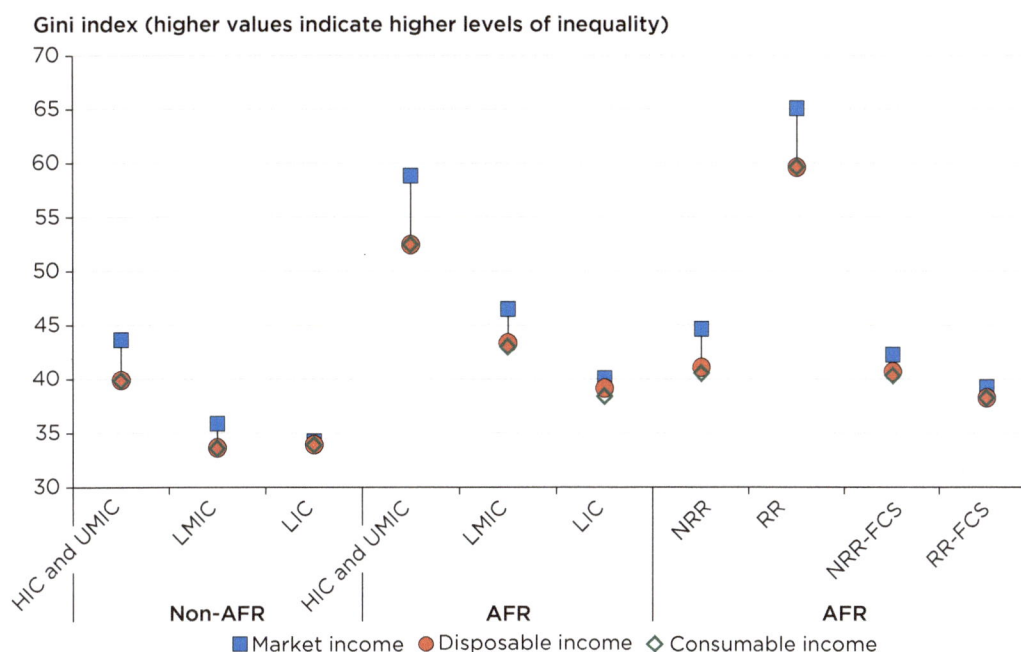

Sources: Original figure for this publication, using estimates based on data from Data Center on Fiscal Redistribution of the Commitment to Equity Institute at Tulane University (https://commitmentoequity .org/datacenter); Organisation for Economic Co-operation and Development; and World Bank.
Note: Prefiscal income, or market income, is the sum of labor and capital income. Disposable income is constructed by adding income from direct transfers and discounting the amounts paid in direct taxes given country-specific tax and benefit policies. Consumable income is defined as disposable income plus indirect subsidies, minus indirect taxes paid on consumption. AFR = Sub-Saharan Africa; FCV = fragility-, conflict-, and violence-affected countries; HIC and UMIC = high- and upper-middle-income countries; LIC = low-income countries; LMIC = lower-middle-income countries; NRR = non-resource-rich countries; RR = resource-rich countries.

higher-income countries redistribute more than lower-income countries worldwide, the reduction in inequality due to taxes, transfers, and subsidies is larger in Africa than the average for non-African countries with comparable income levels. Yet despite this redistributive effort, inequality after fiscal policies in Africa (measured as consumable income) is still higher than prefiscal inequality in comparable countries. Although this is especially true among upper-middle-income countries (UMICs), it is also true for low-income and lower-middle-income countries (LICs and LMICs, respectively). For instance, among LMICs in Africa, the average consumable income Gini is 43, higher than the average market income Gini of 34 for non-African LMICs. This highlights the need to do more to reduce prefiscal inequality across the region, as discussed in previous chapters of this report.

Africa's redistributive capacity is limited by fragility and conflict. FCS countries redistribute much less than non-FCS countries, regardless of whether they are resource rich (refer to figure 5.1). Resource-rich countries tend to start off with higher levels of prefiscal inequality compared with non–resource-rich countries, but despite their natural wealth they have very limited redistribution in an FCS environment. In contrast, non-FCS countries tend to have much higher levels of redistribution and have especially large impacts through their in-kind spending on education and health compared with non-FCS countries.

These averages hide considerable variation in fiscal redistribution across countries. UMICs in Southern Africa have among the highest prefiscal Gini indices in the world, and fiscal redistribution is also very large, reducing inequality between market and consumable income (refer to figure 5.2). When interventions aimed at building

FIGURE 5.2 Impact of taxes, transfers, and subsidies on inequality in each country

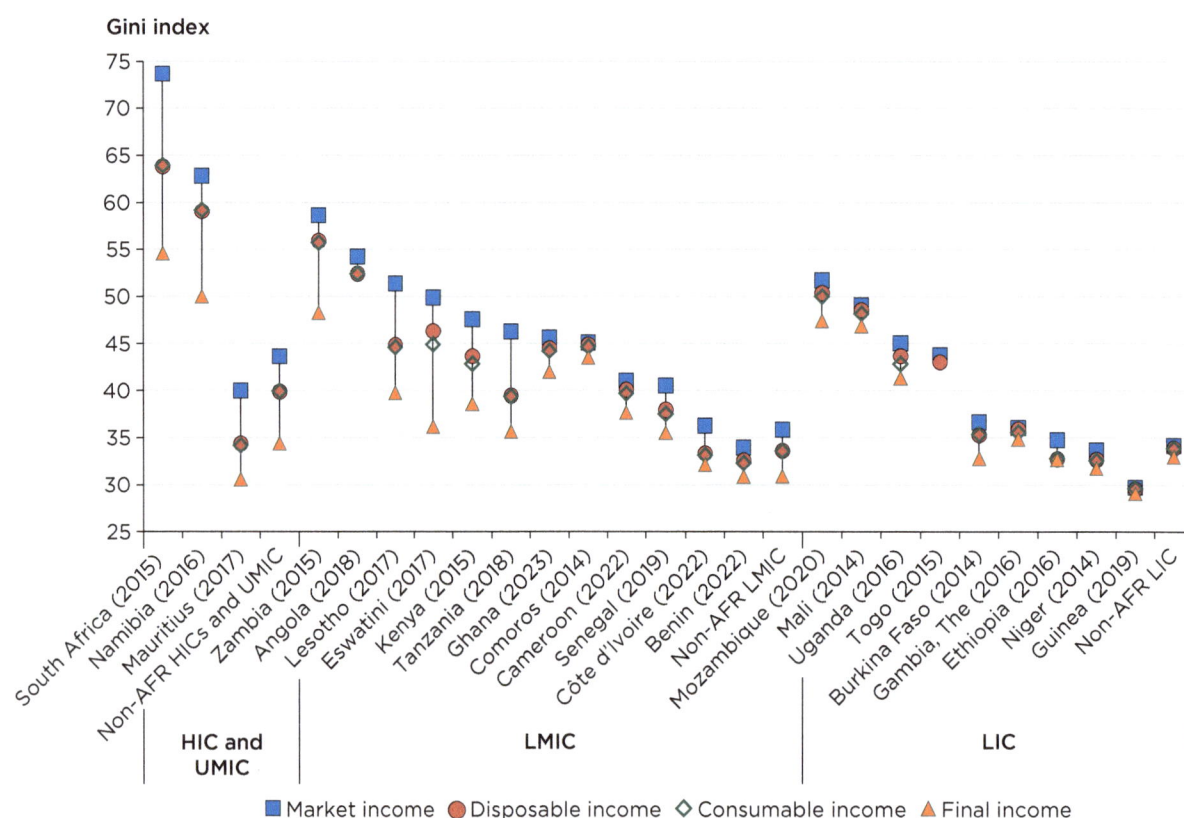

Source: Original figure for this publication based on CEQ studies conducted by the World Bank and the CEQ Institute, Tulane University.
Note: Pensions are treated as government transfers in Mali, Burkina Faso, and Niger. Elsewhere they are treated as deferred savings. Final income values for Angola and Togo are not available. Estimates for Ghana are based on microsimulation for 2023 using 2016/17 data. AFR = Africa; CEQ = Commitment to Equity; HIC = high-income countries; LIC = low-income countries; LMIC = lower-middle-income countries; UMIC = upper-middle-income countries.

productive capacities are considered, such as education and health spending, the decline in Gini (as measured by final income) is even higher, although there are important differences across countries. Despite this redistributive effort, their postfiscal (final) income distribution is still more unequal than the prefiscal inequality of comparable countries outside Africa. Similarly, some LMICs and LICs also have strikingly high levels of prefiscal inequality compared with similar-income countries outside Africa, but the extent to which they redistribute through taxes, transfers, and subsidies varies significantly. LICs are the least able to redistribute in both Africa and other regions; however, here, too, there are important differences across countries. For instance, Uganda has a higher gross domestic product (GDP) per capita than The Gambia. However, its much higher level of prefiscal inequality means that its relatively greater redistribution efforts are far from sufficient to reduce poverty and inequality.

Combined impact of taxes and social spending leads to higher poverty in many African countries in the short run

The increase in short-term poverty that results from the combined effect of taxes, transfers, and subsidies is larger in African countries than in other regions. Poor households in Africa pay far more in taxes than they receive in transfers and subsidies, leading to increases in short-term poverty.[3] Although taxes are a burden to households across the globe, what is significant in Africa is that their impact on poor households is larger than in other regions. Figure 5.3a shows poverty rates before fiscal interventions, and figure 5.3b shows the change in poverty rates after taxes, subsidies, and social transfers. In most countries in Africa, poverty rates increase after fiscal interventions, even in high- and middle-income countries, more so than is seen in countries in other regions with similar levels of development. This occurs because spending on subsidies and social assistance does not make up for the impact that indirect taxes have on increasing the prices of goods and services that low-income households consume, even after accounting for the fact that poorer households largely purchase goods in informal markets. Except for South Africa and Angola, resource-rich countries are no better at protecting poor households than non–resource-rich countries. The negative net impact on poverty in Africa points to the need to ensure that efforts to improve domestic revenue mobilization do not increase poverty further.

FIGURE 5.3 Impact of taxes, transfers, and subsidies on poverty in each country

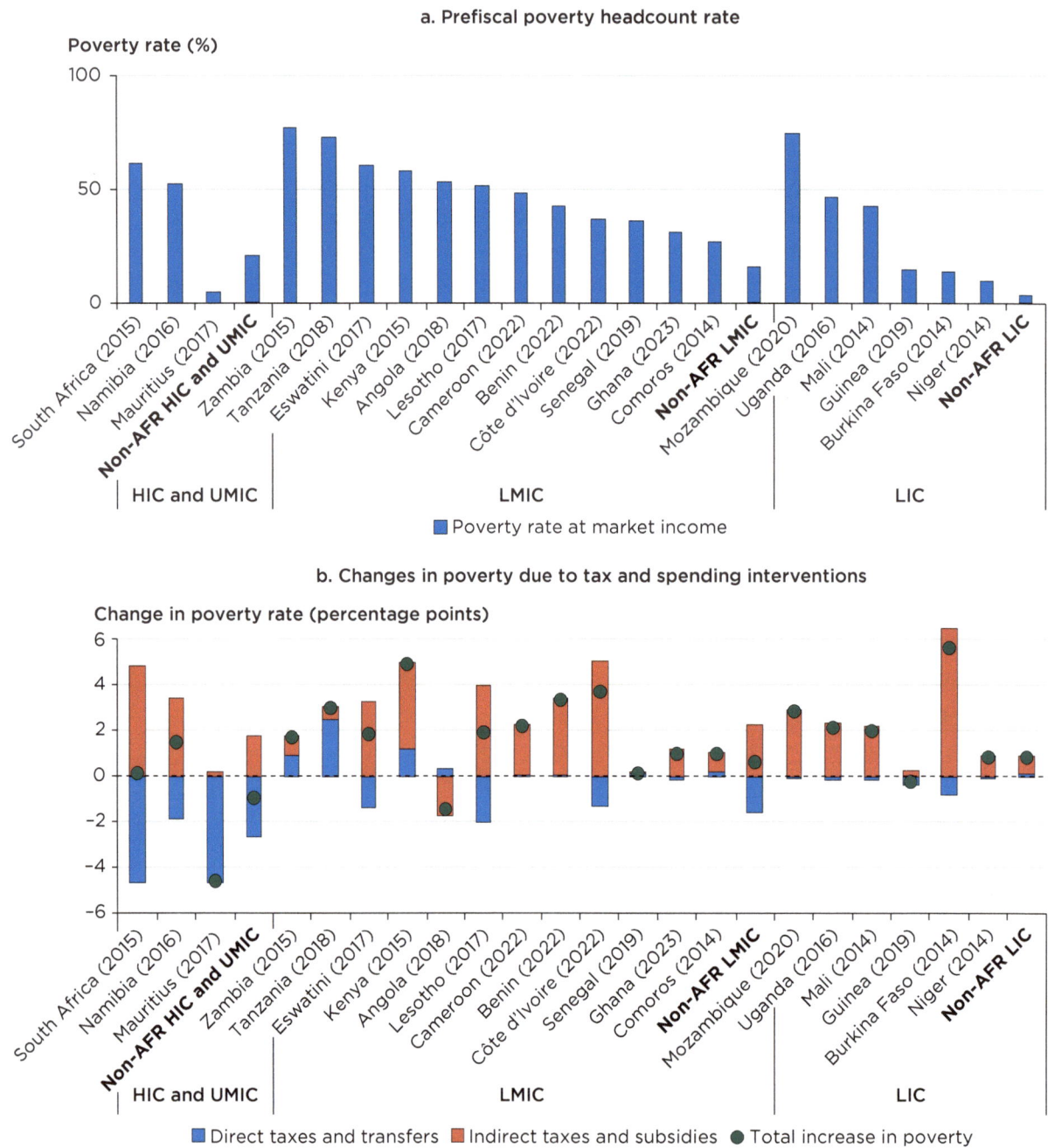

a. Prefiscal poverty headcount rate

Poverty rate (%)

Legend: ■ Poverty rate at market income

b. Changes in poverty due to tax and spending interventions

Change in poverty rate (percentage points)

Legend: ■ Direct taxes and transfers ■ Indirect taxes and subsidies ● Total increase in poverty

Source: Original figure for this publication, using estimates based on data from Data Center on Fiscal Redistribution of the Commitment to Equity Institute at Tulane University (https://commitmentoequity.org /datacenter); Organisation for Economic Co-operation and Development; and World Bank.

Note: The figure combines poverty rates estimated under different PPP thresholds for extreme poverty, given limitations in data availability. The $2.15/day line at 2017 PPP is used for Angola, Benin, Cameroon, Côte d'Ivoire, Ghana, Guinea, Mauritius, Mozambique, Senegal, Uganda, and Zambia. The $1.90/day line at 2011 PPP is used for Comoros, Eswatini, Kenya, Lesotho, Namibia, South Africa, and Tanzania. The $1.25/day line at 2005 PPP is used for Burkina Faso, Mali, and Niger. Pensions are treated as deferred income in all cases except Burkina Faso, Mali, and Niger, where they are treated as government transfers. AFR = Sub-Saharan Africa; HIC and UMIC = high- and upper-middle-income countries; LIC = low-income countries; LMIC = lower-middle-income countries; PPP = purchasing power parity.

Greater redistribution is possible in many middle-income and resource-rich countries

For several African LICs, it is difficult to expect more fiscal redistribution given the very limited size of the state. One metric regularly used to gauge the extent of fiscal redistribution that is needed in a country is the aggregate poverty gap.[4] This measure provides the amount needed to mechanically lift the poor population out of poverty if one were to be able to perfectly compensate households through fiscal redistribution.

This exercise among LICs shows that the resources at their disposal are often insufficient to eliminate poverty at even a theoretical level. In seven of 45 countries with data (Burundi, Central African Republic, Democratic Republic of Congo, Madagascar, Malawi, Mozambique, and Niger), at least 10 percent of GDP (in 2017 prices) would be needed to fill the aggregate poverty gap. By comparison, average tax collections amount to 11.4 percent of GDP in low-income African countries. Because running a government and providing basic public goods is around 15 percent of GDP (World Bank 2022a), it is not realistic to expect poverty reduction to be driven by fiscal redistribution in these LICs (refer to figure 5.4). Similarly, although some countries have wealth in natural resources, these resources are not large enough to address the poverty gap for most natural resource–rich countries (refer to figure 5.5).

FIGURE 5.4 **Marginal tax rate on nonpoor population required to close the poverty gap**

Marginal tax rate on the nonpoor population ($6.85/day) needed to fill the poverty gap for $2.15 a day (%)

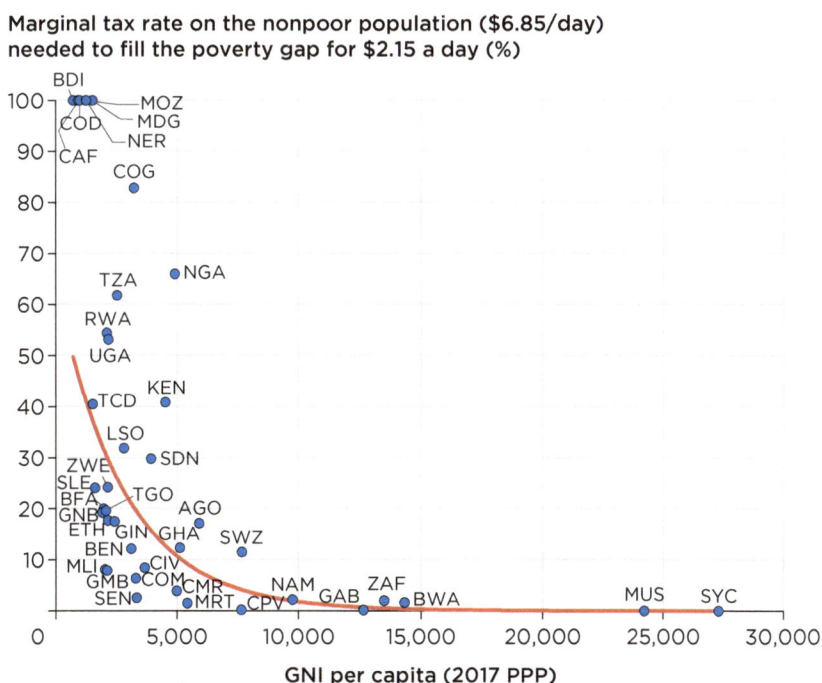

Source: World Bank calculations.
Note: The marginal tax rate on the nonpoor population is capped at 100 percent. GNI = gross national income; PPP = purchasing power parity. For country abbreviations, refer to https://www.iso.org/obp/ui/#search.

FIGURE 5.5 Share of government natural resource revenue required to close the poverty gap

Government natural resource revenue needed to close poverty gap (%)

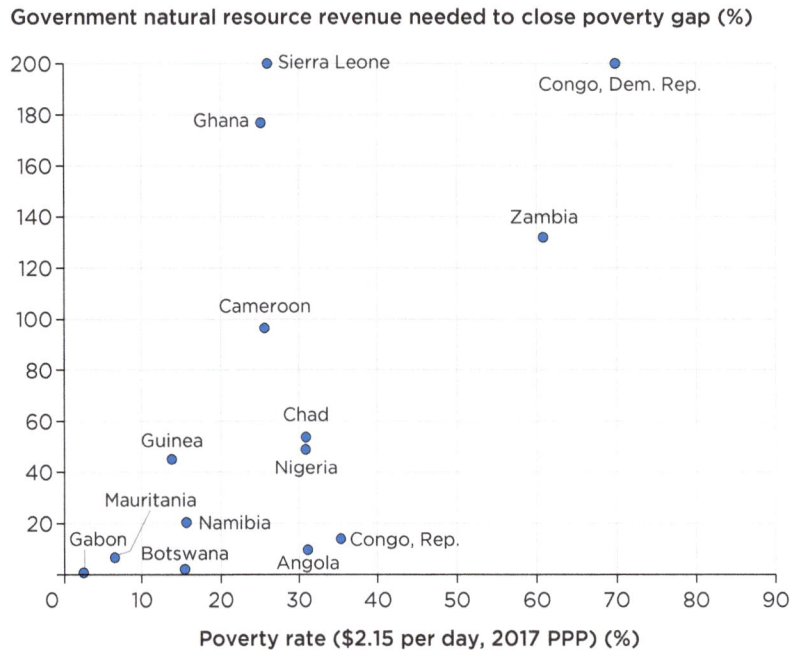

Poverty rate ($2.15 per day, 2017 PPP) (%)

Sources: World Bank poverty gap calculations and UN-WIDER Government Revenue dataset (https://www.wider.unu.edu/database/data-and-resources-grd).
Note: The share of government natural resource revenue needed to close the poverty gap is capped at 200 percent. PPP = purchasing power parity.

For UMICs and some resource-rich countries, however, reasonable taxation of the nonpoor population could raise domestic revenue to close the poverty gap. Closing the poverty gap would imply a marginal income tax rate of less than 10 percent among the nonpoor population in 13 of the 19 LMICs for which there are data, and it would amount to a marginal tax rate of less than 2 percent in the five UMICs for which there are data. Similarly, five of the resource-rich African countries (Angola, Botswana, the Republic of Congo, Gabon, and Mauritania) could close their poverty gap with a direct transfer of 15 percent (or less) of government natural resource revenues. Thus, for a fair number of middle-income African countries, there is room for greater domestic revenue mobilization.

The objective of reducing poverty and inequality through fiscal interventions has become increasingly challenging. The sharp increase in public debt since 2012, combined with a steady decline in official development aid and lower liquidity in international capital markets since mid-2022, has led to very high costs of external borrowing and limited financing options for countries in the region. As of 2023, the median public debt had reached 60 percent of GDP for low- and middle-income countries (refer to spotlight 4 on debt). Moreover, the shift in the composition of Africa's debt resulting from nonconcessional borrowing has increased the overall debt service burden. As a result of both higher primary deficits and debt service, public gross financing needs remain higher than historical averages. Moreover, the shift to nonconcessional debt has led to higher vulnerability to external shocks. In the constrained fiscal environment that these pressures create, greater equity and efficiency in tax and spending policies will be paramount, while the design of policies aimed at domestic resource mobilization must guard against placing an undue burden on the poor.

There is room to improve the efficiency and redistributive impact of government spending

The developing challenges faced by countries in the region and the tight fiscal environment imply that spending choices require careful and deliberate consideration. For many countries, public investment spending is very low relative to current spending, which has potential consequences for the ability of the state to provide key services, spur future growth, and lead to sustained poverty reduction (refer to figure 5.6a). This is especially important for low-income FCS countries and those with limited capacity to redistribute. Moreover, there is scope to improve the composition of spending by reallocating spending to pro-poor sectors and by improving the efficiency of spending in these sectors. For instance, FCS countries dedicate a substantial share of their resources to military spending and energy subsidies but spend much less on health and social assistance (refer to figure 5.6b). Interestingly, among countries that are not FCS, resource-rich countries spend more on education, health, and social assistance than non–resource-rich countries, whereas FCS countries spend more on energy subsidies. Reallocating government spending to sectors that are critical for poor households—such as agriculture, water and sanitation, education, health, and social safety net systems—would make an important difference in the government's ability to redistribute. Moreover, spending in each of these sectors could be made more efficient and meaningful for those at the bottom of the distribution. In this section, we highlight key areas that require special attention, focusing on interventions that lead to fiscal redistribution and have an impact on overall income inequality, namely, taxes, social transfers, and subsidies. Social spending on health, education, and infrastructure has previously been discussed (see chapters 3 and 4).

In addition to improving the efficiency of spending, there is room to improve public expenditure management and financial preparedness for crisis response. Weak public expenditure management systems often result in substantial gaps between the budget allocation process and the actual execution of government spending (for example, see Musiega et al. 2023). As such, even if funding is allocated in an efficient and redistributive manner, this does not guarantee that spending will be redistributive in practice. Medium-term budgeting, transparent public procurement, and careful debt management can generate fiscal space for pro-poor spending, lead to greater trust in government, and allow for better long-term planning (Comelli et al. 2023; Dom et al. 2022). A key aspect of sound expenditure and debt management, as discussed in more detail later, is financial planning for disaster response, which helps to ensure that funds will be available quickly and cost-effectively should a crisis hit (World Bank 2022b).

FIGURE 5.6 Composition of public spending in Africa

a. Public investment expenditure ratio

Share of current expenditures (%)

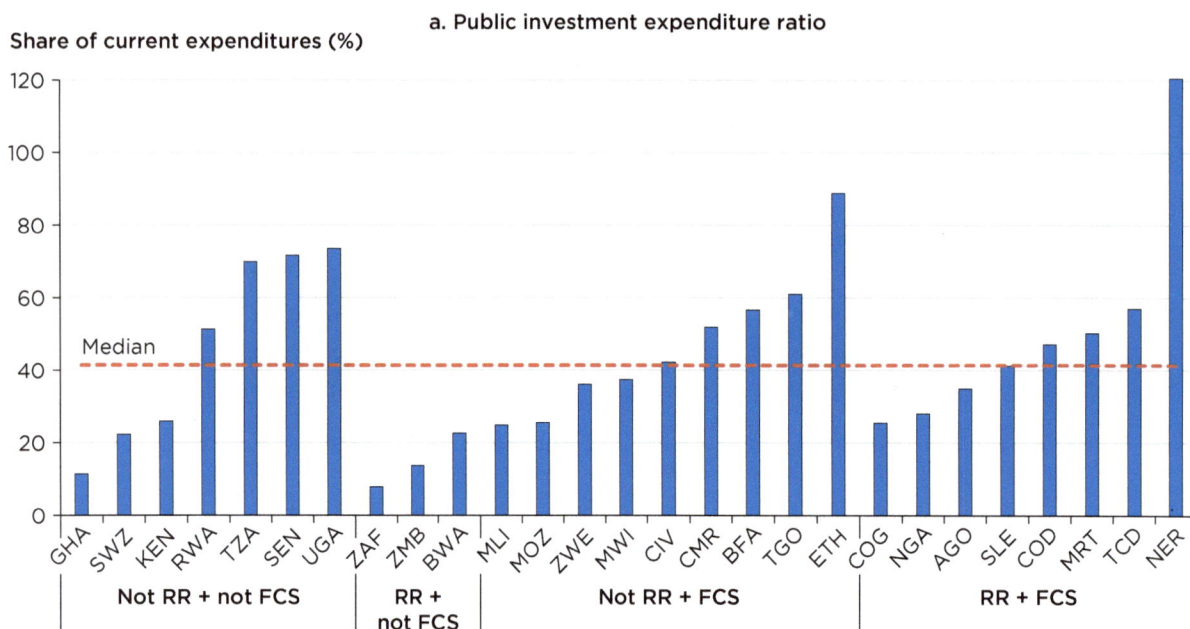

Not RR + not FCS: GHA, SWZ, KEN, RWA, TZA, SEN, UGA
RR + not FCS: ZAF, ZMB, BWA
Not RR + FCS: MLI, MOZ, ZWE, MWI, CIV, CMR, BFA, TGO, ETH
RR + FCS: COG, NGA, AGO, SLE, COD, MRT, TCD, NER

b. Spending by sector, 2021

Share of GDP

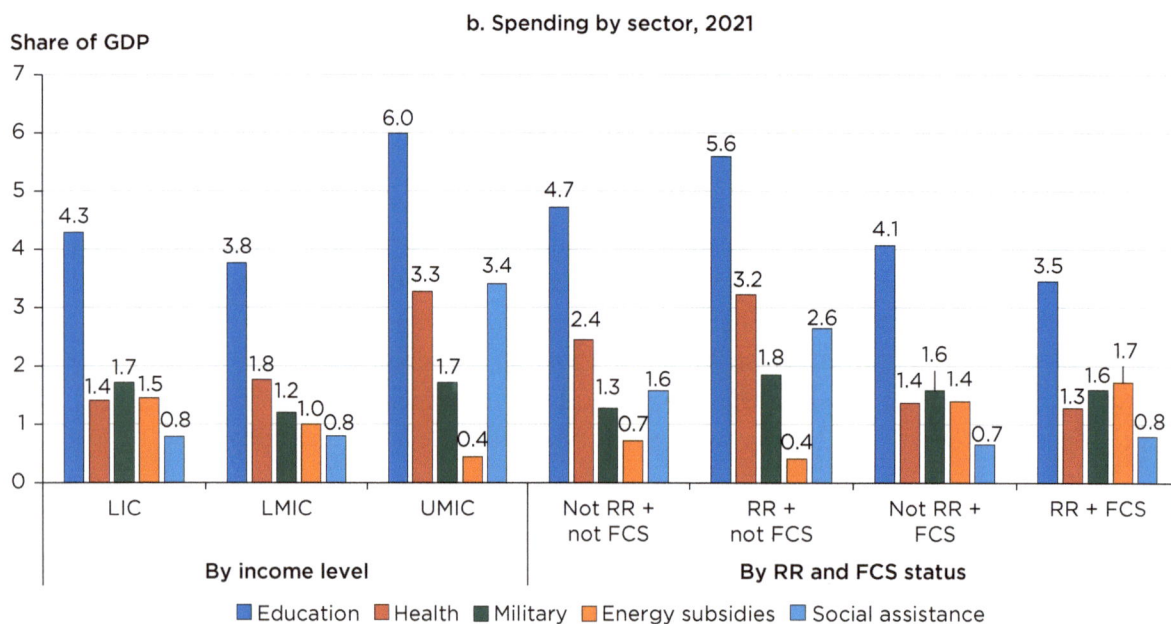

By income level: LIC, LMIC, UMIC
By RR and FCS status: Not RR + not FCS, RR + not FCS, Not RR + FCS, RR + FCS

■ Education ■ Health ■ Military ■ Energy subsidies ■ Social assistance

Sources: Education and military, World Development Indicators database (https://databank.worldbank.org/source/world-development-indicators); health, World Health Organization Global Health Expenditure database (https://apps.who.int/nha/database/Select/Indicators/en); explicit energy subsidies, International Monetary Fund Fossil Fuel Subsidies database January 2024 (https://www.imf.org/en/Topics/climate-change/energy-subsidies); social assistance, Atlas of Social Protection Indicators of Resilience and Equity database (https://www.worldbank.org/en/data/datatopics/aspire).

Note: FCS= fragile and conflict affected situations; GDP = gross domestic product; LIC = low-income countries; LMIC = lower-middle-income countries; RR = resource rich; UMIC = upper-middle-income countries. For country abbreviations, refer to https://www.iso.org/obp/ui/#search.

Subsidies are large and mostly benefit high-income households

African governments spend an important share of their budget on energy and other subsidies. Consumer price subsidies can be enacted relatively easily, without the need to establish complex delivery systems. As such, they are often the tool of choice when a shock hits. This is particularly the case in LICs and LMICs, which spend more on subsidies than they do on social assistance (refer to figure 5.6). Energy subsidies are higher in LICs and FCS countries, and they are larger than other types of subsidies and largely concentrated on electricity and fuel (refer to figure 5.7). Agricultural subsidies in the region, however, are largely concentrated on input subsidies, which differs from what is seen in high-income countries, where the emphasis is on decoupled transfers that provide support to farmers but do not have impacts on trade or production (see, for instance, Cahill 1997; OECD 2006). In contrast to input subsidies, decoupled transfers do not depend on production choices, output levels, or market conditions, nor do they subsidize production activities, inputs, or prices.

FIGURE 5.7 Government spending on energy and fertilizer subsidies (percent of GDP), aggregated by income group and region

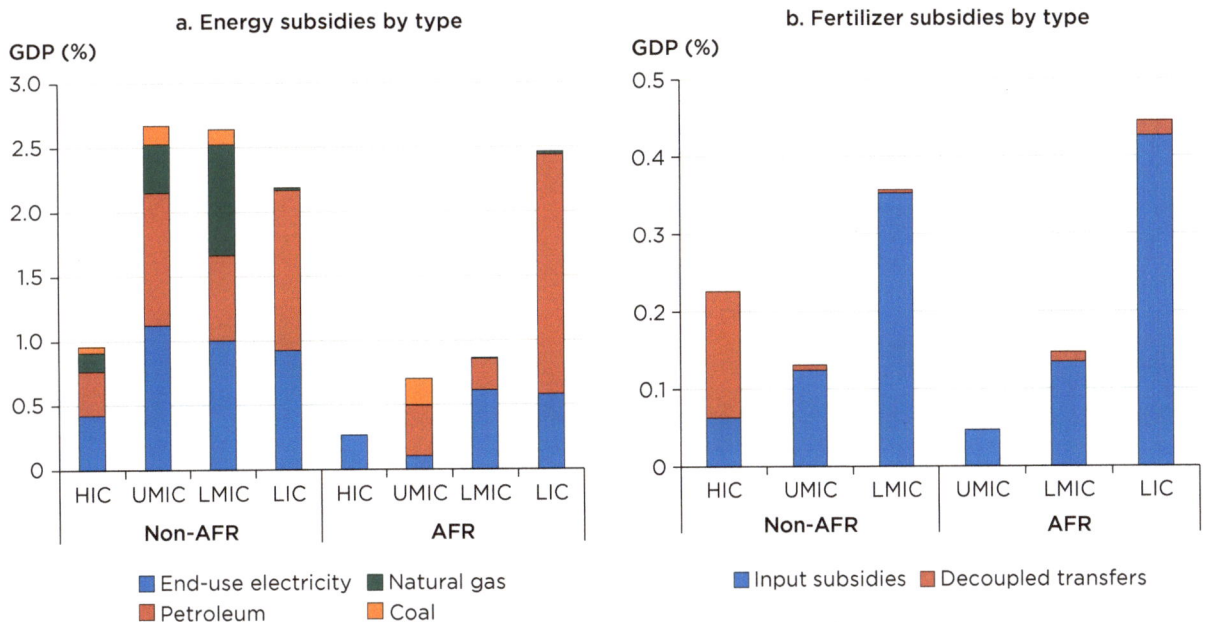

Sources: International Organizations Consortium for Measuring the Policy Environment for Agriculture database (http://www.ag-incentives.org/); energy subsidies, International Institute for Sustainable Development (https://www.iisd.org/).
Note: Agricultural subsidies calculated as averages for 2016–18. Energy subsidies calculated as average subsidies for 2017–19. AFR = Sub-Saharan Africa; GDP = gross domestic product; HIC = high-income countries; LIC = low-income countries; LMIC = lower-middle-income countries; UMIC = upper-middle-income countries.

Given that energy subsidies largely benefit higher-income households, they are inefficient at reducing poverty and inequality. Electricity and fuel subsidies disproportionately benefit richer households because these households consume more. In fact, less than 20 percent of spending on energy subsidies typically benefits the poorest 40 percent of the distribution in African countries (refer to figure 5.8b). Consumer price subsidies are therefore a very inefficient way of increasing the

FIGURE 5.8 Incidence of energy subsidies

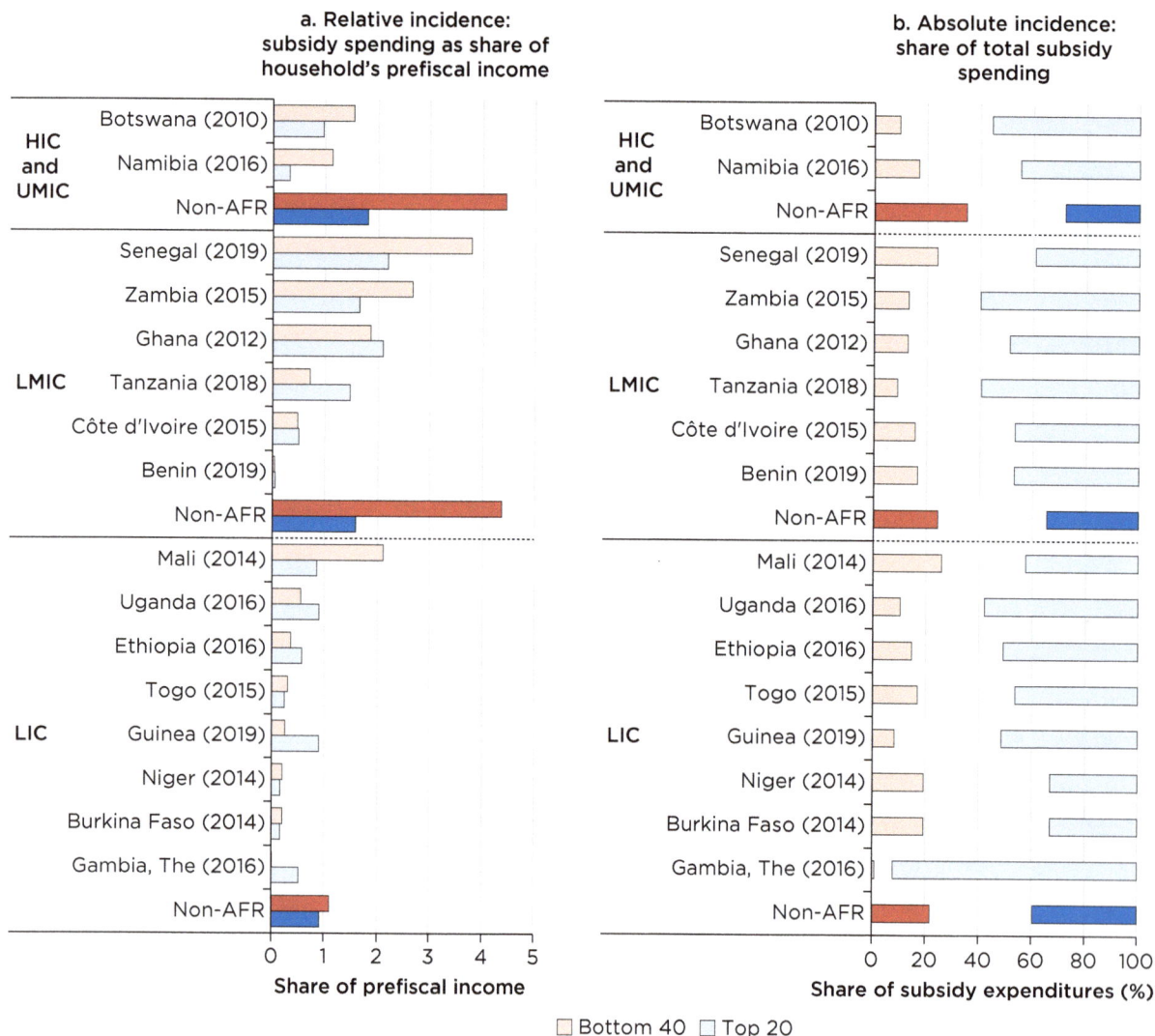

Source: Original figure for this publication based on CEQ studies conducted by the World Bank and the CEQ Institute, Tulane University.
Note: Dark bars indicate average of countries outside Africa for which data are available. Non-AFR LIC aggregate is composed of only Tajikistan. AFR = Sub-Saharan Africa; CEQ = Commitment to Equity; HIC and UMIC = high-income and upper-middle-income countries; LMIC = lower-middle-income countries; LIC = low-income countries.

consumption of the poorest households. Moreover, energy subsidies distort prices so that the resulting overconsumption contributes to global warming, intensifies local air pollution, and generates transport externalities. In fact, when the social and environmental costs of this excess consumption are considered, the size of these subsidies is substantially larger than the explicit budgetary cost (Black et al. 2023). Nevertheless, removing energy subsidies would still hurt poor households because these subsidies make up a nontrivial share of household budgets at the bottom of the distribution (refer to figure 5.8a)—even though these households benefit less than higher-income households. As a result, efforts to remove these subsidies must also compensate the most vulnerable of these households.

Fertilizer subsidies are also inefficient because they do not necessarily lead to higher agricultural productivity and are not always targeted to poor households. A growing number of studies have found that nitrogen application is inefficient and economically unprofitable (Goyal and Nash 2017; Jayne et al. 2018). Crop response rates are highly variable and usually low because smallholder farmers are often unable to use fertilizer efficiently and profitably due to low water availability and poor soil, chronically late deliveries of fertilizer, poor management practices, and insufficient complementary inputs, including extension services. Corruption, elite capture, and resale of government-provided fertilizer for profit also limit the efficiency of these subsidies (Beegle and Christiaensen 2019). Moreover, in some countries, subsidies provided to households in richer deciles tend to be larger than those to households in poorer deciles (where targeting is regressive with respect to asset wealth and landholding size), and the gains in overall food production have been transitory and much smaller than the costs (Jayne et al. 2018). For example, in Tanzania, households in the top 60 percent of the distribution received around seven times more agricultural subsidies than the bottom 40 percent of the distribution in 2018 (World Bank 2023b). Whereas fertilizer use is more intensive at the bottom of the distribution in West African countries, the efficiency of their use is still of concern (Inchauste et al. forthcoming).

Despite their inefficiency, subsidies are more commonly used by African governments than direct transfers to households. Removing subsidies and shifting that spending toward targeted public goods and services would improve efficiency, enhance equity, and limit the environmental impacts of fertilizer and fossil fuel consumption. However, the problem of subsidy removal is not one of expert knowledge about their perverse effects. To some extent, it is one of the only tools available to governments to confront external shocks (refer to box 5.2).

BOX 5.2

Use of subsidies as a response to the price shocks sparked or accelerated by the Ukraine War

Economies in Africa implemented 218 measures across 47 economies between April 2022 and June 2023 in response to the food, fuel, fertilizer, and other price shocks sparked or accelerated by the Ukraine war (Gentilini et al. 2023; refer to table B5.2.1). Subsidies made up 36 percent of measures adopted in Africa, closely followed by social assistance measures (35 percent).

TABLE B5.2.1 Number of measures and share of total

Type of measure	AFR		World		AFR as a share of the global total (%)
	No. of measures	Share of total (%)	No. of measures	Share of total (%)	
Subsidies	79	36	439	33	18
Fuel subsidy	19	9	84	6	23
Fertilizer subsidy	24	11	58	4	41
Food subsidy	23	11	77	6	30
Fee subsidy	13	6	220	17	6
Social assistance	76	35	409	31	19
Cash transfers	45	21	316	24	14
In-kind transfers	19	9	57	4	33
Public works	4	2	8	1	50
School feeding	6	3	11	1	55
Noncontributory pensions	2	1	17	1	12
Tax measures	44	20	258	19	17
Direct taxes	5	2	69	5	7
Indirect taxes	39	18	189	14	21
Trade-related measures	13	6	75	6	17
Labor market programs	4	2	77	6	5
Social insurance	2	1	75	6	3
Total	218	100	1333	100	16

Source: Gentilini et al. 2023.
Note: Sum of row may not add up to total due to rounding. AFR = Sub-Saharan Africa.

Among the 36 economies implementing subsidies, fertilizer subsidies are the most common, with 24 measures recorded across 18 countries, or 30.4 percent of all subsidy measures. Food subsidies are the second-most-used form of intervention, followed by fuel and fee subsidies such as utility discounts, transportation, education, and housing. Cash transfers constitute most social assistance measures (45 measures). Social assistance programs experienced a variety of reforms. Some programs experienced only vertical increases, meaning the benefit size increased (Mauritius), and others expanded horizontally, increasing coverage of beneficiaries (Cabo Verde, Mauritania). In some cases, measures were expanded both horizontally and vertically (Ghana).

Once in place, subsidies are very difficult to remove because of the fear of a public backlash against a possible increase in the cost of living. In some settings, subsidies are seen as citizens' rightful share in the country's natural wealth, a form of compensation for hardships during economic crises, or a way of receiving tangible benefits from the government when trust is low or the government's capacity to deliver better services is weak (Hoy et al. 2023). Moreover, in the presence of multiple stakeholders, including some with vested interests, there are complex political economy challenges to removing them (Inchauste and Victor 2017). To address the politics of reform, consumers first need to see what they get in exchange for rising prices if the process is to be sustained. When subsidies are scaled back, other equally visible and desired benefits need to be scaled up at the same time. Strong communication on the need for price liberalization and reform is important to sustain price increases and can help to build trust in its ability to handle competing interests.

Social assistance is limited by low benefit levels and low coverage

Direct transfers are progressive but often do not have a meaningful impact on poverty and inequality in African countries. This is because social assistance is limited, even when it is well targeted, and therefore has very little impact on poverty. Important exceptions are the Southern African high- and upper-middle-income countries, where targeted direct transfers make up a very large share of household income for the poorest deciles. Outside Southern Africa, direct transfers make up less than 3 percent of prefiscal incomes at the bottom of the distribution.

The limited impact of social assistance in reducing poverty is due to both the limited coverage and the relatively low benefit amount. Outside countries in Southern Africa, coverage of poor households by social safety nets is very low, covering less than 50 percent of the poorest quintile of the population in most countries (refer to figure 5.9). Coverage of the poorest quintile is even lower in countries with higher poverty rates. Moreover, the average benefit amount provided by cash transfer (CT) programs is very low in Africa and in countries outside the southern subregion. Over the course of 2011–19 (the most recent data available), the average CT provided in low-income and LMICs was less than $0.25 per capita (in 2011 PPP terms) and less than $2 a day in UMICs (World Development Indicators). More important, far more resources were directed toward social insurance (for example, pensions for government employees) as opposed to social assistance (for example, CTs targeted to poorer households). As such, the nature of social protection in LICs and LMICs in Africa is that poorer households do not benefit as much as they could if social assistance were prioritized. CEQ analysis in Africa shows that more than 40 percent of social assistance beneficiaries are in the bottom 40 percent of

FIGURE 5.9 **Social safety net coverage of the poorest quintile in Africa, by poverty headcount rate**

**Coverage of social safety net programs
in poorest quintile (percent of population)**

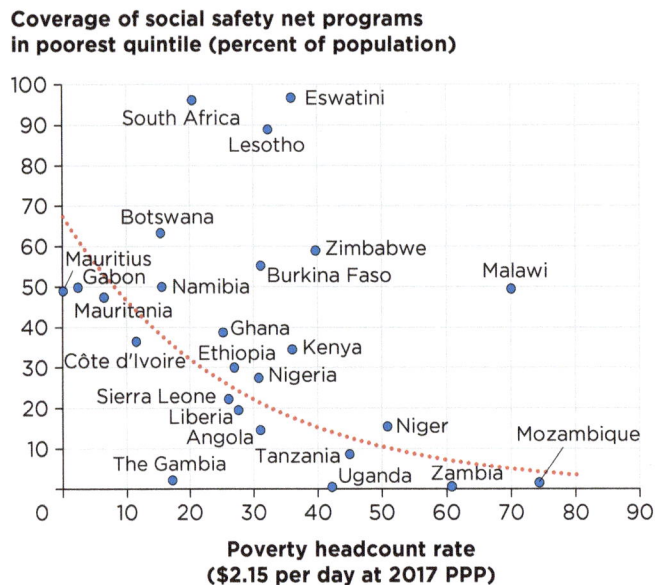

**Poverty headcount rate
($2.15 per day at 2017 PPP)**

Source: Original figure for this publication based on Atlas of Social Protection Indicators of Resilience and Equity (ASPIRE) database (https://www.worldbank.org/en/data/datatopics/aspire), 2011–19.
Note: The dotted line indicates the correlation between the poverty headcount rate and the coverage of social safety net programs among the poorest quintile in each country. PPP = purchasing power parity.

the income distribution in most African countries (refer to figure 5.10), a testament to how well targeted these programs are.

Given the high poverty headcount rates in the region, it is difficult to imagine that social assistance could cover all poor households. However, adaptive social protection (ASP) systems can help to build the resilience of poor and vulnerable households to the impacts of large, covariate shocks, such as natural disasters, economic crises, pandemics, conflict, and forced displacement. By providing transfers and services directly to households affected by shocks, ASP systems can support the capacity of vulnerable households to prepare for, cope with, and adapt to the shocks they face, before, during, and after these shocks occur, thus avoiding long-term scarring effects. Over the long term, by supporting these three capacities, ASP systems can provide a pathway to more resilient households that may otherwise lack the resources to move out of chronically vulnerable situations (refer to box 5.3).

Moreover, CT programs have been shown to have positive development impacts that go beyond direct consumption effects, through diversification of incomes and positive impacts on education and health. When complemented by appropriate investment in service provision, social protection helps build human capital, contributing to improved health and education outcomes (see Baird et al. 2014; Bastagli, Hagen-Zanker, and Sturge 2016; De Walque et al. 2017; Molina Millán et al. 2019). Moreover, well-designed and -implemented social protection systems can facilitate the creation of productive assets; stimulate local economies; and support improved productivity, labor market functioning, and macroeconomic growth (Alderman and Yemstov 2014; Egger et al. 2019; Thome et al. 2016).

FIGURE 5.10 Benefit incidence by income category and region

Absolute incidence (share of total direct transfer spending)

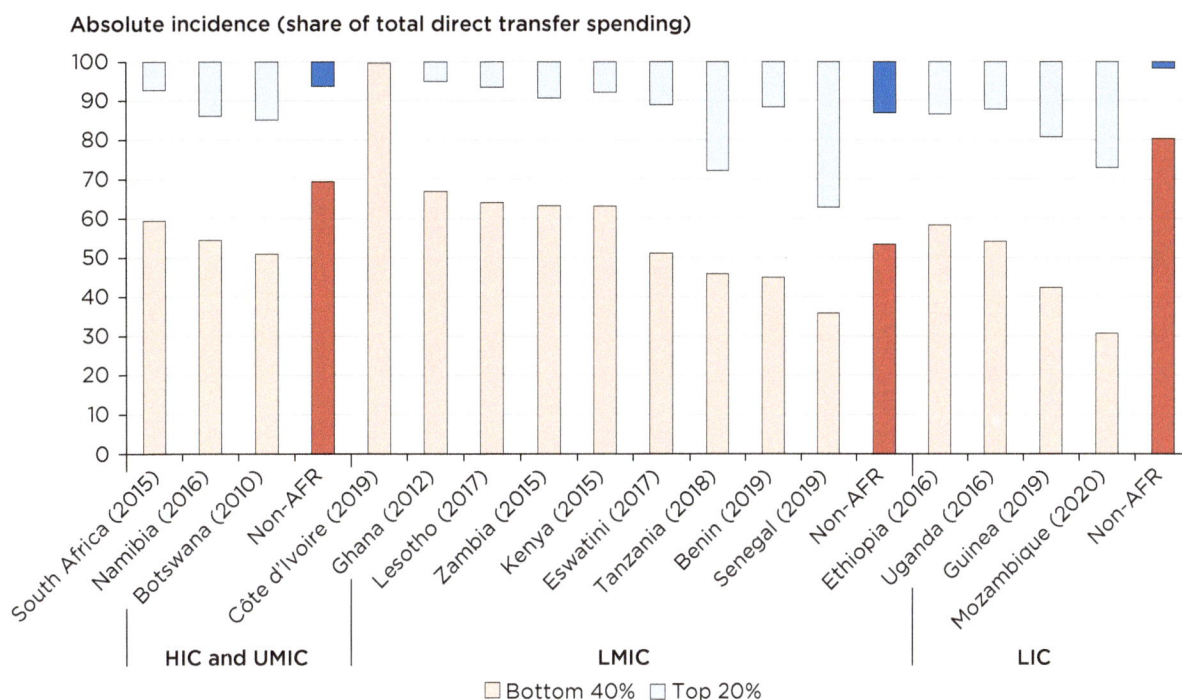

Bottom 40%   Top 20%

Source: Original figure for this publication based on CEQ studies conducted by the World Bank and the CEQ Institute, Tulane University.
Note: AFR = Sub-Saharan Africa; HIC and UMIC = high-income and upper-middle-income countries; LMIC = lower-middle-income countries; LIC = low-income countries. Darker bars indicate average of countries outside Africa for which data are available.

For instance, research in Mali has shown that a year and a half after the end of the safety net program, participants were 57 percent more likely to save and 46 percent more likely to invest in productive assets than nonparticipants (Paul, Dutta, and Chaudhary 2021). In Niger, a year and a half after receiving a productive inclusion program, women's incomes increased by 59–100 percent, and the share coming from nonagriculture activities increased by 62–107 percent. The impacts on education and health were seen in Burkina Faso, where about a year after the safety net program ended, participating children had a school enrollment rate 14.3 percent higher than that of nonparticipants, and children younger than age five years had improved arm circumference ratio (a measure of nutrition). Similarly, in Mali social safety nets increased the chances that a teenage girl enrolled in school would make it into the next grade by 56 percent (Paul, Dutta, and Chaudhary 2021). Moreover, social protection programs can complement cash with additional inputs and service components or links to other sectors. For instance, a multidimensional program in Niger offered women business management training, coaching, and psychosocial activities in addition to cash, which led to increases in consumption, savings, and improvements in women's mental health.[5] Accordingly, economic inclusion programs are seen as an important complement to existing antipoverty efforts. As with any policy intervention, careful design of these programs is important to minimize targeting errors and avoid unintended behavioral responses, but in general these programs have been shown to have positive impacts.[6]

BOX 5.3
Adaptive social protection

Low revenue collection and high poverty rates place a binding constraint on increasing the coverage and benefits of current social protection systems. To optimize social gains, systems should move from a static to an adaptive design. A static system provides fixed direct transfers to a set number of households identified as poor on the basis of a set of observable characteristics. This approach can be expensive in African countries with a large poor population. It may also overlook nonpoor households at risk of poverty or continue supporting households long after they overcome poverty. In contrast, adaptive systems adjust the amount of cash transfers, coverage, and targeting on the basis of evolving circumstances, such as downturns or natural disasters, thus recognizing poverty as dynamic rather than as a fixed household characteristic.

Implementing an adaptive social protection (ASP) system requires transforming how social protection is funded, the core objectives of its programs, and to whom and how the funds are disbursed. Bowen et al. (2020) and Leite et al. (2017) highlight five initial steps to implement an ASP system, with examples from the region:

- *Establish early warning systems*. Ensuring a fast response to households in the aftermath of a shock ameliorates the shock's impact on household welfare (Hill, Skoufias, and Maher 2019). These early systems are usually triggered by real-time data. In Uganda, satellite data are used as an index to trigger earlier responses to drought through the Northern Uganda Social Action Fund's cash-for-work program. Similarly, Ethiopia's rural Productive Safety Net Program uses climate data to define the timing and coverage of its benefits.

- *Expand social registries*. In addition to poor households, social registries should collect information from households that could become poor because of shocks. Leite et al. (2017) find coverage of social registries in Africa is about 30 percent (for example, in the Registre National Unique in Senegal, the Social Register of Mauritius, and the Social Protection Registry for Integrated National Targeting in Sierra Leone), lagging behind the 80 percent coverage observed in Pakistan and the Dominican Republic.

- *Include risk of poverty as part of the targeting*. Social programs should go beyond targeting households that are structurally poor and include households that, despite not being poor today, are at risk of falling into poverty because of a shock. For example, Niger protects these households by using weather and hazard data (rainfall, vegetation, droughts, and price shocks) to design the geographical allocation of its main safety net program.

- *Design programs to enhance resiliency*. Programs should improve how households prepare for, cope with, and adapt to climate change. Policies that increase households' savings, subsidize weather-indexed insurance, and facilitate access to credit will help households prepare for climate shocks. Similarly, policies that provide technical assistance to reduce households' risk and allow them to make adaptation investments (for example, irrigation, weather-resistant seeds, or air conditioning) will help to develop household resiliency.

- *Design disbursement mechanisms*. Because existing social safety nets do not cover all populations, governments have found it helpful to use electronic transfers to bank accounts or mobile phone payments as vehicles to rapidly reach affected households. For instance, Kenya increased access to bank accounts in the country's poorest counties as part of the implementation of its insignia emergency cash program, the Hunger Safety Net Program.

School feeding programs can also serve as a critical safety net. Recent systematic reviews have found that school feeding programs improve the nutrition of their beneficiaries, lead to significant increases in the height and weight of children, boost enrollment, and lead to a significant increase in school attendance (Wang et al. 2021; World Food Programme 2021). Moreover, evidence from Uganda and Burkina Faso shows positive spillovers to household members because nutritional outcomes of younger children (those younger than age five) and adult women improved in communities where in-school cooked meals or take-home rations were provided to schoolchildren (Adelman et al. 2019; Kazianga, de Walque, and Alderman 2014). With complementary inputs, there is also evidence that these interventions can lead to improved learning. For instance, an evaluation of the school feeding program in India found that prolonged exposure to school nutrition led to improvements in math and reading test scores, with effects being most pronounced when complemented by schooling inputs, such as learning materials and teachers in attendance (Chakraborty and Jayaraman 2019). Critically, these programs are a lifeline in times of crisis, preventing negative coping strategies, because nutritious meals reduce anemia and stunting while increasing immunity, particularly for girls and vulnerable children (Aurino et al. 2019; Gelli et al. 2019).

Substituting energy subsidies and redirecting the fiscal savings to better-targeted programs would reduce poverty and inequality

Fiscal microsimulations are often used to assess the potential impact of alternative reform policies using household survey data and detailed modeling of tax and spending policies. To estimate the distributional impact of eliminating energy subsidies (for example, electricity and fossil fuels), fiscal microsimulation models developed for seven African countries by the World Bank are used. During the study period, energy subsidies amounted to 1.8 percent of GDP in Angola, one of Africa's largest oil producers, whereas those in the rest of the countries ranged between 0.02 percent (Kenya) and 1.1 percent (Senegal). In each case, the details of the electricity, fuel, and social assistance systems are modeled in detail, and both the direct impact of subsidies and the indirect effects that occur through input–output linkages are computed.[7] To compensate the population for the elimination of subsidies, half the fiscal savings obtained from the subsidy removal are used to fund four alternative compensation measures.[8] Figure 5.11 shows the change in poverty (panel a) and inequality (panel b) for consumable income using five different simulation scenarios: a removal of subsidies (1) without compensation measures, (2) with a hypothetical universal basic income (UBI) transfer, (3) with a CT directed toward primary and secondary school students enrolled in public schools, (4) with an increase in the coverage of the main CT program, and (5) with an increase in the generosity and coverage of the main CT program, as detailed in annex 5.2. The results for these simulations show the impacts on poverty and inequality and lend clues to the readiness of the existing social assistance systems to mitigate the impact of reform.

FIGURE 5.11 Poverty and inequality effects of removing energy subsidies, by compensation measure

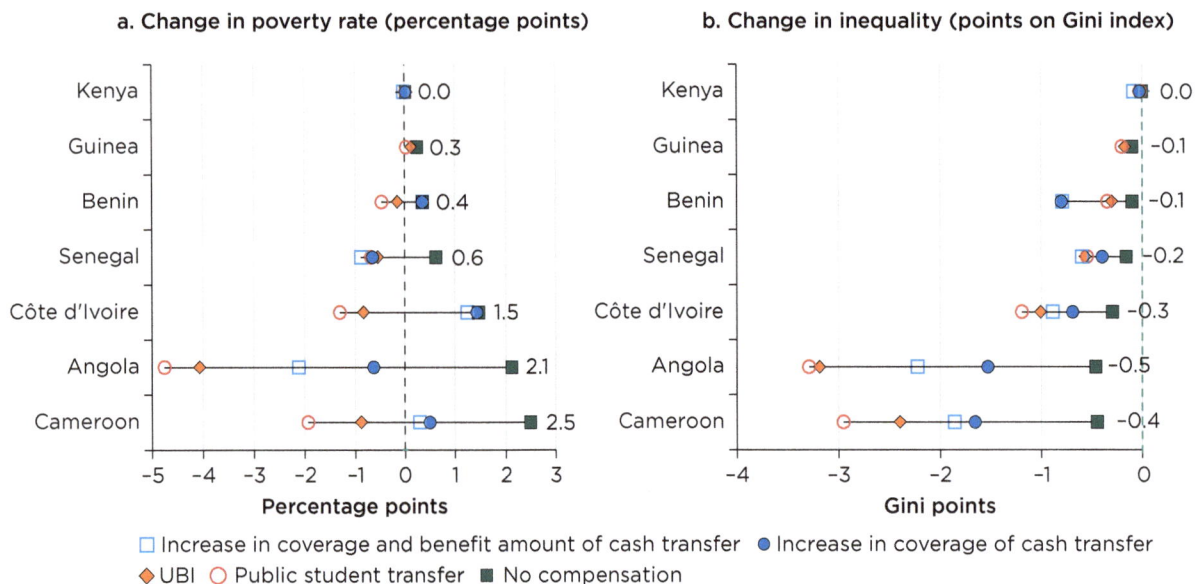

a. Change in poverty rate (percentage points)

b. Change in inequality (points on Gini index)

Legend:
□ Increase in coverage and benefit amount of cash transfer   ● Increase in coverage of cash transfer
◆ UBI   ○ Public student transfer   ■ No compensation

Source: Original figure for this publication, using estimates based on fiscal microsimulation models for each country.
Note: The dashed line indicates 0. The figure shows the change in poverty (panel a) and inequality (panel b) resulting from a change in consumable income under five different simulations. In panel a, the poverty line is defined as $3.65/day at 2017 purchasing power parity. UBI = universal basic income. More detail is provided in annex 5.B.

The removal of energy subsidies is expected to reduce inequality and create moderate increases in poverty. Given the regressive nature of energy subsidies, removing them will slightly reduce inequality in all countries, with the exception of Kenya, where inequality will barely change. The stronger reductions in inequality would happen in Angola and Cameroon, where inequality is expected to decline by almost a half Gini point because of the removal of energy subsidies. This is in line with the relatively large size of fuel subsidies in these countries (refer to figure 5.11). Poverty is expected to increase slightly in all countries, with the exception of Angola, Cameroon, and Côte d'Ivoire, where the expected increase in poverty is expected to be above 1.5 percentage points. This points to the fact that although most of the benefit from energy subsidies goes to high-income households, poor households will nevertheless be affected when subsidies are removed. The relatively modest increase in poverty in these countries is consistent with less well-off households having low levels of direct consumption of energy because of, for example, lack of connectivity to the electricity grid and relatively low levels of ownership of assets that depend on energy (for example, cars and computers, among others). Moreover, part of the impoverishment effect is expected to be driven by the indirect effects that the subsidy removal has on the prices of other goods in these countries.[9]

Redirecting half the fiscal savings into compensation measures would increase the overall capacity of the fiscal system to reduce poverty and inequality. If half the savings from removal of subsidies was spent on compensation measures, this would reduce poverty and inequality more than was possible with energy subsidies in all the countries analyzed, with higher reductions in Angola, Cameroon, Côte d'Ivoire, and Senegal because of the larger budget devoted to subsidies in these countries. Using a UBI or a CT program for public students would in some cases outperform compensation policies that rely on more targeted CTs. These results should not be interpreted as evidence of a weakness in CT programs, but as a weakness in the level of benefits of these programs. For instance, the current benefit level of the CT programs in Angola and Cameroon is so low that expanding it to the whole population (blue circle in figure 5.11) will not exhaust the budget allocated to compensation measures. This result does not change even if the CT's benefits increase by 50 percent (blue squares in figure 5.11). In other words, compensation policies using CT programs result in lower reductions in poverty than a UBI because the low benefits of CT programs limit the amount of fiscal savings that can be mobilized through this policy instrument.[10] This highlights the fact that social protection systems in the region are still far from adequate in protecting poor households, and to make them work, it is essential to increase the size of their benefits and give them the flexibility to work as vehicles to compensate households for the expected welfare loses that will take place during the energy transition.

Improvements in public expenditure management

Beyond changes in expenditure policies, improvements in public expenditure and debt management can make a difference in improving the redistributive impact of spending. Public financial management performance includes budget reliability, transparency of public finances, sound management of assets and liabilities, the extent to which fiscal strategy and budgeting are prepared in line with strategic policy objectives, whether there is predictability and control in budget execution, the strength of accountability and reporting, and external audit and scrutiny (PEFA 2022). In each of these areas, Africa lags other regions (refer to figure 5.12), pointing to potential gaps between policy priorities, including those aimed at improving the redistributive impacts and actual execution of spending. Similarly, improvements in public debt management can generate fiscal savings through lower debt service, resources that can then be used for development objectives. This is increasingly important considering the high levels of debt and debt service in Africa (see spotlight 4 on debt). Improved transparency can promote lower borrowing costs, as episodes of hidden debt coming to light have painfully demonstrated in Mozambique and Zambia (Rivetti 2021).[11] However, greater transparency or improved public expenditure management rules alone will not be effective in changing outcomes unless the underlying power asymmetries are addressed (Gootjes and de Haan 2022; World Bank 2017). For instance, information asymmetries are rarely an accident of history. Rather, the lack of disclosure of information is often the result of powerful actors intentionally withholding information or resisting attempts to make it accessible (Khagram, Fung, and de Renzio 2013). In this context, three key conditions are needed for effective information initiatives: transparency, publicity, and accountability (Naurin 2006). Making information available, accessible, and actionable intrinsically involves addressing the existing power structures that exacerbate structural inequalities (IMF 2023).

Developing a disaster risk management strategy is an important part of ensuring a timely response that can protect poor individuals. As noted in spotlight 1 on climate, substantive evidence shows that receiving a timely response when a crisis hits can make the difference between a quick recovery and long-term scarring for poor and vulnerable individuals (Crossley et al. 2021; Hill et al. 2019). Various risk-financing instruments can be designed to protect government budgets after shocks, targeting specific people or sectors, including the most vulnerable households (World Bank 2022b). The availability of multilateral loans and grants is an opportunity to support anticipatory financial planning, including through the World Bank's Global Risk Financing Facility, the International Development Association's early response financing, and the United Nations' Central Emergency Response Fund. Moreover, to the extent that governments will likely continue to rely on ex post financing in major disasters, sound fiscal management is a precondition to ensure a low cost of borrowing when disaster hits.

FIGURE 5.12 **Public financial management indicators, 2022**

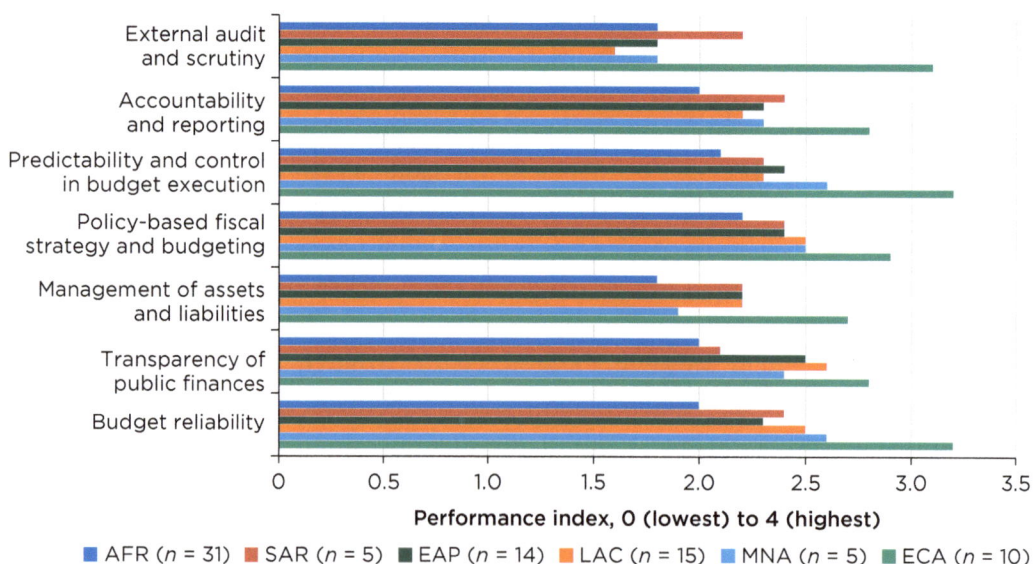

Source: Public Expenditure and Financial Accountability program.
Note: AFR = Sub-Saharan Africa; EAP = East Asia and Pacific; ECA = Europe and Central Asia; LAC = Latin America and the Caribbean; MNA = Middle East and North Africa; SAR = South Asia.

It is possible to raise revenue while protecting the poor

Domestic resource mobilization strategies have a critical role to play in raising the necessary revenue to allow governments to implement policies that reduce inequality of opportunities. The preceding chapters showed the need for greater investments to reduce inequality in building and utilizing productive capacities. Pivotal in this effort is the need for additional government revenue as debt levels mount. Moreover, given the limited fiscal capacity for redistribution and the fact that the net impact of fiscal policies increases poverty in most African countries, the design of policies aimed at domestic revenue mobilization will need to be especially mindful of the poor population. This section discusses several ways for governments to raise revenue without further increasing poverty and inequality in the region. An important part of this discussion is highlighting that the de jure and de facto impacts of revenue mobilization efforts often differ due to low levels of compliance.

Overview of sources of government revenue

Government revenue tends to be a higher share of GDP in richer African countries. On average, LICs in Africa collect less than 15 percent of their GDP in revenue, LMICs collect just over 20 percent, and UMICs collect closer to 30 percent. This pattern is consistent with trends elsewhere in the world because high levels of informality and low levels of compliance, which are partly due to the structure of lower-income economies, make it challenging to raise more taxes (Jensen 2022). On average, non-FCS, resource-rich countries collect almost 30 percent of GDP in revenue, whereas in non-FCS non–resource-rich countries and FCS resource-rich countries, around 20 percent of GDP is collected in revenue (excluding grants). In contrast, just over 10 percent of GDP is collected in revenue (excluding grants) in FCS non–resource-rich countries.

Consumption taxes are the largest source of revenue in poorer countries, whereas richer countries typically raise a higher share of revenue through income taxes. On average, consumption taxes, mainly value added taxes (VATs), are the largest source of revenue in LICs and the second source of revenue in LMICs in Africa (refer to figure 5.13). In contrast, income taxes are the dominant source of revenue in UMICs. Revenue from resources varies depending on whether countries are endowed with large resource deposits. Natural resource revenue makes up around half of revenue in FCS countries that are rich in resources. Taxes that are directly applied to wealth, such as property taxes, tend to feature less prominently in Africa than in other regions (UNU-WIDER 2023). Unsurprisingly, grants are a higher share of revenue in poorer and in FCS countries.

Tax expenditures through exemptions, allowances, deductions, and reduced rates are substantial in Africa. Information on tax expenditures is patchy, in part because

FIGURE 5.13 Types of revenue as a share of GDP in Africa

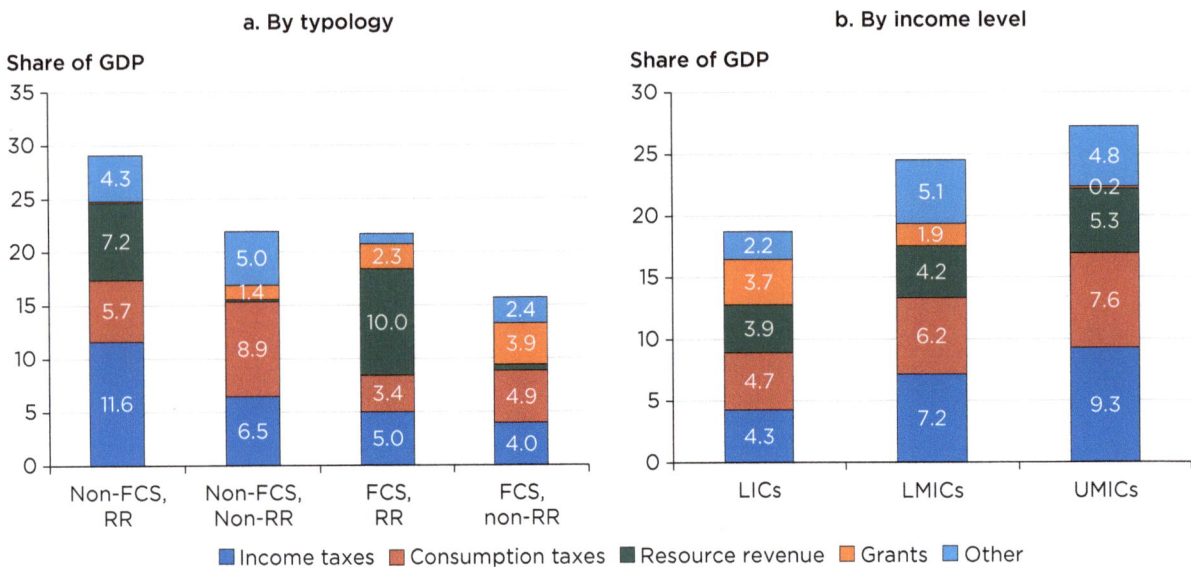

a. By typology

Share of GDP

Non-FCS, RR	Non-FCS, Non-RR	FCS, RR	FCS, non-RR
4.3	5.0	2.3	2.4
7.2	1.4	10.0	3.9
5.7	8.9	3.4	4.9
11.6	6.5	5.0	4.0

b. By income level

Share of GDP

LICs	LMICs	UMICs
2.2	5.1	4.8
3.7	1.9	0.2
3.9	4.2	5.3
4.7	6.2	7.6
4.3	7.2	9.3

■ Income taxes ■ Consumption taxes ■ Resource revenue ■ Grants ■ Other

Source: UNU-WIDER 2023.
Note: FCS = fragile and conflict-affected situations; GDP = gross domestic product; LIC = low-income countries; LMICs = lower-middle-income countries; RR = resource rich; UMICs = upper-middle-income countries.

few African countries transparently report them as part of their national budget. However, recent efforts to build a Global Tax Expenditure Database (https://gted .taxexpenditures.org/), based on government-reported data, demonstrate the potential for additional revenue mobilization in the region. In 2021, tax expenditures amounted to an average of 2.4 percent of GDP and 15.6 percent of revenue, based on data for 22 African countries. About three-quarters of these tax expenditures were forgone revenue from taxes on goods and services, and nearly half of tax expenditures were from forgone VAT, largely in the form of exemptions (as opposed to deductions). In addition, another 12 percent of tax expenditures were based on forgone revenue from taxes on income, of which three-quarters is for corporate income tax (CIT) expenditures, largely in the form of deductions (as opposed to exemptions). These patterns tend to hold across most countries for which there are data. Given the size of these tax expenditures, it is important to assess their policy rationale, whether these instruments are reaching their intended recipients, and the reason for using a tax instrument instead of a more transparent spending instrument. For instance, if the policy rationale for exempting some goods from VAT is to protect those who are poor and vulnerable, it is important to evaluate whether the tax instrument is reaching the intended beneficiaries and whether there are better alternatives to achieve the same objective.

Taxes on consumption

VAT rates in Africa are slightly higher on average than in most parts of the world and typically do not vary substantially across goods and services (Okunogbe and Santoro

FIGURE 5.14 Incidence of indirect taxes as a share of household consumption

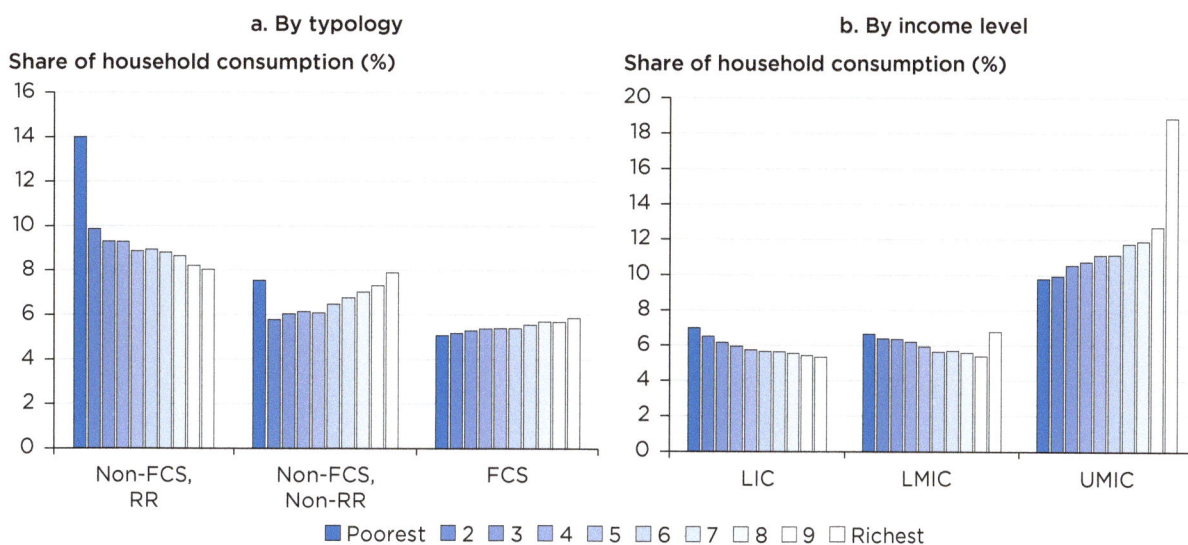

a. By typology

Share of household consumption (%)

b. By income level

Share of household consumption (%)

Legend: ■ Poorest ■ 2 ■ 3 ■ 4 ■ 5 □ 6 □ 7 □ 8 □ 9 □ Richest

Source: Original figure for this publication based on CEQ studies conducted by the World Bank and the CEQ Institute, Tulane University.
Note: Figure excludes South Africa. FCS = fragile and conflict-affected situations; GDP = gross domestic product; LIC = low-income countries; LMICs = lower-middle-income countries; RR = resource rich; UMICs = upper-middle-income countries.

2023). Standard CEQ assessments in 18 African countries show that, on average, indirect taxes (mainly VAT) are largely neutral, because they make up a relatively consistent share of household consumption across the distribution (refer to figure 5.14). However, poorer households in non-FCS countries tend to pay a higher share of household consumption than richer households. Consequently, these types of taxes increase both poverty and inequality in these settings. VAT is more regressive than many types of excise taxes, such as those levied on luxury goods. However, the total amount of revenue collected from VAT far outweighs excise taxes in all African countries with comparable data available (UNU-WIDER 2023).

Recent work suggests that consumption taxes are progressive, once high levels of informality in low- and middle-income countries are considered. Bachas et al. (2023b) show that poorer households are much more likely to purchase goods from informal sellers, and their consumption is consequently less likely to be subject to VAT across a sample of 31 countries (16 of which are in Africa). Moreover, Warwick et al. (2022) show that VAT exemptions largely benefit higher-income households, even when accounting for cascading effects, simply because richer households consume more than low-income households. Combined, these stylized facts have two important implications. First, exemptions to VAT and other consumption taxes based on poverty or equity arguments seem less reasonable because the poorest households are typically not the main beneficiaries. Second, because poorer households tend to purchase goods in informal shops, efforts to increase the number of small businesses that are formally registered will have distributional consequences and are likely to increase the regressivity of consumption taxes.

Removing VAT exemptions and using some of the additional revenue to better target programs would reduce poverty and inequality

Replacing regressive VAT expenditures with direct transfers could help some countries reduce postfiscal inequality.[12] Figure 5.15a leverages fiscal microsimulation models developed by the World Bank to estimate the distributional impact of removing VAT expenditures in seven countries in the region. The simulations apply a standard tax rate with no exemptions or reduced rates for all nonfood products, accompanied by the same four compensation measures that were implemented earlier for the simulations on energy subsidies, as detailed in annex 5.B. All these compensation measures cost no more than half of the fiscal savings obtained from the removal of these tax expenditures. In all cases, higher informality among lower-income households and the cascading effects due to exemptions are accounted for.

FIGURE 5.15 Poverty and inequality effects of removing VAT expenditures, by compensation measure

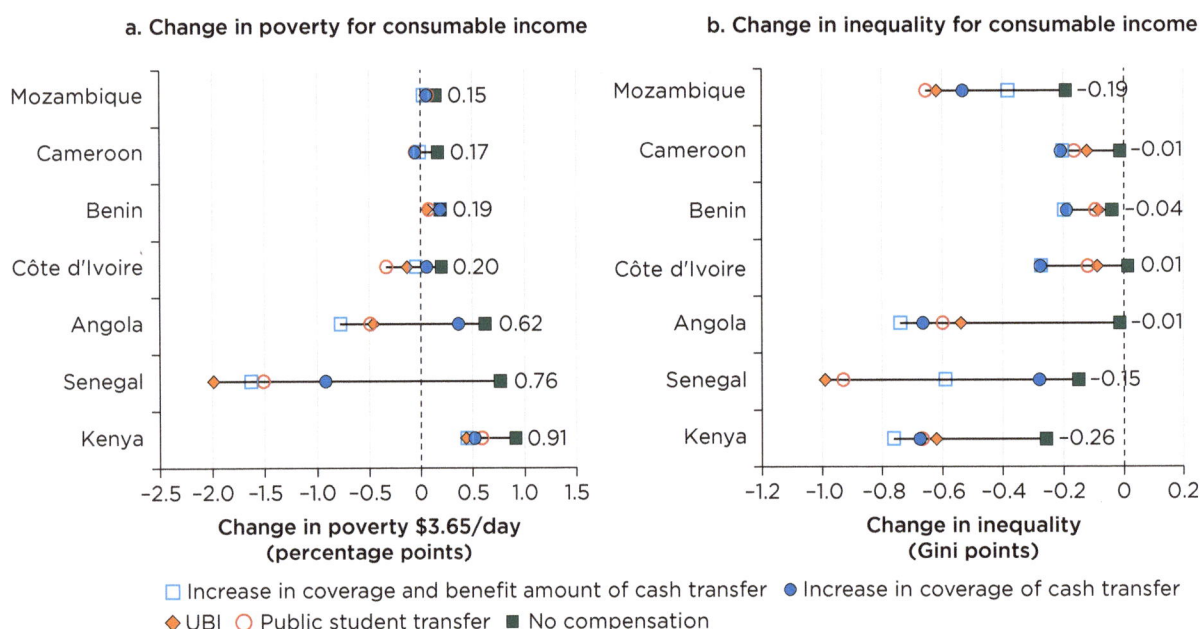

a. Change in poverty for consumable income

b. Change in inequality for consumable income

Change in poverty $3.65/day (percentage points)

Change in inequality (Gini points)

□ Increase in coverage and benefit amount of cash transfer ● Increase in coverage of cash transfer
◆ UBI ○ Public student transfer ■ No compensation

Source: Original figure for this publication based on fiscal microsimulation models conducted by the World Bank in each country.
Note: Changes in poverty and inequality for consumable income were calculated using five different simulations: (1) removal of VAT expenditures without compensation measures (black squares), (2) removal of VAT expenditures with a UBI transfer, (3) removal of VAT expenditures with a cash transfer directed to primary and secondary students enrolled in public schools, (4) removal of VAT expenditures with an increase in the coverage of the main targeted cash transfer program, and (5) removal of VAT expenditures with an increase in the generosity and coverage of the main cash transfer program. More detail is provided in annex 5.B. UBI = universal basic income; VAT = value-added tax.

Removing VAT expenditures is expected to reduce inequality. However, without proper compensation measures, their removal could result in significant increases in poverty. Removing VAT expenditures without a revenue-recycling strategy could increase poverty 0.1–1.0 percentage point (refer to figure 5.15a). The increase in poverty after eliminating tax expenditures is higher than the impacts obtained for the removal of energy subsidies, because poor households spend more on VAT-exempted products than on fuel and electricity. For instance, in Senegal, 5 of 10 people in the bottom 40 percent of the distribution report consuming exempted nonfood items, whereas only 3 of 10 consume electricity. Although eliminating exemptions and removing reduced rates would not make a substantial difference in inequality, compensating measures financed with the additional revenues would have profound impacts on postfiscal inequality (refer to figure 5.15b). The decline in the Gini coefficient with compensation measures is more than the double the decline observed without them in all countries. In general, policies increasing the coverage and benefits of the main CT program are better at reducing poverty and inequality. For instance, in Angola combining the removal of VAT expenditures with the expansion of Kwenda (the main CT program) can result in a reduction in poverty (0.8 percentage point) and inequality (0.73 Gini point). In Senegal, Côte d'Ivoire, and Mozambique, CT programs underperform, which, as explained earlier, suggests not that these countries should opt for implementing UBI or categorical CT programs but that they should work on improving the generosity and coverage of their current programs.

Taxes on household income and wealth

Direct taxes, which primarily consist of personal income taxes (PITs), reduce inequality because they are almost exclusively levied on high-income earners (for example, formal sector employees). PIT regimes are designed in a way to make them progressive in all African countries. This is largely thanks to tax-free income thresholds, below which employees are not required to pay income tax. Recent research shows that one of the main factors in determining how large an impact PIT has on inequality is the income threshold for which the top marginal PIT rate begins and the level of the top marginal PIT rate (McNabb and Oppel 2023). All available CEQ assessments in Africa show that PIT is progressive. In most countries, households in the poorest deciles of the income distribution effectively pay no direct taxes, whereas those in the richest decile of the income distribution pay more than 10 percent of their income in direct taxes. Direct taxes are particularly progressive in resource-rich, non-FCS countries where the richest two deciles pay more than 90 percent of the total amount of direct taxes, whereas less than two-thirds of direct taxes are collected from the richest two deciles in FCS countries (refer to figure 5.16).

FIGURE 5.16 Direct taxes paid by decile

Share of direct taxes paid by decile (%)

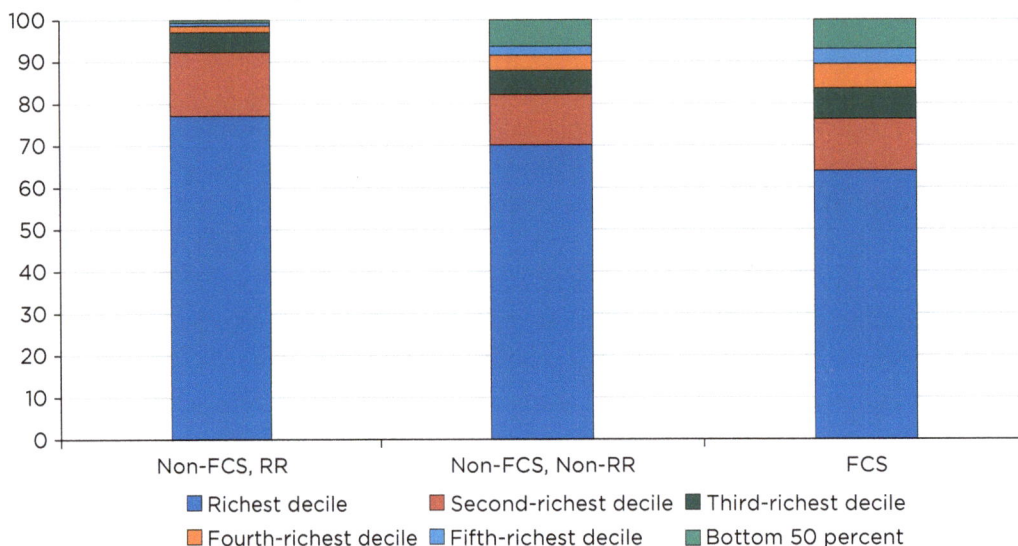

Legend:
- Richest decile
- Second-richest decile
- Third-richest decile
- Fourth-richest decile
- Fifth-richest decile
- Bottom 50 percent

Source: Original figure for this publication based on CEQ studies conducted by the World Bank and the CEQ Institute, Tulane University.
Note: FCS = fragile and conflict-affected situations; RR = resource rich.

Increasing the PIT rate for high-income earners may not be a straightforward way to raise revenue and reduce inequality. Although some evidence suggests that PIT rates are relatively low in Africa (Chancel et al. 2023), efforts to raise the top marginal tax rates have been associated with increased tax evasion, to the point that little additional revenue ends up being raised (Axelson et al. 2024; Jouste et al. 2023). Moreover, increasing the PIT rate increases horizontal inequality between employees and self-employed workers who earn high incomes because the latter are not subject to tax withholding regimes and have more opportunities to evade taxes (Jensen 2022). Finally, as discussed earlier in this chapter (refer to figure 5.4), even dramatically increasing PIT rates may have relatively limited revenue potential because many low-income African countries do not have many rich households.

Property taxes exist in most African countries and could potentially be a more substantial source of government revenue while also reducing inequality. These taxes are required to be paid by wealthier property owners, mainly in urban areas, and are typically collected by subnational governments (except in some Francophone countries). However, country studies, including those from Ghana (Dzansi et al. 2022), the Democratic Republic of Congo (Balán et al. 2020), Senegal (Knebelman 2021), and Uganda (Regan and Manwaring 2023) show that property tax collection remains at 10–20 percent of potential in most African cities. The full revenue potential of property taxes has yet to be realized, partly because of low administrative capacity and a lack of documented property rights (Brockmeyer et al. 2021; Deininger and Goyal 2023; Moore, Prichard, and Fjeldstad 2018). However, growing evidence suggests that even governments with weak capacity can make slight changes to increase revenue (Franzsen and McCluskey 2017; Jibao and Prichard 2016). A particularly promising area is the use of technology to increase the amount collected in property taxes (Dzansi et al. 2022; Okunogbe and Santoro 2023). For example, recent research shows that local government officials often underestimate the value of the wealthiest properties, and technology can address this, which increases revenue and the degree of progressivity of property taxes (Knebelmann, Pouliquen, and Sarr 2023).

Other taxes on the wealth of households (such as net wealth taxes and inheritance taxes) have yet to be implemented by most African governments; however, they are only likely to be a sizable source of revenue in richer countries. Taxes on wealth help to raise revenue and reduce inequality and have been growing in popularity in UMICs (Bergolo, Londoño-Vélez, and Tortarolo 2023). However, relatively limited revenue can be generated by them in LICs, where most households do not have a substantial amount of wealth. In 2022, across Africa (including North Africa), only around 10 percent of the population had more than US$10,000 in total assets and only around 1 percent had wealth above US$100,000 (UBS 2023). In fact, Ghana, Kenya, and South Africa are the only countries in Africa with a total population above 3 million in which more than 10 percent of the population had at least US$10,000 in total assets in 2022 (UBS 2023).

Taxes on business income

Most tax revenue raised from businesses in Africa is through CIT, which does not directly alter household income. However, the indirect effects of CIT on household welfare are notable because businesses can react to these taxes through reductions in employment and wages or increases in prices. In addition, CIT can indirectly influence household welfare by changing how much earnings are distributed to shareholders who, when they are domestically based, are often in the most well-off households (Bilicka, Qi, and Xing 2022). Recent research shows that CIT can play a somewhat redistributive role because some of the richest households in countries that benefit from corporate profits may not pay PIT (because of evasion, low labor income, or both; Fuest and Neumeier 2023). Extensive evidence shows that large businesses adjust their activities to evade tax when CIT is raised, and these changes in operations (such as reducing the size of the workforce) indirectly affect household welfare (Alstadsæter et al. 2023). As such, because of the likely increase in tax evasion, there is potentially limited scope for African governments to dramatically raise revenue by increasing CIT unless it is a coordinated effort with other countries (Alstadsæter et al. 2023).

However, governments could reduce forgone revenue by decreasing tax incentives (or tax expenditures). Although many LICs use tax holidays and income tax exemptions to attract investment, these incentives generally rank low in investment climate surveys as factors that lead to investments taking place. In many cases, there is evidence that investments would have been undertaken even without them, particularly when dealing with investments in sectors that involve location-specific factors, such as natural resources, agglomeration effects, or local markets (IMF et al. 2015; Mansour and Keen 2009; Mataba et al. 2023; Millot et al. 2020). Moreover, the way these incentives are applied is typically inefficient, because many LICs use costly tax holidays and income tax exemptions to attract investment, whereas investment tax credits and accelerated depreciation yield more investment per dollar spent (IMF et al. 2015). Furthermore, these tax expenditures are often discretionary, taking place without a legislative process or other forms of accountability (IMF et al. 2015; Mataba et al. 2023; Waiswa and Rakundo 2023). From an equity perspective, it is unlikely that these instruments would reduce structural inequalities, because there is evidence that tax expenditures result in larger firms paying an effective tax rate well below what is paid by medium-sized firms (Bachas et al. 2023a).

Careful design of simplified tax regimes for micro-, small-, and medium-sized enterprises (MSMEs) can limit their impact on poverty and reduce inequality. MSMEs in Africa are largely unincorporated and are owned and managed by poorer and middle-class households, particularly in urban areas, and the taxes that they pay directly affect household income. Relatively little revenue is collected from MSMEs, even though policy makers direct substantial attention to this issue (Moore 2023). Overwhelmingly, the clear message from the existing literature is that there is limited value in registering new businesses and focusing enforcement efforts on small businesses (De La O et al. 2021; Gallien and van den Boogaard 2021; Hoy, McKenzie, and Sinning 2024). However, there is considerable variation in how simplified tax regimes are designed across the region, and some design features, such as whether there is a tax-free threshold, have substantial implications for the welfare of the poorest households (refer to box 5.4, which provide further details).

BOX 5.4

Simplified tax regimes for micro-, small-, and medium-sized enterprises in Africa

Simplified tax regimes (STRs), often referred to as turnover or presumptive taxes, reduce the compliance costs faced by formal micro-, small-, and medium-sized enterprises (MSMEs) by removing the requirement to pay tax as a share of profits (that is, the typical way in which corporate income tax [CIT] is determined) or to pay tax under the personal income tax regime (which is primarily for labor income). Rather, MSMEs subject to STRs are only required to pay a percentage of total turnover (percentage approach) or a fixed amount that varies on the basis of

(continued)

BOX 5.4

Simplified tax regimes for micro-, small-, and medium-sized enterprises in Africa *(continued)*

turnover thresholds (fixed approach). STRs also help to encourage informal MSMEs to formalize because they can still be fully compliant with their tax obligations without having to accurately calculate their profits. Collectively, around two-thirds of countries in Africa have implemented some form of STRs for MSMEs.

There are several differences in the design features across countries, which have important implications for poverty and equity:

- Turnover of firms is always used as the sole criterion for determining the amount of tax owed. However, some countries (for example, Angola, Cameroon, the Central African Republic, the Democratic Republic of Congo, Ethiopia, Mauritius, and Togo) vary the tax liability depending on the sector, size (for example, whether an MSME has employees or not), or location. These variations can result in horizontal inequality between MSMEs.
- Almost two-thirds of countries with STRs (20 of 32) determine tax liability using a percentage of turnover, around one-third (9 of 32) use a fixed amount (or fee), and the remainder use a combination of these two approaches.[a] In the case of the fixed approach, MSMEs must pay a set lump-sum amount of tax regardless of their turnover—a feature that is quite regressive because smaller firms pay a higher effective tax rate.
- Only around one-half of countries apply a tax-free threshold, for which MSMEs whose turnover is below the threshold are exempt from paying any tax, and the other half require all MSMEs that have any turnover to pay tax. In other words, in one-half of countries, even very small firms with minimal turnover are required to pay tax.
- More than one-third of countries have multiple turnover thresholds where the marginal tax rate is higher when the turnover is higher. As such, they have a progressive tax regime for MSMEs that reduces inequality (however, this complexity may somewhat undermine the purpose of an STR).
- Among countries that have STRs using the percentage approach, the size of the tax rate varies from as low as 1 percent to as high as 35 percent. In fact, in many countries, medium-sized firms (but still well below the CIT threshold) pay the same or higher effective tax rates as large enterprises.

Note: This information was sourced from Hoy et al. 2024, which provides extensive details about simplified tax regimes across Africa.
a. For example, Tanzania and Rwanda use both fixed and percentage approaches, with the former used for businesses with no records and the latter for those that kept records. The effective tax rate is lower for businesses that maintain accurate records of their transactions.

Resource-rich countries vary in the extent to which they capture the rents from commodities

Many African countries are rich in resources; however, few countries collect a substantial share of GDP in revenue from that sector. Resources contribute around 7.5 percent of GDP for the median African country and exceed 10 percent of GDP in 19 countries (World Bank 2023a). However, less than 1 percent of GDP is collected in revenue from resources in the median African country, and only eight countries collect 5 percent or more of GDP in resource revenue (UNU-WIDER 2023).[13] Numerous studies have provided an order of magnitude of just how much more revenue could be obtained from the sector, such as analysis by Cust and Zeufack (2023) that estimates that, on average, countries capture only about 40 percent of the revenue they could potentially collect from resources. More important, many of the changes in tax policy and administration that are proposed to increase revenue are likely to have limited impacts on poverty and may even reduce inequality (for example, see Readhead et al. 2023; World Bank 2023a). This is because resource extraction often takes place in enclaves that have few linkages with most of the population (Savoia and Sen 2021).[14]

A comprehensive review of the types of revenue collection instruments that are used in African countries provides several insights into the revenue potential of the sector (refer to figure 5.17). This analysis of countries in which resource rents exceed 5 percent of GDP is based on the Extractives Industry Transparency Initiative (EITI) database, which provides among the best publicly available information about the instruments used to collect revenue from the resources sector (for example, royalties, CIT, dividends; EITI 2023). First, there is significant variation in the types of instruments that countries use, which highlights the value of governments exploring greater regional harmonization of resource revenue strategies to avoid a race to the bottom between countries (Cust and Zeufack 2023). Second, all countries have some form of fixed instruments (such as royalties and production entitlements) that provide a stable but inflexible source of revenue that does not allow governments to substantially benefit from increases in commodity prices (Albertin et al. 2021). Third, less than half of resource revenue in each country (except for Mozambique) is sourced from instruments that are directly linked to the profitability of the sector (for example, income tax or dividends). This may have contributed to the growing interest in a minimum profit share for governments, whereby they are guaranteed a fraction of the profit generated from resources when they exceed a predefined threshold (ATAF 2023).

FIGURE 5.17 Instruments used to collect revenue from resources sector in each country

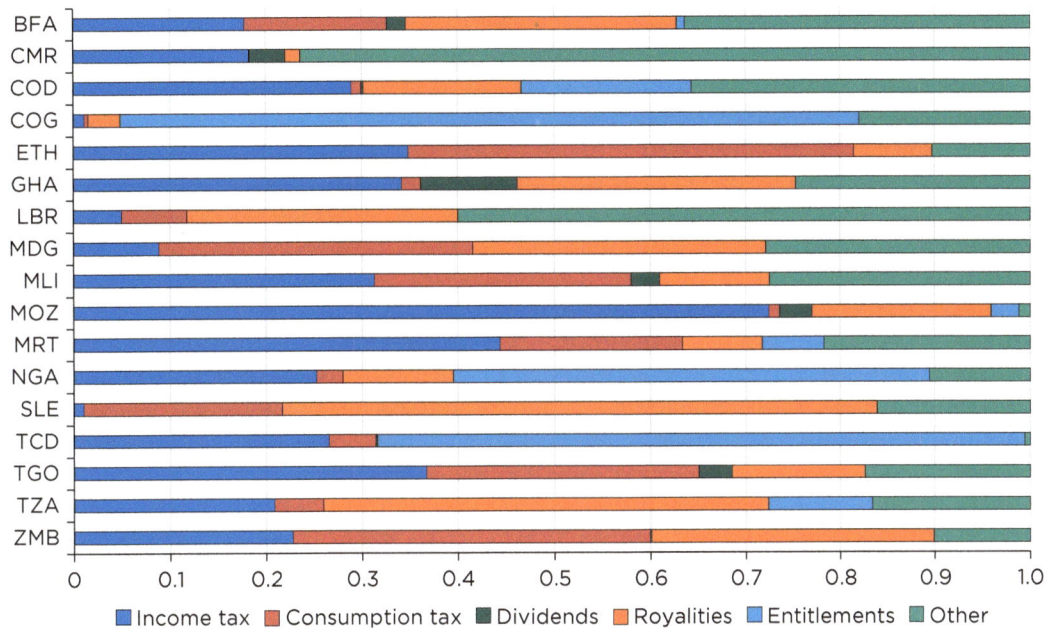

Source: EITI 2023.

Notes: This figure is based on the most recent complete EITI assessment in each country. For country abbreviations, refer to https://www.iso.org/obp/ui/#search.

Improvements in tax enforcement, when not accompanied by improved social spending and service delivery, could lead to increases in poverty and inequality

A government's ability to collect taxes from its citizens is widely considered to be one of the hallmarks of the modern state (Weigel 2020); however, increases in this ability to enforce compliance can lead to increases in poverty and inequality. In many instances, African governments focus on increasing compliance among small informal firms (that is, among firms not registered for VAT or a business tax regime; Moore 2023). However, these enforcement efforts disproportionally target poor individuals, who are much more likely to manage small businesses and consume from the informal sector (Bachas et al. 2023b; Boadway and Sato 2009). Even when these economic activities become formalized, they rarely raise substantial revenue, and sometimes poorer taxpayers end up paying well above their required obligations due to confusion arising from complex tax systems (Gallien and van den Boogaard 2021). For example, Tourek (2022) shows that a large share of registered small businesses in Rwanda paid the same amount in tax each year even after consecutive reductions in the tax rates these firms were required to pay. Rather than governments focusing enforcement activities on small informal sector firms, registered small businesses, or both, growing evidence suggests that simplifying tax administration for these segments of society, such as by using technology, can increase revenue and ensure more equitable tax collection (Aghion et al. 2017; Dzansi et al. 2022; J-PAL 2022).

Efforts to increase the compliance of larger firms and richer individuals provide a more promising way of increasing revenue and reducing inequality. For example, the establishment of large- and medium-sized taxpayer offices (where these taxpayers have a higher chance of being audited) and improvement in the quality of tax collectors has increased revenue in low- and middle-income countries, including in Africa (Basri et al. 2021; Bergeron, Tourek, and Weigel 2023). These studies have shown that improvements in tax administration can increase revenue in a similar order of magnitude as increases in the tax rates themselves. In addition, suggestive evidence across countries shows that improvements in the tax system's progressivity can positively affect the general population's compliance (for example, see Hoy 2022). Relatedly, analysis based on cross-country regressions shows that reductions in inequality and increases in accountability are positively associated with increases in tax capacity in Africa (Dom, Morrissey, and Tagem 2023; Tagem and Morrissey 2023). Although these examples highlight the promise of improving enforcement on wealthier segments of society, this needs to be balanced with the earlier discussion of how these types of taxpayers sometimes increase evasion, often across borders, in the face of greater tax burdens. As such, collective action by governments across countries to boost compliance, such as by establishing a global minimum CIT, may hold considerable potential for raising revenue (Alstadsæter et al. 2023; Cust and Zeufack 2023).

Fiscal policies to unlock the productive potential of poor individuals

For many of the poorest countries in the region, it is difficult to expect more fiscal redistribution given the very limited size of the state. Low-income and fragile or conflict-affected countries (without substantial natural resource rents) often do not have the fiscal capacity to redistribute in a way that would fill the aggregate poverty gap. For these countries, the key development priority is to lay the foundations for economic growth, particularly because they have relatively low levels of prefiscal inequality.

However, for middle-income and some resource-rich countries, relatively modest taxation of the nonpoor population could allow improved fiscal redistribution. Fiscal redistribution reduces inequality in most African countries, but it leads to increases in poverty, largely because the taxes paid outweigh transfers received by households. This need not be the case. This chapter has shown that opportunities exist to improve the efficiency and distributional impact of spending in the region and raise revenue while protecting poor individuals. Reallocating government spending to sectors that are critical for poor households and improving the quality of that spending can help to generate trust, strengthen the social contract, allow for further redistribution, and contribute to poverty reduction.

There are key opportunities for greater efficiency and equity on the spending side. First, subsidies, particularly for energy, are very costly and typically quite regressive. Redirecting these expenditures toward expanding direct transfer programs would considerably reduce poverty in many countries in the region. In contrast, social assistance programs in the region have low coverage and low benefit levels, despite being a very efficient way to reduce poverty and inequality. Programs that target school-age children, such as school feeding programs, could also play a similar role. Adaptive social safety nets should be dramatically expanded to have a meaningful impact on the depth and breadth of poverty. Finally, there is room to improve expenditure and debt management as well as financial planning for disaster response.

There is scope to raise revenue without increasing poverty through targeted changes in the tax system, which could provide a substantial source of government revenue while also reducing inequality. First, tax expenditures, such as VAT exemptions and reduced tax rates, do not substantially reduce poverty and drain already-stretched government budgets. Removing them would raise much-needed revenue that could fund programs for poorer households. Second, the full extent of property taxes has yet to be realized, and other taxes on wealth have yet to be implemented. Third, although there is limited scope to dramatically raise revenue by increasing CITs (because of tax evasion), governments could reduce forgone revenue by decreasing tax incentives. In resource-rich countries, tax instruments should allow governments to benefit from high commodity prices or be directly linked to the profitability of the sector. Further cooperation between governments in the region could assist with reducing tax evasion by multinational firms, and greater harmonization of revenue collection strategies could help to minimize the risk of a race to the bottom between countries. With respect to small- and medium-sized firms, some features of simplified tax regimes, such as a tax-free threshold, can be designed to minimize the impacts on the poorest households. Finally, it is important to note that substantial improvements in tax enforcement, when not accompanied by improved social spending and service delivery, could lead to increases in poverty and inequality.

Annex 5A: Fiscal analysis

This annex details the sample of countries used for the fiscal incidence analyses in chapter 5. The sample consists of 102 countries and 108 observations; six countries have observations from two different sources. There are 72 countries with data sourced from a Commitment to Equity (CEQ) analysis containing Gini and other indicators, and 36 countries have Gini estimates from the Organisation for Economic Co-operation and Development (OECD). The six countries in both samples are Chile, Costa Rica, Poland,

Spain, Türkiye, and the United States. Table 5A.1 summarizes the number of countries per region and source. For this chapter, OECD numbers are used to estimate the average inequality at market income level of high-income and upper-middle-income countries, including OECD countries that are largely excluded from the CEQ sample. All analyses of fiscal redistribution and progressivity, including impacts of fiscal policy on inequality from market income to final income, poverty impacts, marginal contributions, and incidence analyses, are done using exclusively CEQ data. Table 5A.2 lists all the countries in the sample and the data source.

TABLE 5A.1 Country sample size, by region

Source and region	Sample size
CEQ analysis	
ECA	17
LAC	14
EAP	10
NA	1
MNA	5
AFR	24
SAR	1
OECD	36

Source: Original table for this publication based on set of available studies.
Note: CEQ analysis refers to for CEQ exercises produced by the World Bank or the CEQ Institute, Tulane University. The studies from the CEQ Institute are accessible at the CEQ Data Center on Fiscal Redistribution, https://commitmentoequity.org/datacenter. CEQ = Commitment to Equity; EAP = East Asia and Pacific; ECA = Europe and Central Asia; LAC = Latin America and the Caribbean; MNA = Middle East and North Africa; NA = North America; OECD = Organisation for Economic Co-operation and Development; SAR = South Asia; AFR = Sub-Saharan Africa.

TABLE 5A.2 List of countries included in the sample, by source

WEO country name	Year	Source	WEO country name	Year	Source
Albania	2015	CEQ analysis	Indonesia	2017	CEQ analysis
Angola	2018	CEQ analysis	Iraq	2017	CEQ analysis
Argentina	2017	CEQ analysis	Jordan	2017	CEQ analysis
Armenia	2017	CEQ analysis	Kenya	2015	CEQ analysis
Belarus	2015	CEQ analysis	Kyrgyz Republic	2016	CEQ analysis
Benin	2022	CEQ analysis	Lao PDR	2019	CEQ analysis
Bolivia	2015	CEQ analysis	Lesotho	2017	CEQ analysis
Brazil	2018	CEQ analysis	Malaysia	2019	CEQ analysis
Bulgaria	2019	CEQ analysis	Mali	2014	CEQ analysis
Burkina Faso	2014	CEQ analysis	Mauritius	2017	CEQ analysis
Cambodia	2019	CEQ analysis	Mexico	2014	CEQ analysis
Cameroon	2022	CEQ analysis	Moldova	2017	CEQ analysis
Chile	2013	CEQ analysis	Mongolia	2016	CEQ analysis
China	2014	CEQ analysis	Montenegro	2015	CEQ analysis
Colombia	2017	CEQ analysis	Morocco	2017	CEQ analysis
Comoros	2014	CEQ analysis	Mozambique	2020	CEQ analysis
Costa Rica	2020	CEQ analysis	Myanmar	2017	CEQ analysis
Côte d'Ivoire	2022	CEQ analysis	Namibia	2016	CEQ analysis
Croatia	2018	CEQ analysis	Niger	2014	CEQ analysis
Djibouti	2017	CEQ analysis	Pakistan	2019	CEQ analysis
Dominican Republic	2013	CEQ analysis	Panama	2016	CEQ analysis
			Paraguay	2014	CEQ analysis
Egypt, Arab Rep.	2015	CEQ analysis	Poland	2014	CEQ analysis
El Salvador	2017	CEQ analysis	Romania	2016	CEQ analysis
Eswatini	2017	CEQ analysis	Russian Federation	2014	CEQ analysis
Ethiopia	2016	CEQ analysis	Senegal	2019	CEQ analysis
Fiji	2019	CEQ analysis	Serbia	2016	CEQ analysis
Gambia, The	2016	CEQ analysis	South Africa	2015	CEQ analysis
Georgia	2013	CEQ analysis	Spain	2017	CEQ analysis
Ghana	2023	CEQ analysis	Tajikistan	2015	CEQ analysis
Guatemala	2014	CEQ analysis	Tanzania	2018	CEQ analysis
Guinea	2019	CEQ analysis	Thailand	2019	CEQ analysis

(continued)

TABLE 5A.2 List of countries included in the sample, by source *(continued)*

WEO country name	Year	Source	WEO country name	Year	Source
Togo	2015	CEQ analysis	Israel	2019	OECD
Türkiye	2016	CEQ analysis	Italy	2018	OECD
Uganda	2016	CEQ analysis	Japan	2018	OECD
Ukraine	2016	CEQ analysis	Korea, Rep.	2020	OECD
United States	2016	CEQ analysis	Latvia	2020	OECD
Uruguay	2017	CEQ analysis	Lithuania	2019	OECD
Venezuela, RB	2013	CEQ analysis	Luxembourg	2019	OECD
Viet Nam	2018	CEQ analysis	Netherlands	2020	OECD
Zambia	2015	CEQ analysis	New Zealand	2020	OECD
Australia	2020	OECD	Norway	2020	OECD
Austria	2019	OECD	Poland	2018	OECD
Belgium	2019	OECD	Portugal	2019	OECD
Canada	2020	OECD	Slovak Republic	2019	OECD
Chile	2017	OECD	Slovenia	2019	OECD
Costa Rica	2021	OECD	Spain	2019	OECD
Czechia	2019	OECD	Sweden	2020	OECD
Denmark	2019	OECD	Switzerland	2019	OECD
Estonia	2019	OECD	Türkiye	2019	OECD
Finland	2020	OECD	United Kingdom	2020	OECD
France	2019	OECD	United States	2021	OECD
Germany	2019	OECD			
Greece	2019	OECD			
Hungary	2019	OECD			
Iceland	2017	OECD			
Ireland	2018	OECD			

Source: Original table for this publication.
Note: CEQ analysis refers to for CEQ exercises produced by the World Bank or the CEQ Institute, Tulane University. CEQ = Commitment to Equity; OECD = Organisation for Economic Co-operation and Development; WEO = *World Economic Outlook* (International Monetary Fund).

Annex 5B: Fiscal microsimulation modeling

This annex describes the regional simulations implemented in chapter 5.[15] Fiscal microsimulation models were developed by World Bank teams for each country (table 5B.1). In each case, tax and spending interventions are modeled in detail. On the tax side, this includes all value-added tax (VAT) exemptions and reduced rates. On the spending side, it includes direct transfers (cash and near-cash transfer programs) and energy subsidies (for example, electricity and fuel). The analysis on subsidies and VAT exemptions includes both the direct and the indirect effects that occur through input–output linkages. In each case, models are macro-validated to ensure that survey results are consistent with the aggregate taxes and spending observed in administrative data under the baseline scenario.

A baseline and 10 counterfactual scenarios were produced for each country. The scenarios combine an energy subsidy reform or a VAT expenditure reform with alternative compensation measures, as listed in table 5B.2. In each case, the assumption is that half the fiscal savings obtained from the reform would be used to compensate households using different mechanism to target those who are poor and vulnerable. The advantage of undertaking this coordinated analysis is that it can help to assess the relative size of the savings obtained from the reform, as well as the extent to which there is a viable social safety net in place to mitigate the poverty impacts of reform. However, the size of these subsidies and tax expenditures as a share of GDP vary widely—from 1.80 percent in Angola to just 0.02 percent in Kenya. This has implications for the results because countries in which the size of the subsidies is relatively large would be able to expand their current cash transfer to the entire population, whereas countries with relatively low spending on subsidies will have a much lower capacity to compensate the households affected by the reform.

TABLE 5B.1 Fiscal microsimulation models

Country	Survey	Policy year	Reform	Indirect effects	Consumption informality[a]	Cash transfer program[b]
Angola	IDREA 2018–19	2022	Subsidy and VAT expenditures	Yes	Yes	Kwenda
Senegal	EHCVM 2018–19	2019	Subsidy and VAT expenditures	Yes	Yes	PNBSF
Guinea	EHCVM 2018–19	2023	Subsidy	No	Yes	n.a.
Cameroon	ECAM5	2022	Subsidy and VAT expenditures	Yes	Yes	Filet Sociaux
Kenya	KIHBS 2015–16	2022	Subsidy and VAT expenditure	Yes	Yes	CT-OVC
Benin	EHCVM 2021–22	2022	Subsidy and VAT expenditures	Yes	Yes	ACCESS
Cote d'Ivoire	EHCVM 2021–22	2022	VAT expenditures	Yes	Yes	PSSN
Mozambique	IOF 2019–20	2020	VAT expenditures	Yes	Yes	PSSB

Source: Original table for this publication.

Note: ACCESS = Appui aux Communes et Communautés pour l'Expansion des Services Sociaux; CT-OVC = cash transfer for orphans and vulnerable children; ECAMS = Enquête Camerounaise Auprès des Ménages; EHCVM = Enquête Harmonise de Conditions de Vie des Ménages; IDREA = Inquérito Sobre Despesas, Receitas e Emprego em Angola; IOF = Inquérito sobre Orçamento Familiar; KIHBS = Kenya Integrated Household Budget Survey; n.a. = not available; PNBSF = Programme National de Bourses de Sécurité familiale; PSSB = Basic Social Subsidy Program; PSSN = Productive Social Safety Net Project; VAT = value-added tax.

a*Consumption informality* means that the model incorporates the fact that some households do not pay VAT for the goods consumed because of either tax exemptions or tax evasion; refer to Bachas et al. (2023b).

bKwenda is the name of the cash transfer program in Angola. Guinea did not model expansion of its cash transfer program.

TABLE 5B.2 Fiscal microsimulation scenarios

Scenario	Reform	Compensation measures	
		Policy instrument	**Policy changes**
0–0	No reform	No compensation	
1–0	Eliminate energy subsidies	No compensation	
1–1		Universal transfer	Transfer to all population
1–2		Public school	Transfer to students in public schools
1–3		Cash transfer program	Increase of coverage
1–4			Increase of coverage and benefits
2–0	Eliminate VAT exemptions and reduced rates	No compensation policy	
2–1		Universal transfer	Transfer to all population
2–2		Public school	Transfer to students in public schools
2–3		Cash transfer program	Increase of coverage
2–4			Increase of coverage and benefits

Source: Original table for this publication.
Note: The compensation measures will be financed with half the fiscal savings obtained from the reform.
VAT = value-added tax.

Reforms

The key reforms simulated are the elimination of energy subsidies and VAT expenditures:

- *Energy subsidies.* Eliminating energy subsidies implies increasing the price of energy so that final consumers pay market prices for both direct and indirect energy consumption. Notice that estimating indirect energy consumption (through transport services, for instance) requires estimating the impact of eliminating energy subsidies on the price of products that use energy as an input. This is done using country-specific input–output matrices and a "cost-push" model (Coady 2008) to account for impacts on all prices.

- *VAT expenditures.* The second reform eliminates tax expenditures on VAT for all goods and services other than food. This involves two steps: (1) equalizing all reduced and special VAT rates to the standard VAT rate and (2) eliminating VAT exemptions. In all cases, the fiscal microsimulation models take account of the high degree of evasion of indirect taxes in African countries. Following Bachas et al. (2023b), the studies use information on the place of purchase to model heterogeneity in the propensity of households to pay indirect taxes. In addition, potential cascading due to VAT exemptions is modeled in Senegal and Kenya, following the methodology described by Warwick et al. (2022).

Design of compensation policies

In all cases, compensation policies were designed to have the same budget constraint, which is equivalent to a fraction of the fiscal savings generated by the reform. However, depending on the country and policy reform, this binding constraint is not always binding (more details are provided when each compensation measure is explained). Let the budget for the compensation measure be defined as κS_0, where S_0 is the prereform fiscal spending and κ is the fraction of the reform's savings that is being recycled (that is, the recycling parameter). The simulations use a recycling parameter of $\kappa = \frac{1}{2}$, which implies that half the fiscal savings are recycled to finance compensation measures.[16] Prereform spending (S_0) is computed for each reform as follows:

- *Energy subsidies*: S_0 is equal to national spending on energy subsidies, as defined by administrative records (for example, gasoline, diesel, kerosene, liquefied petroleum gas, and electricity, among others).[17]

- *VAT tax expenditure*: S_0 should ideally come from official estimates of the aggregate VAT expenditures. When that was not possible, $S_0 = (\gamma - 1)V$, where γ is obtained from estimating total VAT collected with and without VAT expenditures (exemptions and reduced rates) in the household survey. In particular, γ is the ratio of VAT collected without VAT expenditures (that is, simulated scenario) and VAT collected with VAT expenditures (that is, baseline scenario). V corresponds to the total prereform VAT collected from administrative records for the year the fiscal simulation was deployed.

Four compensation measures were estimated, each varying in terms of their targeting, coverage, and benefits. The first two compensation measures use universal or categorical-based targeting approaches:

- *Universal transfer.* Under this scenario, fiscal savings are used to give a universal cash transfer to all the population. The transfer is made on a per capita basis, and the amount received by each citizen, b^u, is defined by the per capita fiscal savings that are planned to be recycled:

$$b^u = \frac{\kappa S_0}{population},$$

using official population estimates rather than survey estimates.

- *Near-cash transfer to public school students.* Under this scenario, the fiscal savings are used to give a cash transfer to households with children attending public schools, for either primary or secondary education. The transfer is per student and the amount received by each student, b^s, is defined by the per-student fiscal savings that are planned to be recycled:

$$b^s = \frac{\kappa S_0}{students},$$

Transfers to students are limited to those whose age is equal to or lower than the typical age at graduation from high school in each country. The total number of primary and secondary students comes from administrative records. When this figure was not available, survey estimates were used.

The other two compensation measures use a more targeted approach based on the targeting features of the country's insignia cash transfer program. The insignia cash transfer program is the direct transfer program for which it is feasible to increase both its coverage and benefits. When more than one scalable program is available,[18] the simulation selects the program with the highest marginal contribution to poverty. The horizontal expansion of the program is simulated using the program's eligibility and targeting criteria, which, depending on the country, include a geographical and proxy means test targeting close to the official targeting used by the government. This implies that this simulated targeting will inevitably suffer from inclusion and exclusion errors, which in practice would be partially curated by the government through community-based targeting, cross-referencing with administrative data, and other non-model-based mechanisms. This implies that the performance of the models simulated here, in terms of targeting, is expected to be worse for countries that invest more in correcting the errors of a pure model-based approach.

To characterize each of the reforms, it is useful first to define the prereform (that is, D_0^{ct}) and postreform (that is, D_1^{ct}) cost of the insignia cash transfer program as

$$D_0^{ct} = c_0^{ct} \times b_0^{ct}$$

$$D_1^{ct} = c_1^{ct} \times b_1^{ct} = D_0^{ct} + \kappa S_0,$$

where C_0^{ct} and $c_1^{ct} = \Delta c^{ct} + c_0^{ct}$ are the pre- and postreform coverage and b_0^{ct} and $b_1^{ct} = \Delta b^{ct} + b_0^{ct}$ are the pre- and postreform benefit or generosity. The equation that defines D_1^{ct} ensures that the increase in the cost of the cash transfer program is completely financed by the recycled fiscal savings. Also, it guarantees that all the compensation policies have a similar cost. The two compensation policies are characterized as follows:

- *Increase coverage.* This policy increases coverage while keeping the generosity of the cash transfer program constant. This implies an increase in the families receiving the program by

$$\Delta c^{ct} = \frac{\kappa S_0}{b_0}.$$

It is possible that, given the value of the benefit—b_0—the initial budget (κS_0) is enough to expand the main cash transfer program to all potential beneficiaries. This has two implications: first, the cost of this compensation measure is lower than the initial budget; second, this compensation measure becomes similar to a universal transfer scheme with a transfer amount of b_0.

- *Increase amount and coverage.* This compensation measure increases the amount of the cash transfers received by families by 50 percent and increases the coverage with the rest of the compensation budget. This implies that the two following equations are satisfied:

$$\Delta D b^{ct} = 0.5\ b^{ct}$$

$$\Delta c^{ct} = \left(\kappa S_0 - \Delta b^{ct} c_0^{ct}\right)/b_1^{ct}$$

If the initial budget is lower than the cost of increasing benefits by 50 percent, then benefits are increased by the amount that exhausts all the compensation budget, $\Delta b^{ct} = \kappa S_0 / c_0^{ct}$, and keeps coverage constant using the same targeting mechanism as in the original program.

Caveats behind the comparison across compensation measures

The analysis presented highlights the potential benefits of each compensation measure in terms of reducing poverty and inequality and is mostly aimed at noting the lack of efficiency of untargeted tax expenditures and subsidy regimes. However, the simulations are insufficient to fully compare alternative compensation measures for at least three reasons:

- First, the study is agnostic about the actual differences in the cost of implementing each measure. An effective comparison across methods should be based on cost–benefit ratios that, for instance, take into account financial inclusion, coverage of identity documents needed to obtain benefits, and the telecommunications infrastructure needed to implement a universal basic income (UBI; Gentilini et al. 2019). Similarly, in expanding the coverage of a cash transfer program, the size of the social registry and whether it has the capacity to implement the proposed expansion needs to be considered.

- Second, the simulations only address the short-term direct effects of these compensation measures and do not account for their long-term political and fiscal sustainability. It is important to consider that large expansions of cash transfer programs or the implementation of a UBI may not be politically feasible in the long run and could potentially create a more restricted fiscal space for the government, making it more challenging to eliminate these programs. Furthermore, substantial expansions could also lead to behavioral responses that, depending on the direction, could affect poverty through other general equilibrium channels.[19]

- Third, an important distinction across compensation measures lies in the level at which the benefits are distributed. Although cash transfer programs are distributed at the household level, universal approaches are targeted at the individual or public student level. This suggests that regardless of targeting and coverage, there is a unit-level effect that makes UBI and public student–based transfers more effective at reaching poor households than what would happen under cash transfer programs. This effect is explained by the fact that poorer households tend to be larger and have more children attending public schools.

Notes

1. Adopt policies, especially fiscal, wage, and social protection policies, and progressively achieve greater equality.

2. The prefiscal Gini for 78 countries outside Africa, including data for all Organisation for Economic Co-operation and Development (OECD) countries, is 40.8, and the prefiscal Gini for 48 non-African countries from Commitment to Equity (CEQ) studies, which largely exclude OECD European countries, is 41.2. The average for Africa includes 24 countries and is based on CEQ studies. These averages are based on the latest available data.

3. Note that this does not account for in-kind benefits such as education and health services, in line with standard poverty measurement, because households do not know how much is being spent on their behalf, nor can they choose to switch those benefits for higher consumption.

4. The aggregate poverty gap is the monetary value of the gap between the income of poor households and the international poverty line, aggregated across the population.

5. See a summary of the impact evaluation at IPA (2022).

6. For a recent review of the literature on implementation of these programs in developing countries, see Banerjee et al. (2024) and Bastagli et al. (2019).

7. The only exception is Guinea, for which indirect effects are not modeled.

8. Note that although half the savings are aimed at social transfers, in some cases, this budget is not fully exhausted because of the low benefit level of the cash transfer (CT) program. See the later discussion.

9. The indirect effects of the subsidy removal refer to the impact that occurs through the increase in prices of energy-intensive goods—for instance, public transit, manufacturing, and locally produced food. In the case of Angola, for example, fish, the main source of protein, will see a significant price increase if fuel subsidies are eliminated.

10. A secondary reason why CT programs could be outperformed by universal basic income and categorical targeting mechanisms (public student transfers) is the usual undercoverage of targeting mechanisms used to allocate CT, such as the proxy means test. However, this is not the main force explaining the results of these simulations, because the size of subsidies allows CT programs to become almost universal.

11. In 2016, the Tuna Bond case in Mozambique highlighted the dangers of inadequate debt transparency when two large, previously unreported loans totaling US$1.15 billion—equal to about 9 percent of the country's gross domestic product—were revealed. As a result, donor support was frozen, the economy plunged, and the government was forced to make deep cuts in public spending. Similarly, in Zambia, reporting lags and uncertainty about public debt coverage led to speculation about the true level of indebtedness and a sharp increase in bond yields in 2018. For details, see Rivetti (2021).

12. *VAT expenditures* refers to the provisions in the tax code that reduce how much taxpayers owe because of exemptions, deductions, and reduced rates. They are equivalent to the forgone VAT revenue because of these provisions.

13. Most of these countries that collect substantial resource revenue have in recent decades increasingly become dependent on natural resources as a source of revenue, and their fiscal positions are very exposed to changes in commodity prices (Cogneau et al. 2021).

14. However, if companies in the resources sector were to substantially reduce operations because of increases in the amount they need to pay the government, this would have a nontrivial impact on overall economic activity (Havranek, Horvath, and Zeynalov 2016).

15. This section benefits from comments from Mitja Del Bono, Elena Glinskaya, Ambika Sharma, and Ruslan G. Yemtsov.

16. This is an ad hoc threshold selected to ease the comparison across countries; the optimal size of the recycling parameter depends on the country context: size of the spending on subsidies and characteristics of the cash transfer program.

17. Administrative data on energy subsidies are preferred to data obtained from the household surveys for at least two reasons: (1) Household survey data only measure the energy consumed by households, ignoring government energy consumption and exports; (2) consumption measured in household surveys may be underreported, which affects the direct and indirect consumption of energy. Some reasons for underreporting of consumption include undercoverage of specific goods (that is, durables), undercoverage of top income households, and measurement error related to the collection methods.

18. *Scalable* refers to the capacity to which the program can increase its coverage and is evaluated subjectively by the poverty economist of each simulation.

19. For a recent review of these design issues and potential behavioral responses, refer to Banerjee et al. (2024) and Bastagli et al. (2019).

References

Adelman, Sarah, Daniel A. Gilligan, Joseph Konde-Lule, and Harold Alderman. 2019. "School Feeding Reduces Anemia Prevalence in Adolescent Girls and Other Vulnerable Household Members in a Cluster Randomized Controlled Trial in Uganda." *Journal of Nutrition* 149 (4): 659–66.

Aghion, Philippe, Ufuk Akcigit, Matthieu Lequien, and Stefanie Stantcheva. 2017. "Tax Simplicity and Heterogeneous Learning." Working Paper 24049, National Bureau of Economic Research, Cambridge, MA.

Albertin, Giorgia, Boriana Yontcheva, Dan Devlin, Hilary Devine, Marc Gerard, Irena Jankulov Suljagic, Vimal Thakoor, and Sebastian Beer. 2021. "Tax Avoidance in Sub-Saharan Africa's Mining Sector." Departmental Paper 2021/022, International Monetary Fund, Washington, DC.

Alderman, Harold, and Ruslan Yemtsov. 2014. "How Can Safety Nets Contribute to Economic Growth?" *World Bank Economic Review* 28 (1): 1–20. https://doi.org/10.1093/wber/lht011.

Alstadsæter, Annette, Sarah Godar, Panayiotis Nicolaides, and Gabriel Zucman. 2023. *Global Tax Evasion Report 2024*. Paris: EU Tax Observatory. https://www.taxobservatory.eu//www-site/uploads/2023/10/global_tax_evasion_report_24.pdf.

ATAF (African Tax Administration Forum). 2023. *Suggested Approaches to Drafting Domestic Minimum Top-up Tax (DMTT) Legislation*. Pretoria: ATAF. https://events.ataftax.org/index.php?page=documents&func=view&document_id=209.

Aurino, Elisabetta, Jean-Pierre Tranchant, Amadou Sekou Diallo, and Aulo Gelli. 2019. "School Feeding or General Food Distribution? Quasi-Experimental Evidence on the Educational Impacts of Emergency Food Assistance during Conflict in Mali." *Journal of Development Studies* 55 (S1): 7–28.

Axelson, Chris, Antonia Hohmann, Jukka Pirttilä, Roxanne Raabe, and Nadine Riedel. 2024. "Taxing Top Incomes in the Emerging World." Working Paper 232, Southern Africa—Towards Inclusive Economic Development, Helsinki. https://sa-tied.wider.unu.edu/article/taxing-top-incomes-in-the-emerging-world.

Bachas, Pierre, Anne Brockmeyer, Roel Dom, and Camille Semelet. 2023a. "Effective Tax Rates and Firm Size." Policy Research Working Paper 10312, World Bank, Washington, DC.

Bachas, Pierre, Lucie Gadenne, and Anders Jensen. 2023b. "Informality, Consumption Taxes, and Redistribution." *Review of Economic Studies*: rdad095. https://doi.org/10.1093/restud/rdad095.

Baird, Sarah, Francisco H. G. Ferreira, Berk Özler, and Michael Woolcock. 2014. "Conditional, Unconditional and Everything in Between: A Systematic Review of the Effects of Cash Transfer Programmes on Schooling Outcomes." *Journal of Development Effectiveness* 6 (1): 1–43. https://doi .org/10.1080/19439342.2014.890362.

Balán, Pablo, Augustin Bergeron, Gabriel Tourek ,and Jonathan Weigel. 2020. "Land Formalization in Weak States: Experimental Evidence from Urban Property Titling in the D.R. Congo." Unpublished manuscript, Harvard University, Cambridge, MA.

Banerjee, Abhijit, Rema Hanna, Benjamin A. Olken, and Diana Sverdlin Lisker. 2024. "Social Protection in the Developing World." Working Paper 32382, National Bureau of Economic Research, Cambridge, MA. https://www.nber.org/papers/w32382.

Basri, M. Chatib, Mayara Felix, Rema Hanna, and Benjamin A. Olken. 2021. "Tax Administration versus Tax Rates: Evidence from Corporate Taxation in Indonesia." *American Economic Review* 111 (12): 3827–71.

Bastagli, Francesca, Jessica Hagen-Zanker, Luke Harman, Valentina Barca, Georgina Sturge, and Tanja Schmidt. 2019. "The Impact of Cash Transfers: A Review of the Evidence from Low- and Middle-income Countries." *Journal of Social Policy* 48 (3): 569–94. https://doi.org/10.1017 /S0047279418000715.

Bastagli, Francesca, Jessica Hagen-Zanker, and Georgina Sturge. 2016. "Cash Transfers: What Does the Evidence Say?" London: ODI. https://odi.org/en/publications/cash-transfers-what-does-the -evidence-say-a-rigorous-review-of-impacts-and-the-role-of-design-and-implementation -features/.

Beegle, Kathleen, and Luc Christiaensen. 2019. *Accelerating Poverty Reduction in Africa*. Washington, DC: World Bank. http://hdl.handle.net/10986/32354.

Bergeron, Augustin, Gabriel Tourek, and Jonathan Weigel. 2023. "The State Capacity Ceiling on Tax Rates: Evidence from Randomized Tax Abatements in the DRC." Working Paper 31685, National Bureau of Economic Research, Cambridge, MA.

Bergolo, Marcelo, Juliana Londoño-Vélez, and Darío Tortarolo. 2023. "Tax Progressivity and Taxing the Rich in Developing Countries: Lessons from Latin America." *Oxford Review of Economic Policy* 39 (3): 530–49.

Bilicka, Katarzyna, Yaxuan Qi, and Jing Xing. 2022. "Real Responses to Anti-Tax Avoidance: Evidence from the UK Worldwide Debt Cap." *Journal of Public Economics* 214: 104742.

Black, Simon, Antung A. Liu, Ian W. H. Perry, and Nate Vernon. 2023. "IMF Fossil Fuel Subsidies Data: 2023 Update." Working Paper WP/23/169, International Monetary Fund, Washington, DC. https:// www.imf.org/en/Publications/WP/Issues/2023/08/22/IMF-Fossil-Fuel-Subsidies-Data-2023 -Update-537281.

Boadway, Robin, and Motohiro Sato. 2009. "Optimal Tax Design and Enforcement with an Informal Sector." *American Economic Journal: Economic Policy* 1 (1): 1–27.

Bowen, Thomas, Carlo del Ninno, Colin Andrews, Sarah Coll-Black, Ugo Gentilini, Kelly Johnson, Yasuhiro Kawasoe, Adea Kryeziu, Barry Maher, and Asha Williams. 2020. *Adaptive Social Protection: Building Resilience to Shocks*. International Development in Focus. Washington, DC: World Bank. https://openknowledge.worldbank.org/handle/10986/33785.

Brockmeyer, Anne, Alejandro Estefan, Karina Ramírez Arras, and Juan Carlos Suárez Serrato. 2021. "Taxing Property in Developing Countries: Theory and Evidence from Mexico." Working Paper 28637, National Bureau of Economic Research, Cambridge, MA.

Cahill, Sean A. 1997. "Calculating the Rate of Decoupling for Crops under CAP/Oilseeds Reform." *Journal of Agricultural Economics* 48 (3): 349–78.

Chakraborty, Tanika, and Rajshri Jayaraman. 2019. "School Feeding and Learning Achievement: Evidence from India's Midday Meal Program." *Journal of Development Economics* 139: 249–65.

Chancel, Lucas, Denis Cogneau, Amory Gethin, Alix Myczkowski, and Anne-Sophie Robilliard. 2023. "Income Inequality in Africa, 1990–2019: Measurement, Patterns, Determinants." *World Development* 163: 106162.

Coady, David. 2008. "The Distributional Impacts of Indirect Tax and Public Pricing Reforms: A Review of Methods and Empirical Evidence." In *Poverty and Social Impact Analysis by the IMF: Review of Methodology and Selected Evidence*, edited by Robert Gillingham, 33–73. Washington, DC: International Monetary Fund.

Cogneau, Denis, Yannick Dupraz, Justine Knebelmann, and Sandrine Mesplé-Somps. 2021. "Taxation in Africa from Colonial Times to Present: Evidence from Former French Colonies 1900–2018." Working Paper 2021-62, Paris School of Economics, Paris. https://shs.hal.science/halshs -03420664v1/file/WP_202162_.pdf.

Comelli, Fabio, Peter Kovacs, Jimena Jesus Montoya Villavicencio, Arthur Sode, Antonio David, and Luc Eyraud. 2023. "Navigating Fiscal Challenges in Sub-Saharan Africa: Resilient Strategies and Credible Anchors in Turbulent Waters." Departmental Paper 2023/007, International Monetary Fund, Washington, DC.

Crossley, Elle, Debbie Hillier, Michèle Plichta, Niklas Rieger, and Scott Waygood. 2021. "Funding Disasters: Tracking Global Humanitarian and Development Funding for Response to Natural Hazards." Working Paper 8, Centre for Disaster Protection and Development Initiatives, London.

Cust, James, and Albert G. Zeufack. 2023. *Africa's Resource Future: Harnessing Natural Resources for Economic Transformation during the Low-Carbon Transition*. Africa Development Forum. Washington, DC: World Bank.

Deininger, Klaus, and Aparajita Goyal. 2023. "Land Institutions to Address New Challenges in Africa: Implications for the World Bank's Land Policy." Policy Research Working Paper 10389, World Bank, Washington, DC. http://hdl.handle.net/10986/39634.

De La O, Ana L., Donald P. Green, Peter John, Rafael Goldszmidt, Anna-Katharina Lenz, Martin Valdivia, Cesar Zucco, Darin Christensen, Francisco Garfias, Pablo Balán, Augustin Bergeron, Jonathan Weigel, Jessica Gottlieb, Adrienne LeBas, Janica Magat, Nonso Obikili, Jake Bowers, Nuole Chen, Christopher Grady, Matthew Winters, Nikhar Gaikwad, Gareth Nellis, Anjali Thomas, and Susan Hyde. 2021. "Fiscal Contracts? A Six-Country Randomized Experiment on Transaction Costs, Public Services, and Taxation in Developing Countries." Unpublished manuscript. https:// www.dropbox.com/scl/fi/iqv0nkr2g0ae13sw1dg0y/MetaketaII_meta_analysis_2022Oct20. pdf?rlkey=kvocikk5esqwmpopruodr5lqj&e=1&dl=0.

De Walque, Damien, Lia Fernald, Paul Gertler, and Melissa Hidrobo, 2017. "Cash Transfers and Child and Adolescent Development." In *Child and Adolescent Health and Development*, edited by Donald A. P. Bundy, Nilanthi de Silva, Susan Horton, Dean T. Jamison, and George C. Patton, 325–41. 3rd ed. Washington, DC: World Bank. https://doi.org/10.1596/978-1-4648-0423-6_ch23.

Dom, Roel, Anna Custers, Stephen R. Davenport, and Wilson Prichard. 2022. *Innovations in Tax Compliance: Building Trust, Navigating Politics, and Tailoring Reform*. Washington, DC: World Bank. http://hdl.handle.net/10986/36946.

Dom, Roel, Oliver Morrissey, and Abrams M. E. Tagem. 2023. "Taxation and Accountability in Sub-Saharan Africa." WIDER Working Paper 2023/115, UNU-WIDER, Helsinki. https://doi.org /10.35188/UNU-WIDER/2023/423-6

Dzansi, James, Anders Jensen, David Lagakos, and Henry Telli. 2022. "Technology and Tax Capacity: Evidence from Local Governments in Ghana." Working Paper 29923, National Bureau of Economic Research, Cambridge, MA.

Egger, Dennis, Johannes Haushofer, Edward Miguel, Paul Niehaus, and Michael W. Walker. 2019. "General Equilibrium Effects of Cash Transfers: Experimental Evidence from Kenya." Working Paper 26600, National Bureau of Economic Research, Cambridge, MA. https://doi.org/10.3386 /w26600.

EITI (Extractive Industries Transparency Initiative). 2023. "Open Data." Oslo: EITI. https://eiti.org /open-data.

Franzsen, Riël, and William McCluskey, eds. 2017. *Property Tax in Africa: Status, Challenges, and Prospects*. Cambridge, MA: Lincoln Institute of Land Policy.

Fuest, Clemens, and Florian Neumeier. 2023. "Corporate Taxation." *Annual Review of Economics* 15 (1): 425–50.

Gallien, Max, and Vanessa van den Boogaard. 2021. "Rethinking Formalisation: A Conceptual Critique and Research Agenda." Working Paper 127, Institute of Development Studies, Brighton, UK. https://doi.org/10.19088/ICTD.2021.016.

Gelli, Aulo, Elisabetta Aurino, Gloria Folson, Daniel Arhinful, Clement Adamba, Issac Osei-Akoto, Edoardo Masset, Kristie Watkins, Meena Fernandes, Lesley Drake, and Harold Alderman. 2019. "A School Meals Program Implemented at Scale in Ghana Increases Height-for-Age during Midchildhood in Girls and in Children from Poor Households: A Cluster Randomized Trial." *Journal of Nutrition* 149 (8): 1434–42.

Gentilini, Ugo, Mohamed Almenfi, Hrishikesh T. M. M. Iyengar, Giorgia Valleriani, Yuko Okamura, Emilio Raul Urteaga, Sheraz Aziz, Mohammad Farid Al Azim Bin Noruzi, and Margret Chu. 2023. "Tracking Global Social Protection Responses to Inflation." Living Paper, v.5. Social Protection & Jobs Discussion Paper 2305, World Bank, Washington, DC. http://hdl.handle .net/10986/37441.

Gentilini, Ugo, Margaret Grosh, Jamele Rigolini, and Ruslan Yemtsov, eds. 2019. *Exploring Universal Basic Income: A Guide to Navigating Concepts, Evidence, and Practices*. Washington, DC: World Bank.

Gootjes, Bram, and Jakob de Haan. 2022. "Do Fiscal Rules Need Budget Transparency to Be Effective?" *European Journal of Political Economy* 75: 102210.

Goyal, Aparajita, and John Nash. 2017. *Reaping Richer Returns: Public Spending Priorities for African Agriculture Productivity Growth*. Africa Development Forum. Washington, DC: World Bank and Agence Francaise de Developpement. http://hdl.handle.net/10986/25996.

Havranek, Tomas, Roman Horvath, and Ayaz Zeynalov. 2016. "Natural Resources and Economic Growth: A Meta-Analysis." *World Development* 88: 134–51.

Hill, Ruth Vargas, Neha Kumar, Nicholas Magnan, Simrin Makhija, Francesca de Nicola, David J. Spielman, and Patrick S. Ward. 2019. "Ex Ante and Ex Post Effects of Hybrid Index Insurance in Bangladesh." *Journal of Development Economics* 136: 1–17.

Hill, Ruth, Emmanuel Skoufias, and Barry Maher. 2019. *The Chronology of a Disaster: A Review and Assessment of the Value of Acting Early on Household Welfare*. Washington, DC: World Bank. https://openknowledge.worldbank.org/handle/10986/31721.

Hoy, Christopher. 2022. "How Does the Progressivity of Taxes and Government Transfers Impact People's Willingness to Pay Tax? Experimental Evidence across Developing Countries." Policy Research Working Paper 10167, World Bank, Washington, DC.

Hoy, Christopher, Yeon Soo Kim, Minh Nguyen, Mariano Sosa, and Sailesh Tiwari. 2023. "Building Public Support for Reducing Fossil Fuel Subsidies: Evidence across 12 Middle-Income Countries." Policy Research Working Paper. 10615, World Bank, Washington, DC.

Hoy, Christopher, Luke McKenzie, and Mathias Sinning. 2024. "Improving Tax Compliance without Increasing Revenue: Evidence from Population-Wide Randomized Controlled Trials in Papua New Guinea. *Economic Development and Cultural Change* 72 (2). https://doi.org /10.1086/721650.

Hoy, Christopher, Thiago Scot, Alex Oguso, Anna Custers, Daniel Zalo, Ruggero Doino, Jonathan Karver, and Nicolas Orgeira Pillai. 2024. "Trade-Offs in the Design of Simplified Tax Regimes: Evidence from Sub-Saharan Africa." Policy Research Working Paper 10909, World Bank, Washington, DC. https://hdl.handle.net/10986/42165.

IMF (International Monetary Fund). 2023. *Making Public Debt Public—Ongoing Initiatives and Reform Options*. Washington, DC: IMF.

IMF (International Monetary Fund), OECD (Organisation for Economic Co-operation and Development), UN (United Nations), and World Bank. 2015. *Options for Low-Income Countries' Effective and Efficient Use of Tax Incentives for Investment: Tools for the Assessment of Tax Incentives*. Washington, DC: World Bank. http://hdl.handle.net/10986/22924.

Inchauste, Gabriela, Bernardo Atuesta, and Akem Fabinin. forthcoming. *The Distributional Impact of Higher Import Prices in WAEMU+2 Countries*. Washington, DC: World Bank.

Inchauste, Gabriela, and David G. Victor, eds. 2017. *The Political Economy of Energy Subsidy Reform*. Washington, DC: World Bank.

IPA (Innovations for Poverty Action). 2022. "Impact d'un programme public d'inclusion économique sur les ménages pauvres au Niger: Filets sociaux et chemins de sortie de la pauvreté." Washington, DC: IPA. https://poverty-action.org/sites/default/files/publications/FRH-Impact-Dun -Programme-Public-Dinclusion-Economique-JUNE-2022_0.pdf.

Jayne, Thomas S., Nicole M. Mason, William J. Burke, and Joshua Ariga. 2018. "Review: Taking Stock of Africa's Second-Generation Agricultural Input Subsidy Programs." *Food Policy* 75: 1–14. https://doi.org/10.1016/j.foodpol.2018.01.003.

Jensen, Anders. 2022. "Employment Structure and the Rise of the Modern Tax System." *American Economic Review* 112 (1): 213–34.

Jibao, Samuel, and Wilson Prichard. 2016. "Rebuilding Local Government Finances after Conflict: Lessons from a Property Tax Reform Programme in Post-Conflict Sierra Leone." *Journal of Development Studies* 52 (12): 1759–75. https://doi.org/10.1080/00220388.2016.1153073.

Jouste, M., Barugahara, T.K., Ayo, J.O., Pirttilä, J., Rattenhuber, P. 2023. "Taxpayer Response to Greater Progressivity: Evidence from Personal Income Tax Reform in Uganda." WIDER Working Paper 2023/66, UNU-WIDER, Helsinki. https://doi.org/10.35188/UNU-WIDER/2023/374-1.

J-PAL (Abdul Latif Jameel Poverty Action Lab). 2022. "Improving Tax Compliance through Reminder Messages for Taxpayers." *J-PAL Policy Insights*, July. https://www.povertyactionlab.org/policy -insight/improving-tax-compliance-through-reminder-messages-taxpayers.

Kazianga, Harounan, Damien de Walque, and Harold Alderman. 2014. "School Feeding Programs, Intrahousehold Allocation and the Nutrition of Siblings: Evidence from a Randomized Trial in Rural Burkina Faso." *Journal of Development Economics* 106: 15–34.

Khagram, S., A. Fung, and P. de Renzio, eds. 2013. *Open Budgets: The Political Economy of Transparency, Participation, and Accountability*. Washington, DC: Brookings Institution Press. http://www.jstor .org/stable/10.7864/j.ctt1262zx.

Knebelmann, Justine. 2021. "The (Un)Hidden Wealth of the City: Property Taxation under Weak Enforcement in Senegal." Unpublished manuscript, Paris School of Economics, Paris.

Knebelmann, Justine, Victor Pouliquen, and Bassirou Sarr. 2023. "Discretion versus Algorithms: Bureaucrats and Tax Equity in Senegal." Unpublished manuscript. https://drive.google.com /file/d/1EAPqRR7GWkP8PrOVV-uUItsB09NGx7uq/view.

Leite, Phillippe, Tina George, Changqing Sun, Theresa Jones, and Kathy Lindert. 2017. "Social Registries for Social Assistance and Beyond: A Guidance Note and Assessment Tool." Social Protection and Labor Discussion Paper 1704, World Bank, Washington, DC. https:// openknowledge.worldbank.org/handle/10986/28284.

Lustig, Nora, ed. 2022. *Commitment to Equity Handbook: Estimating the Impact of Fiscal Policy on Inequality and Poverty*. 2 vols. New Orleans: Commitment to Equity. https://commitmentoequity.org/.

Mansour, M., and Keen, M. 2009. "Revenue Mobilization in Sub-Saharan Africa: Challenges from Globalization." Working Paper WP/09/157, International Monetary Fund, Washington, DC. https://www.imf.org/external/pubs/ft/wp/2009/wp09157.pdf.

Mataba, Kudzai, Thomas Lassourd, Alexandra Readhead, and Suzy Nikièma. 2023. "Revisiting Tax Incentives as an Investment Promotion Tool: Q&A for Investment Policy-makers." International Institute for Sustainable Development Brief, Winnipeg. https://www.iisd.org/system/files/2023 -10/revisiting-tax-incentives-investment-promotion-tool-policy-makers.pdf.

McNabb, Kyle, and Annalena Oppel. 2023. "Personal Income Tax Reforms and Income Inequality in African Countries." Working paper, ODI, London. https://www.odi.org/en/publications /personal-incometax-reforms-and-income-inequality-in-african-countries/.

Millot, Valentine, Åsa Johansson, Stéphane Sorbe, and Sebastien Turban. 2020. "Corporate Taxation and Investment of Multinational Firms: Evidence from Firm-Level Data." Taxation Working Paper 51, Organisation for Economic Co-operation and Development, Paris.

Molina Millán, Teresa, Tania Barham, Karen Macours, John A. Maluccio, and Marco Stampini. 2019. "Long-Term Impacts of Conditional Cash Transfers: Review of the Evidence." *World Bank Research Observer* 34 (1): 119–59. https://doi.org/10.1093/wbro/lky005.

Moore, Mick. 2023. "Tax Obsessions: Taxpayer Registration and the 'informal sector' in Sub-Saharan Africa." *Development Policy Review* 41 (1): e12649. https://doi.org/10.1111/dpr.12649.

Moore, Mick, Wilson Prichard, and Odd-Helge Fjeldstad. 2018. *Taxing Africa: Coercion, Reform and Development*. London: Zed Books.

Musiega, Anita, Benjamin Tsofa, Lizah Nyawira, Rebecca G. Njuguna, Joshua Munywoki, Kara Hanson, Andrew Mulwa, Sassy Molyneux, Isabel Maina, Charles Normand, Julie Jemutai, and Edwine Barasa. 2023. "Examining the Influence of Budget Execution Processes on the Efficiency of County Health Systems in Kenya." *Health Policy Plan* 38 (3): 351–62. https://doi.org/10.1093/heapol/czac098.

Naurin, Daniel. 2006. "Transparency, Publicity, Accountability: The Missing Links." *Swiss Political Science Review* 12 (3): 90–98.

OECD (Organisation for Economic Co-operation and Development). 2006. "Decoupling: A Conceptual Overview." *OECD Papers* 5 (11). https://doi.org/10.1787/oecd_papers-v5-art37-en.

Okunogbe, Oyebola, and Fabrizio Santoro. 2023. "Increasing Tax Collection in African Countries: The Role of Information Technology." *Journal of African Economies* 32 (Supplement 1): i57–i83. https://doi.org/10.1093/jae/ejac036.

Paul, Boban Varghese, Puja Vasudeva Dutta, and Sarang Chaudhary. 2021. "Assessing the Impact and Cost of Economic Inclusion Programs: A Synthesis of Evidence." Policy Research Working Paper 9536, World Bank, Washington, DC. http://hdl.handle.net/10986/35109.

PEFA (Public Expenditure and Financial Accountability). 2022. *2022 Global Report on Public Financial Management*. Washington, DC: PEFA. https://www.pefa.org/global-report-2022/en/.

Readhead, Alexandra, Viola Tarus, Thomas Lassourd, Ezera Madzivanyika, and Bernd Schlenther. 2023. *The Future of Resource Taxation: 10 Policy Ideas to Mobilize Mining Revenues*. Winnipeg: International Institute for Sustainable Development & African Tax Administration Forum. https://www.iisd.org/publications/guide/future-of-resource-taxation.

Regan, Tanner, and Priya Manwaring. 2023. "Public Disclosure and Tax Compliance: Evidence from Uganda." Discussion Paper CEPDP1937, Centre for Economic Performance, London. https://cep.lse.ac.uk/_NEW/publications/abstract.asp?index=10308.

Rivetti, Diego. 2021. *Debt Transparency in Developing Economies*. Washington, DC: World Bank. http://documents.worldbank.org/curated/en/743881635526394087/Debt-Transparency-in-Developing-Economies.

Savoia, Antonio, and Kunal Sen. 2021. "The Political Economy of the Resource Curse: A Development Perspective." *Annual Review of Resource Economics* 13 (1): 223.

Tagem, Abrams Mbu Enow, and Oliver Morrissey. 2023. "Institutions and Tax Capacity in Sub-Saharan Africa." *Journal of Institutional Economics* 19 (3): 332–47. https://doi.org/10.1017/S1744137422000145.

Thome, Karen, J. Edward Taylor, Mateusz Filipski, Benjamin Davis, and Sudhanshu Handa. 2016. *The Local Economy Impacts of Social Cash Transfers*. Rome: Food and Agriculture Organization of the United Nations. https://www.fao.org/publications/card/en/c/1154dc4a-037a-47f0-855e-66abdea96d57

Tourek, Gabriel. 2022. "Targeting in Tax Behavior: Evidence from Rwandan Firms." *Journal of Development Economics* 158: 102911.

UBS. 2023. *Global Wealth Report*. Union City, NJ: UBS Financial Services. https://www.ubs.com/global/en/family-office-uhnw/reports/global-wealth-report-2023.html.

UNU-Wider. 2023. "UNU-WIDER Government Revenue Dataset." Version 2023. Helsinki: UNU-Wider. https://doi.org/10.35188/UNU-WIDER/GRD-2023.

Waiswa, Ronald, and Solomon Rukundo. 2023. "Strategic Investment Tax Incentives in Africa: The Case of Tax Holidays in Uganda." ICTD Working Paper 161, Institute of Development Studies, Brighton, UK. https://doi.org/10.19088/ICTD.2023.013.

Wang, Dongqing, Sachin Shinde, Tara Young, and Wafaie W. Fawzi. 2021. "Impacts of School Feeding on Educational and Health Outcomes of School-Age Children and Adolescents in Low- and Middle-Income Countries: A Systematic Review and Meta-Analysis. *Journal of Global Health* 11: 04051. https://doi.org/10.7189/jogh.11.04051.

Warwick, Ross, Tom Harris, David Phillips, Maya Goldman, Jon Jellema, Gabriela Inchauste, and Karolina Goraus-Tańska. 2022. "The Redistributive Power of Cash Transfers vs VAT Exemptions: A Multi-Country Study." *World Development* 151: 105742. https://doi.org/10.1016/j.worlddev.2021.105742.

Weigel, Jonathan. 2020. "The Participation Dividend of Taxation: How Citizens in Congo Engage More with the State When It Tries to Tax Them." *Quarterly Journal of Economics* 135 (4): 1849–1903. https://doi.org/10.1093/qje/qjaa019.

World Bank. 2017. *World Development Report 2017: Governance and the Law*. Washington, DC: World Bank. http://hdl.handle.net/10986/25880.

World Bank. 2022a. *Poverty and Shared Prosperity 2022: Correcting Course*. Washington, DC: World Bank. http://hdl.handle.net/10986/37739.

World Bank. 2022b. *World Development Report 2022: Finance for an Equitable Recovery*. Washington, DC: World Bank Group.

World Bank. 2023a. *World Development Indicators*. Washington, DC: World Bank. https://databank .worldbank.org/source/world-development-indicators.

World Bank. 2023b. "Tanzania Economic Update: The Efficiency and Effectiveness of Fiscal Policy in Tanzania." Tanzania Economic Update 19. Washington, DC: World Bank. http://hdl.handle .net/10986/40452.

World Food Programme. 2021. *School Feeding Programs in Low- and Lower-Middle Income Countries: A Focused Review of Recent Evidence from Impact Evaluations*. Rome: World Food Programme. https://www.wfp.org/publications/school-feeding-programmes-low-and-lower -middle-income-countries.

Poverty and Inequality Influencers: Debt

CÉSAR CALDERÓN

Public debt increased sharply in Africa long before the onset of the economic fallout from the COVID-19 pandemic.[1] Over the past two decades, public debt accumulated faster in the prepandemic years. General government gross debt in Africa jumped from 29 percent of gross domestic product (GDP) in 2012 to 53 percent of GDP in 2019. It reached 57 percent of GDP at the height of the pandemic (2020–21) and continued rising, to 61 percent in 2023 (refer to figure S4.1a).[2] In 2023, the median public debt for low-income and middle-income countries in the region reached 60 percent and 61 percent of GDP, respectively. The debt ratio has increased by approximately 31 percentage points of GDP for low-income countries since 2012, and it has expanded by 34 percentage points of GDP for middle-income countries.

As a result of looser global financial conditions and ample financing from China, many countries in the region shifted their borrowing away from traditional concessional financing to market-based and non–Paris Club sources of funding (refer to figure S4.1b). The share of concessional financing in public and publicly guaranteed (PPG) external debt declined from a peak of 42 percent in 2005 to about 26 percent in 2022. In contrast, the share of market-based funding for Africa soared to a peak of 48 percent in 2019 from about 28 percent in 2009. This surge in private sources of external borrowing was mainly driven by the issuance of international bonds, because their share increased from 14 percent in 2009 to 31 percent in 2019. Over the past decade, the composition of public debt has gradually been shifting toward domestic debt, with greater reliance on domestic debt to meet COVID-19–related financing needs. Specifically, estimates suggest that domestic public debt in the region accounted for nearly half of outstanding public debt by the end of 2021.

FIGURE S4.1 Public debt in Africa

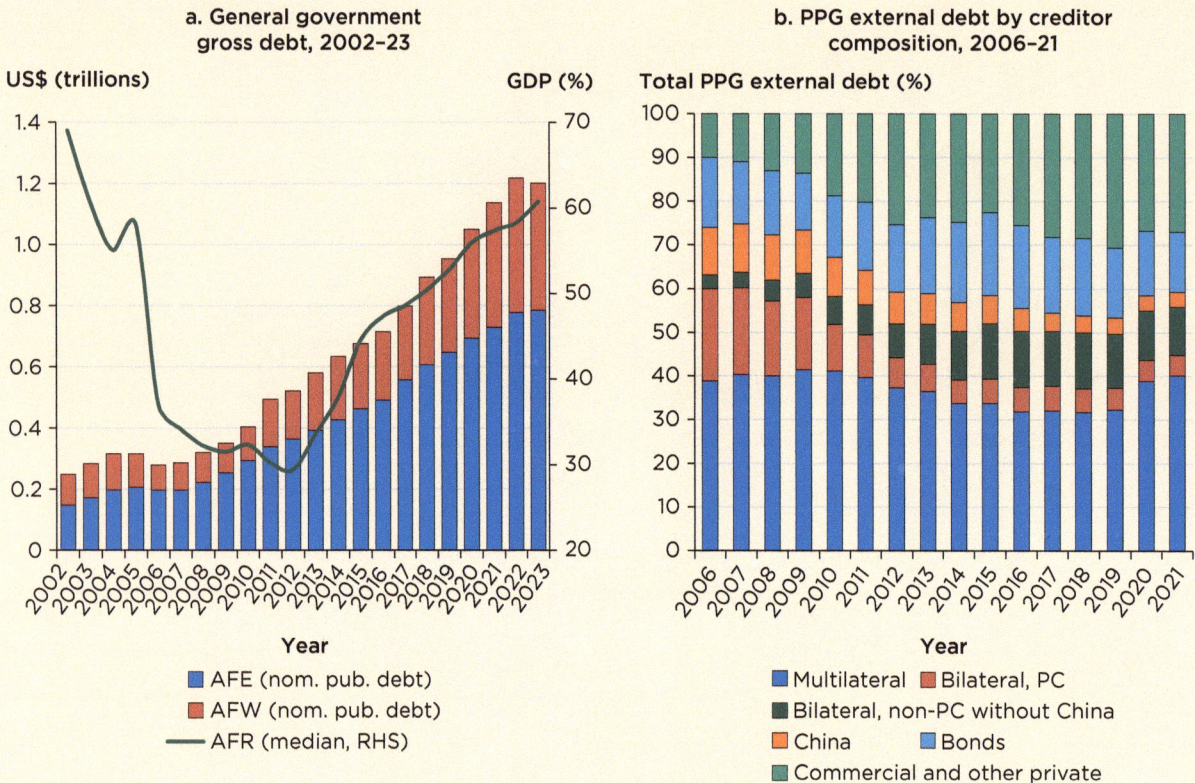

a. General government gross debt, 2002–23

US$ (trillions) / GDP (%)

Legend:
- AFE (nom. pub. debt)
- AFW (nom. pub. debt)
- AFR (median, RHS)

b. PPG external debt by creditor composition, 2006–21

Total PPG external debt (%)

Legend:
- Multilateral
- Bilateral, PC
- Bilateral, non-PC without China
- China
- Bonds
- Commercial and other private

Sources: World Economic Outlook, April 2024, International Monetary Fund (https://www.imf.org/en /Publications/WEO/weo-database/2024/April); International Debt Statistics 2022, World Bank (https://www.worldbank.org/en/programs/debt-statistics/ids).
AFE = Eastern and Southern Africa; AFR = Sub-Saharan Africa; AFW = Western and Central Africa; GDP = gross domestic product; nom. pub. debt = nominal public debt; PC = Paris Club; PPG = public and publicly guaranteed; RHS = right *y* axis.

What has driven the surge of public debt in the region over the past decade? Persistent primary deficits have been the main driver of public debt increases in the region and, particularly, in all low-income countries (refer to figure S4.2a). On average, the public-debt-to-GDP ratio increased from 56 percent in 2015 to 69 percent in 2019 among International Development Association (IDA)–eligible countries in the region. At the onset of the pandemic in 2020, this ratio increased to 78 percent, and it edged down to 75 percent in 2023. Real exchange rate depreciation and wider primary deficits as a result of the 2014–15 collapse in oil prices pushed public debt upward. The pace of debt accumulation decelerated in 2019 thanks to a decline in real interest rates and a slight improvement in fiscal balances. In 2020, however, public debt increased sharply to alleviate the economic fallout from the COVID-19 pandemic. On average, public debt for IDA-eligible countries rose to about 9 percentage points of GDP in 2020, mainly driven by higher deficits and a contraction in economic activity.

FIGURE S4.2 Drivers of public debt and evolution of debt service

a. Drivers of public sector debt accumulation in IDA-eligible AFR countries (% GDP, average)

b. Public debt service ratios in AFR, 2010–22

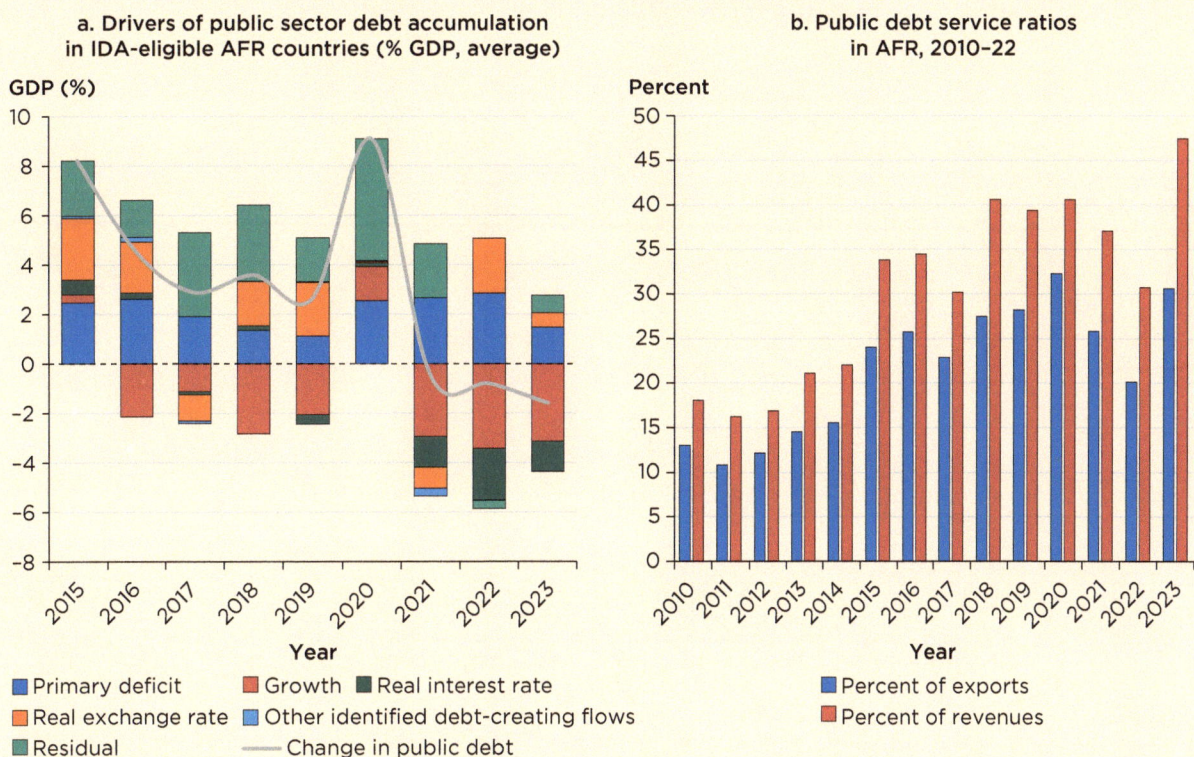

Legend:
- Primary deficit
- Growth
- Real interest rate
- Real exchange rate
- Other identified debt-creating flows
- Residual
- Change in public debt
- Percent of exports
- Percent of revenues

Sources: Panel a, Low-Income Country Debt Sustainability Analysis database as of end of June 2023. Panel b, *World Economic Outlook,* April 2023; World Bank staff calculations.
Note: AFR = Sub-Saharan Africa; GDP = gross domestic product; IDA = International Development Association.

The underlying debt dynamics show that primary deficits have increased the public-debt-to-GDP ratio by nearly 17 percentage points of GDP since 2015 (refer to figure S4.2a). The weakening of African currencies in real terms has contributed to an increase in public debt by 7 percentage points of GDP since 2015—with notable contributions in 2015–16, 2018–19, and 2022. In contrast, real GDP growth has helped contain public debt accumulation, with a cumulative decline of 16 percentage points of GDP since 2015.

The shift in the composition of Africa's debt toward nonconcessional financing has led to a surge in the overall debt service burden and in vulnerability to shocks. The region's debt service levels have steadily increased over the past decade; for instance, public debt service increased by US$97 billion between 2012 and 2023, with the highest increase among Eastern and Southern African countries, for which the increase amounted to US$81 billion. Rising debt service ratios, at a staggering 47 percent of revenues and 31 percent of exports in the region in 2023, are depleting the resources available to support public investments and social programs (refer to figure S4.2b). With stagnant exports, it may also reduce the availability of foreign exchange for essential imports needed for production and investment.

On the back of rising debt levels and increased nonconcessional borrowing, the risk of debt distress among African countries has soared since 2015, and it has been exacerbated since the COVID-19 pandemic. According to the Low-Income Country Debt Sustainability Framework (LIC-DSF), the share of countries in the region at high risk of debt distress expanded from 19 percent in 2015 to 32 percent in 2023.[3] The share of countries in the region already in debt distress increased from 8 percent to 21 percent over the same time period. In sum, more than half of IDA-eligible African countries remain classified as high risk or already in debt distress (refer to figure S4.3a). Additionally, no country in the region that is part of the LIC-DSF has been classified as being at low risk of debt distress since 2021, whereas the share of countries classified as at moderate risk has edged up, from 39 percent in 2021 to 42 percent in 2022 and 47 percent as of December 2023.

FIGURE S4.3 **Risk of debt distress and gross financing needs in Africa**

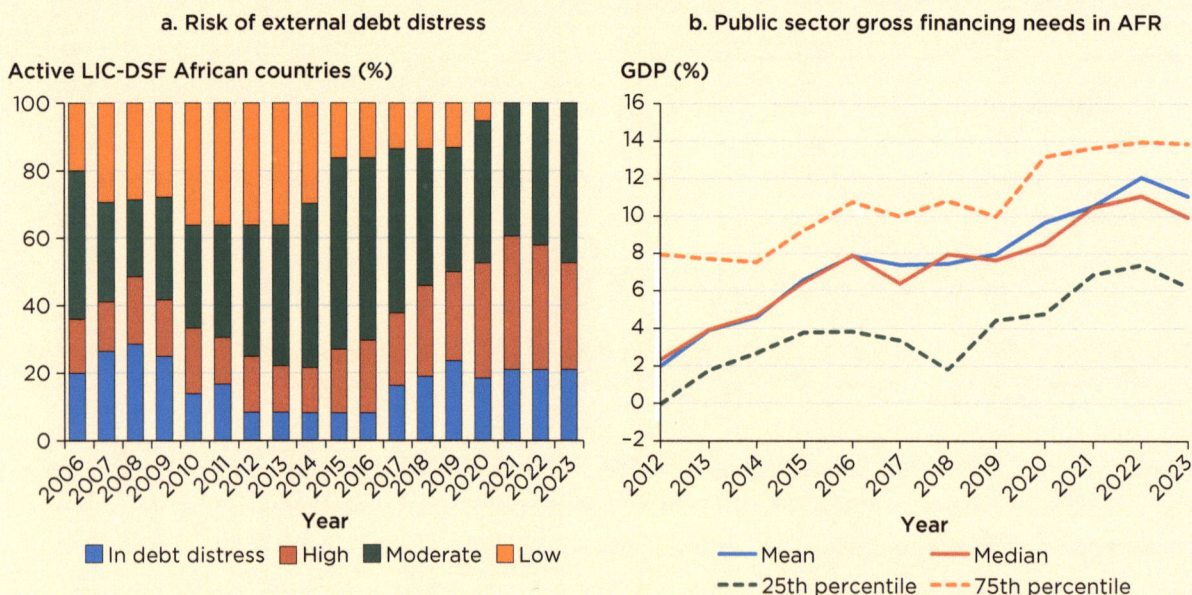

a. Risk of external debt distress

Active LIC-DSF African countries (%)

b. Public sector gross financing needs in AFR

GDP (%)

In debt distress | High | Moderate | Low

Mean | Median | 25th percentile | 75th percentile

Sources: World Bank–International Monetary Fund Low-Income Country Debt Sustainability Framework (LIC-DSF) Analysis database as of end of December 2023; World Bank staff calculations.
Note: AFR = Sub-Saharan Africa; GDP = gross domestic product.

Public gross financing needs (GFN), including primary deficits and debt service, remain higher than historical averages in Africa (refer to figure S4.3b). GFN among governments in the region increased from a median of 2.3 percent of GDP in 2012 to 11 percent in 2022. The median GFN for the region edged down to 10 percent of GDP in 2023. The public GFN exceeded 20 percent of GDP in 2023 for five countries in the region: The Gambia, Ghana, São Tomé and Príncipe, Sierra Leone, and Zambia. Total debt service in the Africa region increased from US$59 billion in 2012 to US$116 billion in 2021, and it increased further to US$156 billion in 2023. This trend signals that other components, such as primary deficits, which remain persistent, are causing the GFN to remain high.

Over the past decade, nearly two-thirds of market-access countries in the region and around one-third of LICs have tapped international markets. In 2018 and 2019, African countries hit record international bond issuances with about US$30 billion each year. On average, sovereign credit ratings deteriorated after 2018, and African countries tapped international markets amid worsening creditworthiness.[4] Furthermore, countries lengthened maturities of new bond issuances at marginally higher costs. International bond issuances stopped in 2020 on account of the COVID-19 crisis but picked up again in 2021, with total issuances of nearly US$10 billion. Several countries (including Angola, Benin, Ghana, Kenya, and Nigeria) issued Eurobonds in 2021 and early 2022. In 2024, Benin, Côte d'Ivoire, and Kenya returned to international capital markets to buy back and refinance Eurobonds and commercial loans falling due. For instance, Côte d'Ivoire placed US$2.6 billion in Eurobonds in January 2024, which represents the first issuance for any African country since April 2022. The issuance consisted of US$1.1 billion in nine-year bonds at 7.875 percent and US$1.5 billion in 13-year bonds at 8.5 percent. In February, Benin raised US$750 million in 14-year bonds at 8.375 percent, and Kenya made a US$1.5 billion issuance at a higher yield and coupon rate (10.375 and 9.75 percent, respectively). International bond issuances came at a higher cost than before the pandemic. For instance, the coupon of the new Eurobond issued by Kenya in February 2024 is 9.75 percent, compared with the 6.875 percent of the Eurobond maturing in 2024.

Currently, tightening global financial conditions—as a result of global contractionary monetary policy to control inflation—have substantially increased sovereign spreads and weakened currencies in the region, thus increasing debt burdens and curtailing access to global capital markets. Additionally, the sell-off of developing countries' Eurobonds and rising investor fears about the global economic environment amplify the risks for African countries facing large Eurobond redemptions. More specifically, bond redemptions will increase starting in 2024 and remain at elevated levels, posing refinancing risk for countries with large bullet redemptions, including Angola (around US$1.7 billion in 2025), Ethiopia (US$1 billion in 2024), and Kenya (US$2 billion in 2024).

Finally, several countries have resorted to debt restructurings to resolve sustainability issues and rebuild fiscal space. Chad, Ethiopia, Ghana, and Zambia applied for external debt treatments under the Common Framework. Progress has been slower than desired. Chad was the first country to reach an agreement with its main creditors (bilateral and the largest private one), in November 2022. The government of Ghana reached an agreement in principle with its Official Creditor Committee (OCC) on the terms of the treatment of official bilateral debt in January 2024. In June 2024, the government reached an agreement in principle with its international bondholders to restructure its dollar bonds. For Zambia, the OCC provided financing assurances, which paved the way for the International Monetary Fund's (IMF's) approval of an Extended Credit Facility–supported program in August 2022. In June 2023, the OCC agreed to restructure US$6.3 billion worth of loans to Zambia, of which more than US$4 billion was owed to the Export–Import Bank of China. An agreement with an ad hoc steering committee of Eurobond holders was reached in March 2024. Bondholders agreed to a nominal reduction in debt payments of 22 percent and to forgo approximately US$840 million in claims. Finally, Ethiopia requested treatment under the Common Framework in February 2021, and an OCC was formed in September of that year. The government reached an agreement with official creditors to suspend debt service in November 2023 and defaulted on its US$1 billion Eurobond after missing a US$33 million coupon payment in December of that year. By the end of July 2024, the birr was allowed to float by the central bank, and the IMF approved a four-year, US$3.4 billion program that paved the way for the country's debt restructuring to move forward.

Notes

1. This spotlight draws heavily from World Bank (2024). Mellany Pintado Vasquez and Mariela Caycho Arce contributed to the narrative and an update of the figures.

2. These figures refer to median public-debt-to-GDP ratios. Looking instead at averages, public debt in Africa increased from 35 percent of GDP in 2005 to 58 percent in 2019, reached 66 percent during 2020–21, and decreased slightly to 63 percent in 2022.

3. Note that the 2023 figure refers to the Low-Income Country Debt Sustainability Framework data available as of the end of December 2023.

4. Senegal was the first low-income country in the region to issue an international bond with an original maturity of 30 years in 2018, followed since then by Côte d'Ivoire, Ghana, Kenya, and Nigeria.

Reference

World Bank. 2024. "Tackling Inequality to Revitalize Growth and Reduce Poverty in Africa." *Africa's Pulse* 29 (April). http://documents.worldbank.org/curated/en/099009304082416318/IDU1e42991 fc157681444f1aa551febfbae741eb.

CHAPTER 6

Policies to Tackle Structural Inequalities and Accelerate Poverty Reduction and Growth

GABRIELA INCHAUSTE AND NISTHA SINHA

Chapter highlights

No country can afford to ignore the presence of inequality and, in particular, the presence of structural inequality that precludes progress toward poverty reduction. This report outlines a set of policies to address the various dimensions of structural sources of inequality that pose a barrier to growth and poverty reduction. These are policies aimed at building productive capacity; addressing market and institutional distortions that limit people, firms, and farms from using their productive capacity; and leveraging fair fiscal policies. Positive change is feasible, as testified by successful episodes of poverty reduction and increased growth across six countries, all of which implemented policies to address structural inequality.

A key insight from this analysis is that policies that address inequality in one dimension will be insufficient to reduce structural inequality in another dimension. Moreover, many of the policies and technical solutions discussed in the preceding chapters for each dimension are not new. However, they will not work in isolation. Removing structural inequalities calls for an integrative strategy—one that recognizes interlinkages, complementarities, and trade-offs. Multisectoral strategies are needed that go well beyond current practice.

Although policy priorities depend on the country context, the interlinkages across the dimensions of inequality mean that careful timing and sequencing of reforms is required. For fragile and conflict-affected situation (FCS) countries, the priority should be on actions that can restore confidence by providing citizen security, jobs, and key basic services, particularly in the conflict-affected areas. For resource-rich countries not affected by conflict, the priority is to promote economic diversification, using their natural resources to reduce inequality in building productive capacity. Countries that are not resource rich and not afflicted by conflict can do more to address structural inequalities across all dimensions.

This is Africa's moment to make a change

It is widely acknowledged that global progress on poverty reduction would be impossible without progress in Africa. The region stands out for its high level of extreme poverty and within-country inequality. At 38 percent, Africa's extreme poverty rate is the highest of all world regions. In fact, more than 60 percent of all people living in extreme poverty in 2022 lived in the region, as many as 460 million people. Moreover, the gap in well-being between Africa and the world has been growing. At the same time, inequality is much higher than expected, given Africa's level of development, with most of that inequality being structural, meaning that it is not just the result of differences in efforts and talents but also of structural distortions.

Progress on poverty reduction without revitalizing economic growth in the region is also impossible. Growth is slowing down, and a lost decade of growth may be imminent, with regional growth between 2015 and 2025 projected to contract at an annual average rate per capita of 0.2 percent (World Bank 2024). Conflict, debt overhang, energy shortages, and currency pressures continue to affect the region's economies. This report focuses on long-term constraints on reducing poverty rather than on short-term fixes that could be swept away with the next crisis or shock.

Three factors make this the right time to act. First, Africa has access to the talent potential of the 8 to 11 million youths expected to enter the labor market every year between 2020 and 2050. Second, the region's large number of resource-rich countries have a valuable source of potential revenue in mineral endowments, including green minerals, that are in high demand to support a global clean energy transition. Third, as a region that has been the home of leapfrog innovations such as mobile money and digital platforms, Africa can leverage digital infrastructure to bring knowledge, information, and services to people, firms, and farms, particularly those located far from capital cities. For instance, the laying down of submarine cables that brought high-speed internet access to Africa improved labor market outcomes for both workers with a high level of education and those with a low level of education in 12 African countries studied (Hjort and Poulsen 2019).

The preceding chapters point to the potential to accelerate poverty reduction and spur growth by tackling structural inequalities. This report has argued that structural inequalities, an outcome of inequality of opportunities and market and institutional distortions, act as a major constraint on reducing inequality and poverty in Africa through several channels. First, structural inequalities contribute to wasted human potential, underused productive capacity, and misallocation of resources that affect the long-term trajectory of growth itself. This is true with respect to inequality of opportunity when it comes to human capital formation, driven by inherited or unalterable characteristics, such as parental socioeconomic status, location of birth, ethnicity, religion, gender, and other such circumstances. Second, when inequality in building productive capacity is combined with market and institutional failures, such as those preventing access to finance or entry into markets, it also affects people's incomes by limiting the opportunities that firms, farms, and workers have to use their productive potential. These inequalities can perpetuate a cycle of low economic mobility and inequality, which in turn weakens the link between economic growth and household well-being. Moreover, drivers of structural inequalities influence the composition of growth and the pace of structural transformation, which also weaken this link. Third, structural inequalities in building and utilizing productive capacities can be reinforced by the limited redistributive power of fiscal policy, which often increases poverty. Fourth, perceptions of inequality, and inequality of opportunity, or "fairness," in particular, can erode support for policies that are good for growth, increasing the risk of social instability. Finally, high levels of inequality tend to amplify the distributional impacts of shocks, increasing the chances that poverty traps will worsen over time.

Addressing structural inequalities calls for an integrative strategy—one that recognizes interlinkages, complementarities, and trade-offs; failure to do so risks trapping the region in a low-growth, high-poverty equilibrium. If economies are distorted enough (as appears to be the case in the region), such that they are producing well below their productive potential, then lifting constraints on productivity can improve efficiency and equity (Cerra, Lama, and Loayza 2021; Duclos and O'Connell 2015; López-Calva and Rodriguez-Castelan 2016). Not only will enabling talented individuals and entrepreneurs to achieve their full potential improve productivity and lead to growth, but it will also reduce poverty and inequality. However, policies that address only one stage of the income generation process will be insufficient to reduce structural inequality and drive poverty reduction. Policies and institutions must be guided by objectives that are overlapping and mutually reinforcing—promoting fairness to create a level playing field and enhancing the productive capacity of those who are disadvantaged.

Addressing structural inequalities has both a functional and an intrinsic justification for public policy intervention. The functional justification is that structural inequalities prevent growth, poverty reduction, and economic development more broadly. The intrinsic justification is the simple principle that circumstances at birth should not matter for a person's chances in life, and market distortions should not misallocate resources away from firms, farms, and workers that can potentially earn high returns.

Lessons from successful episodes: Economic growth with poverty and inequality reduction

Six countries on three continents have achieved three remarkable goals in the past three decades. They have each had episodes in which increases in gross domestic product (GDP) per capita were accompanied by large declines in extreme poverty, and at the same time they have reduced inequality or kept it in check (refer to box 6.1). Remarkably, all six cases feature policies that have, in one way or another, addressed structural inequalities: promoting productive capacity, striving to make the most of everyone's economic potential, and improving the fairness of their fiscal system. During these successful episodes, human development improved. Agricultural productivity strengthened. Export-oriented manufacturing grew.

BOX 6.1

Successful poverty reduction episodes in six countries

- In Bangladesh, extreme poverty (US$2.15/day) fell from more than 40 percent in 1991 to 5 percent in 2022, without an increase in inequality (Gini index around 33), with per capita gross domestic product (GDP) growth rising from 1.5 percent in 1991 to 6.7 percent in 2019.
- Colombia halved extreme poverty from 14.8 to 8.1 percent between 2004 and 2014, reduced inequality (the Gini index of income fell from 57.2 in 2002 to 50.8 in 2017), and experienced an increase in per capita GDP growth from 0.9 percent in 2002 to 3.5 percent in 2014.
- Ethiopia's extreme poverty rate fell from a high of 69 percent in 1995 to 27 percent in 2015, alongside a decline in inequality (the Gini index fell from 44 to 35) and an acceleration of GDP per capita growth from 2.7 percent in 1995 to 7.5 percent in 2015.
- Ghana experienced a halving of extreme poverty from 55 percent in 1998 to 25.2 percent in 2016, accompanied by a moderate increase in inequality (the Gini index rose from 40.1 to 43.5) and an acceleration in per capita GDP growth from 2.2 percent in 1998 to 11 percent in 2011, when oil production began, before falling to 1 percent in 2016.
- Kenya experienced a successful episode between 2005 and 2015, when the extreme poverty rate fell from 36.7 percent to 29.4 percent, inequality declined (the Gini index fell from 46.5 to 40.8), and the per capita GDP growth rate rose from 2.8 percent in 2005 to 5.1 percent in 2010, before falling back to 2.8 percent in 2015.
- Viet Nam eradicated extreme poverty between 1993 and 2022 (extreme poverty fell from 45 percent in 1993 to 1 percent in 2022). The country did not experience a significant increase in income inequality over this period (the Gini index remained close to 36), with high and sustained GDP per capita growth rates (6 percent in 1993 and 7.3 percent in 2022).

Sustaining progress in poverty reduction and growth is difficult, and all six countries have experienced headwinds in recent years from a mix of factors, including COVID-19. In 2024, Ethiopia, Ghana, and Kenya are grappling with high levels of sovereign debt that has undone some of their past success and weakened the link between growth and the pace of poverty reduction. During such reversals, it is important for countries to keep pursuing policies that level the playing field and expand people's opportunities.

These six countries include those that are resource rich, FCS, or both, as well as those that are not. Countries that are resource rich have experienced successful episodes, including oil-exporting Ghana and Colombia. Countries that are not resource rich, including Bangladesh, Kenya, and Viet Nam, have also trodden a similar path. Moreover, some of these countries, such as Colombia and Ethiopia, have done so while emerging from conflict and with fragile institutions. Although each country has charted its own course, there are three common denominators.

First, these six countries have improved the productive capacities of children and youth, universalizing access to opportunities for human development, including education, sanitation, roads, and electricity. In Bangladesh, nongovernmental organizations joined the government in promoting social services to communities, resulting in remarkable progress in the country's human development indicators. Improvements in schooling reduced inequalities between boys and girls and rich and poor individuals. Viet Nam widened access to primary education and health care while investing extensively in paved roads, electricity, piped water, and sanitation. It made great progress in reducing child mortality and child stunting. It did so, in part, by expanding health care, targeting women's and children's health, and promoting family planning. Ghana invested in primary education and saw increases in primary completion rates for boys and girls; improvements in nutrition indicators; and significant improvements in access to sanitation, electricity, and clean water. Ethiopia has expanded access to land user rights, helping to promote investment in agriculture. Although the state owns all land, elected councils have issued user certificates to both women and men.

Second, these countries invested to promote agricultural productivity, created manufacturing jobs, and connected farms and firms to customers, expanding access to good earning opportunities. All these countries were successful in boosting farm output and productivity through a mix of state-led investments along with market-oriented reforms. In Ethiopia, public investments in rural roads led to improvements in agricultural income. Market-friendly financial products, such as microfinance in Bangladesh and mobile money in Kenya, helped to boost financial inclusion and households' ability to cope with shocks. Partial market liberalization of the cocoa sector in Ghana, along with investment in research, disease control, and credit programs, led to increases in agricultural productivity (Chuhan-Pole and Angwafo 2011; Kolavalli and Vigneri 2011; World Bank 2018). Foreign direct investment (FDI) and effective transport and logistics helped to create job opportunities for low-skilled workers, such as in manufacturing in Bangladesh and Viet Nam and in cut flowers in Colombia, Ethiopia, and Kenya. Colombia also enhanced competition by implementing reforms of the liquor monopolies to increase competitiveness and transparency.

Bangladesh and Viet Nam are well known for their success in creating nonagricultural, labor-intensive wage employment opportunities for workers in manufacturing by becoming an attractive destination for FDI. Moreover, Bangladesh's reforms in the 1990s paved the way for greater private sector participation in trade, finance, and land ownership. Structural improvements between the early 1990s and mid-2000s provided a strong impetus for the rapid expansion of export-oriented, labor-intensive, ready-made garment industries. Strong nonagricultural job creation was accompanied by a shift of workers from agriculture to industry and services and from rural to urban areas. Women's employment increased at a faster pace than men's employment and brought millions of women into the workforce, boosting women's economic power.

Third, these six countries ensured macroeconomic stability coupled with spending on productive capacities. Colombia stands out for its ability to harness revenues to expand access to education and health as it emerged from more than a half-century of conflict. Colombia pressed forward with structural reforms at a time when it was enjoying an oil boom. The country used revenues from oil production (3.3 percent of GDP in 2013) and higher economic growth, combined with a series of tax reforms, to expand public spending on universal access to health and education. General government spending on health increased to 5.1 percent of GDP by 2014, and government spending on education represented 4.6 percent of GDP that year. This increased spending was accompanied by improved human development. By 2017, a year after a landmark peace deal, Colombia achieved almost universal health coverage. The average number of years of education also rose from 6.8 to 8.0 between 2005 and 2015.

Policies aimed at tackling structural inequalities

Structural inequalities in Africa are driven by wide-ranging factors, and addressing them requires multisectoral policy approaches aimed at unlocking productive capacity and raising earnings for poor and vulnerable individuals. The factors include market failures (such as in credit markets, as well as lack of competition), inadequate and inequitable public investment (in education, health, and infrastructure, including roads and electricity), small market size (low population density and limited market integration), and high and uninsurable risks (including climate change and conflict). Reducing welfare gaps therefore requires addressing the drivers of structural inequality by building and using productive capacities rather than solely relying on fiscal policy to provide the solutions. This in turn requires policies and institutions to be guided by objectives that are overlapping and mutually reinforcing—promoting fairness to create a level playing field and enhancing the productive capacity of disadvantaged individuals.

This report outlines a set of policies that could address structural inequalities and unleash stronger growth and poverty reduction. Table 6.1 presents a 3 × 4 policy matrix organized around two dimensions. The column heads list the stages of the income generation process presented throughout the report. First-stage policies aim to address the disparities that occur when the productive capacity of individuals is being built, largely before entering markets to obtain an income. Second-stage policies aim to address disparities that arise when people engage in markets to use their productive capacity for income generation. Finally, third-stage fiscal policies aim to provide near-term income relief and generate the resources to build productive capacity for the medium term.

A second dimension, represented by the table's row heads, focuses on the targets of policy interventions: economic and institutional foundations, people, firms and farms, and state effectiveness. This classification is useful, because addressing structural inequalities requires multisectoral policies and actors to unlock the productivity of poor individuals. Because the list of policies that could be classified into the two dimensions is long, policies were selected as priorities if they address market distortions and, for public spending, there is evidence that the marginal value of public funds being invested is high or there are double or triple wins in equity, efficiency, and climate adaptation or resilience.

TABLE 6.1 Policy matrix: Promoting growth and poverty reduction by reducing structural inequalities

	Stage 1: Build productive capacity	Stage 2: Grow better jobs and earning opportunities	Stage 3: Apply fair fiscal policy
Economic and institutional foundations		• Promote macro-fiscal stability • Adopt institutions that enhance the contestability of the decision-making process.	
People	• Invest in expanding and universalizing health care and education (focus on early-childhood interventions and girls). • Target underserved populations and regions when investing in basic (resilient) infrastructure (water, sanitation, or electricity).	• Facilitate low-income workers' job searches (job certification programs). • Build capacity through training for business owners and farmers. • Facilitate female work through gender-equal labor laws and provision of childcare services.	• Implement progressive personal income and property taxes. • Eliminate exemptions to and reduced rates on value-added taxes. • Strengthen adaptive social safety nets. • Consider school feeding programs to reach vulnerable children. • Invest in early warning systems to warn against natural disasters.
Firms and farms	• Invest in skills-building and technical and vocational education programs. Focus on women and youth. • Eliminate regulatory barriers to land or asset registration and property rights. Focus on women. • Encourage investments by smallholders in natural capital (tree planting and soil and forest conservation).	• Create policies to facilitate asset-based microfinance, supply chain financing, and other market-based financial products for small firms and farms. • Connect firms and farms to markets by investing in building and maintenance of spatially connective infrastructure (rural roads and transport and digital and mobile connectivity). • Promote smallholder adoption of agriculture technology (by providing climate information, as well as using other methods) through multisectoral or integrated packages. • Adopt multisectoral policies to foster participation in agricultural or global value chains.	• Tax extractive industries. • Eliminate energy subsidies. • Repurpose agricultural subsidies toward public goods. • Implement tax-free thresholds for small and medium enterprises.

(continued)

TABLE 6.1 Policy matrix: promoting growth and poverty reduction by reducing structural inequalities *(Continued)*

	Stage 1: Build productive capacity	Stage 2: Grow better jobs and earning opportunities	Stage 3: Apply fair fiscal policy
State effectiveness	• Improve service delivery for all; develop shock-resilient delivery plans, particularly for those in underserved locations. • Strengthen local capacity to deliver services.	• Enforce financial consumer protection laws to protect small borrowers. • Design and enforce inclusive market institutions (contract enforcement, competition, and justice). • Adopt and enforce labor standards in firms, particularly those that are part of global value chains.	• Increase tax compliance, particularly among high-income taxpayers. • Improve public expenditures and debt management. • Adopt sovereign disaster risk management practices to protect vulnerable groups. • Promote regional cooperation on taxation of extractive industries and multinational firms.

Source: Original table for this publication.

Economic and institutional foundations

Strong economic foundations are necessary for poverty and inequality reduction at all stages. It is impossible to imagine progress on poverty reduction without macroeconomic stability. In fact, the evidence from the economic crises of the 1980s and 1990s shows that the number of people living in poverty increased by as much as 25 percent during large contractions in output that followed a sovereign debt crisis (Farah-Yacoub et al. 2022). Similarly, in a sample of 131 sovereign debt defaults since 1900, poverty headcount rates exceeded their precrisis levels by roughly 30 percent shortly after a sovereign debt default and remained elevated a decade later (World Bank 2022). Not surprisingly, aggregate economic shocks that weaken the government's ability to provide public goods, such as health care and education, are also associated with a deterioration in human development and social indicators.

Similarly, it is difficult to imagine progress on poverty and inequality reduction without strong institutional foundations. Policy making and implementation do not occur in a vacuum. Rather, they take place in complex political and social settings, in which individuals and groups with unequal power interact within changing rules as they pursue conflicting interests (World Bank 2017). Exclusion, capture, and clientelism are manifestations of power asymmetries that lead to structural inequalities and limited growth, which can in turn lead to conflict and fragility. The distribution of power in society is partly determined by history, but social contracts evolve over time. Positive change is possible through improvements in governance, that is, in the way policy making and policy implementation take place. Efforts to shift the incentives of those with power in favor of positive development outcomes and to enhance the contestability of the decision-making process can mitigate and even overcome power asymmetries to bring about sustainable reductions in poverty (World Bank 2017).

Policies aimed at building productive capacity

Addressing inequality in building productive capacities requires policies that equalize opportunities and strengthen the state's capacity to deliver basic services. Addressing inequality of opportunities requires sectoral policies aimed at ensuring people, firms, and farms can reach their productive potential. This includes investments in health and education as well as expansion of basic services to underserved populations so that individuals benefit regardless of the circumstances in which they were born. From an efficiency point of view, there are clear positive externalities from having a more educated and healthier citizenry, and the market will likely not supply basic services without public intervention. An explicit focus on equity through interventions targeted to underserved populations and regions may bring the best results to those with the lowest coverage in basic services, including electricity, water, and sanitation.

The evidence especially points to high returns to public funds spent on early child interventions and basic education. For instance, a recent cross-country analysis finds large, long-run returns to schooling in low- and middle-income countries compared with high-income countries (Montenegro and Patrinos 2021). Careful evaluations of preprimary investments generate sizable learning gains relative to cost (Holla et al. 2021), as do some structured pedagogical investments (Evans and Yuan 2019). There is also substantial evidence that more educated individuals are also likely to assess and respond to risks more effectively, therefore being better prepared to cope with natural disasters and weather shocks, which is crucial in determining a household's ability to adapt to climate change.[1] When it comes to women and girls, education has far-reaching impacts, influencing factors such as age at first marriage, fertility, productivity, and intergenerational transmission of poverty (World Bank 2023).

The largest positive educational effects come from coordinating reinforcing interventions. Recent analysis for Africa finds that combining teacher training with ongoing teacher support and classroom learning materials for students is most effective in improving learning (Bashir et al. 2018). Similarly, increases in learning time, school feeding programs, and improvements in the process of hiring teachers are important. Student attendance rates increase when cash transfers are combined with improved hygiene in school infrastructure and community-based monitoring.

There is also evidence that investments in basic health interventions have long-term benefits. For instance, basic health interventions such as deworming and providing vitamin A supplements are known to generate large impacts relative to up-front costs (Bhula, Mahoney, and Murphy 2020). Similarly, a recent randomized trial found substantial improvements in child health from a program in Mali that delivered free care for children followed by community health worker visits (Dean and Sautmann 2022). The focus on women's health should include interventions to improve reproductive health and eliminate child marriage and other harmful practices, such as female genital mutilation (FGM). Investments in reproductive health lead to future health care savings, equalize the labor market, and boost economic growth (Canning and Schultz 2012). Increasing the age at first marriage has also been shown to be effective, but only 13 countries in Africa have set the legal age for marriage at 18; 17 have no minimum age, and the rest set a minimum age younger than 18 (World Bank 2023). Similarly, FGM remains prevalent in 33 African countries, with high rates in The Gambia, Guinea, Mali, and Somalia, affecting more than 70 percent of women ages 15 to 19 (UNICEF 2023), which is not only a health risk but has long-term consequences for girls' ability to study, work, and be productive members of society (WHO 2023).

Targeting investments in basic water, sanitation, and electricity to underserved populations and regions is likely to have strong returns. The key rationale for public spending on these basic services is that these are investments that the private sector will likely not make. Moreover, some infrastructure assets are natural monopolies that require some level of government involvement. Investments in clean water and sanitation are a key input to improve health outcomes. Investment in electricity is complementary to efforts to improve health and education, but through its impacts on employment, it is also a precondition for reducing inequality in the labor market (Foster et al. 2023; Mensah 2023). These investments can also reduce gender gaps by limiting the time women spend on household chores, thus improving their paid labor opportunities (Small and van der Meulen Rodgers 2023; World Bank 2023). The cost of providing services largely depends on the goal of increasing access to and quality of services (including the costs of sustainable alternatives), as well as the efficiency of spending (Rozenberg and Fay 2019). Service expansion should consider

- Making the key measure of success hookup rates or actual connections

- Focusing on unserved population living physically close to infrastructure networks

- Developing a better understanding of community needs and demand-side barriers, which is crucial for expanding coverage

- Recovering connection costs by sharing them across the entire customer base or by extending payments over several years instead of through one-time up-front charges (Foster and Briceño-Garmendia 2010).

With regard to interventions to build productive capacities for farms and firms, three areas stand out. First, improving the equity, efficiency, and relevance of technical and vocational education and training (TVET) and higher education will help ensure that the formal TVET systems in the region are responsive to the demand for such skills by firms and farms. Second, expanding land registration and securing property rights are essential interventions to ensure that firms, farms, and workers can maximize their productive capacity. For instance, in Ethiopia and Rwanda, public policy facilitated registration and formalization of use rights that have seen significant payoffs in higher earnings and government revenue mobilization from property taxation. Special attention is needed when inheritance laws or other regulatory barriers limit women's ownership rights, because they have important consequences for women's productive capacity (across 37 countries, only around 8 percent of married women own land or housing, compared with about 25 percent of married men; World Bank 2023b). Finally, efforts to encourage investments in the environment, including tree planting and soil and forest conservation, have been shown to have large positive environmental externalities. Moreover, they can lead to improvements in output, thus promoting growth and, if targeted appropriately, reducing poverty—a triple win (Baquie and Hill 2023; Grosset, Papp, and Taylor 2024).

Enhancing state effectiveness in building productive capacities requires improvements in service delivery, including through strengthened local capacities. This is true with respect to human capital interventions, but it is also true when focusing on efforts to increase resiliency of communities or to improve certainty over land ownership. For instance, high rates of teacher absenteeism reflect challenges in delivering payment, inadequate monitoring, lack of access to transport and health facilities, and heavy school administrative responsibilities. Similarly, health workers' absenteeism and their low ability to correctly diagnose and treat common health conditions is a concern, particularly in rural areas (Gatti et al. 2021). However, even if efforts are in place to train, monitor, and support teachers and health workers, they may be insufficient. Improving public awareness of the unacceptably low levels of learning in selected areas of a country may be used to change teachers' and policy makers' incentives to improve the quality of education. Adding new actors—for example, parents—can change power dynamics as well if parents can credibly enforce sanctions. In all cases, increasing accountability is important for achieving the desired development outcomes (World Bank 2017).

Policies aimed at growing better jobs and earning opportunities

Policies aimed at growing better jobs and earnings opportunities to level the playing field for workers should seek to address market and institutional distortions. Such policies aimed at firms, farms, and workers have three features that are worth noting. First, policies to create a level playing field in the labor market are important for reaping the returns to investments in productive capacities: healthy and better-educated youth entering the labor market will be able to find productive jobs, and agricultural technology adoption will be possible for farmers with land user rights. Second, coordination across a wide range of stakeholders for these reforms will be needed to realize gains from complementarities. Stakeholders in policies aimed at addressing distortions range from authorities who set financial sector policy and competition policy to agencies that manage public investments in infrastructure and line ministries that cover agriculture and rural development. An example of a complementarity is the availability of rural roads that facilitates market access and productivity gains for farmers adopting agricultural technology. Another example is the availability of effective contract enforcement mechanisms that can help unlock farmers' and firms' participation in value chains. Finally, creating buy-in for these reforms will be critical. To the extent that policy reforms lead resources to move out of low-productivity, low-paying sectors to higher-productivity, better-paying sectors, these reforms can have short- to medium-term adjustment effects on firms and farms. Strong institutions and training and job certification policies can help smooth this adjustment. Relatedly, as *World Development Report 2006* points out, some of these reforms, such as enforcing competition or labor standards, can have political economy implications (World Bank 2005).

For workers, addressing market and institutional distortions includes improving signaling about job skills, providing business training, and ensuring women can access work opportunities. Easing workers' cost of traveling to where the jobs are is a promising public policy action, given the evidence from a study of job seekers in urban Ethiopia (Abebe et al. 2021; Franklin 2018). A growing body of evidence shows that job skills certification is a cost-effective intervention in terms of its impact on the employment rate (Abebe et al. 2021; Caria et al. 2024). Skills certification programs can be offered by governments as part of job search assistance policies. The public policy rationale for this is that these programs correct an information failure so that workers can signal their skills to firms and thus reduce an important source of friction in the labor market (Carranza and McKenzie 2023). Business training and personal initiative are effective for microenterprise owners. For instance, the International Labour Organization's Gender and Enterprise Together program appears to be effective in improving business practices for women entrepreneurs (Kenya and Viet Nam) and also in improving their sales (Kenya) (McKenzie et al. 2023). These skills certification programs can be combined with business grants and offered via business competitions aimed at finding firms with the highest productive potential, coordinated by government but potentially cofinanced by development partners or the private sector, provided adequate governance measures are in place (McKenzie 2024). Women face additional sources of friction in the labor market that arise from various legal barriers to work; several countries in the region have recently made progress in removing these barriers and equalizing opportunities. For women, particularly those in urban areas, childcare responsibilities can serve as a barrier to earnings and hours worked. In the Africa region, available data from the World Bank's Women, Business, and the Law Database indicate that no country has specific policies in place for delivery of these services (public or private; Sakhonchik, Elefante, and Niesten 2023).

For firms and farms, addressing market and institutional distortions includes strengthening the financial sector, promoting technology adoption, and investing in key infrastructure whose absence holds back productivity growth and scaling up. Leveraging financial sector policy and strengthening the credit infrastructure are important for facilitating innovation by private sector banks and nonbank institutions to deliver low-cost lending products to small borrowers. Unlike preferential credit policies that target loan products by firm or farm size, reducing the financial sector's cost of delivering credit to small borrowers via market-based products has the advantage of not being distortionary. Needs range from equity financing and venture capital for growth-oriented firms to leveraging financial technology where possible, as well as adaptations to microfinance for microfirms and farms. For farms, there is a promising case for promoting technology adoption via an integrated package of services (including delivering climate-smart information), recognizing that multiple constraints must be alleviated. Public investment in connective infrastructure, particularly rural road construction and maintenance, has been found to have high returns; ensuring strong efficiency of this public spending is key. When complemented by a competitive transport sector, these investments can yield high returns for rural farmers. Finally, a set of multisectoral policies are needed to facilitate firms' and farms' participation in integrated value chains linking firms across sectors. Gains from better domestic market connectivity can be enhanced if firms and farms can access regional markets (via the African Continental Free Trade Area) and international markets (via trade agreements and programs, such as Economic Partnership Agreements with the European Union and the United States' African Growth and Opportunity Act). Strong institutional arrangements are needed to ensure that participating farms, firms, and workers benefit.

The state's role in creating and enforcing inclusive market institutions is central to the effectiveness of these policies. Financial consumer protection laws in the region can be designed to protect consumers while minimizing impacts on the financial sector (Boeddu and Chien 2022). Economic laws and effective justice service delivery are needed to facilitate market transactions, be they between farmers and input providers or between SMEs and financial institutions. Ensuring a level playing field on which state-owned enterprises are present and limiting anticompetitive firm behavior are both needed, through strong competition policy alone or complemented by a competition authority. If the competition authorities are able to function independently, they can be effective in tackling anticompetitive behavior (Büthe and Kigwiru 2020). Effective justice policies for commercial transactions are needed that can accommodate the needs of micro-, small-, and medium-sized enterprises. The improved access to justice these policies will bring can be critical, especially if used to bridge the gap with customary laws, where relevant. Finally, adopting and enforcing labor standards in wage employment and fair treatment of farmers in global value chains is crucial given the potential market power of foreign firms.

Improving the fairness of fiscal policies

Fair fiscal policy requires a domestic revenue mobilization strategy that protects poor individuals and improves the efficiency of public spending. Efforts toward more progressive personal income and property taxation are the cornerstone of a domestic revenue mobilization strategy that protects those who are poor. Efforts to tax individuals with high net worth, including through property taxation, should be pursued. To the extent that indirect taxation will continue to be the main source of revenue for the foreseeable future, the tax base could be broadened through the elimination of exemptions, which largely benefit high-income households because of the presence of informality (Bachas, Gadenne, and Jensen 2023; Warwick et al. 2022). On the spending side, critical to reducing prefiscal inequality are targeted adaptive social assistance and school feeding programs, which can significantly improve the redistributive impact of fiscal policies and at the same time guard against shocks that could prevent children and youth from reaching their full potential. Similarly, establishing early warning systems to prevent long-term human impacts from natural disasters would go a long way toward reducing poverty and inequality.

With respect to firms and farms, fair fiscal policies include market-based solutions to environmental externalities and careful design of simplified tax regimes. Taxation of extractive industries should ensure that firms internalize the social cost of pollution and other environmental impacts. These taxes should allow governments to benefit from high commodity prices, be directly linked to the profitability of the sector, or both. To the extent that countries have simplified tax regimes for small enterprises, these should include a tax-free threshold that can protect the poorest and most vulnerable of these firms. On the spending side, eliminating energy subsidies would improve efficiency, equity, and environmental sustainability, because these subsidies largely benefit higher-income households at a very high fiscal cost and with considerable environmental consequences. Repurposing agricultural subsidies away from fertilizer subsidies toward public goods can be a triple win by improving yields and farm incomes and limiting environmental degradation (Goyal and Nash 2017).

Effective public financial management and tax administration are necessary complements to ensure fair fiscal policy. Improving tax compliance, particularly among high-income taxpayers, would lead to higher revenue while safeguarding poor and vulnerable individuals. Furthermore, pursuing cooperation between governments in the region could lead to greater harmonization on taxation of extractive industries and multinational firms that would minimize the risk of a race to the bottom between countries. Improved public expenditure management includes medium-term budgeting, transparent discussion of tax expenditures as part of the budget process, improved debt management, and elimination of arrears through improvements in public finance controls. Critically, better financial planning for disaster response can ensure that financing will be available quickly and cost-effectively should a crisis hit.

Interlinkages and trade-offs

A key insight from this analysis is that policies that address only one stage of the income generation process will be insufficient to reduce structural inequality and drive poverty reduction. Many of the policies and technical solutions discussed here are not new. However, they will not work in isolation. For instance, policies and efforts aimed at alleviating structural inequalities in building productive capacities that are subsequently not complemented by policies aimed at ensuring that those capacities can be productively employed will not result in greater productivity and poverty reduction. Countries could succeed in improving the education of their workforce, but if market distortions are not addressed, young graduates will have no viable work options to use their skills. Efforts at women's financial inclusion are meaningless if women face legal barriers to owning land and assets that could serve as collateral. Greater trade integration without rural connectivity could risk isolating remote rural areas. Efforts to build job certification programs or setting up industrial parks without minimum labor standards could risk hurting workers. Tax deductions and exemptions aimed at enticing investment will not generate jobs if property rights are unclear. Moreover, without transparency and accountability at all stages, any of these efforts can exacerbate existing structural inequality.

Achieving poverty reduction therefore requires that governments and their partners work in multisectoral and integrated ways, well beyond current practice. Reducing welfare gaps requires addressing the drivers of structural inequality at all stages of the income generation process. This in turn requires that coordinated policies and institutions be guided by objectives that are overlapping and mutually reinforcing—promoting fairness to create a level playing field and enhancing the productive capacity of those who are disadvantaged. In fact, achieving double or triple wins is often only possible when a combination of reforms is simultaneously being implemented. This would certainly be the case for the success of multisectoral and spatially integrated interventions, such as the agricultural value chains in which smallholders and firms participate. Moreover, the timing and sequencing of reforms is critical, particularly when several policies are being pursued. For instance, eliminating energy subsidies would address equity and efficiency concerns while reducing negative climate externalities. However, without complementary social policies, subsidy reforms can lead to increased poverty and ultimately backfire. Sequencing is often critical: for instance, implementation of trade liberalization policies would be meaningful if it were preceded by the removal of distortions in transportation markets. Enhanced coordination across government institutions with multiple and simultaneous implementation efforts are challenging, even in the best of circumstances. Therefore, it is critical that governments strategically prioritize and coordinate their efforts. Sectoral approaches that aim to advance policy reform in isolation are not sufficient to achieve the goal of poverty reduction.

Only in the presence of externalities and market imperfections can one expect win–win policies. As such, this report prioritizes policies in which there are clear externalities, allowing for double wins and even triple wins. For instance, efforts to reduce social tensions and address poverty in former FCS countries could include public works programs in regions previously affected by conflict, focusing on climate adaptation investments, such as rural roads, soil, or forest conservation efforts, thus providing income support while at the same time leading to greater future resilience to climate change. Similarly, investments in early childhood education equalize opportunities, increase productivity and growth, and improve resilience to climate change. However, to achieve these triple wins, coordinated action across multiple sectors is needed.

Moreover, it is important to recognize that there may be short-term policy trade-offs that require careful planning in the timing and sequencing of reform. Domestic revenue mobilization efforts are costly for households, firms, and farms, with potential impacts on productivity and poverty reduction, but they are necessary for the provision of public goods. Similarly, removing fertilizer subsidies could have large impacts on poor farmers, whereas investments in research and technology that could offer higher crop yields at a lower cost take time to mature. Critical intertemporal and intergenerational trade-offs also exist, such as the decision to provide additional funding for social assistance, which addresses poverty today, versus longer-term physical and human capital investments that have the potential to reduce future poverty. Overcoming these challenges necessarily requires integrated policy packages and clarity about the timing and sequencing of complementary reforms.

Civil society and development partners can play an important role in supporting a strategy to address structural inequalities. These partners will also need to work in multisectoral and integrated ways centered on government strategic priorities. Partnerships will be critical to make gains in poverty reduction, through financial as well as technical support. As demonstrated in chapter 5, it is important to acknowledge that for some countries in Africa, domestic revenue mobilization efforts will be insufficient to generate sufficient resources to eliminate poverty and address critical development needs. Given the tight fiscal space, concessional financing for development priorities could play an important role in advancing this agenda. This includes multilateral and bilateral donors, as well as nongovernmental organizations, which are especially needed in the poorest and most fragile environments. Furthermore, in FCS settings, international partners must have a long-term perspective, respond with agility around a narrow and clearly laid-out set of priorities, and have staying power (World Bank 2011).

The private sector is also an important ally in mobilizing capital and delivering critical inputs. For example, private schools can play an important role in ensuring universal high-quality education, especially in fiscally constrained countries, provided sectoral policies are in place to regulate the sector. Similarly, training programs, business competitions, and efforts to promote global value chains will rely on partnerships with the private sector to lead to growth in productivity and greater employment opportunities for the growing population. Creating a level playing field for private sector innovation and investment combined with appropriate supervisory institutions will be essential to attract investments in areas such as digital finance for inclusion.

Policy priorities depend on the country context

One of the most salient features of inequality in Africa is its universality rather than specific differences among countries. As such, no country can afford to ignore the presence of inequality and, in particular, the presence of structural inequality that precludes progress toward poverty reduction. Similarly, macro-fiscal stability is a foundational requirement for all countries, because macroeconomic crises typically lead to large output losses, increases in poverty, and potentially large swings in inequality. Table 6.1 presents a broad menu of policies; however, an in-depth analysis of structural inequality at the country level would be useful to arrive at a robust set of policy priorities specific to each context. Moreover, the interlinkages across dimensions of inequality require careful timing and sequencing of reforms that will vary across country contexts.

The typology based on fragility, conflict, and resource wealth status recognizes that governments' capacity to address structural inequalities will be limited or shaped by these circumstances. Security is a precondition for development, and yet it is absent in many countries in the region. Violent conflict can be seen as the result of three types of breakdowns in governance:

- The unconstrained power of individuals, groups, and governments

- Failed agreements between participants

- The exclusion of relevant individuals and groups from the policy-making process (*World Development Report 2017*, World Bank 2017).

Power-sharing agreements, resource redistribution, dispute settlement, and sanctions and deterrence can potentially prevent, reduce, or end violent conflict. However, any agreement is unlikely to succeed in the long term if it is unable to constrain the power of ruling elites, achieve and sustain agreements, and include relevant individuals and groups. For resource-rich countries, these broad governance constraints can be aggravated by challenges in managing natural resource wealth, including high vulnerability to rent seeking, commodity market fluctuations, Dutch disease, and weak linkages between resource sectors and the rest of the economy. At the same time, natural resource wealth may allow for more ambitious public investment and resource sharing and redistribution, which would help to sustain peace. Countries without natural resources that are afflicted by conflict are likely to be the most constrained, and countries not in conflict or without natural resources are the least constrained. Policy priorities are therefore different across these country contexts.

For FCS countries, the priority should be actions that can restore confidence by providing citizens with security, jobs, and key basic services, particularly in conflict-affected areas. As *World Development Report 2011* noted, "No country or region can afford to ignore areas where repeated cycles of violence flourish and citizens are disengaged from the state" (World Bank 2011, 18). FCS countries that are resource rich are home to 37 percent of the population of Africa, and it is in these countries where the poverty headcount rate is the highest, with an average poverty rate of 46 percent in 2022—17 percentage points higher than in countries with resource wealth that were not in fragility or conflict. Non–resource-rich FCS countries are home to 35 percent of the African population and are where poverty rates have been slowest to decline. In these cases, the priority should be citizen security, underpinned by justice and jobs, both of which can help to restore confidence and prevent future cycles of violence (World Bank 2011). In these settings, programs that support a relationship with the state in insecure areas can be helpful. For instance, it may be possible to fund community-based public works programs addressing infrastructure bottlenecks, such as rural roads. Similarly, vaccination and school feeding programs could provide jobs while investing in the long-term productivity of citizens and increasing their resilience to shocks.

For FCS countries that are resource rich, the challenge is to strengthen the management of their natural resources. In contrast, FCS countries that are not resource rich often do not have sufficient resources to provide even basic services, because their revenue collection is extremely limited and tends to be used to fund current spending. In these settings, agile and speedy international assistance is needed, and national leaders will need to lay clear priorities and demonstrate transparency and accountability standards. In resource-rich FCS countries, the priorities for building confidence in conflict-affected areas are similar, but there is also the challenge of managing the natural resources. This includes efforts toward greater transparency, accountability, and resource sharing. It also includes building a macroeconomic framework that will allow for adequate incentives for diversification.

For resource-rich countries not affected by conflict, the priority is to promote economic diversification, using their natural resources to build productive capacities and facilitate market integration. Resource-rich countries not affected by conflict are home to 7 percent of the population of Africa. Although this group of countries has the lowest poverty rates, they have had an average overall decline in poverty of only 1.2 percent per year over the last two decades. Moreover, these countries have the highest levels of inequality. This high inequality, combined with the fact that nearly 30 percent of their population remains in extreme poverty, suggests that the deleterious effects of the resource curse may be particularly pronounced: Dutch disease and overreliance on imports have led to low economic diversification and created few good economic opportunities. Moreover, although children have relatively high access to schools, much more is needed to improve the quality of education and ensure children have access to basic services. In these cases, in addition to sound natural resource management and a macro framework that incentivizes diversification, more can be done to invest in basic infrastructure that targets poor and underserved populations, opens access to markets, and reduces labor market frictions. In terms of fiscal policies, more could be done to ensure that extractive industries pay taxes commensurate with the social cost of carbon and that those resources are used to address structural inequalities in building and using productive capacities.

Finally, non–resource-rich countries not affected by conflict could address structural inequalities at all stages of the income generation process. These countries are home to 21 percent of the African population and have had the strongest, most sustained declines in poverty reduction. These are also the countries in which children have higher and more equal access to opportunities. However, it is also in these countries where more can be done to address structural inequalities across all stages of the income generation process.

Note

1. See the recent summary in Hill, Nguyen, and Doan (2024).

References

Abebe, Girum, A. Stefano Caria, Marcel Fafchamps, Paolo Falco, Simon Franklin, and Simon Quinn. 2021. "Anonymity or Distance? Job Search and Labour Market Exclusion in a Growing African City." *Review of Economic Studies* 88 (3): 1279–1310. https://doi.org/10.1093/restud/rdaa057.

Bachas, Pierre, Lucie Gadenne, and Anders Jensen. 2023. "Informality, Consumption Taxes, and Redistribution." *Review of Economic Studies* 91 (5): 2604–34. https://doi.org/10.1093/restud/rdad095.

Baquie, S., and R. Hill. 2023. "Improving Water Availability and Restoring Soil Fertility in the Sahel." In *Reality Check: Lessons from 25 Policies Advancing a Low-Carbon Future*, 89–93. Climate Change and Development Series. Washington, DC: World Bank. https://doi.org/10.1596/978-1-4648-1996-4.

Bashir, Sajitha, Marlaine Lockheed, Elizabeth Ninan, and Jee-Peng Tan. 2018. *Facing Forward: Schooling for Learning in Africa*. Africa Development Forum series. Washington, DC: World Bank. https://doi.org/10.1596/978-1-46481260-6.

Bhula, Radhika, Meghan Mahoney, and Kyle Murphy. 2020. *Conducting Cost-Effectiveness Analysis (CEA)*. Cambridge, MA: Massachusetts Institute of Technology, Abdul Latif Jameel Poverty Action Lab. https://www.povertyactionlab.org/resource/conducting-cost-effectiveness-analysis-cea.

Boeddu, Gian, and Jennifer Chien. 2022. "Financial Consumer Protection and Fintech: An Overview of New Manifestations of Consumer Risks and Emerging Regulatory Approaches." Fintech and the Future of Finance Overview Paper, World Bank, Washington, DC. https://thedocs.worldbank.org/en/doc/11ea23266a1f65d9a08cbe0e9b072c89-0430012022/related/Note-5.pdf.

Bosio, Erica. 2023. *Increasing Access to Justice in Fragile Settings*. Washington, DC: World Bank. http://documents.worldbank.org/curated/en/099101123141530374/P17955108fb2a104e0a55e04b0257738ea3.

Büthe, Tim, and Vellah Kedogo Kigwiru. 2020. "The Spread of Competition Law and Policy in Africa: A Research Agenda." *African Journal of International Economic Law* 1 (Fall): 41–83. https://www.afronomicslaw.org/sites/default/files/journal/2021/Bu%C3%8C%C2%88theKigwiru-Spread-of-Competition-Policy-in-Africa-1-AfJIEL-41-2020-2.pdf.

Calice, Pietro. 2020. "Boosting Credit: Public Guarantees Can Help Mitigate Risk during COVID-19." *World Bank Blogs*, May 28. https://blogs.worldbank.org/en/psd/boosting-credit-public-guarantees-can-help-mitigate-risk-during-covid-19?cid=SHR_BlogSiteEmail_EN_EXT.

Canning, David, and T. Paul Schultz. 2012. "The Economic Consequences of Reproductive Health and Family Planning." *Lancet* 380 (9837): 165–71.

Caria, Stefano, Kate Orkin, Alison Andrew, Robert Garlick, Rachel Heath, and Niharika Singh. 2024. "Barriers to Search and Hiring in Urban Labour Markets." *VoxDevLit* 10 (1).

Carranza, Eliana, and David McKenzie. 2023. "Job Training and Job Search Assistance Policies in Developing Countries." Policy Research Working Paper 10576, World Bank, Washington, DC. https://documents.worldbank.org/curated/en/099648409282314225/IDU0376203a30f7ac04c690bd9900b63d1dbfd80.

Cerra, Valerie, Ruy Lama, and Norman V. Loayza. 2021. "Links between Growth, Inequality, and Poverty: A Survey." Working Paper 2021/068, International Monetary Fund, Washington, DC. https://www.imf.org/-/media/Files/Publications/WP/2021/English/wpiea2021068-print-pdf.ashx.

Chuhan-Pole, Punam, and Manka Angwafo. 2011. *Yes Africa Can: Success Stories from a Dynamic Continent*. Washington, DC: World Bank. http://hdl.handle.net/10986/2335.

Dean, Mark, and Anja Sautmann. 2022. "The Effects of Community Health Worker Visits and Primary Care Subsidies on Health Behavior and Health Outcomes for Children in Urban Mali." Policy Research Working Paper 9986, World Bank, Washington, DC. http://hdl.handle.net/10986/37245.

Duclos, Jean-Yves, and Stephen A. O'Connell. 2015. "Is Poverty a Binding Constraint on Growth in Sub-Saharan Africa?" In *Economic Growth and Poverty Reduction in Sub-Saharan Africa*, edited by Andrew McKay and Erik Thorbecke, 54–90. Oxford: Oxford University Press. https://doi.org/10.1093/acprof:oso/9780198728450.001.0001.

Evans, David K., and Fei Yuan. 2019. "Equivalent Years of Schooling: A Metric to Communicate Learning Gains in Concrete Terms." Policy Research Working Paper 8752, World Bank, Washington, DC.

Farah-Yacoub, Juan P., Clemens Graf von Luckner, Rita Ramalho, and Carmen Reinhart. 2022. "The Social Costs of Sovereign Default." Policy Research Working Paper 10157, World Bank, Washington, DC. http://hdl.handle.net/10986/37945.

Foster, Vivien, and Cecilia Briceño-Garmendia. 2010. *Africa's Infrastructure: A Time for Transformation*. Washington, DC: World Bank. https://documents1.worldbank.org/curated/en/246961468003355256/pdf/521020PUB0EPI1101Official0Use0Only1.pdf.

Foster, Vivien, Nisan Gorgulu, Stéphane Straub, and Maria Vagliasindi. 2023. "The Impact of Infrastructure on Development Outcomes: A Qualitative Review of Four Decades of Literature." Policy Research Working Paper 10343, World Bank, Washington, DC. http://hdl.handle.net/10986/39515.

Franklin, Simon. 2018. "Location, Search Costs and Youth Unemployment: Experimental Evidence from Transport Subsidies." *Economic Journal* 128 (614): 2353–79. https://doi.org/10.1111/ecoj.12509.

Gatti, Roberta, Kathryn Andrews, Ciro Avitabile, Ruben Conner, Jigyasa Sharma, and Andres Yi Chang. 2021. *The Quality of Health and Education Systems Across Africa: Evidence from a Decade of Service Delivery Indicators Surveys*. Washington, DC: World Bank. http://hdl.handle.net/10986/36234.

Goyal, Aparajita, and John Nash. 2017. *Reaping Richer Returns: Public Spending Priorities for African Agriculture Productivity Growth*. Africa Development Forum. Washington, DC: World Bank and Agence Francaise de Developpement. http://hdl.handle.net/10986/25996.

Grosset-Touba, Florian, Anna Papp, and Charles A. Taylor. 2024. "Rain Follows the Forest: Land Use Policy, Climate Change, and Adaptation." SSRN, August. https://doi.org/10.2139/ssrn.4333147.

Hill, Ruth, Tran Nguyen, and Miki Khanh Doan. 2024. "The Welfare Impacts of Climate and Climate Policies: A Framework." Unpublished manuscript, World Bank, Washington, DC.

Hjort, Jonas, and Jonas Poulsen. 2019. "The Arrival of Fast Internet and Employment in Africa." *American Economic Review* 109 (3): 1032–79. https://www.doi.org/10.1257/aer.20161385.

Holla, Alaka, Magdalena Bendini, Lelys Dinarte, and Iva Trako. 2021. "Is Investment in Preprimary Education Too Low? Lessons from (Quasi) Experimental Evidence across Countries." Policy Research Working Paper 9723, World Bank, Washington, DC.

Kimura, Yuichi. 2024. "Why Do Overlapping Land Rights Discourage Investment in Agriculture? Customary Land Tenure System in West Africa." MPRA Paper 122183, September 24. https://mpra.ub.uni-muenchen.de/122183/.

Kolavalli, Shashi, and Marcella Vigneri. 2011. "Cocoa in Ghana: Shaping the Success of an Economy." In *Yes, Africa Can: Success Stories from a Dynamic Continent*, edited by Punam Chuhan-Pole and Manka Angwafo, 201–17. Washington, DC: World Bank. https://doi.org/10.1596/978-0-8213-8745-0.

López-Calva, Luis-Felipe, and Carlos Rodriguez-Castelan. 2016. "Pro-Growth Equity: A Policy Framework for the Twin Goals." Poverty and Equity Global Practice Working Paper 091, World Bank, Washington, DC. http://documents.worldbank.org/curated/en/468851524551936188 /Pro-growth-equity-a-policy-framework-for-the-twin-goals.

McKenzie, David. 2024. "Is There Still A Role for Direct Government Support to Firms in Developing Countries?" *New Zealand Economic Papers*, February, 1–6. https://doi.org/10.1080/00779954.2023 .2290484.

McKenzie, David, Christopher Woodruff, Kjetil Bjorvatn, Miriam Bruhn, Jing Cai, Juanita Gonzalez-Uribe, Simon Quinn, Tetsushi Sonobe, and Martin Valdivia. 2023. "Training Entrepreneurs." *VoxDevLit* 1 (3). https://voxdev.org/sites/default/files/2023-11/Training_Entrepreneurs_Issue_3.pdf.

Mensah, Justice Tei. 2023. "Jobs! Electricity Shortages and Unemployment in Africa." *Journal of Development Economics* 167: 103231. https://doi.org/10.1016/j.jdeveco.2023.103231.

Montenegro, Claudio E., and Harry Anthony Patrinos. 2021. "A Data Set of Comparable Estimates of the Private Rate of Return to Schooling in the World, 1970–2014." *International Journal of Manpower* 44(6): 1248–68. https://doi.org/10.1108/IJM-03-2021-0184.

Rozenberg, Julie, and Marianne Fay. 2019. *Beyond the Gap: How Countries Can Afford the Infrastructure They Need while Protecting the Planet*. Sustainable Infrastructure. Washington, DC: World Bank. http://hdl.handle.net/10986/31291.

Sakhonchik, Alena, Marina Elefante, and Hannelore Maria L. Niesten. 2023. *Government Financial Support for Childcare Services: A Study of Regulations in 95 Economies*. Global Indicators Briefs 21. Washington, DC: World Bank. http://documents.worldbank.org/curated/en/099431007202325029 /IDU090ab2deb0038e047160b8cb0dc3650a2d1cf.

Small, Sarah F., and Yana van der Meulen Rodgers. 2023. "The Gendered Effects of Investing in Physical and Social Infrastructure." *World Development* 171: 106347. https://doi.org/10.1016/j .worlddev.2023.106347.

Stanley, Andrew. 2023. "A Demographic Transformation in Africa Has the Potential to Alter the World Order." *Finance and Development*, September. https://www.imf.org/en/Publications/fandd /issues/2023/09/PT-african-century.

UNICEF (United Nations Children's Fund). 2023. "Female Genital Mutilation (FGM): At Least 200 Million Girls and Women Alive Today Living in 31 Countries Have Undergone FGM." Last updated March 2024. https://data.unicef.org/topic/child-protection/female-genital-mutilation/.

Warwick, Ross, Tom Harris, David Phillips, Maya Goldman, Jon Jellema, Gabriela Inchauste, and Karolina Goraus-Tańska. 2022. "The Redistributive Power of Cash Transfers vs VAT Exemptions: A Multi-Country Study." *World Development* 151: 105742. https://doi.org/10.1016/j.worlddev.2021.105742.

World Bank. 2005. *World Development Report 2006: Equity and Development*. Washington, DC: World Bank. http://hdl.handle.net/10986/5988.

World Bank. 2011. *World Development Report 2011: Conflict, Security, and Development*. Washington, DC: World Bank. http://hdl.handle.net/10986/4389.

World Bank. 2017. *World Development Report 2017: Governance and the Law*. Washington, DC: World Bank. http://hdl.handle.net/10986/25880.

World Bank. 2018. *Ghana Priorities for Ending Poverty and Boosting Shared Prosperity: Systematic Country Diagnostic*. Washington, DC: World Bank. http://hdl.handle.net/10986/30974 License: CC BY 3.0 IGO.

World Bank. 2022. *World Development Report 2022: Finance for an Equitable Recovery*. Washington, DC: World Bank. http://hdl.handle.net/10986/36883.

World Bank. 2023. "What Works to Narrow Gender Gaps and Empower Women in Sub-Saharan Africa? An Evidence-Review of Selected Impact Evaluation Studies." World Bank, Washington, DC. https://documents1.worldbank.org/curated/en/099061623110030316/pdf/P1804940a8a04e0ab0988e0e90727152914.pdf.

World Bank. 2024. "Transforming Education for Inclusive Growth." *Africa's Pulse* 30 (October 15). https://hdl.handle.net/10986/20236.

WHO (World Health Organization). 2023. "Female Genital Mutilation." Fact Sheet. WHO, Geneva. https://www.who.int/news-room/fact-sheets/detail/female-genital-mutilation.

www.ingramcontent.com/pod-product-compliance
Lightning Source LLC
Chambersburg PA
CBHW050900210326
41597CB00002B/29